MATHEW BRADY'S
ILLUSTRATED HISTORY OF THE
CIVIL WAR

1861-65

AND THE CAUSES THAT LED UP TO THE GREAT CONFLICT

BY

BENSON J. LOSSING, LL.D.

AND

A CHRONOLOGICAL SUMMARY AND RECORD

OF EVERY ENGAGEMENT BETWEEN THE TROOPS OF THE UNION AND OF THE CONFEDERACY
AND SHOWING THE TOTAL LOSSES AND CASUALTIES TOGETHER
WITH WAR MAPS OF LOCALITIES

COMPILED FROM

THE OFFICIAL RECORDS OF THE WAR DEPARTMENT

ILLUSTRATED

WITH FAC-SIMILE PHOTOGRAPHIC REPRODUCTIONS
OF THE OFFICIAL WAR PHOTOGRAPHS

TAKEN AT THE TIME BY

MATHEW B. BRADY

UNDER THE AUTHORITY OF PRESIDENT LINCOLN AND NOW IN THE POSSESSION OF THE

WAR DEPARTMENT, WASHINGTON, D. C.

FROM WHOM SPECIAL PERMISSION HAS BEEN GRANTED TO REPRODUCE THE SAME TO ILLUSTRATE THIS WORK

FROM THE FAMOUS AND AUTHENTIC BRADY WAR PHOTOGRAPH COLLECTION THERE HAS BEEN SELECTED PORTRAITS OF THE GREAT COMMANDERS AND
LEADERS OF BOTH THE UNION AND CONFEDERATE ARMIES AND NAVIES, AND MANY SCENES OF GREAT HISTORICAL INTEREST,
AND MAKING A MARVELOUS FAC-SIMILE REPRODUCTION OF THE BATTLEGROUNDS, FORTIFICATIONS, THE DEAD AND
WOUNDED, HOSPITALS, AND INCIDENTS OF THE GREATEST CONFLICT THIS COUNTRY HAS EVER KNOWN AND

FITTINGLY COMMEMORATING THE

FIFTIETH ANNIVERSARY OF THE GREAT NATIONAL STRUGGLE

THE ENTIRE WORK, ISSUED IN SIXTEEN SECTIONS, WITH SIXTEEN SEPARATE COLOR PLATES OF
GREAT COMMANDERS IN ACTION AND FAMOUS BATTLE SCENES FROM THE PAINTING
OF H. A. OGDEN AND OTHER FAMOUS ARTISTS OF MILITARY SUBJECTS

GRAMERCY BOOKS
NEW YORK • AVENEL

LOSSING—BRADY—OGDEN

BENSON J. LOSSING, LL. D.

BENSON J. LOSSING, LL. D.—the author of A History of the Civil War 1861–65—was more than a historian, and he was more than an engaging writer, though to be sure he was both of these. He was also a great authority; a court of last resort for facts and data. He knew how to write history and he gathered his material in a manner all his own. Charles Dudley Warner said of him, "In reading the historical works of Lossing, one is amazed that any human being could carry so much information, and yet carry it so lightly. His vast array of facts did not seem to bear him down; he was as buoyant as cork and as light as a feather."

John Morley, in writing of Dr. Lossing, said, "To be interesting and at the same time authentic—to be patriotic and at the same time impartial—to be at once a reader for young and old—this was his peculiar genius, and in this he was supreme."

Brander Matthews said, "He was the most conscientious and thorough writer of history this country has produced."

Sir Walter Besant once said that it is easier to make history than it is to write it, and that it is not so difficult to conduct a battle as it is to describe one. Whether this be literally true or not, there is little doubt that writing history is one thing, and writing history that the world will read is quite another. The power to state facts accurately, and yet to fill them with charm and interest is the gift that has been given to few men. Dr. Lossing had this supreme gift. He wrote a score of fascinating books, and his writing was as graceful and natural as the flight of a bird. He was a veritable wizard of the pen. Such a man was he in his peculiar field that Oliver Wendell Holmes said of him that he had done more than any other man to make history interesting and popular. His History of the Civil War was written at the time when the facts were fresh. Lossing was intimately acquainted with the great leaders of the country. He conversed with President Lincoln, Generals Grant, Sherman, Sheridan, and other great men of the time. He heard them talk and noted what they told him. He secured the stories and opinions of those who had been concerned in what he described. He traveled the country over and visited the scenes and battle-grounds of the great National conflict and was able to tell what he had seen and heard—and with the pen of a genius. As we read, all is alive and real. The events, the battles of the war, the triumphs and defeats are told faithfully and vividly. It was Lossing's purpose to make this history familiar to all, and by doing so, to kindle in this natural, wholesome way the spirit of patriotism. The reader is carried on from page to page, from chapter to chapter, with an ever-compelling interest that makes it difficult to pause. There is nothing tedious or dull; every character is real, and all the thrilling events and scenes seem to be filled with new interest and life. Lossing put his vast learning into this work. He wished it to be regarded as a memorial to him. He died loaded with glory and honors. A dozen great colleges had conferred on him scholarly and honorary degrees, and the Metropolitan Museum of Art in New York City had made him an Honorary Fellow for life.

MATHEW B. BRADY

MATHEW B. BRADY, who photographed the Civil War 1861–65 and sold his wonderful collection of negatives to the United States Government, was unique as a photographic artist. The reproduction of his famous War negatives shows in this History of the Civil War that he was *fifty years in advance of his time*, for many of his photographs compare favorably with the best quality of work to-day. That he was well equipped for this great work is shown by his remarkable career. In the early 50's, he was the representative photographic artist of the day. His studios on Broadway, New York City, were patronized by the famous men and women of the period. The list of famous men and women who posed before his magic camera is too long to receive more than passing mention in this brief notice. A few of the prominent negatives now in the possession of the United States Government may, however, be mentioned, such as portraits of Washington Irving, James Fenimore Cooper, Edgar Allan Poe, Walt Whitman, Charles Dickens, Nathaniel Hawthorne, William Cullen Bryant, John G. Saxe, John Lothrop Motley, and the great authors and poets of the period. Among the ex-presidents may be mentioned the portraits of Abraham Lincoln, Franklin Pierce, James Buchanan, James A. Garfield, while the members of the stage contributed to his marvelous collection of celebrities such portraits as Edwin Booth, Joseph Jefferson, Jenny Lind, Dion Boucicault, J. C. Howard, the actor and father of the first little Eva of "Uncle Tom's Cabin." A few of the famous men and women of the time may be mentioned, as Horace Greeley, Henry Ward Beecher, Clara Barton—the founder of the world-famous Red Cross Society—Edward Everett, Ben Perley Poor, Granville Dodge—the famous engineer—General Sam Houston, Henry Grinnell, famous Arctic Explorer.

This list, taken at random from thousands, shows beyond dispute that Brady was the leader in his profession. The most important of all Brady's work, as General Greeley says, is his marvelous collection of Civil War photographs. It was Brady who left his profitable business to take pictures of the War. He secured permission from President Lincoln, and under the protection of Allan Pinkerton of the Secret Service Bureau, Brady and his men started taking pictures, thinking that the War would not last more than two or three months, but for four long, weary years, they were actively at work throughout the country, and his wonderful collection of negatives of the great historical scenes and portraits of the leaders on both sides now attest to his energetic and remarkable work. It was these negatives that he sold to the United States Government, and by special permission of the War Department, reproductions have been made direct from the originals which so fittingly illustrate, as nothing else could do, the vivid text of Dr. Lossing in this History of the Civil War. General Grant, Butler and Garfield valued this collection at $150,000. As it turns out to-day, this valuation was remarkably conservative. Yet Brady sold the negatives to the Government for $27,840. (See General Greeley's report on page four). The reproduction of these famous negatives at this time by permission of the War Department not only commemorates the fiftieth anniversary of the War for the Nation, but will leave a memorial to Mathew B. Brady for future generations as the photographic genius of his time.

HENRY A. OGDEN stands in the front rank of American painters of Colonial and Military subjects and Army men and scenes. Mr. Ogden's famous battlefield collection of the Civil War is reproduced in colors.

Additional to Mr. Ogden's famous series are eight great battle scenes and naval engagements by Mr. Thulstrup, Davidson, and other artists of military subjects.

[Some additional description and a photograph of Henry A. Ogden were deleted from this edition, to accommodate Library of Congress Cataloging-in-Publication Data. However, these are the only deletions that have been made from this edition.]

Originally published as *A History of the Civil War.*

This edition is published by Gramercy Books, distributed by Random House Value Publishing, Inc., 40 Engelhard Avenue, Avenel, New Jersey 07001.

Printed and bound in the United States of America

Library of Congress Cataloging-in-Publication Data

Lossing, Benson John, 1813-1891.
    Mathew Brady's illustrated history of the Civil War, 1861-65, and the causes that led up to the great conflict / by Benson J. Lossing; Illustrated with facsimile photographic reproductions of the official war photographs, taken at the time by Mathew B. Brady, under the authority of President Lincoln.
        p. cm.
    ISBN 0-517-11979-X
    1. United States—History—Civil War, 1861-1865—Pictorial works. I. Brady, Mathew B., 1823 (ca.)-1896. II. Title.
E468.7.L88 1994
973.7—dc20
                                                    94-14791
                                                    CIP

8765432

PRESIDENT LINCOLN'S ADDRESS AT GETTYSBURG

NOVEMBER 19, 1863

FOUR score and seven years ago our fathers brought forth on this continent a new nation conceived in liberty, and dedicated to the proposition that all men are created equal.   Now we are engaged in a great civil war; testing whether that nation, or any nation so conceived, and so dedicated, can long endure.   We are met on a great battlefield of that war.   We have come to dedicate a portion of that field as a final resting-place for those who here gave their lives that that nation might live.   It is altogether fitting and proper that we should do this.

But, in a larger sense, we cannot dedicate—we cannot consecrate—we cannot hallow—this ground.   The brave men, living and dead, who struggled here, have consecrated it, far above our poor power to add or detract.   The world will little note nor long remember what we say here, but it can never forget what they did here.   It is for us, the living, rather, to be dedicated here to the unfinished work which they who fought here have thus far so nobly advanced.   It is rather for us to be here dedicated to the great task remaining before us—that from these honored dead we take increased devotion to that cause for which they gave the last full measure of devotion—that we here highly resolve that these dead shall not have died in vain—that this nation, under God, shall have a new birth of freedom—and that government of the people, by the people, for the people, shall not perish from the earth.

ABRAHAM LINCOLN

WAR DEPARTMENT LIBRARY,
WASHINGTON, D. C., February 1, 1897.

Extracts from the report of A. W. Greeley, Brigadier-General and Chief Signal Officer in supervisory charge of War Department Library, referring to the photographs in the War Library:

GEN. A. W. GREELEY

By far the greater number, and by all means the most important, of these negatives are those generally known as the *Brady War Photographs*, which reproduce scenes and portraits connected with the War of the Union. From their value, importance, and present condition a brief post-bellum history of these negatives is most appropriate. It appears that on January 29, 1866, the council of the National Academy of Design, D. Huntington, President, adopted a resolution reciting the value of this collection as a reliable authority for art and as illustrative of American History. They strongly recommended the proposal to place the collection permanently in the keeping of the New York Historical Society.

Relative to the proposition of its owner, Mr. Mathew B. Brady, to exhibit the collection temporarily in the galleries of the New York Historical Society, Lieut.-General U. S. Grant, in a letter dated February 3, 1866, spoke of it as "a collection of photographic views of battlefields, etc., *taken on the spot while the occurrences represented were taking place*" and adds, "I knew when many of these representations were being taken, and have in my possession most of them, and I can say that the scenes are not only spirited and correct, but also well chosen. The collection will be valuable to the student and artist of the present generation, but *how much more valuable to future generations*."

Brady in his descriptive circular spoke of the collection as then embracing the results of twenty-five years, including:

First: "Portraits of many distinguished men who figured in the early years of the present century."

Second: "Likenesses of all prominent actors in the war with Mexico."

Third: "Portraits of eminent men and women of the whole country."

Fourth: "Battlefields of the rebellion and its memorable localities with groups and likenesses of the prominent actors."

*　　*　　*　　*　　*　　*　　*　　*　　*　　*　　*　　*　　*

The first active connection of the Government with the Brady collection appears in the action of the Secretary of War William W. Belknap who purchased for the War Department in July, 1874, as shown by his letter of August 7th to the Adjutant-General, a large number of photographic negatives of war views and pictures of prominent men at an expense of $2,840.00.

*　　*　　*　　*　　*　　*　　*　　*　　*　　*　　*　　*　　*

On motion of General Benjamin F. Butler, member of Massachusetts, a paragraph was inserted in the Sundry Civil Appropriation Bill (Act approved March 3, 1873) reading: To enable the Secretary of War to acquire a full and perfect title to the Brady collection of photographs of the War, and to secure and purchase the remainder now in the possession of the artist for $25,000.00. In connection with the amendment, General Butler said:

"The title under which the Secretary of War purchased the part already obtained was acquired for non-payment of storage. It is very doubtful whether the Secretary of War has a valid title."

General James A. Garfield joined Butler in the statement "that the commercial value of the entire collection was $150,000.00 and Garfield stated that the part bought for $2,500.00 covered three-quarters of the collection."

The sum of $25,000.00 thus appropriated was paid April 15, 1875, the voucher reading, "For the Brady collection of photographs of the War and a conveyance of a full and perfect title to the same."

*　　*　　*　　*　　*　　.　　*　　*　　*　　*　　*　　*　　*　　*

The Comptroller said of these Brady negatives, "The photographic views of the War, showing battlefields, military divisions, fortifications, etc., are among the most authentic and valuable records of the Rebellion. The preservation of these interesting records of the War is too important to be intrusted to glass plates, so easily destroyed by accident or design, and no more effective means than printing them can be devised to save them from destruction."

*　　*　　*　　*　　*　　*　　*　　*　　*　　*　　*　　*　　*

This collection cost the United States originally the sum of $27,840.00, and it is a matter of general regret that these invaluable reproductions of scenes and faces connected with the late civil conflict should remain inaccessible to the general public. The features of most of the prominent actors connected with the War of the Union have been preserved in these negatives, where also are portrayed certain physical aspects of the War that are of interest and of historic value, certain artistic processes now lend themselves to suitable reproduction of these photographs which could thus be given permanency, impossible for the deteriorating negatives, at an expense which a few years since would have appeared impossibly small.

General Greeley states further, "It is hoped that recommendations already made by Chief Signal Officer of the Army may at an appropriate time receive the approval of the War Department and that Congress may authorize the reproduction of the most valuable and important photographs."

The War Department has given permission, and furnished photographs of the most valuable and important pictures direct from the Brady negatives, for reproduction as shown in this edition of Lossing's "History of the Civil War."

CONFEDERATE LINES—NORTH OF ATLANTA—BETWEEN PEACH TREE STREET AND CHATTANOOGA R.R., 1864.

THE NEW SOUTH*

THERE was a South of slavery and secession—that South is dead. There is a South of union and freedom—that South, thank God, is living, breathing, growing every hour.

These words, delivered from the immortal lips of Benjamin H. Hill, at Tammany Hall in 1866, true then and truer now, I shall make my text to-night.

Mr. President and Gentlemen—Let me express to you my appreciation of the kindness by which I am permitted to address you. I make this abrupt acknowledgment advisedly, for I feel that if, when I raise my provincial voice in this ancient and august presence, I could find courage for no more than the opening sentence, it would be well if in that sentence I had met in a rough sense my obligation as a guest, and had perished, so to speak, with courtesy on my lips and grace in my heart. Permitted, through your kindness, to catch my second wind, let me say that I appreciate the significance of being the first Southerner to speak at this board, which bears the substance, if it surpasses the semblance, of original New England hospitality, and honors the sentiment that in turn honors you, but in which my personality is lost and the compliment to my people made plain.

* * * * * * * * * * * * *

My friends, Dr. Talmage has told you that the typical American has yet to come. Let me tell you that he has already come. Great types, like valuable plants, are slow to flower and fruit. But from the union of these colonies, Puritans and Cavaliers, from the straightening of their purposes and the crossing of their blood, slow perfecting through a century, came he who stands as the first typical American, the first who comprehended within himself all the strength and gentleness, all the majesty and grace of this republic—Abraham Lincoln.

He was the sum of Puritan and Cavalier, for in his ardent nature were fused the virtues of both, and in the depths of his great soul the faults of both were lost. He was greater than Puritan, greater than Cavalier, in that he was American, and that in his honest form were first gathered the vast and thrilling forces of his ideal government—charging it with such tremendous meaning and elevating it above human suffering that martyrdom, though infamously aimed, came as a fitting crown to a life consecrated from the cradle to human liberty. Let us, each cherishing the traditions and honoring his fathers, build with reverend hands to the type of this simple but sublime life, in which all types are honored, and in our common glory as Americans there will be plenty and to spare for your forefathers and for mine.

Dr. Talmage has drawn for you, with a master's hand, the picture of your returning armies. He has told you how, in the pomp and circumstance of war, they came back to you, marching with proud and victorious tread, reading their glory in a nation's eyes! Will you bear with me while I tell you of another army that sought its home at the close of the late war—an army that marched home in defeat and not in victory—in pathos and not in splendor, but in glory that equalled yours, and to hearts as loving as ever welcomed heroes home! Let me picture to you the footsore Confederate soldier, as, buttoning up in his faded gray jacket the parole which was to bear testimony to his children of his fidelity and faith, he turned his face southward from Appomattox in April, 1865.

Think of him as ragged, half-starved, heavy-hearted, enfeebled by want and wounds, having fought to exhaustion, he surrenders his gun, wrings the hands of his comrades in silence, and lifting his tear-stained and pallid face for the last time to the graves that dot old Virginia hills, pulls his gray cap over his brow and begins the slow and painful journey. What does he find—let me ask you who went to your homes eager to find, in the welcome you had justly earned, full payment for four years' sacrifice—what does he find when, having followed the battle-stained cross against overwhelming odds, dreading death not half so much as surrender, he reaches the home he left so prosperous and beautiful?

He finds his house in ruins, his farm devastated, his slaves free, his stock killed, his barns empty, his trade destroyed, his money worthless, his social system, feudal in its magnificence, swept away; his people without law or legal status, his comrades slain, and the burdens of others heavy on his shoulders. Crushed by defeat, his very traditions are gone. Without money, credit, employment, material or training, and, besides all this, confronted with the gravest problem that ever met human intelligence—the establishing of a status for the vast body of his liberated slaves.

What does he do—this hero in gray with a heart of gold? Does he sit down in sullenness and despair? Not for a day. Surely God, who had stripped him of his prosperity, inspired him in his adversity. As ruin was never before so overwhelming, never was restoration swifter. The soldier stepped from the trenches into the furrow; horses that had charged Federal guns marched before the plow, and fields that ran red with human blood in April were green with the harvest in June; women reared in luxury cut up their dresses and made breeches for their husbands, and, with a patience and heroism that fit women always as a garment, gave their hands to work. There was little bitterness in all this. Cheerfulness and frankness prevailed.

I want to say to General Sherman, who is considered an able man in our parts, though some people think he is a kind of careless man about fire, that from the ashes he left us in 1864 we have raised a brave and beautiful city; that somehow or other we have caught the sunshine in the bricks and mortar of our homes, and have builded therein not one ignoble prejudice or memory.

But what is the sum of our work? We have found out that in the summing up the free negro counts more than he did as a slave. We have planted the schoolhouse on the hill-top and made it free to white and black. We have sowed towns and cities in the place of

---

*It seems appropriate to print in advance of the History of the Civil War extracts from the address delivered by Henry W. Grady, a famous orator and editor of Atlanta, Ga., before the New England Club, New York, December 21, 1886.

theories, and put business above politics. We have challenged your spinners in Massachusetts and your iron-makers in Pennsylvania. We have learned that the $400,000,000 annually received from our cotton crop will make us rich when the supplies that make it are home-raised. We have reduced the commercial rate of interest from twenty-four to six per cent., and are floating four per cent. bonds.

We have learned that one Northern immigrant is worth fifty foreigners; and have smoothed the path to southward, wiped out the place where Mason and Dixon's line used to be, and hung out our latch-string to you and yours. We have reached the point that marks perfect harmony in every household, when the husband confesses that the pies which his wife cooks are as good as those his mother used to bake; and we admit that the sun shines as brightly and the moon as softly as it did before the war. We have established thrift in city and country. We have fallen in love with our work. We have restored comfort to homes from which culture and elegance never departed. We have let economy take root and spread among us as rank as the crabgrass which sprung from Sherman's cavalry camps, until we are ready to lay odds on the Georgia Yankee as he manufactures relics of the battlefield in a one-story shanty and squeezes pure olive oil out of his cotton seed, against any Down-Easter that ever swapped wooden nutmegs for flannel sausage in the valleys of Vermont. Above all, we know that we have achieved in these "piping times of peace" a fuller independence for the South than that which our fathers sought to win in the forum by their eloquence or compel in the field by their swords.

It is a rare privilege, sir, to have had part, however humble, in this work. Never was nobler duty confided to human hands than the uplifting and upbuilding of the prostrate and bleeding South—misguided, perhaps, but beautiful in her suffering, and honest, brave, and generous always. In the record of her social, industrial, and political illustration we await with confidence the verdict of the world.

But what of the negro? Have we solved the problem he presents or progressed in honor and equity toward solution? Let the record speak to the point. No section shows a more prosperous laboring population than the negroes of the South, none in fuller sympathy with the employing and land-owning class. He shares our school fund, has the fullest protection of our laws and the friendship of our people. Self-interest as well as honor demand that he should have this. Our future, our very existence, depend upon working out this problem in full and exact justice.

We understand that when Lincoln signed the Emancipation Proclamation, your victory was assured, for he then committed you to the cause of human liberty, against which the arms of man cannot prevail—while those of our statesmen who trusted to make slavery the corner-stone of the Confederacy doomed us to defeat as far as they could, committing us to a cause that reason could not defend or the sword maintain in sight of advancing civilization.

*   *   *   *   *   *   *   *   *   *   *   *   *

The relations of the Southern people with the negro are close and cordial. We remember with what fidelity for four years he guarded our defenceless women and children, whose husbands and fathers were fighting against his freedom. To his eternal credit be it said that whenever he struck a blow for his own liberty he fought in open battle, and when at last he raised his black and humble hands that the shackles might be struck off, those hands were innocent of wrong against his helpless charges, and worthy to be taken in loving grasp by every man who honors loyalty and devotion.

Ruffians have maltreated him, rascals have misled him, philanthropists established a bank for him, but the South, with the North, protests against injustice to this simple and sincere people.

But have we kept faith with you? In the fullest sense, yes. When Lee surrendered—I don't say when Johnston surrendered, because I understand he still alludes to the time when he met General Sherman last as the time when he determined to abandon any further prosecution of the struggle—when Lee surrendered, I say, and Johnston quit, the South became, and has since been, loyal to this Union.

We fought hard enough to know that we were whipped, and in perfect frankness accept as final the arbitrament of the sword to which we had appealed. The South found her jewel in the toad's head of defeat. The shackles that had held her in narrow limitations fell forever when the shackles of the negro slave were broken. Under the old régime the negroes were slaves to the South; the South was a slave to the system. The old plantation, with its simple police regulations and feudal habit, was the only type possible under slavery. Thus was gathered in the hands of a splendid and chivalric oligarchy the substance that should have been diffused among the people, as the rich blood, under certain artificial conditions, is gathered at the heart, filling that with affluent rapture, but leaving the body chill and colorless.

The old South rested everything on slavery and agriculture, unconscious that these could neither give nor maintain healthy growth. The new South presents a perfect democracy, the oligarchs leading in the popular movement—a social system compact and closely knitted, less splendid on the surface, but stronger at the core—a hundred farms for every plantation, fifty homes for every palace—and a diversified industry that meets the complex need of this complex age.

The new South is enamored of her work. Her soul is stirred with the breath of a new life. The light of a grander day is falling fair on her face. She is thrilling with the consciousness of growing power and prosperity. As she stands upright, full statured and equal among the people of the earth, breathing the keen air and looking out upon the expanded horizon, she understands that her emancipation came because through the inscrutable wisdom of God her honest purpose was crossed, and her brave armies were beaten.

This is said in no spirit of time-serving or apology. The South has nothing for which to apologize. She believes that the late struggle between the States was war and not rebellion; revolution and not conspiracy, and that her convictions were as honest as yours. I should be unjust to the dauntless spirit of the South and to my own convictions if I did not make this plain in this presence. The South has nothing to take back. In my native town of Athens is a monument that crowns its central hill—a plain, white shaft. Deep cut into its shining side is a name dear to me above the names of men—that of a brave and simple man who died in a brave and simple faith. Not for all the glories of New England, from Plymouth Rock all the way, would I exchange the heritage he left me in his soldier's death. To the foot of that I shall send my children's children to reverence him who ennobled their name with his heroic blood. But, sir, speaking from the shadow of that memory which I honor as I do nothing else on earth, I say that the cause in which he suffered and for which he gave his life was adjudged by higher and fuller wisdom than his or mine, and I am glad that the omniscient God held the balance of battle in his Almighty hand and that human slavery was swept forever from American soil, the American Union was saved from the wreck of war.

This message, Mr. President, comes to you from consecrated ground. Every foot of soil about the city in which I live is as sacred as a battleground of the republic. Every hill that invests it is hallowed to you by the blood of your brothers who died for your victory, and doubly hallowed to us by the blood of those who died hopeless, but undaunted in defeat—sacred soil to all of us—rich with memories that make us purer and stronger and better—silent but staunch witnesses, in its red desolation, of the matchless valor of American hearts and the deathless glory of American arms—speaking an eloquent witness in its white peace and prosperity to the indissoluble union of American States and the imperishable brotherhood of the American people.

Now, what answer has New England to this message? Will she permit the prejudice of war to remain in the hearts of the conquerors when it has died in the hearts of the conquered? Will she transmit this prejudice to the next generation that in their hearts which never felt the generous ardor of conflict it may perpetuate itself? Will she withhold, save in strained courtesy, the hand which, straight from his soldier's heart, Grant offered to Lee at Appomattox? Will she make the vision of a restored and happy people, which gathered above the couch of your dying captain, filling his heart with grace; touching his lips with praise, and glorifying his path to the grave—will she make this vision on which the last sign of his expiring soul breathed a benediction, a cheat and delusion? If she does the South, never abject in asking for comradeship, must accept with dignity its refusal; but if she does not refuse to accept in frankness and sincerity this message of good will and friendship, then will the prophecy of Webster, delivered in this very Society forty years ago amid tremendous applause, become true, be verified in its fullest sense, when he said: "Standing hand to hand and clasping hands, we should remain united as we have been for sixty years citizens of the same country, members of the same government united, all united now and forever." There have been difficulties, contentions, and controversies, but I tell you that in my judgment—

> ——"those opened eyes,
> Which, like the meteors of a troubled heaven,
> All of one nature, of one substance bred,
> Did lately meet in th' intestine shock,
> Shall now, in mutual well-beseeming ranks,
> March all one way."

CHAPTER I.

Causes leading to Secession—The Fugitive-Slave Law—Fillmore's administration—Election of General Pierce—Senator Douglas' bill for two vast Territories—Raids in Central America—Struggle begun in Kansas.

IT was believed by superficial thinkers and observers that the Compromise Act of 1850 had quieted, forever, all controversy on the subject of slavery; and during his entire administration, President Fillmore gave his support to all the measures embraced in that act. When his administration closed in the spring of 1853, there seemed to be very little uneasiness in the public mind on the subject of slavery. But it was only the ominous calm that precedes the bursting of a tempest. The moral sense of the people in the free-labor States (and of thousands in the slave-labor States) had been shocked by the passage of the Fugitive-Slave Law, which compelled every person to become a slave-catcher, under certain circumstances, willing or not willing. That law was so much at variance with Christian ethics and the civilization of the age, that a multitude of persons in all parts of the Union yearned to see it wiped from our national statute-books as an ugly blot; and, pondering upon it, many persons who had been indifferent, felt a desire to have a check put upon the further expansion of the system of slavery in our republic.

This feeling, and the supporters of that system not a mere sectional in-collisions in speech, and, civil war. The Fugitive-James M. Mason of Vir-bringing on that terrible

When Mr. Fillmore's ing to a close, nominations made. A Democratic na-bled at Baltimore, in June, Franklin Pierce, of New and William R. King, of dent. A Whig national the same place in the same General Winfield Scott for Graham of North Carolina Democratic nominees were March, 1853, President life. One of the most events of his administra-act of Congress, of a new ton, which was carved out

GENERAL U. S. GRANT, WIFE AND SON AT WINTER QUARTERS, CITY POINT, 1865

avowed intention of the to make it a national and stitution, produced violent finally, a most sanguinary Slave Law, framed by ginia, had much to do with crisis in our history.

administration was draw-for his successor were tional convention assem-1852, nominated General Hampshire, for President, Alabama, for Vice-Presi-convention assembled at month, and nominated President, and William A. for Vice-President. The elected, and on the 4th of Fillmore retired to private important of the closing tion was the creation, by Territory called Washing-of the northern part of

Oregon. The bill for this purpose became a law on the 2d of March, 1853.

General Pierce took the oath of office as President of the United States, upon a platform of New Hampshire pine, which had been erected at the eastern portico of the Capitol. It was administered in the presence of thousands of people, who stood in a storm of driving sleet as witnesses of the august ceremony. President Pierce chose for his cabinet William L. Marcy, Secretary of State; James Guthrie, Secretary of the Treasury; Jefferson Davis, Secretary of War; James C. Dobbin, Secretary of the Navy; Robert McClelland, Secretary of the Interior; James Campbell, Postmaster-General, and Caleb Cushing, Attorney-General.

An unexpected movement now aroused a vehement discussion of the slavery question. In January, 1854, Senator Stephen A. Douglas presented a bill in the Senate for the erection of two vast Territories in mid-continent, to be called, respectively, Kansas and Nebraska. The bill provided for giving permission to the inhabitants of those Territories to decide for themselves whether slavery should or should not exist within their domain. This proposed nullification of the Missouri Compromise produced rancorous controversies in and out of Congress, and the people of the free-labor States became violently excited. After long and bitter discussions in both Houses of Congress, the bill became a law in May following. The people of the North thought they perceived in this measure a determination to make slavery national; and the boast of Robert Toombs, of Georgia, that he would yet "call the roll of his slaves on Bunker Hill," seemed likely not to be an idle one.

In the light of historic events, it is clear to-day, that men who afterward appeared as leaders in the war against our government, were then concocting and executing schemes for the extension of the domains of the slave system. It must expand or suffocate. They contrived and put in motion expeditions for conquering neighboring provinces, in the southwest, under various pretexts, and their acts were unrebuked by our government. They formed a design to conquer parts of Mexico, and also Central America; and the theatre of their first practically successful endeavors was on the northern portion of the great isthmus between North and South America. The first movement was an armed "emigration" into Nicaragua, with peaceful professions, led by Colonel H. L. Kinney. This was followed by an armed invasion by Californians led by William Walker, first, of provinces in Mexico, and then of the state of Nicaragua. Walker also made peaceful professions on landing, but the next day he cast off the mask and attempted to capture a town. He was soon driven out by Nicaraguan troops, and escaped in a schooner. He soon reappeared with a stronger force (September, 1855) when the country was in a state of revolution, and pushed his scheme of conquest so vigorously that he seized the capital of the state (Grenada), in October, and placed one of his followers (a Nicaraguan) in the presidential chair. He also strengthened his power by armed "emigrants" who came from the slave-labor States. The other governments on

HOME OF JEFFERSON DAVIS AT MONTGOMERY, ALA.

the isthmus were alarmed for their own safety, and in the winter of 1856 they formed an alliance for expelling the invaders. Troops from Costa Rica marched into Nicaragua, but were soon driven out by Walker's forces. So firm was his grasp that he caused himself to be elected President of Nicaragua; and the government at Washington hastened to acknowledge the new "nation," by cordially receiving Walker's embassador in the person of a Roman Catholic priest named Vigil. For two years this usurper ruled that state with a high hand, and offended commercial nations by his interference with trade. At length the combined powers on the isthmus crushed him. In May, 1857, he was compelled to surrender the remnant of his army, but escaped himself through the interposition of Commodore Davis of our navy. Late in the same year he reappeared in Central America, when he was seized, with his followers, by Commodore Paulding, and sent to New York as an offender against neutrality laws. The President (Buchanan) *privately* commended Paulding for his action, but for "prudential reasons," as he said, he publicly condemned the commander in a message to Congress, for "thus violating the sovereignty of a foreign country." Walker was allowed to go free, when he fitted out another expedition and sailed from Mobile. He was arrested only for leaving port without a clearance, and was tried and acquitted by the supreme court at New Orleans. Then he went again to Nicaragua, where he made much mischief, and was finally captured and shot at Truxillo.

A SLAVE PEN AT ALEXANDRIA, VA.

Our country was approaching that great crisis which appeared in the dreadful aspect of civil war—a tremendous conflict between Freedom and Slavery for supremacy in the republic. With the enactment and enforcement of the Fugitive-Slave Law and the virtual repeal of the Missouri Compromise Act, in

PONTOON BOATS ON WHEELS

the case of Kansas and Nebraska, the important question was forced upon the attention of the whole people of the land, "Shall the domain of our republic be the theatre of all free or all slave labor, with the corresponding civilization of each as a consequence?" The time had come when one or the other of these social systems must prevail in all parts of the land. Part free and part slave was a condition no longer to be tolerated, for it meant perpetual war. The supporters of the slave-system, encouraged by their recent triumphs, had full faith in their ability to win other and more decisive victories, and did not permit themselves to doubt their ultimate possession of the field, so they sounded the trumpet for their hosts to rally and prepare for the struggle. Kansas was the chosen field for the preliminary skirmishing. It lay nearest to the settled States; it was bordered on the east by a slave-labor State, and it was easy of access from the South. On the surface of society they saw only insignificant ripples of opposition. They began to colonize the Territory; and, flushed with what seemed to be well-assured success, they cast down the gauntlet of defiance at the feet of the friends of free-labor in the nation.

That gauntlet was quickly taken up by their opponents, and champions of freedom seemed to spring from the ground like the harvest from the seed-sowing of dragons' teeth. Enterprising men and women swarmed out of New England to people the virgin soil of Kansas with the hardy children of toil. They were joined by those of other free-labor States in the North and West. The then dominant party in the Union were astonished at the sudden uprising, and clearly perceived that the opponents of slavery would speedily outvote its supporters. Combinations were formed under various names, such as "Blue Lodges," "Friends' Society," "Social Band," "Sons of the South," etc., to counteract the efforts of the "Emigrant Aid Society" of Massachusetts, to gain numerical supremacy in Kansas—a society which had been organized immediately after the passage of the Kansas-Nebraska bill. The supporters of slavery, conscious that their votes could not secure supremacy in Kansas, where the question of slavery or no slavery was to be decided at the ballot-box, organized physical force in Missouri to oppose this moral force. Associations were formed in Missouri, whose members were pledged to be ready, at all times, to assist, when called upon by the friends of slavery in Kansas, in removing from that Territory

CAMP OF THE 50TH NEW YORK ENGINEERS

GENERAL WINFIELD SCOTT
Showing the Present Condition of the Broken Negative in Possession of the War Department.

by force every person who should attempt to settle there "under the auspices of the Northern Emigrant Aid Society."

In the autumn of 1854, A. H. Reeder was sent to govern the Territory of Kansas. He immediately ordered an election of a Territorial legislature, and with that election the struggle for supremacy there was finally begun. Missourians went into Kansas to assist the supporters of slavery there in carrying the election. They went with tents, artillery and other weapons. There were then eight hundred and thirty-one legal voters in the Territory, but there were more than six thousand votes polled. The members of the Legislature were all supporters of slavery; and when they met at Shawnee, on the borders of Missouri, they proceeded to enact laws for upholding slavery in Kansas. These laws were regularly vetoed by Governor Reeder, who became so obnoxious that President Pierce was asked to recall him. The President did so, and sent Wilson Shannon of Ohio, who was an avowed supporter of slavery, to fill Reeder's place.

REAR ADMIRAL H. PAULDING

The actual settlers in Kansas, who were chiefly from the free-labor States, met in mass convention in September, 1855, and resolved not to recognize the laws passed by the illegally elected legislature, as binding upon them. They called a delegate convention to assemble at Topeka on the 19th of October, at which time and place the convention framed a State constitution which was approved by the legal voters of the Territory, and which contained an article making provision for constituting Kansas a free-labor State. Under this constitution they asked Congress to admit that Territory into the Union as a State. By this action the contest between Freedom and Slavery was transferred from Kansas to Washington, for awhile. The prospect of success for the opponents of slavery, in Kansas, was beginning to appear bright, when President Pierce gave the supporters of the institution much comfort by a message to Congress in January, 1856, in which he declared the action of the legal voters, in adopting a State constitution, to be open rebellion.

Throughout the spring and summer of 1856, armed men from other States roamed over Kansas, committing many excesses under pretext of compelling obedience to the laws of the illegal legislature. There was much violence and bloodshed; but during the autumn, the Presidential election absorbed so much of the public attention, that Kansas was allowed a season of rest. At that election there were three parties in the field, each of which had a candidate for the Presidency. One was a party composed of men of all political creeds, who were opposed to slavery. It was called the Republican party, and it assumed powerful proportions at the outset. Another powerful political organization was known as the American or Know-Nothing party, whose chief bond of union was opposition to foreign influence. The Democratic party, dating its organization at the period of the election of President Jackson in 1828, was then the dominant party in the Union. The Democratic candidate for the Presidency was James Buchanan of Pennsylvania; of the Republican party, John C. Fremont of California, and of the American party, Ex-President Fillmore. After an exciting canvass, James Buchanan was elected President, with John C. Breckenridge of Kentucky as Vice-President.

MILITARY RAIL ROAD GUN

ALLAN PINKERTON—PRESIDENT LINCOLN—MAJ. GEN. J. A. MCCLERNAND

CHAPTER II.

A New Era—Skirmishes before the Civil War—The Democratic Party—The Dred Scott Decision—Action of the Supreme Court of the United States—Early Efforts to Restrict Slavery—Slaves in England—The Status of Slavery Here—President Buchanan's Course Foreshadowed—Civil War in Kansas and Civil Government There—Lecompton Constitution Adopted and Rejected—Admission of Kansas as a State—A Judicial Decision Practically Reversed—Reopening of the African Slave-Trade and Action Concerning It—Working of the Fugitive-Slave Law—Action of State Legislatures.

WHEN James Buchanan, of Pennsylvania, was inaugurated the fifteenth President of the United States on the 4th of March, 1857, and chose, for his constitutional advisers, Lewis Cass, Secretary of State; Howell Cobb, Secretary of the Treasury; John B. Floyd, Secretary of War; Isaac Toucey, Secretary of the Navy; Jacob Thompson, Secretary of the Interior; Aaron V. Brown, Postmaster-General, and Jeremiah S. Black, Attorney-General, a new era in the history of the United States was begun. It was the beginning of a great political and social revolution in our republic which entirely and permanently changed the industrial aspects in many of the States of the Union.

CAMP WORK

It was during the administration of Mr. Buchanan that the preliminary skirmishes, moral and physical, which immediately preceded the great Civil War, occurred. Both parties were then putting on their armor and preparing their weapons for the mighty struggle. The political organization by which the new President had been elected had, for some time, coalesced with the friends and supporters of the slave-labor system in their efforts not only to extend the public domain so as to allow the almost indefinite expansion of their cherished institution, but to make it national. That coalition and sympathy were manifested in various ways. The two wings of the Democratic party (one of them leaning toward an anti-slavery policy and called the "Free-Soil Democracy") had been reconciled, and worked together in the national convention at Cincinnati in June, 1856, which nominated Mr. Buchanan for the Presidency. In their resolutions, put forth as a platform of principles, they approved the invasion and usurpation of Walker, in Nicaragua, as efforts of the people of Central America "to regenerate that portion of the continent which covers the passage across the interoceanic isthmus." They approved the doctrine of the "Ostend Manifesto," by resolving that "the Democratic party were in favor of the acquisition of Cuba," and Mr. Buchanan was chosen to be their standard-bearer because of his known sympathy with these movements for the extension of the area and perpetuation of the slave system. Senator A. G. Brown of Mississippi, one of the committee appointed to call upon Mr. Buchanan and officially inform him of his nomination, wrote to a friend, saying: "In my judgment Mr. Buchanan is as worthy of Southern confidence and Southern votes as ever Mr. Calhoun was."

One of the most vitally important skirmishes before the Civil War actually began occurred at about the time of Mr. Buchanan's accession to the Presidency of the Republic. It was of a moral and not of a physical nature, and is known in our judicial history as "the Dred Scott case."

Dred Scott was a young negro slave of Dr. Emerson, a surgeon in the United States Army, living in Missouri. When the latter was ordered to Rock Island, in Illinois, in 1834, he took Scott with him. There Major Taliaferro, of the army, had a feminine slave, and when the two masters were transferred to Fort Snelling (now in Minnesota) next year, the two slaves were married with the consent of the

FIELD TELEGRAPH STATION

LANDING SUPPLIES AT CITY POINT

COMPANY OF 170TH NEW YORK VOLUNTEERS

masters.   They had two children born in the free-labor Territory; and the mother had been bought by Dr. Emerson, who finally took parents and children back to Missouri, and there sold them to a New Yorker. Dred sued for his freedom, on the plea of his involuntary residence in a free-labor State and Territory for several years, and the Circuit Court of St. Louis decided in his favor.   The Supreme Court of Missouri reversed the decision of the inferior court, and it was carried, by an appeal, to the Supreme Court of the United States, then presided over by Roger B. Taney, a Maryland slaveholder.   A majority of that court were in sympathy with the friends of the slave-labor system, and their decision, about to be given in 1856, was, for prudential reasons, withheld until after the Presidential election that year.   When it was known that Buchanan was elected, the decision was made against Scott, but it was not promulgated until after the inauguration of the new President of the Republic.   The decision, through the Chief Justice, declared that any person "whose ancestors were imported into this country and held as slaves" had no right to sue in any court of the United States; in other words, denying any right of citizenship to a person who had been a slave or was the descendant of a slave.

OPEN PONTOON BRIDGE

The only legitimate business of the court was to decide the question of jurisdiction in the case; but the Chief Justice, with the sanction of a majority of the court, further declared that the framers and supporters of the Declaration of Independence did not include the negro race in our country in the great proclamation that "*all* men are created equal;" that the patriots of the Revolution, and their progenitors "for more than a century before," regarded the negroes as beings of an inferior order, and altogether unfit to associate with the white race either in social or political relations; and so far inferior that *they had no rights which the white man was bound to respect*, and that the negro might lawfully be reduced to slavery for his (the white man's) benefit.   The Chief Justice further declared that they were never spoken of except as property; and that in the days of our fathers, even emancipated blacks "were identified in the public mind with the race to which they belonged, and *regarded as a part of the slave population rather than the free.*"

How much at variance with the plain teachings of history were these statements, let our public records testify.   In the English-American colonies, the most enlightened men looked on slavery with great disfavor, as a moral wrong, and they made attempts, from time to time, to limit or eradicate it.   The utterances and writings of men like General Washington, Henry Laurens, Thomas Jefferson, and other slaveholders, and of Dr. Franklin, John Jay and many leading patriots of the Revolution, directly refute the assertion of Judge Taney, that in their time Africans by descent were "never thought or spoken of except as property."   The Declaration of Independence, framed by a slaveholder, was a solemn protest against human bondage in *every* form; and in his original draft of that document, Mr. Jefferson made the protest stronger than the Congress finally approved.

Among the public acts of the fathers of the Republic in favor of human freedom and restriction of the slave-system, was the famous Ordinance of 1787, adopted before the National Constitution was framed, which was the final result of an effort commenced in the Continental Congress in 1784 to restrict slavery.   That effort was made in proposing a plan for the government of a Territory including the whole region west of the old thirteen States, as far south as the thirty-first degree of north latitude, and embracing several of the late slave-labor States.   The plan was submitted by a committee, of which Thomas Jefferson was chairman.   It contemplated the ultimate division of that Territory into seventeen States, eight of them below the latitude of the present city of Louisville, in Kentucky.   Among the rules for the government of that region, reported by Mr. Jefferson, was the following: "That after the year 1800 of the Christian Era, there shall be neither slavery nor involuntary servitude in any of the said States, otherwise than in the punishment of crime, whereof the party shall have been convicted to be personally guilty."   On motion of Carolinians, this clause was stricken out. A majority of the States were in favor of it, but as it required the votes of nine States to carry a proposition, it was not adopted.   This rule, omitting the words "after the year 1800 of the Christian Era," was incorporated in the Ordinance of 1787, above alluded to, and so secured freedom to the territory northward of the Ohio River.

The mother-country, from which a larger portion of the patriots of our Revolution had sprung, had just swept slavery from the dominions of Great Britain, when the old war for independence was a-kindling. It was done by a decision of Chief Justice Mansfield in the case of James Somerset, a native of Africa, who was first carried to Virginia and sold as a slave, then taken to England by his master, and there induced,

LARGEST GUN MOUNTED IN THE WAR

by philanthropic men, to assert his freedom. Chief Justice Mansfield decided that he was a free man. So early as 1597, it was held by the lawyers in England, that "negroes being usually bought and sold among merchants as merchandise, and also being infidels, there might be a property in them sufficient to maintain trover," or the gaining possession of any goods by whatever means. This position was overruled by Chief Justice Holt, who decided that "so soon as a negro lands in England, he is free." It was to this decision that Cowper alluded in his lines:

> "Slaves cannot breathe in England;
> That moment they are free they touch our country,
> And their shackles fall."

BUILDING PONTOON BRIDGE, NEAR BEAUFORT, S. C.

In 1702, Justice Holt also decided that "there is no such thing as a slave by the laws of England;" but in 1729, an opinion was obtained from the crown-lawyer, that negroes legally enslaved elsewhere might be held as slaves in England, and that baptism was no bar to the master's claim. This was a sort of fugitive slave-law for the benefit of the English-American colonists, that was obeyed until the sweeping decision of Chief Justice Mansfield, which would have abolished slavery here had not the Revolution broken out soon afterward.

After Chief Justice Taney had made his declaration about the feelings of our forefathers concerning the negro as a man, he declared that the Missouri Compromise Act and all other acts for the restriction of slavery were unconstitutional; and that neither Congress nor local legislatures had any authority for restricting the spread of the institution all over the Union. The majority of the Supreme Court sustained not only the legitimate decision, but the extra-judicial opinion of the Chief Justice; and the dominant party who had elected Mr. Buchanan assumed that the decision was final—that slavery was a national institution having the right to exist anywhere in the Union, and that Mr. Toombs might legally "call the roll of his slaves on Bunker's Hill." It was assumed by the leaders of that party that, in consequence of the promulgated opinion of five or six fallible men, evidently based upon a perversion of historical facts, the nation was bound to consent to the turning back of the bright tide of Christian civilization into the darker channels of a barbarous age from which it had escaped. To this proposition the conscience of the nation refused acquiescence. Large numbers of the dominant party deserted their leaders, and every lover of freedom was impelled to prepare for the inevitable conflict which this extra-judicial opinion of the highest court in the land would certainly arouse. It being extra-judicial, it was no more binding, in law, upon the people, than was the opinion of any citizen of the Republic.

The new President had been informed of this decision before it was promulgated, and in his inaugural address he foreshadowed his own course in the treatment of the subject. Indeed, that decision was a chief topic of the discourse. He spoke of the measure as one that would "speedily and finally" settle the slavery question, and he announced his intention to cheerfully submit to it, declaring that the question was wholly a judicial one, which only the Supreme Court of the Republic could settle, and that by its decision the admission or rejection of slavery in any Territory was to be determined by the legal votes of the people thereof. "The whole territorial question," he said, "was thus settled upon the principle of popular sovereignty—a principle as

HORSES KILLED BY BURSTING SHELLS

Group of United States Artillery

Confederate Prisoners at Belle Plain

ancient as free government itself." He averred that "everything of a practical nature" had been settled, and he expressed a sincere hope that the long agitation of the subject of slavery was "approaching its end."

Alas! it was only the beginning of the dreadful scenes that marked its end. That decision and opinion of the Chief Justice rekindled the fire spoken of by the Georgian in debate in Congress on the admission of Missouri, which he said, "all the waters of the ocean would not put out, and which only seas of blood could extinguish."

As we have observed, there was actual civil war in Kansas in the earlier portions of 1856. It assumed alarming aspects during the spring and summer of that year, as we have noticed. The actual settlers from free-labor States outnumbered emigrants from elsewhere; and a regiment of young men from Georgia and South Carolina, under Colonel Buford, fully armed, went into the Territory for the avowed purpose of making it a slave-labor State "at all hazards." They were joined by armed Missourians, and for several

FIELD HOSPITAL 1ST DIVISION 2D CORPS

months they spread terror over the land. They sacked the town of Lawrence, and murdered and plundered individuals in various places. Steamboats ascending the Missouri River with emigrants from free-labor States were stopped, and the passengers were frequently robbed of their money; and persons of the same class, crossing the State of Missouri, were arrested and turned back. Lawlessness reigned supreme in all that region. Justice was bound, and there was general defiance of all mandates of right.

The civil war in Kansas, so begun, was more wasteful than bloody, and there was only one battle with any semblance of regularity fought there. That conflict took place on an open prairie. It was waged between twenty-eight emigrants, led by John Brown, of Ossawattamie, and fifty-six armed men under H. Clay Pate, of Virginia. Brown was the victor. Finally, John W. Geary, afterward a major-general, and Governor of Pennsylvania, who succeeded Shannon as chief magistrate of Kansas, by judicious administration of affairs there, smothered the flames of civil war, and both parties worked vigorously with moral forces for the admission of Kansas as a State of the Union, but with ends in view diametrically opposed.

In September, 1857, the friends of the slave-system met in convention at Lecompton, on the Kansas River, and then the Territorial capital, and adopted a State Constitution, in which it was declared that

GENERAL POTTER AND STAFF. MATHEW B. BRADY STANDING BY TREE

"the rights of property in slaves now in the Territory shall in no manner be interfered with," and it forbade any amendment of the instrument until 1864. It was submitted to the votes of the people in December following, but by the terms of the election law then in force, no person could vote *against* the

SIGNAL STATION ON ELK MOUNTAIN

Constitution. The ballots were endorsed: "For the Constitution *with* slavery" and "For the Constitution *without* slavery." In either case, a constitution that would foster and protect slavery would be voted for. The consequence was that a large portion of the friends of the free-labor system refused to vote, and the Lecompton Constitution was adopted by a very large majority.

R. J. Walker, of Mississippi, had now succeeded Governor Geary, and when an election for a new Territorial Legislature occurred, he assured the people that justice should prevail. Encouraged by these assurances of an honest man, the friends of free-labor generally voted, and the law-makers then elected were composed chiefly of

their political friends. They also elected their candidate for Congress. That Legislature ordered the Lecompton Constitution to be submitted to the people of Kansas for their adoption or rejection, and it was rejected by at least ten thousand majority. The President of the Republic, regardless of this expressed will of the people of Kansas, sent the rejected Constitution into Congress, with a message recommending its ratification. "It has been solemnly adjudged by the highest tribunal known to our laws," said President Buchanan, "that slavery exists in Kansas by virtue of the Constitution of the United States. Kansas is, therefore, at this moment as much a slave State as Georgia or South Carolina." Congress did not ratify it, but ordered it to be again submitted to the people of Kansas, when they rejected it by an overwhelming majority. From that hour the controlling political power in Kansas was wielded by the free-labor party.

Their strength steadily increased, and at near the close of January, 1861, just as the great Civil War was a-kindling, that Territory was admitted into the Union as a free-labor State. The Republic was now composed of thirty-four States and several Territories. Six years after the decision of Judge Taney and the majority of the Supreme Court, which declared that it was impossible for a black man to become a citizen, that decision was practically set aside by the issuing of a passport by the Secretary of State, William H. Seward, to the descendant of a slave to travel abroad as a "citizen of the United States."

While the struggle for freedom was going on in Kansas, the friends of the slave-labor system, emboldened by the sympathy of the general government, formed plans for its perpetuity. These plans would practically disregard

A CAMP SCENE

Second Maine Infantry and Encampment

the plain requirements of the National Constitution and the laws made under it. They resolved to reopen the African slave-trade, which had been closed in 1808 by a provision of the Constitution. Leading citizens of Louisiana prepared to engage in it, under the guise of the "African Labor-Supply Association," and captives, as of old, were actually brought across the sea, landed on the shores of the Southern States, and sold into perpetual bondage. Newspapers in the slave-labor States openly defended the measure, and the pulpit uttered its approval.

ARRIVAL OF NEGRO FUGITIVES WITHIN THE LINES

The President of the Presbyterian Theological Seminary at Columbia, South Carolina, Dr. James H. Thornwell, who died at the beginning of the Civil War, declared that it was his conviction that "the African slave-trade was the most worthy of all missionary societies." The "Southern Commercial Convention," held at Vicksburg in May, 1859, resolved that "all laws, State or Federal, prohibiting the African slave-trade, ought to be abolished." A grand jury in Savannah, who were compelled by law to indict several persons charged with complicity in the slave-trade, actually protested against the laws they were sworn to support, saying: "We feel humbled as men in the consciousness that we are freemen but in name, and that we are living, during the existence of such laws, under a tyranny as supreme as that of the despotic governments of the Old World. Heretofore the people of the South, firm in their consciousness of right and strength, have failed to place the stamp of condemnation upon such laws as reflect upon the institution of slavery, but have permitted, unrebuked, the influence of foreign opinion to prevail in their support." A Mississippi newspaper, the *True Southron*, in its earnestness for the cause, suggested the "propriety of *stimulating the zeal of the pulpit by founding a prize for the best sermon in favor of free-trade in negroes*," and the proposition was widely copied, with approval; while in many pulpits "zeal" was exhibited in the service of the slaveholders without the stimulus of an offered prize. And in the United States Senate, John Slidell, of Louisiana, one of the most effective civil leaders among the late Confederates, urged the propriety of withdrawing American cruisers from the coast of Africa, that the slave-traders there might not be molested; and President Buchanan's administration, inspired by men like Slidell, was made to serve the plans of the supporters of the slave-labor system, by protesting against the visitation, by British cruisers, of vessels bearing the American flag, on suspicion that they were "slavers." These visitations were made in accordance with a positive agreement between the two governments, that under such circumstances, visits should be made freely by either party.

This arrangement had been made for the purpose of more effectually suppressing the slave-trade then about to be opened by the "African Labor-Supply Association;" and in the summer of 1858, the British cruisers in the Gulf of Mexico were unusually vigilant. In the course of a few weeks they boarded about forty suspected American vessels. It was this activity, which promised to be an effectual bar to the reviving trade in slaves, that gave a pretext for the President to enter his protest. There was a cry raised against the "odious British doctrine of the right of search," and the British government, for "prudential reasons," put a stop to it. In this case it was only "the end" that "justified the means."

The Fugitive-Slave Law now began to bear bitter fruit, and it soon became one of the most prolific causes of the continually increasing controversies between the upholders and opposers of the slave-labor system. It was made more offensive by the evident intention of the friends of the institution everywhere to *nationalize* slavery; and the perversion of the obvious meaning of the vital doctrine of the Declaration of Independence, by the judicial branch of the government, while the executive branch was ready to lend his tremendous power in giving practical effect to the system, awakened in the breasts of the people of the free-labor States a burning desire to wipe the stain of human bondage from the escutcheon of the Republic. Seizures under the Fugitive-Slave Law were becoming more and more frequent, with circumstances of increasing injustice and cruelty. The business of arresting, and remanding to hopeless slavery, men, women and children, was carried on all over the free-labor States, and the people stood appalled. By that dreadful law, every man was compelled to become a slave-hunter, under certain

WASHINGTON IN THE SIXTIES. ORDNANCE DEPOT AT CITY POINT

conditions; and every kind-hearted woman who might give a cup of cold water or the shelter of a roof to a suffering sister fleeing from intolerable bondage, incurred the penalty of a felony!

This law became a broad cover under which the kidnapping of free persons of color was extensively carried on; and scores of men, women and children, born free, were dragged from their homes and consigned to hopeless bondage. Our public legal records are stained with the revolting details of the workings of the law; and the newspapers of the day contained accounts of many stirring events connected with the execution of it. The following facts will suffice as an illustration:

On a cold day in January, 1856, two slaves, with their wives and four children, all thinly clad, escaped from Kentucky into Ohio. They crossed the frozen river to Cincinnati, closely pursued by the master of three of them, on horseback. In Cincinnati, they were harbored by a colored man. Their retreat was discovered by the pursuing master, who repaired to the house with the United States marshal and his assistants, and demanded their surrender. They refused; and after a desperate struggle, the door was

CAMP OF 114TH PENNSYLVANIA VOLUNTEERS AT BRANDY STATION, VA.

broken open and the fugitives were secured. They had resolved to die rather than be taken back into slavery. The mother of the three children, in despair, tried, first to kill her offspring, and then herself. When she was seized, she had already slain one of her children with a knife—a beautiful little girl, nearly white in complexion—and had severely wounded the other two. A coroner's jury was called, who decided that the frantic mother had killed her child, and it was proposed to hold her for trial under the laws of Ohio. But it was discovered that the Fugitive-Slave Law had been made so absolute by the terms of its enactment and the opinion of the Chief Justice of the United States, that a State law could not interfere with it; so the mother and her surviving companions were remanded into slavery. They were taken across the Ohio River, and all traces of them were lost.

When the hideous character of the Fugitive-Slave Law, in all its aspects, became fully manifest, the public conscience was aroused to action, and righteous men and women all over the slave-labor States, shocked by a spectacle that disgraced a free people pretending to be civilized, protested as loudly as they dared; and the legislatures of several of the free-labor States adopted measures for relieving their citizens from the penalties imposed upon those who should refuse to become slave-catchers.

New York Harbor at the Opening of the War

By the terms of the Fugitive-Slave Law, the sacred right of trial by jury was denied to the man who was alleged to be a slave, and he had no redress. This was logical, for the Chief Justice of the United States had declared that the black man "had no rights which the white man was bound to respect." He had also declared that no State law could inter-fere with the operations of the Fugitive-Slave Act, or with slavery itself. This opinion was directly adverse to the letter and spirit of a statute in the code of the State of New York, which declared the immediate freedom of any slave when brought involuntarily within its borders. The Legislature of that State determined to sustain that statute, and boldly denounced the opinion of the Chief Justice, which denied citizenship to men of color who had descended from slaves. Ohio took similar action, and Maine, Massachusetts, Con necticut, Michigan and Wisconsin took strong ground in favor of the freedom of the slaves with in their borders, without assuming an attitude of actual resistance to the obnoxious act which every citizen was bound to obey so long as it remained unrepealed.

This movement in the Northern States naturally exasperated the slaveholders, and it was used by the politicians among them to create hot indignation in the hearts of the people in the slave-labor States. This, according to the testi-

TRACK AND BRIDGE DESTROYED ON THE VIRGINIA CENTRAL R. R.

mony of a personal friend of the author of the Fugitive-Slave Act (James M. Mason, of Virginia), was precisely what the peculiarly offensive features of that act were intended to effect. It was calculated that it would finally cause resistance to the measure on the part of the people of the free-labor States, and so give a plausible pretext for disunion, rebellion, and civil war, if necessary, on the part of the friends of the slave-labor system. This testimony was given to me orally, while standing among the ruins of Mr. Mason's house at Winchester, in 1866.

SCENE IN CAMP

GENERAL McMAHON'S HEADQUARTERS. 164TH NEW YORK VOLUNTEERS

GENERAL JAMES H. WILSON AND FRIENDS

CHAPTER III.

Public Quiet Broken by John Brown's Raid—Incidents of that Raid and Its Effects—The Republican Party—A Pretext for Revolution —Convention of Democrats at Charleston—Disruption of the Democratic Party—Incidents of the Plan—Nominations for President—Principles of the Parties—Lincoln Elected—Action of the Southern Politicians—Yancey's Mission—Fatal Power of the Politicians.

IN the fall of 1859, the feverishness in the public mind, excited by the vehement discussion of the topic of slavery, had somewhat subsided, when suddenly a rumor went out of Baltimore, as startling as a thunder peal on the genial October air, that the Abolitionists had seized the Government Armory and Arsenal at Harper's Ferry, at the junction of the Shenandoah and Potomac rivers, and that an insurrection of the slaves in Virginia was imminent.

The rumor was true. John Brown, of Ossawatamie, who had fought and won a battle on the Kansas prairie in 1856, had struck a blow at slavery, on Sunday evening, the 16th of October. Brown was a native of Connecticut, in the sixtieth year of his age, and had espoused the cause of the Abolitionists (as the opponents of the slave-labor system, who wished to abolish it, were called) in early life. He was enthusiastic, fanatical and brave. He had been active in the midst of the troubles in Kansas, and had suffered much; and he believed himself to be the destined liberator of the slaves in our Republic. With a few white followers and twelve slaves from Missouri, he went into Canada West, and at Chatham a convention of sympathizers was held in May, 1859, whereat a "Provisional Constitution and Ordinances for the People of the United States" was adopted, not, as the instrument declared, "for the overthrow of any government, but simply to amend and repeal." This was part of a scheme for promoting the uprising of the slaves for obtaining their freedom.

LOADING THE BIG GUN AT FORT CORCORAN

Brown spent the summer of 1859 in preparation for his work. He hired a farm a few miles from Harper's Ferry, where he was known by the name of "Smith." There, one by one, a few followers congregated stealthily; and pikes and other weapons were gathered, and ammunition was provided, with the intention of striking the first blow in Virginia, and arming the insurgent slaves. Under cover of profound darkness, Brown, at the head of seventeen white men and five negroes, entered the village of Harper's Ferry on that fatal Sunday night, put out the street lights, seized the Armory and the railway bridge, and quietly arrested and imprisoned in the Government buildings the citizens found here and there in the streets at the earliest hours of the next morning, each one ignorant of what had happened. The invaders had seized Colonel Washington, living a few miles from Harper's Ferry, with his arms and horses, and liberated his slaves; and at eight o'clock on Monday morning, the 17th of October, Brown and his few followers (among whom were two of his sons) had full possession of the village and Government works. When asked what was his purpose and by what authority he acted Brown replied, "To free the slaves, and by the authority of God Almighty." He felt assured that when the blow should be struck, the negroes of the surrounding country would rise and flock to his standard. He sincerely believed that a general uprising of the slaves of the whole country would follow, and that he would be a great liberator. He was mistaken.

The news of this alarming affair went speedily abroad, and before Monday night Virginia militia had gathered at Harper's Ferry in large numbers. Struggles between these and Brown's little company ensued, in which the two sons of the leader perished. The invaders were finally driven to the shelter of a fire-engine house, where Brown defended himself with great bravery. With one son dead by his side, and another shot through, he felt the pulse of his dying child with one hand, held his rifle with the other and issued oral commands to his men with all the composure of a general in his marquee, telling them to be firm and to sell their lives as dearly as possible.

"That We Here Highly Resolve That These Dead Shall Not Have Died in Vain"—Lincoln

CHRONOLOGICAL SUMMARY AND RECORD

Of Every Engagement Between the Troops of the Union and of the Confederacy, in the Civil War in the United States, Showing the Total Losses and Casualties in Each Engagement—The Whole Collated and Compiled from the Official Records of the War Department at Washington.

APRIL, 1861

12—Bombardment of Fort Sumter, S. C.   No casualties.

15—Evacuation of Fort Sumter, S. C.   *Union* 1 killed, 3 wounded. By premature explosion of cannon in firing a salute to the United States flag.

19—Riots in Baltimore, Md.   6th Mass., 26th Pa.   *Union* 4 killed, 30 wounded.   *Confed.* 9 killed.

MAY, 1861

10—Camp Jackson, Mo.   1st, 3d and 4th Mo. Reserve Corps, 3d Mo. Vols.   *Confed.* 639 prisoners.

Riots in St. Louis, Mo.   5th Mo., U. S. Reserves.   *Union* 4 killed. *Confed.* 27 killed.

JUNE, 1861

1—Fairfax C. H., Va.   Co. B. 2d U. S. Cav.   *Union* 1 killed, 4 wounded. *Confed.* 1 killed, 14 wounded.

3—Philippi, W. Va.   1st W. Va., 14th and 16th Ohio, 7th and 9th Ind. *Union* 2 wounded.   *Confed.* 16 wounded.

10—Big Bethel, Va.   1st, 2d, 3d, 5th and 7th N. Y., 4th Mass. Detachment of 2d U. S. Artil.   *Union* 16 killed, 34 wounded.   *Confed.* 1 killed, 7 wounded.

11—Romney, W. Va.   11th Ind.   *Union* 1 wounded.   *Confed.* 2 killed, 1 wounded.

17—Vienna, Va.   1st Ohio.   *Union* 5 killed, 6 wounded.   *Confed.* 6 killed.

Booneville, Mo.   2d Mo. (three months') Volunteers, Batteries H and L Mo. Light Artil.   *Union* 2 killed, 19 wounded.   *Confed.* 14 killed, 20 wounded.

Edwards Ferry, Md.   1st Pa.   *Union* 1 killed, 4 wounded.   *Confed.* 15 killed.

18—Camp Cole, Mo.   Home Guards.   *Union* 15 to 25 killed, 25 to 52 wounded.   *Confed.* 4 killed, 20 wounded.

26—Patterson Creek or Kelley's Island, Va.   11th Ind.   *Union* 1 killed, 1 wounded.   *Confed.* 7 killed, 2 wounded.

27—Matthias' Point, Va.   Gunboats *Pawnee* and *Freeborn*.   *Union* 1 killed, 4 wounded.

JULY, 1861

2—Falling Waters, Md., also called Haynesville or Martinsburg, Md.   1st Wis., 11th Pa.   *Union* 8 killed, 15 wounded.   *Confed.* 31 killed, 50 wounded.

5—Carthage or Dry Forks, Mo.   3d and 5th Mo., one battery of Mo. Artil. *Union* 13 killed, 31 wounded.   *Confed.* 30 killed, 125 wounded, 45 prisoners.

Newport News, Va.   1st Co. 9th N. Y.   *Union* 6 wounded.   *Confed.* 3 wounded.

6—Middle Creek Fork or Buckhannon, W. Va.   One Co. 3d Ohio.   *Union* 1 killed, 6 wounded.   *Confed.* 7 killed.

7—Great Falls, Va.   8th N. Y.   *Union* 2 killed.   *Confed.* 12 killed.

8—Laurel Hill or Bealington, W. Va.   14th Ohio, 9th Ind.   *Union* 2 killed, 6 wounded.

10—Monroe Station, Mo.   16th Ill., 3d Ia., Hannibal (Mo.) Home Guards. *Union* 3 killed.   *Confed.* 4 killed, 20 wounded, 75 prisoners.

11—Rich Mountain, Va.   8th, 10th and 13th Ind., 19th Ohio.   *Union* 11 killed, 35 wounded.   *Confed.* 60 killed, 140 wounded, 100 prisoners.

12—Barboursville or Red House, Va.   2d Ky.   *Union* 1 killed.   *Confed.* 10 killed.

Beverly, W. Va.   4th and 9th Ohio.   *Confed.* 600 prisoners.

14—Carrick's Ford, W. Va.   14th Ohio, 7th and 9th Ind.   *Union* 13 killed, 40 wounded.   *Confed.* 20 killed, 10 wounded, 50 prisoners.

16—Millsville or Wentzville, Mo.   8th Mo.   *Union* 7 killed, 1 wounded. *Confed.* 7 killed.

17—Fulton, Mo.   3d Mo. Reserves.   *Union* 1 killed, 15 wounded.

Scarrytown, W. Va.   2d Ky., 12th and 21st Ohio, 1st Ohio Battery. *Union* 9 killed, 38 wounded.

Martinsburg, Mo.   One Co. of 1st Mo. Reserves.   *Union* 1 killed, 1 wounded.

Bunker Hill, Va.   Detachment of Gen. Patterson's command.   *Confed.* 4 killed.

18—Blackburn's Ford, Va.   1st Mass., 2d and 3d Mich., 12th N. Y., Detachment of 2d U. S. Cav., Battery E 3d U. S. Artil.   *Union* 19 killed, 38 wounded, 26 wounded.   *Confed.* 15 killed, 53 wounded.

18 and 19—Harrisonville and Parkersville, Mo.   Van Horne's (Mo.) Battalion, Cass Co. Home Guards.   *Union* 1 killed.   *Confed.* 14 killed.

21—Bull Run or Manassas, Va.   2d Me., 2d N. H., 2d Vt., 1st, 4th and 5th Mass., 1st and 2d R. I., 1st, 2d and 3d Conn., 8th, 11th, 12th, 13th, 16th, 18th, 27th, 29th, 31st, 32d, 35th, 38th, and 39th N. Y., 2d, 8th, 14th, 69th, 71st and 79th N. Y. Militia, 27th Pa., 1st, 2d and 3d Mich., 1st and 2d Minn., 2d Wis., 1st and 2d Ohio, Detachments of 2d, 3d and 8th U. S. Regulars, Battalion of Marines, Batteries D, E, G and M, 2d U. S. Artil., Battery E, 3d Artil., Battery D, 5th Artil., 2d R. I. Battery, Detachments of 1st and 2d Dragoons.   *Union* 481 killed, 1,011 wounded, 1,460 missing and captured.   *Confed.* 269 killed, 1,483 wounded.   *Confed.* Brig.-Gens. Bee and Barton killed.

22—Forsyth, Mo.   1st Ia., 2d Kan., Stanley Dragoons, Totten's Battery. *Union* 3 wounded.   *Confed.* 5 killed, 10 wounded.

24—Blue Mills, Mo.   5th Mo. Reserves.   *Union* 1 killed, 12 wounded.

26—Lane's Prairie, near Rolla, Mo.   Home Guards.   *Union* 3 wounded. *Confed.* 1 killed, 3 wounded.

27—Fort Fillmore, N. Mex.   7th U. S. Inft. and U. S. Mounted Rifles, in all 400 men, captured by Confederates.

AUGUST, 1861

2—Dug Springs, Mo.   1st Ia., 3d Mo., five batteries of Mo. Light Artil. *Union* 4 killed, 37 wounded.   *Confed.* 40 killed, 41 wounded.

3—Messilla, N. Mex.   7th U. S. Inft. and U. S. Mounted Rifles.   *Union* 3 killed, 6 wounded.   *Confed.* 12 killed.

5—Athens, Mo.   Home Guards, 21st Mo.   *Union* 3 killed, 8 wounded. *Confed.* 14 killed, 14 wounded.

Point of Rocks, Md.   28th N. Y.   *Confed.* 3 killed, 2 wounded.

7—Hampton, Va.   20th N. Y.   *Confed.* 3 killed, 6 wounded.

8—Lovettsville, Va.   19th N. Y.   *Confed.* 1 killed, 5 wounded.

10—Wilson's Creek, Mo., also called Springfield and Oak Hill.   6th and 10th Mo. Cav., 2d Kan. Mounted Vols., one Co. of 1st U. S. Cav., 1st Ia., 1st Kan., 1st, 2d, 3d and 5th Mo., Detachments of 1st and 2d U. S. Regulars, Mo. Home Guards, 1st Mo. Light Artil., Battery F 2d U. S. Artil.   *Union* 223 killed, 721 wounded, 291 missing.   *Confed.* 265 killed, 800 wounded, 30 missing.   *Union* Brig.-Gen. Nathaniel Lyon killed.

Potosi, Mo.   Mo. Home Guards.   *Union* 1 killed.   *Confed.* 2 killed, 3 wounded.

17—Brunswick, Mo.   5th Mo. Reserves.   *Union* 1 killed, 7 wounded.

19—Charlestown or Bird's Point, Mo.   22d Ill.   *Union* 1 killed, 6 wounded. *Confed.* 40 killed.

20—Hawk's Nest, W. Va.   11th Ohio.   *Union* 3 wounded.   *Confed.* 1 killed, 3 wounded.

26—Cross Lanes or Summerville, W. Va.   7th Ohio.   *Union* 5 killed, 40 wounded, 200 captured.

27—Ball's Cross Roads, Va.   Two Co.'s 23d N. Y.   *Union* 1 killed, 2 wounded.

28 and 29—Fort Hatteras, N. C.   9th, 20th and 99th N. Y. and Naval force. *Union* 1 killed, 2 wounded.   *Confed.* 5 killed, 51 wounded, 715 prisoners.

29—Lexington, Mo.   Mo. Home Guards.   *Confed.* 8 killed.

31—Munson's Hill, Va.   Two Cos. 23d N. Y.   *Union* 2 killed, 2 wounded.

SEPTEMBER, 1861

1—Bennett's Mills, Mo.   Mo. Home Guards.   *Union* 1 killed, 8 wounded.

Boone C. H., W. Va.   1st Ky.   *Union* 6 wounded.   *Confed.* 30 killed.

2—Dallas, Mo.   11th Mo.   *Union* 2 killed.

Dry Wood or Ft. Scott, Mo.   5th and 6th Kan., one Co. of 9th Kan. Cav., 1st Kan. Battery.   *Union* 4 killed, 9 wounded.

Beher's Mills.   13th Mass.   *Confed.* 3 killed, 5 wounded.

10—Carnifex Ferry.   9th, 10th, 12th, 13th, 28th and 47th Ohio.   *Union* 16 killed, 102 wounded.

11—Lewinsville, Va.   19th Ind., 3d Vt., 65th N. Y., 79th N. Y. Militia. *Union* 6 killed, 8 wounded.

12—Black River, near Ironton, Mo.   Three Cos. 1st Ind. Cav.   *Confed.* 5 killed.

12 and 13—Cheat Mountain, W. Va.   13th, 14th, 15th and 17th Ind., 3d, 6th, 24th and 25th Ohio, 2d W. Va.   *Union* 9 killed, 12 wounded. *Confed.* 80 wounded.

13—Booneville, Mo.   Mo. Home Guards.   *Union* 1 killed, 4 wounded. *Confed.* 12 killed, 30 wounded.

14—Confederate Privateer *Judah* destroyed near Pensacola, Fla., by the U. S. Flag-ship *Colorado*.   *Union* 3 killed, 15 wounded.

15—Pritchard's Mills, or Darnestown, Va.   28th Pa., 13th Mass.   *Union* 1 killed.   *Confed.* 8 killed, 75 wounded.

12 to 20—Lexington, Mo.   23d Ill., 8th, 25th and 27th Mo., 13th and 14th Mo. Home Guards, Berry's and Van Horne's Mo. Cav., 1st Ill. Cav. *Union* 42 killed, 108 wounded, 1,624 missing and captured.   *Confed.* 25 killed, 75 wounded.

17—Morristown, Mo.   5th, 6th and 9th Kan. Cav., 1st Kan. Battery. *Union* 2 killed, 6 wounded.   *Confed.* 7 killed.

Blue Mills, Mo.   3d Ia.   *Union* 11 killed, 39 wounded.   *Confed.* 10 killed, 60 wounded.

18—Barboursville, W. Va.   Ky. Home Guards.   *Union* 1 killed, 1 wounded. *Confed.* 7 killed.

21 and 22—Papinsville or Osceola, Mo.   5th, 6th and 9th Kan. Cav.   *Union* 17 killed.

(Continued in Section 2)

Born April 27, 1822.　　GENERAL ULYSSES SIMPSON GRANT　　Died at Mt. McGregor, N. Y., July 23, 1885.

CHAPTER III.—Continued.

ON Monday evening, Colonel Robert E. Lee arrived at Harper's Ferry, with ninety United States marines and two pieces of artillery. The doors of the engine-house were forced open, and Brown and

his followers were captured. He was speedily indicted for murder and treason; was found guilty, and on the 3d of December (1859) he was hanged at Charlestown, not far from the scene of his exploits. The most exaggerated reports of this raid went over the land. Terror spread throughout Virginia. Its governor (Henry A. Wise) was excited almost to madness, and declared that he was ready to make war on all the free-labor States. In a letter to President Buchanan, written on the 25th of November, he declared he had authority for believing that a conspiracy to rescue John Brown existed in Ohio, Pennsylvania, New York and other States.

Brown was suspected of being an emissary of the Abolitionists, and attempts were made to implicate leaders of the Republican party and the inhabitants of the free-labor States generally in a scheme for liberating the slaves. A committee of the United States Senate, with the author of the Fugitive-Slave Law (James M. Mason) at its head, was appointed to investigate the subject. The result was positive proof that Brown had no accomplices and only about twenty-five followers.

INFLATING PROF. LOWE'S WAR BALLOON

John Brown's attempt to free the slaves was a crazy one in itself, and utterly failed, but it led to events that very soon brought about the result he so much desired. His bitterest enemies acknowledged that he was sincere, and a real hero, and he became, in a manner, the instrument of deliverance of millions from bondage. His effort aroused the slumbering party spirit of the combatants for and against slavery to great activity, and at the beginning of 1860, a remarkable and growing strength of the Republican party was everywhere manifested. Its central idea of universal freedom attracted powerful and influential men from all other political parties, for it bore a standard around which persons differing in other things might gather in perfect accord.

The elections held in 1858 and 1859 satisfied the opponents of this party that they were rapidly passing to the position of a hopeless minority, and that the domination in the National Councils which the friends of the slave-system had so long enjoyed would speedily come to an end.

The sagacious leaders of the pro-slavery party in the South, who had been for years forming plans and preparing a way for a dissolution of the Union, so as to establish the great slave-empire of their dreams within the Golden Circle (to be noticed presently), believed that they would not be able to elect another President of their choice, and that the time had come for the execution of their destructive scheme. A pretext more plausible than that of the violations of the Fugitive-Slave Act at the North afforded them, must be had, for that act had become too odious in the estimation of righteous men and women in all parts of the Union to inspire them with a desire for its maintenance. No such pretext existed, and the politicians in

FAMOUS WAR BALLOON "INTREPID"

Prof. Lowe's Balloon Gas Generators Nos. 7 and 8

the slave-labor States deliberately prepared to create one, which, they knew, would be powerful. At that time they were in full alliance with the Democratic party of the North, which was then in power. If it should remain a unit and the fraternal relations with the Southern wing of the party should continue undisturbed, there might be a chance for the supremacy of the coalition awhile longer. But there were omens already of a speedy dismemberment of the Democratic party, for the Fugitive-Slave Law and the attempt to nationalize slavery had produced wide-spread defection in their ranks. A large portion of that party, led by Senator Stephen A. Douglas, showed a proclivity toward independent action, and even of affiliation with the Republican party on the subject of slavery; and the hopes of the friends of that system, of the undivided support of the Northern Democracy, vanished.

In view of this impending crisis, the Southern politicians deemed it expedient to destroy absolutely all unity in the Democratic party and make it powerless, when the Republicans might elect their candidate for the Presidency in the fall of 1860. Then would appear the pretext for a revolution—the election of a *sectional* President. Then the plausible war-cry

NAVAL BATTERY IN FRONT OF YORKTOWN

might be raised—"No sectional President! No Northern domination! Down with the Abolitionists!" This would appeal to the hearts and interests of the Southern people, especially to the slave-holding class, "fire the Southern heart," and produce, as they believed, a "solid South" in favor of breaking up the old Republic and forming an empire whose "corner-stone should be slavery." With this end in view, leading politicians in the South, who afterward appeared conspicuous among the confederated enemies of the National Government during the Civil War, entered the Democratic National Convention assembled at Charleston, South Carolina, on the 23d of April, 1860, for the purpose of nominating a candidate for the Presidency of the United States and setting forth an embodiment of political principles.

On the appointed day, almost six hundred chosen representatives of the Democratic party assembled in Convention in the hall of the South Carolina Institute, in Charleston, and chose Caleb Cushing, of Massachusetts, their chairman. It was evident from the first hour after the organization of the Convention that the spirit of Mischief was there enthroned; and observing ones soon discovered omens of an impending tempest which might topple from its foundations the organization known as the Democratic party.

The choice of Mr. Cushing as chairman was very satisfactory to the friends of the slave-system in the Convention. He was a statesman of great experience, and then sixty years of age; a scholar of wide and varied culture, and a sagacious observer of men. Because he had joined the Democratic party at the time of Mr. Tyler's defection; had been a conspicuous advocate of the war with Mexico and other measures for the extension and perpetuation of the system of slavery, he was regarded by the Southern men in the Convention as their fast political friend and coadjutor; but when they made war upon the unity of the Republic the next year, he gave his influence in support of the National Government.

Mr. Cushing, in his address on taking the chair in the Convention, declared it to be the mission of the Democratic party "to reconcile popular freedom with constituted order" and to maintain "the sacred reserved rights of the sovereign States." He declared that the Republicans were "laboring to overthrow the Constitution" and "aiming to produce in this

ROBERT TOOMBS OF THE FIRST
CONFEDERATE CABINET

JOHN BROWN'S FORT AT HARPER'S FERRY

country a permanent sectional conspiracy—a traitorous sectional conspiracy—of one-half of the States of the Union against the other half; who, impelled by the stupid and half-insane spirit of faction and fanaticism, would hurry our land on to revolution and to civil war." He declared it to be the "high and noble part of the Democratic party of the Union to withstand—to strike down and conquer—these banded enemies of the Constitution."

These utterances were warmly applauded by the Convention, excepting by the extreme pro-slavery wing. *They* did not wish to "strike down" the Republican party. They had a more important scheme to foster. It was their wish to "strike down" the Democratic party, for the moment, by dividing it. They had come instructed to demand from the Convention a candidate and an avowal of principles which should promise a guaranty for the speedy recognition by the National Government and the people, in a

DEPARTURE FROM THE OLD HOMESTEAD

practical way, of the system of slavery as a national institution. They knew that the most prominent candidate before the Convention, for the nomination, was Stephen A. Douglas of Illinois, who was committed to an opposing policy, and that he and his friends would never vote for such a "platform"—such an avowal of principles. They also knew that his rejection by the representatives of the slaveholders would split the Democratic party, and they resolved to act in accordance with these convictions. They held the dissevering wedge in their

own hands, and they determined to use it with effect.

A committee composed of one delegate from each State was appointed to prepare a platform of principles for the action of the Convention. A member from Massachusetts (Mr. Butler) proposed in that committee to adopt the "Cincinnati Platform" agreed to by the Convention that nominated Mr. Buchanan, and which committed the Democratic party to the doctrine of "Popular Sovereignty;" that is to say, the doctrine of the right of the people of any

GROUP OF N. Y. 71ST VOLUNTEERS

Territory of the Republic to decide whether slavery should or should not exist within its borders. Now was offered the opportunity for entering the dissevering wedge, and it was applied. When the vote was taken on the proposition of Mr. Butler, it was rejected by seventeen States (only two of them free-labor States) against fifteen. This was followed on the part of the majority by an offer to adopt the "Cincinnati Platform," with additional resolutions declaring in the spirit of Judge Taney's opinion, that Congress nor any other legislative body had a right to interfere with slavery *anywhere*, or to impair or destroy the right of property in slaves by any legislation. This proposition virtually demanded of the Democratic party the recognition of slavery as a sacred, permanent and national institution.

It was now clearly perceived that the politicians of the slave-labor States were united, evidently by pre-concert, in a determination to wring from the people of the free-labor States further and more revolting concessions to the greed of the pro-slavery faction for political domination. The manhood of the minority was evoked, and they resolved that the limit of concession was reached, and that they would yield no further. That minority, composed wholly of delegates from the free-labor States, and representing a

GENERAL VIEW OF HARPER'S FERRY

majority of the Presidential electors (172 against 127), offered to adopt the "Cincinnati Platform," and a resolution expressing a willingness to abide by any decision of the Supreme Court of the United States on questions of Constitutional law.   They also offered to adopt another resolution, denouncing the laws

BRIDGE ACROSS CHICKAHOMINY RIVER

passed by Northern legislatures in opposition to the Fugitive Slave Act.   Mr. Butler opposed making even these concessions to their arrogant demands.   The consequence was, the committee went into the Convention with three reports—a majority and minority report, and a report from Mr. Butler.

The debate upon these reports was opened by the chairman of the majority committee (Mr. Avery of North Carolina), who assured the Convention that if the doctrine of Popular Sovereignty should be adopted as the doctrine of the Democratic party, the members of the Convention from the slave-labor States and their constituents, would consider it as dangerous and subversive of their rights, as the adoption of the principle of Congressional interference or prohibition.   The debate continued until the 29th (April, 1860), and on the morning of the 30th the vote was taken in the presence of an immense audience with which the hall was packed.   Mr. Butler's report was first acted upon, and rejected.   Then the minority report was presented by Mr. Samuels of Iowa, and adopted by a decided majority.   Preconcerted rebellion immediately lifted its head, and the delegates from Alabama, led by L. Pope Walker (afterward the Confederate Secretary of War), seceded and left the Convention.

This secession was followed by delegates from the other slave-labor States, and they all reassembled at St. Andrew's Hall to prepare for an independent political organization. The disruption of the Democratic party represented in the Convention was now complete. The slavery question had split it beyond hope of restoration; an event which had been provided for, in secret, by the politicians. When D. G. Glenn, of the Mississippi delegation, announced the secession of the representatives from that State, he said: "I tell Southern members, and, for them, I tell the North, that in less than sixty days you will find a united South standing side by side with us." These utterances called forth long and vehement cheering, especially from the South Carolinians; and that night Charleston was the theatre of great rejoicings, for the leaders there comprehended the significance of the movement.

On the following day, the

MAP OF HARPER'S FERRY

GENERAL GEORGE B. McCLELLAN

seceders, with James A. Bayard of Delaware at their head, organized what they called a "Constitutional Convention;" sneered at the body they had left, as a "Rump Convention," and on the 3d of May adjourned to meet in Richmond, Virginia, in June. The regular Convention also adjourned, without making a nomination, to meet at Baltimore on the 18th of June.

The seceders reassembled in Richmond on the 11th of June. Robert Toombs and other Congressmen had issued an address from Washington city, urging the Richmond Convention to refrain from all important action there, but to adjourn to Baltimore, and there re-enter the Convention from which they had withdrawn, and, if possible, defeat the nomination of Mr. Douglas. This high-handed measure was resorted to; and when the Richmond Convention adjourned, most of the delegates hastened to Baltimore, and claimed the right to re-enter the Convention from which they had formally withdrawn. The South Carolina delegates remained in Richmond to watch the course of events and manage the scheme.

BRIDGE BUILT BY THE 15TH N. Y. ENGINEERS
CHICKAHOMINY RIVER

At the appointed time the regular Convention assembled at Baltimore, with Mr. Cushing in the chair. The question arose as to the right of the seceders to re-enter the Convention. Some were favorable to their admission; others proposed to admit them provided they would pledge themselves to abide by the decision of the majority. A stirring time ensued, and the matter was referred to a committee, a majority of whom reported in favor of admitting Douglas delegates from the slave-labor States in place of the seceders. In the course of a vehement debate that ensued, a slave-trader from Georgia warmly advocated the policy of reopening the African slave-trade, and his sentiments were loudly applauded. The majority report was adopted, when a large number of delegates from the border slave-labor States withdrew. This was followed the next morning (June 23, 1860) by the withdrawal of Mr. Cushing and a majority of the Massachusetts delegation. "We put our withdrawal before you," Mr. Butler said, "upon the simple ground, among others, that there has been a withdrawal, in fact, of a majority of the States; and further (and that perhaps more personal to myself) upon the ground that I will not sit in a convention where the African slave trade, which is piracy by the laws of my country, is approvingly advocated."

Vice-President Tod, of Ohio, now took Mr. Cushing's place at the head of the Convention, which proceeded to nominate Stephen A. Douglas, of Illinois, for President by an almost unanimous vote. Herschel V. Johnson of Georgia was afterward nominated for Vice-President. Meanwhile the seceders, young and old, had reassembled, called Mr. Cushing to the Chair, denominated their body the National Democratic Convention, and proceeded to nominate John C. Breckenridge of Kentucky for President, and Joseph Lane of Oregon for Vice-President. A recent political organization calling themselves the "National Constitutional Party" had already nominated (May 9, 1860) John Bell of Tennessee for President, and Edward Everett of Massachusetts for Vice-President. A week later (May 16) a vast concourse of Republicans assembled in an immense building erected for the purpose in Chicago, and called the "Wigwam," nominated Abraham Lincoln of Illinois for President, and Hannibal Hamlin of Maine for Vice-President.

By a series of resolutions, the Republican Convention took a position in direct antagonism to the avowed principles of the friends of the slave-system and the extra-judicial opinion of Chief-Justice Taney. They declared that each State had absolute control over its own domestic affairs; that the new political dogma, averring that the National Constitution, of its own force, carried slavery into the Territories of the Republic, was a dangerous political heresy, revolutionary in its tendency, and subversive of the peace and harmony of the country; that the normal condition of all the territory of the United States is that of freedom, and that neither Congress, nor a Territorial legislature, nor any individuals have authority to give legal existence to slavery in any Territory of the Union; and that the reopening of the African slave-trade, then recently commenced in the Southern States, as we have seen, under cover of the National flag, was a crime against humanity, and a burning shame to our country and age.

There were now four candidates for the Presidency in the field. The Democratic party was hopelessly

BATTERY AT ANNAPOLIS

split in twain.   The Douglas wing made no positive utterances concerning the status of slavery in the Territories; and the party led by Bell and Everett declined to express any opinions upon any subject. Their motto was—*The Constitution of the Country, the Union of the States, and the Enforcement of the Laws.*

SCENE AT SAVAGE STATION, JUNE, 1862

Only the earnest and determined wing of the Democratic party led by Breckenridge and of the Republican party led by Lincoln, showed a really aggressive spirit born of absolute convictions. The Southern portion of the former had resolved to nationalize slavery or destroy the Union; the latter declared that there was "an irrepressible conflict between freedom and slavery," and that the Republic could not exist "half slave and half free."   This was the real issue; and after one of the most exciting political campaigns ever witnessed in our country, from June until November, Mr. Lincoln was elected Chief Magistrate of the United States by a large majority over the other candidates, with Mr. Hamlin as Vice-President. An analysis of the popular vote showed that three-fourths of the whole number were given to men opposed to the extension of slavery.   This significant fact notified the friends of the slave-system that the days of their political domination in the councils of the nation had ended, perhaps forever, and they acted accordingly.

Such is a brief outline history of the conspiracy of Southern politicians to divide the Democratic party; give victory to the Republican party; cause the election of a "sectional President," and so afford a plausible pretext for a premeditated attempt to dissolve the Union and destroy the Republic.   Thus far their schemes had worked to their satisfaction; it now remained for them to "fire the Southern heart" and produce a "solid South" in favor of emancipation from what they were pleased to call the tyranny of a "sectional party" led by a "sectional President."   This accomplished, they would be ready to raise the arm to give the fatal blow to the existence of the Republic.

The leading men who brought upon the Southern people and those of the whole country the horrors of a four-years Civil War, with all its terrible devastation of life, property and national prosperity, were few in number, but wonderfully productive of their kind.   They were then, or had been, connected with the National Government, some as legislators and others as cabinet ministers.   They were not so numerous at first, said Horace Maynard, a loyal Tennesseean, in a speech in Congress, "as the figures on a chess-board.   There are those within reach of my voice," he said, "who also knew them, and can testify to their utter perfidy; who have been the victims of their want of principle, and whose self-respect has suffered from their insolent and overbearing demeanor.   No Northern man was ever admitted to their confidence, and no Southern man unless it became necessary to keep up their numbers; and then not till he was thoroughly known by them, and known to be thoroughly corrupt.   They, like a certain school of ancient philosophers, had two sets of principles or doctrines—one for outsiders and one for themselves; the one was 'Democratic principles' for the Democratic party, the other was for their own and without a name. Some Northern men and some Southern men were, after a fashion, petted and patronized by them, as a gentleman throws from his table a bone, or a choice bit, to a favorite dog; and they imagined they were conferring a great favor thereby, which would be requited only by the abject servility of the dog.   To hesitate, to doubt, to hold back, to stop, was to call down a storm of wrath that few men had the nerve to encounter, and still fewer the strength to withstand.   Not only in political circles, but in social life, their rule was inexorable, their tryanny absolute.   God be thanked for the brave men who had the courage to meet them and bid thcm defiance, first at Charleston in April, 1860, and then at Baltimore, in June! To them is due the credit of declaring war against this intolerable despotism."

During the canvass in the summer and autumn of 1860, pro-slavery politicians traversed the free-labor States and disseminated their views without hindrance.   Among the most daring and outspoken of these was William L. Yancey of Alabama, who was a fair type of politicians in other Southern States who, by vehemence of manner and sophistry in argument, misled the people.   He was listened to with patience by the people of the North, and was treated kindly everywhere; and when he returned to the South, he labored incessantly with tongue and pen to stir up the people to rebellion, saying in substance, as he had

GROUP OF 22D NEW YORK VOLUNTEERS

written two years before: "Organize committees all over the Cotton States; fire the Southern heart; instruct the Southern mind; give courage to each other; and at the proper moment, by one organized, concerted action, precipitate the Cotton States into revolution."

The "proper moment" was near at hand. Mr. Lincoln was elected by a large majority over each candidate, and was chosen in accordance with the letter and spirit of the National Constitution; yet,

EXAMINING PASSES AT GEORGETOWN FERRY

because he received nearly a million of votes less than did all of his opponents combined, the cry was raised by the Southern politicians, that he would be a usurper when in office because he had not received a majority of the aggregate votes of the people; that his antecedents, the principles of the Republican platform, the fanaticism of his party and his own utterances, all pledged him to wage an unrelenting warfare upon the system of slavery and rights of the slave-labor States, with all the powers of the National Government at his command. They said, in effect, to the people, through public oratory, the pulpit, and the press, "Your rights and liberties are in imminent danger—'to your tents, O Israel!'"

While these alarming assertions were fearfully stirring the inhabitants of the Southern States, the politicians were rejoicing because their plans were working so admirably, and they immediately set about the execution of their long-cherished scheme for the dissolution of the Union. All active loyalty to the Government was speedily suppressed by an organized system; and the promise of a North Carolina Senator (Clingman), that Union men should be hushed by "the swift attention of Vigilance Committees," was speedily fulfilled. In this work the Press and the Pulpit were powerful auxiliaries; and by these accepted oracles of wisdom and truth, thousands of men and women were led into an attitude of rebellion against their government. To quiet their scruples the doctrine of "State Supremacy" had been, for a long time, vehemently preached by the politicians and their allies, and the people were made to believe that their allegiance was primarily due to their respective States, and not to the National Government. "Perhaps there never was a people," wrote a resident of a slave-labor State in the third year of the Civil War that ensued, "more bewitched, beguiled and befooled, than we were when we drifted into this rebellion."

CHAPTER IV.

The Pretext for Disunion—True Reasons—State-Rights Associations—Desires for a Royal Government and Aristocratic Privileges—Early Preparations for Disunion—Secret Conferences—Sentiments of Virginians—Congratulatory Despatches on Lincoln's Election—Excitement in Charleston—Public Offices Abdicated—A State Convention Authorized—Secret Doings of Secessionists—Movements in South Carolina—State Supremacy and Its Effects—Events in Georgia—Toombs and Stephens—Movements toward Secession in Various States—Southern Methodists—Initial Steps for Disunion in South Carolina—Dishonorable Propositions—Vigilance Committees—Secession Assured.

THERE is direct evidence to prove that the politicians of South Carolina and elsewhere had been making preparations for revolt many years, and that the alleged violations of the Fugitive-Slave Act and the election of Mr. Lincoln were made only pretexts for stirring up "the common people" to support and do the fighting for them. The testimony of speakers in the Convention at Charleston that declared the secession of that State from the Union was clear and explicit. "It is not an event of a day," said Robert Barnwell Rhett, one of the most violent declaimers of his class; "it is not anything produced by Mr. Lincoln's election, or by the non-execution of the Fugitive-Slave Law. It is a matter which has been gathering head for thirty years. . . . In regard to the Fugitive-Slave Law, I myself doubted its constitutionality, and doubted it on the floor of the Senate when I was a member of that body. The States, acting in their sovereign capacity, should be responsible for the rendition of slaves. This was our best security." Another member of the Convention (Francis S. Parker) said: "It is no spasmodic effort that has come suddenly upon us; it has been gradually culminating for a long period of thirty years." John A. Inglis, the chairman of the committee that drew up the South Carolina Ordinance of Secession,

GENERAL BENJAMIN F. BUTLER

said: "Most of us have had the matter under consideration for the last twenty years." And Lawrence M. Keit, one of the most active of the younger politicians, declared: "I have been engaged in this movement ever since I entered political life."

When President Buchanan in his annual message in December, 1860, declared that "the long-continued and intemperate interference of the Northern people with the question of slavery in the Southern States" had produced the estrangement which had led to present troubles, the assertion was claimed by the poli-ticians in the slave-labor States to be untrue. Senator Hammond, of South Carolina, had declared in a speech in October, 1858, that the discussion of slavery at the North had been very useful to them. After speaking of the great value of slavery to the cotton States, he observed: "Such has been for us the happy results of the Abolition discussion. So far our gain has been immense from this contest, savage and malignant as it has been. Now we have solved already the question of emancipation [from connection with the Northern States] by this re-examination and exposition of the false theories of religion, political economy, which embarrassed the fathers in their days. At the North and in Europe, they cried havoc, and let loose upon us all the dogs of war. And how stands it now? Why, in this very quarter of a century, our slaves have doubled in numbers, and each slave has more than doubled in value." In July, 1859, Alexander H. Stephens,

BLOCK HOUSE NEAR AQUEDUCT BRIDGE, POTOMAC RIVER

of Georgia, said he was not one of those who believed that the South had sustained any injury by these agitations. "So far," he said, "from the institution of African slavery in our section having been weakened or rendered less secure by the discussion, my deliberate judgment is that it has been greatly strengthened and fortified." Earl Russell, the British Premier, in a letter to Lord Lyons at Washington, in May, 1861, said that one of the Confederate commissioners told him that "the principal of the causes which led to secession was not slavery, but the very high price which, for the sake of protecting Northern manufactures, the South was obliged to pay for the manufactured goods which they required."

De Bow's Review was the acknowledged organ of the slave interest. In its issue for February, 1861, George Fitzhugh, a leading publicist of Virginia, commenting on the President's message, said: "It is a gross mistake to suppose that Abolition is the cause of dissolution between the North and the South. The Cavaliers, Jacobites and the Huguenots who settled the South, naturally hate, contemn, and despise the Puritans who settled the North. The former are master races; the latter a slave race, the descendants of the Saxon serfs." Mr. Fitzhugh added: "Our women are far in advance of our men in their zeal for disunion. They fear not war, for every one of them feels confident that when their sons or husbands are called to the field, they will have a faithful body-guard in their domestic servants. Slaves are the only body-guard to be relied on. . . . They [the women] and the clergy lead and direct the disunion movement." The *Charleston Mercury*, edited by a son of Barnwell Rhett, and the chief organ of the conspirators of South Carolina, scorning the assertion that anything so harmless as "Abolition twaddle" had caused any sectional feelings, declared, substantially, that it was an abiding consciousness of the degradation of the "chivalric Southrons" being placed on an equality in government with "the boors of the North" that made "Southern gentlemen" desire disunion. It said haughtily, "We are the most aristocratic people in the world. Pride of caste, and color, and privilege makes every man an aristocrat in feelings."

It was by men of this cast of mind that "Southern Rights" associations were formed, and were fostered for nearly thirty years before the Civil War, with disunion as their prime object. The feeling of contempt for the Northern *masses* among the "chivalric Southrons" was more intense in South Carolina than elsewhere. The self-constituted leaders of the people there, who hated democracy and a republican form of government, who yearned for the pomps of royalty and the privileges of an hereditary aristocracy, and who had persuaded themselves and the "common people" around them that they were superior to

GENERAL DAVID B. BIRNEY

all others on the continent as patterns of gentility, refinement, courtly manners, grace and every characteristic of the highest ideal of chivalry, had for many years yearned for separation from the vulgar North. William H. Trescott, who was Assistant Secretary of State under Buchanan, and one of the most active members of the "Southern Rights Association" of South Carolina (the avowed object of which was the destruction of the unity of the Republic), said, in an address before the South Carolina Historical Society in 1859: "More than once has the calm self-respect of old Carolina breeding been caricatured by the consequential insolence of vulgar imitators."

ENGINEER CORPS MAKING CORDUROY ROADS

This was the common tone of thought among the leading South Carolinians. Dr. Russell, writing to the London *Times* at the close of April, 1861, said: "Their admirations on the English model, for privileged classes, and for a landed aristocracy and gentry, is undisguised and apparently genuine. Many would go back to-morrow, if we could.' An intense affection for the love of British habits for British sentiment, civilization and literature distinguish the inhabitants in their descent from three islands, whose fortunes they still follow, and with whose members they maintain, not unfrequently, familiar relations, regard with an aversion which it is impossible to give an idea of to one who has not seen its manifestations, the people of New England and the population of the Northern States, whom they regard as tainted beyond cure with the venom of Puritanism." There was a prevailing voice, Dr. Russell wrote, that said, "If we could only get one of the royal race of England to rule over us, we should be content." That sentiment, he wrote, "varied a hundred ways, has been repeated to me over and over again."

So early as May, 1851, when there were active preparations in South Carolina for revolt, Muscoe R. H. Garnett, of Virginia, wrote to Mr. Trescott, then a leader of the "Southern Rights Association" in the first-named State, expressing his fears that Virginia would not consent to engage in the movement. The Legislature did not favor it, but he expressed the hopeful opinion that the law-makers did not reflect the sentiments of the people of the State. "In the East, at least," he said, "the great majority believe in the right of secession, and feel the deepest sympathy with Carolina in opposition to measures which they regard as she does. But the West—West Virginia—here is the rub!—*only sixty thousand slaves to four hundred and ninety-four thousand whites!* When I consider this fact, and the kind of argument which we have heard in this body, I cannot but regard with the greatest fear the question, whether Virginia would assist Carolina in such an issue. I must acknowledge, my dear sir, that I look to the future with almost as much apprehension as hope. You will object to the term *Democrat*. Democracy, in its original philosophical sense, is incompatible with slavery and the whole system of Southern society. . . . I do not hesitate to say that if the question is raised between Carolina and the Federal Government, and the latter prevails, the last hope of Republican government and, I fear, of Southern civilization is gone."

The restless spirits of South Carolina continued to confer secretly with the politicians of the slave-labor States on the subject of disunion; and finally, in November, 1859, the Legislature of that State openly resolved that "the commonwealth was ready to enter, together with other slave-holding States, or such as desire prompt action, into the formation of a Southern Confederacy." The Carolinians were specially anxious to secure the co-operation of the Virginians; and in January following, at the request of the Legislature, the governor of the State sent C. G. Memminger as a special commissioner to Virginia, for the purpose of enlisting its representatives in the scheme of disunion. With protestations of attachment to the Union, Mr. Memminger invited the Virginians to co-operate in a convention of delegates from slave-labor States to "take action for their defence;" in other words, to secede from the Union. He made an able plea, addressed to their reason, their passions, and their prejudices, and concluded by saying, "I have delivered into the keeping of Virginia the cause of the South." But the Virginians did not desire a Southern Confederacy wherein free-trade in African slaves would prevail, for it would seriously interfere

OFFICERS OF THE 4TH NEW YORK VOLUNTEERS

with the profitable inter-state traffic in negroes. So they hesitated; and in an autograph letter before me, Mr. Memminger wrote to the editor of the *Charleston Mercury*, that the Democratic party in Virginia was "not a unit," that "Federal politics" made that "great State comparatively powerless," and that he saw "no men who would take the position of *leaders in a revolution.*"

GENERAL ROBERT E. LEE

I have cited these few utterances from speakers and writers who were participants or contemporaries with the actors in the events of the late Civil War, that the reader may have a key to the real causes which brought about that war. These seem to have been chiefly a desire on the part of the slave-holders to be freed from social and political contact with the people of the free-labor States (whom they regarded as less cultivated, refined, chivalric and civilized than themselves), with perfect freedom to extend and perpetuate the system of slave-labor, and revive, without hindrance, the African slave-trade. Notwithstanding the *Charleston Mercury*, at the beginning, gave greater prominence to the first-named cause, after more than three years of war (February, 1864), it was constrained to say: "South Carolina entered into this struggle *for no other purpose than to maintain the institution of slavery.* Southern independence has no other object or meaning. . . . Independence and slavery must stand or fall together."

When the election of Mr. Lincoln was certified, the political leaders in South Carolina were eager to begin the contemplated revolution. To be prepared for immediate action, an extraordinary session of the Legislature was assembled at Columbia on the 5th of November; and as the news of the result of the election went over the land, the governor of the State received congratulatory despatches from other commonwealths wherein the politicians were in

"THOSE WHO GAVE THEIR LIVES THAT THE NATION MIGHT LIVE"—LINCOLN

SCENES IN CAMP, ARMY OF THE POTOMAC, AUGUST TO DECEMBER, 1863

sympathy with the Secessionists. "North Carolina will secede," a despatch from Raleigh said. "A large number of Bell men have declared for secession; the State will undoubtedly secede," said another from the capital of Alabama. Another from Milledgeville, Georgia, said: "The hour for action has come. This State is ready to assert her rights and independence. The leading men are eager for the business." "There is a great deal of excitement here," said a despatch from Washington city; "several extreme Southern men, in office, have donned the palmetto cockades and declared themselves ready to march South." A

CHRIST CHURCH, ALEXANDRIA, VA., WHERE WASHINGTON ATTENDED

despatch from Rich-mond said: "If your State se-cedes, we will send you troops and volunteers to aid you." "Placards are posted about the city," said a message from New Orleans, "calling a convention of those favorable to the organi-zation of a corps of minute-men." A second mes-sage from Washington said: "Be firm; a large quantity of arms will be shipped South from the Arsenal here to-mor-row. The President is perplexed. His feelings are with the South, but he is afraid to assist them openly." So was revealed the

fact that simultaneous action in favor of disunion had been preconcerted. As these despatches came, one after the other, to Columbia, and were immediately forwarded to Charleston, a blaze of pleasurable excitement was kindled among the citizens of the latter place. The palmetto flag, the emblem of the sovereignty of the State, was everywhere displayed. From the thronged streets went up cheer after cheer for a Southern Confederacy. All day long on the 7th of November, when it was known that Mr. Lincoln was elected, the citizens were harangued in the open air and in public halls, the speakers portraying the glories of State independence. Flags and banners, martial music, and the roar of cannon attested the general joy; and that night blazing bonfires and illuminations lighted up the city. Multitudes of palmetto cockades (made of blue silk ribbon, with a button in the centre bearing the figure of a palmetto tree) were worn in the streets of Charleston. Public offices under the Government of the United States were closed, or transferred to the "sovereign State" of South Carolina, in the most formal manner. On the 7th of November, Judge McGrath, of the United States District Court, solemnly resigned his office, saying to the jurors: "For the last time I have, as judge of the United States, administered the laws of the United States within the limits of South Carolina. So far as I am concerned, the temple of justice raised under the Constitution of the United States is now closed." He then laid aside his judicial gown and retired. The collector of customs at Charleston resigned at the same time; so also did the attorney-general. So it was that before a convention to consider the secession of the State from the Union had been authorized, the Secessionists, with plans matured, acted as if disunion had been already accomplished.

The Legislature of South Carolina assembled at Columbia on the day after Mr. Lincoln's election, when joint resolutions of both houses providing for a State Convention to consider the withdrawal of the State from the Union were offered. Some of the more cautious members counselled delay, but they were overborne by the more fiery zealots, who did not wish the popular excitement caused by the election to cool before the decisive step should be taken. One of the latter (Mr. Mullins, of Marion), in a speech against delay and waiting for the co-operation of other States, revealed the fact that an overwhelming majority of the inhabitants of the State were opposed to the schemes of the politicians. He also revealed the important fact that emissaries had been sent to Europe to prepare the way for aid and recognition by foreign governments of the contemplated Southern Confederacy. "We have it from high authority,"

General Winfield Scott Hancock

he said, "that the representative of one of the imperial powers of Europe [France], in view of the prospective separation of one or more of the Southern States from the present Confederacy, has made propositions in advance for the establishment of such relations between it and the government about to be established in this State, as will insure to that power such a supply of cotton for the future as their increasing demand for that article will require." He urged the importance of immediate action. "If we wait for co-operation," he said, "Slavery and State rights will be abandoned; State sovereignty and the cause of the South lost forever." James Chestnut, a member of the United States Senate, recommended immediate secession; and W. W. Boyce, of the National House of Representatives, said: "I think the only policy for us is to arm as soon as we receive authentic intelligence of the election of Lincoln. It is for South Carolina, in the quickest manner and by the most direct means, to withdraw from the Union."

Other members of the Legislature were equally vehement; and on the 12th of November (1860) an act was passed authorizing a Convention. The Legislature also formulated the doctrine of "State Sovereignty" or State Supremacy, in a resolution that declared that a "Sovereign State" of the Union had a right to secede from it, adopting as its own the doctrine that the States of the Union are not subordinate to the National Government; were not created by it, and do not belong to it; that *they* created

CAPTURED GUNS AT WASHINGTON ARSENAL

the National Government; from them it derives its powers; to them it is responsible, and when it abuses the trust reposed in it, they, as equal sovereigns, have a right to resume the powers respectively delegated to it by them. This is the sum and substance of the doctrine of State Supremacy ("State Rights," as it was adroitly called) which dwarfs patriotism to the narrow dimensions of a single State, denationalizes the American citizen, and opposes the fundamental principles upon which the founders of the Republic securely built our noble superstructure of a free, powerful and sovereign Commonwealth. And it perverts the plain meaning of the Preamble to the National Constitution, which declares that the *people* (not States) of the whole country had given vitality to that fundamental law of the land, and to the nation. James Madison, one of the founders of the Republic, in a letter to Edmund Randolph in April, 1787, wrote: "I hold it for a fundamental point, that an individual independence of the States is utterly irreconcilable with the idea of aggregate sovereignty." And Washington wrote in a letter to John Jay, in March, 1787, on the subject of the National Constitution: "A thirst for power, and the bantling—I had liked to have said the *monster*—sovereignty, which have taken such fast hold of the States individually, will, when joined by the many whose personal consequence in the line of State politics will, in a manner, be annihilated, form a strong phalanx against it."

The politicians in other slave-labor States followed the example of South Carolina in immediate preparations for secession. Robert Toombs, then a National Senator, was one of the chief conspirators

HEADQUARTERS OF GEN. J. H. WARD.

HEADQUARTERS 1ST BRIGADE HORSE ARTILLERY.

HEADQUARTERS OF 1ST BRIGADE HORSE ARTILLERY.

HEADQUARTERS 1ST BRIGADE HORSE ARTILLERY

against the life of the nation, and by violent harangues aided materially in bringing upon his State (Georgia) the awful calamities of war.   In a speech at Milledgeville on the 13th of November, he exclaimed, "Withdraw your sons from the army, from the navy, and from every department of the Federal public service. Keep your own taxes in your own coffers.   Buy arms with them, and throw the bloody spear into this den of incendiaries and assassins [the Northern people], and let God defend the right. . . . . *Twenty years of labor, and toils, and taxes, all expended upon preparation*, would not make up for the advantage the enemy would gain if the rising sun on the 5th of March should find you in the Union.   Then strike while it is yet time."   Then he cried: "I ask you to give me the sword; for if you do not give it to me, as God lives, I will take it myself!"   In the war that ensued, the sword was given him, with the commission of a brigadier-general; and it is on record that Mr. Toombs, acting upon the maxim that "Prudence is the better part of valor," was never known to remain longer than he was compelled to in a place of danger to himself.   On the following evening, Alexander H. Stephens, a man of conservative views and equal

COMPANY OF INDIANA VOLUNTEERS

courage, in a speech in favor of the Union, exposed the many misstatements of Mr. Toombs, and touched the fiery Georgian and others to the quick, with the Ithuriel spear of truth, when he said: "Some of our public men have failed in their aspirations; that is true, and from that comes a great part of our troubles."

The Georgia Legislature followed the example of South Carolina in ordering a Convention to consider secession.   So, also, did the Legislatures of Mississippi and Alabama.   L. Q. C. Lamar, a representative in Congress of the people of the first-named State, submitted to the inhabitants, before the close of November, a plan for a Southern Confederacy; and a few days before the election of delegates to the Alabama Convention, the Conference of the "Methodist Church South," sitting at Montgomery, resolved that they believed "African Slavery, as it existed in the Southern States of the Republic, to be a wise, humane and righteous institution, approved of God, and calculated to promote, in the highest possible degree, the welfare of the slave." They also resolved: "Our hearts are with the South; and should they ever need our hands to assist in achieving our independence, we shall not be found wanting in the hour of danger."

The politicians of Florida, with those of Louisiana and Texas, followed in the wake of the leaders in the other four States named, in preparing for secession, all of them asserting the right of their respective

BATTERY NO. 4 IN FRONT OF YORKTOWN

States to secede because they had "created the National Government." The fallacy of this claim is apparent when we remember that Mississippi, Alabama, Louisiana, Texas and Florida did not exist, even in territorial form, as parts of the Union, when the National Government was created, and that three of them belonged to foreign governments at that time. North Carolina, one of the original thirteen States, joined South Carolina and Georgia, her ancient sisters, in providing for a Convention; and the governors of all the slave-labor States, excepting those of Delaware and Maryland, who had been elected by the Democratic party, showed their readiness to act in concert with the Secessionists. It was soon ascertained that the President of the Republic, and a majority of his cabinet, were ready to declare that the National Constitution did not give the Chief Magistrate authority to stay the arm of insurrection or rebellion by coercive measures.

Such is a brief outline history of the preparations by politicians in the slave-labor States, for marshalling a combined host for the overthrow of the Republic. The important initial step was taken by those of South Carolina. When the Legislature authorized a Convention, orators of every grade immediately

VIEWS OF FORT PULASKI

went out to harangue the people in all parts of the State. Motley crowds of men, women and children—Caucasian and African—listened, in excited groups, at cross-roads, court-houses, and other usual gathering places. Every speech was burdened with complaints of "wrongs suffered by South Carolina in the Union;" her right and her duty to leave it; her power to "defy the world in arms;" and the glory that would illumine her whole domain in that near future when her independence of the thralls of the "detested Constitution" should be secured. Their themes were as various as the character of their audiences. One of their orators, addressing the slaveholders in Charleston, said: "Three thousand millions of property is involved in this question; and if you say at the ballot-box that South Carolina shall not secede, you put into the sacrifice three thousand millions of your property. . . . . The Union is a dead carcass, stinking in the nostrils of the South. . . . . Ay, my friends, a few weeks more, and you will see floating from the fortifications the ensign that now bears the Palmetto, the emblem of a Southern Confederacy." The *Charleston Mercury* called upon all natives of South Carolina in the army or navy to resign their commissions and join in the revolt. "The mother looks to her sons," said this fiery organ of sedition, "to protect her from outrage. . . . . She is sick of the Union—disgusted with it, upon any terms within the range of the widest possibility." This call was responded to by the resignation of the commissions of many South Carolinians;

CENTRAL SIGNAL STATION WASHINGTON, D. C.

and the leaders in the revolutionary movements in that State, seemingly unable to comprehend the principles of honor and fidelity—the highest virtues of a soldier—boasted that "not a son of that State would prove loyal to the old flag." They were amazed when men like the late Admiral Shubrick, a native of South Carolina, refused to do the bidding of disloyal politicians, while they commended the action of Lieutenant J. R. Hamilton of the navy, another "son" of South Carolina, who, at Fortress Monroe, issued a circular letter to his fellow "Southrons" in the marine service, in which, after writing much of honor, counselled them to follow his example, to engage in plundering the Government, in these words: "What the South asks of you now is, to *bring with you every ship and man you can*, that we may use them against the oppressors of our liberties, and the enemies of our aggravated but united people."

Vigilance committees were speedily organized to discover and suppress every anti-secession sentiment and movement in South Carolina; and before the close of November these committees were in active operation, clothed with extraordinary powers, as "guardians of Southern rights." Their officers possessed full authority to decide all questions brought before them, and their decision was "final and conclusive." The patrols had power to arrest all suspicious white persons and bring them before the Executive Committee for trial; to suppress all "negro preachings, prayer-meetings, and all congregations of negroes that may be considered unlawful by the patrol companies," the latter having unrestricted authority to "correct and punish all slaves, free negroes, mulattoes and mestizoes, as they may deem proper."

The powers of these vigilance committees were soon felt. Northern men suspected of feelings opposed to the secession movements were banished from the State, and some who were believed to be "Abolitionists" were tarred and feathered. The committees having authority to persecute, soon made the expressed sentiment in South Carolina "unanimous in favor of secession;" and the *Charleston Mercury* was justified in saying to the army and navy officers from that State, in the service of the Republic, when calling them home: "You need have no more doubt of South Carolina's going out of the Union than of the world's turning round. *Every man that goes to the Convention will be a pledged man*—pledged for immediate separate State secession, in any event whatever."

This promise was uttered before the members of the Convention had been chosen. Everything had been arranged by the politicians; the *people* had nothing to do with it. The *Southern Presbyterian*, a theological publication of wide influence, issued at Columbia, said, on the 15th of December, that it was well known that every member of the Convention was pledged to pass an ordinance of secession, and added: "It is a matter for devout thankfulness that the Convention will embody the very highest wisdom and character of the State; private gentlemen, judges of her highest legal tribunals and ministers of the Gospel." Even almost the very day when the ordinance of secession would be adopted was known to those who were engaged in the business. In a letter to me, written on the 13th of December, the late William Gilmore Simms, the distinguished South Carolina scholar, said: "In ten days more South Carolina will have certainly seceded; and in a reasonable interval after that event, if the forts in our harbor are not surrendered to the State, they will be taken."

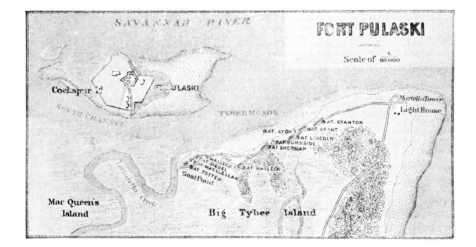

FORT PULASKI

CHRONOLOGICAL SUMMARY AND RECORD—Continued

SEPTEMBER, 1861—*Continued from Section 1*

22—Eliott's Mills or Camp Crittenden, Mo. 7th Ia. *Union* 1 killed, 5 wounded.

23—Romney or Hanging Rock, W. Va. 4th and 8th Ohio. *Union* 3 killed, 50 wounded. *Confed.* 35 killed.

25—Chapmansville, W. Va. 1st Ky., 34th Ohio. *Union* 4 killed, 9 wounded. *Confed.* 20 killed, 50 wounded.

26—Lucas Bend, Ky. Stewart's Cavalry. *Confed.* 4 killed.

29—Camp Advance, Munson's Hill, Va. 69th Pa., through mistake, fire into the 71st Pa., killing 9 and wounding 25.

OCTOBER, 1861

3—Greenbrier, W. Va. 24th, 25th and 32d Ohio, 7th, 9th, 13th, 14th, 15th and 17th Ind., Battery G, 4th U. S. Artil., Battery A, 1st Mich. Artil. *Union* 8 killed, 32 wounded. *Confed.* 100 killed, 75 wounded.

4—Alamosa, near Ft. Craig, N. Mex. Mink's Cav. and U. S. Regulars. *Confed.* 11 killed, 30 wounded.
Buffalo Hill, Ky. *Union* 20 killed. *Confed.* 50 killed.

8—Hillsborough, Ky. Home Guards. *Union* 3 killed, 2 wounded. *Confed.* 11 killed, 29 wounded.

9—Santa Rosa, Fla. 6th N. Y., Co. A 1st U. S. Artil., Co. H 2d U. S. Artil., Co.'s C and E 3d U. S. Inft. *Union* 14 killed, 29 wounded. *Confed.* 350 wounded.

12—Cameron, Mo. James' Cav. *Union* 1 killed, 4 wounded. *Confed.* 8 killed.
Upton Hill, Mo. 39th Ind. *Confed.* 5 killed, 3 wounded.
Bayles' Cross Roads, La. 79th N. Y. *Union* 4 wounded.

13—Beckwith Farm (12 miles from Bird's Point), Mo. Tuft's Cav. *Union* 2 killed, 5 wounded. *Confed.* 1 killed, 2 wounded.
West Glaze, also called Shanghai, or Henrytown, or Monday's Hollow, Mo. 6th and 10th Mo. Cav. Fremont Battalion Cav. *Confed.* 62 killed.

15—Big River Bridge, near Potosi, Mo. Forty men of 38th Ill. *Union* 1 killed, 6 wounded, 33 captured. *Confed.* 5 killed, 4 wounded.
Lime Creek, Mo. 13th Ill. Inft., 6th Mo. Cav. *Confed.* 63 killed, 40 wounded.

16—Bolivar Heights, Va. Parts of 28th Pa., 3d Wis., 13th Mass. *Union* 4 killed, 7 wounded.
Warsaw, Mo. *Confed.* 3 killed.

17 to 21—Fredericktown and Ironton, Mo. 17th, 20th, 21st, 33d and 38th Ill., 8th Wis., 1st Ind. Cav., Co. A 1st Mo. Light Artil. *Union* 6 killed, 60 wounded. *Confed.* 200 wounded.

19—Big Hurricane Creek, Mo. 18th Mo. *Union* 2 killed, 14 wounded. *Confed.* 14 killed.

21—Ball's Bluff, also called Edwards Ferry, Harrison's Landing, Leesburg, Va. 15th, 20th Mass., 40th N. Y., 71st Pa., Battery B, R. I. Artil. *Union* 223 killed, 226 wounded. *Confed.* 36 killed, 264 wounded, 445 captured and missing. *Union* Acting Brig.-Gen. E. D. Baker killed.

22—Buffalo Mills, Mo. *Confed.* 17 killed.

23—West Liberty, Ky. 2d Ohio, 1st and Loughlin's Ohio Cav., 1st Ohio Artil. *Union* 2 wounded. *Confed.* 10 killed, 5 wounded.
Hodgeville, Ky. Detach. 6th Ind. *Union* 3 wounded. *Confed.* 3 killed, 5 wounded.

25—Zagonyi's Charge, Springfield, Mo. Fremont's Body Guard and White's Prairie Scouts. *Union* 18 killed, 37 wounded. *Confed.* 106 killed.

26—Romney or Mill Creek Mills, W. Va. 4th and 8th Ohio, 7th W. Va., Md. Volunteers, 2d Regt. of Potomac Home Guards, and Ringgold (Pa.) Cav. *Union* 2 killed, 15 wounded. *Confed.* 20 killed, 15 wounded, 50 captured.
Saratoga, Ky. 9th Ill. *Union* 4 wounded. *Confed.* 8 killed, 17 wounded.

27—Plattsburg, Mo. *Confed.* 8 killed.
Spring Hill, Mo. 1st Co. of 7th Mo. Cav. *Union* 5 wounded.

29—Woodbury and Morgantown, Ky. 17th Ky., 3d Ky. Cav. *Union* 1 wounded.

NOVEMBER, 1861

1—Renick, Randolph Co., Mo. *Union* 14 wounded.

6—Little Santa Fé, Mo. 4th Mo., 5th Kan. Cav., Kowald's Mo. Battery. *Union* 2 killed, 6 wounded.

7—Belmont, Mo. 22d, 27th, 30th and 31st Ill., 7th Ia., Battery B 1st Ill. Artil., 2d Co. 15th Ill. Cav. *Union* 90 killed, 173 wounded, 235 missing. *Confed.* 261 killed, 427 wounded, 278 missing.
Galveston Harbor, Tex. U. S. Frigate *Santee* burned the *Royal Yacht.* *Union* 1 killed, 8 wounded. *Confed.* 3 wounded.
Port Royal, S. C. Bombardment by U. S. Navy. *Union* 8 killed, 23 wounded. *Confed.* 11 killed, 39 wounded.

9—Piketown or Fry Mountain, Ky. 2d, 21st, 33d and 59th Ohio, 16th Ky. *Union* 4 killed, 26 wounded. *Confed.* 18 killed, 45 wounded, 200 captured.

10—Guyandott, W. Va. Recruits of 9th W. Va. *Union* 7 killed, 20 wounded. *Confed.* 8 killed, 10 wounded.
Gauley Bridge, W. Va. 11th Ohio, 2d Ky. Cav. *Union* 2 killed, 16 wounded.

11—Little Blue, Mo. 110 men of the 7th Kan. Cav. *Union* 7 killed, 9 wounded.

12—Occoquan Creek, Va. Detach. 1st N. Y. Cav. *Union* 3 killed, 1 wounded.

17—Cypress Bridge, Ky. *Union* 10 killed, 15 wounded.

18—Palmyra, Mo. Detach. 3d Mo. Cav. *Confed.* 3 killed, 5 wounded.

19—Wirt C. H., W. Va. Detach. 1st W. Va. Cav. *Confed.* 1 killed, 5 wounded.

23—Ft. Pickens, Pensacola, Fla. Cos. C and E 3d U. S. Inft., Cos. G and I 6th N. Y., Batteries A, F and L 1st U. S. Artil., and C, H and K 2d U. S. Artil. *Union* 5 killed, 7 wounded. *Confed.* 5 killed, 93 wounded.

24—Lancaster, Mo. 21st Mo. *Union* 1 killed, 2 wounded. *Confed.* 13 killed.

26—Little Blue, Mo. 7th Kan. Cav. *Union* 1 killed, 1 wounded.
Drainesville, Va. 1st Pa. Cav. *Confed.* 2 killed.

29—Black Walnut Creek, near Sedalia, Mo. 1st Mo. Cav. *Union* 15 wounded. *Confed.* 17 killed.

DECEMBER, 1861

3—Salem, Mo. Detach. 10th Mo. Cav. *Union* 6 killed, 10 wounded. *Confed.* 16 killed, 20 wounded.
Vienna, Va. Detach. 3d Pa. Cav. *Union* all captured. *Confed.* 1 killed.

4—Anandale, Va. 30 men of 3d N. J. *Union* 1 killed. *Confed.* 7 killed.
Dunksburg, Mo. Citizens repulse raiders. *Confed.* 7 killed, 10 wounded.

11—Bertrand, Mo. 2d Ill. Cav. *Union* 1 wounded.

13—Camp Allegheny or Buffalo Mountain, W. Va. 9th and 13th Ind.. 25th and 32d Ohio, 2d W. Va. *Union* 20 killed, 107 wounded. *Confed.* 20 killed, 96 wounded.

17—Rowlett's Station, also called Mumfordsville or Woodsonville, Ky. 32d Ind. *Union* 10 killed, 22 wounded. *Confed.* 33 killed, 50 wounded.

18—Milford, also called Shawnee Mound, or Blackwater, Mo. 27th Ohio, 8th, 18th, 22d and 24th Ind., 31st Kan., 1st Ia. Cav., Detach. U. S. Cav., 2 Batteries of 1st Mo. Lt. Artil. *Union* 2 killed, 8 wounded. *Confed.* 1,300 captured.

20—Drainesville, Va. 1st, 6th, 9th, 10th and 12th Pa. Reserve Corps, 1st Pa. Artil., 1st Pa. Cav. *Union* 7 killed, 61 wounded. *Confed.* 43 killed, 143 wounded.

21—Hudson, Mo. Detach. 7th Mo. Cav. *Union* 5 wounded. *Confed.* 10 killed.

22—Newmarket Bridge, near Newport News, Va. 20th N. Y. *Union* 6 wounded. *Confed.* 10 killed, 20 wounded.

24—Wadesburg, Mo. Mo. Home Guards. *Union* 2 wounded.

28—Sacramento, Ky. 3d Ky. Cav. *Union* 1 killed, 8 wounded. *Confed.* 30 killed.
Mt. Zion, Mo. Birge's Sharpshooters, 3d Mo. Cav. *Union* 5 killed, 63 wounded. *Confed.* 25 killed, 150 wounded.

JANUARY, 1862

1—Port Royal, S. C. 3d Mich., 47th, 48th and 79th N. Y., 50th Pa. *Union* 1 killed, 10 wounded.

4—Huntersville, Va. Detachments of 25th Ohio, 2d W. Va. and 1st Ind. Cav. *Union* 1 wounded. *Confed.* 1 killed, 7 wounded.
Bath, Va., also including skirmishes at Great Cacapon Bridge, Alpine Station and Hancock. 39th Ill. *Union* 2 killed, 2 wounded. *Confed.* 30 wounded.
Calhoun, Mo. *Union* 10 wounded. *Confed.* 30 wounded.

7—Blue Gap, near Romney, Va. 4th, 5th, 7th and 8th Ohio, 14th Ind., 1st W. Va. Cav. *Union* 2 killed. *Confed.* 15 killed.
Jennies' Creek, Ky., also called Paintsville. Four Cos. 1st W. Va. Cav. *Union* 3 killed, 1 wounded. *Confed.* 6 killed, 14 wounded.

8—Charleston, Mo. 10th Ia. *Union* 8 killed, 16 wounded.
Dry Forks, Cheat River, W. Va. One Co. of 2d W. Va. Cav. *Union* 6 wounded. *Confed.* 6 killed.
Silver Creek, Mo., also called Sugar Creek, and Roan's Tan Yard. Detachments of 1st and 2d Mo., 4th Ohio, 1st Iowa Cav. *Union* 5 killed, 6 wounded. *Confed.* 80 wounded.

9—Columbus, Mo. 7th Kan. Cav. *Union* 5 killed.

10—Middle Creek and Prestonburg, Ky. 40th and 42d Ohio, 14th and 22d Ky. *Union* 2 killed, 25 wounded. *Confed.* 40 killed.

19 and 20—Mill Springs, Ky., also called Logan's Cross Roads, Fishing Creek, Somerset and Beech Grove. 9th Ohio, 2d Minn., 4th Ky., 10th Ind., 1st Ky. Cav. *Union* 38 killed, 194 wounded. *Confed.* 190 killed, 160 wounded. *Confed.* Gen. F. K. Zollikoffer killed.

22—Knob Noster, Mo. 2d Mo. Cav. *Union* 1 killed.

29—Occoquan Bridge, Va. Detachments of 37th N. Y. and 1st N. J. Cav. *Union* 1 killed, 4 wounded. *Confed.* 10 killed.

FEBRUARY, 1862

1—Bowling Green, Ky. One Co. of 2d Ind. Cav. *Confed.* 3 killed, 2 wounded.

6—Fort Henry, Tenn. U. S. Gunboats *Essex, Carondelet, Saint Louis, Cincinnati, Conestoga, Tyler* and *Lexington.* *Union* 40 wounded. *Confed.* 5 killed, 11 wounded.

8—Linn Creek, Va. Detachment of 5th W. Va. *Union* 1 killed, 1 wounded. *Confed.* 8 killed, 7 wounded.
Roanoke Island, N. C. 21st, 23d, 24th, 25th and 27th Mass., 10th Conn., 9th, 51st and 53d N. Y., 9th N. J., 51st Pa., 4th and 5th R. I., U. S. Gunboats *Southfield, Delaware, Stars and Stripes, Louisiana, Hetzel, Commodore Perry, Underwriter, Valley City, Commodore Barney, Hunchback, Ceres, Putnam, Morse, Lockwood, J. N. Seymour, Granite, Brinker, Whitehead, Shawseen, Pickett, Pioneer, Hussar, Vidette, Chasseur.* *Union* 35 killed, 200 wounded. *Confed.* 16 killed, 39 wounded, 2,527 taken prisoners.

10—Elizabeth City or Cobb's Point, N. C. U. S. Gunboats *Delaware, Underwriter, Louisiana, Seymour, Hetzel, Shawseen, Valley City, Putnam, Commodore Perry, Ceres, Morse, Whitehead* and *Brinker.* *Union* 3 killed.

13—Blooming Gap, Va. 8th Ohio, 7th W. Va., 1st W. Va. Cav. *Union* 2 killed, 5 wounded. *Confed.* 13 killed.

14—Flat Lick Fords, Ky. 49th Ind., 6th Ky. Cav. *Confed.* 4 killed, 4 wounded.

14, 15 and 16—Fort Donelson, Tenn. 17th and 25th Ky., 11th, 25th, 31st, and 44th Ind., 2d, 7th, 12th and 14th Iowa, 1st Neb., 58th and 76th Ohio, 8th and 13th Mo., 8th Wis., 8th, 9th, 11th, 12th, 17th, 18th, 20th, 28th, 29th, 30th, 31st, 41st, 45th, 46th, 48th, 49th, 57th and 58th Ill., Batteries B and D 1st Ill. Art., D and E 2d Ill. Artil., four Cos. Ill. Cav., Birge's Sharpshooters and six gunboats. *Union* 446 killed, 1,735 wounded, 150 missing. *Confed.* 231 killed, 1,007 wounded, 13,829 prisoners. *Union* Maj.-Gen. John A. Logan wounded.

(Continued in Section 3)

GUNBOAT AT ALEXANDRIA

CHAPTER V.

Secession Convention in South Carolina—Proceedings of the Convention—Ordinance of Secession Adopted—Public Excitement—Signing the Ordinance—Anxiety of the Loyal People—Secretary Cobb's Schemes—President's Message: Its Tone and Reception—The Attorney-General's Opinion—Movements of the People and the Clergy—Proceedings in South Carolina—Declaration of Independence—Nationality of South Carolina Proclaimed—Events in Charleston Harbor—Secretary Floyd's Treachery—Transfer of Troops to Fort Sumter—The Secessionists Foiled—Floyd Succeeded by Holt.

ON the 3d of December, 1860, delegates to the State Convention of South Carolina were chosen. They met at Columbia, the capital, on the 17th, and chose David F. Jamison president of their body. When he was about to administer an oath to the delegates, a serious difficulty was presented.

The Constitu-provided that, the Constitution That require-leaders in the away by ex-come here to port one." The the object of without the scious that the them to be an and their acts binding upon President addressed the taking the chair, saying: "I can-

tion of the State of South Carolina on such occasions, an oath to support of the United States must be taken. ment was like a cobweb before the movement; and the difficulty was swept Governor Adams, who said: "We have break down a government, not to sup-delegates were all of one mind concerning their assemblage; so they proceeded solemnity of an oath of any kind, con-fundamental law of their State declared unlawful body, were not any one.

Jamison briefly Convention on and closed by not offer you movement, than ment of the to dare! and words were the Convention, was raging as an ately proposed delegates (W. P. shall be sneered chivalry of proof against first train the Charleston.

anything better, in inaugurating this the words of Danton at the commence-French Revolution: 'To dare! and again without end to dare!'" These brave followed by considerable excitement in for intelligence came that the small-pox epidemic in Columbia. It was immedi-to adjourn to Charleston. One of the Miles) begged them not to flee. "We at," he said; and exclaimed, "Is this the South Carolina?" But chivalry was not fear of the loathsome disease, and by the next morning, the delegates all fled to

PARAPET AND SEA VIEW, FORT SUMTER

The Convention proceeded to business by appointing several committees to consider various subjects, such as the relations of South Carolina to the United States in regard to public property within the limits of that State, and commercial relations; also their connection with the people of other slave-holding States. A committee was also chosen, with John A. Inglis as chairman, to report the form of an ordinance of secession. After debating some questions, and proposing a provisional government for the States that might follow the example of South Carolina in seceding; to send commissioners to Washington city to negotiate with the National Government for the cession of its property within the State of South Carolina, and to elect delegates to meet others from slave-labor States for the purpose of forming a Southern Con-

Major Robert Anderson

federacy, the proper committee reported an ordinance of secession in the following words, in accordance with the theory of State supremacy:

"We, the people of the State of South Carolina, in convention assembled, do declare and ordain, and it is hereby declared and ordained, that the ordinance adopted by us in convention, on the 23d day of May, in the year of our Lord one thousand seven hundred and eighty-eight, whereby the Constitution of the United States was ratified, and also all acts and parts of acts of the General Assembly of the State, ratifying amendments of the said Constitution, are hereby repealed, and the Union now subsisting between South Carolina and other States, under the name of the United States of America, is hereby dissolved."

DESTRUCTION OF RAIL ROAD ROLLING STOCK ON THE ORANGE AND ALEXANDRIA R. R.

It was noon on the 20th of December, 1860, when this ordinance was submitted. At a quarter before one o'clock, it was adopted by the unanimous voice of the Convention, one hundred and sixty-nine delegates voting in the affirmative. They were then assembled in St. Andrew's Hall. It was proposed that the members should walk in procession to Institute Hall, and there, at seven o'clock in the evening, in the presence of the constituted authorities of the State and of the people, to sign it—"the great Act of Deliverance and Liberty."

The cry at once went forth, *"The Union is dissolved!"* It was echoed and re-echoed in the streets of Charleston, and was sent upon the wings of lightning all over the Republic. Placards announcing the fact were posted throughout the city of Charleston, and again the people of that town were almost wild with excitement. All business was suspended, and huzzas for a "Southern Confederacy" filled the air. Women appeared in the streets with secession bonnets, the invention of a Northern milliner in Charleston. Flags waved; church-bells pealed merrily, and cannon boomed; and some enthusiastic young men went to the grave of John C. Calhoun, in St. Philip's church-yard, and forming a circle around it, made a solemn vow to devote their "lives, their fortunes and their sacred honor" to the cause of "South Carolina independence."

Before night the ordinance of secession was engrossed on a sheet of parchment; and at the appointed time, in the evening, Institute Hall was crowded with eager spectators to witness the signing of the instrument. Back of the president's chair was suspended a banner of cotton cloth, on which was painted a significant device. At the bottom was a mass of broken and discolored blocks of hewn stones, on each of which were the name and arms of a free-labor State. Rising from this mass were two columns made of perfect blocks of stone, each bearing the name and arms of a slave-labor State. The keystone of an arch that crowned the two columns had the name and arms of South Carolina upon it, and it bore a figure of Calhoun. In the space between the columns was a palmetto tree, with a rattlesnake coiled around its trunk, and on a ribbon the words, "Southern Republic." Beneath all, in large letters, were the significant words, *"Built from the Ruins."*

This flag foreshadowed the designs of the Secessionists to overthrow the Republic and build an empire

General Hatch's Headquarters, Charleston, S. C.

upon its ruins whose corner-stone should be slavery. To that end the members of the Convention proceeded to sign the ordinance in the presence of the governor of the State, the members of the Legislature, and other dignitaries of the land. When the act was finished there was deep silence. Then the Rev. Dr. Bachman, with white flowing locks, advanced on the platform whereon the president sat, and with uplifted hands implored Almighty God to bless the people engaged in the act and to favor the undertaking. Then President Jamison exhibited the instrument to the people, read it, and said: "The Ordinance of Secession

TRANSPORTS ON THE JAMES, MONITOR IN THE DISTANCE

has been signed and ratified, and I proclaim the State of South Carolina an independent commonwealth." The people shouted their approval; and so closed the first great act in the terrible drama of the great Civil War. A few months afterward, every building in Charleston in which public movements for the destruction of the Union had taken place was accidentally destroyed by fire; and late one evening in 1866, after the "Confederate States of America," organized in Montgomery early in 1861, had become a thing of the past, I heard the mournful voice of a screech-owl in the blackened tower of the Circular Church which stood within a few rods of the grave of Calhoun in St. Philip's church-yard.

In the meantime, the National capital had become the theatre of stirring events. The proceedings of the Southern politicians had been watched by the loyal people of the country with intense interest and anxiety, especially by the mercantile and manufacturing classes. To these the Southern planters and merchants were indebted to the amount of full two hundred million dollars, and at the middle of November, remittances from the South had almost ceased, owing to various causes. Howell Cobb, one of the most active of the secret enemies of the Republic, was then Mr. Buchanan's Secretary of the Treasury, and had adroitly managed to strike a paralyzing blow at the public credit, months before Mr. Lincoln's election. When he entered the cabinet in 1857, he found the Government coffers so overflowing, that the treasury notes next due were bought in; in the autumn of 1860, the treasury was empty, and he was in the market as a borrower of money to carry on the ordinary operations of the Government. His management had created such distrust in financial circles, that he was compelled to pay ruinous premiums at a time when money was never more abundant in the country.

This wrecking of the Government by destroying its credit was a part of Cobb's financial scheme for the benefit of his associate Secessionists. Another of his schemes for the supposed benefit of the South was foreshadowed in a letter (the original is before me), written by William H. Trescott, then Assistant Secretary of State, to the editor of the *Charleston Mercury*, dated "Washington, Nov. 1, 1860." In that letter, by permission of Mr. Cobb, Mr. Trescott gives that gentleman's views concerning the situation. After some remarks about deferring overt acts of rebellion until the 4th of March following, Mr. Trescott wrote: "Mr. Cobb desires me to impress upon you his conviction that any attempt to precipitate the actual issue upon this Administration will be most mischievous—calculated to produce differences of opinion and destroy unanimity. *He thinks it of great importance that the cotton crop should go forward at once, and that the money should be in the hands of the people, that the cry of popular distress shall not be heard at the outset of this move.*" Mr. Cobb's motive for his recommendation is made apparent by the fact that it was a common practice for the cotton planter to receive pay for his crops in advance. The crop then to "go forward" was already paid for. The money to be received on its delivery was for the *next year's crop, which would never be delivered.* It was a deliberate scheme to cheat Northern men out of many millions of dollars—a scheme which the honest cotton-growers would not have sanctioned had they been aware of it. But in this, as in all other plans then ripening for a rebellion, the politicians would not trust the people with their secrets.

The meeting of the Thirty-sixth Congress on the 3d of December, drew the attention of the whole people to the National capital. It was an event of solemn interest to the nation. To the Annual Message of the President the public looked eagerly for a definite expression of the views of the Government on the

INTRENCHMENTS AT CITY POINT

all-absorbing topic. The people sat down to read it with hope, and arose from its perusal with grievous disappointment. Faint-heartedness and indecision appeared in almost every paragraph. After arguing that the election of a President who was distasteful to the people of one section of the country afforded no excuse for the offended ones to rebel, he declared that certain acts of Northern State Legislatures in opposition to the Fugitive-Slave Law were violations of the Constitution, and if not repealed "the injured States, after

having first used all peaceful and Constitutional means to ob- tain redress, would be justified in revolutionary re- sistance to the Government." The Secessionists could ask no more. The President then considered the right of secession, and the relative powers of the National Govern- ment. Be- fore preparing this portion of his message, he turned to the Attorney-General (Jeremiah S. Black) for advice. It was given in ample measure on the 20th of Novem- ber, in not less than three thousand words. It gave much "aid and comfort" to the enemies of the Union, for it yielded everything possessed an to them. It declared, in substance, that any State there was no inherent right to secede, and when it had seceded, tion to com- power known to the Constitu- argued that pel it to return to the Union. He had virtually by an act of secession a State public; and disappeared as a part of the Re- the power of the National Gov- ernment being only auxiliary to State life and force, National troops would certainly use wholly illegal." It seemed "be out of place, and their an attempt to force the people to the Attorney-General that the laws of the Republic and to of a State into submission to troy it, would be making war desist from attempts to des- would be converted into alien upon them, by which they pelled to act accordingly." He enemies, and would "be com-

virtually to counselled the President, to become suffer this concrete Republic faction, or disintegrated by the fires of rather than the blows of actual rebellion, disposal, for to use force legitimately at his ty and life. the preservation of its integri- ing the ad- The weak President, accept- doctrine into vice of the Attorney-General, incorporated the of its dan- a portion of his Message; but, apparently conscious against gerous tendency, he uttered some brave words heresy dan- secession as a crime, and State Supremacy as a doctrine gerous to the nationality of the Republic—a Confederacy which, if practically carried out, would make "the the first ad- a rope of sand, to be penetrated and dissolved by In this verse wave of public opinion in any of the States. may resolve manner," he truly said, "our thirty-three States lics, each themselves into so many jarring and hostile repub- whenever one retiring from the Union without responsibility, a course. By any sudden excitement might impel them to such fragments in this process a Union might be entirely broken into toil, priva- a few weeks, which cost our fathers many years of tion, and blood to establish."

VIEWS OF FORT BEAUREGARD, BAY POINT, S. C., NOVEMBER, 1861

Seemingly alarmed at his own outspoken convictions, and the offence it might give his Southern friends, the perplexed President proposed to conciliate them by allowing them to infuse deadly poison into the blood of their intended victim, which would more slowly but as surely accomplish their purpose. To do this he proposed an "explanatory amendment" to the Constitution on the subject of slavery, which would give to the enemies of the Union everything which they demanded, namely, the elevation of the slave-system to the dignity of a National institution, and thus sap the very foundations of our free Government.

HOSPITAL NO. 15 BEAUFORT, S. C., DECEMBER, 1864

This amendment was to consist of an express recognition of the right of property in slaves in the States where slavery then existed or might thereafter exist; of the recognition of the duty of the National Government to protect that right in all the Territories throughout their territorial existence; the recognition of the right of the slave-owner to every privilege and advantage given him in the Fugitive-Slave Law; and a declaration that all the State laws impairing or defeating that law were violations of the Constitution, and consequently null and void.

This Message, so indecisive and inconsistent, alarmed the people and pleased nobody. When a motion was made in the National Senate for its reference, it was spoken lightly of by the friends and foes of the Union. Senator Clingman, of North Carolina, who first sounded the trumpet of disunion in the Upper House, declared that it fell short of stating the case then before the country. Senator Wigfall, of Texas, said he could not understand it; and in the course of debate a few weeks afterward, Senator Jefferson Davis said that diplomacy is he continued, to reach any When the coun- being formed, power ever to we have the trate. One policy . . . . either subordinate to Government, bound to enforce as a State Rights

GEN. McLAWS, C.S.A.

JEFFERSON DAVIS, C. S. A.

it had "all the characteristics of a diplomatic paper, for said to abhor certainty, as nature abhors a vacuum; and," "it is not within the power of man fixed conclusion from that Message. try was agitated, when opinions are when we are drifting beyond the return," he said, "this is not what right to expect from a Chief Magis- or the other he ought to have taken of a Federalist, that every State is the Federal and he was its authority; or Democrat, which Constitution ernment to have brought another, and, safer than it is." said that if he secession, it was Union; that is secede. The He goes on to

GENERAL WILCOX, C. S. A.

he professed to be, holding that the gave no power to the Federal Gov- coerce a State. The President should his opinion to one conclusion or to-day, our country would have been

Senator Hale, of New Hampshire, understood the meaning of the Message on the subject of this:—"South Carolina has just cause for seceding from the the first proposition. The second is, that she has no right to third is, that we have no right to prevent her from seceding. represent this as a great and powerful country, and that no State has a right to secede from it; but the power of the country, if I understand the President, consists in what Dickens makes the English constitution to be—a power to do anything at all. Now I think it was incumbent on the President of the United States to point out definitely and to recommend to Congress some rule of action, and to tell us what he recommended us to do. But, in my judgment, he has entirely avoided it. He has failed to look the thing in the face. He has acted like the ostrich, which hides her head, and thereby thinks to escape danger."

So thought the people, who perceived that no reliance could be placed upon the arm of the Executive in defending the integrity of the Union. Had they then comprehended the fearful proportions of the imminent danger, they would have almost despaired. Patriotic men wrote to their representatives in Congress, asking them to be firm, yet conciliatory; and clergymen of every sect exhorted their people to be "firm in faith, patient in hope, careful in conduct and trustful in God." More than forty of the leading clergymen of various denominations in New York, New Jersey and Pennsylvania, united in sending forth a Circular Letter on New Year's day, 1861, making an appeal to the Churches. "We cannot doubt," they said, "that a spirit of candor and forbearance, such as our religion prompts, and the exigencies of the times demand, would render the speedy adjustment of our difficulties possible, consistently with every Constitutional right. Unswerving fealty to the Constitution justly interpreted, and a prompt return to its spirit and requirements whenever these may have been divergent from either, would seem to be the first duty of citizens and legislators. It is our firm, and, we think, intelligent conviction, that only a very inconsiderable fraction of the people of the North will hesitate in the discharge of their Constitutional obligations; and that whatever enactments are found to be in conflict therewith, will be annulled." This well-meant missive operated only as the mildest soothing-syrup; the disease was too malignant and wide-spread to be touched by anything but the probe and cautery.

JEFFERSON DAVIS' HOUSE IN RICHMOND

JEFFERSON DAVIS' HOUSE AT DAVIS RUN, MISSISSIPPI

While the National Legislature were tossing upon the suddenly raised surges of disunion, and the people of the free-labor States were listening with breathless anxiety to the roar of the tempest at the Capitol, the noise of the storm in the far South was like the portentous bellowing of distant thunder. It was raging vehemently in South Carolina. The Convention at Charleston, after passing the Ordinance of Secession, appointed commissioners to proceed to Washington to treat for the possession of public property within the limits of South Carolina. They also issued an Address to the people of the other slave-labor States, and a Declaration of the causes which impelled South Carolina to leave the Union. In

SUTLER'S CAMP, FIRST BRIGADE HORSE ARTILLERY

the former, they said: "South Carolina desires no destiny separate from yours. To be one of a great slave-holding Confederacy, stretching its arms over territory larger than any power in Europe possesses, with a population four times greater than that of the whole United States when they achieved their independence of the British empire; with productions which make our existence more important to the world than that of any other people inhabiting it; with common institutions to defend and common dangers to encounter, we ask your sympathy and confederation. . . . . All we demand of other people, is to be let alone to work out our own high destinies. . . . . United, we must be a great, free and prosperous people, whose renown must spread throughout the civilized world, and pass down, we trust, to the remotest ages. We ask you to join in forming a *Confederacy of Slave-holding States*." In their declaration of causes for the separation, they failed to point out a single act of wrong on the part of the Government they were intending to destroy, and it consisted chiefly of complaints that the Northern people did not look upon slavery with favor; were opposed to the Fugitive-Slave Law, and did not believe a decision of the Supreme Court of the United States was superior in authority to the Divine Law.

On the day when that Declaration was adopted, the governor of South Carolina (Pickens) issued a proclamation declaring the sovereignty, freedom and independence of that State, and that it was vested with national functions. The proclamation closed with the words—"Given under my hand, the 24th of December, 1860, and in the eighty-fifth year of the sovereignty and independence of South Carolina." Then, with perfect consistency, the Charleston newspapers published intelligence from the other States of the Union, under the head of "Foreign News." A small medal was struck to commemorate the secession of the State, and a banner for the new empire was adopted, composed of red silk, bearing a blue silk cross with fifteen white stars, the number of the slave-labor States. The Convention appointed one commissioner to each of the States to invite the politicians to send delegates to meet those of South Carolina at Montgomery, Alabama, to form a Southern Confederacy; authorized Governor Pickens, as chief magistrate

Defence of Washington, Fort Totten, View of Interior

of the new nation, to receive ambassadors, consuls, etc., from foreign countries, and took other measures for organizing a national government. The governor chose cabinet ministers, and the South Carolina nation began its brief career.

"A nationality!" exclaimed the London *Morning Star*, when commenting upon this Declaration of the sovereignty of South Carolina. "Was there ever, since the world began, a nation constituted of such materials—a commonwealth founded on such a basis? The greatest empire of antiquity is said to have grown up from a group of huts, built in a convenient location by fugitive slaves and robber huntsmen. But history nowhere chronicles the establishment of a community of slaveholders solely upon the alleged

AN AMBULANCE TRAIN

right of maintaining and enlarging their property in man. Paganism at least protected the Old World from so monstrous a scandal upon free commonwealths, by shutting out the idea of a common humanity and of individual rights derivable from inalienable duties."

Charleston harbor now became the theatre of stirring events. John B. Floyd of Virginia, one of the leading conspirators, was then Secretary of War, and was secretly weakening the physical power of the Government by stripping the arsenals of the North of their arms and ammunition, and strengthening the Secessionists by filling the arsenals of the South with an abundance of weapons. Of course he paid no attention to the words of General Winfield Scott, the chief of the army, when, so early as the close of October, he observed signs of incipient insurrection in South Carolina, and recommended the strengthening of the forts near Charleston. And when, at the close of the same month, Colonel Gardiner, in command of the fortifications near that city, attempted to increase his supply of ammunition, Floyd removed him, and in November placed Major Robert Anderson, a meritorious officer in the war with Mexico, in his place. That loyal Kentuckian at once perceived by various acts, the designs of the Secessionists to seize the fortifications in the harbor, and he urged his Government to strengthen them with men and munitions of war, especially Fort Moultrie, in which he was placed with a feeble garrison. But his constant warnings were unheeded, even when he wrote: "The clouds are threatening, and the storm may burst at any moment. I need not say to you how anxious I am, indeed determined, as far as honor will permit, to avoid collision with the people of South Carolina. Nothing will, however, be better calculated to prevent bloodshed, than our being found in such an attitude that it would be madness and folly to attack us." He continually begged the War Department to give him more strength, and send him explicit instructions; and when he found his warnings treated with contemptuous silence, he wrote: "Unless otherwise directed, I shall make future communications through the regular channel—the General-in-Chief."

Anderson did not know that he was addressing an enemy and not a protector of his Government, who was working with all his might to destroy the Republic. On the very day when the patriotic Major wrote to Floyd, the treacherous Secretary sold ten thousand Government muskets to an agent of the

Headquarters Co. F, 11th Rhode Island Volunteers, Miners Hill, Virginia

Officers of the 61st New York Infantry

Secessionists of Georgia. Eight days before he had sold five thousand to the State of Virginia; and vast numbers were sent to other slave-labor States. The *Mobile Advertiser*, the organ of the Secessionists in Alabama, exultingly declared that within twelve months one hundred and thirty-five thousand muskets had been quietly transferred from the Northern Arsenal at Springfield (Mass.) alone, to those in the Southern States. "We are much obliged to Mr. Floyd," said the *Advertiser*, "for the foresight he has thus displayed in disarming the North and equipping the South for this emergency. There is no telling the quantity of arms and munitions which were sent South from other arsenals. There is no doubt but that *every man in the South who can carry a gun can now be supplied from private or public sources.*" Floyd also attempted to supply the Secessionists with heavy guns, but loyal men prevented the outrage.

VIEWS AT BEAUFORT, S. C., AND HILTON HEAD

Secretary Floyd found Anderson too loyal for his purpose, but it was too late to displace him, so he left him to his own feeble resources, satisfied that the military companies then in process of organization in South Carolina, would be able to seize the forts in Charleston harbor in good time. Moultrie was weak, and many of the little garrison in Sumter were known to be disloyal. The latter fort was by far the stronger and more important work; and as evidence hourly increased, especially after the passage of the Ordinance of Secession, that the South Carolinians intended to seize Fort Sumter, Anderson, being commander of *all* the forts in the harbor, resolved to transfer the garrison in Fort Moultrie into that of Sumter, and abandon the former. It was a delicate undertaking, for the Secessionists had watchboats out upon the waters.

Anderson revealed his secret to only three or four of his most trusted officers. Then he resorted to stratagem to get the women and children first into Fort Sumter. They were taken in a vessel, with ample provisions, to Fort Johnson on James Island, where, under pretext of difficulty in finding quarters for them, they were detained on board until evening. Three guns fired at Fort Moultrie was to be the signal for consigning them immediately to Fort Sumter. The movement was regarded by the people of Charleston as a natural and prudent measure of Anderson, who, they knew, believed they were about to attack Fort Moultrie, and so all suspicion was allayed.

At the close of that evening, while the almost full-orbed moon was shining brightly, the greater portion of the little garrison at Moultrie embarked for Sumter. The three guns were fired; the women and children were quickly taken from before Fort Johnson to Sumter, and the movement was successful. Two or three officers remained at Fort Moultrie to spike the cannon, to destroy the gun-carriages, and to cut down the flag-staff, that no secession banner might float from the peak from which the National flag had so long fluttered. When the soldiers and their families and many weeks' provision were safely within the granite walls of Fort Sumter, Major Anderson wrote to the Secretary of War—"I have the honor to report that I have just completed, by the blessing of God, the removal to this fort, of all my garrison except the surgeon, four North Carolina officers and seven men."

NEAR GEORGETOWN FERRY.

NEAR AQUEDUCT BRIDGE.

GEORGETOWN D.C.

BRIDGE NEAR CHAIN BRIDGE POTOMAC

AQUEDUCT BRIDGE POTOMAC

VIEWS ON THE POTOMAC RIVER

The telegraph conveyed from the Secessionists to Floyd the astounding intelligence long before Anderson's despatch reached him. It flashed back the angry words of the dismayed and foiled conspirator: "Intelligence has reached here this morning [December 27] that you have abandoned Fort Moultrie, spiked your guns, burnt the carriages and gone to Fort Sumter. It is not believed, because there is no order for any such movement. Explain the meaning of this report." Anderson calmly replied by telegraph: "The telegram is correct. I abandoned Fort Moultrie because I was certain that if attacked my men must have been sacrificed, and the command of the harbor lost. I spiked the guns and destroyed the carriages to keep the guns from being turned against us. If attacked, the garrison would never have surrendered without a fight."

PONTOON BRIDGE AND RUINS OF STONE BRIDGE ACROSS THE POTOMAC
AT BERLIN, OCTOBER, 1862

The soldiers in Sumter wished to fling out the National ensign defiantly before the dawn next morning; but Anderson, who was a devout man, wishing to impress upon his followers the lesson that upon God alone they were to rely in the great trial that was evidently before them, would not consent to the act until the return of the absent chaplain. He came at noonday, when the whole company in the fort gathered around the flagstaff, not far from a huge cannon. The commander, with the halyards in his hand, knelt at the foot of the staff, when the chaplain earnestly invoked the sustaining power of the Almighty. A loud Amen! fell from the lips of many; and then the brave Major hoisted the flag to the top of the staff. It was greeted with hearty cheers, and the band saluted it with the air of "Hail Columbia."

A boat now approached the fort from Charleston. It conveyed a messenger who bore to Major Anderson a demand from Governor Pickens, that the former should immediately leave Fort Sumter, and return to Fort Moultrie. The demand was courteously refused; and Anderson was denounced as a "traitor to the South," he being a native of Kentucky, a slave-labor State. The conspirators in Charleston and Washington were enraged. At the very moment when the flag was flung to the breeze over Sumter, Secretary Floyd, in cabinet meeting, was demanding of the President permission to withdraw Anderson from Charleston harbor. The President refused. A storm suddenly arose which produced a disruption in the cabinet, and Floyd was succeeded by Joseph Holt, a loyal Kentuckian, who wrote to Major Anderson that his movement in transferring the garrison from Moultrie to Sumter, "was in every way admirable, alike for its humanity and patriotism as for its soldiership." Words of cheer came for the Major from other quarters. The Legislature of Nebraska, sitting two thousand miles away from Fort Sumter, telegraphed to him "A Happy New Year;" and cannon were fired in several places in honor of the event.

CHAPTER VI.

Heroism of Major Anderson—His Wife and Peter Hart—Robbery in the Interior Department—Flight of Secretary Floyd—Cabinet Changes—South Carolina Commissioners in Washington—Attempt to Reinforce and Supply Fort Sumter—Inauguration of Civil War at Charleston—Language of the Politicians—The People Bewildered—Fate of Leaders—"Secession" in Other States—Seizure of Public Property—Northern Sympathizers—Plan of the Secessionists—Dix's Order—Action in the Border States—Concessions— Peace Convention—Adams's Proposition—Convention at Montgomery—Establishment of a Southern Confederate Government.

MAJOR ANDERSON and his little band of soldiers were in extreme peril from the hour when they entered Fort Sumter. His friends knew that he was exposed to treachery within and fierce assault from without, and were very anxious. His devoted wife, daughter of General Clinch of Georgia, was an invalid in New York. She resolved to go to her husband with a faithful servant whom he might trust if she could find him. It was Peter Hart, who had been a sergeant with Anderson in Mexico, and was warmly attached to his person. After much search Mrs. Anderson found he was attached to the police force in New York, and she sent for him. He came, accompanied by his wife. "I have sent for you,"

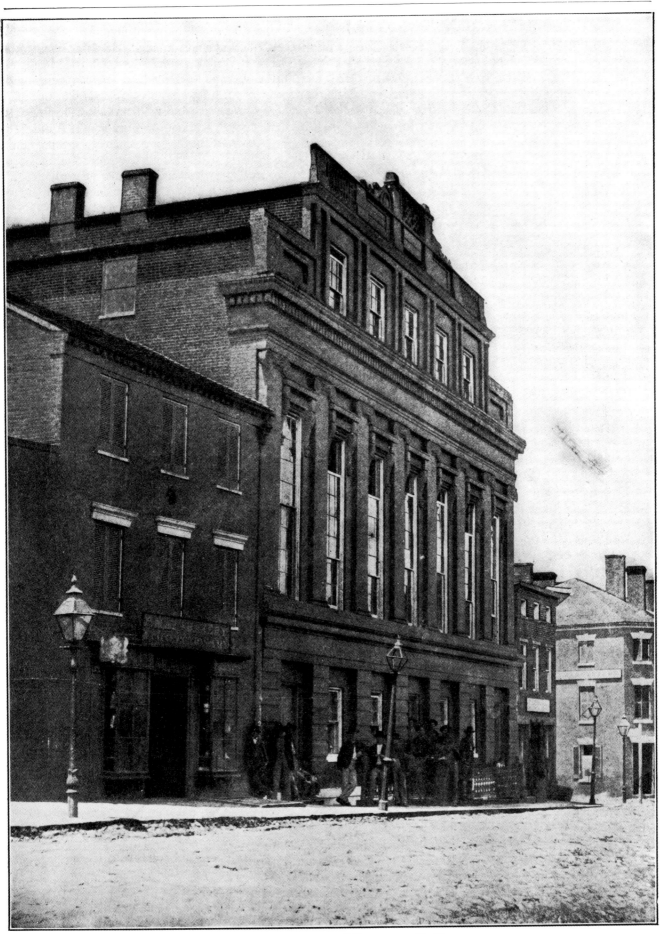

FORREST HALL PRISON, WASHINGTON, D. C.

said Mrs. Anderson, "to ask you to do me a favor." "Anything Mrs. Anderson wishes, I will do," was Hart's prompt reply. "But it may be more than you imagine," Mrs. Anderson said. Hart again replied, "Anything Mrs. Anderson wishes." "I want you to go with me to Fort Sumter," she said. Hart looked at his wife a moment, and then promptly responded, "I will go, madame." Then the earnest woman said, "But, Hart, I want you to *stay* with the major. You will leave your family, and give up a good situation." Again Hart glanced inquiringly toward his wife, and perceiving consent in her expression, he quickly replied, "I will go, madame." "But, Margaret," said Mrs. Anderson, turning to Hart's wife, "what do *you* say?" "Indade, ma'am, and its Margaret's sorry she can't do as much for you as Pater can," was the reply of the warm-hearted woman.

Twenty-four hours after this interview, Mrs. Anderson, contrary to the advice of her physician, started by railway for Charleston, accompanied by Peter Hart in the capacity of a servant. From Thursday night until Sunday morning, when she arrived at Fort Sumter, she neither ate, drank, nor slept. In the cars in southern Virginia and through the Carolinas, her ears were frequently assailed by curses of her husband and threats of violence against him, by men to whom the delicate, pale-faced woman, the wife of the man they hated, was a stranger. On Sunday morning, after some difficulty, she procured permission to visit Fort Sumter with Peter Hart. As the little boat touched the wharf of the fortress near the sallyport, and the name of Mrs. Anderson was announced to the sentry, the major, informed of her presence, rushed out, and clasped her in his arms with the exclamation, in a vehement whisper intended for her ear only, "My glorious wife!" "I have brought you Peter Hart," she said. "The children are well; I return to-night." She then partook of refreshments, and after resting a few hours, she was on her way back to New York, where she was threatened with brain fever a long time.

CITY OF CHARLESTON FROM TOP OF ORPHAN ASYLUM

She had given her husband the most faithful friend and assistant, under all circumstances, in the fort, during the three months of severe trial that ensued. She had done what the Government would not or dared not do—not *sent* but *took* a most valuable reinforcement to Fort Sumter.

While excitement was vehement in Washington because of events in Charleston harbor, it was intensified by a new development of bad faith or crime in the Department of the Interior, of which Jacob Thompson, of Mississippi, was chief. The safe of the Department was rifled of bonds to the amount of $800,000, which composed the Indian Trust Fund. The wildest rumors prevailed as to the amount abstracted, making it millions. It was known that Cobb had impoverished the Treasury, and the public was inclined to believe that plunder was a part of the business of the cabinet, for Secretary Floyd was deeply implicated in the Bond robbery. The public held Floyd and Thompson responsible for the crime. The grand jury of Washington city indicted Floyd for "malfeasance in office, complicity in the abstraction of the Indian Trust Fund, and conspiracy against the Government; and a committee of the House of Representatives mildly reported that Floyd's conduct was irreconcilable with purity of motives, and faithfulness to public trusts." But before the action of the grand jury and the report of the committee were known, the offending Secretary of War had fled to Virginia, where he was received with open arms by the Secessionists, and made a military leader with the commission of brigadier-general. His place in the cabinet was filled, as we have observed, by Joseph Holt, a loyal Kentuckian.

General Cass, the Secretary of State, had resigned, and Mr. Black, the Attorney-General, took his place, when the last-named office was filled by Edwin M. Stanton, afterward the efficient Secretary of War. John A. Dix, a staunch patriot of New York, was called to the head of the Treasury Department, and Secretary Thompson left the Department of the Interior and returned to Mississippi to help his fellow Secessionists make war on the Republic. These changes in the cabinet caused the loyal people of the country to breathe freer and indulge in hope.

At the same time there was another cause for excitement in the National capital. R. W. Barnwell, James H. Adams and James L. Orr, appointed commissioners by the Convention of South Carolina to treat for the disposition of the property of the National Government within the borders of that State,

FORT LINCOLN, WASHINGTON, D. C.

THE LIGHT HOUSE.

THE LINCOLN GUN.

AT FORTRESS MONROE

arrived at Washington, took a house for the transaction of diplomatic business, and made Wm. H. Trescott their Secretary. With the formality of foreign ministers, they announced their presence to the President of the Republic, and set forth the objects of their mission in haughty language, and prepared for a long line of negotiations. The business was cut short by the refusal of the President to receive them in any other capacity than as private gentlemen. Their demands had been uttered in a manner so insulting, that the President was justly indignant, and wrote them a letter, courteous in tone but severe in its facts, which called from them a most insolent rejoinder. This

communication was these words: "This dent, is of such a it." Thus ended between the Presi-bassadors from a placed in an attitude Government. These "ministerial resi-turned home to en-with all their might,

returned to them, indorsed with paper, just presented to the Presi-character that he declines to receive the "diplomatic correspondence" dent of the Republic and the em-State which its politicians had of rebellion against the National embassadors, after occupying their dence" ten days, left it and re-gage in the work of the Secessionists excepting Mr. Orr.

With more loyal elements composing his cabinet, President Buchanan now seemed to act more decidedly in support of the National authority; and listening to the counsels of Generals Dix and Scott,

and other patriotic men, he determined to send reinforcements and supplies to Fort Sumter. The *Star of the West*, a merchant steamship, was employed for the purpose; and, in order to mislead spies in New York, she was cleared from that port for Savannah and New Orleans. But the secret of her destination, revealed to Secretary Thompson while he was writing his resignation, was telegraphed by him to Charleston; and when, on the morning of the 9th of January, 1861, she entered that harbor with the National flag flying, she was fired upon from redoubts which the Secessionists, now become insurgents, had erected on the shores. Her commander displayed a large American ensign, but the assailants had no respect for the insignia of the Union; and after receiving seventeen shots, chiefly in her rigging, and being unarmed with artillery, the *Star of the West* turned about, put to sea, and returned to New York. This movement had been watched by the garrison at Fort Sumter, with eager curiosity at first, until it was evident that the steamship was in the Government employ bringing relief to the fort, when the guns of the fortress, all shotted, were brought to bear on the batteries of the insurgents. Anderson was not aware of the changed condition of affairs at Washington, and, restrained by positive orders not to act until attacked, he withheld fire. Had he known that his act would have been approved by

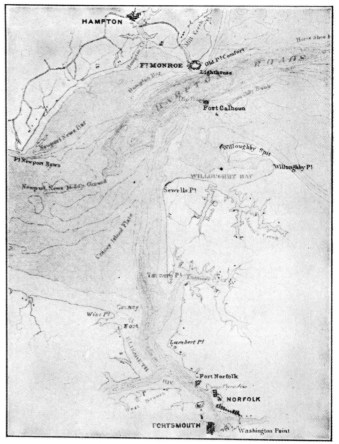

HAMPTON ROADS

GRAPE VINE BRIDGE BUILT BY UNITED STATES ENGINEERS

his Government, he would have silenced the hostile batteries and received the soldiers and supplies on board the *Star of the West* into Fort Sumter. This overt act of the insurgents was the beginning of the terrible Civil War that followed.

The South Carolinians struck the first blow (which rebounded so fearfully), and gloried in it. The commander of the battery on Morris Island (Major Stevens) that caused the *Star of the West* to put to sea, loudly boasted of his feat in humbling the flag of his country. The Legislature of the State resolved that they had learned "with pride and pleasure of the successful resistance of the troops of the State, acting under orders of the governor, to an attempt to reinforce Fort Sumter. The *Charleston Mercury* exclaimed: "Yesterday, the 9th of January, will be remembered in history. Powder has been burnt over the decree of our State, timber has been crashed, perhaps blood spilled.

"The expulsion of the *Star of the West* from Charleston harbor yesterday morning was the *opening of the ball of revolution.* We are proud that our harbor has been so honored. We are more proud that the State of South Carolina, so long, so bitterly, so contemptuously reviled and scoffed at, above all others, should thus proudly have thrown back the scoff of her enemies. Intrenched upon her soil, she has spoken from the mouth of her cannon and not from the mouths of scurrilous demagogues, fanatics and scribblers. Contemned, the sanctity of her waters violated with hostile purpose of reinforcing enemies in our harbor, she has not hesitated to *strike the first blow* full in the face of her insulters. Let the United States Govern-

SCENES AT HILTON HEAD AND PORT ROYAL, SOUTH CAROLINA

ment bear, or return it at its good will, the blow still tingling about its ears—the fruit of its own bandit temerity. We would not exchange or recall that blow for millions! It has wiped out half a century of scorn and outrage. Again South Carolina may be proud of her historic fame and ancestry, without a blush upon her cheek for her own present honor. The haughty echo of her cannon has ere this reverberated from Maine to Texas, through every hamlet of the North, and down along the great waters of the southwest. The decree has gone forth. Upon each acre of the peaceful soil of the South, armed men will spring up as the sound breaks upon their ears; and it will be found that every word of our insolent foe has been, indeed, a dragon's tooth sown for their destruction. And though grizzly and traitorous ruffians may cry on the dogs of war, and treacherous politicians may lend their aid in deceptions, South Carolina will stand under her own palmetto-tree, unterrified by the snarling growls or assaults of the one, undeceived or deterred by the wily machinations of the other. And if that red seal of blood be still lacking to the parchment of our liberties, and blood they want—blood they shall have—and blood enough to stamp it all in red. For, by the God of our fathers, the soil of South Carolina *shall be free!*"

Such was the language of the Declaration of War against the Union by the politicians of South Carolina—arrogant, boastful, savage. Unmindful of the wisdom of the injunction of the king of Israel, "Let not him that girdeth on his harness boast himself as he that putteth it off," they proceeded in hot haste, in the spirit of their Declaration, to inaugurate Civil War, and to drag the peaceful inhabitants of the other slave-labor States into its horrid vortex. The people, whose rights they had violated and whose sovereignty they had usurped, were stunned and bewildered by the violence of these self-constituted leaders, and they found themselves and their millions of property at the mercy of madmen who, as the sequel proved, were totally unfit to lead in the councils of a free, intelligent and patriotic community. Four years after the war so boastfully begun by these political leaders in South Carolina, Charleston was a ghastly ruin, in which not one of these men remained; Columbia, the capital of the State, was laid in ashes;

COMPANY A 9TH INDIANA VOLUNTEERS

VIEWS ON THE JAMES RIVER

every slave within the borders of the Republic was liberated; society in the slave-labor States was wholly disorganized; the land was filled with the mourning of the deceived and bereaved people; and a large number of those who signed the Ordinance of Secession and so brought the curse of war's desolation upon the innocent inhabitants of most of the Southern States, became fugitives from their homes, utterly ruined. I would gladly draw the veil of oblivion over the folly and wrong-doing of these few crazy leaders, for they were citizens of our common country; but justice to posterity requires that their actions should be made warning beacons to others who, in like manner, contemplate rebellion against the divine law of the Golden Rule, and a total disregard of the rights of man.

GENERAL H. A. WISE, C. S. A.

The South Carolina politicians now made frantic appeals to those of other slave-labor States to follow their example, and bind the people hand and foot by ordinances of secession. During the first thirty days of the year 1861, the politicians in six of the other States responded by calling conventions and passing ordinances of secession, in the following order: Mississippi, on the 9th of January; Florida, on the 10th; Alabama, on the 11th; Georgia, on the 19th; Louisiana, on the 26th and Texas on the first of February. At the same time the Secessionists of Virginia were anxious to enroll their State among the seceders; and under the control of ex-Governor Henry A. Wise, and of others in Maryland under leaders unknown to the public, large numbers of "Minute-men" were organized and drilled for the special purpose of seizing Washington city and the Government Buildings and archives—a prime object of the conspirators against the life of the nation. Acting upon the suggestions of the politicians of South Carolina, those of other States caused the seizure of forts, arsenals and other property of the United States within the borders of the slave-labor States. In Louisiana the Arsenal, Mint, Custom-house and Post-office, with all their contents, were seized and turned over to the State authorities, while the President, evidently bound by ante-election pledges, dared not interfere. The insurgents everywhere were encouraged by the leaders of the Administration party in the North, by language such as was used at a large Democratic meeting held in Philadelphia on the 16th of January, 1861, when one of the resolutions adopted, echoing the sentiments of the decision of the Attorney-General, declared: "We are utterly opposed to any such compulsion as is demanded by a portion of the Republican party; and the Democratic party of the North will, by all constitutional means, and with its moral and political influence, oppose any such extreme policy, or a fratricidal war thus to be inaugurated." And a Democratic State Convention held at the capital of Pennsylvania, on the 22d of February, 1861, said by a resolution: "We will, by all proper and legitimate means, oppose, discountenance and prevent any attempt on the part of the Republicans in power, to make any armed aggressions upon the Southern States, especially so long as laws [meaning those concerning the Fugitive-Slave Act] contravening their rights shall remain unrepealed on the statute books of Northern States, and so long as the just demands of the South shall continue to be unrecognized by the Republican majorities in those States, and unsecured by proper amendatory explanations of the Constitution."

Such moral "aid and comfort" everywhere given by Northern politicians, made the insurgents believe that there would be such a fatally "divided North" that their schemes might be consummated with ease, and they did not pause in their mad career. They at once set about executing, with boldness and energy, their preconcerted plans as set forth in the following words by one of them: "We intend to take possession of the army and navy, and of the archives of the Government; not allow the electoral votes to be counted; proclaim Buchanan provisional president if he will do as we wish; if not, choose another; seize the Harper's Ferry Arsenal and the Norfolk Navy-yard simultaneously and sending armed men down from the former and armed vessels up from the latter, take possession of Washington city and establish a new government." Many seizures were made; and the value of the public property thus appropriated to the use of the insurgents, before the close of Buchanan's administration, was estimated at $30,000,000.

A defiant spirit now prevailed all over the South. When General Dix, the loyal Secretary of the Treasury, sent a special agent of his department to secure from seizure revenue cutters at New Orleans and Mobile, with special orders for their commanders, the captain (Breshwood) of one of them at the former port, haughtily refused to obey. When the agent telegraphed to the Secretary a notice of this disobedience, the latter immediately sent his famous despatch: "Tell Lieutenant Caldwell to arrest Captain Breshwood, assume the command of the cutter, and obey the order through you. If Captain Breshwood,

VIEWS OF ARTILLERY

after arrest, undertakes to interfere with the command of the cutter, tell Lieutenant Caldwell to consider him as a mutineer. *If any one attempts to pull down the American flag, shoot him on the spot!*"

This vigorous order was the first sign given by the Executive Government at Washington of a real determination to quell the rising insurrection; and it gave hopes to the friends of the Union who had observed, with great anxiety, the President of the Republic sitting with his hands folded in passive acquiescence while its enemies were preparing to destroy it. But the conspirators in New Orleans, who had control of the telegraph, did not allow the despatch to pass. The revenue cutter fell into the hands of the insurgents; and two days afterward the National Mint and Custom-house at New Orleans, with all

CONFEDERATE DEAD IN FRONT OF FORT ROBINETTE, CORINTH

the coin and bullion to $536,000, were and the precious coffers of the State of While events in the month of January, more toward armed tional Government, States became fully danger to the Union. also deeply agitated, flicting sentiments, class of Unionists in were speedily over- of the Secessionists; see and Missouri were under the banner of eracy, by their poli- with Kentucky, bore dreadful conflict that en- Maryland were in a one time. The patriotic the latter fast to her loyal commonwealths; Magoffin of Kentucky, politician, failing to drag sion, procured for it an "neutrality" that was habitants than a positive or the other. Governors Harris of Tennessee and with their associate poli- committed their respective States to the fortunes of the enemies of the Union.

they contained, amounting seized by the Secessionists, metals were placed in the Louisiana. the slave-labor States, in 1861, were tending more and rebellion against the Na- the people of the free-labor aroused to the impending The Border States were at the same time, by con- for there was a very large each of them. But these borne by the violence and Virginia, Tennes- finally arranged the Southern Confed- ticians, and these, the brunt of the sued. Kentucky and doubtful position at Governor Hicks kept moorings among the but Governor who was an adroit that State into seces- attitude of so-called far worse for the in- position on one side Letcher of Virginia, Jackson of Missouri, ticians, formally

Meanwhile the loyal people of the Northern States were holding public meetings and counteracting, as far as they might, the revolutionary proceedings of their opponents North and South. They loved peace and desired friendship, and were willing to make almost any concessions to the enemies of the Government that did not involve their honor. When, as the politicians in State after State adopted ordinances of secession, and their respective representatives in both Houses of Congress abdicated their seats and hurled defiance and threats in the face of the Government and its supporters, the latter patiently yielded, and showed a willingness to conciliate the arrogant leaders of the Secessionists. So early as the 27th of December, Charles Francis Adams, a representative of Massachusetts—a commonwealth against which the fiercest maledictions of the slave-holders had been hurled for years—offered a resolution in the House of Representatives, "That it is expedient to propose an amendment to the Constitution, to the effect that no future amendments of it in regard to slavery shall be made unless proposed by a slave State, and ratified by all the States." And so eager were the loyal men for reconciliation, that when the authorities of Virginia proposed a General Convention at the National capital (which was called a Peace Conference), they readily agreed to the measure and appointed delegates to it, albeit many wise men doubted the sincerity of the proposers and regarded it as a plan to gain time for the perfecting of plans for seizing Washington city.

BATTERY HAYES—SEVEN 300 POUND PARROTTS.

BATTERIES AGAINST FORT WAGNER

BATTERY REYNOLDS, FIVE TEN-INCH SIEGE MORTARS.

BATTERY WEED, FIVE TEN-INCH SIEGE MORTARS.

The Peace Conference assembled at the National capital on the 4th of February, 1861, in which delegates from twenty-one States appeared.   Ex-President John Tyler of Virginia was appointed chairman

GENERAL JOHN A. DIX

of the Convention.   "Your patriotism," he said, in taking the chair, "will surmount the difficulties, however great, if you will but accomplish one triumph in advance, and that is triumph over *party*.   And what is party, when compared to the work of rescuing one's country from danger?

The Convention heartily reciprocated these patriotic words.   Efforts were made in the Convention to have an amendment to the National Constitution adopted, that would nationalize slavery.   It failed, and a compromise was effected by adopting an article that should *preserve* slavery.   With this compromise, Mr. Tyler and his Virginia friends professed to be satisfied.   "I cannot but hope," he said, in his closing speech before the Convention, "that the blessing of God will follow and rest upon the result of your labors, and that such result will bring to our country that quiet and peace which every patriotic heart so earnestly desires. . . . . It is probable that the result to which you have arrived is the best that, under all the circumstances, could be expected.   So far as in me lies, therefore, I shall recommend its adoption."   The politicians at Richmond seem not to have responded kindly to this sentiment, and Mr. Tyler was compelled to change his views; for, thirty-six hours after the adjournment of the Convention, in a speech in the Virginia capital, he denounced the Peace Convention, and declared that "the South" had nothing to hope from the Republican party.   Thenceforth he gave his whole influence for the promotion of disunion.

On the day when the Peace Convention assembled at Washington city, a band of men, professing to represent the people of six of the "seceded States," met at Montgomery, in Alabama, to form a Southern Confederacy. They were chosen by the Secession Conventions of South Carolina, Georgia, Alabama, Mississippi, Louisiana, and Florida; and it is a notable fact that the *people* of these States were not allowed to act in the matter.   The politicians would not trust them, and took the whole management of public affairs into their own hands.   Not a single ordinance of secession was ever submitted to the *people* for ratification or rejection; and the delegates that met at Montgomery, forty-two in number, assembled wholly without the sanction of the *people*.   Nevertheless, they proceeded as if they were a body of representatives, legally chosen by the inhabitants to perfect their plans.   Howell Cobb, of Georgia, was chosen to preside, who, in a short speech, declared that they represented "sovereign and independent States;" that the separation was a "fixed and irrevocable fact—perfect, complete, and perpetual. . . . With a consciousness of the justice of our cause," he said, "and with confidence in the guidance and blessings of a kind Providence, we will this day inaugurate for the South a new era of peace, security, and prosperity."

FAC-SIMILE COPY OF GENERAL DIX'S DISPATCH

VIEWS OF CONFEDERATE FORTIFICATIONS

CHRONOLOGICAL SUMMARY AND RECORD—Continued

FEBRUARY, 1862—*Continued from Section 2*

17—Sugar Creek or Pea Ridge, Mo. 1st and 6th Mo., 3d Ill. Cav. *Union* 5 killed, 9 wounded.

18—Independence, Mo. 2d Ohio Cav. *Union* 1 killed, 3 wounded. *Confed.* 4 killed, 5 wounded.

21—Ft. Craig or Valverde, N. Mex. 1st N. Mex. Cav., 2d Col. Cav., Detachments of 1st, 2d and 5th N. Mex., and of 5th, 7th and 10th U. S. Inft., Hill's and McRae's Batteries. *Union* 62 killed, 140 wounded. *Confed.* 150 wounded.

24—Mason's Neck, Occoquan, Va. 37th N. Y. *Union* 2 killed, 1 wounded.

26—Keytesville, Mo. 6th Mo. Cav. *Union* 2 killed, 1 wounded. *Confed.* 1 killed.

MARCH, 1862

2—Pittsburg Landing, Tenn. 32d Ill. and U. S. Gunboats *Lexington* and *Tyler*. *Union* 5 killed, 5 wounded. *Confed.* 20 killed, 200 wounded.

3—New Madrid, Mo. 5th Iowa, 59th Ind., 39th and 63d Ohio, 2d Mich. Cav., 7th Ill. Cav. *Union* 1 killed, 3 wounded.

5—Occoquan, Va. Detachment of 63d Pa. *Union* 2 killed, 2 wounded.

6, 7 and 8—Pea Ridge, Ark., including engagements at Bentonville, Leetown and Elkhorn Tavern. 25th, 35th, 36th, 37th, 44th and 59th Ill., 2d, 3d, 12th, 15th, 17th, 24th, and Phelps' Mo., 8th, 18th and 22d Ind., 4th and 9th Iowa, 3d Iowa Cav., 3d and 15th Ill. Cav., 1st, 4th, 5th and 6th Mo. Cav., Batteries B and F 2d Mo. Light Artil., 2d Ohio Battery, 1st Ind. Battery, Battery A 2d Ill. Artil. *Union* 203 killed, 972 wounded, 174 missing. *Confed.* 1,100 killed, 2,500 wounded, 1,600 missing and captured. *Union* Brig.-Gen. Asboth and Actg. Brig.-Gen. Carr wounded. *Confed.* Brig.-Gen. B. McCulloch and Actg. Brig.-Gen. James McIntosh killed.

7—Fox Creek, Mo. 4th Mo. Cav. *Union* 5 wounded.

8—Near Nashville, Tenn. 1st Wis., 4th Ohio Cav. *Union* 1 killed, 2 wounded. *Confed.* 4 killed.

9—Mountain Grove, Mo. 10th Mo. Cav. *Union* 10 killed, 2 wounded. Hampton Roads, Va. 20th Ind., 7th and 11th N. Y., U. S. Gunboats *Monitor*, *Minnesota*, *Congress* and *Cumberland*. *Union* 261 killed, 108 wounded. *Confed.* 7 killed, 17 wounded.

10—Burke's Station, Va. One Co. 1st N. Y. Cav. *Union* 1 killed. *Confed.* 3 killed, 5 wounded.
Jacksborough, Big Creek Gap, Tenn. 2d Tenn. *Union* 2 wounded. *Confed.* 2 killed, 4 wounded.

11—Paris, Tenn. Detachments of 5th Iowa and 1st Neb. Cav., Battery K 1st Mo. Art. *Union* 5 killed, 5 wounded. *Confed.* 10 killed.

12—Lexington, Mo. 1st Iowa Cav. *Union* 1 killed, 1 wounded. *Confed.* 9 killed, 3 wounded.
Near Lebanon, Mo. *Confed.* 13 killed, 5 wounded.

13—New Madrid, Mo. 10th and 16th Ill., 27th, 39th, 43d and 63d Ohio, 3d Mich. Cav., 1st U. S. Inft., Bissell's Mo. Engineers. *Union* 50 wounded. *Confed.* 100 wounded.

14—Newberne, N. C. 51st N. Y., 8th, 10th and 11th Conn., 21st, 23d, 24th, 25th and 27th Mass., 9th N. J., 51st Pa., 4th and 5th R. I. *Union* 91 killed, 466 wounded. *Confed.* 64 killed, 106 wounded, 413 captured.

16—Black Jack Forest, Tenn. Detachments of 4th Ill. and 5th Ohio Cav. *Union* 4 wounded.

18—Salem or Spring River, Ark. Detachments of 6th Mo. and 3d Iowa Cav. *Union* 5 killed, 10 wounded. *Confed.* 100 killed, wounded and missing.

21—Mosquito Inlet, Fla. U. S. Gunboats *Penguin* and *Henry Andrew*. *Union* 8 killed, 8 wounded.

22—Independence or Little Santa Fe, Mo. 2d Kan. *Union* 1 killed, 2 wounded. *Confed.* 7 killed.

23—Carthage, Mo. 6th Kan. Cav. *Union* 1 wounded.
Winchester or Kearnstown, Va. 1st W. Va., 84th and 110th Pa., 5th, 7th, 8th, 29th, 62d and 67th Ohio, 7th, 13th and 14th Ind., 39th Ill., 1st Ohio Cav., 1st Mich. Cav., 1st W. Va. Artil., 1st Ohio Artil., Co. E 4th U. S. Artil. *Union* 103 killed, 440 wounded, 24 missing. *Confed.* 80 killed, 342 wounded, 269 prisoners.

26—Warrensburg or Briar, Mo. Sixty men of 7th Mo. Militia Cav. *Union* 1 killed, 22 wounded. *Confed.* 9 killed, 17 wounded.
Humansville, Mo. Co. B 8th Mo. Militia Cav. *Union* 5 wounded. *Confed.* 15 wounded.

26, 27 and 28—Apache Cañon or Glorietta, near Santa Fe, N. Mex. 1st and 2d Colo. Cav. *Union* 32 killed, 75 wounded, 35 missing. *Confed.* 36 killed, 60 wounded, 93 missing.

28—Warrensburg, Mo. 1st Ill. Cav. *Union* 3 killed, 1 wounded. *Confed.* 15 killed.

APRIL, 1862

2—Putnam's Ferry, near Doniphan, Mo. 21st and 38th Ill., 5th Ill. Cav., 16th Ohio Battery and Col. Carlin's Brigade. *Confed.* 3 killed.

4—Great Bethel, Va. Advance of 3d Corps Army of Potomac. *Union* 4 killed, 10 wounded.
Crump's Landing or Adamsville, Tenn. 48th, 70th and 72d Ohio, 5th Ohio Cav. *Union* 2 wounded. *Confed.* 20 wounded.

6 and 7—Shiloh or Pittsburg Landing, Tenn. Army of Western Tennessee, commanded by Maj.-Gen. U. S. Grant, as follows: 1st Div., Maj.-Gen. J. A. McClernand; 2d Div., Maj.-Gen. C. F. Smith; 3d Div., Brig.-Gen. Lew. Wallace; 4th Div., Brig.-Gen. S. A. Hurlbut; 5th Div., Brig.-Gen. W. T. Sherman; 6th Div., Brig.-Gen. B. M. Prentiss. Army of the Ohio commanded by Maj.-Gen. D. C. Buell, as follows: 2d Div., Brig.-Gen. A. M. D. Cook; 4th Div., Brig.-Gen. W. Nelson; 5th Div., Brig.-Gen. T. L. Crittenden, 21st Brigade of the 6th Div., Gunboats *Tyler* and *Lexington*. *Union* 1,735 killed, 7,882 wounded, 3,956 captured. *Confed.* 1,728 killed, 8,012 wounded, 959 captured. *Confed.* Maj.-Gen. A. S. Johnson, commander-in-chief, and Brig.-Gen. A. H. Gladden killed; Maj.-Gen. W. S. Cheatham and Brig.-Gen. C. Clark, B. R. Johnson, and J. S. Bowen wounded; *Union* Maj.-Gen. W. T. Sherman and W. H. L. Wallace wounded and B. M. Prentiss captured.

8—Island No. 10, Tenn. Maj.-Gen. Pope's command and the Navy, under Flag-officer Foote. *Confed.* 17 killed, 3,000 prisoners.
Near Corinth, Miss. 3d Brigade 5th Div. Army of Western Tennessee and 4th Ill. Cav. *Confed.* 15 killed, 25 wounded, 200 captured.

9—Owen's River, Cal. 2d Cal. Cav. *Union* 1 killed, 2 wounded.

10—Ft. Pulaski, Ga. 6th and 7th Conn., 3d R. I., 46th and 48th N. Y., 8th Maine, 15th U. S. Inft., Crew of U. S. S. *Wabash*. *Union* 1 killed. *Confed.* 4 wounded, 360 prisoners.

11—Huntsville, Ala. Army of the Ohio 3d Div. *Confed.* 200 prisoners.
Yorktown, Va. 12th N. Y., 57th and 63d Pa. *Union* 2 killed, 8 wounded.

12—Little Blue River, Mo. *Confed.* 5 killed.
Monterey, Va. 75th Ohio, 1st W. Va. Cav. *Union* 3 wounded.

14—Pollocksville, N. C. *Confed.* 7 wounded.
Diamond Grove, Mo. 6th Kan. Cav. *Union* 1 wounded.
Walkersville, Mo. 2d Mo. Militia Cav. *Union* 2 killed, 3 wounded.
Montavallo, Mo. Two Cos. 1st Iowa Cav. *Union* 2 killed, 6 wounded. *Confed.* 2 killed, 10 wounded.

15—Pechacho Pass, Ariz. 1st Cal. Cav. *Union* 3 killed, 3 wounded.

16—Savannah, Tenn. *Confed.* 5 killed, 65 wounded.
White Marsh or Wilmington Island, Ga. 8th Mich., Battery of R. I. Light Artil. *Union* 10 killed, 35 wounded. *Confed.* 5 killed, 7 wounded.
Lee's Mills, Va. 3d, 4th and 6th Vt., 3d N. Y. Battery and Battery of 5th U. S. Artil. *Union* 35 killed, 129 wounded. *Confed.* 20 killed, 75 wounded, 50 captured.

17—Holly River, W. Va. *Union* 3 wounded. *Confed.* 2 killed.

18—Falmouth, Va. 2d N. Y. Cav. *Union* 5 killed, 16 wounded. *Confed.* 19 captured.
Edisto Island, S. C. 55th Pa., 3d N. H., U. S. S. *Crusader*. *Union* 3 wounded.

18 to 28.—Forts Jackson and St. Philip, and the capture of New Orleans, La. Commodore Farragut's fleet of war vessels and mortar boats, under Commander D. D. Porter. *Union* 36 killed, 193 wounded. *Confed.* 185 killed, 197 wounded, 400 captured.

19—Talbot's Ferry, Ark. 4th Iowa Cav. *Union* 1 killed. *Confed.* 3 killed.
Camden, N. C., also called South Mills. 9th and 89th N. Y., 21st Mass., 51st Pa., 6th N. H. *Union* 12 killed, 98 wounded. *Confed.* 6 killed, 19 wounded.

23—Grass Lick, W. Va. 3d Md., Potomac Home Brigade. *Union* 3 killed.

25—Fort Macon, N. C. U. S. Gunboats *Daylight*, *Georgia*, *Chippewa*, the bark *Gemsbok* and Gen. Parkes's division. *Union* 1 killed, 11 wounded. *Confed.* 7 killed, 18 wounded, 450 captured.

26—Turnback Creek, Mo. 5th Kan. Cav. *Union* 1 killed.
Neosho, Mo. 1st Mo. Cav. *Union* 3 killed, 3 wounded. *Confed.* 30 wounded, 62 prisoners.
In front of Yorktown, Va. Three Cos. 1st Mass. *Union* 3 killed, 16 wounded.

27—Horton's Mills, N. C. 103d N. Y. *Union* 1 killed, 6 wounded. *Confed.* 3 wounded.

28—Paint Rock Railroad Bridge. Twenty-two men of 10th Wis. *Union* 7 wounded.
Cumberland Mountain, Tenn. 16th and 42d Ohio, 22d Ky.
Monterey, Tenn. 2d Iowa Cav. *Union* 1 killed, 3 wounded. *Confed.* 5 killed.

29—Bridgeport, Ala. 3d Div. Army of the Ohio. *Confed.* 72 killed and wounded, 350 captured.

MAY, 1862

1—Clarke's Hollow, W. Va. Co. C 23d Ohio. *Union* 1 killed, 21 wounded.

3—Farmington, Miss. 10th, 16th, 22d, 27th, 42d and 51st Ill., 10th and 16th Mich., Yates's (Ill.) Sharpshooters, 2d Mich. Cav., Battery C 1st Ill. Artil. *Union* 2 killed, 12 wounded. *Confed.* 30 killed.

4—Licking, Mo. 24th Mo., 5th Mo., Militia Cav. *Union* 1 killed, 2 wounded.
Cheese Cake Church, Va. 3d Pa., 1st and 6th U. S. Cav.

5—Lebanon, Tenn. 1st, 4th and 5th Ky. Cav., Detachment of the 7th Pa. *Union* 6 killed, 25 wounded. *Confed.* 66 prisoners.
Lockridge Mills or Dresden, Ky. 5th Iowa Cav. *Union* 4 killed, 16 wounded, 68 missing.
Williamsburg, Va. 3d and 4th C———— Army of the Potomac. *Union* 456 killed, 1,400 wounded, 372 m————. *Confed.* 1,000 killed, wounded, and captured.

7—West Point or Eltham's Landi——, Va. 16th, 31st and 32d N. Y., 95th and 96th Pa., 5th Maine, 1s. Mass. Artil., Battery D 2d U. S. Artil. *Union* 49 killed, 104 wounded, 41 missing.
Somerville Heights, Va. 13th Ind. *Union* 2 killed, 7 wounded, 24 missing.

8—McDowell or Bull Pasture, Va. 25th, 32d, 75th and 82d Ohio, 3d W. Va., 1st W. Va. Cav., 1st Conn. Cav., 1st Ind. Battery. *Union* 28 killed, 225 wounded. *Confed.* 100 killed, 200 wounded.
Glendale, near Corinth, Miss. 7th Ill. Cav. *Union* 1 killed, 4 wounded. *Confed.* 30 killed and wounded.

9—Elkton Station, near Athens, Ala. Co. E 37th Ind. *Union* 5 killed, 43 captured. *Confed.* 13 killed.
Slatersville or New Kent C. H., Va. 98th Pa., 2d R. I., 6th U. S. Cav. *Union* 4 killed, 14 wounded. *Confed.* 10 killed, 14 wounded.

10—Fort Pillow, Tenn. U. S. Gunboats *Cincinnati* and *Mound City*. *Union* 3 wounded. *Confed.* 2 killed, 1 wounded.

11—Bloomfield, Mo. 1st Wis. Cav. *Confed.* 1 killed.

13—Monterey, Tenn. Part of Brig.-Gen. M. L. Smith's Brigade. *Union* 2 wounded. *Confed.* 2 killed, 3 wounded.

(Continued in Section 4)

BATTERIES AGAINST FORT SUMTER

CHAPTER VI.—Continued.

MAJOR ROBERT ANDERSON

I T was soon found that perfect harmony could not be expected to prevail in that Convention. There were too many ambitious men there to promote serenity of thought and manner, and the sweetness of concord. They were nearly all aspirants for high positions in the new empire about to be formed; and each felt himself, like Bottom the Weaver, capable of sustaining any character, from that of a "Lion" to "Moonshine." The South Carolina politicians were particularly clamorous for honors and emoluments. Their State, they said, had taken the lead—struck the first blow—in the revolution, and they deserved the highest seats. Judge McGrath, who laid aside his official robes at Charleston, sent word that he would like to put them on again at Montgomery as Attorney-General. R. Barnwell Rhett, one of the most violent of the politicians, thought himself particularly fitted to be Secretary of War; and because his claims were not allowed, he wrote complaining letters to his son, the editor of the *Charleston Mercury*, some of the originals of which are now before me, and are rich in revelations of disappointed ambition. On the 16th of February, Rhett said in a letter, written at Montgomery: "They have not put me forward for office, it is true. I have two enemies in the [South Carolina] delegation. *One* friend, who, I believe, wants no office himself, and will probably act on the same principle for his friend—and the rest, personally, are indifferent to *me*, whilst some of them are not indifferent to *themselves*. There is no little jealousy of me by a part of them, and they will never agree to recommend me to any position whatever under the Confederacy. I expect nothing, therefore, from the delegation, lifting me to position. Good-bye, my dear son." Rhett and men of his way of thinking had counselled violence and outrage from the beginning, but they were restrained in the Convention by more sensible men like Stephens and Hill of Georgia, Brooks of Mississippi, and Perkins of Louisiana.

The sessions of the Convention were mostly held in secret. A committee of thirteen was appointed, with C. G. Memminger as chairman, to report a plan for a provisional Confederate government, and it was agreed to call the Convention a "Congress." The Legislature of Alabama voted a loan of half a million dollars to enable the Secessionists to set the new government in motion; and on the same day (February 7, 1861), the committee reported a plan, the basis of which was the National Constitution with some important modifications. They gave the name of the government organized under it the *Confederate States of America*. This was a misnomer; for no States as States were parties to the affair; it was only a confederation of politicians without the sanction of the people.

The constitution of the provisional government was adopted by the unanimous "vote of the States" on the 8th of February. On the following day, the members of the Convention took the oath of allegiance to the *Confederate States of America;* and then they proceeded to elect Jefferson Davis of Mississippi provisional president, and Alexander H. Stephens of Georgia vice-president of the Confederacy. The vast multitude who thronged the

GENERAL P. G. T. BEAUREGARD, C. S. A.

PRESIDENT LINCOLN'S FIRST CABINET: 1. SIMON CAMERON, SECRETARY OF WAR. 2. GIDEON WELLS, SECRETARY OF THE NAVY. 3. SALMON P. CHASE, SECRETARY OF THE TREASURY. 4. HANNIBAL HAMLIN, VICE-PRESIDENT. 5. WILLIAM H. SEWARD, SECRETARY OF STATE. 6. CALEB B. SMITH, SECRETARY OF THE INTERIOR. 7. EDWARD BATES, ATTORNEY-GENERAL.

State-House received the announcement of the election with vehement applause, and the same evening Mr. Stephens was serenaded. In a brief speech he predicted a glorious career for the Confederacy, if it should be supported by "the virtue, intelligence, and patriotism of the people." Alluding to the slave-system, he said: "With institutions, so far as regards their organic and social policy, in strict conformity to nature and the laws of the Creator, whether read in the Book of Inspiration or the great Book of Manifestations around us, we have all the natural elements essential to the highest attainment in the highest degree of power and glory. These institutions have been much assailed, and it is our mission to vindicate the great truths on which they rest, and with them exhibit the highest type of civilization which it is possible for human society to reach."

MAJ. ALLAN PINKERTON, SECRET SERVICE HEADQUARTERS

Having appointed standing committees, the Convention proceeded to choose a committee to report a form for a permanent government for the Confederacy, and they and the members warmly discussed the subject of a proper national flag and seal. Almost daily, various devices were sent in; and finally they decided that the national flag should consist of two red and one white stripe of equal width, running horizontally, with a blue union spangled with seven white stars, for, since the beginning of their session, Texas had joined the Confederacy, making seven States in their union. This flag, under which the insurgent hosts

rushed to battle, was first displayed over the State-House at Montgomery on the 4th of March, 1861. The Confederate government never possessed a *seal*, the emblem of sovereignty. One which they had ordered from England arrived at Richmond just as the Confederacy was broken up, in April, 1865, and was never used.

When Jefferson Davis was apprised, at his home near Vicksburg, of his election to the presidency, he hastened to Mont-

GROUP AT SECRET SERVICE HEADQUARTERS

gomery, where he was received with great enthusiasm, on the 15th of February. He was welcomed with the thunder of cannon and shouts of a great multitude; and at the railway station he made a speech, in which he briefly reviewed the then position of the South. He declared that the time for compromises had passed. "We are now determined," he said, "to maintain our position, and make all who oppose us smell Southern powder and feel Southern steel. . . . We will maintain our rights and our government at all hazards. We ask nothing; we want nothing; and will have no complications. If the other States join our Confederacy, they can freely come in on our terms. Our separation from the old Union is complete, and no compromise, no reconciliation can now be entertained." He was inaugurated on the 18th, when he chose for his constitutional advisers, Robert Toombs, Secretary of State; Charles G. Memminger, Secretary of the Treasury; Le Roy Pope Walker, Secretary of War; Stephen R. Mallory,

PRESIDENT OF THE SENATE AND FIRST CONFEDERATE CABINET.

FOUNTAIN AND STREET IN MONTGOMERY, ALA.

JEFFERSON DAVIS' FIRST CABINET

Secretary of the Navy, and John H. Reagan, Postmaster-General. Judah P. Benjamin was appointed Attorney-General. So was inaugurated the government known as the *Confederate States of America*, which carried on war against the life of our Republic for more than four years.

CHAPTER VII.

Lunacy—Yielding to Necessity—Wild Dreams of the Future—Boasting—The Confederates Prepare for War—Permanent Constitution Adopted—Adjournment of the Montgomery Convention—Principles of the New Government Expounded—Lincoln and Davis—Lincoln's Journey to the Capital—Narrative of His Escape—His Inauguration and Inaugural Address—Duties of the Administration —Condition of the Army and Navy—Benton's Prophecy—Confederate Commissioners at the Capital—The Virginians—Attempt to Relieve Fort Sumter and the Result.

THERE were symptoms of real lunacy among some of the leaders in the revolutionary movement, especially in South Carolina. When that new "nation" was only nine days old, a correspondent of the Associated Press wrote that it had been proposed to adopt for it a new system of civil time, to show its independence. Only a week after the organization of the Southern Confederacy at Montgomery,

U. S. INFANTRY CAMP

the editor of the *Charleston Courier* wrote: "The South *might*, under the new Confederacy, treat the disorganized and demoralized Northern States as *insurgents*, and deny them recognition. But if peaceful division ensues, the South, *after taking the Federal Capitol and archives*, and being recognized as the government *de facto* by all foreign powers, can, if they see proper, recognize the Northern Confederacy or Confederacies, and enter into treaty stipulations with them. Were this not done, it would be difficult for the Northern States to take a place among the nations, and their flag would not be respected or recognized." There was much "wild talk" of that sort; and the venerable James L. Pettigru of Charleston, who remained a firm friend of the Union in spite of the madmen around him, was justified when, on being asked by a stranger in the streets of the city, "Where is the lunatic asylum?" he said, as he pointed alternately to the east, "It is there;" to the west, "It is there;" to the north, "It is there;" and to the south, "It is there; the whole State of South Carolina is a lunatic asylum."

Notwithstanding the same arrogant and world-defying spirit was superficially manifested in the councils of the Confederacy at Montgomery, they were compelled to bow to the behests of prudence and expediency, and, abandoning the position that they would have *free trade* with all the world whereby the riches of the earth would fall at their feet, they proceeded not only to impose a tariff upon imports, but regarding "King Cotton" as immortal and omniscient, they even went so far as to propose an export duty on the great staple of the Gulf States. Howell Cobb, who proposed it, said: "I apprehend that we are conscious of the power we hold in our hands, by reason of our producing that staple so necessary to the

VIEWS OF FORT SUMTER

world. I doubt not that power will exert an influence mightier than armies or navies. We know that by an embargo we could soon place not only the United States, but many of the European powers, under the necessity of electing between such a recognition of our independence as we require, or domestic convulsions at home." Of this supposed omnipotent power, and the superior courage and prowess in arms of the people of the slave-labor States, the leaders were continually boasting. Senator Hammond, of South Carolina, a wealthy slaveholder and a son of a New England schoolmaster, writing to a feminine relative in Schenectady, New York, on the 5th of February, 1861, after alluding to the dissolution of the Union, and saying, "We absolve you, by this, from all the sins of slavery, and take upon ourselves all its supposed sin and evil, openly before the world, and in the sight of God," remarked: "Let us alone. Let me tell you, my dear cousin, that if there is any attempt at war on the part of the North, we can soundly thrash them on any field of battle." "One Southron is equal to five Yankees in a fight!" exclaimed Yancey, in a speech at Selma. And the Convention at Montgomery proceeded to prepare for testing the relative strength of the two sections.

President Davis was authorized to accept one hundred thousand volunteers for six months, and to borrow $15,000,-000 at the rate of eight per cent. interest a year. Provision was made for a navy and a postal revenue; and Davis was authorized to assume control of "all military operations between the Confederate States" or any of them, and powers foreign to them. The Convention recommended the several States to cede the forts and all other public establishments within their limits to the Confederate States; and P. G. T. Beaure-

DEFENCES OF WASHINGTON

gard, a Louisiana creole, who had abandoned his flag, was appointed brigadier-general and ordered from New Orleans to the command of the insurgents at Charleston. Early in March a permanent constitution for the Confederacy was adopted; and a commission was appointed to proceed to Washington and make a settlement of all questions at issue between the "two governments," while the Confederate secretary of the treasury prepared to establish custom-houses along the frontiers of the Confederate States. After agreeing, by resolution, to accept a portion of the money belonging to the United States which Louisiana had unlawfully seized, the Convention adjourned. Their proceedings were never published, but constitute a part of the "Confederate archives" in the possession of the National Government.

Meanwhile Mr. Stephens, the vice-president of the Confederacy, had assumed the office of expounder of the principles upon which the new government was founded. In a speech at Savannah, on the 21st of March, 1861, he declared that the immediate cause of the rebellion was African Slavery—the rock, he said, on which Mr. Jefferson declared the Union would split; but he doubted whether Mr. Jefferson understood the truth on which that rock stood. He believed the founders of the Republic held erroneous views on the subject of slavery, and that it was a false assumption of the fathers, put forth in the Declaration of Independence, that "*all* men are created equal." He declared that the corner-stone of the new Confederacy rested "upon the great truth, that the negro is not equal to the white man; that slavery—

OFFICERS ON DECK OF PHILADELPHIA.

DECK AND TURRET OF KAATSKILL.

QUARTER DECK OF PAWNEE.

QUARTER DECK OF PAWNEE.

The "Pawnee," the "Philadelphia" and the "Kaatskill"

subordination to the superior race—is his natural and normal condition. It is upon this truth," he said, "on which our fabric is firmly planted; and I cannot permit myself to doubt the ultimate success of a full recognition of this principle throughout the civilized world." Then, to give strength to his declaration that slavery was the corner-stone of the new fabric, he rather irreverently quoted the words of the Apostle

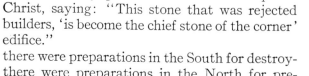

applied to by the first in our new While ing the Union serving it. In in the latter, persuade the really organ- Jefferson Da- be inaugu- Montgomery, Southern Lincoln was Illinois to the stalled Chief divided Re- justice, and South, in his inaugural address: friends. We must not be ene- have strained, it must not break mystic chords of memory, field and patriot grave to every all over this broad land, will yet when again touched, as surely angels of our nature." They

Jefferson Davis was then Abraham Lincoln was fifty-two. was, in person, sinewy and light, the middle height, and erect in Lincoln was tall, thin, large- six feet four inches in height. ewy, easily lifting five hundred pounds. His were disproportionately long, and there was no movements. The features of Davis were regu- defined; his face was thin and much wrinkled; sightless, and the other was dark and piercing Lincoln's features were angular; his forehead eyes were dark gray and very expressive, alter- ling with fun and subdued into sadness. and Davis were both natives of Kentucky, life Davis was taken to Mississippi. Raised in parative luxury, he was educated at the West tary Academy. He served in the army in Mex- father-in-law, General Zachary Taylor; held a place in the National Congress, and was Presi-

INTERIOR VIEWS OF FORT SUMTER

Christ, saying: "This stone that was rejected builders, 'is become the chief stone of the corner' edifice."

there were preparations in the South for destroy- there were preparations in the North for pre- the former section, they were chiefly material; they were chiefly moral, for it was difficult to loyal people that the Southern politicians would ize an armed rebellion. At the time when vis was moving from his home in Mississippi to rated president of the Southern Confederacy at and to declare "all who oppose us shall smell powder and feel Southern steel," Abraham moving from his home in National capital, to be in- Magistrate of the whole un- public, with sublime faith in to say to the North and the "We are not enemies, but mies. Though passion may our bonds of affection. The stretching from every battle- living heart and hearthstone swell the chorus of the Union they will be, by the better were nearly equal in age. about fifty-four years of age; Mr. Davis a little above posture; Mr. boned, and He was sin- legs and arms grace in his lar and well one eye was in expression. was high; his nately spark- Mr. Lincoln but in early ease and com- Point Mili- ico under his distinguished dent Pierce's

Secretary of War. Lincoln was born in obscurity; passed his early days in poverty, laboring with his hands on a farm, in the forest, or as a flat-boatman on the Mississippi. He had settled with his father in Illinois, where he, self-taught, studied law and rose to distinction at the bar, and in the esteem of his fellow-citizens. Davis was a keen politician; calm, reticent, audacious, polished, cold, sagacious, rich in experience in the arts of the partisan and the affairs of statecraft, possessed of great concentration of purpose, an imperious will, abounding pride, and much executive ability. Lincoln was as open as the day; loved truth supremely, and country above party; abhorred trickery and deception; possessed great

SHOWING EFFECT OF TEN DAYS BOMBARDMENT.

SHOWING DESTRUCTION OF OUTER WALLS. NOV. 10.

SHOWING EFFECT OF TRIAL SHOTS FROM THE FEDERAL BREACHING BATTERIES.

SCENES SHOWING EFFECT OF BOMBARDMENT AT FORT SUMTER

firmness of will and a childlike reliance upon God; read the Bible and Shakespeare more than any other books; with extraordinary conversational powers and exuberant mirthfulness manifested in sparkling jests, stories and anecdotes, at appropriate times. He was, at one time, a representative in the National Congress; and on all occasions appeared as a representative American, illustrating by his own career, in a

most conspicuous and distinguished manner, cent and elevating operations of republican and institutions. His last words, when he his home at Springfield, Illinois, after allu- Washington, whose seat he was about to feel that I cannot succeed without the same which sustained him, and on the same Being I place my reliance for support; and I my friends, will all pray that I may receive assistance without which I cannot succeed, which success is certain."

the benefi- government parted from ding to occupy: "I Divine aid Almighty hope you, that Divine but with

On his journey to the National capital New York, Philadelphia and Harrisburg, was everywhere greeted with affection and was in Philadelphia on ton's birthday, and with his raised the American flag the consecrated old State- the presence of a vast as- people. There, where the pendence was adopted and an extraordinary speech, in his views of the moral power ment, and declared his belief of justice enunciated in it, saved from ruin. "But," he country cannot be saved principle, I I would *on this spot* My friends, but what I and, if it be mighty God, than four in Inde- sinated be- principles of A plot murder Mr. through at Washing- existence of ger to meet danger. The President's 1864, and in much

by way of Mr. Lincoln respect. He Washing- own hands high above House, in semblage of Declaration of Inde- proclaimed, he made which he expounded of that great instru- that by the principles our Republic might be exclaimed, "if this without giving up this was about to say rather *be assassinated than surrender it. . . .* I have said nothing am willing to live by, the pleasure of Al- die by." A little more years afterward, his body lay in state pendence Hall. He had been assas- cause he had firmly supported the the Declaration of Independence! had been formed in Baltimore to Lincoln while he should be passing that city. General Scott and others ton were so well satisfied of the such a plot, that they sent a messen- Mr. Lincoln and warn him of his story of his escape was given by the own lips to the writer in December, was substantially as follows, though greater detail: He arrived in Phila-

VIEWS OF FORTRESS MONROE

delphia on the 21st of February, where he agreed to stop over night, and hoist the flag on Independence Hall the next morning. That evening an intimate friend of his from Chicago (Mr. Judd) invited Mr. Lincoln to his room in the Continental Hotel, where he met Mr. Allan Pinkerton, a shrewd detective from Chicago. They told Mr. Lincoln of the plot. Mr. Pinkerton had been engaged several days in Baltimore in ferreting it out. It was fully discovered, but he could not learn the names of the conspirators.

ARMY HOSPITAL NEAR WASHINGTON, D. C.

Mr. Lincoln had made arrangements to go to Harrisburg from Philadelphia, to meet the Pennsylvania Legislature there, and from that capital to proceed through Baltimore to Washington. His friends urged him to go on that night through Baltimore to the capital, and so evade the murderers; but he determined to adhere to his engagements, for he could not believe there was a conspiracy to kill him.

FORT JOHNSON, JAMES ISLAND

When returning to his room at the Continental, Mr. Lincoln met a son of Senator Seward, the messenger sent to give him warning. He said the Washington police had discovered the plot, but they were not aware of the work of Mr. Pinkerton. Then Mr. Lincoln was satisfied that there was danger. After hoisting the flag at the State-House the next morning, he went to Harrisburg, in company with Mr. Sumner and others, dined, and waited for the time to return to Philadelphia, for he determined to go back to that city, and immediately on to Baltimore, instead of leaving Harrisburg the next morning for that place, according to the public arrangements. Mr. Judd, meanwhile, had obtained such control of the telegraph at Harrisburg, that no communication could pass to Baltimore and give the conspirators a knowledge of the change in arrangements. In New York Mr. Lincoln had been presented with a fine beaver hat, and in it had been placed a soft wool hat. He had the hats in a box in his room. He had never worn a soft wool hat in his life; so, after making arrangements for Mr. Lamon (afterward marshal of the District of Columbia), whom nobody knew, and Mr. Judd, to accompany him, Mr. Lincoln put on an old overcoat he had with him, and with the soft hat in his pocket, he walked out the back door of the hotel where he was stopping, bareheaded, without exciting any special curiosity. "Then I put on the soft hat and joined my friends," said Mr. Lincoln, "for I was not the same man." They returned to Philadelphia, where they found a despatch from Pinkerton, at Baltimore, that it was doubtful whether the conspirators had courage to execute their scheme; but as the arrangements had been made, they went on in a special train. "We were a long time in the station at Baltimore," said the President. "I heard people talking around, but no one particularly observed me. At an early hour on Saturday morning, at about the time I was expected to leave Harrisburg, I arrived in Washington."

Mr. Lincoln was warmly welcomed by his friends in Washington city, and when, at an early hour after his arrival (February 23, 1861), he called on President Buchanan, the latter could hardly believe his eyes. He gave the President-elect a cordial welcome. So also did General Scott, who, the Secessionists thought, would join them because he was a Virginian; but he was loyal to the core, and had filled Washington city with troops in such numbers, it was supposed, that serious interference with Mr. Lincoln's inauguration was made impossible. That ceremony took place on Monday, the 4th of March, 1861. Chief Justice Taney administered the oath. There was no disturbance. The scheme of the Secessionists to prevent Mr. Lincoln's inauguration had been frustrated, but the plan of the Confederates to ultimately seize the National capital was still a cherished one. Only about six hundred troops were there, but as they had been gathered in small numbers at a time from various points, and kept concealed, the Secessionists believed there were many thousands of them; and when the small number was revealed on the first of March, it was too late to call together the "minute-men" of Maryland and Virginia. Meanwhile President Buchanan had been greatly harassed by the Secessionists. Governor Pickens had demanded of Major Anderson the surrender of Fort Sumter. Anderson

CHARLES A. DANA, ASSISTANT SECRETARY OF WAR

OFFICERS OF THE 164TH AND 170TH NEW YORK VOLUNTEERS

refused; whereupon the governor sent J. W. Hayne, the attorney-general of South Carolina, to Washington, to make the same demand. The President's course was vacillating; and in this, as in other matters, he resolved to cast the responsibility upon his successor. The Secessionists had failed to accomplish, through the arts of diplomacy, a recognition by the National Government of the sovereignty of any States; and their efforts ceased early in February. Mr. Buchanan left the chair of state for private life a deeply humiliated and sorrowing man. On bidding Senator Fitzpatrick good-bye, and with the consciousness of rare opportunities for winning glory and renown as a patriot forever lost, he said: "The current of public opinion warns me that we shall never meet again on this side the grave. I have tried to do my duty to both sections, and have displeased both. I feel isolated in the world."

President Lincoln, standing at the east front of the Capitol, like Saul among the prophets, head and shoulders above other men, read his inaugural address in a clear, loud voice, in the ears of a vast multitude of people, who heard him distinctly, and who greeted its sentences with cheer after cheer. It had been waited for by the loyal people of the land with the greatest anxiety, for it was expected to foreshadow the policy of the new adminis- tration. And so it did. It gave no uncertain sound. To the people of the slave- labor States he first ad- dressed a few assuring words in which he said: "I have no purpose, directly or in- directly, to interfere with the institution of slavery in the States where it exists. I believe I have no lawful right to do so, and I have no inclination to do so." He read a resolution of the Re- publican Convention that nominated him, which de- clared that the rights of the States, in order that they might control their own in- stitutions, should be main- tained inviolate, and de- nouncing as a high crime the invasion by an armed force of any State or Terri- tory, "no matter under what pretext." He reiterated these sentiments as his own; assured the people that "the prosperity, peace, and secu- rity of no section" were to be "in any wise endan- gered by the new incoming Administration," and fur- ther that every section of the Union should have equal protection without favor to any.

FORT MOULTRIE AFTER BOMBARDMENT

Mr. Lincoln then dis- cussed the political struc- ture and character of the Republic, showing that the Union is older than the Constitution; that it is necessarily *perpetual;* that there is no inherent power in the whole or in part to terminate it, and that the secession of a State was impossible. Assuming that the Republic was unbroken, he declared that, to the extent of his ability, he should take care, as the Consti- tution required him to do, that the laws should be executed in all the States, performing that duty as far as practicable, unless his "rightful masters, the American people," should withhold the requisite means, or, in some authoritative manner, direct the contrary. "I trust this will not be regarded as a menace," he continued, "but only as the declared purpose of the Union that it will constitutionally defend and maintain itself. In doing this," he added, "there need be no bloodshed or violence; and there shall be none, unless it be forced upon the National authority." He declared that the power confided to him should be used "to hold, occupy, and possess the property and places belonging to the Government, and to collect the duties and imposts."

So, in a frank, generous, kindly manner, did Mr. Lincoln avow his determination to perform the duties of the Chief Executive of the nation, according to his convictions and his ability. He had said in a speech at Trenton, on his way from New York to Philadelphia: "I shall do all that may be in my power to promote a peaceful settlement of all our difficulties. The man does not live who is more devoted to peace than I am—no one who would do more to preserve it; *but it may be necessary to put the foot down firmly.*" The *Springfield Journal,* published at the home of Mr. Lincoln, and his accredited "organ," had said weeks before: "If South Carolina violates the law [by obstructing the collection of the revenue], then comes the tug of war. The President of the United States, in such an emergency, has a plain duty to perform. Mr. Buchanan may shirk it, or the emergency may not exist during his administration. If not, then the Union will last through his term of office. If the overt act, on the part of South Carolina, takes place on or after the 4th of March, 1861, then the duty of executing the laws will devolve upon

DISTANT VIEW OF FORT SUMTER

Mr. Lincoln." So felt all the loyal people of the land; and they were strengthened by hope, given in the promise of his inaugural address that he should faithfully do his duty.

In that address, the President also declared that he should "endeavor, by justice, to reconcile all discontents;" and he asked the enemies of the Government to point to a single instance where "any right, plainly written in the Constitution," had ever been denied. He then showed the danger of the precedent established by secession, for it might lead to infinite subdivisions by discontented minorities. "Plainly," he said, "the central idea of secession is anarchy." He referred to the impossibility of a dissolution of the Union, physically speaking; and contemplating a state of political separation of the sections, he asked, significantly, "Can treaties be more faithfully enforced among aliens than laws can among friends?" He reminded them that their respective territories must remain "face to face;" that they could not "fight always," and that the causes of feuds would continue to exist. He begged his countrymen to take time for serious deliberation. "Such of you," he said, "as are now dissatisfied, still have the old Constitution unimpaired, and, on the sensitive point, the laws of

BERMUDA HUNDRED LANDING

your own framing under it; while the new Administration will have no immediate power, if it would, to change either. . . . In your hands, my dissatisfied fellow-countrymen, and not in mine, is the momentous issue of Civil War. The Government will not assail you. You can have no conflict without being yourselves the aggressors. You have no oath registered in Heaven to destroy the Government; whilst I shall have the most solemn one to preserve, protect, and defend it."

The Secessionists would listen to no words of kindness, of justice, or of warning; they had resolved to destroy the Union at all hazards; and the prophecy of Thomas H. Benton, uttered in 1857, was speedily fulfilled. He knew their schemes, for they had long tried to enlist him in them. "So long as the people of the North," he said to Senator Wilson, "shall be content to attend to commerce and manufactures, and accept the policy and rule of the disunionists, they will condescend to remain in the Union; but should the Northern people attempt to exercise their just influence in the nation, they would attempt to seize the Government or disrupt the Union; but," he said, with terrible emphasis, "*God and their own crimes will put them in the hands of the people.*"

Mr. Lincoln chose for his constitutional advisers, Wm. H. Seward of New York, Secretary of State; Salmon P. Chase of Ohio, Secretary of the Treasury; Simon Cameron of Pennsylvania, Secretary of War; Gideon Welles of Connecticut, Secretary of the Navy; Caleb Smith of Indiana, Secretary of the Interior; Montgomery Blair of Maryland, Postmaster-General; and Edward Bates of Missouri, Attorney-General. With these men Mr. Lincoln began his eventful administration. With the close of the "Inauguration Ball," the night before these appointments were made, ended the poetry of his life; after that it was all the prose of care, anxiety, and incessant labor incident to the daily life of a conscientious head of a nation in a state of civil war. The plain meaning of his inaugural address was distorted by the Confederates to inflame the minds of the people in the slave-labor States. It was misrepresented and maligned, and the people were bewildered. Meanwhile the President and his cabinet went calmly at work to ascertain the condition of the ship of state. Means were planned for replenishing the exhausted Treasury and to strengthen the public credit. The condition of the Army and Navy was contemplated with great solicitude, for it was evident that the Confederates had resolved on war. Of the twenty forts in the slave-labor States, all but four had been seized by them. Every arsenal there was in their possession. The entire regular force of the

BRIGADIER-GENERAL A. J. SLEMMER

Pontoon Bridge, Valley of the Potomac

John Cabin Bridge Over the Potomac River

Republic, in soldiers, was sixteen thousand men, and these were mostly on the Western frontiers, guarding the settlers against the Indians; and of this small number, General David E. Twiggs had treacherously surrendered between two and three thousand, with munitions of war, into the hands of the Texan insurgents, so early as the middle of February.

CITY OF CHARLESTON, S. C., FROM THE TOP OF MILLS HOUSE

The little National navy, like the army, had been placed far beyond the reach of the Government, for immediate use. It consisted of ninety vessels of all classes, but only forty-two were in commission. Twenty-eight, carrying an aggregate of nearly nine hundred guns, were lying in ports, dismantled, and could not be made ready for sea, some of them, in several months. Most of those in commission had been sent to distant seas; and the entire available force for the defence of the whole Atlantic coast of the Republic was the *Brooklyn*, 25, and the store-ship *Relief*, of two guns. The *Brooklyn* drew too much water to enter Charleston harbor, where war had begun, with safety; and the *Relief* had been ordered to the coast of Africa with stores for the squadron there. Many of the naval officers were born in slave-labor States; so also were those of the army; and many of both arms of the service deserted their flag at the critical moment, and joined the enemies of their Government. The amazing fact was presented that Mr. Buchanan's Secretaries of War and Navy had so disposed the available military forces of the Republic that it could not command their services at the critical moment when the hand of its enemy was raised to destroy its life. The public offices were swarming with disloyal men, and for a full month the President, knowing the importance of having faithful instruments to work with, was engaged in relieving the Government of these unfaithful servants. He wisely strengthened his arm by calling to his aid loyal men, before he ventured to strike a blow in defence of the threatened National authority.

We have observed that the Convention at Montgomery appointed commissioners to treat with the National government upon matters of mutual interest. Two of these (John Forsyth and Martin J. Crawford) arrived in Washington city on the 5th of March (1861), and asked for an "unofficial interview" with the Secretary of State. It was declined, when they sent him a sealed communication setting forth the object of their mission as representatives of "a government perfect in all its parts, and endowed with all the means of self-support," and asking for an opportunity to "present their credentials" at an early day. This communication—this adroit attempt to obtain a recognition of the sovereignty of the Confederate States from the National Government—failed. In a "memorandum" which he sent to them, the Secretary referred to the principles laid down in the inaugural address, and, like Mr. Lincoln, he declared the doctrine that no State as a State had seceded or could secede, and that, consequently, the "Confederate States government" had no legal existence. The commissioners remained more than a month in Washington, and then, after giving the Secretary (Mr. Seward) a lecture on the theory of government, they left for home on the day when the South Carolinians proceeded to attack Fort Sumter.

Among the first questions that demanded the attention of the new Administration was, "Shall Fort Sumter be reinforced and supplied?" They were anxious for peace, and the question was kept in abeyance until late in March, when Gustavus V. Fox (afterward the efficient Assistant Secretary of the Navy) was sent to Charleston harbor to ascertain the exact condition of things there. He found that Major Anderson had sufficient supplies to last him until the 12th of April, and it was understood between them that if not supplied, he must surrender or evacuate the fort at noon on that day. On his return to Washington Mr. Fox reported to the President that if succor was to be afforded to Anderson, it must be before the middle of April. The President, anxious for peace, and not to bring on a collision with the South Carolina insurgents, had listened favorably to urgent advice to abandon Sumter and not precipitate hostilities. The Virginia State Convention was then in session considering the propriety of leaving the Union. Mr. Lincoln sent for a professed Union man in that body, and said to him, "If your Convention shall adjourn, instead of staying in session menacing the Government, I will immediately direct Major Anderson to evacuate Fort Sumter." Had the Virginia politicians wanted peace, this request would have been complied with. On the contrary, this professed Virginia Unionist replied, "Sir, the United States must

TRANSPORTATION OF SUPPLIES

instantly evacuate Fort Sumter and Fort Pickens, and give assurances that no attempt will be made to collect revenue in the Southern ports."

This virtual demand for the President to recognize the Southern Confederacy as an independent nation caused him to "put the foot down firmly." He ordered an expedition to be sent to Charleston harbor immediately, under the direction of Mr. Fox (who had offered a plan for such action), with provisions and troops for Fort Sumter. Fox sailed from New York with a squadron of eight vessels, on the 9th of April, but only three reached the vicinity of Charleston harbor, which they could not enter because of a terrible storm that was sweeping over the ocean in that region. While these vessels (the *Baltic*, carrying the troops, and the *Pawnee* and *Harriet Lane*) were buffeting the tempest, the insurgents attacked Fort Sumter with bomb-shells and solid shot, with great fury. For three months after the expulsion of the *Star of the West*, Anderson had been kept in suspense by the temporizing policy of his Government. He had seen forts and batteries piled around Fort Sumter for its destruction, and had been compelled to keep his own great guns muzzled, waiting for an attack. Nearly all that time he was menaced daily with

FORT PUTNAM, CHARLESTON, S. C.

hostilities; abused by the Southern press; misrepresented by the Northern newspapers, and yet was forced to passively endure his situation until his supplies were exhausted. He had sent away the women and children to New York, in February, and had calmly awaited the course of events.

Meanwhile the leaders in the revolutionary movement were impatient to begin their destructive work. They were vehemently urging Virginia and other Border States to openly and practically espouse their cause. They feared the cooling effects of delay and hesitation, and anxiously sought a pretext for firing the first gun. The crisis was reached on the morning of the 8th of April, when President Lincoln, with the most generous fairness, telegraphed to Governor Pickens that he was about to send relief to Fort Sumter. It produced the most intense excitement in Charleston. Beauregard, who was in command of the armed insurgents there, sent the message to Montgomery, to which L. Pope Walker, the Confederate Secretary of War, replied on the 10th, ordering him to demand the evacuation of the fort. "If this is refused," he said, "proceed, in such manner as you may determine, to reduce it." Beauregard replied, "The demand will be made to-morrow."

Aqueduct Bridge, Potomac River

CHAPTER VIII.

Virginians in Charleston—A Cry for Blood—Events in Charleston—Siege of Fort Sumter—Incidents of the Struggle—Evacuation of the Fort—Joyful Feelings in Charleston—Gratitude of the Loyal People Displayed—Honors to Major Anderson—Attempts to Capture Fort Pickens—Honors to Lieutenant Slemmer—President's Call for Troops—Responses to the Call—Uprising of the Loyal People—Boastings of the Northern Press—A Fatal Mistake—Interpretations of Scripture—Proclamations and Counter-Proclamations—Privateering Recommended to the Confederates—Action of the Confederate Congress—Privateers Commissioned.

THE hesitation of Virginia to join the Confederacy gave the leaders in South Carolina many misgivings as to her "patriotism;" but two of her sons, who were in Charleston at this crisis, gave them assurance of her "fidelity to the cause." These were Edmund Ruffin, a gray-haired old man, and Roger A. Pryor, a young lawyer, who had served a term in the National Congress. Pryor was serenaded on the evening of the 10th of April (1861), and in response to the compliment he made a characteristic speech. "Gentlemen," he said, "I thank you especially that you have at last annihilated this cursed Union, reeking with corruption and insolent with excess of tyranny. Thank God it is at last

ARMY HOSPITAL, NEAR WASHINGTON

blasted and riven by the lightning wrath of an outraged and indignant people. Not only is it gone, but gone forever. . . . Do not distrust Virginia. As sure as to-morrow's sun will rise upon us, just so sure will Virginia be a member of the Southern Confederacy. And I will tell you, gentlemen," said Mr. Pryor with great vehemence of manner, "what will put her in the Southern Confederacy in less than an hour by Shrewsbury clock—*strike a blow!* The very moment that blood is shed, old Virginia will make common cause with her sisters of the South."

This cry for blood was telegraphed to Montgomery, when a member of the Alabama Legislature (Mr. Gilchrist) said to Davis and his cabinet: "Gentlemen, unless you sprinkle blood in the faces of the people of Alabama, they will be back in the old Union in less than ten days." Beauregard was at once ordered to shed blood if necessary, and so "fire the Southern heart." That officer sent a deputation to Major Anderson to demand the immediate surrender of Fort Sumter. The supplies for the garrison were nearly exhausted, and Anderson replied: "I will evacuate the fort in five days if I do not receive controlling instructions from my Government." Davis knew better than Anderson that vessels were on their way with supplies for the fort, and he instructed Beauregard to act accordingly. So, at a little past three o'clock in the morning of the 12th of April, that officer announced to Anderson, that within one hour the batteries, which then formed a semi-circle around Sumter, would open upon the fort. The military in Charleston had been summoned to their posts early in the evening, in anticipation of this movement, and a call was made by telegraph to the surrounding country to send four thousand men into the city.

At the appointed hour the heavy booming of a cannon on James Island awakened the sleepers in Charleston, and the streets were soon thronged with people. From the broad throat of a mortar a fiery

VIEWS OF BEAUFORT, PORT ROYAL, HILTONS HEAD, S. C.

bomb-shell sped through the black night and exploded over Sumter.   After a brief pause, another heavy gun at Cumming's point, on Morris Island, sent a large round-shot that struck against the granite wall of the fort with fearful force.   That gun was fired by the white-haired Virginian (Ruffin), who had begged the privilege of firing the first shot against Sumter.   He boasted of the deed so long as he lived.   In the early summer of 1865, when he was over seventy years of age, he deliberately blew off the top of his head with his gun, declaring in a note which he left—"I cannot survive the liberties of my country."   His shot was followed by a tempest of shells and balls from full thirty cannons and mortars which opened at once upon the fort, but which elicited no response until about seven o'clock in the morning.   Then, by a judicious arrangement of the little garrison, the great guns of Sumter were enabled to play upon all the hostile batteries at the same time, under the skillful directions of Captain Doubleday, Surgeon Crawford, and Lieutenant Snyder.   Doubleday and Crawford afterward became distinguished major-generals.   But

Lt. John C. Davis   Capt. Abner Doubleday   Capt. J. G. Foster
Asst. Surgeon S. W. Crawford   Lt. Truman Seymour

it was evident, after four hours of hard and skillful labor at the guns, that Fort Sumter could not seriously injure the works opposed to it.   On Cumming's Point was an iron-plated battery that was absolutely invulnerable to missiles hurled upon it from Fort Sumter.

A fearful contest had now begun.   The walls and parapets of the fort were soon shattered; its *barbette* guns were dismounted, and its barracks and officers' quarters were set on fire.   News of the relief squadron had reachd the garrison, and Surgeon Crawford bravely ascended to the parapet to look for it.   He distinctly saw the three ships struggling with the storm outside the bar.   Their near presence nerved the hearts and muscles of the soldiers, but their hopes were vain.   The little squadron was compelled to leave the band of brave men in Sumter without relief.

All that day the assault continued, and all that night, which was dark and stormy, a sluggish bombardment of the fort was kept up; and when, on the following morning (April 13, 1861), on which the sun rose in unclouded splendor, it was renewed with increased vigor, the wearied garrison of not more than seventy men found their supplies almost exhausted.   In three days they must be starved out.   On that morning the last parcel of rice had been cooked, and nothing but salted pork was left to be eaten. Red-hot shot were making havoc among the wooden structures of the fort.   The flames spread, and the heat was intolerable.   The fire threatened the magazine, and ninety barrels of powder were rolled into the sea.   The smoke and heat were so stifling that the men were often compelled to lie upon the ground with wet cloths over their faces to enable them to breathe.   The old flag was kept flying until a shot cut its staff, and it fell to the ground at a little past noon.   It was caught up, carried to the ramparts, and there replanted by Sergeant Peter Hart, Major Anderson's faithful servant and friend.

When the flag of Sumter fell, the insurgents shouted, for they regarded its downfall as a token of submission.   A boat instantly shot out from Cumming's Point, bearing an officer who held a white

FORT JOHNSON, CHARLESTON, S. C.

handkerchief on the point of his sword as a flag of truce. He landed at the wharf at Fort Sumter, and, hurrying to the nearest port-hole, begged a soldier to let him in. The faithful man refused. "I am General Wigfall, of Beauregard's staff, and want to see Major Anderson!" he cried. The soldier said, "Stand there until I can call the commander." "For God's sake," cried Wigfall, "let me in! I can't stand out here in the firing." He ran around to the sallyport, but was there confronted by its blazing ruins. Then the poor fellow, half dead with fright, ran around the fort waving his white handkerchief

MONITOR IN TRENT'S REACH, JAMES RIVER, 1861

toward his fellow-insurgents, to prevent their firing; but it was in vain. At last, out of sheer pity, he was allowed to crawl into a port-hole, after giving up his sword, where he was met by some of the officers of the fort. He told them who he was; that he had been sent by Beauregard to stop the firing, and begged them piteously to raise a white flag. "You are on fire," he said, "and your flag is down." He was interrupted by one of the officers, who said, "Our flag is not down," and Wigfall saw it where Peter Hart had replaced it. "Well, well," he said, "I want to stop this." Holding out his sword and handkerchief, he said to one of the officers, "Will you hoist this?" "No, sir," was the reply; "it is for you, General Wigfall, to stop them." "Will any of you hold this out of the embrasure?" he asked. No one offering the service, he said, "May I hold it there?" "If you wish to," was the cool reply. Wigfall sprang into the embrasure and waved the handkerchief several times, when a shot striking near him, he scampered away. He then begged some one else to hold it for him. At length consent was given to hoist a white flag over the ramparts, for the sole purpose of holding a conference with Major Anderson, who was sent for. Wigfall repeated his false story that he had come from Beauregard, and on assuring Anderson that the latter acceded to the major's terms—the evacuation of the fort on the 15th—that officer allowed the white flag to be hoisted, and Wigfall left. Seeing this, a deputation came from Beauregard, who informed the commander of the fort that Wigfall had not seen their chief in two days. Indignant because of the foul deception, Anderson declared the white flag should immediately come down, but he was persuaded to leave it until a conference could be held with Beauregard. Wigfall was a National Senator from Texas, and was one of the most insolent and boastful men on the floor of Congress. Soon after this ridiculous display of his mendacity and cowardice, he disappeared from public life, shorn of the confidence and respect of his more honorable associates. He was on Jefferson Davis's staff for a while.

The conference with Beauregard resulted in an arrangement for the evacuation of Fort Sumter; and on Sunday, the 14th of April, 1861, the little garrison, with their private property, went on board a small steamboat that took them to the *Baltic* that lingered outside the bar, in which they were conveyed to New York. Major Anderson *evacuated* the fort, but did not *surrender* it; and he carried away with him the garrison flag, which, just four years afterward, tattered and torn, was again raised by the hands of that gallant officer (then a major-general) over all that remained of Fort Sumter—a heap of ruins.

Governor Pickens had watched the bombardment of the fort on Saturday with a telescope, and that evening he addressed the excited multitude in Charleston, saying: "Thank God the war is open, and

GENERAL VIEWS OF CULPEPPER, AUGUST, 1862

COLONEL BRAXTON BRAGG, C.S.A., LATER MAJOR-GENERAL

we will conquer or perish. . . . We have humbled the flag of the United States. I can here say to you, it is the first time in the history of this country that the Stars and Stripes have been humbled. That proud flag was never lowered before to any nation on the earth. It has triumphed for seventy years; but to-day, the 13th of April, it has been humbled, and humbled before the glorious little State of South Carolina." On the following day, the holy Sabbath, the fall of Fort Sumter was commemorated in the churches of Charleston. The venerable bishop of the diocese of the Protestant Episcopal church was led by the rector of St. Philip's to the sacred desk, where he addressed a few words to the people. Speaking of the battle, he said, "Your boys were there, and mine were there, and it was right they should be there." Bishop Lynch, of the Roman Catholic church, spoke exultingly of the result of the conflict; and a *Te Deum* was chanted in commemoration of the event in the cathedral of St. John and St. Finbar, where he was officiating.

The loyal people of the free-labor States were loud in their praises of Major Anderson and his men for their gallant defence of the fort; and their gratitude was shown by substantial tokens. The citizens of Taunton, Massachusetts, and of Philadelphia, each presented Major Anderson with an elegant sword, richly ornamented. The citizens of New York presented a beautiful gold medal, and the authorities of that city gave him the freedom of the corporation in an elegant gold box. The Chamber of Commerce caused a series of medals to be struck in commemoration of the defence, to be presented to Major Anderson and his whole command; and from legislative bodies and other sources he received pleasing testimonials. Better than all, the President of the United States gave the major, by commission, the rank and pay of a brigadier-general in the army.

While hostilities against Fort Sumter were occurring, movements were made for the capture of strong Fort Pickens, on Santa Rosa Island, commanding the entrance to the harbor of Pensacola, in Florida. Near it were two inferior forts (Fort Barrancas, built by the Spaniards, and Fort McRee); and near Pensacola was a navy-yard.

A DEAD CONFEDERATE SOLDIER IN THE TRENCHES.

INTERIOR VIEW.

A DEAD CONFEDERATE SOLDIER IN THE TRENCHES.

VIEW ON PARAPET.

ENTRANCE TO MINE.

CONFEDERATE DEAD IN THE TRENCHES AND OTHER VIEWS

Group of Unknown Federal Officers—Who Can Recognize Them?

CHRONOLOGICAL SUMMARY AND RECORD—Continued

MAY, 1862—*Continued from Section 3*

15—Linden, Va. One Co. of 28th Pa. *Union* 1 killed, 3 wounded, 14 missing.

Fort Darling, James River, Va. U. S. Gunboats *Galena, Port Royal, Naugatuck, Monitor* and *Aroostook*. *Union* 12 killed, 14 wounded. *Confed.* 7 killed, 8 wounded.

Chalk Bluffs, Mo. 1st Wis. Cav. *Union* 1 killed, 3 wounded.

Butler, Bates Co., Mo. 1st Iowa Cav. *Union* 3 killed, 1 wounded.

15, 16 and **18**—Princeton, W. Va. Gen. J. D. Cox's Division. *Union* 30 killed, 70 wounded. *Confed.* 2 killed, 14 wounded.

17—In front of Corinth, Miss. Brig.-Gen. M. L. Smith's Brigade. *Union* 10 killed, 31 wounded. *Confed.* 12 killed.

19—Searcy Landing, Ark. Detachments of 3d and 17th Mo. and 4th Mo. Cav., Battery B 1st Mo. Light Artil. *Union* 18 killed, 27 wounded. *Confed.* 150 killed and missing.

Clinton, N. C. *Union* 5 wounded. *Confed.* 9 killed.

21—Phillip's Creek, Miss. 2d Div. Army of Tennessee. *Union* 3 wounded.

22—Florida, Mo. Detachment 3d Iowa Cav. *Union* 2 wounded.

Near New Berne, N. C. Co. I 17th Mass. *Union* 3 killed, 8 wounded.

23—Lewisburg, Va. 36th and 44th Ohio, 2d W. Va. Cav. *Union* 14 killed, 60 wounded. *Confed.* 40 killed, 66 wounded, 100 captured.

Front Royal, Va. 1st Md., Detachments of 29th Pa., Capt. Mapes' Pioneers, 5th N. Y. Cav., and 1st Pa. Artil. *Union* 32 killed, 122 wounded, 750 missing.

Buckton Station, Va. 3d Wis., 27th Ind. *Union* 2 killed, 6 wounded. *Confed.* 12 killed.

Ft. Craig, New Mex. 3d U. S. Cav. *Union* 3 wounded.

24—New Bridge, Va. 4th Mich. *Union* 1 killed, 10 wounded. *Confed.* 60 killed and wounded, 27 captured.

Chickahominy, Va. Davidson's Brigade of 4th Corps. *Union* 2 killed, 4 wounded.

25—Winchester, Va. 2d Mass., 29th and 46th Pa., 27th Ind., 3d Wis., 28th N. Y., 5th Conn., Battery M 1st N. Y. Artil., 1st Vt. Cav., 1st Mich. Cav., 5th N. Y. Cav. *Union* 38 killed, 155 wounded, 711 missing.

27—Hanover C. H., Va. 12th, 13th, 14th, 17th, 25th and 44th N. Y., 62d and 83d Pa., 16th Mich., 9th and 22d Mass., 5th Mass. Artil., 2d Maine Artil., Battery F 5th U. S. Artil., 1st U. S. Sharpshooters. *Union* 53 killed, 344 wounded. *Confed.* 200 killed and wounded, 730 prisoners.

Big Indian Creek, near Searcy Landing, Ark. 1st Mo. Cav. *Union* 3 wounded. *Confed.* 5 killed, 25 wounded.

Osceola, Mo. 1st Iowa Cav. *Union* 3 killed, 2 wounded.

28—Wardensville, Va. 3d Md., Potomac Home Brigade, 3d Ind. Cav. *Confed.* 2 killed, 3 wounded.

29—Pocataligo, S. C. 50th Pa., 79th N. Y., 8th Mich., 1st Mass. Cav. *Union* 2 killed, 9 wounded.

30—Booneville, Miss. 2d Iowa Cav., 2d Mich. Cav. *Confed.* 2,000 prisoners.

Front Royal, Va. 1st R. I. Cav. *Union* 5 killed, 8 wounded. *Confed.* 156 captured.

31—Neosho, Mo. 10th Ill. Cav., 14th Mo. Cav. (Militia). *Union* 2 killed, 3 wounded.

Near Washington, N. C. 3d N. Y. Cav. *Union* 1 wounded. *Confed.* 3 killed, 2 wounded.

31 and **June 1**—Seven Pines and Fair Oaks, Va. 2d Corps, 3d Corps and 4th Corps, Army of the Potomac. *Union* 890 killed, 3,627 wounded, 1,222 missing. *Confed.* 2,800 killed, 3,897 wounded, 1,300 missing. *Union* Brig.-Gen'ls O. O. Howard, Naglee, and Wessells wounded. *Confed.* Brig.-Gen. Hatton killed, Gen. J. E. Johnson and Brig.-Gen. Rhodes wounded, Brig.-Gen. Pettigrew captured.

JUNE, 1862

1 and **2**—Strasburg and Staunton Road, Va. 8th W. Va., 60th Ohio, 1st N. J. Cav., 1st Pa. Cav. *Union* 2 wounded.

3—Legare's Point, S. C. 28th Mass., 100th Pa. *Union* 5 wounded.

4—Jasper, Sweden's Cove, Tenn. 79th Pa., 5th Ky. Cav., 7th Pa. Cav., 1st Ohio Battery. *Union* 2 killed, 7 wounded. *Confed.* 20 killed, 20 wounded.

Blackland, Miss. 2d Iowa Cav., 2d Mich. Cav. *Union* 5 killed, 14 wounded.

5—Tranter's Creek, N. C. 24th Mass., Co. I 3d N. Y. Cav., Marine Artil. *Confed.* 7 killed, 11 wounded.

6—Memphis, Tenn. U. S. Gunboats *Benton, Louisville, Carondelet, Cairo,* and *St. Louis;* and Rams *Monarch* and *Queen of the West*. *Confed.* 80 killed and wounded, 100 captured.

Harrisonburg, Va. 1st N. J. Cav., 1st Pa. Rifles, 6th Ohio, 8th W. Va. *Union* 63 missing. *Confed.* 17 killed, 50 wounded. *Confed.* Gen. Ashby killed.

8—Cross Keys or Union Church, Va. 8th, 39th, 41st, 45th, 54th and 58th N. Y., 2d, 3d, 5th and 8th W. Va., 25th, 32d, 55th, 60th, 73d, 75th and 82d Ohio, 1st and 27th Pa., 1st Ohio Battery. *Union* 125 killed, 500 wounded. *Confed.* 42 killed, 230 wounded. *Confed.* Brig.-Gens. Stewart and Elzey killed.

9—Port Republic, Va. 5th, 7th, 29th and 66th Ohio, 84th and 110th Pa., 7th Ind., 1st W. Va., Batteries E 4th U. S. and A and L 1st Ohio Artil. *Union* 67 killed, 361 wounded, 574 missing. *Confed.* 88 killed, 535 wounded, 34 missing.

10—James Island, S. C. *Union* 3 killed, 13 wounded. *Confed.* 17 killed, 30 wounded.

11—Monterey, Owen Co., Ky. Capt. Blood's Mounted Provost Guard, 13th Ind. Battery. *Union* 2 killed. *Confed.* 100 captured.

12—Waddell's Farm, near Village Creek, Ark. Detachment of 9th Ill. Cav. *Union* 12 wounded. *Confed.* 28 killed and wounded.

13—Old Church, Va. 5th U. S. Cav. *Confed.* 1 killed.

James Island, S. C. *Union* 3 killed, 19 wounded. *Confed.* 19 killed, 6 wounded.

14—Turnstall Station, Va. *Union* 4 killed, 8 wounded. Bushwackers fire into railway train.

16—Secessionville or Fort Johnson, James Island, S. C. 46th, 47th and 79th N. Y., 3d R. I., 3d N. H., 45th, 97th and 100th Pa., 6th and 7th Conn., 8th Mich., 28th Mass., 1st N. Y. Engineers, 1st Conn. Artil., Battery E 3d U. S. and I 3d R. I. Artil., Co. H 1st Mass. Cav. *Union* 85 killed, 472 wounded, 138 missing. *Confed.* 51 killed, 144 wounded.

17—St. Charles, White River, Ark. 43d and 46th Ind., U. S. Gunboats *Lexington, Mound City, Conestoga* and *St. Louis*. *Union* 105 killed, 30 wounded. *Confed.* 155 killed, wounded and captured.

Warrensburg, Mo. 7th Mo. Cav. (Militia). *Union* 2 killed, 2 wounded.

Smithville, Ark. *Union* 2 killed, 4 wounded. *Confed.* 4 killed, 4 wounded, 15 prisoners.

18—Williamsburg Road, Va. 16th Mass. *Union* 7 killed, 57 wounded. *Confed.* 5 killed, 9 wounded.

21—Battle Creek, Tenn. 2d and 33d Ohio, 10th Wis., 24th Ill., 4th Ohio Cav., 4th Ky. Cav., and Edgarton's Battery. *Union* 4 killed, 3 wounded.

22—Raceland, near Algiers, La. 8th Vt. *Union* 3 killed, 8 wounded.

23—Raytown, Mo. 7th Mo. Cav. *Union* 1 killed, 1 wounded.

25—Oak Grove, Va., also called Kings School House and The Orchards. Hooker's and Kearney's Divisions of the Third Corps, Palmer's Brigade of the Fourth Corps, and part of Richardson's Division of the Second Corps. *Union* 51 killed, 401 wounded, 64 missing. *Confed.* 65 killed, 465 wounded, 11 missing.

Germantown, Tenn. 56th Ohio. *Union* 10 killed.

Little Red River, Ark. 4th Iowa Cav. *Union* 2 wounded.

26 to **29**—Vicksburg, Miss. U. S. Fleet, under command of Commodore Farragut. No casualties recorded.

26 to **July 1**—The Seven Days' Retreat. Army of the Potomac, Maj.-Gen. Geo. B. McClellan commanding, including engagements known as Mechanicsville or Ellison's Mills on the 26th, Gaines' Mills or Cold Harbor and Chickahominy on the 27th, Peach Orchard and Savage Station on the 29th, White Oak Swamp, also called Charles City Cross Roads, Glendale, Nelson's Farm, Frazier's Farm, Turkey Bend and New Market Cross Roads on the 30th and Malvern Hill on July 1st.

Union—First Corps, Brig.-Gen. McCall's Div., 253 killed, 1,240 wounded, 1,581 missing.

Second Corps, Maj.-Gen. E. V. Sumner, 187 killed, 1076 wounded, 848 missing.

Third Corps, Maj.-Gen. Heintzleman, 189 killed, 1,051 wounded, 833 missing.

Fourth Corps, Maj.-Gen. E. D. Keyes, 69 killed, 507 wounded, 201 missing.

Fifth Corps, Maj.-Gen. Fitz-John Porter, 620 killed, 2,460 wounded, 1,198 missing.

Sixth Corps, Maj.-Gen. Franklin, 245 killed, 1,313 wounded, 1,179 missing.

Cavalry, Brig.-Gen. Stoneman, 19 killed, 60 wounded, 97 missing.

Engineers' Corps, 2 wounded, 21 missing.

Total, 1,582 killed, 7,709 wounded, 5,958 missing.

(Maj.-Gen. Sumner and Brig.-Gens. Mead, Brook and Burns, wounded.)

Confed.—Maj.-Gen. Hager's Division, 187 killed, 803 wounded, 360 missing.

Maj.-Gen. Magruder's Division, 258 killed, 1,495 wounded, 30 missing.

Maj.-Gen. Longstreet's Division, 763 killed, 3,929 wounded, 239 missing.

Maj.-Gen. Hill's Division, 619 killed, 3,251 wounded.

Maj.-Gen. Jackson's Division, 966 killed, 4,417 wounded, 63 missing.

Maj.-Gen. Holmes' Division, 2 killed, 52 wounded.

Maj.-Gen. Stuart's Cavalry, 15 killed, 30 wounded, 60 missing.

Artillery, Brig.-Gen. Pendleton, 10 killed, 34 wounded.

Total, 2,820 killed, 14,011 wounded, 752 missing.

Brig.-Gens. Griffith, killed, and Anderson, Featherstone and Pender wounded.

27—Williams Bridge, Amite River, La. 21st Ind. *Union* 2 killed, 4 wounded. *Confed.* 4 killed.

Village Creek, Ark. 9th Ill. Cav. *Union* 2 killed, 30 wounded.

Waddell's Farm, Ark. Detachment 3d Iowa Cav. *Union* 4 killed, 4 wounded.

29—Willis Church, Va. Cavalry advance of Casey's Division, Fourth Corps. *Confed.* 2 killed, 15 wounded, 46 captured.

30—Luray, Va. Detachment of Cavalry of Brig.-Gen. Crawford's Command. *Union* 1 killed, 3 wounded.

JULY, 1862

1—Boonville, Miss. 2d Iowa Cav., 2d Mich. Cav. *Union* 45 killed and wounded. *Confed.* 17 killed, 65 wounded.

Morning Sun, Tenn. 57th Ohio. *Union* 4 wounded. *Confed.* 11 killed, 26 wounded.

3—Haxals or Elvington Heights, Va. 14th Ind., 7th W. Va., 4th and 8th Ohio. *Union* 8 killed, 32 wounded. *Confed.* 100 killed and wounded.

6—Grand Prairie, near Aberdeen, Ark. 24th Ind. *Union* 1 killed, 21 wounded. *Confed.* 84 killed and wounded.

7—Bayou Cache, also called Cotton Plant, Round Hill, Hill's Plantation and Bayou de View. 11th Wis., 33d Ill., 8th Ind., 1st Mo. Light Artil., 1st Ind. Cav., 5th and 13th Ill. Cav. *Union* 7 killed, 57 wounded. *Confed.* 110 killed, 200 wounded.

8—Black River, Mo. 5th Kan. Cav. *Union* 1 killed, 3 wounded.

9—Hamilton, N. C. 9th N. Y. and Gunboats *Perry, Ceres* and *Shawseen*. *Union* 1 killed, 20 wounded.

Aberdeen, Ark. 24th, 34th, 43d and 46th Ind. Casualties not recorded.

Tompkinsville, Mo. 3d Pa. Cav. *Union* 4 killed, 6 wounded. *Confed.* 10 killed and wounded.

(Continued in Section 5)

EFFECT OF EXPLOSION OF 32-POUND SHELL FROM MASSACHUSETTS HEAVY ARTILLERY

CHAPTER VIII.—Continued

THE military works were in charge of Lieutenant Adam Slemmer, and the naval establishment was under Commodore Armstrong. Slemmer was informed that an attempt to seize the military works would be made as soon as the Florida politicians should declare the secession of that State; and he took measures accordingly. Perceiving it to be impossible to hold all the works with his small garrison, he,

MAJOR-GENERAL JOHN E. WOOL

like Major Anderson, abandoned the weaker ones and transferred his people and supplies to the stronger Fort Pickens. That was on the 10th of January, 1861, the day on which the Florida Convention passed the Ordinance of Secession. On the same morning, about five hundred insurgents of Florida, Alabama, and Mississippi appeared at the gate of the navy-yard and demanded its surrender. Armstrong was powerless, for three-fourths of the sixty officers under his command were disloyal. Commander Farrand was actually among the insurgents who demanded the surrender, and Flag-Officer Renshaw immediately ordered the National standard to be pulled down. The post, with ordnance stores valued at $156,000, passed into the hands of the authorities of Florida; and Forts Barrancas and McRee were taken possession of by the insurgents.

Lieutenant Slemmer, deprived of the promised aid of the naval establishment, was now left to his own resources. The fort was one of the strongest on the Gulf Coast. There were fifty-four guns in position, and provisions for five months within it; but the garrison consisted of only eighty-one officers and men.

Two days after the seizure of the navy-yard near Pensacola, a demand was made by insurgent leaders for the surrender of Fort Pickens. Lieutenant Slemmer refused compliance. Three days later (January 15) Colonel W. H. Chase of Massachusetts, who was in command of all the insurgents in that region, obtained an interview with Slemmer, and tried to persuade him to "avoid bloodshed" by quietly surrendering the fort, saying in conclusion: "Consider this well, and take care that you will so act as to have no fearful recollections of a tragedy that you might have avoided; but rather to make the present moment one of the most glorious, because Christian-like, of your life." The wily serpent could not seduce the patriot, and Slemmer did make that a glorious moment of his life by refusing to give up the fort. On the 18th, another demand was made for the surrender of the fort and refused, and a siege of that stronghold was begun.

The number of insurgents at Pensacola rapidly increased, and the new Administration resolved to send relief to Fort Pickens. A small squadron was dispatched from New York for the purpose; and Lieutenant J. L. Worden of the navy was sent overland to Pensacola, with orders to Captain Adams, in command of some vessels off Fort Pickens, to throw reinforcements into that work immediately. Worden reached Pensacola on the 10th of April, where Colonel Braxton Bragg was in chief command of the Confederates. He had observed great excitement and preparations for war on his journey, and fearing arrest, Worden had made himself well acquainted with the contents of the despatches, and then tore them up. He frankly told Bragg that he was sent by his Government with orders to Captain Adams, and that they were not written, but oral. That officer gave the lieutenant a pass for his destination. His message was timely delivered, for Bragg was

MAJOR-GENERAL BENJAMIN F. BUTLER

COMPANY OF INDIANA VOLUNTEERS

COMPANY OF INDIANA VOLUNTEERS FROM BROKEN BRADY NEGATIVE

on the point of attacking the fort. The reinforcements were thrown in, and the plan was foiled. Worden returned to Pensacola, and was permitted to take the cars for Montgomery, Alabama, when Bragg was informed by a spy that Fort Pickens had been reinforced. Mortified by his stupid blunder in allowing

COLONEL E. E. ELLSWORTH

Worden to pass to and from the squadron, he violated truth and honor by telegraphing to the Confederate government at Montgomery that Worden had practised falsehood and deception in gaining access to the squadron, and recommended his arrest. He was seized on the 15th of April and cast into the common jail, where he was treated with scorn by the Confederates, and kept a prisoner until November following, when he was exchanged. Worden had acted with the utmost frankness and the nicest sense of honor in the whole matter. He was the first prisoner-of-war held by the insurgents.

A few days after the reinforcement of Fort Pickens, two vessels, bearing several hundred troops and ample supplies, under Colonel Harvey Brown, appeared there, when Lieutenant Slemmer and his brave little band, worn down by fatigue and continued watchfulness, were relieved, and sent to Fort Hamilton, near New York, to rest. The grateful people honored them. The President gave Slemmer the commission of major, and afterward of brigadier; and the New York Chamber of Commerce also caused a series of bronze medals to be struck as presents to the commander and men of the brave little garrison. Reinforcements continued to be sent to Fort Pickens; and the number of the insurgents intended to assail it also increased, until, in May, they numbered over seven thousand. But events of very little importance occurred in that vicinity during the ensuing summer.

On Sunday morning, the 14th of April, 1861, the tidings of the dishonoring of the National standard in Charleston harbor was telegraphed over the land, and created the wildest excitement everywhere, North and South. The loyal people were indignant; the disloyal people were jubilant. I was in New Orleans on that day. The sound of Sabbath-bells was mingled with the martial-music of fife and drum. Church-goers and troops in bright uniforms were seen in almost every street, the latter gathering for an immediate expedition against Fort Pickens. All faces beamed with gladness, and the pulpits overflowed with words of loyalty to the Southern Confederacy. At the North, the loyal hearts of the patriotic people beat vehemently with emotion; and everywhere the momentous question was asked, What next? It was not long unanswered, for within twenty-four hours after Major Anderson went out of Fort Sumter, the President of the United States issued a stirring call for seventy-five thousand troops to suppress the rising rebellion. In that proclamation (April 15, 1861) the President declared that for some time combinations in several of the States (which he named), "too powerful to be suppressed by the ordinary course of judicial proceedings or by the powers vested in the marshals by law," had opposed the laws of the Republic; and therefore, by virtue of power vested in him, he called out the militia of the Union, to the number just mentioned, and appealed to the patriotism of the people in support of the measure. In the same proclamation he summoned the National Congress to meet at Washington city on the 4th day of July next ensuing, to consider the crisis. At the same time the Secretary of War sent a despatch to the governors of all the States excepting those mentioned in the President's proclamation, requesting each of them to cause to be detailed from the militia of his State the quota designated in a table which he appended, to serve as infantrymen or riflemen for the period of three months, unless sooner discharged.

This call of the President and the requisition of the Secretary of War were responded to with enthusiasm in the free-labor States; but in six of the eight slave-labor States not omitted in the call, they were treated with scorn. The exceptions were Delaware and Maryland. In the other slave-labor States, disloyal governors held the reins of power. Governor Letcher of Virginia replied: "I have only to say that the militia of this State will not be furnished to the powers at Washington for any such use or purpose as they have in view. Your object is to subjugate the Southern States, and a requisition made upon me for such an object will not be complied with. You have chosen to inaugurate Civil War, and, having

HARPER'S FERRY, AFTER EVACUATION

done so, we will meet it in a spirit as determined as the Administration has exhibited toward the South." Governor Ellis of North Carolina answered: "Your despatch is received, and if genuine, which its extraordinary character leads me to doubt, I have to say in reply, that I regard the levy of troops made by

CHAIN BRIDGE OVER THE POTOMAC

the Administration for the purpose of subjugating the States of the South, as in violation of the Constitution and a usurpation of power. I can be no party to this wicked violation of the laws of the country, and to this war upon the liberties of a free people. You can get no troops from North Carolina." Governor Magoffin of Kentucky answered: "Your despatch is received. I say emphatically that Kentucky will furnish no troops for the wicked purpose of subduing her sister Southern States." Governor Harris of Tennessee said: "Tennessee will not furnish a single man for coercion; but fifty thousand, if necessary, for the defence of our rights or those of our Southern brethren." Governor Rector of Arkansas replied, "In answer to your requisition for troops from Arkansas, to subjugate the Southern States, I have to say that none will be furnished. The demand is only adding insult to injury. The people of this Commonwealth are freemen, not slaves, and will defend, to the last extremity, their honor, their lives and property against Northern mendacity and usurpation." Governor Jackson of Missouri responded: "There can be, I apprehend, no doubt that these men are intended to make war on the seceded States. Your requisition, in my judgment, is illegal, unconstitutional and revolting in its objects, inhuman and diabolical, and cannot be complied with. Not one man will the State of Missouri furnish to carry on such an unholy crusade."

It was reported from Montgomery that Mr. Davis and his compeers received Mr. Lincoln's call for troops "with derisive laughter." Mr. Hooper, the Secretary of the Montgomery Convention, in reply to the question of the agent of the Associated Press at Washington, "What is the feeling there?" said:

> "Davis answers, rough and curt,
> With Paixhan and petard,
> Sumter is ours and nobody hurt,
> We tender old Abe our Beau-regard."

And on the day after the call was made (April 16), the *Mobile Advertiser* contained the following advertisement in one of its inside business columns:

"75,000 COFFINS WANTED."

"PROPOSALS will be received to supply the Confederacy with 75,000 black coffins.
☞ No proposals will be entertained coming north of Mason and Dixon's line.
"Direct to   JEFF. DAVIS, Montgomery, Alabama."

This ghastly joke showed the temper of the political leaders in that region. But this feeling of boastfulness and levity was soon changed to seriousness, for there were indications of a wonderful uprising of the loyal people of the free-labor States in defence of the Union. Men, women, and children shared in the general enthusiasm. Loyalty was everywhere expressed, as if by preconcert, by the unfurling of the National flag. That banner was seen all over the land in attestation of devotion to the Union—in halls of justice and places of public worship. It was displayed from flagstaffs, balconies, windows, and even from the spires of churches and cathedrals. It was seen at all public gatherings, where cannon roared and orators spoke eloquently for the preservation of the Republic; and *red, white, and blue*—the

CAPTAIN OTIS AND COMPANY OF 22D NEW YORK VOLUNTEERS AT HARPER'S FERRY

COMPANY E, NEW YORK VOLUNTEERS

colors of our flag in combination—were the hues of ornaments worn by women in attestation of their loyalty. And when it was evident to the people of the free-labor States that the National capital was in danger, organized military bands were seen hurrying to the banks of the Potomac for the defence of Washington city.

The foolish boastings of the Southern newspapers were imitated by some of the members of the Northern press. "The nations of Europe," one said, "may rest assured that Jeff. Davis & Co. will be swinging from the battlements at Washington, at least by the 21st of July. We spit upon a later or longer-deferred justice." Another said: "Let us make quick work. The 'rebellion,' as some people term it, is an unborn tadpole. Let us not fall into the delusion, noted by Hallam, of mistaking a 'local commotion' for revolution. A strong, active 'pull together' will do our work effectually in thirty days."

And still another of sense can for that this much- ing will end in a Northern people vincible. The band of ragamuf- like chaff before approach." And with particular s p e e c h, said: get out of the war of the West. battle, and suc- two or three farthest. Illinois South by herself. matter being us. . . . The crushed out be- blage of Con-

Neither sec- hended the ear-

CONTRABANDS AND TOLLER'S HOTEL

said: "No man a moment doubt ado-about-noth- month. The are simply in- rebels—a mere fins — will fly the wind, on our a Chicago paper, c r a z i n e s s of "Let the East way; this is a We can fight the cessfully, within months at the can whip the We insist on this turned over to rebellion will be fore the assem- gress."

tion compre- nestness a n d

prowess of the other—the pluck that always distinguished the American people, North and South. Each, in its pride, felt a contempt for the other, each believing the other would not fight. This was a fatal misapprehension, and led to sad results. Each party appealed to the Almighty to witness the rectitude of its intentions, and each was quick to discover omens of Heaven's approval of its course. When, on the Sunday after the President's call for troops went forth, the first lesson in the morning service in the Protestant Episcopal churches of the land on that day contained this battle-call of the prophet: "Proclaim ye this among the Gentiles: Prepare for war; wake up the mighty men; let all the men of war draw near; let them come up; beat your ploughshares into swords, and your pruning-hooks into spears; let the weak say, I am strong," the loyal people of Boston, New York, and Cincinnati said: "See, how Revelation summons us to the conflict!" and the insurgents of Charleston, Mobile, and New Orleans answered: "It is equally a call for us," adding: "See how specially we are promised victory in another Scripture lesson in the same church, which says: 'I will remove off from you the *Northern Army*, and will drive him into a land barren and desolate, with his face toward the East sea, and his hinder part toward the utmost sea. . . . Fear not, O land! be glad and rejoice; for the Lord will do great things.'"

Two days after the President's call was promulgated, the chief of the Southern Confederacy issued a proclamation, in which, after declaring that Mr. Lincoln had announced the intention of invading the "Confederate States" for "the purpose of capturing its fortresses and thereby subverting its independence, and subjecting the free people thereof to the dominion of a foreign power," he invited all persons who felt so disposed to enter upon a course of legalized piracy called "privateering," and to depredate on the commerce of the United States. This proclamation was immediately followed by another from the President, declaring his intention to employ a competent force to blockade all the ports which were claimed to belong to the Southern Confederacy; also warning all persons who should engage in privateering under the sanction of a commission from the insurgent chief, that they would be held amenable to the laws of the United States for the prevention and punishment of piracy.

26TH NEW YORK VOLUNTEERS

The "Congress of the Confederate States" had been summoned to meet at Montgomery on the 29th of April (1861), and a few days after the session began, an act was passed declaring that war existed between the seven "seceded" States and the United States, and authorized Mr. Davis to employ the power of their section to "meet the war thus commenced, and to issue to private armed vessels commissions or letters of marque and general reprisal, in such form as he shall think proper, under the seal of the

DRILLING IN THE FORT

Confederate States, against the vessels, goods, and effects of the Government of the United States, and of the citizens or inhabitants of the States and Territories thereof." They also offered a bounty of twenty dollars for each person who might be on board of an armed vessel of the United States that should be destroyed by a Confederate privateer—in other words, a reward for the destruction of men, women, and children. "Happily for the credit of humanity," says a historian of the war, "this act has no parallel on the statute-book of any civilized nation." Mr. Davis did not wait for this authority, but several days before the assembling of his "Congress," he issued commissions for privateering, signed by himself, and Robert Toombs, as secretary. With these hostile proclamations of Mr. Lincoln and Mr. Davis, the great Conflict was fairly begun.

CHAPTER IX.

The Virginia Convention—Union Sentiments Suppressed by Violence—Ordinance of Secession Passed—Bad Faith—Virginia Annexed to the Confederacy—The People Disfranchised—The National Capital To Be Seized—Davis's Professions—Poetic Comments on Them—Events at Harper's Ferry and Gosport Navy-Yard—Response to the Call for Troops—Massachusetts Sends Troops to Washington—Attack upon Them in Baltimore—Critical Situation of the Capital—The President and Maryland Secessionists— Prompt and Efficient Action of General Wool—Union Defence Committee—General Butler's Operations in Maryland—He Takes Possession of Baltimore—Events at the Capital—Preparations for the Struggle.

AT this time Virginia had passed through a fiery ordeal and lay prostrate, bound hand and foot by her disloyal sons, at the feet of the Southern Confederacy. A State Convention assembled at the middle of February, and remained in session more than two months. A large majority of the members were animated by a sincere love for the Union, especially those from the mountain districts in Western Virginia; and even so late as a fortnight before its adjournment, an Ordinance of Secession was defeated by a vote of eighty-nine against forty-five. Yet the conspirators persevered with hope, for they saw one after another of weak Union members converted by their sophistry.

The crisis was reached when Edmund Ruffin fired his gun at Fort Sumter. "That gun," said a telegraphic despatch from Charleston, "will do more in the cause of secession in Virginia than volumes of stump speeches." So it did. It set bells ringing and cannon thundering in the Virginia capital, and

FORTIFICATIONS

ADMIRAL DAHLGREN AND OFFICERS ON DECK OF "PAWNEE"

produced the wildest excitement in and out of the Convention. "The war has begun; what will Virginia do?" asked Governor Pickens, by telegraph. Governor Letcher replied, "The Convention will determine." That determination was speedily made. When, on Monday the 15th of April, the President's call for troops to suppress the rising rebellion was read in the Convention, that body was shaken by a fierce tempest of contending passions. Reason and judgment fled, and the stoutest Union men bent before the storm like reeds in a gale. Yet when the Convention adjourned that evening, and the question was pending, Shall Virginia secede at once? there was a strong majority in favor of Union.

The conspirators were now desperate. They perceived that the success of their grand scheme, the seizure of the National capital, depended upon the action of Virginia at that crisis. Richmond was then in the hands of an excited populace ready to do the bidding of the leading politicians, and the latter resolved to act with a high hand. They perceived that the absence of ten Union members from the Convention would give a majority for secession. Accordingly ten of them were waited upon by the conspirators on that evening, and informed that they must choose between three modes of action, namely, to vote for secession, absent themselves, or be hanged. They saw that resistance to these desperate men would be vain, and they absented themselves. These violent proceedings awed other Union men in the Convention,

SCENE ON THE JAMES RIVER

and on Wednesday the 17th of April, 1861, an Ordinance of Secession was adopted. Unlike the conventions of other "seceding" States, it referred the Ordinance to the people to vote on at a future day. But this show of respect for the popular will was not sincere. A despatch was immediately sent to Jefferson Davis, telling him that Virginia was "out of the Union"; and within twenty-four hours after the passage of the Ordinance, and while it was yet under cover of an injunction of secrecy, Governor Letcher set in motion expeditions to capture the Arsenal at Harper's Ferry, and the Navy-yard at Gosport, opposite Norfolk, preparatory to the seizure of the National capital. Davis sent his lieutenant, Alexander H. Stephens, from Montgomery to Richmond, to urge the Convention to violate its faith pledged to the people, and to formally annex Virginia to the Confederacy without their consent. This was done within a week after the passage of the Ordinance of Secession, and a month before the day appointed for the people to vote upon it.

Stephens arrived in Richmond on the evening of the 23d of April. The Convention appointed a commission, with ex-President Tyler at its head, to treat with this representative of the "Confederacy" for the annexation of Virginia to that league. The act was accomplished the next day. The "treaty" provided that "the whole military force and military operations" of Virginia, "offensive and defensive, in the impending conflict with the United States," should be under the chief control of Jefferson Davis. Then they adopted and ratified the "Provisional Constitution of the Confederacy;" appointed delegates to the "Confederate Congress;" authorized the banks of the State to suspend specie payments; made

SCENES AND VIEWS IN YORKTOWN

provision for the establishment of a navy for Virginia; made other provisions for waging war on the Union, and invited the "government at Montgomery" to make Richmond its future seat. All this was done in spite of the known will of the people; and when the day approached for them to express that will by the ballot, they found themselves tied hand and foot by an inexorable despotism. James M. Mason, one of the most active of the Virginia conspirators, issued a manifesto, in which he declared his State to be out of the old Union; that a rejection of the Ordinance of Secession would be a violation of a sacred pledge given to the Confederacy by the politicians; and said, concerning those who could not conscientiously vote to separate Virginia from the Union, "Honor and duty alike require that they should not vote on the question; and if they retain such opinions, *they must leave the State.*" Submission or banishment was the alternative. Mason simply repeated the sentiments of Jefferson Davis in another form: "All who oppose us shall smell Southern powder, and feel Southern steel."

When the vote was finally taken on the 23d of May, it was in the face of bayonets. Terror reigned all over Eastern Virginia. Unionists were compelled to fly for their lives before the instruments of the civil and military power at Richmond, for the "Confederate government" was then seated there. By these means the enemies of the Union were enabled to report a majority of over one hundred thousand votes of Virginians in favor of secession, the vote being given by the voice and not by the secret ballot.

COMPANY DRILL

Then the governor of South Carolina, with selfish complacency, said to his people: "You may plant your seed in peace, for Old Virginia will have to bear the brunt of the battle." And so she did much of the time. Her politicians offered her back to the burden which the Gulf States had rolled from their own shoulders, and a most grievous one it was.

Prodigious efforts were now made for the seizure of the National capital. On his journey to Richmond, Alex. H. Stephens had harangued the people at various points, and everywhere raised the cry, "On to Washington!" That cry was already resounding throughout the slave-labor States. Troops were marshaling for the service, in Virginia; and already Carolina soldiers were treading its soil. The Southern press, everywhere, urged the measure with the greatest vehemence. On the day when Stephens arrived in Richmond, one of the newspapers of that city said: "There never was half the unanimity among the people before, nor a tithe of the zeal upon any subject, that is now manifested to take Washington and drive from it every Black Republican who is a dweller there. From the mountain tops and valleys to the shores of the sea, there is one wild shout of fierce resolve to capture Washington city, at all and every human hazard." Yet in the face of the universal chorus, "On to Washington!" Mr. Jefferson Davis, president of the Southern Confederacy, speaking more to Europe than to his people, said to his congress at Montgomery: "We profess solemnly, in the face of mankind, that we desire peace at any sacrifice save that of honor. . . . In independence we seek no conquest, no aggrandizement, no cession of any kind from the States with which we have lately confederated. *All we ask is to be let alone*—those who never held power over us, should not now attempt our subjugation by arms."

Harper's Ferry, at the confluence of the Potomac and Shenandoah rivers, where their combined

VIEWS ON THE JAMES RIVER

waters flow through the Blue Ridge, in Virginia, had been for years the seat of an Armory and Arsenal of the United States, where almost ninety thousand muskets were usually stored. At the time we are considering, the post was in charge of Lieutenant Roger Jones, with some dismounted dragoons and a few other soldiers. Warned of impending danger, Jones was vigilant; and he prepared for any sudden emergency by laying a train of gunpowder for the destruction of the Government property, if necessary. When, late in the evening of the 18th of April, about two thousand Virginia militia were within a mile of the post and were pressing on to seize it, Jones fired his trains, and in a few minutes the Government buildings were all in flames, and the little garrison of forty men were crossing the covered railway bridge into Maryland, in a successful flight to Carlisle Barracks, in Pennsylvania. The insurgents were foiled in their attempt to secure a large quantity of fire-arms; but they seized Harper's Ferry as an important point for future hostile operations. In May, full eight thousand Confederate troops were there.

DOCK AT HILTON HEAD, BUILT BY SOLDIERS

The expedition against the Navy-yard at Gosport was more successful. It was situated on the Elizabeth River, opposite Norfolk, and at that time contained two thousand pieces of heavy cannon fit for service, and a vast amount of munitions of war, naval stores, and materials for ship-building. In the waters near and on the stocks were several vessels-of-war, which the Secessionists attempted to secure by sinking obstructions in the river below to prevent their sailing out. This was done on the day before the Virginia Ordinance of Secession was adopted. The post was in command of Commodore C. S. McCauley, who, soothed and deceived by false professions of loyalty by the officers of Southern birth under him, delayed taking action to protect the Navy-yard and the vessels until it was too late. When the action of the officers at Pensacola was known, these men said to the Commodore, "You have no Pensacola officers here; we will never desert you; we will stand by you until the last, even to the death;" yet these men all resigned when the Virginia Ordinance of Secession was passed, abandoned their flag, and joined the forces under General Taliaferro, commander of the Virginia troops in that region, who arrived at Norfolk on the evening of the 18th of April to attempt the seizure of the naval station. Believing an immediate effort would be made to seize the vessels, McCauley ordered them to be scuttled and sunk, and this was done. At that critical moment, Captain Paulding of the navy arrived in the *Pawnee* as the successor of McCauley, and perceiving all the vessels but the *Cumberland* beyond recovery, he ordered them and all the public property at the Navy-yard to be burned or otherwise destroyed. This destruction was only partially accomplished. About seven million dollars' worth of property disappeared; but the insurgents gained a vast number of heavy guns with which they waged war afterward. They also saved some of the vessels. Among the latter was the *Merrimac*, which was afterward converted by the Confederates into a powerful iron-clad vessel. This important post was held by the insurgents until early in May the following year, when it was recovered by General Wool.

So secretly had the Confederates prepared for the seizure of the National capital that the sudden development of their strength was amazing. The Government was made painfully aware that its call for troops had not been made an hour too soon.

TURRET AND PART OF DECK OF ORIGINAL MONITOR, SHOWING DENTS MADE
BY POINTED SHOT FROM THE GUNS OF THE MERRIMAC

MONITOR ON THE JAMES

OFFICERS ON DECK OF MONITOR

There was a general impression that Washington city was to be the first point of serious attack, and toward it vast numbers of armed men eagerly pressed to the protection of the President, his cabinet, the Government archives, and the Capitol. Within three days after the call, full one hundred thousand young men had dropped their implements of labor to prepare for war.

GROUP OF CONTRABANDS

Those of Massachusetts were first ready. Early in the year Governor Andrew had put the militia of the State on a sort of war footing, and five thousand volunteers were drilled in armories. He invited the other New England States to do likewise, and they complied, in a degree. When, on the day the President called for seventy-five thousand men, Senator Henry Wilson telegraphed to Governor Andrew to send twenty companies immediately to Washington, they were ready. A few hours later the requisition of the Secretary of War reached the governor, and before sunset four regiments at different points were ordered to muster on Boston Common. They were all there the next day, in charge of Brigadier-General Benjamin F. Butler; and it was arranged for the Sixth Regiment, Colonel Jones of Lowell, to go forward at once to Washington, through New York, Philadelphia, and Baltimore.

On the day (April 18) when the insurgents expected to seize the arms at Harper's Ferry, five companies of Pennsylvanians passed through Baltimore for the capital. They were slightly attacked by the mob in that city. They were the first of the loyal troops to reach Washington city, and were quartered in the Capitol. The Secessionists of Maryland were then active, and were determined to place their State as a barrier across the pathway of troops from the North and East. Their governor (Hicks) was a loyal man, but the mayor of Baltimore was not, and the chief of police (Kane) was an ally of the disloyal leaders. When the Pennsylvanians had passed through the city, rumors came that a regiment from Massachusetts were approaching; and when, on the following day (April 19, 1861), the latter were marching from one railway station to another, in Baltimore, they were violently assailed with missiles of every sort by an excited populace numbering full ten thousand persons. The mayor, alarmed at the furious whirlwind that his political friends had raised, vainly attempted to control it. With a large body of the police, most of whom did not share in the treason of their chief (Kane), he tried to quell the disturbance, but his power was inoperative. The fight in the streets was severe. Three of the troops (the Sixth Massachusetts) were killed or mortally wounded, and in defence of their own lives they slew nine citizens of Baltimore. This tragedy produced intense excitement all over the country. There the first blood was shed in the terrible conflict that ensued. For a moment the indignation of the loyal people was so hot, that the city seemed doomed to swift destruction. A cry went forth, "Lay it in ashes!" and Bayard Taylor wrote:

"Bow down in haste thy guilty head!
    God's wrath is swift and sure;
The sky with gathering bolts is red.
Cleanse from thy skirts the slaughter shed
Or make thyself an ashen bed,
    O Baltimore!"

The troops from Pennsylvania and Massachusetts were not too soon in the National capital; for all communication between Washington and the North, by railway and telegraph, was cut off for a week after the affray in Baltimore. On the night of the riot the bridges of the railway running northward from that city were burned, and the telegraph wires were cut, under the sanction of its mayor and chief of police; and the President of the United States and other officers of government, civil and military, at the capital, were virtually prisoners in the hands of the enemies of their country. The capital was swarming with them; and these, with the Minute-men of Maryland, were barely restrained from violence by the Pennsylvania and Massachusetts soldiers in Washington.

The Maryland Secessionists now declared that no more troops should pass through that State to Washington; and the mayor of Baltimore, with the sanction of Governor Hicks, sent a committee to

Clerks at Commissary depot.

Quartermasters Office.

Wharves

Wharves

AQUIA CREEK LANDING

Group at Hospital

Officers at Landing

Employees at Quartermaster's Wagon Camp.

SCENES AT AQUIA CREEK LANDING

MAP OF RICHMOND AND PART OF VIRGINIA

GENERAL VIEW OF HARPER'S FERRY

GREAT FALLS. POTOMAC RIVER

President Lincoln to tell him of this decision. The President received them courteously, and yielded much for the sake of peace, proposing to have the troops go by water to Annapolis, and thence march through the sparsely settled country to the capital. The Secessionists would not yield an iota of their demand that "no United States soldier should tread the soil of Maryland." Governor Hicks, a sincere Unionist, but not in robust bodily health and almost seventy years of age, was overborne by the violent Secessionists in official position, and was made their passive instrument in some degree. He was induced to make the degrading proposition that Lord Lyons, the British minister at Washington, "be requested to act as mediator between the contending parties in our country." In the name of the President, Mr. Seward reminded the governor that when the capital was in danger in 1814, as it was now, his State gladly welcomed the United States troops everywhere on its soil, for the defence of Washington. This mildly drawn but stinging rebuke of the chief magistrate of a State that professed to be a member of the Union, gave the Secessionists notice that no degrading propositions would, for a moment, be entertained by the Government.

Still another delegation went from Baltimore to the President to give him advice in the interest of

INTERIOR OF FORT

the Secessionists. They represented the theological element of Baltimore society, and were led by Rev. Dr. Fuller of the Baptist Church. When that gentleman assured the President that he might secure peace by recognizing the independence of the "seceded" States; that they would never be a part of the Union again, and expressed a hope that no more troops would be allowed to pass through Maryland, the President listened patiently, and then said significantly: "I *must* have troops for the defence of the capital. The Carolinians are now marching across Virginia to seize the capital, and hang me. What am I to do? I *must* have troops, I say; and as they can neither crawl under Maryland nor fly over it, they must come across it." The deputation returned to Baltimore, and the Secessionists of that city never afterward gave suggestions or advice to President Lincoln.

The critical situation of the capital created intense anxiety throughout the free-labor States. All communication between Washington and the rest of the world was cut off. General Scott could not send an order anywhere. What was to be done? That question was promptly answered by the veteran General John E. Wool. He hastened from his headquarters in Troy, New York, to the presence of the governor of the State (Morgan) at Albany, and they went immediately to the city of New York. Wool was the commander of the Eastern Department of the Army, which included the whole country eastward of the Mississippi River. He and the governor held a conference with the "Union Defence Committee," composed of some of the leading citizens of New York, with General John A. Dix as chairman and William M. Evarts as secretary. A plan of action for the relief of the capital was formed and put into

PICKET OUTPOST, SHOWING BRADY'S PHOTOGRAPHIC OUTFIT

immediate operation. Wool, unable to communicate with the General-in-Chief (Scott), assumed the responsibility of ordering the movements of troops, providing for the safety of Fortress Monroe, and sending forward immediate military relief and supplies for the menaced capital. The governors of a dozen States applied to him for relief and munitions of war, as he was the highest military authority then accessible; and he assisted in arming no less than nine States. By his prodigious and judicious labors in connection with the liberal "Union Defence Committee" of New York, the *capital was saved*.

The destruction of bridges north of Baltimore prevented troops from passing that way. So the Seventh Regiment of New York, Colonel Ellsworth's New York Fire Zouaves and some Massachusetts troops, under General B. F. Butler, proceeded to Annapolis by water, and saved the frigate *Constitution* there, which was about to be seized by the Secessionists. Butler took possession of the railway between Annapolis and Washington, and first opened communication with the capital; and on the 25th of April he took possession of the Relay House, nine miles from Baltimore, where the Baltimore and Ohio railway turns toward Harper's Ferry. While he was there, over nine hundred men, with a battery, under Colonel F. E. Patterson, sailed from Philadelphia and landed near Fort McHenry, at Baltimore, in the presence

COMPANY UNRECOGNIZED

of the mayor of the city, Chief of Police Kane and many of his force, and a vast crowd of excited citizens. Latent Unionism in Maryland was then astir, and shouts of welcome greeted the Pennsylvanians. That was on the 9th of May—three weeks after the attack on the Massachusetts troops in the streets of Baltimore. These were the first troops that had passed through since, and were the pioneers of tens of thousands of Union soldiers who streamed through that city during the war that ensued. Though the Maryland Legislature shielded, by special law, the leaders in the murderous assault on the troops on the 19th of April, from punishment, no such violence was ever attempted afterward.

General Scott had planned a ponderous expedition for seizing and holding Baltimore. It was to consist of twelve thousand men divided into four columns, who were to approach that city from four different points at the same time. General Butler saw that a swifter movement was necessary to accomplish that end. He obtained permission of General Scott to attempt the seizure of some arms and ammunition said to be concealed in Baltimore, and to arrest some Secessionists there. Baltimore was in the Department of Annapolis, of which Butler was commander, and the permission implied the use of troops. Having promised Colonel Jones, of the Sixth Massachusetts Regiment, that his men should again march through Baltimore, he summoned that regiment from the capital to the Relay House. With these and a few other troops, and two pieces of artillery well manned, in all a little more than a thousand men, he entered cars headed toward Harper's Ferry. They ran up the road a short distance, and then backed slowly past the Relay House and into Baltimore early in the evening, just as a heavy thunderstorm

Scenes in the Camp of the Army of the Potomac, 1862

burst upon the city. Few persons were abroad, and the citizens were ignorant of this portentous arrival. The mayor was soon afterward apprised of it, and sent a note to General Butler inquiring what he meant by thus threatening the peace of the city by the presence of a large body of troops.

When the mayor's message arrived at the station, Butler and his men had disappeared in the gloom. Well piloted, they marched to Federal Hill, an eminence that commanded the city. The rain fell copiously; the rumble of the cannon-wheels was mingled with that of the thunder, and was mistaken for it, and the lightning played around the points of their bayonets. In his wet clothing, at near midnight, General Butler sat down and wrote a proclamation to the citizens of Baltimore, assuring all peaceable citizens full protection, and intimating that a much larger force was at hand to support the Government in its efforts to suppress the rebellion. This proclamation (dated May 14, 1861) was published in a city paper (the *Clipper*) the next morning, and gave the people of Baltimore the first intimation that their town was in of National troops. In

the actual possession a single night, a little men had accom- cious leader, what to do with twelve definite time. The eral-in-Chief was of- action of a subordi- for acting without his removal from the ment. The good- President did remove to a more extended ations, with a higher From that time, troops were pass freely through Balti- the North; and at the mid- the National capital was so tected that it was regarded ly safe from capture by the

The contest had now as- dignity of Civil War. The erates were putting forth all gies to meet the forces called by the President of the Re- vis summoned his "con- have observed, to meet at ery on the 29th of April, to ures for prosecuting the war, and defensive. At that time erates had seized property

more than a thousand plished, under an auda- General Scott proposed thousand men in an in- jealous pride of the Gen- fended by the superior nate. He reproved him orders, and demanded Depart- natured Butler, but field of oper- commission. enabled to more from dle of May, well pro- as absolute- insurgents. sumed the Confed- their ener- to the field public. Da- gress," as we Montgom- take meas- offensive the Confed- belonging to

DEAD MEN TELL NO TALES, BUT THIS PICTURE TELLS A TALE THAT CANNOT BE FORGOTTEN

the United States valued at $40,000,000, and had forty thousand armed men in the field, more than one-half of whom were then in Virginia, and forming an irregular line from Norfolk to Harper's Ferry. At the beginning of May they had sent emissaries abroad to seek recognition and aid from foreign governments. They had extinguished the lamps of the light-houses, one hundred and thirty-three in number, all along the coasts of the Republic, from Hampton Roads to the Rio Grande, and had commissioned numerous "privateers" to prey upon the commerce of the United States. Encouraged by their success at

Long Bridge Across the Potomac

View of Georgetown

Charleston, they were then besieging Fort Pickens, as we have observed, and were using prodigious exertions to obtain possession of the National capital.

The magnitude of the disaffection to the National Government was now more clearly perceived; and the President, satisfied that the number of militia called for would not be adequate for the required service against the wide-spreading rebellion, issued a proclamation on the 3d of May, calling for sixty-four thousand volunteers for the army, and eighteen thousand for the navy, to "serve during the war." Fortress Monroe, a very important fort in Southeastern Virginia, and Fort Pickens, near Pensacola, were reinforced; and the blockade of the Southern ports, from which "privateers" were preparing to sail, was proclaimed. Washington city was made the general rendezvous of all troops raised eastward of the Alleghany mountains. These came flocking thither by thousands, and were quartered in the Patent-Office building and other edifices, and the Capitol was made a vast citadel. Its legislative halls, the rotunda, and other rooms were filled with soldiery; so also was the great East Room in the President's house. The basements of the Capitol were converted into store-rooms for barrels of flour, beef and pork, and other commissary stores. The vaults under the broad terrace on its western front were converted into bakeries, where sixteen thousand loaves of bread were baked each day.

Before the summer of 1861 had fairly begun, Washington was an immense garrisoned town, and strong fortifications were growing upon the hills that surround it. The States westward of the Alleghanies were also pouring out their thousands of armed men, who were gathered at appointed rendezvous; and every department of the National Government was active in preparation for the great conflict of mighty hosts that were to fight, one party for freedom and the other for slavery.

ALEXANDRIA, FROM CAMP OF 44TH NEW YORK VOLUNTEERS

CONFEDERATE WOUNDED AT SMITH'S BARN, DR. HURD OF THE 14TH INDIANA IN ATTENDANCE

CHAPTER X.

Defection of Colonel Lee—Temptation and Fall—First Invasion of Virginia—Death of Colonel Ellsworth—Blockade of the Potomac—
Engagement at Sewall's Point—Loyalty in Western Virginia—Action of the Secessionists—Conventions—Creation and Admission
of a New State—Troops from Beyond the Ohio—The First Battle on Land—Attitude of the Border States—Kentucky Unionism—
Events in Missouri—General Lyon—The Governor of Missouri Raises the Standard of Revolt—Movements in Tennessee—
Pillow and Polk—Change in the Confederate Seat of Government—Jefferson Davis in Virginia—His Reception in Richmond.

THE Confederates acquired much strength at the beginning, by the defection of Colonel Robert E. Lee, an accomplished engineer officer in the National army, and one who was greatly beloved and thoroughly trusted by the General-in-Chief, Scott. Temptation assailed him in the form of an offer of the supreme command of the military and naval forces of his native State, Virginia. It was rendered more potent by the doctrine of State supremacy; and it so weakened his patriotism that he

MAJOR-GENERAL BUTLER AND STAFF

yielded to the tempter. And when the Convention of Virginia passed an Ordinance of Secession, he resigned his commission, deserted his flag, and took up arms against his Government, saying, in the common language of men of the State-supremacy school: "I must go with my State." He had lingered in Washington city for a week after the evacuation of Fort Sumter; and received from General Scott, without giving a hint of his secret determination, all information possible from that confiding friend, concerning the plans and resources of the Government, to be employed in suppressing the rebellion. With this precious treasury of important knowledge, Lee hastened to Richmond, and was cordially received there, with marks of great distinction, by the vice-president of the Confederacy and officers of his State, and was informed that the supreme command of the forces of the Commonwealth was committed to his care.

No man had stronger inducements to be a loyal and patriotic citizen than Robert E. Lee. His associations with the founders of the Republic he tried to destroy were very strong. He was a son of that "Lowland Beauty" who was the object of Washington's first love. His father was glorious "Legion Harry" of the Revolution, whose sword had been gallantly used in gaining the independence of the American people; and he had led an army to crush an insurrection. Colonel Lee's wife was a great-granddaughter of Mrs. Washington. And his beautiful home, called Arlington, near Washington city, inherited from the adopted son of Washington, was filled with plate, china and furniture that had been used by the beloved patriot at Mount Vernon.

OFFICERS OF A NEW YORK REGIMENT—DO YOU KNOW THEM?

ORDNANCE YARD, MORRIS ISLAND, S. C.

CHRONOLOGICAL SUMMARY AND RECORD—Continued

JULY, 1862—*Continued from Section* 4

11—Williamsburg, Va. *Confed.* 3 killed.

Pleasant Hill, Mo. 1st Iowa Cav., Mo. Militia. *Union* 10 killed, 19 wounded. *Confed.* 6 killed, 5 wounded.

12—Lebanon, Ky. 28th Ky., Lebanon Home Guards (Morgan's Raid). *Union* 2 killed, 65 prisoners.

Near Culpepper, Va. 1st Md., 1st Vt., 1st W. Va., 5th N. Y. Cav. *Confed.* 1 killed, 5 wounded.

13—Murfreesboro', Tenn. 9th Mich., 3d Minn., 4th Ky. Cav., 7th Pa. Cav., 1st Ky. Battery. *Union* 33 killed, 62 wounded, 800 missing. *Confed.* 50 killed, 100 wounded.

14—Batesville, Ark. 4th Iowa Cav. *Union* 1 killed, 4 wounded.

15—Attempt to destroy 4th Wis., Gunboats *Carondelet, Queen of the West, Tyler* and *Essex. Union* 13 killed, 36 wounded. *Confed.* 5 killed, 9 wounded.

Apache Pass, Ariz. 2d Cal. Cav. *Union* 1 wounded.

Fayetteville, Ark. Detachment of Cavalry, under command of Maj. W. H. Miller. *Confed.* 150 captured.

Near Decatur, Tenn. Detachment of 1st Ohio Cav. *Union* 4 wounded.

17—Cynthiana, Ky. 18th Ky., 7th Ky. Cav., Cynthiana, Newport, Cincinnati and Bracken Co. Home Guards (Morgan's Raid). *Union* 17 killed, 34 wounded. *Confed.* 8 killed, 29 wounded.

18—Memphis, Mo. 2d Mo. Cav., 9th and 11th Mo. State Militia. *Union* 13 killed, 35 wounded. *Confed.* 23 killed.

20 to September 20—Guerrilla Campaign in Missouri. Gen. Schofield's Command. *Union* 77 killed, 156 wounded, 347 missing. *Confed.* 506 killed, 1,800 wounded, 560 missing.

23—Florida, Mo. Two Cos. 3d Iowa Cav. *Union* 22 wounded. *Confed.* 3 killed.

Columbus, Mo. 7th Mo. Cav. *Union* 2 wounded.

24—Trinity, Ala. Co. E 31st Ohio. *Union* 2 killed, 11 wounded. *Confed.* 12 killed, 30 wounded.

Near Florida, Mo. 3d Iowa Cav. *Union* 1 killed, 2 wounded. *Confed.* 1 killed, 12 wounded.

24 and 25—Santa Fe, Mo. 3d Iowa Cav. *Union* 2 killed, 13 wounded.

25—Courtland Bridge, Ala. Two Cos. 10th Ky., two Cos. 1st Ohio Cav. *Union* 100 captured.

25 and 26—Mountain Store and Big Piney, Mo. Three Cos. 3d Mo. Cav., Battery L 2d Mo. Artil. *Confed.* 5 killed.

26—Young's Cross Roads, N. C. 9th N. J., 3d N. Y. Cav. *Union* 7 wounded. *Confed.* 4 killed, 13 wounded.

Greenville, Mo. 3d and 12th Mo. Militia Cav. *Union* 2 killed, 5 wounded.

28—Bayou Barnard, Ind. Ter. 1st, 2d and 3d Kan. Home Guards, 1st Kan. Battery. No casualties recorded.

Moore's Mills, Mo. 9th Mo., 3d Iowa Cav., 2d Mo. Cav., 3d Ind. Battery. *Union* 19 killed, 21 wounded. *Confed.* 30 killed, 100 wounded.

29—Bollinger's Mills, Mo. Two Cos. 13th Mo. *Confed.* 10 killed.

Russelville, Ky. 7th Ind., Russelville Home Guards. *Union* 1 wounded.

Brownsville, Tenn. One Co. 15th Ill. Cav. *Union* 4 killed, 6 wounded. *Confed.* 4 killed, 6 wounded.

30—Paris, Ky. 9th Pa. Cav. *Confed.* 27 killed, 39 wounded.

31—Coggins' Point, opposite Harrison's Landing, Va. U. S. Gunboat Fleet. *Union* 10 killed, 15 wounded. *Confed.* 1 killed, 6 wounded.

AUGUST, 1862

1—Newark, Mo. Seventy-three men of the 11th Mo. State Militia. *Union* 4 killed, 4 wounded, 60 captured. *Confed.* 73 killed and wounded.

2—Ozark or Forsythe, Mo. 14th Mo. State Militia. *Union* 1 wounded. *Confed.* 3 killed, 7 wounded.

Orange C. H., Va. 5th N. Y. Cav., 1st Vt. Cav. *Union* 4 killed, 12 wounded. *Confed.* 11 killed, 52 captured.

Clear Creek or Taberville, Mo. Four Cos. 1st Iowa Cav. *Union* 5 killed, 4 wounded. *Confed.* 11 killed.

Coahomo Co., Miss. 11th Wis. *Union* 5 wounded.

3—Sycamore Church, near Petersburg, Va. 3d Pa. Cav., 5th U. S. Cav. *Union* 2 wounded. *Confed.* 6 wounded.

Chariton Bridge, Mo. 6th Mo. Cav. *Union* 2 wounded. *Confed.* 11 killed, 14 wounded.

Jonesboro', Ark. 1st Wis. Cav. *Union* 4 killed, 2 wounded, 21 missing.

Lauguelle Ferry, Ark. 1st Wis. Cav. *Union* 17 killed, 38 wounded.

4—Sparta, Tenn. Detachments of 4th Ky. and 7th Ind. Cav. *Union* 1 killed.

White Oak Swamp Bridge, Va. 3d Pa. Cav. *Confed.* 10 wounded, 28 captured.

5—Baton Rouge, La. 14th Me., 6th Mich., 7th Vt., 21st Ind., 30th Mass., 9th Conn., 4th Wis., 2d, 4th and 6th Mass. Batteries. *Union* 82 killed, 255 wounded, 34 missing. *Confed.* 84 killed, 316 wounded, 78 missing. *Union* Brig.-Gen. Thomas Williams killed.

Malvern Hill, Va. Portion of Hooker's Div., Third Corps and Richardson's Div., Second Corps and Cavalry, Army of the Potomac. *Union* 3 killed, 11 wounded. *Confed.* 100 captured.

6—Montevallo, Mo. 3d Wis. Cav. *Union* 1 wounded, 3 missing.

Beech Creek, W. Va. 4th W. Va. *Union* 3 killed, 8 wounded. *Confed.* 1 killed, 11 wounded.

Kirksville, Mo. Mo. State Militia. *Union* 28 killed, 60 wounded. *Confed.* 128 killed, 200 wounded.

Matapony or Thornburg, Va. Detachment of King's Division. *Union* 1 killed, 12 wounded, 72 missing.

Tazewell, Tenn. 16th and 42d Ohio, 14th and 22d Ky., 4th Wis. Battery. *Union* 3 killed, 23 wounded, 50 captured. *Confed.* 9 killed, 40 wounded.

7—Trenton, Tenn. 2d Ill. Cav. *Confed.* 30 killed, 20 wounded.

8—Panther Creek, Mo. 1st Mo. Militia Cav. *Union* 1 killed, 4 wounded.

9—Stockton, Mo. Col. McNeil's command of Mo. State Militia. *Confed.* 13 killed, 36 missing.

Cedar Mountain, Va., also called Slaughter Mountain, Southwest Mountain, Cedar Run and Mitchell's Station. Second Corps, Maj.-Gen. Banks; Third Corps, Maj.-Gen. McDowell. Army of Virginia, under command of Maj.-Gen. Pope. *Union* 450 killed, 660 wounded, 290 missing. *Confed.* 229 killed, 1,047 wounded, 31 missing. *Union* Brig.-Gens. Augur, Carroll, and Geary wounded. *Confed.* Brig.-Gen. C. S. Winder killed.

10—Nueces River, Tex. Texas Loyalists. *Union* 40 killed. *Confed.* 8 killed, 14 wounded.

10 to 13—Grand River, Lee's Ford, Chariton River, Walnut Creek, Compton Ferry, Switzler's Mills and Yellow Creek, Mo. 9th Mo. Militia. *Union* 100 killed and wounded.

11—Independence, Mo. 7th Mo. Militia Cav. *Union* 14 killed, 18 wounded, 312 missing.

Helena, Ark. 2d Wis. Cav. *Union* 1 killed, 2 wounded.

Wyoming C. H., W. Va. Detachment of 37th Ohio. *Union* 2 killed.

Kinderhook, Tenn. Detachments of 3d Ky. and 1st Tenn. Cav. *Union* 3 killed. *Confed.* 7 killed.

12—Galatin, Tenn. 2d Ind., 4th and 5th Ky., 1st Pa. Cav. *Union* 30 killed, 50 wounded, 200 captured. *Confed.* 6 killed, 18 wounded.

13—Galatin, Tenn. 13th and 69th Ohio, 11th Mich., drove the Confederates from the town with slight loss.

Clarendon, Ark. Brig.-Gen. Hovey's Div. of the 13th Corps. *Confed.* 700 captured.

15—Merriweather's Ferry, Tenn. One Co. 2d Ill. Cav. *Union* 3 killed, 6 wounded. *Confed.* 20 killed.

16—Lone Jack, Mo. Mo. Militia Cav. *Union* 60 killed, 100 wounded. *Confed.* 110 killed and wounded.

18—Capture of Rebel steamer *Fairplay*, near Milliken's Bend, La. 58th and 76th Ohio. *Confed.* 40 prisoners.

19—Clarksville, Tenn. 71st Ohio. *Union* 200 captured.

White Oak Ridge, near Hickman, Ky. 2d Ill. Cav. *Union* 2 wounded. *Confed.* 4 killed.

20—Brandy Station, Va. Cavalry of Army of Virginia. *Confed.* 3 killed, 12 wounded.

Edgefield Junction, Tenn. Detachment of 50th Ind. *Confed.* 8 killed, 18 wounded.

Union Mills, Mo. 1st Mo. Cav., 13th Ill. Cav. *Union* 4 killed, 3 wounded. *Confed.* 1 killed.

21—Pinckney Island, S. C. *Union* 3 killed, 3 wounded.

22—Courtland, Tenn. 42d Ill. *Union* 2 wounded. *Confed.* 8 killed.

23—Big Hill, Madison Co., Ky. 3d Tenn., 7th Ky. Cav. *Union* 10 killed, 40 wounded and missing. *Confed.* 25 killed.

23 to 25—Skirmishes on the Rappahannock at Waterloo Bridge, Lee Springs, Freeman's Ford and Sulphur Springs, Va. Army of Virginia, under Maj.-Gen. Pope. *Confed.* 27 killed, 94 wounded. *Union* Brig.-Gen. Bohlen captured.

23 to Sept. 1—Pope's Campaign in Virginia. Army of Virginia. *Union* 7,000 killed, wounded and missing. *Confed.* 1,500 killed, 8,000 wounded.

24—Dallas, Mo. 12th Mo. Militia Cav. *Union* 3 killed, 1 wounded.

Coon Creek or Lamar, Mo. *Union* 2 killed, 22 wounded.

25 and 26—Fort Donelson and Cumberland Iron Works, Tenn. 71st Ohio, 5th Iowa Cav. *Union* 31 killed and wounded. *Confed.* 30 killed and wounded.

Bloomfield, Mo. 13th Ill. Cav. *Confed.* 20 killed and wounded.

26—Rienzi and Kossuth, Miss. 2d Iowa Cav., 7th Kan. Cav. *Union* 5 killed, 12 wounded.

27—Bull Run Bridge, Va. 11th and 12th Ohio, 1st, 2d, 3d and 4th N. J. *Union* Brig.-Gen. G. W. Taylor mortally wounded.

Kettle Run, Va. Maj.-Gen. Hooker's Div. of Third Corps. *Union* 300 killed and wounded. *Confed.* 300 killed and wounded.

28—Readyville or Round Hill, Tenn. 10th Brigade Army of Ohio. *Union* 5 wounded.

28 and 29—Groveton and Gainesville, Va. First Corps, Maj.-Gen. Sigel, Third Corps, Maj.-Gen. McDowell, Army of Virginia, Hooker's and Kearney's Division of Third Corps, and Reynolds' Division of First Corps, Army of Potomac, Ninth Corps, Maj.-Gen. Reno. *Union* 7,000 killed, wounded and missing. *Confed.* 7,000 killed, wounded and missing.

29—Manchester, Tenn. Two Cos. 18th Ohio, one Co. 9th Mich. *Confed.* 100 killed and wounded.

30—Second Battle of Bull Run or Manassas, Va. Same troops as engaged at Groveton and Gainesville on the 28th and 29th, with the addition of Porter's Fifth Corps. *Union* 800 killed, 4,000 wounded, 3,000 missing. *Confed.* 700 killed, 3,000 wounded.

Bolivar, Tenn. 20th and 78th Ohio, 2d and 11th Ill. Cav., 9th Ind. Art. *Union* 5 killed, 18 wounded, 64 missing. *Confed.* 100 killed and wounded.

McMinnville, Tenn. 26th Ohio, 17th and 58th Ind., 8th Ind. Battery. *Confed.* 1 killed, 20 wounded.

Richmond, Ky. 12th, 16th, 55th, 66th, 69th and 71st Ind., 95th Ohio, 18th Ky., 6th and 7th Ky. Cav., Batteries D and G Mich. Art. *Union* 200 killed, 700 wounded, 4,000 missing. *Confed.* 250 killed, 500 wounded.

31—Medon Station, Tenn. 45th Ill., 7th Mo. *Union* 3 killed, 13 wounded, 43 missing.

Yates' Ford, Ky. 94th Ohio. *Union* 3 killed, 10 wounded.

(*Continued in Section* 6)

CONFEDERATE BATTERIES AT HOWLETT HOUSE, TRENT'S REACH, JAMES RIVER

CHAPTER X.—Continued.

COLONEL, LATER GENERAL, LEW WALLACE

THESE considerations, so calculated to expand the generous soul with National pride and make the possession of citizenship of a great nation a cherished honor and privilege, seem to have had no influence with Colonel Lee. The narrow political creed of his class of thinkers taught no broader doctrines of citizenship than the duty of allegiance to a petty State whose flag is utterly unknown beyond our shores—an insignificant portion of a great Republic whose flag is honored and respected on every sea and in every port of the civilized world. Acting upon these narrow views, Colonel Lee said, "I must go with my State;" and going, he took with him precious information which enabled him to make valuable suggestions to the insurgents concerning the best methods for seizing the National capital. In time Colonel Lee became the general-in-chief of all the armies in rebellion against his Government, at whose expense he had been educated in the art of war.

Colonel Lee advised the Virginians to erect a battery of heavy guns on Arlington Heights, not far from his own home, which would command the cities of Washington and Georgetown. They were about to follow this advice, when, late in May, their plans were frustrated by the General-in-Chief, who sent National troops across the Potomac to the Virginia shore by way of the Long Bridge at Washington, and the Aqueduct Bridge at Georgetown, to take possession of Alexandria and Arlington Heights. Ellsworth's New York Fire Zouaves went to Alexandria in two schooners, at the same time, to be assisted by a third column that crossed the river at the Long Bridge.

The troops that first passed the Long Bridge constructed a battery at the Virginia end of it, which they named Fort Runyon, in compliment to General Runyon of New Jersey, who was in command of a part of them. The troops that passed Aqueduct Bridge were led by General Irwin McDowell; and upon the spot where Lee proposed to erect a battery of siege-guns, to destroy the capital, the troops erected a redoubt to defend it, which they named Fort Corcoran, in compliment to the commander of an Irish regiment among them. These were the first redoubts constructed by the National troops in the Civil War; and this was the initial movement of the Government forces in opening the first campaigns of that war. It occurred on the morning of the 24th of May, 1861.

The troops sent by land and water reached Alexandria about the same time, and took possession of the city. They seized the Orange and Alexandria railway station and much rolling stock, with some Virginia cavalry who were guarding it. The Secessionists in the city were defiant; and one of them, the keeper of a tavern, persisted in flying the Confederate flag over his house. The impetuous young Ellsworth proceeded to pull it down with his own hands, when the proprietor shot him dead, and was killed, in turn, by one of the Zouaves. This tragedy caused great bitterness in both sections of the country for a time.

Meanwhile the Confederates had erected batteries on the Virginia shores of the Potomac River to obstruct its navigation by National vessels. They had also cast up redoubts near Hampton Roads, not far from Fortress Monroe. Captain J. H. Ward was

COLONEL B. F. KELLEY

COMPANY OF INFANTRY NEAR HARPER'S FERRY

sent to the Roads with a flotilla of armed vessels. The insurgents then possessed Norfolk, and had erected a battery on Sewall's point at the mouth of the Elizabeth River, where, on the morning of the 20th of May, when Ward's vessels appeared in the Roads, there were about two thousand Confederate soldiers. Ward opened the guns of his flag-ship (the *Freeborn*) upon the battery. It was soon silenced, and the insurgents were dispersed. Then Ward proceeded immediately up the Potomac toward Washington, after reporting to Commodore Stringham, and patrolled that important stream. At Aquia Creek, about sixty miles below Washington, he encountered some heavy batteries, and a sharp but indecisive engagement ensued on the first of June. Soon afterward, in an attack upon other batteries at Matthias's Point, the flotilla was repulsed, and Captain Ward was killed. At that place and vicinity the Confederates established batteries which defied the National vessels on those waters; and for many months, the Potomac, as a highway for supplies for the army near Washington, was effectively blockaded by them.

The Union element in the Virginia Secession Convention was chiefly from Western Virginia, a mountain district, where the slave-labor system had not been profitable; and the loyalty of the people there to the old flag gave the Virginia conspirators much uneasiness. At the very beginning the Confederates perceived the importance of holding possession of that region, and so control the Baltimore and Ohio Rail-way that traversed it, and connected Maryland with the teeming West. For that purpose troops were sent from Richmond to restrain the active patriotism of the people, when the latter flew to arms under the leader-ship of Colonel B. F. Kelley, a native of New Hamp-shire, who set up his stand-ard near Wheeling, where an important political movement had already ta-ken place which later divi-ded the State.

Before the adjournment of the Convention at Rich-mond the inhabitants of Western Virginia perceived the necessity of making a bold stand for the Union and their own independence of the oligarchy that ruled the State in the interests of the slaveholders. This first meeting was held at Clarks-burg, on the line of the Bal-timore and Ohio railway, on the 22d of April. John S.

NEWS BOYS IN CAMP

Carlisle, a member of the Convention then sitting at Richmond, offered a resolution at that meeting (which was adopted) calling a Convention of delegates at Wheeling on the 13th of May. Similar meetings were held at other places. One at Kingswood, Preston county, declared that the separation of Western from Eastern Virginia was essential to the maintenance of their liberties. They also resolved to elect a representative to sit in the National Congress; and at a mass Convention held at Wheeling on the 5th of May, it was resolved to sever all political connection with the conspirators at Richmond.

The Convention of delegates met at Wheeling on the 13th of May. The National flag was unfurled over the Custom-House there with appropriate demonstrations of loyalty; and in the Convention the chief topic of discussion was the division of the State and the formation of a new Commonwealth composed of forty or fifty counties of the mountain region. It was asserted in the Convention that the slave oligarchy eastward of the mountains, and in all the tide-water counties, wielded the political power of the State, and used it for the promotion of their great interest, in the levying of taxes, and in lightening their own burdens at the expense of the labor and thrift of the citizens of West Virginia. These considerations, and an innate love for the Union, produced such unanimity of sentiment that the labors of the secret emissaries of the conspirators, and of the open service of recruiting officers were almost fruitless in Western Virginia. The Convention itself was a unit in feeling and purpose; but it was too informal in its character to take decisive action upon the momentous question of a division of the State. So, after condemning the Ordi-nance of Secession, a resolution was adopted, calling a Provisional Convention, at the same place, on the 11th of June, unless the people should vote adversely to that Ordinance, at the appointed time.

The proceedings at Wheeling alarmed the conspirators. They expected an immediate revolt in that region; and Governor Letcher ordered Colonel Porterfield, who was in command of State troops at Grafton, to seize and carry away the arms at Wheeling belonging to the United States, and to use them in arming such men as might rally around his flag. He also told Porterfield that it was "advisable to cut off telegraphic communication between Wheeling and Washington, so that the disaffected at the former

MARYLAND HEIGHTS, HARPER'S FERRY

place could not communicate with their allies at headquarters." Letcher added: "If troops from Ohio or Pennsylvania shall be attempted to be passed on the railroads, do not hesitate to obstruct their passage by all means in your power, even to the destruction of the road and bridge."

As we have observed, the people in Eastern Virginia, under the pressure of the bayonet, ratified the Ordinance of Secession. The Provisional Convention assembled at Wheeling on the appointed day, when about forty counties were represented. The meeting was held in the Custom-house, with Arthur Boreman president, and G. L. Cranmer secretary. A Bill of Rights, reported by J. S. Carlile, was adopted; all allegiance to the Southern Confederacy was denied; a resolution was passed declaring the determination of the inhabitants of Virginia never to submit to the Ordinance of Secession, but to maintain the rights of the Commonwealth in the Union; and all citizens who had taken up arms against the National Government were exhorted to lay them down and return to their allegiance. An Ordinance was reported and adopted vacating all the offices in the State held by State in hostility to the General Govern- also providing for a Provisional gov- the election of officers for a period of also requiring all officers of the State, towns, to take an oath of allegiance tional Government. This move- formally deposed Governor Letcher officers in rebellion against the Na- ernment, but not a secession from purely revolution- Convention adopted of independence of ernment of Virginia, signed by fifty-six on the 19th a Pro- g a n i z e d b y t h e pont, Provisional Polsley, lieutenant- Council of five mem- (June 20, 1861) the tion from Eastern lution adopted by

Mr. Pierrepont He at once notified States that an insur- formidable to be and called for aid ment to suppress it. borrowed money for

PICKET POST, BULL RUN.

GENERAL BEAUREGARD'S HEADQUARTERS

CONFEDERATE FORTIFICATIONS AT MANASSAS JUNCTION.

officers acting ment, and ernment and six months; counties and to the Na- ment, which and all State tional Gov- the State, was ary. T h e a declaration the old gov- which was members; and visional government was or- choice of Francis H. Pierre- governor of the State; Daniel governor, and an Executive bers. On the following day necessity of ultimate separa- Virginia was favored by reso- unanimous vote. was a bold and energetic man. the President of the United rection in Virginia was too suppressed by local power, from the National Govern- He organized the militia, and the public service on the

pledge of his own private fortune. He upheld the "restored government" against the extraordinary efforts of the conspirators at Richmond to crush the new organization and enslave the loyal people. A Legislature was chosen, and at its session, begun at Wheeling on the 1st of July, John S. Carlile and Waitman G. Willie were chosen to represent the restored Commonwealth in the National Congress. Finally a convention of delegates, held in November, 1861, adopted a new

CONFEDERATE FORTIFICATIONS AT MANASSAS

State Constitution, in which Slavery was prohibited; and on 3d of May following, the people who voted upon it, ratified it.

The Legislature, at a called session, approved of a division of the State, and the establishment of a new Commonwealth. All the legal requirements having been complied with, the western counties, by Act of Congress, organized under a constitution, were admitted into the Union under the title of the State of *West Virginia*, on the 20th of June, 1863; and Arthur J. Boreman was chosen governor of the new Commonwealth. At midsummer, Old Virginia presented the curious political spectacle of Letcher, at Richmond, claiming authority over the *whole* State; Pierrepont, at Alexandria, claiming authority over the whole old State excepting West Virginia, and Boreman, at Wheeling, the chief executive of the new Commonwealth, as legal governor.

The Unionists of Western Virginia needed help from the beginning; for the regiment that gathered around Colonel Kelley at Wheeling, though full eleven hundred strong, were too few to withstand the

GROUP AT ARLINGTON

Confederate forces sent against them. Already General George B. McClellan, who had been called to the command of the Ohio troops, was assigned to the head of the Department of the Ohio, which included Western Virginia. With Ohio and Indiana troops he crossed the Ohio River. These, with Kelley's Virginians, moved on Grafton and drove Porterfield and his Confederates to Philippi, closely pursued by his foes. After a sharp engagement at the latter place, on the 2d of June, the Confederates were dispersed, and, for a while, matters were quiet in that region. Kelley was severely wounded in the battle at Philippi. That was the first conflict on land after the President's call for troops.

While events in Western Virginia were assuming the character of open warfare between armed forces, others of great importance were occurring westward of the Alleghany Mountains; for, so early as the beginning of June, civil war had begun wherever the system of slavery prevailed. Political leaders in the "Border States"—slave-labor States bordering on free-labor States—took a position which finally brought great distress upon the inhabitants of those Commonwealths. A large class of these leaders professed to be friends of the Union, but *conditionally*. They would be its friends so long as the National Government did not interfere with slavery, nor "attempt to bring back the seceded States;" in other words, they were friends of the Republic so long as its Government did not raise a finger for the salvation of its life. When the President's call for troops to suppress the rebellion appeared, the *Louisville Journal*, the organ of the professed Unionists of Kentucky, hastened to say: "We are struck with mingled amazement and

DESTRUCTION OF THE RAIL ROAD AT MANASSAS

indignation. The policy announced in the proclamation deserves the unqualified condemnation of every American citizen. It is unworthy, not merely of a statesman, but of a man. It is a policy utterly hare-brained and ruinous. If Mr. Lincoln contemplated this policy in his inaugural address, he is a guilty

GENERAL ROBERT PATTERSON

dissembler; if he conceived it under the excitement aroused by the seizure of Fort Sumter, he is a guilty Hotspur. In either case, he is miserably unfit for the exalted position in which the enemies of the country have placed him. Let the people instantly take him and his administration into their own hands, if they would rescue the land from bloodshed, and the Union from sudden and irretrievable destruction." And at a large "Union meeting" at Louisville, over which James Guthrie and other leading men in the State held control, it was resolved that "Kentucky reserved to herself the right to choose her own position; and that, while her natural sympathies are with those who have a common interest in the protection of slavery, she still acknowledges her loyalty and fealty to the Government of the United States, which she will cheerfully render *until that Government becomes aggressive, tyrannical, and regardless of our rights in slave property*." They declared that the States were peers of the National Government; and gave the world to understand that the latter should not be allowed to "use sanguinary or coercive" measures to "bring back the seceded States." The "Kentucky State Guard," which the governor had organized for the benefit of the Secessionists, were commended by this Union meeting as "the bulwark of the safety of the Commonwealth," and its members were enjoined to remember that they were "pledged equally" to fidelity to the United States and Kentucky.

The "Guard" was placed under the command of Captain Simon B. Buckner of the National army, who was then evidently in the secret service of the Confederacy, for he used his position effectively in seducing large numbers of the members of the "Guard" from their allegiance to the old flag, and sending them as recruits to the Confederate armies. It was not long before he led a large portion of them into the camp of the enemy, and he became a Confederate major-general. Then the *Louisville Journal*, that had so savagely condemned the President, more savagely assailed Buckner with curses, saying: "Away with your pledges and assurances—with your protestations, apologies and proclamations—at once and altogether! Away, parricide! Away, and do penance for-ever!—be shriven or slain—away! You have less palliation than Attila—less boldness, magnanimity and nobleness than Coriolanus. You are the Benedict Arnold of the day! you are the Cataline of Kentucky! Go, thou miscreant!" And when in February, 1862, Buckner and some of the "State Guard" were captured at Fort Donelson, and he was sent to Fort Warren, Boston, many of those who were deceived by the pretence that the "Guard" were the "bulwark of the Commonwealth," demanded his delivery to the authorities of Kentucky, to be tried for treason against the State. That was after the Legislature of that State had refused to favor the scheme of the disloyal governor, and Kentucky was feeling the effects of its peculiar "neutrality;" a sort of Unionism that caused Missouri and Kentucky to become battle-fields, and to suffer untold miseries. Their soil was trodden and ravaged by contending armies, which had no respect for what was known as "Kentucky neutrality," for, in the hands of the Secessionists it was only an adroit scheme to mislead and confuse the people, a large majority of whom were sincerely attached to the Union.

Although the slaves were not more than one-tenth of the population of Missouri and the best interests of the State were allied to free-labor, the Slave power, wielded by the most active politicians, had such potential influence that it controlled the destiny of that State. By these the election of Claiborne T. Jackson, governor of Missouri, was effected, and he was now one of the most active of the Secessionists. His political friends formed a plan for placing the militia of the State under his absolute control for the benefit of the Confederacy. The chief leader in this scheme was D. M. Frost, of New York, a graduate of West Point, who was commissioned a brigadier and placed at the head of that militia. Frost resolved to seize the Arsenal at St. Louis, and hold possession of that chief city of the Mississippi Valley; and for this purpose he formed a camp near the town with the pretext of disciplining the men under his command. At that time the military post at St. Louis was in charge of Captain Nathaniel M. Lyon, who was vigilant and brave; and when he was satisfied of Frost's treacherous designs, he marched out with a large number of volunteers, surrounded the insurgent camp, and made the leader and his followers prisoners.

Views on the James River

It was now late in May, and the Secessionists in Missouri took open issue with the National Government. The latter, satisfied that it was the design of the Confederates to hold military possession of that State and of Kentucky, fortified Cairo, Illinois, at the confluence of the Ohio and Mississippi rivers. It was made impregnable, and became of immense importance to the Union cause; for there some of the land and naval expeditions which performed signal service in the valley of the Mississippi were fitted out.

FORT BEAUREGARD, NEAR MANASSAS

General W. S. Harney, a conservative in feeling, was at the head of the Department of the West, with his quarters at St. Louis. He returned to his post, after a brief absence, when the excitement was at its height. Wishing to preserve peace, he made a compact with the insurgent leaders not to employ the military arm so long as they should preserve public order. The loyal people were alarmed, for they would not trust the promises of the Secessionists. Happily for the Union cause, the National Government did not sanction the compact. Appreciating the great services of Lyon, he was commissioned a brigadier, and at the close of May he succeeded Harney with the title of Commander of the Department of Missouri.

Early in June, General Lyon, Colonel Blair and others, held a conference with Governor Jackson and General Price, on the subject of pacification. Jackson demanded the disbanding of the Home Guard, composed of loyal Missourians, and the withdrawal of National troops from the State. Lyon peremptorily refused, when Jackson and Price returned to Jefferson City, the State capital. The Legislature had placed the purse and sword of Missouri in the hands of the governor; and on the 12th of June (1861) he issued a proclamation calling into active service fifty thousand of the militia, and raised the standard of revolt, with General Sterling Price as military leader. At the same time he ordered his son to destroy two important railway bridges, and cut the telegraph wires between St. Louis and the State capital. Then began those movements of troops within the borders of Missouri which continued almost incessantly during the entire period of the war, with the most disastrous results to the peace and prosperity of the State. At the same time the disloyal governor of Tennessee (Isham G. Harris) had placed that State in military relations to the Confederacy, similar to that of Virginia, and was working in concert with Jackson. General Gideon J. Pillow, an indifferent leader, was placed in chief command of the troops of both States, and with these he made an unsuccessful effort to seize Cairo. He was soon superseded by Leonidas Polk, a graduate of West Point, and then Bishop of the Protestant Episcopal Church in the Diocese of Louisiana, who had been commissioned a major-general, and became an earnest leader of Confederate armies in the West.

Civil War had now begun in earnest; and in all parts of the Union, North and South, hosts of armed men were marshaling for the dreadful struggle that ensued. The Confederate government, in order to be nearer the National capital, their coveted object, had resolved to leave Montgomery and make their headquarters at Richmond; while their forces, designed for the capture of Washington, were gathering in large numbers, under General Beauregard, at Manassas, about thirty miles from that city. The president of the Confederacy (Jefferson Davis) left Montgomery for Virginia, on Sunday the 26th of May, with the intention, it was said, of taking command of the Confederate troops there, in person. He was accompanied by his favorite aid, General Wigfall of Fort Sumter fame, and by Robert Toombs, his secretary of state. His journey was a continual ovation. At every railway station, men, women, and children greeted him with enthusiasm. A reporter of the *Richmond Enquirer* was sent to chronicle the events of the journey, whose admiration of the "presidential party" was very pronounced. He spoke of the "flute-like voice" of Davis, and of the excessive modesty of Wigfall and Toombs. "In vain he [Wigfall] would seek some remote part of the cars," said the chronicler; "the crowd hunted him up, and the welkin rang with rejoicings as he addressed them in his emphatic and fervent style of oratory." Of Toombs, he said: "He, too, sought to avoid the call, but the echo would ring with the name of 'Toombs! Toombs!' and the sturdy

Building Winter Quarters at City Point

Georgia statesman had to respond." On the southern verge of Virginia, some of the State riflemen, designed as an escort to the president, joined the party. With every step the popularity of their "chief magistrate" seemed to be more and more manifest, for the people felt that "the mantle of Washington had fallen gracefully upon his shoulders." At Goldsboro', "the Hall," said the reporter, "was thronged with beautiful girls, and many were decking him with garlands of flowers, while others fanned him. It was a most interesting occasion. Never were a people more enraptured with their chief magistrate."

At Richmond, Davis was received with equal enthusiasm; and at the Fair-ground he addressed an immense multitude of people. With a consciousness of power, he spoke bitter words against the Government whose kindness he had ever experienced. He flattered the vanity of the Virginians by reminding them that they had been chosen to "smite the invaders;" and he assured them there was "not one true

A BATTERY IN ACTION

son of the South who was not ready to shoulder his musket, to bleed, to die, or to conquer in the cause of liberty here. . . . We have now reached the point," he continued, "where, arguments being exhausted, it only remains for us to stand by our weapons. When the time and occasion serve, we shall smite the smiter with manly arms, as did our fathers before us, and as becomes their sons. To the enemy we leave the base acts of the assassin and incendiary. To them we leave it to insult helpless women; to us belongs vengeance upon man." The Virginians were too insane with passion to resent his virtual reiteration of the selfish words of Pickens: "You may plant your seed in peace, for Old Virginia will have to bear the brunt of the battle;" and they actually rejoiced with pride in the fact that, as he said, upon every hill around their State Capitol were "camps of soldiers from every State in the Confederacy." They purchased an elegant residence for the use of their president, and furnished it sumptuously. There he lived, and exercised the powers of his office for almost four years.

CHAPTER XI.

Beauregard's Proclamation—Insurgents at Harper's Ferry—Exploits of an Indiana Regiment—Events on the Virginia Peninsula—Battle at Big Bethel—National Troops on the Upper Potomac—The Capital in Danger—A Gunpowder Plot—Action of England and France "Punch's" Epigram—Conduct of Great Britain and the Western European Powers—Russia—Meeting of Congress—Department Reports—Appropriations—Increase of the Navy—Enthusiasm of the People—Women's Work—Miss Dix—Benevolent Work in Philadelphia.

THE fulfillment of the prediction that "Poor Old Virginia will have to bear the brunt of battle," had now begun. Beauregard was in command of a constantly increasing force at Manassas, at the beginning of June, and there was a general belief that under the instruction of President Davis, he would attempt the seizure of the capital. In characteristic words, he sent forth a proclamation calculated to "fire the Southern heart." "A reckless and unprincipled tyrant," he said, "has invaded your soil." He assured them that Lincoln had thrown "Abolition hosts" among them, and were murdering and

CAMP OF CONFEDERATE PRISONERS

imprisoning their citizens, confiscating and destroying property, and "committing other acts of violence and outrage too revolting to humanity to be enumerated. All rules of civilized warfare are abandoned, and they proclaim by these acts, if not on their banners, that their war-cry is 'Beauty and Booty.' All that is dear to men—your honor and that of your wives and daughters, your fortune and your lives—are involved in the momentous contest." No man knew better than Beauregard that, at that moment, the only National troops in Virginia, excepting those in the loyal western portion, were the handful of men holding Arlington Heights, the Long Bridge, Alexandria and the village of Hampton near Fortress Monroe, in a merely defensive attitude, against thousands of insurgents who were marshaling under that leader for the avowed purpose of seizing the National capital. He knew that the only "murder" and "outrage" yet committed by National troops was the single act of killing the assassin of Colonel Ellsworth. The author of the proclamation was noted throughout the war for ridiculous boastings, official mendacity, and conspicuous military failures.

OLD CAPITAL PRISON, WASHINGTON, D. C.

Late in May, Joseph E. Johnston, a captain of Topographical Engineers and a meritorious officer who had deserted his flag and accepted the commission of brigadier-general from its enemies, took command of the insurgent troops at Harper's Ferry and in the Shenandoah Valley. At the same time General Robert Patterson, a veteran of two wars, was gathering troops at Chambersburg, in Pennsylvania, to attack Johnston. He moved forward with fifteen thousand men early in June, under instructions from General Scott to "attempt nothing without a clear prospect of success," as the enemy were "strongly posted and equal in numbers." Already, as we have observed, the insurgents had been smitten at Philippi, in Western Virginia; and just as Patterson began his march, an Indiana Zouave Regiment, led by Colonel Lewis Wallace, struck the Confederates a blow at Romney, in that mountain region, which gave them great alarm. That regiment, one of the best disciplined in the field, had been chafing under forced inaction in Southern Indiana, and Wallace urged their employment in active service. He was gratified by being ordered to Cumberland, to report to General Patterson. In less than three days after the receipt of the order, they had traversed Indiana and Ohio; received their ammunition at Grafton, in Western Virginia, and were at Cumberland. Resting a single day, Wallace proceeded to strike a band of insurgents at Romney; and on the night of the 10th of June, 1861, led by a competent guide, the regiment made a silent march along a rough and perilous mountain-path, but did not reach the vicinity of the insurgents until late in the evening of the 12th. They at once attacked the Confederates with such skill and bravery, that they fled to the shelter of the forests, followed by all the villagers, excepting the few negroes. In the space of twenty-four hours, Wallace and his men had traveled eighty-four miles (forty-six of them on foot), engaged in a brisk skirmish, and returned; "and what is more," wrote Colonel Wallace in his report, "my men are ready to repeat it to-morrow." This dash caused Johnston to evacuate Harper's Ferry, for he believed the assailants to be the advance of a much larger force. He moved up the Valley, and took post near Winchester.

While the campaign was thus opening in Western Virginia, stirring events were occurring near Fortress Monroe. The possession of that post was of the first importance to both parties; and Colonel J. B. Magruder, who had deserted his flag, was sent down the Virginia Peninsula, with a considerable force, to attempt its seizure. General B. F. Butler, who was then in command of the Department of Virginia and North Carolina, with his headquarters at Fortress Monroe, took measures to oppose him. General E. W. Pearce was placed in command of an expedition that was to march in two columns against the insurgents. He was to lead, from near Hampton, Duryea's Fifth (Zouave) New York Regiment, and Townsend's Third, to Little Bethel, where he was to be joined by detachments from Colonel Phelps's command at

Winter Quarters and Corduroy Road

Newport News. The latter were composed of battalions of Massachusetts and Vermont troops, Bendix's Germans of New York, known as the Steuben Rifle Regiment, and a battery of two light field-pieces in charge of Lieutenant John T. Greble of the regular army, with eleven artillery men.

Both columns marched at about midnight. An order to secure mutual recognition was neglected, and as the columns approached in the gloom, they mistook each other for enemies, and fired, killing and maiming some of the men. The mistake was instantly discovered, and the combined columns pressed on toward Magruder's fortifications at Big Bethel. The noise of the firing had been heard there, which caused the scattered Confederates to concentrate their forces in time to meet the Nationals. A sharp engagement ensued. The Nationals were repulsed; and just as Lieutenant Greble ordered his field-pieces to be made ready for the retreat, a cannon-ball struck his temple a glancing blow, and he fell dead. So perished, at the very opening of the great Civil War, the first of the officers of the regular army who fell in that conflict. Generous, brave and good, Lieutenant Greble was beloved by all who knew him. His body was carried to Philadelphia, his native city, where it lay in state one day, in Independence Hall, and was buried with military honors in Woodland Cemetery. Major Theodore Winthrop, an accomplished young officer, was also killed at Bethel, while bravely contending with the insurgents. He was a member of General Butler's staff, and his military secretary. When Butler was informed of the action, he proceeded to join the expedition in person, but at Hampton he received tidings of the disaster. It was a result which alarmed and mortified the nation; but the public mind was soon absorbed in the contemplation of far greater and more momentous movements. The failure at Bethel was undoubtedly chargeable more to a general eagerness to do, without experience in doing, than to any special shortcomings of individuals.

GENERAL W. S. ROSECRANS

For a month after the dash on Romney, Wallace and his men were in a perilous situation; but by boldness and audacity of action, a wholesome fear of the Zouaves was created among the Confederates.

GENERAL J. D. COX

By ceaseless activity they guarded the Baltimore and Ohio Railway for more than a hundred miles; and so distinguished were their services, unaided, that General Patterson wrote to Wallace: "I begin to doubt whether the Eleventh Indiana needs reinforcements." Wallace was soon afterward commissioned a brigadier-general of volunteers.

When Johnston abandoned Harper's Ferry, General Patterson, who had received intimations that he was expected to cross the Potomac, pushed his columns forward from Hagerstown and threw about nine thousand troops across the river at Williamsport, where it was fordable. These were led by General George Cadwallader, who commanded five companies of cavalry. At that moment Scott telegraphed to Patterson to send him all his regular troops and a few others under his command. This order was repeated; and again it was repeated early in the morning of the 17th, when the General-in-Chief said: "We are pressed here; send the troops I have twice called for, without delay." Patterson obeyed, but was compelled to call back the remainder of his force into Maryland.

The danger hinted at by the General-in-Chief was great indeed. Beauregard was preparing to move on the capital before the assembling of Congress on the 4th of July. The Confederate government, aided by the Secessionists of Virginia and Maryland,

Pontoon Bridge Between Georgetown and Anacosta Island

were employing every means in their power to accomplish that end. Washington was swarming with enemies, open and secret. Plotters were at work. The Confederate archives at the capital reveal some ugly facts; among others, that the Confederate secretary of war received a proposition to blow up the Capitol with gunpowder that should be conveyed secretly to its crypts, some time between the 4th and 5th of July, when Congress would be in session and possibly the President might be present. The proposition was entertained, and directions were given for a conference between the conspirators and Judah P. Benjamin, the Confederate attorney-general. This scheme for wholesale murder was abandoned then, and Congress assembled quietly at the appointed time.

When Congress met (July 4, 1861) the public welfare demanded immediate and energetic action, and that legislation should be confined to providing means for the salvation of the Republic. Our foreign relations were in a critical state. Confederate emissaries at European courts had created a general impression among statesmen and publicists, that our nation was only a league of States that might be dissolved when a member became dissatisfied. They had magnified the power and unity of the Confed-

GENERAL R. S. GARNETT, C. S. A.   GENERAL W. H. MORRIS

eracy, and had made the free-trade in cotton to France. The belief soon Republic was hopelessly resentatives at Wash-respective governments were hopelessly dismem-public sentiment in amazed at the seeming islating as if the Union, had a future. Some of widen the breach, and the United States by jealous of our expanding and regarded our repub-ment as a standing men-monarchies of the old

Great Britain and equally anxious for the and they entered into a in concert. They even other European govern-standing, with the ex-would concur with them. ning of our difficulties, friendly powers had

most tempting offer of Great Britain and became general that the shattered. Foreign rep-ington wrote to their that the United States bered; and leaders of Europe affected to be folly of Congress in leg-"one and inseparable," them were anxious to so diminish the power of disunity; for they were greatness as a nation, lican form of govern-ace of the unstable world.

France seemed to be overthrow of the Union, secret agreement to act went so far as to apprise ments of this under-pectation that the latter So, at the very begin-these two professedly clandestinely entered

into a combination for arraying all Europe on the side of the insurgents, and giving them moral and material aid. Our loyal people could not, at first, comprehend the unfriendly acts and tone of the British government and the chief representatives of the British people, until the touchstone of Montesquieu's assertion was applied: "Other nations have made the interests of commerce yield to those of politics; the English, on the contrary, have ever made political interests give way to those of commerce." And the traditional philanthropy of the English in behalf of the slave made the following notable epigram of the London *Punch* appear to us, at first, like a good-natured slander:

> "Though with the North we sympathize,
>   It must not be forgotten,
> That with the South we've stronger ties
>   Which are composed of cotton,
> Whereof our imports 'mount unto
>   A sum of many figures;
> And where would be our calico
>   Without the toil of niggers?
>
> The South enslaves their fellow-men,
>   Whom we love all so dearly,
> The North keeps commerce bound again,
>   Which touches us more nearly.
> Thus a divided duty we
>   Perceive in this hard matter—
> Free-trade or sable brothers free?
>   O, will we choose the latter?"

RUINS OF BRIDGE AT BLACKBURN'S FORD

BRIDGE ACROSS BULL RUN - BUILT BY ENGINEERS OF McDOWELL'S CORPS

BATTLEFIELD OF MANASSAS

MRS. SPINNER'S HOUSE NEAR CENTREVILLE

This epigram gave the key to the secret motives of the English government. The astute Frenchman, Count Gasparin, clearly perceived them. He knew the seductive influence of the bribe of free cotton on a manufacturing people like those of Great Britain; and nearly two months before her public acts in favor of the insurgents were manifested, he gave this warning: "Let England beware! It were better for her to lose Malta, Corfu and Gibraltar, than the glorious position which her struggle against Slavery and the Slave-trade has secured her in the esteem of the nations. Even in an age of armored frigates and rifled cannon, the chief of all powers, thank God! is moral power. Woe to the nation that disregards it, and consents to immolate its principles to its interests! From the beginning of the present conflict the enemies of England, and they are numerous, have predicted that the cause of cotton will weigh heavier in her scales than the cause of justice and liberty. They are preparing to judge her by her conduct in the American crisis. Once more, let her beware!"

GENERAL N. P. BANKS

The British ministry did not heed the warning. So early as the 9th of May (1861), Lord John Russell, the Minister for Foreign Affairs, said in Parliament, in reply to the question, What position has the government intended to take? "The Attorney and Solicitor-General and the Queen's Advocate and the Government have come to the opinion that the Southern Confederacy of America, according to those principles which seem to them to be just principles, must be treated as a belligerent." This was preparatory to an open recognition of the independence of the Confederacy, a motion for which was then pending in Parliament. The Queen and her beloved husband, the Prince Consort, felt a real friendship for the Americans, who had treated their son, the Prince of Wales, so kindly only a few months before, but she yielded to ministerial pressure, and on the 13th of May issued a proclamation of neutrality, in which belligerent rights were accorded to the insurgents, and a virtual acknowledgment of the Confederation as a national power. It was followed in the British Parliament, and among the Tory classes and in the Tory newspapers of the realm, by the most dogmatic assertions that the Republic of the West was hopelessly crumbling into ruins, and was unworthy of respectful consideration.

All this was done with unseemly haste, before Mr. Charles Francis Adams, chosen by the new Administration to represent the United States at the Court of St. James, had presented his credentials. When that event occurred, and the tone of Mr. Adams's instructions was known, the British ministry paused, and took counsel of prudence and expediency. Mr. Adams had been instructed by the American Secretary of State (Mr. Seward) especially to counteract the influence of Confederate agents at court. "You will in no case," said the instructions, "listen to any suggestions of compromise by this Government, under foreign auspices, with its discontented citizens. If, as the President does not at all apprehend, you shall unhappily find her Majesty's government tolerating the applications of the so-called Confederate States, or wavering about it, you will not leave them to suppose, for a moment, that they can grant that application and remain the friends of the United States. You may even assure them promptly, in that case, that if they determine to recognize, they may at the same time prepare to enter into an alliance with the enemies of this Republic. You, alone, will represent your country at London, and you will represent the whole of it there. When you are asked to divide that duty with others, diplomatic relations between the government of Great Britain and this Government will be suspended, and will remain so until it shall be seen which of the two is most strongly intrenched in the confidence of their respective nations and of mankind."

The high position taken by Mr. Seward, in the name of his Government, in that able letter of instructions, was doubtless one

GENERAL IRWIN McDOWELL

Maj Gen. C. S. Hamilton.

Maj Gen. Frank P. Blair.

Major-General A. J. Smith

Horrors of War

of the chief causes for the fortunate delay of the British government in the matter of recognizing the independence of the Southern Confederacy. Its puissance was increased by the manifest opposition of the great mass of the "common people" of Great Britain, to the unfriendly conduct of their government and the ruling classes toward the real Government of the United States. The friendly attitude of Russia toward the United States was another cause for delay. The cautious Emperor of the French followed Great Britain, and on the 17th of June issued a decree according belligerent rights to the Confederates; so also

BVT. MAJOR-GENERAL E. B. TYLER

did the Queen of Spain proclaim and entered upon a scheme with seeds of monarchical institutions Republic was about to expire. nized the insurgents as belliger- enlightened Emperor of Russia strike the shackles from almost dominions, instructed (July 10) to say: "In every event, the the most cordial sympathy on the during the important crisis which The powers of Western Europe, a promised ally of the Republic of

the neutrality of her government, Napoleon III. for replanting the in America now that the great The King of Portugal also recog- ents, on the 29th of July; but the (Alexander II.), who was about to forty million slaves in his own his representative at Washington American nation may count upon part of our most august master it is passing through at present." regarding the Russian Emperor as the West, behaved prudently.

It was on Thursday, the 4th fourth anniversary of the Declara- Thirty-seventh Congress assem- extraordinary session. It was a country. Civil War was kindling miles of the Republic, and ene- acing its Capitol and its archives the sound of great guns, armies pose; and secret emissaries of the trusted with errands of deadliest

of July, 1861, and the eighty- tion of Independence, when the bled at the National capital, in critical time in the history of our over a quarter of a million square mies of the nation's life were men- with utter destruction. Within were then gathering for that pur- Confederacy, it was believed, in- mischief, were prowling about the

halls of Congress and the President's house. As promptly as the militia of the country, the members of the National Legislature had responded to the President's call. Twenty-three States were represented in the Senate, and one hundred and fifty-four members of the Lower House were present on the first day of the session, while ten slave-labor States were not represented. In both Houses there was a large working majority of Unionists; yet there was a considerable faction who sympathized with the Confederates in their application of the doctrine of State-supremacy and in opposition to coercive measures.

The President, in his message, after setting forth the causes of trouble, the acts of the insurgents, and the necessity for giving strength to the Executive arm, said: "It is now recommended, that you give the legal means for making this contest a short and decisive one; that you place at the control of the Government, for the work, at least four hundred thousand men and four hundred millions of dollars." That number of men constituted only one-tenth of those of proper age for military service in the regions where, apparently, all were willing to engage; and the sum of money asked for was less than a twenty-third part of the money value owned by the men who seemed willing to devote the whole.

The President's message was accompanied by important reports from three heads of departments. The Secretary of War (Simon Cameron) recommended the enlistment of men for three years; appropria- tions for extraordinary expenses; the appointment of an Assistant Secretary of War, and an increase of the clerical force in his department. The Secretary of the Treasury (Salmon P. Chase) asked for $240,- 000,000 for war purposes, and $80,000,000 for the current expenses of the Government. He proposed to raise these amounts by three different methods. For the civil service, he proposed to procure a revenue by increased duties on specified articles and a system of internal taxation; for war purposes, by a National loan in the form of Treasury notes, bearing an interest of one cent a day on fifty dollars, or in bonds, made redeemable at the pleasure of the Government after a period not exceeding thirty years, and bearing an interest not exceeding six per centum a year. He further recommended the issue of Treasury notes for a smaller amount.

The Secretary of the Navy (Gideon Wells), who had been compelled to resort to extraordinary measures to save the Republic, asked Congress to sanction his acts; to authorize the appointment of an Assistant Secretary of the Navy, and to appoint commissioners to inquire into the expediency of using iron-clad steamers or floating batteries.

POST OFFICE, HEADQUARTERS OF THE ARMY OF THE POTOMAC

The suggestions of the President and the heads of departments were followed by prompt action on the part of Congress. They at once made provisions for the sinews of war and to strengthen the arm of the Chief Magistrate of the Republic. They approved of the President's call for militia and volunteers. They authorized the raising of five hundred thousand troops; and they made an appropriation of $500,000,000 to defray the expenses of the kindling Civil War. They carried out the suggestions of the Secretary of the Treasury concerning methods for procuring the money, by increased taxes and the issue of interest-bearing Treasury notes or bonds. Each House was purged of disloyal members by the expulsion of ten Senators and one Representative. The Secretary of the Navy was upheld by Congress; and, putting forth extraordinary exertions to increase the naval force of the country, he purchased, before the close of

A BATTERY ON DRILL

the year, and put into commission, no less than one hundred and thirty-seven vessels, and contracted for the building of a large number of substantial steamships for sea service. He called attention to the importance of iron-clad vessels; and so promptly were his requisitions for recruits complied with, that no vessel was ever detained for more than two or three days by want of men. Two hundred and fifty-nine officers had resigned or been dismissed from the service for disloyalty since the 4th of March, and several vessels were sent to sea without a full complement of officers; but the want was soon supplied, for many retired officers, who had engaged in civil pursuits, now came to the aid of their country in its hour of need, and were re-commissioned. Many masters and mates were appointed from the commercial marine. The Naval School and public property at Annapolis had been removed to Newport, Rhode Island, for safety, and the seminary found temporary accommodations in Fort Adams there.

When Congress met, there were about three hundred thousand Union troops in the field, and the enthusiasm of the people in the free-labor States was at fever heat. They contributed men, money and soldiers, with lavish generosity. Women, animated by their natural zeal in labors of mercy, went to work with busy fingers preparing lint and bandages for the wounded, and hospital garments for the sick and maimed. In tens of thousands of households in the land, women and children might be seen engaged in the holy toil; while hundreds of the gentler sex, many of whom had been tenderly nurtured in the lap of ease and luxury, hastened to hospitals in camps and towns, and there, with saintly self-sacrifice, they performed the duties of nurse, night and day, and administered, in every way, with all the tenderness of affectionate mothers and sisters, to the wants of the sick, the wounded, and the dying.

Associated efforts in this benevolent work were first organized by Miss Dorothea L. Dix, a woman extensively known in our country for her labors of love in behalf of the poor, the unfortunate, and the afflicted. Perceiving war to be inevitable, she offered her services to the Government gratuitously, in organizing a system for providing comfort for the sick and wounded soldiers. They were accepted. Only eight days after the President's call for troops, the Secretary of War proclaimed: "Be it known to all whom it may concern, that the free services of Miss D. L. Dix are accepted by the War Department, and that she will give, at all times, all necessary aid in organizing military hospitals for the care of all the sick or wounded soldiers, aiding the chief surgeons by supplying nurses and substantial means for the comfort and relief of the suffering; also, that she is fully authorized to receive, control, and disburse special supplies bestowed by individuals or associations for the comfort of their friends or the citizen soldiers from all parts of the United States." Surgeon-General R. C. Wood, recognizing the ability of Miss Dix for the

Bridge Built by Troops on O. & A. R.R., United States Military Railway

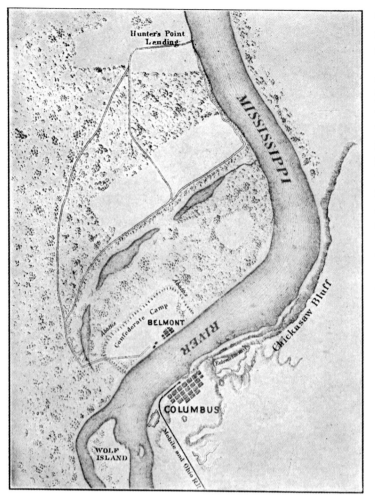

MAP OF BELMONT AND VICINITY

task she had volunteered to perform, publicly requested all women who offered their services as nurses to report to her.

"Like an angel of mercy," says an historian of the war, "this self-sacrificing woman labored day and night throughout the entire war for the relief of the suffering soldiers, without expecting or receiving any pecuniary reward. She went from battle-field to battle-field when the carnage was over; from camp to camp, and from hospital to hospital, superintending the operations of the nurses, and administering with her own hands physical comforts to the suffering, and soothing the troubled spirits of the invalid or dying soldier with a voice low, musical and attractive, and always burdened with words of heartfelt sympathy and religious consolation. . . . Yet she was not the only Sister of Mercy engaged in this holy work. She had hundreds of devoted, earnest, self-sacrificing co-workers of the gentler sex all over the land, serving with equal zeal in the camp and hospitals of National and Confederate armies; and no greater heroism was displayed by soldiers in the field than was exhibited by these American women everywhere."

The firemen of Philadelphia also did noble work. When sick and wounded soldiers began to be brought to the Government hospitals in Philadelphia, the Medical Department often found it difficult to provide vehicles to take them from the vessels to their destination, and there was much suffering on account of delays. The sympathetic firemen of the city made arrangements to give a signal when invalid soldiers arrived, when they would turn out with wagons to convey them to the hospitals. Finally, the Northern Liberties Engine Company had a fine ambulance constructed for the purpose. Other fire companies of the city followed the example; and in these ambulances, one hundred and twenty thousand soldiers were conveyed tenderly from vessels to the hospitals, during the war.

CHAPTER XII.

Confederates in Virginia—National Troops in Western Virginia—McClellan's Campaign—Secessionists Repressed in Baltimore—Confederate Privateers—Troops near Washington—Manassas Junction—Patterson Crosses the Potomac—Movements of National Troops—Battle at Blackburn's Ford—Battle of Bull Run and Its Effects—War in the West—General Lyon's Campaign—Military Operations in Missouri—Death of Lyon—Union Movement—Movements of a Disloyal Governor.

THE gathering of Confederate troops at Manassas, under Beauregard, required prompt and vigorous action on the part of the Government. The main Confederate army was there. Johnston was at Winchester, with a large body, ready to reinforce Beauregard at any moment, unless prevented by General Patterson, who was at Martinsburg early in July, with eighteen thousand Nationals, keenly watching the movements of the Confederates. From their grand encampment at Manassas, the latter had sent out detachments along the line of the Upper Potomac from Georgetown to Leesburg, menacing various points, and foraging. At Vienna they had a severe skirmish (June 17) with an Ohio regiment, and were repulsed; and there the flag of the "Sovereign State of South Carolina" was first seen on a battle-field. The Confederates soon returned and took possession of Vienna and Falls Church Village, and the latter became famous for stirring scenes afterward. It was ten days after this event that Captain Ward, of the *Freeborn*, was killed at Matthias Point.

GENERAL HEINTZELMAN ENTERTAINING FRIENDS AT CONVALESCENT CAMP, ALEXANDRIA

The Confederates now put forth all their available strength to hold the mountain regions of Virginia. The Baltimore and Ohio Railway was guarded by National troops; and about twenty thousand of these from Ohio, Indiana and Virginia, were at Grafton, under the command of General George B. McClellan, at the beginning of July.   Porterfield had been superseded by General R. S. Garnett, in command of the

HEADQUARTERS OF GENERAL MC DOWELL NEAR MANASSAS JULY 1862

Confederate forces in Western Virginia, with his headquarters at Beverly and outlying posts at Bealington, Philippi, Buckhannon and Romney.   In the Great Kanawha region, a considerable body of Confederates were led by Ex-Governor H. A. Wise, where he was confronted by Ohio troops under General J. D. Cox.   At the same time McClellan began offensive operations.   He led ten thousand men to attack Garnett at Laurel Hill, near Beverly; and sent four thousand men under General T. A. Morris toward the same point, by way of Philippi.   Another body under General Hill was sent to a point eastward of Philippi, to prevent the escape of the insurgents over the Alleghany Mountains to join Johnston at Winchester in the Shenandoah Valley.

When the Nationals approached Garnett's position, it was ascertained that Colonel John Pegram, with a considerable body of strongly intrenched Confederates, was Gap in the rear of his immediately dis- in Rich Mountain (afterward General) chief.   McClellan W. S. Rosecrans, patched Colonel with a body of Ohio and Indiana foot soldiers and a troop of cavalry, in light marching order, to dislodge Pegram.   By a circuitous and perilous mountain march in the darkness, and under a heavy rain-storm, they made their way to the top of a ridge of Rich Mountain, above Pegram's camp and only a mile from it (July 11, 1861); but they were not unobserved. Pegram had discovered their approach, and now attacked them furiously with nine hundred men armed with muskets and cannon. A severe engagement ensued.   The Confederates were repulsed; and for his gallantry on that occasion Rosecrans was commis-

YELLOW HOSPITAL, MANASSAS, JULY 1862.

OUR PHOTOGRAPHER NEAR MANASSAS, JULY 1862.

sioned a brigadier-general.   The National troops were in a perilous situation on Rich Mountain, for Pegram confronted them with an overwhelming force.   McClellan had heard the sounds of battle, and pushed forward with troops for their relief.   Pegram did not wait to be attacked, but stole away in the night, and so uncovered Garnett's rear.   Advised of this fact, Garnett also withdrew in the darkness, leaving most of his cannon, tents and wagons behind, and fled toward Huttonsville.   Headed off by McClellan, his forces were scattered in the mountains of the Cheat River region.   Meanwhile Pegram and six hundred of his followers had surrendered (July 14) to McClellan.

GENERAL F. P. BLAIR AND STAFF

CHRONOLOGICAL SUMMARY AND RECORD—Continued

(Continued from Section 5)

SEPTEMBER, 1862.

1—Britton's Lane, Tenn. 20th and 30th Ill., 4th Ill. Cav., Foster's (Ohio) Cav., Battery A 2d Ill. Art. *Union* 5 killed, 51 wounded, 52 missing. *Confed.* 179 killed, 100 wounded.

Chantilly, Va. McDowell's Corps, Army of Virginia. Hooker's and Kearney's Divisions of Third Corps, Army of Potomac, Reno's Corps. *Union* 1,300 killed, wounded, and missing. *Confed.* 800 killed, wounded, and missing. *Union* Maj.-Gen. Kearney and Brig.-Gen. Stevens killed.

2—Vienna, Va. 1st Minn. *Union* 1 killed, 6 wounded.

3—Slaughterville, Ky. Foster's (Ohio) Cav. *Confed.* 3 killed, 2 wounded, 25 captured.

6—Washington, N. C. 24th Mass., 1st N. C., 3d N. Y. Cav. *Union* 8 killed, 36 wounded. *Confed.* 30 killed, 100 wounded.

7—Poolesville, Md. 3d Ind. and 8th Ill. Cav. *Union* 2 killed, 6 wounded. *Confed.* 3 killed, 6 wounded.

Clarksville or Rickett's Hill, Tenn. 11th Ill., 13th Wis., 71st Ohio, 5th Iowa Cav., and two batteries. No casualties recorded.

9—Columbia, Tenn. 42d Ill. *Confed.* 18 killed, 45 wounded.

Des Allemands, La. 21st Ind., 4th Wis. *Confed.* 12 killed.

10—Cold Water, Miss. 6th Ill. Cav. *Confed.* 4 killed, 80 wounded.

Fayetteville, W. Va. 34th and 37th Ohio, 4th W. Va. *Union* 13 killed, 80 wounded.

12 to 15—Harper's Ferry, Va. 39th, 111th, 115th, 125th and 126th N. Y. Militia, 32d, 60th, and 87th Ohio, 9th Vt., 65th Ill., 1st h Ind., 1st and 3d Md. Home Brigade, 8th N. Y. Cav., 12th Ill. Cav., 1st Md. Cav., four Batteries of Artil. *Union* 80 killed, 120 wounded, 11,583 missing and captured. *Confed.* 500 killed and wounded.

14—Turner's and Crampton's Gap, South Mountain, Md. First Corps, Maj.-Gen. Hooker; Sixth Corps, Maj.-Gen. Franklin; Ninth Corps, Maj.-Gen. Reno. *Union* 443 killed, 1,806 wounded. *Confed.* 500 killed, 2,343 wounded, 1,500 captured. *Union* Maj.-Gen. Reno killed. *Confed.* Brig.-Gen. Garland killed.

14 to 16—Mumfordsville, Ky., 18th U. S. Inft., 28th and 33d Ky., 17th, 50th, 60th, 67th, 68th, 74th, 78th, and 89th Ind., Conkle's Battery, 13th Ind. Artil. and Louisville Provost Guard. *Union* 50 killed, 3,566 captured and missing. *Confed.* 714 killed and wounded.

17—Durhamville, Tenn. Detachment of 52d Ind *Union* 1 killed, 10 wounded. *Confed.* 8 killed.

Antietam or Sharpsburg, Md. First Corps, Maj.-Gen. Hooker; Second Corps, Maj.-Gen. Sumner; Fifth Corps, Maj.-Gen. Fitz-John Porter; Sixth Corps, Maj.-Gen. Franklin; Ninth Corps, Maj.-Gen. Burnside; Twelfth Corps, Maj.-Gen. Williams; Couch's Div., Fourth Corps; Pleasanton's Div. of Cav. *Union* 2,010 killed, 9,416 wounded, 1,043 missing. *Confed.* 3,500 killed, 16,399 wounded, 6,000 missing. *Union* Brig.-Gen. Mansfield killed, Maj.-Gens. Hooker and Richardson, and Brig.-Gens. Rodman, Weber, Sedgwick, Hartsuff, Dana, and Meagher wounded. *Confed.* Brig.-Gens. Branch, Anderson, and Starke killed, Maj.-Gen. Anderson, Brig.-Gens. Toombs, Lawton, Kipley, Rodes, Gregg, Armstead, and Ransom wounded.

19 and 20—Iuka, Miss. Stanley's and Hamilton's Divisions, Army of the Mississippi, under Maj.-Gen. Rosecrans. *Union* 144 killed, 598 wounded. *Confed.* 263 killed, 692 wounded, 561 captured. *Confed.* Brig.-Gen. Little killed and Whitfield wounded.

20—Blackford's Ford, Sheppardstown, Va. Fifth Corps, Griffith's and Barnes' Brigades. *Union* 92 killed, 131 wounded, 103 missing. *Confed.* 33 killed, 231 wounded.

30—Newtonia, Mo. 1st Brigade Army of Kansas, 4th Brigade Mo. Militia Cav. *Union* 50 killed, 80 wounded, 115 missing. *Confed.* 220 killed, 280 wounded.

OCTOBER, 1862.

1—Floyd's Ford, Ky. 34th Ill., 77th Penna., 4th Ind. Cav. No casualties recorded.

Sheperdstown, Va. 8th Ill., 8th Penna., 3d Ind. Cav., Pennington's Battery. *Union* 12 wounded. *Confed.* 60 killed.

3 and 4—Corinth, Miss. McKean's, Davies', Hamilton's, and Stanley's Divisons, Army of the West. *Union* 315 killed, 1,812 wounded, 232 missing. *Confed.* 1,423 killed, 5,692 wounded, 2,248 missing. *Union* Brig.-Gens. Hacklemans killed and Oglesby wounded.

5—Metamora, on Big Hatchie River, Miss. Hurlburt's and Ord's Divisions. *Union* 500 killed and wounded. *Confed.* 400 killed and wounded.

7—La Vergne, Tenn. Palmer's Brigade. *Union* 5 killed, 9 wounded, *Confed.* 80 killed and wounded, 175 missing.

8—Perryville, Ky. First Corps, Army of the Ohio, Maj.-Gen. McCook, and Third Corps, Brig.-Gen. Gilbert. *Union* 916 killed, 2,943 wounded, 489 missing. *Confed.* 2,500 killed, wounded, and missing. *Union* Brig.-Gens. J. S. Jackson and Terrill killed. *Confed.* Brig.-Gens. Cleburne, Wood, and Brown wounded.

10—Harrodsburg, Ky. Union troops, commanded by Lieut.-Col. Boyle, 9th Ky. Cav. *Confed.* 1,600 captured.

11—La Grange, Ark. Detach. 4th Iowa Cav. *Union* 4 killed, 13 wounded.

17—Lexington, Ky. Detach. 3d and 4th Ohio Cav. *Union* 4 killed, 24 wounded, 350 missing.

18—Haymarket, Va. Detach. 6th Iowa Cav. *Union* 1 killed, 6 wounded, 23 captured.

22—Pocotaligo or Yemassee, S. C. 47th, 55th, and 76th Penna., 48th N. Y., 6th and 7th Conn., 3d and 4th N. H., 3d R. I., 1st N. Y. Engineers, 1st Mass. Cav., Batteries D and M 1st U. S. Artil. and E 3d U. S. Artil. *Union* 43 killed, 258 wounded. *Confed.* 14 killed, 102 wounded.

23—Waverly, Tenn. 83d Ill. *Union* 1 killed, 2 wounded. *Confed.* 40 killed and wounded.

24—Grand Prairie, Mo. Two Battalions Mo. Militia Cav. *Union* 3 wounded. *Confed.* 8 killed, 20 wounded.

28—Clarkson, Mo. Detach. 2d Ill. Artil. *Confed.* 10 killed, 2 wounded.

NOVEMBER, 1862.

1—Philomont, Va. Pleasanton's Cavalry. *Union* 1 killed, 14 wounded. *Confed.* 5 killed, 10 wounded.

2 and 3—Bloomfield and Union, Loudon Co., Va. Pleasanton's Cavalry. *Union* 2 killed, 10 wounded. *Confed.* 3 killed, 15 wounded.

3—Harrisonville, Mo. 5th and 6th Mo. Cav. *Union* 10 killed, 3 wounded. *Confed.* 6 killed, 20 wounded.

5—Barbee's Cross Roads and Chester Gap, Va. Pleasanton's Cavalry. *Union* 5 killed, 10 wounded. *Confed.* 36 killed.

Nashville, Tenn. 16th and 51st Ill., 69th Ohio, 14th Mich., 78th Pa., 5th Tenn. Cav., 7th Pa. Cav. *Union* 26 wounded. *Confed.* 23 captured.

6—Garrettsburg, Ky. 8th Ky. Cav. *Confed.* 17 killed, 85 wounded.

7—Big Beaver Creek, Mo. 10th Ill., two Cos. Mo. Militia Cav. *Union* 300 captured.

Marianna, Ark. 3d and 4th Iowa, 9th Ill. Cav. *Union* 3 killed, 20 wounded. *Confed.* 50 killed and wounded.

8—Hudsonville, Miss. 7th Kan. Cav., 2d Iowa Cav. *Confed.* 16 killed, 185 captured.

17—Gloucester, Va. 104th Pa. *Union* 1 killed, 3 wounded.

18—Rural Hills, Tenn. 8th Ky. Cav. *Confed.* 16 killed.

24—Beaver Creek, Mo. 21st Iowa, 3d Mo. Cav. *Union* 6 killed, 10 wounded. *Confed.* 5 killed, 20 wounded.

26—Summerville, Miss. 7th Ill. Cav. *Confed.* 28 captured.

28—Cane Hill, Boston Mountain, and Boonsboro', Ark. 1st Division Army of the Frontier. *Union* 4 killed, 36 wounded. *Confed.* 75 killed, 300 wounded.

Hartwood Church, Va. 3d Pa. Cav. *Union* 4 killed, 9 wounded, 200 missing.

DECEMBER, 1862.

1—Charleston and Berryville, Va. 2d Div. 12th Corps. *Confed.* 5 killed, 18 wounded.

5—Coffeeville, Miss. 1st, 2d, and 3d Cav. Brigades, Army of the Tennessee. *Union* 10 killed, 54 wounded. *Confed.* 7 killed, 43 wounded.

Helena, Ark. 30th Iowa, 29th Wis. *Confed.* 8 killed.

7—Prairie Grove or Fayetteville, Ark. 1st, 2d, and 3d Divisions Army of the Frontier. *Union* 167 killed, 798 wounded, 183 missing. *Confed.* 300 killed, 1,200 wounded and missing.

Hartsville, Tenn. 106th and 108th Ohio, 104th Ill., 2d Ind. Cav., 11th Ky. Cav., 13th Ind. Battery. *Union* 55 killed, 1,800 captured. *Confed.* 21 killed, 114 wounded.

9—Dobbin's Ferry, Tenn. 35th Ind., 51st Ohio, 8th and 21st Ky., 7th Ind. Battery. *Union* 5 killed, 48 wounded.

11—Little Bear Creek, Ala. 52d Ill. *Union* 1 killed, 2 wounded. *Confed.* 11 killed, 30 wounded.

12 to 18—Foster's expedition to Goldsboro', N. C. 1st, 2d, and 3d Brigades of First Division and Wessell's Brigade of Peck's Division, Dep't of North Carolina. *Union* 90 killed, 478 wounded. *Confed.* 71 killed, 268 wounded, 400 missing.

13—Fredericksburg, Va. Army of the Potomac, Maj.-Gen. Burnside; Second Corps, Maj.-Gen. Couch; Ninth Corps, Maj.-Gen. Wilcox. Right Grand Div., Maj.-Gen. Sumner; First Corps, Maj.-Gen. Reynolds; Sixth Corps, Maj.-Gen. W. F. Smith. Left Grand Div., Maj.-Gen. Franklin; Fifth Corps, Maj.-Gen. Butterfield; Third Corps, Maj.-Gen. Stoneman. Center Grand Div., Maj.-Gen. Hooker. *Union* 1,180 killed, 9,028 wounded, 2,145 missing. *Confed.* 579 killed, 3,870 wounded, 127 missing. *Union* Brig.-Gens. Jackson and Bayard killed and Gibbons and Vinton wounded. *Confed.* Brig.-Gen. T. R. R. Cobb killed and Maxey Gregg wounded.

14—Kingston, N. C. 1st, 2d and 3d Brigades 1st Div. and Wessell's Brigade of Peck's Division, Dep't of North Carolina. *Union* 40 killed, 120 wounded. *Confed.* 50 killed, 75 wounded, 400 missing.

18—Lexington, Tenn. 11th Ill. Cav., 5th Ohio Cav., 2d Tenn. Cav. *Union* 7 killed, 10 wounded, 124 missing. *Confed.* 7 killed, 28 wounded.

20—Holly Springs, Miss. 2d Ill. Cav. *Union* 1,000 captured.

Trenton, Tenn. Detachments 122d Ill., 7th Tenn. Cav., and convalescents. *Union* 1 killed, 250 prisoners. *Confed.* 17 killed, 50 wounded.

21—Davis's Mills, Miss. Six Cos. 25th Ind., two Cos. 5th Ohio Cav. *Union* 3 wounded. *Confed.* 22 killed, 50 wounded, 20 missing.

24—Middleburg, Miss. 115 men of 12th Mich. *Union* 9 wounded. *Confed.* 9 killed, 11 wounded.

Glasgow, Ky. Five Cos. 2d Mich. Cav. *Union* 1 killed, 1 wounded. *Confed.* 3 killed, 3 wounded.

25—Green's Chapel, Ky. Detachment of 4th and 5th Ind. Cav. *Union* 1 killed. *Confed.* 9 killed, 22 wounded.

26—Bacon Creek, Ky. Detachment 2d Mich Cav. *Union* 23 wounded.

27—Elizabethtown, Ky. 91st Ill. 500 men captured by Morgan.

Dumfries, Va. 5th, 7th and 66th Ohio, 12th Ill. Cav., 1st Md. Cav., 6th Maine Battery. *Union* 3 killed, 8 wounded. *Confed.* 25 killed, 40 wounded.

28—Elk Fork, Tenn. 6th and 10th Ky. Cav. *Confed.* 30 killed, 176 wounded, 51 missing.

28 and 29—Chickasaw Bayou, Vicksburg, Miss. Army of Tennessee. Maj.-Gen. W. T. Sherman—Brig.-Gens. G. W. Morgan's, Frederick Steele's, M. L. Smith's, and A. J. Smith's divisions of the right wing. *Union* 191 killed, 982 wounded, 756 missing. *Confed.* 207 wounded. *Union* Maj.-Gen. M. L. Smith wounded.

30—Wautauga Bridge and Carter's Station, Tenn. 7th Ohio Cav., 9th Pa. Cav. *Union* 1 killed, 2 wounded. *Confed.* 7 killed, 15 wounded, 273 missing.

Jefferson, Tenn. Second Brigade 1st Division Thomas's corps. *Union* 20 killed, 40 wounded. *Confed.* 15 killed, 50 wounded.

(Continued in Section 7)

CONFEDERATE BATTERIES ON THE JAMES RIVER ABOVE DUTCH GAP

CHAPTER XII.—Continued.

THE other fugitives were pursued by General Morris, accompanied by Captain H. W. Benham (McClellan's chief engineer), and were overtaken at Carricksford, on a branch of the Cheat River. There a sharp engagement occurred, when Garnett was killed and his forces were dispersed. Another portion of Garnett's troops had fled toward Staunton, pursued to the summit of the Cheat Range, where

GENERAL T. F. "STONEWALL" JACKSON, C. S. A.

an Indiana regiment established an outpost. Meanwhile Cox had driven Wise out of the Kanawha region, and at the middle of July (1861) the war in Western Virginia seemed to be at an end. On the 19th, McClellan said, in a dispatch to the War Department, "We have completely annihilated the enemy in Western Virginia. Our loss is about thirteen killed and not more than forty wounded; while the enemy's loss is not far from two hundred killed; and the number of prisoners we have taken will amount to at least one thousand. We have captured seven of the guns of the enemy, in all."

The Confederates were not disposed to abandon the granary that would supply Eastern Virginia, without another struggle. General Robert E. Lee succeeded Garnett in the chief command in that region. John B. Floyd, the treacherous National Secretary of War, had succeeded Wise as a leader; but he, too, was now superseded by a better man, and after a while the war in the mountain region of Virginia was renewed. McClellan had been called to the command of the Army of the Potomac, and was succeeded in Western Virginia by General Rosecrans.

At the beginning of June, it was manifest that a powerful combination of Secessionists in Baltimore were preparing to act with the armed insurgents in Virginia, in efforts to seize the National capital. The Legislature of the State were in sympathy with the Confederates, and a committee of that body assured Jefferson Davis that the people of Maryland were with him in sentiment. The National Government took energetic measures to avert the evil. General N. P. Banks was appointed to the command of the Department of Annapolis, with his headquarters in Baltimore; and he was so satisfied of a conspiracy ripening there, that he sent a force of armed men into the city, who arrested Chief of Police Kane and put him into Fort McHenry. At the same time Banks proclaimed that he had appointed Colonel (afterward General) John R. Kenly, of the First Regiment of Maryland Volunteers, provost-marshal. Kenly was a well-known and highly respected citizen of Baltimore, and acted with wisdom and energy. He was put at the head of the Police Department; but the old Board of Police Commissioners, who were Secessionists, refused to acknowledge him and defied the Government. They were arrested and sent as prisoners of State to Fort Warren in Boston Harbor, and very soon afterward the Unionists of Maryland were encouraged to assert their loyalty. Banks withdrew the troops, and thereafter Maryland was justly counted one of the loyal States of the Union; yet for three years the Confederates were deceived by a belief that the people were Secessionists at heart. But the delusion was dispelled when, in 1863, General Lee invaded the State, set up his standard, and expected thousands would rally around it. On the contrary, he lost manifold more men by desertion than he gained by recruiting.

We have observed that Jefferson Davis issued commissions to

GENERAL J. E. B. STUART, C. S. A.

MAP OF THE BATTLE OF BULL RUN AND VICINITY

RUINS OF BRIDGE AT BULL RUN

privateers, and that a Confederate naval bureau was established. The first vessel of the Confederate navy was named the *Lady Davis;* and when the National Congress assembled on the 4th of July, there were no less than twenty Confederate armed vessels afloat and depredating upon the commerce of the United States. So early as the 1st of June they had sent twenty vessels, captured on the sea, into the port of New Orleans alone, as prizes. One of these privateers (the *Savannah*) was captured, and her crew were tried and condemned as pirates; but the Government found it expedient to treat them as prisoners of war. Another (the *Petrel*) went out of Charleston harbor and mistaking the United States frigate *Lawrence* for a richly-laden merchantman, attempted to capture her. She opened her ports, and instantly the *Petrel* became a wreck. A flash of fire, a thunder-peal, the crash of timbers and engulfment in the sea, was the experience of a minute for her crew, four of whom were drowned, while the vessel went swiftly to the bottom of the ocean. Other privateers active during the war will be noticed hereafter.

It was now midsummer, 1861. A large body of troops were gathered around the National capital. General Irwin McDowell was in command of the Department of Virginia, with his headquarters at Arlington House. At Manassas Junction, about halfway between the eastern range of the Blue Ridge and the Potomac at Alexandria, and thirty miles from Washington, were about forty thousand Confederate troops. It was considered the strongest military position between Washington and Richmond, and is connected with the capital of Virginia and the fertile Shenandoah Valley by railways. It was fortified by strong redoubts on which were mounted heavy Dahlgren guns, which the insurgents had seized at the Gosport Navy-yard, and these were managed by naval officers who had deserted their flag. At Winchester, Johnston had almost as strong a force, to prevent McClellan and his troops issuing from the mountain region and joining General Patterson on the Potomac River.

GENERAL J. A. McCLERNAND

The loyal people had become impatient because of the delay of the troops at the capital in moving against the insurgents. They were delighted when, on the afternoon of the 16th of July, the telegraph spread the news over the land that fifty thousand soldiers, under General McDowell, had begun to move toward Manassas, leaving fifteen thousand behind to guard the capital. They were in five divisions, commanded respectively by Brigadier-Generals Daniel Tyler and Theodore Runyon, and Colonels David Hunter, Samuel P. Heintzelman, and Dixon S. Miles. The Confederate forces against whom they moved were distributed along Bull Run, a tributary of the Occoquan, from Union Mills, where the Orange and Alexandria Railway crosses the stream, to the stone bridge on the Warrenton turnpike, a distance of about eight miles, with reserves near Manassas Junction. They also had an outpost at Centreville, and slight fortifications at Fairfax Court-House, ten miles from their main army, in the direction of Washington.

General Patterson was at Martinsburg, charged with the duty of keeping General Johnston from reinforcing Beauregard. He had crossed the Potomac at Williamsport on the 2d of July; and near Falling Waters, his advance-guard under Colonel Abercrombie, chiefly composed of Wisconsin and Pennsylvania troops, horse and foot, with a section of battery, encountered Johnston's advance led by "Stonewall" Jackson, assisted by J. E. B. Stuart and his afterward famous cavalry corps. They fought sharply for half an hour, when Colonel George H. Thomas's brigade, coming to the support of Abercrombie, caused the Confederates to flee. They were hotly pursued five miles, when a heavy Confederate force appearing, the chase was abandoned. On the following

GENERAL H. W. SLOCUM

VIEWS IN CAMP NEAR CUMBERLAND LANDING—ARMY OF THE POTOMAC

day General Patterson and his army entered Martinsburg, and were speedily reinforced by troops under General Sandford of New York. There he remained in enforced inaction for a fortnight.

The aged General Scott was too feeble in mind and body to take command in the field, and that

Colonel E. D. Baker

imbecility caused disaster. The duty devolved upon General McDowell. The latter ordered General Tyler to advance to Vienna on the evening of the 16th of July; and early the next morning the remainder of the army moved in four columns, with the intention, by making feints, to throw the Confederates off their guard, gain their rear, seize the railway, and compel both Beauregard and Johnston to fall back from their positions, so menacing to the seat of Government. But spies and traitors, yet swarming in Washington, kept Beauregard continually advised not only of the movements, but of the intentions of the National troops. There were traitors, evidently, in possession of the secrets of the office of the General-in-Chief, for a copy of a military map was found in a deserted Confederate camp only two days after the original was completed.

McDowell's columns moved by different roads, without much opposition. They entered the village of Fairfax Court-House unopposed; and when they approached Centreville, the Confederates fled. The Nationals were in high spirits, for it appeared as if the march to Richmond would be a pleasant excursion. But Beauregard was alluring them into a perilous position, as they found, on the 18th, when General Tyler made a reconnaissance in force at Blackburn's Ford, on Bull Run, which was guarded by General James Longstreet with a strong force of men and concealed batteries. A severe conflict ensued, in which Michigan, Massachusetts, and New York troops, with Ayers's battery, were engaged. At length the Nationals, defeated, withdrew to Centreville; and McDowell was satisfied that his plan for gaining the rear of the Confederates was impracticable.

The affair at Blackburn's Ford revealed the strength of the Confederates, and McDowell perceived the necessity for an immediate and vigorous attack upon the enemy, for the term of enlistment of about ten thousand of his troops was about to expire. He then had thirty-five thousand men under his immediate command. These were massed around Centreville ready to move; but for want of needed supplies they were detained until the close of the 20th, when the army had begun to melt away from the cause just mentioned.

At two o'clock the next morning (July 21, 1861) the troops moved from Centreville in three columns, the moon shining brightly, to attack the left flank of the Confederates. General Tyler, with the brigades of Schenck and Sherman, and the batteries of Ayres and Carlisle, moved on the Warrenton turnpike toward the stone bridge, leaving Miles and Richardson to watch and guard Blackburn's Ford. The object was to make a feigned attack near the bridge, while the two columns of Hunter and Heintzelman should cross Bull Run at Sudley Church, and fall upon the Confederate left. These movements were very slow; and General McDowell, who was ill, and in a carriage, becoming impatient, mounted his horse and with his cavalry escort, commanded by Colonel A. G. Brackett, he rode forward, passed the two columns toiling along a rough forest road, and first entered the open field which became a battle-ground.

Meanwhile important movements had been made on the Confederate side, of which McDowell was ignorant. When he advanced to Fairfax Court-House, Beauregard informed Davis, at Richmond, of the movement, who ordered Johnston to hasten to join the forces at Manassas with the army of the Shenandoah. It was necessary for Johnston to fight and defeat Patterson or elude

Colonel James A. Mulligan

Ford and Pontoon Bridge at Bull Run

"Quaker" Guns at Centreville, Va., Battle of Bull Run

him. He accomplished the latter, and with six thousand infantry he hastened to Manassas, where he arrived at noon on the 20th, the remainder of his army following at a slower pace. This reinforcement made Beauregard's army outnumber McDowell's by four thousand men, and being strongly fortified, he had an important advantage. Johnston, the senior in rank, took chief command.

General Tyler opened the memorable battle by firing a shell among the Confederates near the stone bridge, commanded by Colonel Evans. Others followed; and Beauregard, believing it to be a real attack, sent reinforcements to Evans. At the same time Johnston ordered a quick and vigorous attack upon McDowell's left wing at Blackburn's Ford, not doubting, because of the superior force of Confederates in that quarter, that they would win a complete victory. The assailants were led by General Ewell. The movement miscarried; and from an eminence Johnston and Beauregard watched the opening conflict with great anxiety. A cloud of dust seen far to the northward gave Johnston apprehensions that Patterson,

when he discovered the given chase or was ha-
Colonel Evans was nonade below was only of heavy columns o'clock scouts told him ley Church. It was Hampshire and Massa- and Reynolds, the whole pared to meet them; was sent forward to as- Nationals appeared in battle began. Only a vale separated the com- Evans's line began to Bee advanced with fresh strength. The National ble, and Colonel Burn- Colonel Andrew Porter

departure of the army of the Shenandoah, had stening to reinforce McDowell. soon satisfied that Tyler's attack and the can- a feint. He had been informed of the march through the forests on his left, and before ten that one column was crossing Bull Run at Sud- Hunter's, composed of Rhode Island, New chusetts troops, with the batteries of Griffin led by Colonel Burnside. Evans at once pre- and General Bee, who commanded reserves,

GENERAL J. M. BRANNON

sist him. Very soon the the open field, and a small stream in a little batants. Hard pressed, waver, when General troops and gave it line then began to trem- side called for h e l p. responded by sending a George Sykes.

GENERAL J. J. REYNOLDS

was severely wounded when the youthful took command of the up with his men and his line again began to man's column appeared; under Colonel Corcoran, timely; for the Nation- were nearly exhausted. ment under Colonel H.

battalion of regular infantry under Major
The battle now raged furiously. Hunter and Colonel Slocum of Rhode Island was killed, Sprague, governor of the little Commonwealth, troops from that State. At length Porter came poured such a heavy fire upon Evans's left, that bend. At that moment the head of Heintzel- also Sherman's brigade, whom Tyler had sent, to assist Burnside. These reinforcements were als, who had been on their feet since midnight,
A furious charge made by a New York regi-

W. Slocum, shattered the bending Confederate line, and the troops fled in confusion to a plateau whereon General T. J. Jackson had just arrived with reserves. "They are beating us back!" exclaimed General Bee. "Well, sir," calmly replied Jackson, "we will give them the bayonet!" Bee was encouraged. "Form! form!" he cried to the fugitives. "There stands Jackson like a stone wall." The effect of these words was wonderful. Their flight was checked, and order was soon brought out of confusion. Ever afterward, the calm general was called "Stonewall Jackson."

It was now noon. Alarmed by the unexpected strength of the Nationals, Johnston and Beauregard sent bodies of troops, under Holmes, Early, and Ewell, in the direction of the sounds of battle, four miles distant. The two commanders hastened to the plateau, when Johnston, the chief by seniority, after reorganizing the shattered columns, left Beauregard in command on the field and hastened to a position from which he had a view of the whole area of operations and of the country toward Manassas, whence reinforcements from the Shenandoah Valley were momentarily expected. Without these, he had small hope of success. From his new position he also sent forward reinforcements; and at two o'clock in the afternoon, when the conflict was renewed, the Confederates had ten thousand soldiers, with twenty-two heavy guns in battle order on the plateau. Meanwhile the Nationals had been preparing for the struggle. At one o'clock they had gained possession of the Warrenton Turnpike, the grand objective of the march

COLUMBIA, S. C., AFTER BOMBARDMENT

against the Confederate left; but their enemies must be driven from the plateau before victory would be secured.   To accomplish this five brigades, namely, Porter's, Howard's, Franklin's, Wilcox's and Sherman's, with the batteries of Ricketts, Griffin and Arnold, and cavalry under Major Palmer, were to turn the Confederate left, while Keyes was sent to annoy them on the right.

COLONEL RIKER   GENERAL PATTERSON
GENERAL NAGLEE   GENERAL PALMER

Colonel Heintzelman accompanied McDowell as his lieutenant on the field, and his division began the attack. They pressed forward in the face of a storm of balls from batteries, and gained possession of a portion of the plateau. There was an elevation near that commanded the whole plateau, and McDowell ordered Ricketts and Griffin to plant their batteries upon it, with the immediate support of Ellsworth's Fire Zouaves, under Colonel Farnham. It was accomplished, while New York, Massachusetts and Minnesota troops took a position to the left of the batteries. As the artillery and Zouaves went boldly forward in the face of a severe fire from the enemy, they were suddenly attacked on the flank by Alabamians in ambush, and then by two companies of Stuart's Black-horse cavalry, in the rear. The Zouaves recoiled, and the horsemen dashed entirely through the shattered column. Colonel Farnham rallied his men, and with some assistance they attacked the Confederate horsemen so furiously that they were dispersed.

When the Zouaves gave way, Heintzelman ordered up a Minnesota regiment to the support of the batteries. Suddenly the Confederates, in overwhelming force, delivered a murderous fire that disabled the batteries by prostrating the men, when the struggle for the plateau became fearful.   Both sides suffered dreadfully.   Johnston heard of the slaughter and lost heart.   He had ordered Early up, at eleven o'clock, with three fresh regiments, but they did not come.   It was now three o'clock.   "Oh for four regiments!" said Johnston bitterly, to Colonel Cocke. His wish was more than satisfied.   Just then he saw a cloud of dust in the direction of the Manassas Gap Railway.   It was caused by a part of his own Shenandoah army, four thousand strong, under General E. Kirby Smith.   They were received with joy, and were ordered into action immediately.   Beauregard's force was almost doubled by these and other fresh troops; and the blow that now smote McDowell's troops, just as they were about to grasp the palm of victory, was sudden, unexpected, heavy, and overpowering.   In fifteen minutes the Nationals were swept from the plateau.   As regiment after regiment gave way and hurried toward the turnpike in confusion, panic seized others, and at four o'clock a greater portion of the National army were flying across Bull Run toward Centreville.   With many it was not a retreat, but a disorderly rout.   They left behind them over three thousand men killed, wounded, or made prisoners.   The Confederates lost over two thousand.   The Confederate congress had assembled at Richmond the day before; and Jefferson Davis, who arrived on the battle-field just as the flight began, sent back to his associates an exultant shout of victory, by the telegraph.   It was echoed, in varying notes, over the Confederacy, while the vanquished army was hastening, in fragments, back to the defence of the capital.   For a moment the gloom of deep despondency settled upon the hearts of the loyal portion of the nation.

The gravity of the occasion was so little appreciated, that when it was known at Washington that McDowell was to attack Beauregard on Sunday, the 21st, scores of men, and even women—Congressmen, officials of every grade, and plain citizens—went out in carriages as to a spectacular show for amusement.

A REGIMENT IN CAMP

DUTCH GAP CANAL ON THE JAMES, CUT BY GENERAL B. F. BUTLER

Passes from military commanders were like tickets to a Roman gladiatorial combat in the circus; and the vicinity of the battle-field was gay, on Sunday morning, with civilians, who indulged in wine and cigars at the headquarters of Colonel Miles at Centreville. The heights there were crowded with spectators, and as the battle went on, and bombs "bursted in air," their cheeks were made to glow with delicious excitement. Before night those cheeks were made pale by terror as the crowd of spectators rushed back, pell-mell, toward places of safety, pursued by the Confederates. Soldiers and citizens and well-dressed women were mingled in picturesque confusion in the line of fugitives who crowded the highways. In several places the roads were blocked with overturned vehicles or abandoned cannon; and horses and human kind seemed equally eager to escape from the whirlwind of destruction that followed in fury behind them for a while. But the pursuit of the Confederates was soon stayed by misinformation. Had they pressed on, their coveted prize, the National capital, might have been in their possession before Monday morning.

The battle at Bull Run depressed the loyal people only for a moment, and there was a quick rebound from despair to hope. Another uprising by the loyalists in favor of the Union took place, and the gaps in the National armies were more than filled within a fortnight by new recruits. The Confederates were weakened by their victory, for it gave them undue confidence in their strength and prowess, and made them neglect to profit by it. But circumstances soon afterward caused a "solid South" to be arrayed against the National Government, and the Confederate armies were wonderfully sustained by the people of the whole South.

General G. H. Thomas

General Patterson was unjustly censured for his failure to hold Johnston at Winchester or to reinforce McDowell. When the truth was made known by positive testimony, it appeared clear that he did all an obedient soldier, bound by instructions, could do under the circumstances, and the public mind was satisfied, and made no further criticism.

While the events we have just considered were occurring in the East, the war was making rapid progress in the West, especially in Missouri, where General Lyon, as we have seen, had taken vigorous measures to quell the rebellion. The disloyal governor of Missouri, who raised the standard of revolt at Jefferson City, fled westward with troops who were led by General Price, and took a stand near Booneville. There they were attacked by Lyon and defeated, when they retreated toward the southwestern portion of Missouri, and halted not far from the Arkansas border. Lyon now held military control over the whole region northeast of a line from Booneville to ward of the Missouri River, and the Arkansas border, thus giving to the Government the important points of St. Louis, Hannibal, St. Joseph, and Bird's Point on the Mississippi, as bases of operations, with railways and rivers for transportation. General Lyon remained about a fortnight at Booneville preparing for a vigorous campaign against the insurgents whom Jackson was gathering around him in southwestern Missouri. He issued a proclamation which quieted the people and strengthened the Union cause, for he assured them that his Government had no other end in view than the maintenance of its authority over the persons and property of the whole people of the State.

On the 1st of July (1861) there were at least ten thousand loyal troops in Missouri, and as many more might have been thrown into it from camps in Illinois, in the space of forty-eight hours. At the same time, Colonel Franz Sigel, a German soldier and patriot, was pushing eager soldiers toward insurgent camps on the borders of Kansas and Arkansas. On the 5th of July he encountered a considerable force under Jackson and Brigadier-General Rains, near Carthage. Their force was much greater in number than his own, and after a sharp fight he was pressed back and retreated in good order to Springfield. Lyon, who was then at the head of a small force, eighty miles from Springfield, satisfied of Sigel's peril, hastened forward to his relief, by forced marches, and encamped not far from him on the 13th of July and took command of the combined forces. In the meantime troops from Texas under Generals McCulloch, Rains, Pearce and McBride, had joined Price, making his whole force about twenty thousand men. They were now marching on Springfield. To confront them Lyon had not more than six thousand men, horse and foot (the former about five hundred in number), and eighteen pieces of artillery. With this

St. Michael's Church After Bombardment, Charleston, S. C.

GENERAL W. T. SHERMAN

comparatively feeble force Lyon went out to meet his enemies, and at Dug Springs, about nineteen miles west from Springfield, they met and fought a desperate battle on the 2d of August. The Confederates were led by General Rains. So furious was the charge of Lyon's cavalry, in the engagement, led by Captain Stanley, that Confederate prisoners seriously inquired: "Are they men or devils?" The Confederates were beaten and fled to Wilson's Creek, about ten miles south of Springfield, where they encamped on the evening of the 9th wearied and half-starved.

The Confederates anxiously sought rest and refreshment, but Lyon would not grant them the boon. Before the dawn the next morning he marched against them in two columns, one led by himself to fall upon their front; the other, under Sigel, twelve hundred strong, with six field-pieces, to attack their rear. A battle began at an early hour. Lyon's column bore the brunt of the conflict. His words and deeds inspired his men to fight valiantly. Wherever the storm of battle was raging fiercest, there Lyon was seen. Very early in the severe engagement, his horse was shot under him. Then he received a wound in the leg. Another in the head soon followed and partially stunned him. Mounting the horse of one of Major Sturgis's orderlies, and placing himself at the head of Kansas troops, he swung his hat over his head, and called upon the men to follow. While dashing forward with a determination to gain the victory, a rifle-ball passed through his body, near his heart, and he expired in a few minutes. The conflict continued about two hours longer, and at eleven o'clock it ceased, the Confederates, discomfited, withdrawing from the field. The loss of the Nationals in the battle was between twelve and thirteen hundred, and of the Confederates full three thousand. The former fell back to Springfield, and the next morning (August 11) the whole Union force, under the general command of Sigel, retreated from Springfield to Rolla, one hundred and twenty-five miles in the direction of St. Louis, safely conducting a Government train valued at $1,500,000.

When Governor Jackson set up the standard of revolt at the capital of Missouri, the loyal men of the Commonwealth tried to stay the hand of secession. They had held a State Convention in February, at which no openly avowed disunionist appeared. That Convention reassembled at Jefferson City on the 22d of July, and declared the government of which Jackson was the head to be illegal. They organized a provisional government for service until a permanent one might be established by the people. The Convention issued an address to the inhabitants, in which the treason of the governor was exposed. Meanwhile General Pillow, by invitation of the governor, had entered the Commonwealth at the head of Tennessee troops to act in concert with M. Jefferson Thompson, the leader of the State militia. The shallow Pillow, vain as he was incompetent, assumed the pompous title of "Liberator of Missouri," and dated his orders and despatches, "Headquarters Army of Liberation." Missouri was not annexed to the Confederacy; but persons claiming to represent that State sat in the Confederate Congress at Richmond during a greater part of the period of the Civil War.

GENERAL J. C. FREMONT

VIEW OF HAMPTON, VIRGINIA

VIEW OF CAMP—ARMY OF THE POTOMAC

CHAPTER XIII.

Fremont in Missouri—Siege and Fall of Lexington—Kentucky Neutrality Violated by the Confederates—Events in Eastern Kentucky— Buckner's Raid—Fremont Superseded—Battle at Belmont—Military Movements in Northwestern Virginia—Lee, Floyd and Wise— Civil War Ended in West Virginia—Capture of Hatteras Forts—Events near Fort Pickens and Southwest Pass—Operations on the Coast of South Carolina—McClellan in Command—"On to Richmond!"—Boldness of the Confederates—They are Pushed Back— Battle at Ball's Bluff.

JOHN C. FREMONT, the eminent explorer and meritorious soldier, who was in Europe when the war began, after purchasing arms for the Government there, hastened home and was commissioned major-general of volunteers. On the 6th of July, he was appointed to the command of the Department of Missouri, with his headquarters at St. Louis, where, in consequence of General Lyon having taken the field in person, he found everything in confusion. He entered upon his duties with vigor. He caused St. Louis to be fortified; and Bird's Point, opposite Cairo, on the Mississippi, was made secure from the operations of the Confederates.

When, on the death of General Lyon and the retreat of the National troops from Springfield toward St. Louis, Fremont perceived the secession element in Missouri to be strong and defiant, he took the civil as well as the military power in his department into his own hands, and soon caused his opponents to act with circumspection. He proclaimed martial law, and assured the disaffected that it would be vigorously enforced. His energy created many jealousies; and such misrepresentations were laid before his Government that his actions, which, at the outset, promised the best results, were restrained, and the wholesome rigors of martial law were entirely removed.

Fremont had already formed a plan for ridding not only Missouri, but the whole Mississippi Valley, of armed insurgents, and for opening the navigation of the great river which was then obstructed by Confederate batteries at Memphis and elsewhere. His plan

GENERAL HEINTZELMAN AND STAFF

contemplated the capture or dispersion of troops under General Price, in Missouri, and the seizure of Little Rock, the capital of Arkansas. By so doing Fremont expected to turn the position of the forces under Pillow and others, in the vicinity of New Madrid, cut off their supplies from the southwest and compel them to retreat, at which time a flotilla of gunboats then a-building near St. Louis might descend the Mississippi and assist in military operations against the batteries at Memphis. In the event of this movement being successful, he proposed to push on toward the Gulf of Mexico, with his army, and take possession of New Orleans.

After the battle of Wilson's Creek, General McCulloch, the Texan leader, abandoned General Price, because they could not agree, when the latter, in sole command, called upon the Secessionists to fill up his ranks. They responded with alacrity; and at the middle of August, Price moved northward in the direction of Lexington, which was situated in a curve of the Missouri River. It occupied an important position, and was garrisoned by less than three thousand troops under Colonel James A. Mulligan. Early in September, when Price had reached its vicinity, Mulligan resolved to defend the place, with his small army, and cast up intrenchments around his camp. At that time a larger Union force was at the State capital, under Colonel Jefferson C. Davis, and General John Pope was coming down from the country northward of the Missouri River, with five thousand more. Price perceived his danger, and pressing vigorously forward, besieged Lexington on the 11th of September, with twenty thousand men, which number soon increased to twenty-five thousand, by reinforcements. Mulligan was inadequately supplied with heavy guns and ammunition to sustain a siege; and after a gallant defence of the post against overwhelming numbers, until the morning of the 20th, he was compelled to surrender. This disaster was

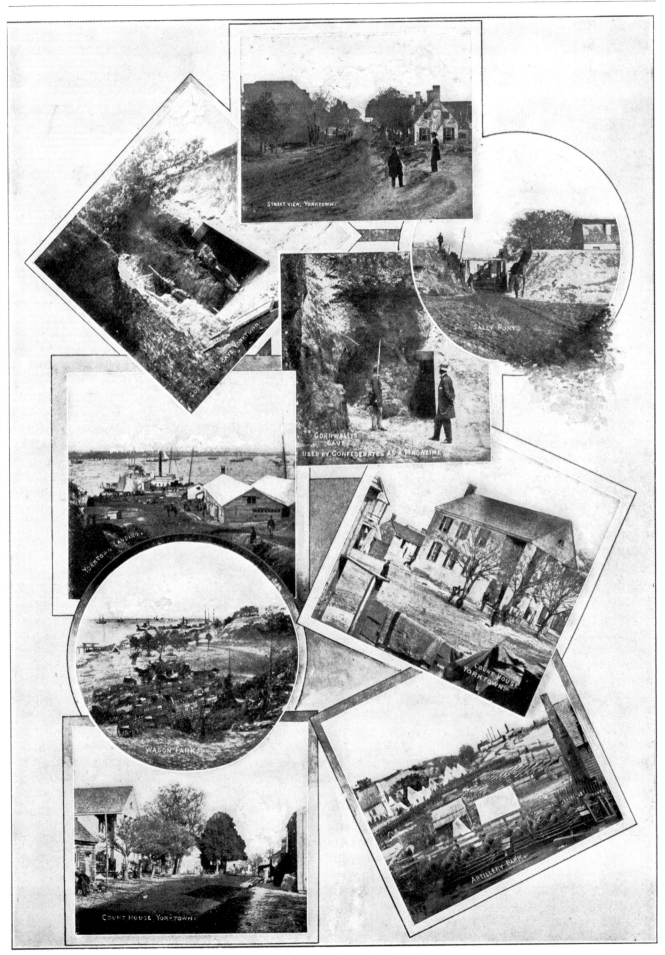

SCENES IN AND NEAR YORKTOWN

severely felt by the Unionists; and Fremont, resolving to retrieve it, at once put in motion an army of more than twenty thousand men to drive Price and his followers out of Missouri.

GENERAL T. R. ANDERSON, C. S. A.

Early in the summer the disloyal governor of Kentucky declared that arrangements had been made at Cincinnati, with General McClellan, that neither National nor Confederate troops should enter Kentucky. McClellan denied the truth of the assertions; but for several months the neutrality of Kentucky was as much respected as if such an arrangement was in force; and the purposes of the governors of Kentucky and Tennessee were promoted, for it gave them more time to prepare for war. In the meantime Pillow had been unsuccessfully trying to capture Cairo by military operations in Missouri. He urged the seizure of the bluff at Columbus, in Western Kentucky, from which he believed he might take Cairo in reverse, turn its guns upon Bird's Point, drive out and disperse the Nationals, and so make a free passage for the Confederates to St. Louis. The solemn pledges of his masters to respect Kentucky neutrality, restrained Pillow; but in September (1861) the Confederates resolved to violate that neutrality. General (Bishop) Polk seized the strong position at Columbus, with a considerable body of troops, under the pretext that National forces were preparing to occupy that place. The Confederate secretary of war publicly telegraphed to Polk to withdraw his troops; and at the same time Jefferson Davis privately telegraphed to him to hold on, saying: "The necessity must justify the means." So Columbus was held by the Confederates. The loyal members of the Kentucky Legislature requested the governor to call out the militia of the State to expel the invaders, and asked the National Government to aid him. The governor did nothing; but General Ulysses S. Grant, then in command of the district around Cairo, took military possession of Paducah, in Northern Kentucky, at the mouth of the Tennessee River. The seizure of Columbus by the Confederates opened the way to all the horrors of war which Kentucky suffered; and the occupation of Paducah by National troops ended the "neutrality" of that State. Thenceforth Kentucky was numbered among the loyal States.

On the day after Polk seized Columbus, a Confederate force under General Zollicoffer (formerly a member of Congress) invaded Kentucky from East Tennessee, where the loyalists were suffering peculiar hardships at the hands of the Secessionists. At the same time, Simon B. Buckner, who had been placed in command of the professed "neutral" *Kentucky State Guard*, formed a Confederate camp in Tennessee, just below the Kentucky border, and, acting in co-operation with Polk and Zollicoffer, attempted to seize Louisville. He was foiled by the vigilance of General Anderson (late of Fort Sumter), who was in command there, with General W. T. Sherman as his lieutenant. Buckner fell back to Bowling Green, on the Nashville and Louisville Railroad, and there established a camp as a nucleus of a powerful Confederate force that was gathered soon afterward.

Buckner's raid and the invasion of Zollicoffer aroused the Unionists of Eastern Kentucky, who flew to arms under various leaders. In an attack upon a camp of Kentucky, Indiana and Ohio troops, under Colonel Garrard, at the Rock Castle Hills, a picturesque region of the Cumberland Mountains, Zollicoffer was repulsed, on the 21st of October. Further eastward, near Piketon, the capital of Pike county, a Confederate force under John S. Williams was dispersed by some Union troops under General William Nelson, early in November. These successes inspirited the loyalists of East Tennessee with hopes of a speedy deliverance from their oppressors; but they were compelled to wait long for relief, for toward the close of 1861 the Confederates had established a firm military foothold in Tennessee, and occupied a considerable portion of Southern Kentucky from the Cumberland

HARD TACK

Sand Bag Defences and Bursted Gun

Mountains to the Mississippi River, along a line about four hundred miles in length. They also occupied a greater portion of Missouri, south of the Missouri River.

Fremont was censured for his failure to reinforce Mulligan. The public knew very little of his embarrassments at that time. Pressing demands came for reinforcements, from General Grant at Paducah. Cries for help were heard at various points in his department; and a peremptory order was received from General Scott to forward five thousand troops immediately to Washington city, notwithstanding McClellan (who was in chief command there) had seventy thousand men within easy call. Fremont's forces did not, at any time, number more than fifty-six thousand, and these were scattered over his department. Chafing under unjust complaints, he proceeded to put his plan for ridding the Mississippi Valley of Confederate troops into operation at once. On the 27th of September, he put more than twenty thousand soldiers (five thousand of them cavalry) in motion under the respective commands of Generals Hunter, Pope, Sigel, McKinstry and Asboth, accompanied by eighty-six heavy guns. These five columns were moving southward early in October; and on the 11th, when his army was thirty thousand strong, Fremont wrote to his Government: "My plan is New Orleans straight; I would precipitate the war forward, and end it soon and victoriously."

GEN. AND MRS. GEO. B. McCLFLLAN

Fremont felt confident of success. His army were in high spirits, and small victories were won by his detachments in various places. He had strengthened the forces in Eastern Missouri, so that St. Louis was safe; and General Hardee at Greenville, and General Pillow near New Madrid, dared not advance. He knew the bitterness of his political enemies, and the jealousies of envious men; and he was in continual expectation of interference with his plans. That interference soon came. False accusers, public and private, had such influence in the military councils at Washington that, just after his superb body-guard of one hundred and fifty cavalry, led by Zagonyi, a Hungarian, had charged upon and routed about two thousand Confederates, foot and horse, at Springfield, Fremont received an order from General Scott, directing him to turn over his command to General Hunter, then some distance in the rear. Hunter arrived just as the troops were about to attack Price. He countermanded Fremont's orders for battle; and nine days afterward General H. W. Halleck was placed in command of the Department of Missouri. The disappointed and disheartened army were turned back, and made a retrograde march to St. Louis in sullen sadness. Fremont was afterward presented with an elegant sword, inscribed: "*To the Path-finder, by the Men of the West.*"

Just before he was deprived of his command, Fremont ordered General Grant to move a co-operative force along the line of the Mississippi River. It was promptly done. A column, about three thousand strong, and composed chiefly of Illinois volunteers, under General John A. McClernand, went down from Cairo in transports and the wooden gunboats *Tyler* and *Lexington* to menace Columbus by attacking the post at Belmont opposite; and at the same time another column, under General C. F. Smith, marched from Paducah to menace Columbus in the rear. Grant accompanied McClernand's column. The troops were landed on the morning of November 7th, three miles above Belmont, and pushed on for that post, while the gunboats opened fire upon Columbus. General Polk, still in command there, acted with vigor and promptness. He sent Pillow across the river with troops to reinforce the garrison at Belmont. In a sharp battle that ensued, the Nationals won the victory, but, exposed to a sharp fire of artillery on the bluff at Columbus that position was untenable; so, giving three cheers for the Union, they set fire to the Confederate camp, and

BULL RUN

withdrew with captured men, horses, and artillery. But Polk determined not to let the victors escape. He opened seven of his heaviest guns upon them, and at the same time sent over fresh troops under General Cheatham, and crossed over himself with two regiments, making the whole Confederate force about five

DECK OF MONITOR AND GROUP OF OFFICERS

GROUP OF UNIDENTIFIED OFFICERS

thousand. There was a desperate struggle; but Grant fought his way back to his transports, and escaped under cover of a fire from the gunboats. These were admirably handled in the engagement respectively by Commanders Walke and Stemble. The Nationals lost about five hundred men, and the Confederates over six hundred.

We have observed that the Confederates, though defeated in Western Virginia in the summer of 1861, resolved not to relinquish possession of that granary without another struggle. It occurred in the autumn of that year. The troops left by Garnett and Pegram were placed in charge of General Robert E. Lee, and early in August he was at the head of about sixteen thousand fighting men. John B. Floyd, the late Secretary of War, was sent with some troops to reinforce those under General Wise, and to take the chief command in the region of the Gauly River. Lee made his headquarters at Huntersville, in Pocahontas county, and he placed a strong guard on Buffalo Mountain, at the crossing of the Staunton turnpike. Much was expected from Floyd, for he promised

GENERAL W. S. HARNEY   GENERAL C. P. STONE
GENERAL C. W. STANFORD   GENERAL W. S. MORRIS

much. It was expected that he would move swiftly down the Kanawha Valley, and drive General Cox across the Ohio River; while Lee should disperse the army of ten thousand men under Rosecrans, McClellan's successor, at Clarksburg, on the Baltimore and Ohio Railroad, and so open a way for an invading force of Confederates into the States of Maryland, Pennsylvania and Ohio. Floyd made his headquarters a few miles from Summerville.

Early in September, Rosecrans marched southward in search of Floyd. He scaled the Gauly Mountains with great difficulty, and on the 10th found his foe at Carnifex Ferry on the Gauly River. Rosecrans fell upon the Ex-Secretary furiously, and for three hours they fought desperately. The contest ceased at twilight; and during the night Floyd stole away under cover of darkness, and did not halt until he reached the summit of Big Sewell Mountain, thirty miles distant. Meanwhile the Nationals under General J. J. Reynolds, whom Rosecrans had left to confront Lee in the Cheat Mountain region, were watching the roads and passes of the more westerly of the Alleghany range of hills. They observed that Lee's scouts were very active, and that he was evidently preparing to strike a blow somewhere. Finally the object of his movements was made clear, which was to attack the Nationals at Elkwater, and the outpost of Indiana troops on the summit of Cheat Mountain, so as to secure the Pass and have a free communication with the Shenandoah Valley, at Staunton. For that object Lee marched from Huntersville on the night of the 11th of September, with nine thousand men and nearly a dozen pieces of artillery, to strike the post at Elkwater, the Summit and the Pass at the same moment. A storm was sweeping over the mountains and favored the enterprise. But it was unsuccessful. Lee was repulsed at Elkwater and the Summit, when he withdrew and joined Floyd on Big Sewell Mountain between the forks of the Kanawha. Their combined forces numbered about twenty thousand men, and they were there confronted by about ten thousand Nationals under Rosecrans, assisted by Generals Cox, Schenck, and Benham.

Very soon afterward, General Lee, whose campaign had been a failure, was recalled and sent to Georgia. He was succeeded by Floyd. The incompetent Wise was also recalled. Floyd, as chief commander in Western Virginia, took post on New River, from which he was driven by Rosecrans on the 12th of November, and was pursued about fifty miles. Then he retired from the army, but reappeared

PROVOST MARSHALL'S OFFICE, ALEXANDRIA

in command at Fort Donelson not long afterward. Vigorous movements made by Generals Kelly and Milroy, toward the close of the year, were successful in dispersing the Confederate troops in Northwestern Virginia. A successful expedition sent against a Confederate post at Huntersville (Lee's old quarters) by Milroy closed the campaign of 1861, in that region, and armed rebellion was effectually crushed in West Virginia.

In the summer of 1861, the Confederates built two forts on Hatteras Island, off the coast of North Carolina, which guarded the entrance to Hatteras Inlet, through which the British blockade runners had begun to carry in supplies to the insurgents. General B. F. Butler, then in command at Fortress Monroe, proposed the sending of a land and naval force against these forts. It was undertaken late in August; and when, toward the close of summer (just after the village of Hampton had been laid in ashes by Virginia troops under Magruder), Butler was succeeded in command at Fortress Monroe by the veteran General

John E. Wool, the former volunteered to command the land forces for the purpose. An expedition, composed of eight transports and war-ships under Commodore Stringham, bearing almost nine hundred land troops commanded by Butler, left Hampton Roads for Hatteras Inlet on the 26th of August, and on the morning of the 28th the vessels of war opened fire upon the forts (Hatteras and Clarke) and some of the troops were landed. An assault by both arms of the service was kept up until the 29th, when the forts were surrendered, and the expedition returned to

"THEY DIED THAT THE UNION MIGHT LIVE"

garrison the captured siege, Mr. Fiske, acting General Butler, per- deed. When one of the abandoned, he swam heavy breakers, with Weber, who was on the tered the evacuated books and papers con- information. These he age, strapped it high and swam back with The information they assailants great advan-

Hampton Roads, leaving a portion of Colonel Hawkins's New York Zouaves, with their commander, to post. During the aide-de-camp to formed a gallant forts (Clarke) was ashore, through orders for Colonel island. Fiske en- fort, and found taining valuable formed into a pack- upon his shoulders, them to the ship. contained gave the tages.

The victory at Hatteras finally led to important results, as we shall perceive hereafter. The politicians of North Carolina had annexed that State to the Confederacy. A conciliatory address to the inhabitants, issued by Colonel Hawkins, led to a Convention on the Eastern Shore, which, on the 16th of November, 1861, adopted a declaration of independence of the Confederacy. It promised so much good that President Lincoln authorized the election of a Congressman from that district. But the heel of despotic power soon crushed this germ of active loyalty among four thousand inhabitants, and it almost disappeared for a time.

We have observed that Fort Pickens, on Santa Rosa Island off the harbor of Pensacola, was saved from the insurgents early in 1861, by the vigilance and bravery of Lieutenant Slemmer. He was furloughed for rest, and Colonel Harvey Brown took his place. The garrison was reinforced from time to time. In June, Wilson's Zouaves from New York arrived on Santa Rosa Island to assist in the defence of the fort, which the Confederates ardently coveted. The latter had gathered in large numbers on the main; and in October they attempted to surprise and capture Wilson's troops, on a dark night, landing and rushing

INTERIOR VIEW.

PARROTT GUN DISMOUNTED BY CONFEDERATE FIRE

VIEW FROM COX'S LANDING

VIEW FROM NORTH SIDE — JAMES RIVER.

INTERIOR VIEW

VIEWS OF FORTIFICATIONS

BATTERY No. 4 IN FRONT OF YORKTOWN

upon their camp with the cry of "Death to Wilson! No quarter!" The Zouaves fought desperately in the gloom, and, with the aid of men from the fort, drove the assailants to their boats. The Confederates lost one hundred and fifty men; the Nationals, sixty-four. Wilson's camp was burned by the enemy, and that was the most that the assailants achieved.

These events were followed, late in November, by a severe cannonade and bombardment of the Confederate works on the main, by Fort Pickens and war-vessels. There were seven thousand men under General Braxton Bragg, encamped behind these works and in a curved line from the Navy-yard to Fort McRee, a distance of about four miles. The works consisted of forts and batteries. In the course of forty-eight hours after the bombardment was begun, most of the heavy guns of the Confederates were silenced, and a greater portion of the Navy-yard, and the villages of Wolcott and Warrington adjoining, were laid in ashes by shells from Fort Pickens. After that, for a few weeks, quiet prevailed in Pensacola Bay, when it was broken by another artillery duel on the 1st of January, 1862. It lasted about twelve hours, but with very little damage to either party.

Meanwhile a speck of war had appeared at the Southwest Pass at the mouth of the Mississippi River. Captain J. S. Hollins of the National navy, who had deserted his flag, was in command there of a Confederate "ram" — an iron-clad gunboat with a sharp and heavy iron beak to crush or punch holes in the sides of wooden vessels. It was called Manassas. With this formidable monster, which might have been very mischievous in competent hands, Hollins attacked the National blockading squadron under Captain Pope; but he was soon driven up the river to Fort Jackson, after doing slight damage to one or two of the vessels of the National Navy.

SUDLEY'S FORD, BULL RUN

Late in the same month (October, 1861), another more formidable land and naval armament left Hampton Roads for a destination unknown to all but the chief commander. It was composed of fifty war-ships and transports commanded by Admiral S. F. Dupont, and fifteen thousand land troops under General W. T. Sherman. Dupont's flag-ship, the *Wabash*, led the way out to sea, and each ship sailed under sealed orders to be opened in case of the dispersion of the fleet. A terrible tempest smote them off Cape Hatteras, and very soon only one vessel could be seen from the deck of the flag-ship. The sealed orders were opened, by which each commander was directed to rendezvous at Port Royal entrance, on the coast of South Carolina. There all but four transports, which were lost, were gathered around the *Wabash* on the evening of the 4th of November. Fortunately no human life perished with the transports lost.

The entrance to Port Royal Sound is between Hilton Head and Phillips's Island, and was guarded by a battery on each, erected by the Confederates. Within the Sound was a small flotilla of armed vessels commanded by the veteran Commodore Tattnall, late of the United States navy, who had espoused the Confederate cause. On the morning of the 7th of November, Dupont's ships attacked the guarding forts, the guns of which were soon silenced, when the fleet moved into the Sound and drove Tattnall's vessels into shallow water. The National forces took possession of Port Royal Island and the neighboring ones, and found them deserted by the planters and their families. Most of the slaves remained. They had refused to follow their masters, who tried to frighten them by horrible stories about the people of the North—the "Yankees"—who, they told them, were coming to steal and sell the negroes in Cuba, or to kill them and bury them in the sand. The colored people did not believe these tales; and when the National ships approached, and the masters and mistresses of the slaves fled in terror, these simple people —men, women, and children—stood in groups on the sea-shore, with little bundles of clothing in their hands, desiring to go on board.

The last efforts of the Confederates to defend the Sea Islands below Charleston, where the most valuable cotton was raised, was made at Port Royal Ferry, between Port Royal Island and the main, on the 1st of January, 1862. After a severe conflict the Confederates were defeated and dispersed. Dupont, in the meantime, had taken possession of Big Tybee Island, near Fort Pulaski, at the mouth of the Savannah River; and before the close of 1861, the National authority was supreme over the coast islands from Warsaw Sound to the mouth of the North Edisto River. A fleet of twenty old wooden ships,

Battery Abbott
Interior View.

Fort Burnham
View from Earthworks

Redoubt Zabriskie,
Exterior View.

Fort Burnham
View from Earthworks.

Redoubt Zabriskie
Exterior View.

Fort Burnham
Bomb Proof Quarters.

Interior View.

Fort Burnham,
Previously Confederate
Fort Harrison.

Federal Earthworks
on Left of
Bermuda Hundred Line
near Point of Rocks.

Battery Abbott,
on Trents Beach, James River.

Fortifications and Batteries

chiefly whalers, heavily laden with rough blocks of granite, which had been sent from New England to be sunk in the four channels of the entrance to Charleston harbor, and so assist in the blockade services, arrived at their destination at about this time. It was when this "stone fleet" approached, that a fire which laid a large portion of Charleston in ashes (an event already mentioned) was raging. Quicksands swallowed the "stone fleet," and its services were of very little account.

We have seen that General McClellan was called from Western Virginia to take charge of the army of the Potomac, as the forces around Washington were called after the battle of Bull Run. He assumed command on the 27th of July. He brought to the service youth, a spotless moral character, robust health, a sound theoretic military education with some practical experience, untiring industry, the prestige of recent success in the field, and the unlimited confidence of the loyal people. He found at his disposal about fifty thousand infantry, less than one thousand cavalry, six hundred and fifty artillerymen, and thirty pieces of cannon. He was very popular, and was called a "Young Napoleon;" and when on the 1st of November, 1861, General Scott resigned his place as General-in-Chief of the armies, McClellan was appointed to fill that office.

The act was hailed as a promise of a speedy termination of the conflict, for he had said that the war should be "short, sharp, and decisive." He thoroughly reorganized the army which had been shattered by the terrible blow of Bull Run; and it was believed that Richmond, which had become the Confederate capital, would be in the possession of the National troops before the close of September. But such was not to be.

The Confederates under General Johnston remained encamped at Manassas, and were compelled to be idle for want of cavalry and adequate subsistence; while the National army was hourly increasing in strength at the rate of two thousand men a day from the teeming free-labor States, with ample supplies of munitions of war. Beauregard urged Johnston to attack the National fortifications which were rising around Washington, but the wise leader prudently refused; and while the hearts of the loyal people yearned to see a forward movement, and some of the newspapers raised and prolonged the insane cry of "On to Richmond!" the civil and military leaders of the Government, remembering the disaster at Bull Run, were circumspect and cautious. For several months these two principal armies lay within thirty miles of each other, the quiet of camp life broken only by an

BATTLEFIELD, THORBURN'S HOUSE AND MATTHEWS HOUSE AT BULL RUN

occasional skirmish or midnight alarm. Detachments of Confederates reconnoitering, sometimes approached within a few miles of Washington; and they held possession of Munson's Hill, within six miles of the dome of the Capitol, as the bird flies. They also kept up the blockade of the Potomac River by batteries on the Virginia shore, already alluded to—a state of things not only perilous to the capital and the army that surrounded it, but exceedingly disgraceful to that great army. So felt the Government, and in September it was resolved to remove these obstructions.

McClellan was ordered to co-operate with the naval force on the river, in the necessary business; but his unfortunate habit of procrastination paralyzed the efforts of the naval commanders, and the

Scenes on Bull Run

blockade was kept up until the Confederates voluntarily abandoned their position in front of Washington, in the spring of 1862.

When the Government ordered the removal of the blockade of the Potomac, the National troops began to push back the Confederate advance on the Virginia side of the river. Late in September the latter retired from Munson's Hill; and struggles for the possession of the Upper Potomac occurred at Lewinsville in Virginia, and Darnestown in Maryland. In these struggles the Nationals won the victory; and by the middle of October (1861) they occupied a line from Fairfax Court-House well up toward Leesburg, and the most advanced outpost of the Confederates was at or near Centreville. Meanwhile

DR. LETTERMAN, MEDICAL DIRECTOR AND OTHER OFFICERS

some National troops had crossed the Potomac at Harper's Ferry to seize some wheat, when they were men-aced by a large body of Confederates. Colonel (afterward General) Geary went over with reinforcements for the invaders, and on the hills back of the village he had a severe engage-ment with the insur-gents, and repulsed them. Then all the Nationals recrossed the river with their spoils.

This event was soon followed by a more im-portant one at Ball's Bluff on the Upper Po-tomac. The left wing of the Confederate army was commanded by General (late Colonel) Evans. It lay at Lees-burg, and was con-fronted by a National force, commanded by General Charles P. Stone, who were en-camped between Con-rad's and Edwards's ferries. His headquarters were at Poolesville. Misinformation had caused a belief that the Confederates had left Leesburg at a little past the middle of October, when McClellan ordered General McCall, who commanded the advance of the right of the National forces in Virginia, to move forward and occupy Drainsville. At the same time he ordered General Stone to co-operate with General McCall, which he did by making a feint of crossing the river at the two ferries above named, on the afternoon of Sunday the 20th of October. At the same time a part of a Massachusetts regiment, under Colonel Devens, was ordered to take post on Harrison's Island in the Potomac, abreast of Ball's Bluff. Devens went with four companies in flat-boats taken from the Chesapeake and Ohio Canal. Three thousand men com-manded by Colonel E. D. Baker, a member of the National Senate, acting as a brigadier, were held in readiness as a reserve, in the event of a battle.

These movements of the Nationals caused an opposing one on the part of the Confederates, who had watched their antagonists with keen vigilance, at a point of concealment not far off. Misinformed as to the position of the insurgents, and supposing McCall to be near enough to give aid, if necessary, Stone, on the morning of the 21st, ordered some Massachusetts troops under Colonels Lee and Devens, to cross to the Virginia main, from Harrison's Island, to reconnoitre. They did not find the foe in the neighborhood. But Evans, unperceived, lay near with a strong force; and when the detachment fell back to the vicinity of Ball's Bluff, he attacked them. It was at a little past noon. Colonel Baker had been sent to Harrison's Island, with his reserves, invested with discretionary power to withdraw or reinforce the other troops. He concluded to go forward, supposing the forces of McCall and others to be near; and on reaching the field he took the chief command by virtue of his rank. Very soon afterward he was instantly killed by a bullet that pierced his brain. His troops, unsupported by others, were crushed by a superior force. Pressed back to the verge of the bluff and down the declivity, they fought desperately for a while at twilight, for they had no means for transportation across the swollen flood. They were soon overpowered. A large number of the Nationals were made prisoners, and many perished in trying to escape by swimming in the dark. Some were shot in the water, and others were drowned. A large flat-boat, overloaded with the wounded and others, was riddled by bullets, and sank. In this affair, the Nationals lost full one thousand men and two pieces of artillery. The loss of Colonel Baker was irreparable. He was a genuine patriot, an acute statesman, and eloquent orator. His death caused sadness wherever his worth was appreciated.

HOUSE AND ROOM IN WHICH "STONEWALL" JACKSON DIED

CHRONOLOGICAL SUMMARY AND RECORD—Continued

DECEMBER, 1862—*Continued from Section 6.*

Parker's Cross Roads or Red Mound, Tenn. 18th, 106th, 119th and 122d Ill., 27th, 39th and 63d Ohio, 50th Ind., 39th Iowa, 7th Tenn., 7th Wis. Battery. *Union* 23 killed, 139 wounded, 58 missing. *Confed.* 50 killed, 150 wounded, 300 missing.

31 to Jan. 2—Murfreesboro' or Stone River, Tenn. Army of the Cumberland, Maj.Gen. Rosecrans. Right Wing, McCook's Corps; Center, Thomas's Corps; Left Wing, Crittenden's Corps. *Union* 1,533 killed, 7,245 wounded, 2,800 missing. *Confed.* 14,560 killed, wounded and missing. *Union* Brig.-Gen. Sill killed and Kirk wounded. *Confed,* Brig.-Gens. Raines and Hanson killed and Chalmers and Davis wounded.

JANUARY, 1863

1—Galveston, Tex. Three Cos. 42d Mass., U. S. Gunboats *Westfield, Harriet Lane, Owasco, Sachem, Clifton,* and *Coryphœus. Union* 600 killed, wounded and missing. *Confed.* 50 killed and wounded.

7 and 8—Springfield, Mo. Mo. Militia, convalescents and citizens. *Union* 14 killed, 144 wounded. *Confed.* 40 killed, 206 wounded and missing. *Union* Brig.-Gen. Brown wounded.

11—Fort Hindman, Ark. Thirteenth Corps, Maj.-Gen. McClernand; Fifteenth Corps, Maj.-Gen. Sherman and gunboats Mississippi squadron. *Union* 129 killed, 831 wounded. *Confed.* 100 killed, 400 wounded, 5,000 prisoners.

Hartsville or Wood's Fork, Mo. 21st Iowa, 99th Ill., 3d Iowa Cav., 3d Mo. Cav., Battery L 2d Mo. Artil. *Union* 7 killed, 64 wounded. *Confed.* Brig.-Gen. McDonald killed.

14—Bayou Teche, La. 8th Vt., 16th and 75th N. Y., 19th Conn., 6th Mich., 21st Ind., 1st La. Cav., 4th and 6th Mass. Battery, 1st Maine Battery, and U. S. Gunboats *Calhoun, Diana, Kinsman* and *Estrella. Union* 10 killed, 27 wounded. *Confed.* 15 killed. *Union* Commodore Buchanan killed. *Confed.* Gunboat *Cotton* destroyed.

24—Woodbury, Tenn. Second Division Crittenden's Corps. *Union* 2 killed, 4 wounded. *Confed.* 35 killed, 100 missing.

30—Deserted House or Kelly's Store, near Suffolk, Va. Portion of Maj.-Gen. Peck's forces. *Union* 24 killed, 80 wounded. *Confed.* 50 wounded.

31—Rover, Tenn. 4th Ohio Cav. *Confed.* 12 killed, 12 wounded, 300 captured.

FEBRUARY, 1863

3—Fort Donelson or Cumberland Iron Works, Tenn. 83d Ill., 2d Ill. Artil., one battalion 5th Iowa Cav. *Union* 16 killed, 60 wounded, 50 missing. *Confed.* 140 killed, 400 wounded, 130 missing.

14—Brentsville, Va. 1st Mich. Cav. *Union* 15 wounded.

16—Near Romney, W. Va. Detachments 116th and 122d Ohio. *Union* 72 wounded and captured.

21—Prairie Station, Miss. 2d Iowa Cav. *Union* 1 killed, 3 wounded.

24—Mississippi River below Vicksburg. U. S. Gunboat *Indianola. Union* 1 killed, 1 wounded. *Confed.* 35 killed.

MARCH, 1863

1—Bradyville, Tenn. 3d and 4th Ohio Cav., 1st Tenn. Cav. *Union* 1 killed, 6 wounded. *Confed.* 5 killed, 27 wounded, 100 captured.

4—Skeet, N. C. 3d N. Y. Cav. *Union* 3 killed, 15 wounded. *Confed.* 28 wounded.

4 and 5—Thompson's Station, also called Spring Hill and Unionville, Tenn. 33d and 85th Ind., 22d Wis., 19th Mich., 124th Ohio, 18th Ohio Battery, 2d Mich. Cav., 9th Penna. Cav., 4th Ky. Cav. *Union* 100 killed, 300 wounded, 1,306 captured. *Confed.* 150 killed, 450 wounded.

8—Fairfax C. H., Va. Brig.-Gen. Stoughton and thirty-three men captured by Mosby in his midnight raid.

10—Covington, Tenn. 6th and 7th Ill. Cav. *Confed.* 25 killed.

13 to April 5—Fort Pemberton, Miss. Thirteenth Corps, Brig.-Gen. Ross; Seventeenth Corps, Brig.-Gen. Quimby, U. S. Gunboats *Chillicothe* and *DeKalb.* Casualties not recorded.

14—Port Hudson, La. Maj.-Gen. Banks' troops and Admiral Farragut's fleet. *Union* 65 wounded.

16 to 22—Expedition up Steele's Bayou and at Deer Creek, Miss. 2d Division Fifteenth Corps, Maj.-Gen. Sherman, gunboat fleet, Admiral Porter. Casualties not recorded.

17—Kelly's Ford, Va. 1st and 5th U. S. Regulars, 3d, 4th and 16th Penna., 1st R. I., 6th Ohio, 4th N. Y. Cav., 6th N. Y. Battery. *Union* 9 killed, 35 wounded. *Confed.* 11 killed, 88 wounded.

20—Vaught's Hill, near Milton, Tenn. 105th Ohio, 101st Ind., 80th and 123d Ill., 1st Tenn. Cav., 9th Ind. Battery. *Union* 7 killed, 48 wounded. *Confed.* 63 killed, 300 wounded.

22—Mt. Sterling, Ky. 10th Ky. Cav. *Union* 4 killed, 10 wounded. *Confed.* 8 killed, 13 wounded.

24—Danville, Ky. 18th and 22d Mich., 1st Ky. Cav., 2d Tenn. Cav., 1st Ind. Battery.

Ponchatoula, La. 127th and 165th N. Y., 9th Conn., 14th and 24th Maine, 6th Mich. *Union* 6 wounded. *Confed.* 3 killed, 11 wounded.

25—Brentwood, Tenn. Detachment 22d Wis. and 19th Mich. *Union* 1 killed, 4 wounded, 300 prisoners. *Confed.* 1 killed, 5 wounded.

Franklin and Little Harpeth, Tenn. 4th and 6th Ky. Cav., 9th Penna. Cav., 2d Mich. Cav. *Union* 4 killed, 19 wounded, 40 missing.

28—Pattersonville, La. Gunboat *Diana* with Detachment of 12th Conn. and 160th N. Y. on board. *Union* 4 killed, 14 wounded, 99 missing.

29—Somerville, Tenn. 6th Ill. Cav. *Union* 9 killed, 29 wounded.

30—Dutton's Hill or Somerset, Ky. 1st Ky. Cav., 7th Ohio Cav., 44th and 45th Ohio Mounted Vol. *Union* 10 killed, 25 wounded. *Confed.* 290 killed, wounded and missing.

Point Pleasant, W. Va. One Co. 13th W. Va. *Union* 1 killed, 3 wounded. *Confed.* 20 killed, 25 wounded.

30 to April 4—Washington and Rodman's Point, N. C. Maj.-Gen. Foster's command. Casualties not recorded.

APRIL, 1863

2 and 3—Woodbury and Snow Hill, Tenn. 3d and 4th Ohio Cav. *Union* 1 killed, 8 wounded. *Confed.* 50 killed and wounded.

7—Bombardment Fort Sumter, S. C. South Atlantic squadron; *Keokuk, Weehawken, Passaic, Montauk, Patapsco, New Ironsides, Catskill, Nantucket* and *Nahant. Union* 2 killed, 20 wounded. *Confed.* 4 killed, 10 wounded.

10—Franklin and Harpeth River, Tenn. 40th Ohio and portion of Granger's Cavalry. *Union* 100 killed and wounded. *Confed.* 19 killed, 35 wounded, 83 missing.

Antioch Station, Tenn. Detachment 10th Mich. *Union* 8 killed, 12 wounded.

12 to 14—Irish Bend and Bisland, La., also called Indian Ridge and Centreville. Nineteenth Corps, Grover's, Emory's, Weitzel's Divisions. *Union* 350 killed, wounded and missing. *Confed.* 400 wounded, 2,000 missing and captured.

12 to May 4—Siege of Suffolk, Va. Troops, Army of Virginia and Department of North Carolina. *Union* 44 killed, 202 wounded. *Confed.* 500 killed and wounded, 400 captured.

15—Dunbar's Plantation, La. 2d Ill. Cav. *Union* 1 killed, 2 wounded.

17 to May 2—Grierson's expedition from La Grange, Tenn., to Baton Rouge, La. 6th and 7th Ill. Cav., 2d Iowa Cav. *Confed.* 100 killed and wounded, 500 prisoners.

18 and 19—Hernando and Coldwater, Miss. Portion of Sixteenth Corps, detachment of Artil., 2d Brigade Cavalry Division. Casualties not recorded.

20—Patterson, Mo. 3d Mo. Militia Cav. *Union* 12 killed, 7 wounded, 41 missing.

24—Tuscumbia, Ala. Sixteenth Corps, 2d Division. Maj.-Gen. Dodge.

White Water, Mo. 1st Wis. Cav. *Union* 2 killed, 6 wounded.

26—Cape Girardeau, Mo. 32d Iowa, 1st Wis. Cav., 2d Mo. Cav., Batteries D and L 1st Mo. Lt. Artil. *Union* 6 killed, 6 wounded. *Confed.* 60 killed, 275 wounded and missing.

27 to May 3—Streight's Raid, Tuscumbia, Ala., to Rome, Ga., including skirmishes at Day's Gap, April 30th; Black Warrior Creek, May 1st and Blount's Farm, May 2d. 3d Ohio, 51st and 73d Ind., 80th Ill., Mounted Inft., two Cos. 1st Ala. Cav. *Union* 12 killed, 69 wounded, 1,466 missing and captured.

27 to May 8—Stoneman's Cavalry Raid in Virginia.

29—Fairmount, W. Va. Detachments 106th N. Y., 6th W. Va. and Va. Militia. *Union* 1 killed, 6 wounded. *Confed.* 100 killed and wounded.

Grand Gulf, Miss. Gunboat fleet. *Union* 26 killed, 54 wounded.

30—Spottsylvania C. H., Va. 6th N. Y. Cav. *Union* 58 killed and wounded.

30 and May 1—Chalk Bluff and St. Francois River, Mo. 2d Mo. Militia, 3d Mo. Cav., 1st Iowa Cav., Battery E 1st Mo. Lt. Artil. *Union* 2 killed, 11 wounded.

MAY, 1863

1—Port Gibson, Miss. (the first engagement in Grant's Campaign against Vicksburg). Thirteenth Corps, Maj.-Gen. McClernand, and 3d Division Seventeenth Corps, Maj.-Gen. McPherson. *Union* 130 killed, 718 wounded. *Confed.* 1,150 killed and wounded, 500 missing. *Confed.* Brig.-Gen. Tracy killed.

1—LaGrange, Ark. 3d Iowa Cav. *Union* 3 killed, 9 wounded, 30 missing.

Monticello, Ky. 2d Tenn. Cav., 1st Ky. Cav., 2d and 7th Ohio Cav., 45th Ohio and 112th Ill. Mounted Inft.

1 to 4—Chancellorsville, Va., including battles of Sixth Corps at Fredericksburg and Salem Heights. Army of the Potomac, Maj.-Gen. Hooker; First Corps, Maj.-Gen. Reynolds; Second Corps, Maj.-Gen. Couch; Third Corps, Maj.-Gen. Sickles; Fifth Corps, Maj.-Gen. Meade; Sixth Corps, Maj.-Gen. Sedgwick; Eleventh Corps, Maj.-Gen. Howard; Twelfth Corps, Maj.-Gen. Slocum. *Union* 1,512 killed, 9,518 wounded, 5,000 missing. *Confed.* 1,581 killed, 8,700 wounded, 2,000 missing. *Union* Maj.-Gen. Berry and Brig.-Gen. Whipple killed, Devens and Kirby wounded. *Confed.* Brig.-Gen. Paxton killed, Lieut.-Gen. T. J. Jackson, Maj.-Gen. A. P. Hill, Brig.-Gens. Hoke, Nichols, Ramseur, McGowan, Heth, and Pender wounded.

3—Warrenton Junction, Va. 1st W. Va. Cav., 5th N. Y. Cav. *Union* 1 killed, 16 wounded. *Confed.* 15 wounded.

4—Siege of Suffolk, Va., raised. (See April 12.)

11—Horse Shoe Bend, Ky. Detachment commanded by Col. R. T. Jacobs. *Union* 10 killed, 20 wounded, 40 missing. *Confed.* 100 killed, wounded, and missing.

12—Raymond, Miss. Seventeenth Corps, Maj.-Gen. McPherson. *Union* 69 killed, 341 wounded. *Confed.* 969 killed and wounded. *Confed.* Gen. Telghman killed.

13—Hall's Ferry. 2d Ill. Cav. *Confed.* 12 killed.

14—Jackson, Miss. Fifteenth Corps, Maj.-Gen. Sherman; Seventeenth Corps, Maj.-Gen. McPherson. *Union* 40 killed, 240 wounded. *Confed.* 450 killed and wounded.

16—Champian Hills, Miss. Hovey's Div. Thirteenth Corps and Seventeenth Corps. *Union* 426 killed, 1,842 wounded, 189 missing. *Confed.* 2,500 killed and wounded, 1,800 missing.

17—Big Black River, Miss. Carr's and Osterhaus's Divisions, Thirteenth Corps, Maj.-Gen. McClernand. *Union* 29 killed, 242 wounded. *Confed.* 600 killed and wounded, 2,500 captured.

18 to July 4—Siege of Vicksburg. Thirteenth Corps, Fifteenth Corps, and Seventeenth Corps, commanded by Maj.-Gen. U. S. Grant, and gunboat fleet, commanded by Admiral Porter. Assault on Fort Hill on May 19th and general assault on the 20th, in which *Confed.* Brig.-Gen. Green was killed. Three divisions of the Sixteenth Corps and two divisions of the Ninth Corps, and Maj.-Gen. Herron's Division were then added to the besieging forces. *Union* 545 killed, 3,688 wounded, 303 missing. *Confed.* 21,277 killed, wounded, and missing.

20 to 28—Clendenin's raid, below Fredericksburg, Va. 8th Ill. Cav. *Confed.* 100 prisoners.

(Continued in Section 8.)

General A. E. Burnside in Camp

CHAPTER XIV.

FOR the space of almost two months after the battle at Ball's Bluff, the ears of the loyal people were vexed with the unsatisfying announcement made every morning, "All is quiet along the Potomac!"

A WOUNDED BOY

The autumn was dry and the roads in Virginia were never in a better condition for the movement of troops, and particularly of heavy artillery. Washington seemed to be perfectly secure, and there was an ample supply of troops not only for its defence, but to make an easy conquest of Richmond. At the close of the year (1861) there were full two hundred thousand men in the Army of the Potomac, while the Confederates that opposed them were never more than sixty thousand strong. The politicians sneeringly called the latter a mob, and plain people naturally wondered how such a rabble could hold so large an army of disciplined soldiers, under a "young Napoleon" who had promised that the war should be "short, sharp, and decisive," so long and so tightly in and near the National capital. They were impatient because of the delay in the promised forward movement of the Army of the Potomac; and there was a sense of relief that amounted to joyfulness, when, at near Christmas, the monotony was broken for a moment by a fight at Drainsville between the brigade of Nationals under Gen. E. O. C. Ord, and a smaller force of Confederate foragers led by Colonel J. E. B. Stuart, the famous cavalry leader. The excitement was only momentary. The Confederates, worsted in the sharp conflict, fled, and the people were again teased with the daily croon—"All is quiet along the Potomac!" Their hearts were becoming sick with hopes deferred, when two events occurred which awakened the liveliest feelings of satisfaction in the public mind. These were the capture of two Confederate embassadors and leading conspirators, and the permanent lodgement of the National power on the coast of North Carolina.

We have seen that the Confederates, at an early period in the contest, sent diplomatic agents to European courts. These proved to be incompetent, and the Confederate government undertook to correct the mistake by sending two of their ablest men to represent their cause at the courts of Great Britain and France, respectively. These were James M. Mason, of Virginia, author of the Fugitive-Slave Act, and John Slidell, who was deeply interested in the scheme for opening the African slave-trade. The embassadors, each accompanied by a "secretary of legation," left Charleston harbor on a stormy night (the 12th of October, 1861), eluded the blockading squadron, and landed at Havana, Cuba, where they were cordially greeted by the British consul and other sympathizers. There they embarked for St. Thomas, in the British mail-steamer *Trent*, intending to go to England in the regular packet from the latter port.

PRISON CAMP, OFFICERS' QUARTERS, ELMIRA, N. Y.

PRISON CAMP, GUARDHOUSE. ELMIRA, N. Y.

While the *Trent* was on her way to St. Thomas, and when off the northern coast of Cuba, she fell in with the American war-ship *San Jacinto*, Captain Wilkes, then on his way home from the coast of Africa. He touched at Havana, where he heard of the movements of the Confederate embassadors. Satisfied

CAPTAIN, LATER COMMANDER WILKES

that the English rule concerning neutrals and belligerents would justify him in seizing these two men on board the *Trent*, and transferring them to his own vessel, he had gone out in search of that steamship. He found her on the 8th of November, and brought her to by a shell fired across her bow. Then he sent Lieutenant Fairfax, a kinsman of Mason, on board the *Trent* to demand the delivery of the embassadors and their secretaries to Captain Wilkes. The officers of the *Trent* protested, and the embassadors refused to leave the ship unless forced by physical power to do so. Lieutenant Greer and a few marines were sent to the aid of Fairfax, who then took Mason by the shoulder and placed him in a boat belonging to the *San Jacinto*. Then the lieutenant returned for Slidell. The passengers were greatly excited. They gathered around him, some making contemptuous allusions to the lieutenant, and some crying out, "Shoot him!" The daughter of Slidell slapped Fairfax in the face three times as she clung to the neck of her father. The marines were called, and Slidell and the two secretaries were compelled to go, when the *Trent* proceeded on her voyage to St. Thomas. The captive embassadors were conveyed to Boston and confined in Fort Warren, as prisoners of State.

The act of Captain Wilkes was applauded by all loyal men. It was in exact accordance with the British interpretation of the law of nations, as exhibited theoretically and practically by that government, yet it made a great ado about the "outrage." By most of the writers on international law in the United States, instructed by the doctrines and practices of Great Britain, the essays of British publicists, the decision of British courts, and by the law as laid down by the Queen's recent proclamation, the act of Captain Wilkes was decided to be abundantly justified; yet, with the same "unseemly haste" that characterized the issuing of the royal proclamation on the 13th of the previous May, the British government prepared for war. It did not wait for a communication on the subject to be received from the United States, but made extensive provisions for hostilities preparatory to sending a peremptory demand for the release of the prisoners; and the Tory press of Great Britain, conducted in the interest of the government, abused the Americans without stint. A single specimen from the columns of the London *Times* will suffice. Speaking of the courteous and accomplished gentleman, Captain Wilkes, the London *Times* said: "He is, unfortunately, but too faithful a type of a people in whose foul mission he is engaged. He is an ideal Yankee. Swagger and ferocity, built upon a foundation of vulgarity and cowardice—these are his characteristics, and these are the most prominent marks by which his countrymen, generally speaking, are known all over the world. To bully the weak, to triumph over the helpless, to trample on every law of country and custom, wilfully to violate the most sacred interests of human nature, to defy as long as danger does not appear, and, as soon as real peril shows itself, to sneak aside and run away—these are the virtues of the race which presumes to announce itself as the leader of civilization and the prophet of human progress in these latter days. By Captain Wilkes, let the Yankee breed be judged."

While the British government was preparing for war, and our Congress was officially thanking Captain Wilkes for his conduct, and other public bodies were bestowing honors upon him, our Government, acting upon the wise counsel of President Lincoln,

GENERAL A. E. BURNSIDE

NASHVILLE FROM THE CAPITOL

and true to its long-cherished principles, proceeded to disavow the act of Wilkes and to release the prisoners. That act was in violation of a principle for the maintenance of which, as we have seen, the

MAJOR-GENERAL E. R. S. CANBY

United States went to war with Great Britain—the principle that the flag of a neutral vessel is a protection to all beneath it. A few hours after the news of the capture reached Washington, the calm and thoughtful President said to the writer: "I fear the traitors will prove to be white elephants. We must stick to American principles concerning the rights of neutrals. We fought Great Britain, for insisting, by theory and practice, on the right to do precisely what Captain Wilkes has done. If Great Britain shall now protest against the act, and demand their release, we must give them up, apologize for the act as a violation of our doctrine, and thus forever bind her to keep the peace in relation to neutrals, and so acknowledge she has been wrong for at least sixty years." Under the instructions of the President, the Secretary of State (Mr. Seward) acted in accordance with these utterances. The prisoners were released, and the British people blushed for shame because of the impotent bluster of their government, when the fact was promulgated by the American minister, Mr. Adams. Then the London *Times*, which had called most vehemently for war on "the insolent Republic," in speaking of the demand of the British government for the release of the embassadors, super-ciliously declared that they were "worthless booty;" and added, "England would have done as much for two negroes." The embassadors were treated, in England, with a coolness that amounted to contempt, and they soon passed into obscurity.

The British government acted not only unwisely but dishonorably in the matter. Lord John Russell, the Foreign Secretary, wrote to Lord Lyons, the British minister at Washington, to demand from our Government the liberation of the captives and "a suitable apology for the aggressions which had been committed;" and if the demand should not be speedily complied with, to leave Washington, with all the members of the legation. On the day of the date of Earl Russell's despatch, Mr. Seward wrote a confidential note to Mr. Adams, calling attention to the fact that Captain Wilkes did not act under orders from his Government, and expressed a hope that the British government would consider the subject in a friendly manner. He gave Mr. Adams permission to read his note to Lord Russell and the Prime Minister. Mr. Adams did so; and yet the British government, with this voluntary assurance that a satisfactory arrangement of the difficulties might be made, continued its preparations for war with vigor, to the alarm and distress of the people. The fact that such assurance had reached the government was not only suppressed, but, when rumors of it were whispered, it was semi-officially denied. And when the fact could no longer be concealed, it was, by the same authority, affirmed, without a shadow of justice, that Mr. Adams had suppressed it, at the same time suggesting, as a reason, that the American minister might profit by the purchase of American stocks at panic prices!

When the excitement, in our country, caused by the "*Trent* affair," was subsiding, early in 1862, public attention was attracted by the fitting out of a third naval armament at Hampton Roads. It was composed of over one hundred war-vessels and transports commanded by Commodore L. M. Goldsborough, and bearing sixteen thousand land troops under General Ambrose E. Burnside, of Rhode Island. The armament left the Roads on the 11th of January (1862), with its destination unknown except

GENERAL FRANZ SIGEL

VIEWS TAKEN AT NASHVILLE

DECK OF GUNBOAT "ARAGO"

to proper officers. That destination was Roanoke Island and Pamlico Sound, on the coast of North Carolina. Off Cape Hatteras the fleet encountered a heavy gale, and it was several days before the whole armament had entered the Inlet.

GENERAL McINTOSH, C. S. A.
KILLED AT THE BATTLE OF PEA RIDGE

The Confederates had strongly fortified Roanoke Island with batteries that commanded the Sounds on each side of it. There was also a fortified camp that extended across a narrow part of the island. These fortifications were garrisoned by North Carolina troops then under the command of Colonel H. M. Shaw, and mounted about forty guns. They had also placed obstructions in the channel leading to the island; and above them, in Croatan Sound, was a flotilla of small gunboats—a sort of "mosquito fleet" like Tattnall's in Port Royal Sound—commanded by Lieutenant W. F. Lynch, late of the National navy. Preparations were made for an attack by land and sea, the first week in February. Goldsborough drew up his fleet of seventy vessels in Croatan Sound, and opened a bombardment upon the batteries. It was kept up all the afternoon, the flotilla and the batteries responding to Goldsborough's guns. At midnight, while a cold storm of wind and rain was sweeping over the land and water, about eleven thousand troops were landed on the island, many of them wading ashore. These were New England, New York, and New Jersey troops. They were without shelter, and were drenched. At dawn, led by General J. G. Foster (Burnside's lieutenant), they moved forward to attack the line of intrenchments that crossed the island. The Confederates, far inferior in number, made a gallant defence, going from redoubt to redoubt as one after another fell into the hands of the Nationals. They made a vigorous stand in a well-situated redoubt that was approached by a causeway. There was to be the last struggle in defence of the line. At the head of a part of Hawkins's Zouaves, Major Kimball (a veteran of the war with Mexico) undertook to take it by storm. Colonel Hawkins was then leading a flank movement with a part of his command. Seeing Major Kimball pushing forward, the Colonel joined him, when the whole battalion shouted, "Zou! Zou! Zou!" and pressed to the redoubt. The affrighted Confederates fled and were pursued by Foster five or six miles, when they surrendered, and Roanoke Island passed into the possession of the National forces, with three thousand prisoners and forty-two cannon. The Confederate flotilla went up Albemarle Sound, followed by National gunboats under Commodore Rowan.

Near Elizabeth, not far from the Dismal Swamp, Rowan attacked the flotilla and some land batteries, driving the Confederates from both, when Lynch and his followers retired into the interior. Then the United States flag was placed upon a shore battery, and this was the first portion of the main of North Carolina that was "repossessed" by the Government. Other portions of the coast of that State were speedily recovered; and on the 18th of February, 1862, Burnside and Goldsborough issued a proclamation jointly to the inhabitants of eastern North Carolina, assuring them that the Government forces were there not as enemies but as friends, and inviting them to separate themselves from the Confederacy and to return to their allegiance. This disaster, worked by the National forces, produced great depression throughout the Confederacy, for it exposed nearly the whole of the North Carolina main, and opened a way by which Norfolk might be smitten in the rear.

Let us now return to the Mississippi Valley, where we left Fremont's disappointed army sullenly marching back to St. Louis.

Late in 1861, the Department of Missouri was enlarged, and General H. W. Halleck was appointed to the command of it. General Hunter was assigned to the Department of Kansas; General Don Carlos Buell to that of the Ohio, and General E. R. S. Canby to that of New Mexico.

GENERAL ZOLLICOFFER C. S. A.

FALLING WATER BRIDGE, NASHVILLE AND CHATTANOOGA RAILROAD, 107 FEET HIGH

Halleck's headquarters were at St. Louis, and he restrained the Secessionists with a vigorous hand. Since the retrograde movement of Hunter, with Fremont's army, Price had been gathering a Confederate force in Missouri, and General John Pope was placed in command of a considerable body of troops to oppose him. Pope acted with great vigor and skill. He made a short, sharp, and effective campaign. Detachments from his army struck some blows here and there that were telling. One was inflicted by troops under General J. C. Davis, on the Blackwater, near Milford, which gave a stunning blow to the insurgents in that State. Davis found the enemy in a wooded bottom opposite his own forces. He carried a well-guarded bridge by storm, and struck the Confederates so hard that they fled in much confusion; and when they were closely pursued, they surrendered, in number about thirteen hundred, cavalry and infantry. The spoils of victory were eight hundred horses and mules, a thousand stand of arms, and over seventy wagons loaded with tents, baggage, ammunition, and supplies of every kind. In a brief space of time, the power of the insurgents in that quarter was paralyzed, and Halleck complimented Pope on his "brilliant campaign."

Pope had not only prevented organized troops from joining Price, but had compelled the latter to withdraw to the borders of Arkansas for supplies and safety. Feeling strengthened by Pope's success, Halleck prepared to put forth more vigorous efforts to suppress the insurrection. On the 3d of December he declared martial law in St. Louis; and, by a subsequent proclamation, he extended that system of rule

PONTOON BRIDGE ON THE RAPPAHANNOCK

to all railroads and their vicinities. Meanwhile, Price, relieved from immediate danger, and being promised reinforcements from Arkansas, moved back to Springfield, and there concentrated about twelve thousand men, halted his army, and prepared to spend the winter there. Halleck sent troops in that direction under General S. R. Curtis, assisted by Generals Davis, Sigel, Asboth, and Prentiss. They moved in three columns early in February (1862), when Price fled southward, and did not halt until he reached a good position in northern Arkansas. Curtis pursued him, and drove him further south; and Halleck was enabled to write to his Government, late in February, that he had "purged Missouri," and that the flag of the Union was "waving in triumph over the soil of Arkansas." The campaign in Missouri, for a few months, had been very active, beginning with Lyon's pursuit of the fugitive governor and his followers. From June, 1861, until late in February, 1862, there had been fought on Missouri soil sixty battles and skirmishes, with an aggregate loss on both sides, in killed, wounded and prisoners, of about twelve thousand men.

Curtis crossed the Arkansas line on the 18th of February in pursuit of Price, and had driven him and his followers over a range of hills known as the Boston Mountains. He then fell back and encamped in a strong position in the vicinity of Pea Ridge, a spur of the Ozark Mountains. In the meantime Price had been joined by General Earl Van Dorn, a dashing young officer, who was his senior in rank and now took the chief command. Forty heavy guns thundered a welcome. "Soldiers!" cried Van Dorn, in response, "behold your leader! He comes to show you the way to glory and immortal renown. He comes to hurl back the minions of the despots at Washington, whose ignorance, licentiousness, and brutality are equalled only by their craven natures. They come to free your slaves, lay waste your plantations, burn your villages, and abuse your loving wives and beautiful daughters."

Van Dorn came from western Arkansas with Generals McCulloch, McIntosh, and Pike. The latter

PONTOON BRIDGE AT DEEP BOTTOM ON THE JAMES

LOCOMOTIVE ON THE UNITED STATES MILITARY RAILROAD

was a New Englander and poet, who had joined the Confederate army on the borders of the Indian country with a body of savages whom he had lured into the service.   The whole insurgent force now numbered twenty-five thousand; the National troops, soon to measure strength with them, did not exceed eleven thousand men in number with fifty pieces of artillery.

When, on the 5th of March (1862), Curtis's scouts told him of the swift approach of the Confederates in overwhelming force, he concentrated his little army in the Sugar Creek Valley.   He perceived his perils, but there was only the alternative to fight or make a disastrous retreat. Choosing the former, he prepared to meet the foe from whatever quarter he might approach.   Meanwhile Van Dorn, by a quick and stealthy movement, flanked Curtis and gained his rear; and on the morning of the 7th he advanced to attack the Nationals, not doubting his ability to vanquish them and seize their train of two hundred wagons.   He found Curtis in battle order, his first and second division being on his left and commanded by Generals Asboth and Sigel; the third, under General Davis, composing his centre, and the fourth, commanded by Colonel Carr, formed his right.   His line of battle extended about four miles, and was confronted by the heavy Confederate force with only a broad and deep ravine covered with fallen trees separating the two armies.   The battle was opened toward noon by a simultaneous attack by the Nationals and Confederates.   A very severe conflict ensued, which continued a greater part of the day with varying fortunes to each party, the lines of strife swaying like a pendulum.   Generals McCulloch and McIntosh of the Confederates were killed, and the slaughter on both sides was dreadful.

BRIG.-GENERAL JAMES A. GARFIELD

At night the Confederates fired the last shot, but the Nationals held the field, slept on their arms, and anxiously awaited the dawn to renew the battle.

Both armies lay among the dead and dying that night.   At dawn (March 8, 1862) the conflict was renewed, when the Nationals hurled such a destructive tempest of shot and shell upon the Confederates, that the latter soon broke and fled in almost every direction in wildest confusion.   The Confederate army, so strong, and confident of victory twenty-four hours before, was broken into fragments.   The losses of each were about the same.   Curtis's was thirteen hundred and eighty men.   Pike's Indians, who had been maddened with liquor before the battle, tomahawked and scalped a number of the Nationals, and were the first to fly from the field, in terror.

While Halleck was purging Missouri of armed insurgents, Hunter, with his headquarters at Fort Leavenworth, was vigorously at work suppressing the insurrection on the borders of Kansas.   Active and armed rebellion was now co-extensive with the slave-labor States.   Civil War was kindling in General Canby's Department of New Mexico.   An attempt was there made to attach that Territory to the Confederacy by the method employed by General Twiggs in Texas, when he betrayed the National forces under his command.   Disloyal officers had been sent by Secretary Floyd, for that purpose, a year before the insurrection broke out; but failing to corrupt the troops (for not one of the twelve hundred men abandoned his flag), and incurring their hot displeasure, these leaders fled from their wrath toward Texas.   On the borders of that State they found the commander and other officers of Fort Fillmore ready to co-operate with them. These men led out their unsuspecting men and betrayed them into the power of Texan insurgents.

Miguel A. Otero, the representative of New Mexico in the National Congress, was in practical, active sympathy with the Secessionists; and the success of the Confederate cause in that quarter seemed to be assured, until Canby appeared and raised the standard of the Union, in strength. Around it the loyal people of the Territory gathered; and his regular troops, New Mexican levies, and volunteers, gave him a force sufficient to meet over two thousand Texans, most of them rough rangers under Colonel H. H. Sibley, a Louisianian, who invaded the Territory at the middle of February.   He had twenty-three hundred followers, many of them veterans who had much experience in fighting the Indians.

COMMODORE A. H. FOOTE

FORT NEGLEY

Canby was then at Fort Craig, on the Rio Grande. Sibley issued a proclamation to the people of New Mexico, in which he denounced the National Government, and demanded from the inhabitants allegiance to the Confederacy and support for his troops. Feeling confident of success, he moved slowly

OFFICERS ON DECK OF MONITOR

toward Fort Craig to attack Canby, when he was astonished to find the general prepared to meet him. He perceived that his light field-pieces would have no effect upon the fort. Unable to retreat or to remain with safety, and unwilling to leave a well-garrisoned post behind him, Sibley was perplexed. At length he forded the Rio Grande, and took a position out of reach of Canby's guns, for the purpose of drawing out the latter. In this he was successful. After some skirmishing, there was a severe conflict at Valverde, about seven miles from the fort, on the 21st of February. Canby was about to make a general advance, with an assurance of victory, when about a thousand Texans, horse and foot, armed with carbines, revolvers and bowie-knives, suddenly burst from a thick wood and attacked two of the National batteries commanded respectively by Captains McRea and Hall. The cavalry were repulsed; but the insurgent infantry pressed forward while the grape-shot were making fearful lanes through their ranks, and captured the battery of McRea. The brave captain defended his guns with great courage. Seated upon one of them, he fought the assailants with a pistol until he was shot dead. At length the Nationals, panic-stricken by the fierceness of the charge, broke and fled, and did not halt until they reached the shelter of Fort Craig. That flight was one of the most disgraceful scenes of the war; and Canby was compelled to see the victory snatched from him, just as it seemed to be secured. But Sibley, alarmed at the sudden and unexpected development of Canby's strength by accessions to his ranks, hurried toward Santa Fe, the capital of the Territory, which he captured but could not hold; and he was soon afterward driven over the mountains into Texas. The Civil War now extended from Maryland in the northeast to New Mexico in the southwest, and was everywhere marked by the vigor and malevolence which generally distinguish such wars.

While these events were occurring westward of the Mississippi, others of great importance had been in progress immediately eastward of its waters, where efforts had been made to expel the Confederates from Kentucky and release Tennessee from their grasp. The region of southern and western Kentucky was then held by the Confederates. They were commanded by an able officer and veteran soldier, A. S. Johnston, who was in charge of the Confederate Western Department, with his headquarters at Nashville. Under the shadow of his military power the Secessionists of Kentucky had met in Convention in November, 1861, and performed the farce of declaring the State to be independent. They passed an ordinance of secession; organized a provisional government; chose George W. Johnson provisional governor; appointed delegates to the Confederate congress at Richmond, and called Bowling Green the State capital. Fifty-one counties were represented in that "Sovereignty Convention" by about two hundred men, without the sanction of the people. At the same time General Johnston had concentrated a large force at Bowling Green, and strengthened the position of Polk at Columbus. General Hardee superseded General Buckner; and General Zollicoffer was firmly planted at Cumberland Gap, the chief passage between Eastern Kentucky and East Tennessee. Between the extremes of the Confederate line across Kentucky were fortified posts, the most important of which were Fort Donelson on the Cumberland River, and Fort Henry on the Tennessee River.

Early in the year, General Buell had organized a large force at Louisville and its vicinity, by which he was enabled to strengthen various

GENERAL C. F. SMITH

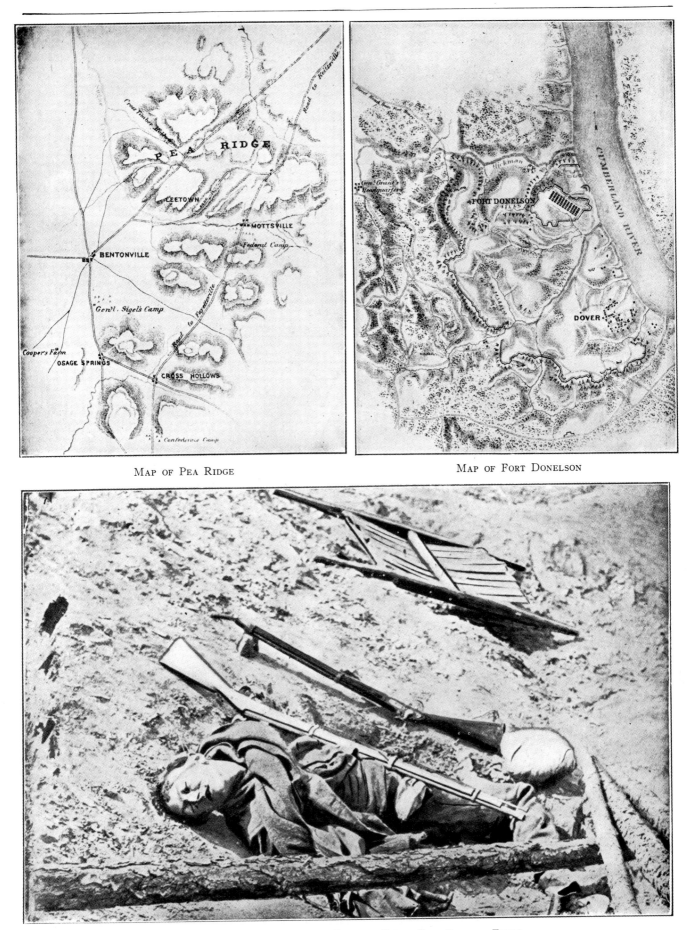

MAP OF PEA RIDGE

MAP OF FORT DONELSON

NO WORDS ARE NEEDED FOR THE STORY THIS PICTURE TELLS

advanced posts, and throw forward, along the line of the Nashville and Louisville Railway, a large force destined to break the Confederate line across the State. The whole number of troops under his command was one hundred and fourteen thousand, arranged in four columns, commanded respectively by Brigadier-Generals Alexander McDowell McCook, Ormsby M. Mitchell, George H. Thomas and Thomas L. Crittenden acting as major-generals, and aided by twenty brigade commanders. These troops, who were citizens of States northward of the Ohio River, with loyalists of Kentucky and Tennessee, occupied an irregular line across the first-named State, almost parallel with that of the Confederates.

General McCook was sent, with fifty thousand troops, down the railway toward Bowling Green, and pushed back the Confederate outposts to the south side of the Green River, at Mumfordsville, where a sharp contest occurred, when the insurgents were compelled to move on to Bowling Green. In the

GENERAL U. S. GRANT

meantime stirring events were occurring in eastern Kentucky. On the 7th of January (1862) a body of Confederates under Hum-phrey Marshall were struck by Union troops, infantry and cavalry, led by Colonel James A. Garfield, near Prestonburg, on the Big Sandy River. The Confed-erates were dispersed and disheartened, and there Marshall's military career ended. The gallant services rendered by Garfield on that occasion won for him the commission of a brig-adier-general. A few days later (January 19) a more important event occurred on the borders of the Cum-berland River, further west-ward, at Beech Grove, near Mill Spring. Near there General Zollicoffer had es-tablished a strongly in-trenched camp; but early in January he was super-seded in command by Gen-eral George B. Crittenden, his senior in rank. To Gen-eral Thomas was assigned the duty of attacking this force, and if successful there to push on over the Cum-berland Mountains, into East Tennessee, where the Secessionists were persecu-ting the Union people with-out stint. When he was within ten miles of the Con-federate camp, Thomas made preparations for bat-tle. The Confederates had marched to meet the Nationals. They were led by Zollicoffer, and at early dawn on the 18th of Jan-uary, the hostile troops met. A severe battle was fought, with great persistency on both sides, for the winner would gain an immense advantage for his cause. Thomas won the battle after a fierce contest, in which Zollicoffer was slain; and the discomfited Confederates fled into northeastern Tennessee, suffering intensely for lack of food and shelter in their flight across an almost barren-country.

This blow effectually severed the Confederate line in Kentucky, and opened the way for a series of successful movements by which the insurgents were soon driven out of that State, and also Tennessee. The loss of the Nationals was two hundred and forty-seven men; and of the Confederates, three hundred and forty-nine. The spoils of victory were twelve pieces of artillery, a large amount of munitions of war, and more than a thousand horses, with wagons, intrenching tools, camp equipage, etc. For their bravery in the battle of Mill Spring or Somerset, the President publicly thanked General Thomas and his men. They had paralyzed the power of the Confederate line eastward of Bowling Green, and shortened it full one-half. The bulk of the insurgents and their chief fortifications were then between Nashville and Bowling Green, and the Mississippi River. The defeat was severely felt by the Confederates. They perceived the urgent necessity for a bold, able, and dashing commander in the west, and supposing Beauregard to be such an one, he was ordered to Johnston's Department late in January (1862), and General G. W. Smith, who had been an active Democratic politician in New York City, was appointed to succeed him at Manassas.

The Confederates attributed their disaster at Mill Spring to the misconduct of the leader of the troops, General Crittenden. Some loudly accused him of treachery to the Confederate cause; while others, more charitable and better informed, charged his intemperate habits with the calamity. It was acknowledged by all to be an almost irretrievable misfortune.

When Beauregard left the army at Manassas, he issued a characteristic address to the troops,

GENERAL DAVID HUNTER

expressing a hope that he would be among them again, soon.   "I am anxious that my brave countrymen here in arms," he said, "fronting the haughty array and muster of Northern mercenaries, should thoroughly appreciate the exigency."   In allusion to the disquietude that was manifested by them because of their long enforced inaction, he said that it was no time for that army "to stack their arms, and furl, even for a brief period, the standards they had made glorious by their manhood."   But they were much dispirited by the defeat of their armies at Mill Spring, and this was deepened by the capture of Roanoke Island soon afterward.   This feeling amounted almost to despair when a more important reverse to their arms occurred on the Tennessee and Cumberland rivers at the middle of February.

CONTRABAND CAMP NEAR MANCHESTER, VA.

CHAPTER XV.

A Gunboat Fleet—Expedition against Forts Henry and Donelson—Capture of Forts Henry and Hieman—Naval Expedition up the Tennessee—Its Discoveries—Army Reorganized—Siege of Fort Donelson—Change in Temperature—Engagements on Land and Water—A Desperate Measure Attempted—Council of War—Cowardice—Surrender of Fort Donelson—Army Postal Service—Panic at Nashville—Surrender of the City—Provisional Government for Tennessee—Events on the Mississippi River—Siege and Capture of Island Number Ten—Movement toward Corinth—National Army at Pittsburg Landing—Buell's Army on the March.

WHEN the Confederate line in Kentucky was broken, the National Government determined to concentrate the forces of Halleck and Buell for a great forward movement to push the Confederates toward the Gulf of Mexico.   Fremont's plan for providing gunboats for the western rivers, to co-operate with the armies, had been carried out.   Twelve of these vessels (some of them covered with iron plates) had been constructed at St. Louis and Cairo, and at the close of January these were armed with one hundred and twenty-six heavy guns and some lighter artillery, and were placed under the command of flag-officer A. H. Foote of the National navy.   When everything was in readiness, some feints were made to deceive the Confederates.   These were reconnaissances down each side of the Mississippi River from Cairo; and Thomas feigned a movement in force against East Tennessee.

In the meantime an expedition against Fort Henry on the Tennessee River, and Fort Donelson on the Cumberland River, where those streams approach each other to within a distance of about twelve miles, had been prepared.   The land troops were placed under the command of General U. S. Grant, assisted by General C. F. Smith.   Commodore Foote was called to the Tennessee with his flotilla of gunboats; and at dawn on the 3d of February, 1862, a portion of that flotilla was only a few miles below Fort Henry, on that stream, and the land troops were disembarking from transports.   The fort lay at the bend of the stream, on the right bank, and its guns commanded a reach of the river for about two miles.   It was armed with seventeen guns, twelve of which could sweep the river.   At the time we are considering, the garrison in the fort and troops encamped around it numbered less than three thousand, commanded by General Tilghman, of Maryland, a graduate of the West Point Academy.   Grant and

THE INTELLIGENT CONTRABAND, "JOHN HENRY," A WELL-REMEMBERED SERVANT

CONFEDERATE WINTER QUARTERS, CENTREVILLE, VA., 1862

Foote had asked and obtained permission of Halleck to attack Fort Henry, and that was the task which they attempted on the morning of the 3d of February.

Both arms of the service proceeded to strike Fort Henry simultaneously. The land force was composed of the divisions of McClernand and Smith. The armed flotilla in hand consisted of the gunboats *Essex*, *St. Louis*, *Carondelet* and *Cincinnati*. The river below Fort Henry had been strewn with torpedoes, but these were successfully fished up before the attack. Opposite Fort Henry was Fort Hieman, situated upon a great hill, from which artillery might be brought to bear upon assailants of the former. To silence its batteries, a portion of the land troops went up that side of the river, while others proceeded to gain a point between Forts Henry and Donelson. The flotilla moved forward and opened the contest at noon on the 6th, and before the land troops could reach a position to co-operate, the fort, with its little garrison, had been surrendered to Foote. A tremendous rain-storm, with thunder and wind, which occurred the night before, had made the roads so heavy, and so swelled the little streams, that the march of the troops was difficult and slow. The garrison made a gallant defence; but at the end of one hour's conflict, they were compelled to strike their flag. Fort Hieman was also surrendered. This was a naval victory of great importance, because it proved the efficiency of gunboats on the narrow western rivers in co-operation with land forces. Therefore the fall of Fort Henry was hailed as a most happy omen of the success of the Union cause. Halleck telegraphed to McClellan: "Fort Henry is ours! the flag of the Union is re-established on the soil of Tennessee. It will never be removed!" The Secretary of the Navy wrote to Foote: "The country appreciates your gallant deeds; and this department desires to convey to you and your brave associates its profound thanks for the service you have rendered."

GENERAL JOHN A. LOGAN
GENERAL R. J. OGLESBY

This victory inflicted a severe blow upon the power of the Confederates. It gave to the Nationals the possession of formidable and important posts; also a firm footing in the vicinity of stronger Fort Donelson and in the rear of Columbus, on the Mississippi. There was now no obstacle to the river navy in its passage up the Tennessee to the fertile regions of northern Alabama toward the heart of the Confederacy. Thitherward Foote sent Lieutenant-Commander S. L. Phelps, on the night after the capture of the fort, with three vessels, to reconnoitre the borders of the river. Those vessels went steadily onward, seizing Confederate property, as far up as Florence, in Alabama, at the foot of the Mussel Shoals. The reconnaissance was a perfect success, for it discovered the weakness of the Confederacy in that region, and developed a most gratifying evidence of genuine Union feeling among the inhabitants of Tennessee which had been repressed by Confederate despotism. Phelps was assured that nothing but the dreadful reign of terror kept thousands from manifesting their love for the old flag. The report of Phelps's reconnaissance was very cheering, and it was determined to attack Fort Donelson, near Dover, the capital of Stewart County, Tennessee. It was a formidable work, situated with a front on the high left bank of the Cumberland River, among hills furrowed by deep ravines, and its irregular lines of outlying intrenchments covering about one hundred acres. General Grant reorganized his army in three divisions, under Generals McClernand, Smith, and Lewis Wallace; and Commodore Foote hurried back to Cairo with three of his gunboats to take his mortar-boats to the Cumberland River to assist in the attack on Fort Donelson.

The divisions of McClernand and Smith left Fort Henry on the morning of the 12th of February (1862), and marched for Fort Donelson, leaving Wallace with a brigade to hold the vanquished forts on the Tennessee. They invested Fort Donelson the same evening; and after some picket-firing the next morning, General Grant resolved to wait for the arrival of the flotilla (bearing troops that would complete Wallace's division) before making a general attack. On the same morning Ex-Secretary Floyd arrived from Virginia, with troops, and superseded General Pillow, who was in command of Fort Donelson. Floyd and Pillow were materially assisted by General S. B. Buckner, a better soldier than either of them, but he was subordinate to both of the inefficient commanders. All that day (February 13th) there was skirmishing, and toward evening an unexpected enemy appeared in the form of severe frost. The morning had dawned in uncommon splendor, and the air was as balmy as that of late spring; but toward evening a violent rain-storm arose, the temperature fell, and before morning the ground became frozen almost as hard as iron and everything was mailed in ice. The National troops were bivouacked without tents, and

Docks at Aquia Creek

they dared not light fires for fear of exposing themselves to the guns of the fort. They were without sufficient food and clothing, and their sufferings were so dreadful that they anxiously awaited the dawn and expected reinforcements.

BATTERY ON THE JAMES IN WINTER

General Grant perceived the peril of his situation, and had sent to General Wallace to bring his troops over from the Tennessee. The latter moved at daybreak on the 14th, the ground encrusted with frozen sleet and the air filled with drifting frost. These troops were in high spirits. With cheering and singing of songs they pressed forward, and at noon their commander dined with General Grant on crackers and coffee. Meantime the armored flotilla, with the transports, had arrived, and Wallace's division was perfected. It was immediately posted between the divisions of McClernand and Smith, and so the thorough investment of the fort was completed. At three o'clock that afternoon, the *Carondelet*, Captain Walke, began the assault on Fort Donelson, and was soon joined by the *St. Louis*, *Pittsburg*, and *Louisville*. Unarmored vessels formed a second line; and the flotilla boldly attacked the water-batteries, but without much effect. The mortar-boats had not arrived; and never were war-vessels exposed to a more tremendous pounding than were the four armored gunboats in this fight by missiles from the shore batteries. They received, in the aggregate, one hundred and forty wounds, and fifty-four men were killed or wounded. Foote was compelled to withdraw, when he hastened to Cairo to have damages repaired, and to bring up a competent naval force to assist in carrying on the siege. Grant resolved to await Foote's return and for expected reinforcements.

The night of the 14th was an anxious one for both parties. The Confederates, perceiving their peril, held a council of war. Floyd's opinion was that the fort was untenable with less than fifty thousand men to defend it; and that the garrison might be saved only by a *sortie* the next morning to rout or destroy the investing army, or to cut through it and escape to the open country in the direction of Nashville. This desperate measure was attempted at five o'clock on the morning of the 15th, by about ten thousand men, led by Pillow and Buckner, the former striking McClernand on the right of the Nationals, and the latter prepared to attack Wallace in the centre. Pillow had boasted that he would "roll the enemy in full retreat over upon Buckner, when the latter, attacking them on the flank and rear, would cut up the Federals and put them completely to rout." The attack was quick and furious; but the troops that first received the shock of battle (Oglesby's brigade), maintained their ground gallantly until their ammunition began to fail. Relief was sent, but the pressure was so great that the whole line gave way excepting the extreme left held by Colonel John A. Logan's Illinois regiment, which stood as firm as a wall and prevented a panic. The good service of the light batteries of Taylor, McAllister and Dresser, made the Confederate line recoil again and again. But fresh troops continually strengthened it, until at length the whole of McClernand's division were in great peril. Then he called upon Wallace for help, and it was given so effectually, that after a hard and skillful struggle on the part of the Nationals, with the Confederate forces of Buckner and Pillow combined, the latter were compelled to fall back to their trenches. "I speak advisedly," wrote Colonel Hillyer (Grant's aide-de-camp) to Wallace, the next day, "God bless you! You did save the day on the right."

In the meantime General Smith had been smiting the Confederate right such telling blows, that when darkness fell upon the scene, the Nationals were victorious and the vanquished Confederates were imprisoned within their trenches, unable to escape.

Finding themselves closely held by Grant, the question, "How shall we escape?" was a paramount one in the minds of the Confederates, especially of Floyd and Pillow. They were both terror-stricken by the impending danger of falling into the hands of their outraged Government. At midnight, Floyd, Pillow, and Buckner held a private council at Pillow's quarters in Dover,

CONFEDERATE "QUAKER" GUNS

where it was concluded that the garrison must be surrendered. "But, gentlemen," said Floyd nervously, "*I* cannot surrender; you know my position with the Federals; it won't do, it won't do." Pillow then

GROUP OF SCOUTS AND GUIDES

OFFICE OF ASSISTANT QUARTERMASTER

said: "I will not surrender myself nor my command—*will die first.*" "Then," said Buckner, coolly, "I suppose, gentlemen, the surrender will devolve upon me." The terrified Floyd said, quickly, "General, if you are put in command, will you allow me to take out, by the river, my brigade?" "If you will move

COMMODORE HENRY WALKE

before I offer to surrender," Buckner replied. "Then, sir," answered Floyd, "I surrender the command." Pillow, who was next in rank, and to whom Floyd offered to transfer the command, quickly exclaimed, "I will not accept it—I will never surrender." As he spoke he turned toward Buckner, when the latter, with the courage, the manliness and the honor of a soldier, said: "I will accept, and share the fate of my command."

Within one hour after that conference, Floyd, with a part of his Virginians, deserted his companions-in-arms and fled up the river, toward Nashville, in a steamboat. At the same time Pillow sneaked away in the darkness, after declaring he would "die" before he would surrender, and finally escaped to his home in Tennessee. History affords no meaner picture than this. The indignant authorities at Richmond suspended both the cowards from command; and an epigrammatist of the day wrote as follows concerning Floyd's escape:

"The thief is a coward by Nature's law;
    Who betrays the State, to no one is true:
And the brave foe at Donelson saw,
    Their light-fingered Floyd was light-footed too."

Early the next morning—the Christian Sabbath—Buckner asked for the appointment of commissioners to agree upon terms of surrender. Grant replied: "No terms other than unconditional and immediate surrender can be accepted. I propose to move immediately upon your works." This answer was followed by the speedy surrender of the fort, and of thirteen thousand five hundred men as prisoners of war; and the spoils of victory were three thousand horses, forty-eight field-pieces, seventeen heavy guns, twenty thousand muskets, and a large quantity of military stores. This catastrophe greatly dispirited the Confederates; and from the time when the fact became known in Europe, no court ever entertained an idea of recognizing the independence of the Southern Confederacy. It was estimated that during the siege the Confederates lost two hundred and thirty-seven killed and one thousand wounded. The estimated loss of the Nationals was four hundred and forty-six killed, seventeen hundred and fifty-five wounded, and one hundred and fifty who were made prisoners, and who, being sent across the river, were not recaptured.

The admirably arranged army mail-service was begun at Forts Henry and Donelson, under the auspices of General Grant, to whom it was suggested by Colonel A. H. Markland, special agent of the National Post-office. In the following letter to me, dated "July 30, 1866," General Grant gives a brief account of its origin:

"DEAR SIR—

"Among the subjects that occupied my mind when I assumed command at Cairo, in the fall of 1861, was the regular supply of mails to and from the troops; not only those in garrison, but those on the march when active movements should begin. When I commenced the movement on Fort Henry, on January 7, 1862, a plan was proposed by which the mails should promptly follow, and as promptly be sent from the army. So perfect was the organization that the mails were delivered to the army immediately upon its occupation of the fort. Within one hour after the troops began to march into Fort Donelson, the mail was being distributed to them from the mail wagons. The same promptness was always observed in the armies under my command, up to the

A BOW GUN

period of the final disbandment. It is a source of congratulation that the postal service was so conducted, that officers and men were in constant communication with kindred and friends at home, and with as

DECK OF GUNBOAT AND CREW

much regularity as the most favored in the large cities of the Union. The postal system of the army, so far as I know, was not attended with any additional expense to the service. The system adopted by me was suggested and ably superintended by A. H. Markland, special agent of the Post-office Department.

"Respectfully,　　"U. S. GRANT, *General.*"

The chaplain of each regiment was recognized at first as "Regimental Postmaster." Afterward, the mails were "brigaded." They were placed in canvas bags at the General Post-office and sent to each brigade, under charge of military authority. The Post-office Department had no further control of the army mails after they left the office at Washington city. The regularity with which the great armies of Grant, Sherman, Thomas and others in the West, as well as those in the Atlantic States, were supplied with mails, under the general superintendence of Colonel Markland, was marvelous. He and his assistants encountered dangers as appalling as those to which the soldiers were exposed—perils from bullets, fatigue and privations—yet they never lost a mail by capture, over which they had personal control. The mail was nearly always in advance of the armies, or moving in a direction to meet them. The number of letters thus carried was enormous. "For months," wrote Mr. S. J. Bowen, the Postmaster of Washington city, in a letter to me dated July 26, 1866, "we received and sent an average of

CONFEDERATE PRISONERS AT BELLE PLAIN

250,000 military letters per day. It is believed that this number was exceeded after General Sherman's army reached Savannah, and up to the time of the review of the troops in this city in the month of May, 1865." He says that the vast number of packages of clothing and articles of every kind which were sent by the mails, reached their destination as regularly as if the recipient lived in a large city. The only loss of any moment which this extra service inflicted upon the Post-office Department, was in mail-bags. "It is estimated," wrote Mr. Bowen, "that at least thirty thousand of these were sent out which never found their way back to this office, though every effort was made by us to have them returned." This army mail-service presents one of the moral wonders of the great conflict; and its value, in keeping whole armies in continual communication with friends at home, is incalculable. It was a powerful preventive of that terrible home-sickness with which, at first, raw troops are often prostrated; and it brought the sweet influence of the domestic circle to bear most powerfully in strengthening the men against the multifarious temptations of army life.

It was clearly perceived by General A. S. Johnston, that the fall of Fort Donelson rendered Bowling Green and Columbus untenable, and their evacuation was ordered to take place immediately. The troops at Bowling Green, who were menaced by the swiftly approaching advance of Buell's army under the energetic General Mitchel, were ordered to retire to Nashville. They did so, in haste, after destroying their property at Bowling Green valued at half a million dollars, and were followed by the *Army of the Ohio.* At the same time National gunboats ascended the Cumberland River and co-operated with troops marching on that place. These movements created a fearful panic among the Secessionists. The governor of Tennessee (Harris) was made almost crazy by alarm. He rode through the streets of Nashville, with

Provost Marshall's 3d Army Corps

Sutler's Camp, 50th New York Engineers

his horse at full speed, crying out that the papers in the Capitol must be removed, for he well knew what evidences of his treason they contained. He and his guilty compeers gathered as many of the archives as possible and fled by railway to Memphis, while officers of the banks in Nashville bore away the specie

PROFESSOR LOWE IN HIS BALLOON "INTREPID"
WATCHING BATTLE OF SEVEN PINES

from the vaults of those institutions. Citizens with their most valuable possessions that were portable, crowded the stations of railways that extended to Decatur and Chattanooga. Every kind of wheeled vehicle was brought into requisition, and the price of hack hire was raised to twenty-five dollars an hour. The authorities gave up all as lost. The public stores were thrown wide open, and everybody was allowed to carry off provisions and clothing without hindrance. The panic was more intense because of the sudden reaction from joy occasioned by a foolish boast of Pillow, on Saturday, that victory for the Confederates was sure. It was followed by a despatch from him while the armies were yet struggling and the Confederates had gained a slight advantage, in which he said: *"Enemy retreating! Glorious result! Our boys following and peppering their rear!! A complete victory!!"* The people were comfortably seated in the churches, and the ministers were prepared to preach congratulatory sermons, when the astounding news of the fall of Fort Donelson and the cowardly desertion of the post by Floyd and Pillow reached them. Pillow's act was a crushing commentary on his foolish boast, and the people pronounced his doom of disgrace before the authorities at Richmond had promulgated it.

Johnston and his troops moved rapidly southward from Nashville, and the city was surrendered to the Nationals by the municipal authorities, on the 26th of February, 1862. These events, following so closely upon the capture of Roanoke Island and the operations in its vicinity, produced great alarm throughout the Confederacy. The loyal people of the land were elated; and the Confederates being virtually expelled from Tennessee, the State government abdicated by its fugitive governor, and much latent loyalty being displayed, the National Government proceeded to re-establish civil government there. Andrew Johnson, of East Tennessee, was appointed provisional governor with the military rank of brigadier-general, and he entered upon his duties, at Nashville, on the 4th of March, 1862.

The Mississippi River now became the theatre of stirring events. Beauregard, as we have observed, had been sent West, and was now in command of troops on the borders of the mighty stream, above Memphis; and, obedient to orders from Richmond, he directed General Polk to evacuate Columbus, and transfer his troops and as much of the munitions of war as possible to places of greater safety. New Madrid, Madrid Bend, and Island Number Ten were chosen for this purpose. Meanwhile Commodore Foote had put in motion a fleet of gunboats on the Mississippi, and accompanying transports bore two thousand troops under General W. T. Sherman. When, on the 4th of March, this armament approached Columbus, the Union flag was seen floating there. It had been unfurled the previous evening by a scouting party of Illinois troops from Paducah, who found the fortifications deserted. Sherman left a garrison at Columbus, and Foote returned to Cairo to prepare for a siege of New Madrid and Island Number Ten, which constituted the key to the Lower Mississippi. The Confederates at the former place were commanded by General McCoun, and those on Island Number Ten were under the charge of General Beauregard, in person, who sent forth pompous proclamations to the inhabitants. He called for bells wherewith to make cannon, and there was a liberal response. "In some cities," wrote a Confederate soldier, "every church gave up its bells. Court-houses, public institutions, and plantations sent theirs. And the people furnished large quantities of old brass of every description—andirons, candlesticks, gas-fixtures, and even

REFUGEES

A Company of Zouaves and Band

door-knobs. I have seen wagon-loads of these lying at depots waiting shipment to the foundries." They were all sent to New Orleans. There they were found by General Butler, who sent them to Boston, where they were sold at auction.

General Pope, dispatched from St. Louis by General Halleck, drove the Confederates from New

CONFEDERATE MAGAZINE, YORKTOWN

Madrid on the night of the 13th of March. They fled to Island Number Ten, which then became the chief object of attack by the Nationals. Beauregard had thoroughly fortified it, and Foote attacked it with heavy guns and mortars on the morning of the 16th of March. The siege went on with varying fortunes for both parties until early in April. While Foote was pounding and rending the fortifications of Beauregard, Pope at New Madrid was chafing with impatience to participate in the siege. His guns easily blockaded the river (there a mile wide, and then flowing at the rate of seven or eight miles an hour); but he desired to cross it to the peninsula and attack the Island in the rear, and so insure its capture with its dependencies, their garrisons and munitions of war. But the Tennessee shore was lined with batteries garnished with heavy guns; and until these could be silenced, it would be madness to attempt to cross the river with any means at Pope's command. Pope was at his wits' end, when General Schuyler Hamilton made the extraordinary proposition to cut a canal from the bend of the Mississippi, near Island Number Eight, across the neck of a swampy peninsula, to the vicinity of New Madrid, of sufficient capacity to allow the passage of gunboats and transports, and thereby effectually flank Island Number Ten, and insure its capture. Hamilton offered to do the work with his division of soldiers, and to have it completed in the space of a fortnight. Pope sanctioned the measure, and it was performed in nineteen days under the direction of Colonel Bissell of the Engineers. The labor was most fatiguing. The canal was twelve miles long, one-half the distance through a growth of heavy timber, where a way was made, fifty feet wide, by sawing off trees in some places four feet under water.

Meanwhile Foote had not been idle, but made preparations for closer assaults than the long reach of great guns and mortars afforded. On the night of the first of April an expedition composed of Illinois troops and seamen, to the number of one hundred, proceeded to take one of the seven formidable redoubts on the Kentucky shore, and were successful. This daring feat was followed, on the night of the 3d, by another. Pope had frequently called upon Foote to send gunboats to his assistance. At length the gallant Captain Walke, of the *Carondelet*, obtained permission of his commander to attempt to run by the Confederate batteries with his vessel. The feat was successfully performed at midnight while a fearful thunder-storm was raging. The flashes of lightning revealed her passage to the commanders of

batteries on the shore, and she was compelled to run the gauntlet of a tremendous cannonade from them all. The *Carondelet* did not return a shot. Only after she had reached a place of safety below were her guns heard; then three of them announced to anxious Commodore Foote that she had escaped all perils. She was welcomed by the troops at New Madrid with wildest huzzas.

Perceiving the peril that awaited them when the canal should be completed, the Confederates sunk steamboats in the channel of the river to prevent gunboats descending it, and they unsuccessfully attempted to escape. After the *Carondelet* had passed the batteries, Beauregard was satisfied that the siege must end in disaster and he was not disposed to bear the responsibility.

BATTERY MAGRUDER, C. S. A., YORKTOWN

Scenes at Yorktown

CHRONOLOGICAL SUMMARY AND RECORD—Continued

MAY, 1863—Continued from Section 7

21—Middleton, Tenn. 4th Mich., 3d Ind., 7th Pa., 3d and 4th Ohio and 4th U. S. Cav., 39th Ind. Mounted Inft. Casualties not recorded.

25—Near Helena, Ark. 3d Iowa and 5th Kan. Cav. *Union* 10 killed, 14 wounded.

27—Lake Providence, La. 47th U. S. Colored. *Union* 1 killed, 1 wounded.

27 to July 9—Siege of Port Hudson, La. *Union* 500 killed, 2,500 wounded. *Confed.* 100 killed, 700 wounded, 6,408 prisoners. *Union* Brig.-Gens. W. T. Sherman and H. E. Paine wounded.

JUNE, 1863

4—Franklin, Tenn. 85th Ind., 7th Ky. Cav., 4th and 6th Ky. Cav., 9th Pa. Cav., 2d Mich. Cav. *Union* 25 killed and wounded. *Confed.* 200 killed and wounded.

5—Franklin's Crossing, Rappahannock River, Va. 26th N. J., 5th Vt., 15th and 50th N. Y. Engineers, supported by 6th Corps. *Union* 6 killed, 35 wounded.

6 to 8—Milliken's Bend, La. 23d Iowa and three regts. colored troops. (No quarter shown.) *Union* 154 killed, 223 wounded, 115 missing. *Confed.* 125 killed, 400 wounded, 200 missing.

9—Monticello and Rocky Gap, Ky. 2d and 7th Ohio Cav., 1st Ky. Cav., 45th Ohio and 2d Tenn. Mounted Inft. *Union* 4 killed, 26 wounded. *Confed.* 20 killed, 80 wounded.

Beverly Ford and Brandy Station, Va. 2d, 3d, and 7th Wis., 2d and 33d Mass., 6th Maine, 86th and 104th N. Y., 1st, 2d, 5th, and 6th U. S. Cav., 2d, 6th, 8th, 9th, and 10th N. Y. Cav., 1st, 6th, and 17th Pa. Cav., 1st Md., 8th Ill., 3d Ind., 1st N. J., 1st Maine Cav. and 1st W. Va. Cav. *Union* 500 killed, wounded, and missing. *Confed.* 700 killed, wounded, and missing.

11—Middleton, Va. 87th Pa., 13th Pa. Cav., Battery L, 5th U. S. Artil. *Confed.* 8 killed, 42 wounded.

13 and 15—Winchester, Va. 2d, 67th, and 87th Pa., 18th Conn., 12th W. Va., 110th, 116th, 122d, and 123d Ohio, 3d, 5th, and 6th Md., 12th and 13th Pa. Cav., 1st N. Y. Cav., 1st and 3d W. Va. Cav., Battery L 5th U. S. Artil., 1st W. Va. Battery, Baltimore Battery, one Co. 14th Mass. Heavy Artil. *Union* 3,000 killed, wounded, and missing. *Confed.* 850 killed, wounded, and missing.

14—Martinsburg, Va. 106th N. Y., 126th Ohio, W. Va. Battery. *Union* 200 missing. *Confed.* 1 killed, 2 wounded.

16—Triplett's Bridge, Ky. 15th Mich., 10th and 14th Ky. Cav., 7th and 9th Mich. Cav., 11th Mich. Battery. *Union* 15 killed, 30 wounded.

17—Aldie, Va. Kilpatrick's Cavalry. *Union* 24 killed, 41 wounded, 89 missing. *Confed.* 100 killed.

Westport, Mo. Two Cos. 9th Kan. *Union* 14 killed, 6 wounded.

Capture of rebel gunboat *Atlanta* by U. S. ironclad *Weehawken.* *Confed.* 1 killed, 17 wounded, 145 prisoners.

20—Rocky Crossing, Miss. 5th Ohio Cav., 9th Ill. Mounted Inft. *Union* 7 killed, 28 wounded, 30 missing.

20 and 21—La Fourche Crossing, La. Detachments 23d Conn., 176th N. Y., 26th, 42d, and 47th Mass., 21st Ind. *Union* 8 killed, 40 wounded. *Confed.* 53 killed, 150 wounded.

21—Upperville, Va. Pleasanton's Cavalry. *Union* 94 wounded. *Confed.* 20 killed, 100 wounded, 60 missing.

22—Hill's Plantation, Miss. Detachment of 4th Iowa Cav. *Union* 4 killed, 10 wounded, 28 missing.

23—Brashear City, La. Detachments of 114th and 176th N. Y., 23d Conn., 42d Mass., 21st Ind. *Union* 46 killed, 40 wounded, 300 missing. *Confed.* 3 killed, 18 wounded.

23 to 30—Rosecrans' Campaign. Murfreesboro to Tullahoma, Tenn., including Middleton, Hoover's Gap, Beech Grove, Liberty Gap, and Gray's Gap. Army of the Cumberland: Fourteenth, Twentieth, and Twenty-first Corps, Granger's Reserve Corps, and Stanley's Cavalry. *Union* 85 killed, 462 wounded. *Confed.* 1,634 killed, wounded, and captured.

28—Donaldsonville, La. 28th Maine and convalescents, assisted by gunboats. *Confed.* 39 killed, 112 wounded, 150 missing.

29—Westminster, Md. Detachments 1st Del. Cav. *Union* 2 killed, 7 wounded. *Confed.* 3 killed, 15 wounded.

30—Hanover, Pa. Cavalry Corps. *Union* 12 killed, 43 wounded. *Confed.* 75 wounded, 60 missing.

JULY, 1863

1 to 3—Gettysburg, Pa. Army of the Potomac, Maj.-Gen. Geo. G. Meade First Corps, Maj. Gen. Reynolds; Second Corps, Maj.-Gen. Hancock Third Corps, Maj.-Gen. Sickles; Sixth Corps, Maj.-Gen. Sedgwick; Eleventh Corps, Maj.-Gen. Howard; Twelfth Corps, Maj.-Gen. Slocum; Cavalry Corps, Maj.-Gen. Pleasanton. *Union* 2,834 killed, 13,709 wounded, 6,643 missing. *Confed.* 3,500 killed, 14,500 wounded, 13,621 missing. *Union* Maj.-Gen. Reynolds, Brig.-Gens. Weed, Zook, and Farnsworth killed; Maj.-Gens. Sickles and Hancock, Brig.-Gens. Paul, Rowley, Gibbons, and Barlow wounded. (Gen. Lucius Fairchild, Commander-in-Chief Grand Army of the Republic, lost his arm on the first day.) *Confed.* Maj.-Gen. Pender, Brig.-Gens. Gurnett, Barksdale, and Semmes killed; Maj.-Gens. Hood, Trimble, and Heth, Brig.-Gens. Kemper, Scales, Anderson, Hampton, Jones, Jenkins, Pettigrew, and Posey wounded.

1 to 26—Morgan's raid into Kentucky, Indiana, and Ohio, finally captured at New Lisbon, Ohio, by Brig.-Gen. Shackleford's Cavalry. *Union* 22 killed, 80 wounded, 790 missing. *Confed.* 86 killed, 385 wounded, 3,000 captured.

4—Helena, Ark. Maj.-Gen. Prentiss's Division of Sixteenth Corps and gunboat *Tyler.* *Union* 57 killed, 117 wounded, 32 missing. *Confed.* 173 killed, 687 wounded, 776 missing.

4 and 5—Bolton and Birdsong Ferry, Miss. Maj.-Gen. Sherman's forces. *Confed.* 2,000 captured.

4 and 5—Monterey Gap and Smithsburg, Md., and Fairfield, Pa. Kilpatrick's Cavalry. *Union* 30 killed and wounded. *Confed.* 30 killed and wounded, 100 prisoners.

5—Lebanon, Ky. 20th Ky. *Union* 9 killed, 15 wounded, 400 missing. *Confed.* 3 killed, 6 wounded.

6—Quaker Bridge, N. C. 17th, 23d, and 27th Mass., 9th N. J., 81st and 158th N. Y., Belger's and Angel's Batteries.

Hagerstown and Williamsport, Md. Kilpatrick's Cavalry.

7 and 9—Iuka, Miss. 10th Mo. and 7th Kan. Cav. *Union* 5 killed, 3 wounded.

7 to 9—Boonsboro, Md. Buford's and Kilpatrick's Cavalry. *Union* 9 killed, 45 wounded.

9 to 16—Jackson, Miss., including engagements at Rienzi, Bolton Depot, Canton, and Clinton. 9th, 13th, 15th, and part of 16th Corps. *Union* 100 killed, 800 wounded, 100 missing. *Confed.* 71 killed, 504 wounded, 764 missing.

10 to Sept. 6—Siege of Fort Wagner. Morris Island, S. C. Troops Department of the South, under command of Maj.-Gen. Gilmore, and U. S. Navy under Admiral Dahlgren. *Union* 1,757 killed, wounded, and missing. *Confed.* 561 killed, wounded, and missing.

12—Ashby Gap, Va. 2d Mass. Cav. *Union* 2 killed, 8 wounded.

13—Yazoo City, Miss. Maj.-Gen. Herron's Division and three gunboats. *Confed.* 250 captured.

Jackson, Tenn. 9th Ill., 3d Mich. Cav., 2d Iowa Cav., and 1st Tenn. Cav. *Union* 2 killed, 20 wounded. *Confed.* 38 killed, 150 wounded.

Donaldsonville, La. Portions of Weitzel's and Grover's Divisions, Nineteenth Corps. *Union* 450 killed, wounded, and missing.

13 to 15—Draft riots in New York City, in which over 1,000 rioters were killed.

14—Falling Waters, Md. 3d Cav. Division Army of the Potomac. *Union* 29 killed, 36 wounded. *Confed.* 125 killed and wounded, 1,500 prisoners. *Confed.* Maj.-Gen. Pettigrew killed.

14—Elk River, Tenn. Advance of the Fourteenth Corps Army of the Cumberland. *Union* 10 killed, 30 wounded. *Confed.* 60 killed, 24 wounded, 100 missing.

Near Bolivar Heights, Va. 1st Conn. Cav. *Confed.* 25 killed.

15—Pulaski, Ala. 3d Ohio and 5th Tenn. Cav. *Confed.* 3 killed, 50 missing.

Halltown, Va. 16th Pa. and 1st Maine Cav. *Union* 25 killed and wounded. *Confed.* 20 killed and wounded.

16—Sheppardstown, Va. 1st, 4th, and 16th Pa., 10th N. Y. and 1st Maine Cav. *Confed.* 25 killed, 75 wounded.

17—Honey Springs, Ind. Ter. 2d, 6th, and 9th Kan. Cav., 2d and 3d Kan. Batteries, 2d and 3d Kan. Indian Home Guards. *Union* 17 killed. 60 wounded. *Confed.* 150 killed, 400 wounded.

Wytheville, W. Va. 34th Ohio, 1st and 2d W. Va. Cav. *Union* 17 killed, 61 wounded. *Confed.* 75 killed, 125 missing.

Canton, Miss. 76th Ohio, 25th and 31st Iowa, 3d, 13th and 17th Mo., 2d Wis. Cav., 5th Ill. Cav., 3d and 4th Iowa Cav., one battery of artillery. Casualties not recorded.

18 to 21—Potter's Cavalry Raid to Tar River and Rocky Mount, N. C. 3d and 12th N. Y. Cav., 1st N. C. Cav. *Union* 60 wounded.

18 to 26—Morgan's Raid into Kentucky, Indiana, and Ohio pursued and captured by Brig.-Gens. Hobson and Shackleford's Cavalry, including skirmishes at Burkesville, Columbia, Green River Bridge, Lebanon, and Bradenburg, Ky., Corydon and Vernon, Ind., capture of the larger part at Buffington Island, Ohio, and final capture at New Lisbon, Ohio, on the 26th. *Union* 33 killed, 97 wounded, 805 missing. *Confed.* 795 killed and wounded, 4,104 captured.

21 to 23—Manassas Gap and Chester Gap, Va. Cavalry advance and Third Corps Army of the Potomac. *Union* 35 killed, 102 wounded. *Confed.* 300 killed and wounded.

26—Pattacassey Creek, N. C. Brig.-Gen. Heckman's troops. *Union* 3 killed, 17 wounded.

30—Irvine, Ky. 14th Ky. Cav. *Union* 4 killed, 5 wounded. *Confed.* 7 killed, 18 wounded.

AUGUST, 1863

1 to 3—Rappahannock Station, Brandy Station, and Kelly's Ford, Va. Brig.-Gen. Buford's Cav. *Union* 16 killed, 134 wounded.

3—Jackson, La. 73d, 75th, and 78th U. S. Colored Troops. *Union* 2 killed, 2 wounded, 27 missing.

5—Dutch Gap, James River, Va. U. S. Gunboats *Commodore Barney* and *Cohassett.* *Union* 3 killed, 1 wounded.

7—New Madrid, Mo. One company 24th Mo. *Union* 1 killed, 1 wounded.

9—Sparta, Tenn. Cavalry Army of the Cumberland. *Union* 6 killed, 25 wounded.

13—Grenada, Miss. 9th Ill., 2d Iowa Cav., 3d Mich. Cav., 3d, 4th, 9th, and 11th Ill. Cav. Casualties not recorded.

Pineville, Mo. 6th Mo. Militia. *Confed.* 65 wounded.

14—West Point, White River, Ark. 32d Iowa, with U. S. Gunboats *Lexington*, *Cricket*, and *Mariner.* *Union* 2 killed, 7 wounded.

21—Quantrell's plunder and massacre of Lawrence, Kansas, in which 140 citizens were killed and 24 wounded. *Confed.* 40 killed.

Coldwater, Miss. 3d and 4th Iowa Cav., 5th Ill. Cav. *Union* 10 wounded.

24—Coyle Tavern, near Fairfax C. H., Va. 2d Mass. Cav. *Union* 2 killed, 4 wounded.

25 to 30—Averill's Raid in W. Va. *Union* 3 killed, 10 wounded, 60 missing.

26—Rocky Gap, near White Sulphur Springs, Va. 3d and 8th W. Va., 2d and 3d W. Va. Cav., 14th Pa. Cav. *Union* 16 killed, 113 wounded. *Confed.* 156 killed and wounded.

25 to 31—Brownsville, Bayou Metoe and Austin, Ark. Davidson's Cavalry. *Union* 13 killed, 72 wounded.

SEPTEMBER, 1863

1—Barbee's Cross Roads, Va. Detachment 6th Ohio Cav. *Union* 2 killed, 4 wounded.

Devil's Back Bone, Ark. 1st Ark., 6th Mo. Militia, 2d Kan. Cav., 2d Ind. Battery. *Union* 4 killed, 12 wounded. *Confed.* 25 killed, 40 wounded.

(Continued in Section 9)

COPYRIGHT, 1912 BY THE WAR MEMORIAL ASSOCIATION

GRANT IN THE WILDERNESS, MAY 5, 1864

SHERIDAN AT FIVE FORKS   APRIL 1, 1865

SHERMAN AT KENESAW MOUNTAIN, OCTOBER 4, 1864

THOMAS AT CHICKAMAUGA, SEPTEMBER 20, 1863

HOOKER AT CHANCELLORSVILLE, MAY 3, 1863

MEADE AT GETTYSBURG, JULY 2, 1863

McCLELLAN AT ANTIETAM, SEPTEMBER 17, 1862

BURNSIDE AT FREDERICKSBURG, DECEMBER 13, 1862

BATTLE OF SHILOH, APRIL 6 AND 7, 1862

SIEGE OF VICKSBURG. MAY 18 TO JULY 4, 1863

COPYRIGHT, 1888, BY L. PRANG & CO., BOSTON

SIEGE OF VICKSBURG

BATTLE OF GETTYSBURG, JULY 1 TO 3, 1863

SIEGE OF ATLANTA

SIEGE OF ATLANTA. JULY 28 TO SEPTEMBER 2, 1864

FARRAGUT ON THE HARTFORD AT MOBILE BAY, AUGUST 5, 1864

KEARSARGE SINKING THE ALABAMA, JUNE 19, 1864

BATTLE OF SPOTTSYLVANIA.

BATTLE OF SPOTTSYLVANIA. MAY 8 TO 21, 1864

COPYRIGHT 1887, BY L. PRANG & CO., BOSTON

First Iron Clad Gunboat Built in America. Built for the Quartermaster's Department, Armed, Supplied, Officered and Manned by the Army and Navy Jointly. After the Capture of Forts King and Donelson, Island No. 10 and Memphis, It Was Transferred to the Navy Department. This note given by General M. C. Meigs.

CHAPTER XV.—Continued.

AFTER turning over the command on the Island to General McCall, and leaving the troops on the Kentucky and Tennessee shores in charge of General McCoun, Beauregard, with a considerable number of the best soldiers, departed for Corinth to check a formidable movement of National troops through middle Tennessee toward northern Alabama and Mississippi. McCall, on assuming the command, issued

a flaming proclamation; but within thirty-six hours he and his troops prepared to escape from the Island. They were interrupted in their movements by General Pope's forces under Generals Stanley, Hamilton, and Paine; and Island Number Ten, with the troops, batteries and supports on the main, were surrendered to the Nationals on the 8th of April. Over seven thousand men were surrendered prisoners of war; and the spoils of victory were one hundred and twenty-three cannons and mortars, seven thousand small arms, many hundred horses and mules, four steamboats afloat, and a very large amount of ammunition.

The fall of Island Number Ten was a calamity to the Confederacy from which it never recovered. It produced widespread alarm in the Southern States; for it appeared probable that Memphis, one of their strongholds on the Mississippi, where they had immense workshops and armories, would soon share the fate of Columbus, and that National war-vessels would speedily patrol the great river from Cairo to New Orleans. Martial law was proclaimed at Memphis, and the specie in the banks there was taken to places of supposed safety. Troops that guarded the city and panic-stricken residents proposed to lay the town in ashes if it could

COMMODORE A. H. FOOTE, U. S. N.   not be saved from "northern invaders." The zeal of these madmen was cooled by the sensible Mayor Park, who publicly proclaimed that "he who attempts to fire his neighbor's house, or even his own whereby it endangers his neighbor's, regardless of judge, jury, or the benefit of clergy, I will have him hung to the first lamp-post, tree, or awning." At Vicksburg, preparations were made for flight, and the disloyal inhabitants of New Orleans were oppressed with fearful forebodings of impending calamity. The governor of Louisiana, who was a leading Secessionist, issued a despairing appeal to the people. "An insolent and powerful foe is already at the castle gate," he said. "The current of the mighty river speaks to us of his fleets advancing for our destruction, and the telegraph wires tremble with the news of his advancing columns. In the name of all most dear to us, I entreat you to go and meet him." But there was little disposition to comply with the governor's wishes; and when a letter from Beauregard, which he sent by his surgeon-general, making an urgent demand for New Orleans to send five thousand troops to him, at once, "to save the city," was read to the First and Second City Brigades, who were called out, their reply was, "We decline to go." Their city then needed defenders below instead of above it.

It seemed as if the plan devised by Fremont was about to be successfully carried out. Curtis had already broken the military power of the Confederacy west of the Mississippi, at the battle of Pea Ridge; and a heavy force was then making its way up the Tennessee toward Alabama and Mississippi, and had, at the moment of the surrender of the famous Island, achieved a most important victory on the left bank of that stream not a score of miles from Corinth. Curtis, after the battle and the flight of the vanquished Confederates, finding no enemy to fight in that region, gave his army ample time to rest, and then marched in a southeasterly direction toward the Mississippi River and encamped at Batesville, the capital of Independence county, Arkansas, on the White River.

After the capture of Fort Donelson, General Grant had prepared to push toward Corinth, an important position on the line of the Charleston and Memphis Railway. Troops had been sent up the Tennessee River; and finally, at the beginning of April, the main body of Grant's army were encamped between Pittsburgh Landing, on the left bank of that stream, and the Shiloh Meeting-House, the latter in the forest two miles from the river. The grand objective was Corinth. There the Mobile and Ohio Railway intersected the Charleston and Memphis

COMMANDER C. S. BOGGS, U. S. N.

General M. C. Meigs

GENERAL T. W. SHERMAN

roads. The seizure of that point, as a strategic position of vital importance, was Grant's design. It would give the National forces control of the great railway communication between the Mississippi and the East, and the border slave-labor States and the Gulf of Mexico. It would also facilitate the capture of Memphis, toward the accomplishment of which Foote was now bending his energies, and it would add strength to the movements of Curtis in Arkansas.

In the meantime General Buell's army had slowly made preparations to march southward and join Grant's forces, which were, at first, encamped at Savannah, on the right bank of the Tennessee; but it was not until near the close of March, when Grant's position had become really perilous, that Buell left Nashville. He sent part of his force under General Mitchel in the direction of Huntsville, in northern Alabama, to seize and hold the Charleston and Memphis Railway; while the main body, composed of the divisions of Generals Thomas, McCook, Nelson, Crittenden and T. J. Wood, moved more to the westward by way of Columbia, at which place the troops left the railway and marched slowly toward the Tennessee River.

CHAPTER XVI.

The Nationals and Confederates at Shiloh—Battle of Shiloh: Its Events and Results—The Confederate Retreat to Corinth—Siege and Capture of Corinth—General Mitchel's Raid into Alabama—Recovered Territory—Raid upon a Railway—Capture of Memphis—Capture of New Berne and Fort Macon—Events on the Coast of North Carolina—Siege and Capture of Fort Pulaski—Conquests on the Southern Coasts—Expedition against New Orleans—Capture of Forts on the Mississippi—Destruction of the Confederate Flotilla—Seizure of New Orleans—Hatred of General Butler.

GENERAL BEAUREGARD, who had left Island Number Ten with a considerable body of Confederate troops, and had hastened to Corinth to prepare for resisting the grand movement of the Nationals southward, now confronted the latter near Shiloh Meeting-House with a very large force. He had been joined by the troops under General A. S. Johnston that fled from Nashville, and that officer was now Beauregard's chief lieutenant, assisted by Generals Polk, Hardee, Bragg, and Breckenridge. With these expert leaders, the Confederates came up from Corinth in a heavy rain-storm in separate columns, and concentrated a few miles from Shiloh Meeting-House. They came so stealthily that they were within four miles of the National camp before they were discovered by Grant's sentinels. There they halted on the 5th of April, 1862, to await the arrival of Van Dorn and Price, who were approaching Memphis with a large force from central Arkansas. Already the Confederate army of eleven thousand men at Corinth a short time before had increased to forty thousand men.

Intelligence came of Buell's march to join Grant, and on the evening of the 5th it was resolved to strike the Nationals before the dawn next morning, for it was evident the latter were not aware of the near presence of the strong force of the Confederates. At a council of war that made this decision, Beauregard, pointing toward the Union army, said: "Gentlemen, we sleep in the enemy's camp to-morrow night." At that time General W. T. Sherman's division was lying in the woods near Shiloh Meeting-House. General Prentiss's division was planted across the road leading directly to Corinth, and General McClernand's division was behind Prentiss's right. In the rear of these and between them and Pittsburg Landing lay General Hurlburt's division, and that of General Smith led by General W. H. L. Wallace. General David Stuart's brigade of Sherman's division lay upon a road leading to Hamburg, above Pittsburg Landing, and General Lewis Wallace, with his division, was at Crump's Landing, several miles below, observing Confederate movements at Purdy, and covering the river connections between Pittsburg Landing

GENERAL S. A. HURLBURT

GENERALS BURNSIDE, HANCOCK AND STAFF OFFICERS

GENERAL FITZJOHN PORTER AND STAFF AT HARRISON'S LANDING, AUGUST, 1862

COLONEL LOCKE (Standing), MAJOR KIRKLAND (Sitting), MAJOR MONTEITH, GENERAL FITZJOHN PORTER, DOCTOR MCMILLAN, CAPTAIN MCQUADE, COLONEL NORTON, CAPTAIN MASSA

and Savannah. To the latter place General Halleck forwarded supplies for the National army. So little was an attack by the Confederates suspected, that no intrenchments had been cast up by the Nationals, and Buell's army was marching leisurely across Tennessee.

Almost the first intimation of the near presence of the Confederates was the wild cry of pickets flying into camp and a sharp attack upon Sherman's troops by Hardee's division, before the day had fairly dawned on Sunday morning, the 6th of April. Some of the officers were slumbering; some were dressing; a portion of the troops were washing and cooking, and others were eating breakfast. Screaming shells crashed through the forest, and bullets whistled among the tents. Hardee's troops poured into the camp of the bewildered Nationals, fighting desperately, driving half-dressed and half-armed troops before them,

GENERAL U. S. GRANT

and dealing death and terror on every hand. Fearful results followed. Prentiss's division was next attacked. His column was shattered; himself and a large portion of his followers were made prisoners, and his camp was occupied by the Confederates. The struggle soon became general, and for ten hours the battle raged, with varying fortunes on both sides. General W. H. L. Wallace of the Nationals and General Johnston of the Confederates had been killed, and the slaughter on both sides had been severe. The National army was pushed back to the Tennessee River, then brimfull with a spring flood, and the Union troops. The victorious Confederates occupied all the Union camps excepting that of the slain Wallace, where General McArthur was now in command. In the rear of this division the smitten army had now gathered in a space not more than four hundred acres in extent, on the verge of the river. They could be pushed back no further; and so certain was General Beauregard of his final triumph, that he telegraphed a shout of victory to headquarters at Richmond. General Grant had directed the storm on the National side with great skill, but his forces, at twilight, were in a most perilous position. A single vigorous blow, then given by Beauregard, might have justified his shout of victory; but he dealt a feeble one, that was parried by the guns of two boats, the Tyler and Lexington, which had just appeared, and by those of a hastily formed battery on the shore.

Grant's safety was fully assured when, at evening, the van of the slow-moving army of Buell appeared on the opposite shore of the Tennessee, and other portions of it came up the river during the night. At midnight General Lewis Wallace arrived with his division, and then the palm of victory was snatched from the hands of Beauregard.

In the morning twilight of the 7th, Wallace opened the contest anew on the Confederate left, where Beauregard commanded in person. Others soon joined in the battle, and it became general all along the line. The Confederates fought gallantly, but were speedily pushed back by a superior force; and when they perceived that all was lost, they fled, under a storm of blinding sleet and cold rain, to the heights of Monterey in the direction of Corinth. They were covered, in their retreat, by a rear-guard of twelve thousand men, commanded by Ex-President Breckenridge. The Confederates had lost over ten thousand men in the engagement, of whom full three thousand died during the retreat of nine miles. Fifteen thousand Nationals were killed, wounded, or made prisoners. The slain on the battle-field were soon buried, the dead horses were burnt, and the hospital-vessels sent down the Tennessee by the Nationals were crowded with the sick and maimed. Beauregard's shattered army fell back to Corinth, and Grant was about to pursue and capture it, when General Halleck, his superior in rank, who had come up from St. Louis and took the supreme command, caused the impatient troops to loiter until the Confederates, recuperated, were prepared for another contest.

Twenty days after the battle, Halleck and his army had advanced nine miles toward Corinth; and a week later (May 3) they were near that place, making vigorous use of pickaxe and spade in piling up

ADMIRAL DAVID D. PORTER

fortifications for prosecuting a siege. This labor continued twenty-seven days longer, interrupted by frequent sorties from Corinth, when the Confederates were driven from their advanced batteries, and Halleck prepared for a sanguinary conflict the next day. The Confederates had been much strengthened by delay; but Beauregard was not disposed to fight the *Grand Army of the Tennessee*, as it was now called. All the night of the 29th of May, the National sentinels had heard and reported the unceasing roar of moving cars at Corinth; and at daybreak, just as Halleck sent out skirmishers to "feel the enemy," the earth was shaken by a series of explosions, and dense columns of smoke rose above the town. There was no enemy to "feel." Beauregard had evacuated Corinth during the night, burnt and blown up whatever of stores he could not carry away, and fled, in haste, to Tupelo, many miles southward from Corinth, where he left General Bragg in command, and retired to mineral springs in Alabama, for the restoration of his impaired health. Halleck took possession of Corinth, and was soon afterward called to Washington to perform the duties of General-in-Chief of all the armies of the Republic. He left General

Thomas in command at enlarged powers. General Corinth, and General Grant of his old army, with Buell was ordered to join Grant.

When General Buell energetic General Mitchel left the more cautious Buell, pushed on vigorously. On sixty miles from Nashville, There he left the railway, train, he crossed the State Huntsville on the morning up the railway at each end into the place. The unsus-the horses' hoofs in the tants, wrote an eye-witness, dow, exclaiming, with ing tongue, 'They come! come!' Men rushed into

moved from Nashville to meet Grant, he sent the southward, as we have observed. After Mitchel his was a sort of independent command, and he the 4th of April, he was at Shelbyville, Tennessee, where he established a depository of supplies. and after rapid marches with a light supply-line on the 10th into Alabama, and was in front of of the 11th before the dawn. Fatigue parties tore of the town, while the cavalry marched directly picious sleepers were awakened by the clatter of streets. The surprise was complete. The inhabi-

GENERAL R. S. EWELL, C. S. A.

women fainted, the children screamed, the time a scene of perfect terror reigned." The tory were seventeen locomotives, more than a a large amount of supplies of every kind; also one By it Mitchel secured the control of the Charles-from Tuscumbia on the west to Stevenson on the hundred miles. He also won the control of the the same distance. Mitchell met with no

This work was accomplished without the when Corinth fell into the possession of the Na-June, all Kentucky, western and middle Ten-sissippi and northern Alabama, were recovered was confidently expected that East Tennessee leased from the power of the insurgents; but

GENERAL EDW. J. JOHNSTON, C. S. A.

"flocked to door and win-blanched cheek and falter-they come! the Yankees the streets half-dressed, the darkies laughed, and for a spoils of this bloodless vic-hundred passenger cars, and hundred and sixty prisoners. ton and Memphis Railway east, a distance of about one Tennessee River for about resistance.

loss of a single man; and tionals at the beginning of nessee, and northern Mis-from the Confederates. It would be immediately re-General Buell, who had now

joined Mitchel, would not listen to the earnest entreaties of that officer, to add that loyal and sorely oppressed region to the emancipated territory. The way had been prepared by General Negley and others. Negley had climbed over the almost impassable mountains northeast of Stevenson, driven the Confederates from Jasper (June 7), and appeared on the Tennessee River opposite Chattanooga. He needed only a little help to enable him to seize and hold that key to East Tennessee and Northern Georgia. The help was refused by General Buell. When, at the middle of June, the East Tennesseeans saw the insurgents evacuate Cumberland Gap, voluntarily, they surely expected the long-hoped-for deliverance, by the advent of National troops; but Buell refused to walk in at that open door. That cautious leader and the fiery Mitchel could not work in harmony, and the latter was now transferred to another field of duty.

Mitchel had performed important services for the National cause by the exercise of judicious audacity. He smote so swiftly and effectually, that he appalled his enemies; and one of the most daring enterprises undertaken during the war was put in motion by that general. It was an effort to break up railway communication between Chattanooga and Atlanta. For this purpose he employed J. J. Andrews, who

HEADQUARTERS OF THE ARMY OF THE POTOMAC IN FRONT OF YORKTOWN

GENERALS STONEMAN, NAGLEE AND OTHER OFFICERS AT HEADQUARTERS OF THE ARMY OF THE POTOMAC

had been in the secret service of General Buell. With twenty-two picked men Andrews walked to Marietta in the guise of Confederate citizens of Kentucky seeking in Georgia freedom from persecution. At Marietta they took the cars for a station not far from the foot of the Great Kenesaw Mountain, and there, while the conductor and engineer were at breakfast, they uncoupled the engine, tender and a box-car, from the passenger train, and started up the road at full speed, answering questions where they were compelled to stop by saying they were conveying powder to Beauregard. They had passed several trains before they began their destructive work. Then the next train that reached the broken spot had its engine reversed and became a pursuer. Onward they sped with the speed of a gale, passing other trains, when, at an important curve in the road, after destroying the track, Andrews said, exultingly, " Only one more train to pass, boys, and then we will put our engine to full speed, burn the

bridges after us, dash and on to Mitchel, at

The exciting chase The pursued, having pursuers, were fleetest; lost in stopping to cut up the track, that at were prevented from suers were close upon lubricating oil became was the speed of the en-journals on which the melted. Fuel failing, pelled to leave their from Chattanooga. tangled woods of Chick-man-hunt was organ-passes were picketed; men and foot-soldiers,

through Chattanooga, Huntsville." continued many miles. less burden than the but so much time was telegraph wires and tear length the pursued doing either, for the pur-them. Finally their exhausted; and such gines that the brass axles revolved were the fugitives were con-conveyance fifteen miles They took refuge in the amauga Creek. A great ized. The mountain and thousands of horse-with several blood-

MAJOR-GENERAL D. M. PRENTISS
GENERAL S. R. CURTIS   GENERAL J. B. CARR

hounds, scoured the country in all directions. The whole party were finally captured, and thus ended one of the most exciting events in human history. The sequel was that Andrews and seven of his companions were hanged. To each of the survivors of that daring raid, the Secretary of War presented a bronze medal, in token of approval.

While these events were occurring in the interior of Tennessee, Commodore Foote had been busy on the Mississippi River. He went down that stream from Island Number Ten, with his armed vessels, and transports bearing Pope's army, to attempt the capture of Memphis, but was confronted at the first Chickasaw Bluffs, eighty miles above that city, by a Confederate flotilla under Captain Hollins, and three thousand troops under General Jeff. Thompson, who occupied a military work on the bluff, called Fort Pillow, then in command of General Villepigue, an accomplished engineer. Foote began an attack on the 14th; but General Pope's troops, who had landed on the Arkansas shore, could not co-operate because the country was flooded. Pope was soon called by Halleck to Shiloh, and the navy was left to do the best it could. Foote was soon obliged to turn over the command to Captain C. H. Davis, on account of the painfulness of his foot from a wound received at Fort Donelson.

On the 10th of May, Hollins, who had reorganized his flotilla, attacked Foote, and was assisted by the heavy guns of Fort Pillow, but the Confederate vessels were repulsed. For a fortnight afterward the belligerent fleets watched each other, when a "ram" squadron, prepared by Colonel Charles Ellet, Jr. (the builder of the Niagara Suspension Bridge), joined Foote's flotilla, and prepared to attack the foe. The Confederates, having heard of their disaster at Corinth, fled precipitately to Memphis on the 4th of June. Two days afterward the National flotilla won a victory over the Confederate squadron in front of that city, when Memphis passed into the possession of the Union forces, and it was speedily occupied by troops commanded by General Lewis Wallace. For a short time after these events, there was a lull in the storm of war westward of the Alleghany Mountains.

We left General Burnside and Commodore Rowan in Albemarle Sound after the capture of Roanoke Island and Elizabeth City and vicinity, preparing to make other important movements on the coast of North Carolina. They appeared in the Neuse River, eighteen miles below New Berne, on the evening of the 12th of March (1862); and early the next morning National troops led by Generals Foster, Reno and Parke, about fifteen thousand strong, were landed and marched against the defences of that town.

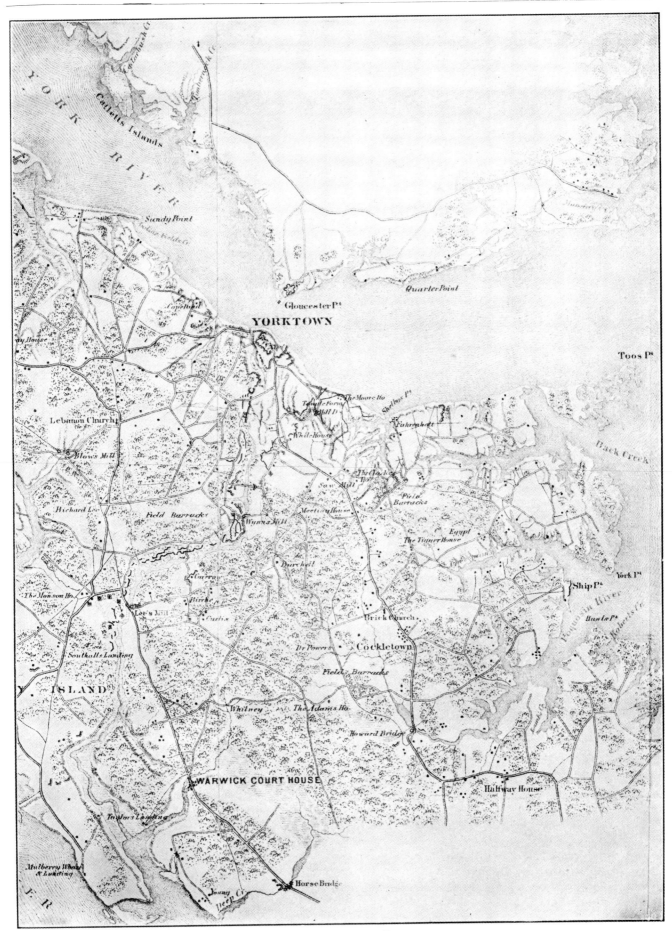

MAP OF YORKTOWN AND VICINITY

The Confederates, under General Branch, who were inferior in numbers, occupied a strongly intrenched position.   The Nationals moved against them at daylight on the morning of the 14th.   The Confederates sustained a severe battle with great bravery and skill until, closely pressed on all sides by superior numbers,

GENERAL G. H. THOMAS

they broke, and fled across the Trent closely pursued by Foster.   They burned the bridges behind them, and so escaped, leaving their killed and wounded and two hundred men, who were made prisoners.   The Nationals then took possession of New Berne; when General Parke proceeded to capture Fort Macon, on a point of Bogue Island near the entrance to Beaufort harbor.   In this enterprise the National troops were assisted by gunboats controlled by Commander Samuel Lockwood. The garrison made but slight resistance, and on the 25th of April, it was surrendered.   At the same time the National troops under General Reno were quietly taking possession of important places on the coast of North Carolina, and threatening Norfolk in the rear.   Plymouth, Winton and Washington were occupied by the National forces.   Garrisons for these places so widely dispersed Burnside's troops, that he could no longer make aggressive movements, and he remained quietly in his department until he was summoned to Fortress Monroe at the middle of July.   He held almost undisputed sway over the coast region from the Dismal Swamp to the Cape Fear River.

At the close of 1861, the National authority (as we have observed) was supreme along the Southern coast from Warsaw Sound, below the Savannah River, to the North Edisto well up toward Charleston.   At the close of the year, General T. W. Sherman, in command in that region, directed his chief engineer, General Q. A. Gillmore, to reconnoitre Fort Pulaski, and report upon the feasibility of a bombardment of it.   It was done, and Gillmore reported that it might be reduced by planting batteries of rifled guns and mortars on Big Tybee Island southeast of Cockspur Island, on which the fort stood.   Explorations were made to discover some channel by which gunboats might get in the rear of the fort, and a New York regiment was sent to occupy Big Tybee Island.   A channel was found, and land troops under General Viele, borne by gunboats commanded by Captain John Rodgers, went through it to reconnoitre.   Another expedition composed of land troops under General Wright, and gunboats commanded by Fleet-Captain Davis, were sent by Admiral Dupont up to the Savannah River, by way of Warsaw Sound, Wilmington River and St. Augustine Creek, in rear of Fort Pulaski.   The gunboats of Rodgers and Davis had a skirmish with Tattnall's "mosquito" fleet; and having accomplished their object, the whole National force returned to Hilton Head, to the great relief of the inhabitants of Savannah, who supposed the expedition was abandoned.   Soon afterward, however, the Nationals made a lodgement on Jones's Island, and erected a heavy battery at Venus's point, also a smaller one on Bird Island, and so effectually closed the Savannah River in the rear of Fort Pulaski.   It was absolutely blockaded near the close of February (1862); and on the 8th of March General David Hunter arrived as successor of General Sherman in command of the Department of the South, and he and Commodore Dupont, who was in command of the navy on that coast, acted in concert.

With great skill General Gillmore had planted his siege-guns on Big Tybee Island that commanded the fort; and on the 10th of April (1862), after Hunter had demanded its surrender and the commander of the fortress had refused compliance, thirty-six heavy rifled cannons and mortars were opened upon it under the direction of Generals Gillmore and Viele. It was gallantly defended until the 12th, when it was so battered that it was untenable, and it was surrendered.   This was an important victory, for it enabled the Nationals to close the port of Savannah against the blockade-runners, which had become numerous and bold all along our coast.

In the meantime Commodore Dupont and General Wright had been making easy conquests on the coast of Florida.   Early in February they captured Fort Clinch, on Amelia Island, which the Confederates had seized, and drove the insurgents from Fernandina.   The Confederates speedily abandoned their other forts along the coast of Florida

GENERAL DON C. BUELL

General Meade and Other Generals of the Army of the Potomac

Military Commission

and Georgia, which the Nationals took possession of; and a flotilla of gunboats and transports, bearing land troops under Lieutenant T. H. Stevens, went up the St. John's River and captured Jacksonville on the 11th of March. St. Augustine was taken possession of at about the same time by Commander C. P. Rodgers, and the alarmed Confederates abandoned Pensacola and all their fortifications on the main opposite Fort Pickens. When Dupont returned to Port Royal, he found General T. W. Sherman in possession of Edisto Island; and before the first anniversary of the evacuation of Fort Sumter, the whole coast from Cape Hatteras to Perdido Bay west of Fort Pickens, excepting at Charleston and its immediate vicinity, had been abandoned by the Confederates.

At the beginning of 1862 the National Government had determined to repossess itself of the important positions of Mobile, New Orleans, Baton Rouge and Galveston, by which it might maintain the National supremacy over the attempt the occupancy jamin F. Butler was the Department of the these points, and com-of proposed operations. operate with the navy prise; and as the first was New Orleans, he the coast of Mississippi, land and naval forces. at Fortress Monroe. ness, he visited Wash-the President, he said: take New Orleans or you Secretary Stanton said: New Orleans is made Butler embarked at his wife, his staff, and troops, in the magnifi-

GENERAL W. NELSON
GENERAL T. L. CRITTENDEN   GENERAL A. M. MITCHELL
GENERAL A. G. McCOOK

Lower Mississippi, and of Texas. General Ben-placed in command of Gulf, which included prised the whole theatre He was directed to co-in the important enter-object of the expedition suggested Ship Island, off as a rendezvous for the He gathered his troops When all was in readi-ington, and on leaving "Good-bye; we shall will never see me again." "The man who takes a lieutenant-general." Fortress Monroe, with about fourteen thousand cent steamship *Missis-*

sippi. He suffered vexatious delays at Port Royal; and it was thirty days before he reached Ship Island, a desolate sand-bar, without a house; and only a few charred boards could be found to make a shanty for the shelter of Mrs. Butler. General Phelps was there with Massachusetts and Connecticut troops, and had strengthened an unfinished fort on the Island. Admiral Farragut had also arrived with a naval force; also a fleet of bomb-vessels commanded by Commodore David D. Porter, prepared to co-operate with the land and naval forces.

At a short bend in the Mississippi River, seventy-six miles from its passage into the Gulf of Mexico, were two forts—Jackson and St. Philip. These, with some fortifications above and obstructions in the river below, seemed to the Confederates to make the stream absolutely impassable by vessels of an enemy; and they believed New Orleans, where there were ten thousand insurgent troops under General Mansfield Lovell (a former politician of New York), to be perfectly safe from invasion. The people continued their occupations, as usual; and one of the journals said: "Our only fear is, that the northern invaders may not appear. We have made such extensive preparations to receive them that it were vexation if their invincible armada escapes the fate we have in store for it." The test was soon made.

General Butler and the two naval commanders arranged a plan for the capture of New Orleans, which comprehended an attack on the forts below the city, first, by Porter's bomb-vessels, Farragut with his stronger vessels remaining as a reserve until the guns of the fort should be silenced. Failing in this, Farragut was to attempt to run by the forts, clear the river of Confederate vessels, isolate the forts and cut off their supplies and supports. Then General Butler was to land his troops in the rear of Fort St. Philip (the weaker one), and attempt to carry it by assault. This done, the land and naval forces were to press on toward New Orleans. The general command of the river defences of the Confederates was intrusted to General J. K. Duncan, formerly an office-holder in New York.

On the 17th of April the fleets of Farragut and Porter were in the river, with the former as chief commander of the naval forces; and Butler, with about nine thousand troops, was at the Southwest Pass. The fleets comprised forty-seven armed vessels, and these, with transports bearing troops, went up the river, Porter's mortar-boats leading. When these approached the forts, their hulls were besmeared with Mississippi mud; and the masts, yards and rigging were so covered with the branches of trees, that under

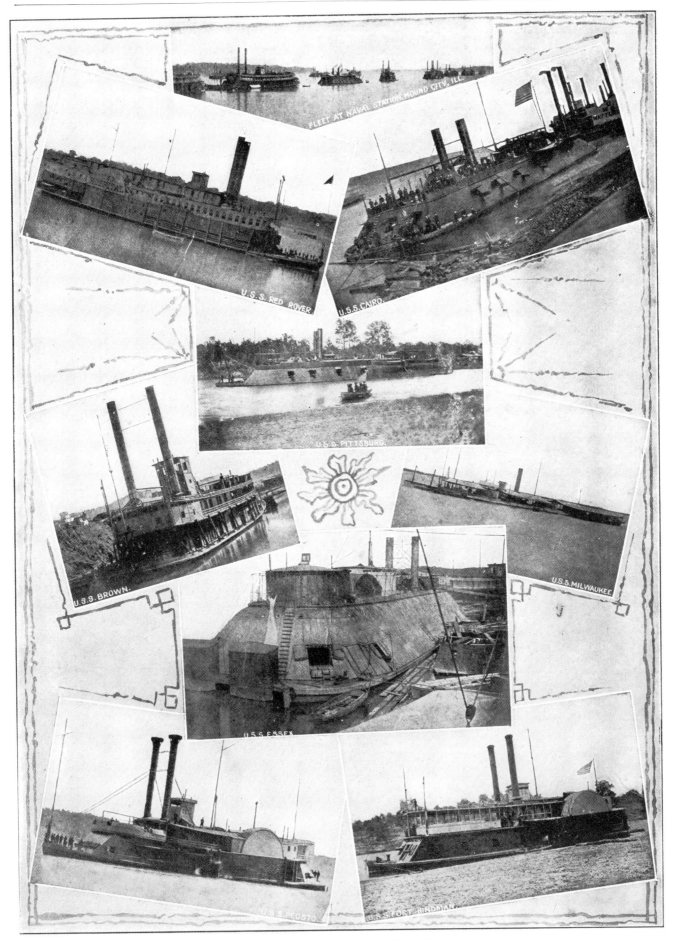

MISSISSIPPI RIVER FLEET OF IRON CLAD GUNBOATS

this disguise they were enabled to take a position near the forts unsuspected. As when "Birnam Wood" moved "toward Dunsinane," the stratagem was successful. The Mississippi was full to the brim; and a boom and other obstructions near Fort Jackson were swept away by the flood.

A battle was begun on the morning of the 18th (April, 1862), by a shot from Fort Jackson. Porter's mortar-boats responded. The latter were supported by the gunboats; but after pounding the fortifications several days, Farragut, satisfied that he could not reduce them, prepared to run by them in the night of the 23d. The mortar-boats led the way, and the remainder of the navy followed, gallantly breasting the swift-flowing current that went over the river banks and flooded every bayou. The perilous passage of the forts was begun at two o'clock in the morning. The mortar-boats were to cover the movement of the gunboats. Farragut, in his flag-ship *Hartford*, with two other strong vessels, was destined to keep near the right bank of the river and fight Fort Jackson; while Captain Theodorus Bailey, commanding eight gunboats, was to keep closely to the eastern bank and fight Fort St. Philip. To Captain Bell was assigned the duty of attacking the Confederate fleet above the forts, with six gunboats.

The night was intensely dark, and a tremendous battle was waged between the mortar-boats and the forts. The gunboats as they came up gave the latter heavy broadsides of grape and canister shot, which drove the garrison from their barbette guns. The scene soon became ribile. Fire-rafts, sent down by the Confederates, blazed "rams" plunged against the National vessels with terrible force. (Farragut's flag-ship), which was a wooden vessel, was set on were soon extinguished. The fleet had scarcely passed the forts by a large flotilla of "rams" and gunboats. A grand and awful noise of twenty mortars and two hundred and sixty great guns, made a terrific sound. The explosion of shells that struck ground, shook the land and water like an earthquake. "Combine," wrote an eye-witness, "all that you ever heard of thunder, and add to it all that you have ever seen of lightning, and you have, perhaps, a conception of the scene," in the darkness before daylight.

GENERAL
SCHUYLER
HAMILTON

grand and ter-fearfully, and The *Hartford* fire, but the flames when it was assailed scene followed. The afloat and ashore, deep in the oozy

GENERAL
G. W. CULLUM

In that fearful struggle, the Nationals were victorious. From the fore-rigging of his ship Farragut had watched the combat through his night-glass, and conducted it as far as possible. Within the space of half an hour after the National vessels had left their anchorage, the forts were passed, the great struggle had occurred, and eleven vessels—nearly the whole of the Confederate flotilla—were destroyed. For a while Captain Bailey sustained the fight with the Confederate flotilla almost unsupported, when Captain Boggs came to his assistance with the gunboat *Varuna*, which immediately became the chief object of the wrath of the enemy. In his report Captain Boggs said that immediately after passing the forts, he found himself "amid a nest of rebel steamers." The *Varuna* rushed in among them (for the river was too narrow to permit her to avoid them), and fired broadsides right and left as she passed. The first one that received her fire was crowded with troops. Its boiler was exploded, and the vessel was run ashore. The *Varuna* ran three other gunboats ashore, and had desperate struggles with the "rams," until, badly wounded, she began to sink, when her commander tied her bow to trees and took out her crew and the wounded, while his latest antagonist was burning to the water's edge. So ended one of the fiercest combats of the war. It was "short, sharp, and decisive." In that struggle on the bosom of the river, the Nationals lost only thirty killed and not more than one hundred and twenty-five wounded. The fleet, after the fight, rendezvoused at Quarantine, just above Fort St. Philip, and that was the first public property "repossessed" by the Government, in Louisiana.

GENERAL W. H. L. WALLACE

COMMANDER WILLIAM JEFFRIES AND OFFICERS OF MONITOR   CREW ON DECK OF THE ORIGINAL MONITOR

SMOKE STACK OF CONFEDERATE RAM RIDDLED BY SHOTS

While the battle was raging near the forts, General Butler landed his troops, and in small boats they went through narrow and shallow bayous in the rear of Fort St. Philip. The alarmed garrison mutinied, spiked the guns, and sallying out surrendered to Butler's pickets, declaring that they had been pressed into the service, and would fight no more. Porter had continued to bombard Fort Jackson, and after the fall of Fort St. Philip, it was surrendered to that officer with nearly one thousand men.

COMMANDER FRANKLIN BUCHANAN,
C. S. N., COMMANDING THE
"MERRIMAC"

Meanwhile Farragut (who had thirteen vessels in safety above the forts) had gone up to New Orleans with his fleet, where a fearful panic prevailed, for the inhabitants had heard of the disasters below. Drums were beating; soldiers were seen hurrying to and fro; merchants had fled from their stores; women without bonnets and brandishing pistols were seen in the streets crying, "Burn the city! Burn the city! Never mind us! Burn the city!" Military officers impressed vehicles into the service of carrying cotton to the levees to be burned; and specie to the amount of $4,000,000 was sent out of the city by railway. Millions worth of other property, with a large number of citizens, had left the doomed town, among them General Twiggs, who betrayed his troops in Texas. Like Floyd, he feared the wrath of his injured Government, and fled, leaving behind him the two swords which had been awarded him for gallantry in Mexico, to fall into the hands of the invaders. And when, on the 25th of April, 1862, Farragut approached the city with nine vessels, General Lovell and his troops fled, the torch was applied to the cotton on the levee, and along the river front for miles a sheet of roaring flames burst forth. In that conflagration fifteen thousand bales of cotton, a dozen large ships and as many fine steamboats, with unfinished gunboats and other large vessels, were burnt. The value of cotton, sugar, and other products destroyed was immense. The citizens were held in durance by Farragut's guns, until the arrival of General Butler on the first of May, when the latter landed with his troops, took formal possession of the defenceless town, and made his headquarters at the St. Charles hotel. Butler ruled New Orleans with the rigor of martial law. Informed that a man named Mumford had pulled down the National flag where Farragut had unfurled it over the Mint, and had treated it in derision, Butler caused his arrest and his immediate trial on a charge of treason. He was convicted and hanged; the only man who has ever suffered death for that crime since the establishment of our National Government.

The loss of New Orleans was a terrible blow for the Confederates. "It annihilated us in Louisiana," wrote a Confederate historian, "diminished our resources and supplies by the loss of one of the greatest grain and cattle countries within the limits of the Confederacy, gave to the enemy the Mississippi River with all its means of navigation for a base of operations, and finally led, by plain and irresistible conclusions, to our virtual abandonment of the great and fruitful valley of the Mississippi."

The loss of New Orleans produced the greatest irritation in the public mind throughout the Confederacy, and the rigor of Butler's rule there excited the most violent personal hatred of the general. When he was about to leave New Orleans, Jefferson Davis, the chief of the Confederacy, issued a proclamation in which he pronounced Butler to be "a felon deserving of capital punishment"; and he ordered that he should not be "treated simply as a public enemy of the Confederate States of America, but as an outlaw, and common enemy of mankind"; and that, "in the event of his capture, the officer in command of the capturing force, do cause him to be immediately executed, by hanging." He also ordered that the same treatment should be awarded to all commissioned officers serving under Butler. A "Georgian" offered a reward of $10,000 "for the infamous Butler." Richard Yeadon, a prominent citizen of Charleston, publicly offered a reward of $10,000 "for the capture and delivery of the said Benjamin F. Butler, dead or alive, to any Confederate authority." A "Daughter of South Carolina," in a letter to the *Charleston Courier*, said: "I propose to spin the thread to make the cord to execute the order of our noble

COMMANDER JOHN L. WORDEN, U.S.N.,
COMMANDING THE "MONITOR"

DECK OF MONITOR IN THE JAMES RIVER

President Davis, when old Butler is caught; and my daughter asks that she may be allowed to adjust it around his neck." And Paul R. Hayne, a South Carolina poet, wrote:

> "Yes! but there is *one who shall not die*
> *In battle harness!* One for whom
> Lurks in the darkness silently
> Another and a sterner doom!
> A warrior's end should crown the brave;
> For *him*, swift cord and felon's grave!"

CHAPTER XVII.

Army of the Potomac—Armies Ordered to Move—McClellan's Plan of Operations—Evacuation of Manassas—"Promenade" of the Union Army—McClellan Relieved—The "Monitor" and "Merrimac"—Events in the Shenandoah Valley—Battle at Kernstown—Army of the Potomac on the Peninsula—Siege of Yorktown—Magruder's Strategy—Battle at Williamsburg—Tardy Movements—McClellan and the President—Capture of Norfolk—Military Events in the Valley—Battles at Winchester, Cross Keys and Port Republic—The "White House"—On the Chickahominy—Confederate Government Rebuked—Fatal Hesitation—Battle at Fair Oaks—Stuart's Raid.

WHILE great activity prevailed in the valley of the Mississippi, the *Grand Army of the Potomac*, under General McClellan, had been lying almost inactive much of the time, in the vicinity of the National capital. It had, however, been growing in numbers and discipline; and early in 1862, it was composed of full two hundred thousand men. The battles of Ball's Bluff and Drainsville, already mentioned, had prevented its rusting into absolute immobility; and the troops were gladdened, from time to time, by promises of an immediate advance upon the Confederates at Manassas. On account of that expectation, very little had been done toward

placing the troops in winter quarters, and much suffering and discontent were the consequence. Efforts were made by many officers to break the monotony of camp-life; and the Secretary of War (Mr. Cameron) permitted the musical Hutchinson family to visit the camps and sing their simple and stirring songs. They were diffusing sunshine through the gloom of the army by delighting crowds of soldiers who listened to their sweet melody, when their career was suddenly checked by the following order:

"By direction of General McClellan, the permit given to the 'Hutchinson Family' to sing in the camps, and their pass to cross the Potomac, are revoked, and they will not be allowed to sing to the troops."

Why not? Because a few of the officers of the army were afraid of offending the confederated slaveholders, and the Hutchinsons had been guilty

GENERAL J. L. RENO   GENERAL J. G. FOSTER
GENERAL J. C. PARKE

of singing Whittier's stirring song, then lately written, to the tune of Luther's Hymn, "Ein feste burg ist unser Gott," in which, among eight similar verses, was the following:

> "What gives the wheat-fields blades of steel?
> What points the rebel cannon?
> What sets the roaring rabble's heel
> On th' old star-spangled pennon?
> What breaks th' oath
> Of th' men o' th' South?
> What whets the knife
> For the Union's life?
> Hark to the answer: *Slavery*."

On the 13th of January, 1862, the energetic Edwin M. Stanton succeeded Simon Cameron, as Secretary of War, and infused new life into the service. The people had become impatient; and the President, satisfied that longer delay was unnecessary, issued a general order on the 27th of January, in which he directed a simultaneous forward movement of "all the land and naval forces of the United States against the insurgent forces on the 22d day of February next ensuing. This order sent a thrill of joy through the hearts of the loyal people, and it was heightened when the President ordered McClellan to move

ADMIRAL FARRAGUT AND CAPTAIN DRAYTON ON U. S. S. HARTFORD

GROUP OF OFFICERS ON DECK OF MONITOR AFTER A HUNTING TRIP. WHO CAN RECOGNIZE THEM?

against the inferior force of Confederates at Manassas. Instead of obeying, McClellan remonstrated, and proposed to take his army to Richmond by the circuitous route of Fortress Monroe and the Peninsula, between the York and James rivers, instead of attempting, with his large and well-equipped army, to press

ADMIRAL D. G. FARRAGUT, U. S. N.

the Confederates back to their Capital. The President strongly urged the trial of the direct movement, as less expensive in time and money, and less perilous to the army; but McClellan so steadily resisted this plan, that the patient Lincoln consented to submit the matter to a council of officers. They decided in favor of McClellan's plan by a vote of eight to four. The President acquiesced, but with many misgivings, which the result justified. The General-in-Chief had declared that he intended to wait for the forces in the West to gain victories before he should move upon Richmond. Well, the *Grand Army of the Potomac* had not fairly inaugurated its campaign in the spring of 1862, before the active little army of General Grant, and the forces under Generals Pope, and Buell, and Mitchel, and the gunboats of Foote, had accomplished far more in the West than McClellan ever dreamed of being possible.

Informed that McClellan (who would not trust his commander-in-chief with his military secrets) intended to take to the Peninsula nearly the entire *Grand Army of the Potomac*, the President issued an order on the 8th of March, that no change of base in the operations of that army should be made without leaving a competent force for the protection of the Capital, that not more than fifty thousand troops should be removed toward the Peninsula until the navigation of the Potomac from Washington to the Chesapeake should be freed from the enemy's batteries and other obstructions; that the new movement should begin as early as the 18th of March and that the army and navy should co-operate in an immediate attack upon the Confederate batteries on the Potomac. Meanwhile the Confederates at Manassas had retired, and were falling back toward Richmond, in fear of the execution of the President's order to move upon them on the 22d of February. When McClellan heard of this evacuation he crossed the Potomac and ordered his whole army to advance, not, as he afterward explained, to pursue the alarmed fugitives and to take Richmond, but to give his own army a little active experience "preparatory to the campaign!" After making a grand display of power at abandoned Manassas and a little beyond, the army moved back to Alexandria. This "promenade" (as one of McClellan's aids, a scion of the royal Orleans family of France called it) of the *Grand Army of the Potomac* disappointed the people and disgusted the President, who, satisfied that McClellan's official burdens were greater than he could profitably bear, kindly relieved him of the chief care of the armies, on the 11th of March, giving him command of the *Department of the Potomac*.

At the moment when the Confederates evacuated Manassas, a strange naval battle occurred in Hampton Roads. The insurgents had raised the *Merrimac*, one of the vessels that was sunk in the river at Norfolk, and had converted it into an iron-clad warrior, which they named *Virginia*, commanded by Captain Buchanan of our navy. On the 8th of March, this vessel attacked and destroyed the wooden sailing frigates *Congress* and *Cumberland*, at the mouth of the James River, and it was expected she would annihilate other transports and war vessels in Hampton Roads, the next morning. Anxiously the army and navy officers in that vicinity passed the night of the 8th. There seemed to be no competent human agency near to arrest the impending disaster, when, at a little past midnight, a strange craft entered the Roads, from the sea, unheralded and unknown. It appeared like a floating platform, sharp at both ends, lying almost level with the surface of the water, and having a round tower made of heavy iron. This tower was pierced for two guns. It was twenty feet in diameter, and about ten feet in height above the platform; and it was made to revolve so as to bring its heavy guns within to bear upon an object, independently of the position of the vessel. This strange craft had been constructed at New York, under the direction of the eminent civil engineer and scientist, Captain John Ericsson, and took the name, so appropriate after its first display of power, of *Monitor*. The little vessel was in command of Lieutenant John L. Worden of

CAPTAIN PERCIVAL DRAYTON, U. S. N.

Mississippi Fleet of Iron Clad Gunboats

the navy, and had been towed to the Roads, after encountering a heavy gale and rolling sea, by a steamship. It was her trial trip.

On his arrival, Worden reported to the flag-officer in the Roads, and learning the situation of affairs there, he promptly prepared to meet the iron-clad monster from Norfolk the next morning—the Sabbath. That morning dawned brightly, and in the gray twilight (March 9, 1862), the *Merrimac* was seen sweeping out of the Elizabeth River on its destructive errand. The *Monitor*, like a little David, moved to meet the Confederate Goliath, whose commander looked with contempt upon the "floating cheese-box," as he called his strange antagonist; but he soon found it to be a citadel, strong and well filled with destructive energy. Her revolving turret was invulnerable to the heaviest shot and shell thrown by her antagonist, and they glanced from the tower like pebbles from granite. The conflict that ensued was terrific. The ponderous missiles hurled from the *Monitor* soon bruised the *Merrimac* so fatally, that she fled up to Norfolk, her wounded commander confounded by the energy of his mysterious little antagonist. The *Merrimac* did not venture out again. The gallant Worden, who was regarded as the savior of his country at a critical moment, was severely injured by having cement around the "peep-hole" in the turret, through which he was watching his antagonist, thrown violently in his face by a heavy shot that struck that point. He was afterwards rewarded with the commission of Admiral.

GENERAL EGBERT L. VIELLE

The exploit of the *Monitor* seemed to promise safety to National vessels navigating the James River; and McClellan prepared to transfer the Army of the Potomac to Fortress Monroe, which place he designed to make a base of supplies for his army while marching on Richmond. To secure Washington city, it was necessary to hold the Confederates in check in the Shenandoah Valley, where they were led by the zealous and gallant "Stonewall Jackson." He had been defeated by the dashing General Lander, at Blooming Gap, on the 14th of February; and when Johnston and his Confederates evacuated Manassas, Jackson had taken post at Winchester. General N. P. Banks was then in command of National troops near Harper's Ferry, destined for operations in the Shenandoah Valley; and when Jackson went further up that valley, he sent General Shields in pursuit. Shields soon turned back, and with a considerable body of troops encamped at Winchester. Jackson, reinforced, came down the valley in force, infantry and cavalry, and attacked Shields at Kernstown just west of Winchester. Shields had only about seven thousand men, and twenty-four heavy guns. The battle that ensued (March 22, 1862) was short and severe. Shields was badly wounded. The Confederates were defeated, and fled up the valley closely pursued by Banks, who remained in that region to watch the insurgents while McClellan should move upon Richmond.

It was not until April when the Army of the Potomac began its campaign on the Virginia Peninsula.

GENERAL QUINCY A. GILLMORE

General McClellan had transferred a larger part of that army to Fortress Monroe, leaving about seventy-three thousand troops for the defence of Washington. At the beginning of April there were one hundred and twenty-one thousand men at Fortress Monroe (exclusive of the forces of General Wool), and a large portion of these now moved, in two columns, up the Peninsula; one column under General Heintzelman marching near the York River, and another under General Keyes, near the James River. A comparatively small Confederate force, under General J. B. Magruder, had formed a fortified line across the Peninsula, in the pathway of the Nationals; and by skillful tricks, Magruder so deceived McClellan as to the number of the Confederates, that the invaders were kept at bay, below Yorktown, nearly a month, while their leader was calling for reinforcements to enable him to break through the opposing line. Yorktown was regularly besieged under the direction of General Fitz John Porter, though the number of the Nationals was ten times as large as that of the Confederates. An attempt to carry the intrenchments on the Warwick River, by a division under General Smith of Keyes's column, caused a sharp engagement. It failed; and finally Magruder fell back to a line of strong intrenchments in front of Williamsburg,

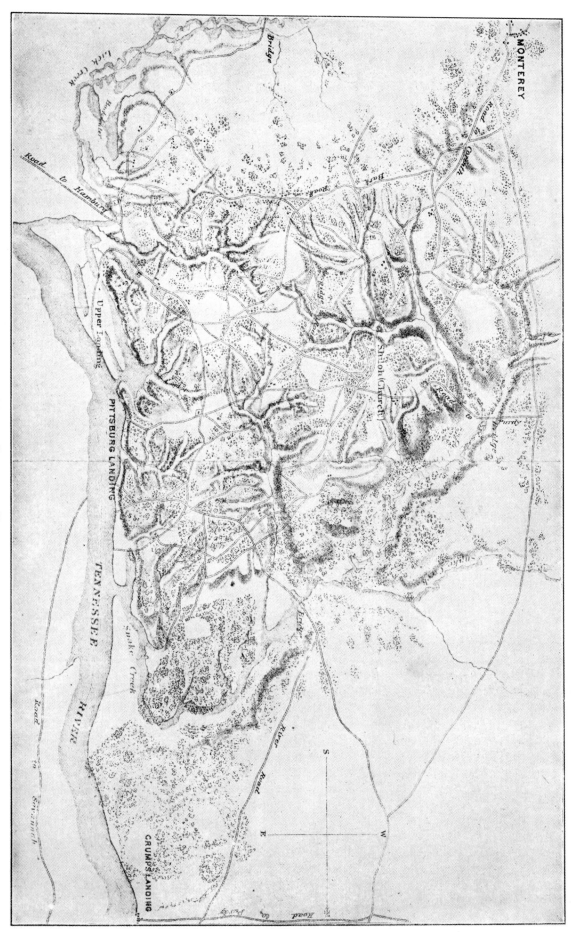

MAP OF SHILOH AND VICINITY

where, on the 3d of May, he wrote, after describing his strategy: "Thus, with five thousand men, exclusive of the garrison, we stopped and held in check over one hundred thousand of the enemy. . . . I was amused when I saw McClellan, with his magnificent army, begin to break ground before miserable

earthworks [at Yorktown] defended by only eight thousand men." General Sumner, with the main body of the Nationals, had pursued the Confederates to Williamsburg, while McClellan remained at Yorktown to forward troops under General Franklin up the York River, to strike the left flank of the insurgents.

General Joseph E. Johnston, who had hastened to the Peninsula after the evacuation of Manassas, was now in chief command in front of McClellan. Leaving a strong guard at Williamsburg to check the pursuers, Johnston fell back with his main army toward Richmond, with the intention of fighting the Nationals when they should approach that city. But he was compelled to fight sooner than he expected, for gallant and energetic men—Generals Hooker, Kearney and Hancock—attacked that rear-guard on the 5th of May. Hard pressed, Johnston sent back a large portion of his army to help them. A sanguinary battle followed. Hooker began the assault, knowing a large body of troops were within supporting distance, and for full nine hours he bore the brunt of the battle. Then Kearney came to his aid, and, Hancock having turned the flank of the Confederates, the

CAMP OF GENERAL ANDREW PORTER
IN FRONT OF YORKTOWN

latter precipitately retreated. In this perilous movement they were led by General James Longstreet, the ablest and best of the Confederate leaders in the war.

On the morning after the conflict, McClellan came upon the battle-field, just as the victors were about to press on in pursuit of the fugitives, who had left about eight hundred of their wounded behind them in their flight. He had kept Franklin so long at Yorktown, that the latter could not flank the Confederates; and now, when the latter were flying evidently in a panic, the Commander-in-Chief would not allow a pursuit, but moved leisurely forward during the next ten or twelve days, reaching the Chickahominy River when Johnston was safely encamped beyond it. Experts on both sides declared, that had a vigorous pursuit followed the events at Williamsburg, the Confederate army might have been captured or dispersed. Franklin had secured a firm foothold at near the head of the York River, which was made the base of supplies for the Army of the Potomac in its earlier operations against Richmond. In the battle at Williamsburg, the Nationals lost twenty-two hundred men, of whom four hundred and fifty-six were killed. The Confederate loss was about one thousand.

More than a month, after General McClellan arrived at Fortress Monroe, had been consumed in moving only thirty-six miles toward Richmond, and the army had suffered fearful losses by sickness. Very few perished by the weapons of the enemy during the month's siege of Yorktown, "but disease," said General J. G. Barnard, McClellan's chief engineer, in his report at the close of the campaign, "took a fearful hold of the army; and toil and hardships, unredeemed by the excitement of combat, impaired their *morale*. We did not carry with us from Yorktown so good an army as we took there. Of the bitter fruits of that month gained by the enemy, we have tasted to our heart's content." Twenty of the thirty days that the army lay before Yorktown were marked by heavy thunder-showers, following in quick succession. The troops, wearied and overheated by labor, lay on the damp ground at night, and were chilled. "In a short time," wrote Dr. Marks, a participant, "the sick in our hospitals were numbered by thousands, and many died so suddenly that the disease had all the aspects of a plague."

One cause of McClellan's tardy advance was his constant fear of not having troops enough to meet the energetic Johnston. Before his army left Washington, Blenker's division of ten thousand men were taken from it to strengthen Fremont, who was in command of the Mountain Department beyond the Blue Ridge; and soon afterward McDowell's army corps were detached from McClellan's immediate command, and its leader instructed to report directly to the Secretary of War. McDowell

GENERAL HORATIO G. WRIGHT

OLD CITY HALL, NEW ORLEANS, WHERE THE OFFICERS OF THE
FLEET DEMANDED THE SURRENDER OF THE CITY

GENERAL BENJAMIN F. BUTLER'S HEADQUARTERS AT NEW ORLEANS

HORRORS OF WAR

was ordered to a position where he might assist in the defence of the Capital, or in an attack upon Richmond, as circumstances might require. General Wool, with his ten thousand men at Fortress Monroe, was also made independent of McClellan's orders, although, like McDowell, he was directed to co-operate with the Army of the Potomac as far as possible.

General McClellan, perceiving these indications of a lack of implicit confidence in his judgment, and feeling that he might be denied support at any time, startled the President on the 7th of April by telegraphing to the Secretary of War that he had only eighty-five thousand effective men, and might be called upon to confront one hundred thousand Confederates. He had just reported that he had over one hundred thousand effective troops. The President asked him to explain, and urged him to strike the foe before they should gather in greater strength on his front. Instead of that, McClellan continued to halt and complain of a want of troops. The President urged him to act. "The country will note—it is now noting," Mr. Lincoln said, "that the present hesitation to move upon an intrenched enemy is but the story of Manassas repeated." The President expressed the kindest feelings toward the general, and closed his letter with the remark, "But you must act." Still he hesitated and complained; and although, at the close of April, just before the Confederates evac-

GENERAL JEFFERSON C. DAVIS

uated Yorktown, he reported one hundred and twelve thousand soldiers on the Peninsula fit for duty, he complained that the lack of McDowell's force prevented Franklin striking the fugitives from Williamsburg on the flank. It is asserted that the chief cause of the failure was McClellan's hesitancy in deciding whether he should smite the Confederates on their front, or flank them, until it was too late to attempt either.

The veteran General John E. Wool had now been in command at Fortress Monroe for some time. He felt certain that the Confederate soldiers might easily be driven out of Norfolk; and after the affair at Williamsburg he obtained leave to make an effort to dislodge them. Having made a personal reconnaissance, he crossed Hampton Roads and landed a few regiments in the rear of Confederate works below that city. General Huger, in command at Norfolk, had already perceived his peril, with Burnside in his rear and McClellan on his flank, and he retreated. So Wool gained a bloodless victory on the 9th of May. The Confederate vessels in the James River hastened toward Richmond. The Confederates set fire to the battered *Merrimac*, and the troops fled from the city of Norfolk. A flotilla of National gunboats, commanded by Commodore Rodgers, chased the Confederate vessels as far as Drewry's Bluff, eight miles below Richmond, where a strong fort and river obstructions checked the pursuers.

COMMODORE ROWAN

COLONEL C. W. LeGENDRE

The wisdom of detaching McDowell's corps from the Army of the Potomac was soon made apparent. After the departure of Johnston, with his troops, from Manassas, which relieved Washington from immediate danger, McDowell advanced to Fredericksburg, with thirty thousand men, to assist McClellan or cover the Capital, as he might be ordered. Fremont among the mountains and Banks in the Shenandoah Valley had, in the aggregate, about the same number of troops; and at the beginning of May, Stonewall Jackson had been joined by the skillful General Ewell, near Harrisonburg, in the upper part of the Valley. Ewell was ordered to hold Banks, while General Robert E. Lee, who had been recalled from Georgia, should push across the Rappahannock with a strong column and cut off all communication between Winchester and Alexandria.

While Jackson was watching Banks he was startled by the approach of one of Fremont's brigades under General Milroy, evidently for the purpose of joining the Nationals in the Valley. Jackson immediately moved against Milroy; and at McDowell, west of Staunton, he struck the brigade a severe blow on the 8th of May. A sharp engagement occurred, lasting about five hours. Neither party won a victory. The Nationals lost in killed and wounded two hundred and fifty-six men, and the

GENERAL BENJAMIN F. BUTLER, FROM A BROKEN BRADY NEGATIVE IN POSSESSION OF THE WAR DEPARTMENT

Confederates, four hundred and sixty-one. Notwithstanding it was a drawn battle, Jackson sent a note to Ewell the next morning, saying: "Yesterday, God gave us the victory at McDowell."

Meanwhile General Banks had been pressed back by Ewell, to Strasburg; and a fortnight later

HEADQUARTERS OF GENERAL MAGRUDER AT YORKTOWN

(May 23d) a National force under Colonel J. R. Kenly, of Baltimore, was captured or dispersed at Front Royal by the combined troops of Jackson and Ewell. Perceiving his peril, Banks fled down the Shenandoah Valley in swift marches, pursued by twenty thousand Confederates, and won the race to Winchester, where he made a stand with seven thousand men, ten Parrott guns, and a battery of 6-pound smooth-bore cannon. There he was attacked by Ewell, on the 25th of May. Contemplating the contingency of a retreat, he had sent his trains toward the Potomac. Very soon Jackson approached with an overwhelming force, when Banks ordered a retreat, after his troops had fought gallantly for several hours. It was done in a masterly manner. They were pursued as far as Martinsburg, where the chase was ended. The Nationals reached the Potomac, at Williamsport, where, on the hill-sides, the wearied troops rested behind a thousand blazing camp-fires that night. The National capital was now in real danger, and it could only be relieved from peril by the retreat or capture

of the Confederates in the Shenandoah Valley. McDowell sent a force over the Blue Ridge to intercept them if they should retreat, and Fremont pressed on from the west, toward Strasburg, with the same object in view. Perceiving the threatened danger, Jackson fled up the Valley with his whole force, hotly pursued by the Nationals; and at Cross Keys, beyond Harrisonburg, Fremont overtook Ewell, when a sharp but indecisive battle occurred on the 7th of June. Jackson was then at Port Republic, beyond the Shenandoah River, only a few miles distant, so closely pressed by troops under Generals Carroll and Tyler, that he called upon Ewell for help. The latter retired from Cross Keys under cover of night, closely followed by the vigilant Fremont; but Ewell fired the bridge over the Shenandoah near Port Republic, before his pursuer could reach that stream. Jackson, having overwhelming numbers, routed the Nationals after a severe battle at Port Republic, and then the latter retraced their steps toward Winchester. So ended the second great race of contending troops in the Shenandoah Valley.

General McClellan, with the head of his pursuing army, reached the "White House," at the head of navigation of the Pamunkey River, on the 16th of May. The "White House" and surrounding lands belonged to General Robert E. Lee's wife, which she inherited from Mrs. Washington. It was not the "White House" in which the first months of Washington's married life were spent, for that had been burned more than thirty years before. It was a modern dwelling near the spot; but by McClellan's order it was carefully protected from harm, not a sick soldier being allowed to find shelter beneath its

roof. From that point, the general pressed forward to Cold Harbor, near the Chickahominy River, where he made his headquarters, within nine miles of Richmond. General Casey's division of General Keyes's corps crossed the river, and occupied heights on the Richmond side of the stream, supported by troops under General Heintzelman. Along the line of the Chickahominy the armies of McClellan and Johnston confronted each other toward the close of May, separated by a narrow stream liable to a sudden overflow of its banks and filling of the adjacent swamps. There the two commanders waited for decisive results in the Shenandoah Valley, each expecting reinforcements from that region.

In the meantime the Confederate government at Richmond, alarmed by the approach of the Nationals by land and water, had prepared to fly into South Carolina. They had actually sent their "archives" to Columbia, and to Lynchburg, in Virginia.

WHITE HOUSE LANDING

ORDERLIES AND SERVANTS AND GROUP AT PHOTOGRAPHER'S TENT, YORKTOWN

EMBARKATION AT YORKTOWN FOR WHITE HOUSE LANDING
GENERALS FRANKLIN, SLOCUM, BARRY AND NEWTON

GENERAL ANDREW PORTER AND STAFF
AND STAFF OFFICERS

CHRONOLOGICAL SUMMARY AND RECORD—Continued

SEPTEMBER, 1863—*Continued from Section* 8

5—Limestone Station, Tenn. Five Cos. 100th Ohio. *Union* 12 killed, 20 wounded, 240 missing. *Confed.* 6 killed, 10 wounded.

8—Night attack on Fort Sumter, S. C. Four hundred and thirteen marines and sailors, commanded by Commander Stevens, U. S. N. *Union* 3 killed, 114 missing.

9—Cumberland Gap, Tenn. Shackleford's Cavalry. *Confed.* 2,000 captured.

10—Little Rock, Ark. Maj.-Gen. Steele's troops and Davidson's Cavalry.

11—Ringgold, Ga. Advance of Twenty-first Corps. *Union* 8 killed, 19 wounded. *Confed.* 3 killed, 18 missing.

12—Sterling's Plantation, La. Battery E 1st Mo. Artil. *Union* 3 killed, 3 wounded. *Confed.* 10 killed, 40 wounded, 75 missing.

13—Culpeper, Va. 1st, 2d, and 3d Divisions, Cavalry Corps Army of the Potomac. *Union* 3 killed, 40 wounded. *Confed.* 10 killed, 40 wounded, 75 missing.

Lett's Tan Yard, near Chickamauga, Ga. Wilder's Mounted Brigade. *Union* 50 killed and wounded. *Confed.* 10 killed, 40 wounded.

14—Rapidan Station, Va. Cavalry Army of the Potomac. *Union* 8 killed, 40 wounded.

Vidalia, La. 2d Mo. *Union* 2 killed, 4 wounded. *Confed.* 6 killed, 11 wounded.

19—Rapidan Station, Va. Buford's Cavalry. *Union* 4 killed, 19 wounded.

19 and 20—Chickamauga, Ga. Army of the Cumberland, Maj.-Gen. Rosecrans; Fourteenth Corps, Maj.-Gen. Thomas; Twentieth Corps, Maj.-Gen. McCook; Twenty-first Corps, Maj.-Gen. Crittenden, and Reserve Corps, Maj.-Gen. Granger. *Union* 1,644 killed, 9,262 wounded, 4,945 missing. *Confed.* 2,389 killed, 13,412 wounded, 2,003 missing. *Union* Brig.-Gen. Lytle killed, and Starkweather, Whittaker, and King wounded. *Confed.* Brig.-Gens. Preston, Smith, Deshler, and Helm killed, and Maj.-Gen. Hood, Brig.-Gens. Adams, Gregg, Brown, McNair, Bunn, Preston, Clerburne, Benning, and Clayton wounded.

21—Bristol, Tenn. Shackleford's and Foster's Cavalry. Casualties not recorded.

22—Madison C. H., Tenn. 1st Division Buford's Cav. *Union* 1 killed, 20 wounded.

Blountsville, Tenn. Foster's 2d Brigade Cav. *Union* 5 killed, 22 wounded. *Confed.* 15 killed, 50 wounded, 100 missing.

Rockville, Md. 11th N. Y. Cav. *Confed.* 34 killed and wounded.

26—Calhoun, Tenn. Cavalry Army of the Ohio. *Union* 6 killed, 20 wounded, 40 wounded.

27—Moffat's Station, Ark. Detachment 1st Ark. *Union* 2 killed, 2 wounded. *Confed.* 5 killed, 20 wounded.

29—Near Morganzia, La. 19th Iowa, 26th Ind. *Union* 14 killed, 40 wounded, 400 missing.

OCTOBER, 1863

1—Anderson's Gap, Tenn. 21st Ky. *Union* 38 killed and wounded.

2—Anderson's Cross Roads, Tenn. McCook's Cavalry Corps. *Union* 70 killed and wounded. *Confed.* 200 killed and wounded.

3—McMinnville, Tenn. 4th Tenn. *Union* 7 killed, 31 wounded, 350 missing. *Confed.* 23 killed and wounded.

4—Neosho, Mo. Three Cos. 6th Mo. Militia Cav. *Union* 1 killed, 14 wounded, 43 missing.

5—Stockade at Stone River, Tenn. One Co. 19th Mich. *Union* 6 wounded, 44 captured.

Glasgow, Ky. 37th Ky. Mounted Inft. *Union* 3 wounded, 100 missing. *Confed.* 13 wounded.

6—Quantrell's attack on the escort of Maj.-Gen. Blunt, at Baxter Springs, Ark., robbing and murdering the prisoners. *Union* 54 killed, 18 wounded, 5 missing.

7—Near Farmington, Tenn. 1st, 3d, and 4th Ohio Cav., 2d Ky. Cav., Long's 2d Cav. Division, and Wilder's Brigade Mounted Inft. *Union* 15 killed, 60 wounded. *Confed.* 10 killed, 60 wounded, 240 missing.

10—Rapidan, Va. Buford's Cavalry. *Union* 20 wounded.

James City, also called Robertson's Run, Va. Pleasanton's Cavalry. *Union* 10 killed, 40 wounded.

Blue Springs, Tenn. Ninth Corps Army of the Ohio and Shackleford's Cav. *Union* 100 killed, wounded, and missing. *Confed.* 66 killed and wounded, 150 missing.

11—Henderson's Mill, Tenn. 5th Ind. Cav. *Union* 11 wounded. *Confed.* 30 killed and wounded.

Colliersville, Tenn. 66th Ind., 13th U. S. Reg. *Union* 15 killed, 50 wounded.

12—Jefferson, Va. 2d Cavalry Division Army of the Potomac. *Union* 12 killed, 80 wounded, 400 missing.

12 and 13—Ingham's Mills and Wyatts, Miss. 2d Iowa Cav. *Union* 45 killed and wounded. *Confed.* 50 killed and wounded.

Culpeper and White Sulphur Springs, Va. Cavalry Corps Army of the Potomac. *Union* 8 killed, 46 wounded.

Merrill's Crossing to Lamine Crossing, Mo. Mo. Enrolled Militia, 1st Mo. Militia Battery, 1st, 4th, and 7th Mo. Militia Cav. *Union* 16 killed. *Confed.* 53 killed, 70 wounded.

Blountville, Tenn. 3d Brigade of Shackleford's Cavalry. *Union* 6 wounded. *Confed.* 8 killed, 26 wounded.

Bulltown, Va. Detachments of 6th and 11th W. Va. *Confed.* 9 killed, 60 wounded.

14—Auburn, Va. Portion of 1st Division Second Corps. *Union* 11 killed, 42 wounded. *Confed.* 8 killed, 24 wounded.

Bristoe Station, Va. Second Corps, portion of 5th Corps, 2d Cavalry Division Army of the Potomac. *Union* 51 killed, 329 wounded. *Confed.* 750 killed and wounded, 450 missing. *Union* Brig.-Gen. Malone killed. *Confed.* Brig.-Gens. Cooke, Posey, and Kirkland wounded.

15—McLean's Ford or Liberty Mills, Va. New Jersey Brigade of Third Corps. *Union* 2 killed, 25 wounded. *Confed.* 60 killed and wounded.

15 to 18—Canton, Brownsville, and Clinton, Miss. Portion of Fifteenth and Seventeenth Corps. *Confed.* 200 killed and wounded.

16—Cross Timbers, Mo. 18th Iowa. *Confed.* 2 killed, 8 wounded.

17—Tampa Bay, Fla. Destruction of two blockade runners by U. S. Gunboats *Tahoma* and *Adele*. *Union* 3 killed, 10 wounded.

18—Charlestown, W. Va. 9th Md. *Union* 12 killed, 13 wounded, 379 missing.

Berryville, Va. 34th Mass., 17th Ind. Battery. *Union* 2 killed, 4 wounded. *Confed.* 5 killed, 20 wounded.

19—Buckland Mills, Va. 3d Division of Kilpatrick's Cav. *Union* 20 killed, 60 wounded, 100 missing. *Confed.* 10 killed, 40 wounded.

20 and 22—Philadelphia, Tenn. 45th Ohio Mounted Inft., 1st, 11th, and 12th Ky. Cav., 24th Ind. Battery. *Union* 20 killed, 80 wounded, 354 missing. *Confed.* 15 killed, 82 wounded, 111 missing.

21—Cherokee Station, Ala. 1st Division Fifteenth Corps. *Union* 7 killed, 37 wounded. *Confed.* 40 killed and wounded.

22—Beverly Ford, Va. 2d Penna. and 1st Me. Cav. *Union* 6 killed.

25—Pine Bluff, Ark. 5th Kan. and 1st Ind. Cav. *Union* 11 killed, 27 wounded. *Confed.* 53 killed, 164 wounded.

26—Cane Creek, Ala. 1st Division Fifteenth Corps. *Union* 2 killed, 6 wounded. *Confed.* 10 killed, 30 wounded.

Vincent's Cross Roads, or Bay Springs, Miss. 1st Alabama (Union) Cav. *Union* 14 killed, 25 wounded.

27—Brown's Ferry, Tenn. Detachment of 2d Brigade, 2d Division of Fourth Corps. *Union* 5 killed, 21 wounded.

Wauhatchie, Tenn. Eleventh Corps and 2d Division of Twelfth Corps. *Union* 77 killed, 339 wounded. *Confed.* 300 killed, 1,200 wounded.

28—Leiper's Ferry, Tenn. 11th and 37th Ky., 112th Ill. *Union* 2 killed, 5 wounded.

29—Cherokee Station, Ala. First Division of Fifteenth Corps. Casualties not recorded.

NOVEMBER, 1863

3—Centerville and Piney Factory, Tenn. Detachments from various regiments, under Lieut.-Col. Scully. *Confed.* 15 killed.

Grand Coteau, La. 3d and 4th Divisions of Thirteenth Corps. *Union* 26 killed, 124 wounded, 576 missing. *Confed.* 60 killed, 320 wounded, 65 missing.

3 and 4—Colliersville, and Moscow, Tenn. Cavalry Brigade of Sixteenth Corps. *Union* 6 killed, 57 wounded. *Confed.* 100 missing.

6—Rogersville, Tenn. 7th Ohio Cav., 2d Tenn. Mounted Inft., 2d Ill. Battery. *Union* 5 killed, 12 wounded, 650 missing. *Confed.* 10 killed, 20 wounded.

Droop Mountain, Va. 10th W. Va., 28th Ohio, 14th Penna. Cav., 2d and 5th W. Va. Cav., Battery B, W. Va. Artil. *Union* 31 killed, 94 wounded. *Confed.* 50 killed, 250 wounded, 100 missing.

7—Rappahannock Station, Va. 5th Wis., 5th and 6th Maine, 49th and 119th Penna., 121st N. Y., supported by balance of Sixth and portion of Fifth Corps. *Union* 370 killed and wounded. *Confed.* 11 killed, 98 wounded, 1,629 missing.

Kelly's Ford, Va. 1st U. S. Sharpshooters, 40th N. Y., 1st and 20th Ind., 3d and 5th Mich., 110th Penna., supported by remainder of Third Corps. *Union* 70 killed and wounded. *Confed.* 5 killed, 59 wounded, 295 missing.

8—Clarksville, Ark. 3d Wis. Cav. *Union* 2 killed.

Muddy Run, near Culpeper, Va. 1st Division Cavalry Division Army of the Potomac. *Union* 4 killed, 25 wounded.

11—Natchez, Miss. 58th U. S. Colored. *Union* 4 killed, 6 wounded. *Confed.* 4 killed, 8 wounded.

13—Trinity River, Cal. Two Cos. 1st Battalion Cal. Inft. *Union* 2 wounded.

14—Huff's Ferry, Tenn. 111th Ohio, 107th Ill., 11th and 13th Ky., 23d Mich., 24th Mich. Battery. *Union* 100 killed and wounded.

Rockford, Tenn. 1st Ky. Cav., 45th Ohio Mounted Inft. *Union* 25 wounded.

Marysville, Tenn. 11th Ky. Cav. *Union* 100 killed and wounded.

15—Loudon Creek, Tenn. 111th Ohio. *Union* 4 killed, 12 wounded. *Confed.* 6 killed, 10 wounded.

16—Campbell's Station, Tenn. Ninth Corps, 2d Division of Twenty-third Corps, Sanders' Cav. *Union* 60 killed, 340 wounded. *Confed.* 570 killed and wounded.

17—Mount Jackson, Va. 1st N. Y. Cav. *Union* 2 killed, 3 wounded. *Confed.* 27 missing.

17 to Dec. 4—Siege of Knoxville, Tenn. Army of the Ohio, commanded by Maj.-Gen. Burnside, complete casualties not recorded. At Fort Sanders, Nov. 29th, the losses were, *Union* 20 killed, 80 wounded. *Confed.* 80 killed, 400 wounded, 300 captured.

19—Union City, Tenn. 2d Ill. Cav. *Union* 1 killed. *Confed.* 11 killed, 53 captured.

23 to 25—Chattanooga, Lookout Mountain, Orchard Knob and Missionary Ridge, Tenn. Fourth and Fourteenth Corps, Army of the Cumberland, Maj.-Gen. Geo. H. Thomas; Eleventh, Geary's Division of the Twelfth, and the Fifteenth Corps Army of the Tennessee, Maj.-Gen. W. T. Sherman. *Union* 757 killed, 4,529 wounded, 330 missing. *Confed.* 361 killed, 2,181 wounded, 6,142 missing.

24—Sparta, Tenn. 1st Tenn. and 9th Penna. Cav. *Confed.* 1 killed, 2 wounded.

26 to 28—Operations at Mine Run, Va., including Raccoon Ford, New Hope. Robertson's Tavern, Bartlett's Mills and Locust Grove. First Corps. Second Corps, Third Corps, Fifth Corps, Sixth Corps, and 1st and 2d Cavalry Divisions Army of the Potomac. *Union* 100 killed, 400 wounded. *Confed.* 100 killed, 400 wounded.

(*Continued in Section* 10)

President Lincoln and General McClellan at Antietam—Their Last Interview

CHAPTER XVII.—Continued.

THE Virginia Legislature, disgusted with the cowardice and perfidy of President Davis and his colleagues, passed resolutions (May 14) calling upon them to defend Richmond at all hazards, and resolved, with a clearness that deprived the trembling government of every excuse but fear, that "the President be assured that whatever destruction or loss of property of the State or individual shall thereby result, will be cheerfully submitted to." It is

A COOK HOUSE

believed that this act was inspired by General Johnston, who saw with indignation the railroad bridge at Richmond covered with plank, for facilitating the flight of artillery across them, and a train of cars in constant readiness for the flight of Davis and his cabinet.

The first collision between the two armies near the Chickahominy occurred on the 23d and 24th of May, one at New Bridge and the other at and near Mechanicsville, less than eight miles from Richmond. The Confederates were driven beyond the Chickahominy at Mechanicsville, and a large part of the Nationals took possession of the Richmond side of the stream. This bold dash was followed the next morning by a stirring order by McClellan for an immediate advance on Richmond. The loyal people rejoiced. He had said to the Secretary of War, ten days before, "I will fight the enemy, whatever their force may be, with whatever force we may have." Everything was in readiness for an advance and every circumstance was favorable, for panic had seized the inhabitants in Richmond, and the Confederate troops were not sanguine of a successful defence. But the over-cautious general hesitated until the golden opportunity was lost forever. This chronic hesitancy President Lincoln evidently anticipated, for about the time when McClellan issued his inspiring order, the former, anxious for the safety of the Capital, telegraphed to the general, "I think the time is near when you must either attack Richmond or give up the job and come to the defence of Washington."

For several days afterward, operations on the flank of the great army made the sum of its action. General Fitz John Porter was sent to Hanover Court-House with a considerable force to keep the way open for McDowell to join the army, which McClellan persistently demanded. Porter had some sharp skirmishes near the Court-House, and cut railway communications with Richmond, all but the important one with Fredericksburg. The general telegraphed to the Secretary of War, that Washington was not in danger, and that it was "the policy and the duty of the Government" to send him "all the well-drilled troops available." When the raids on the Confederate communications had been effected, Porter rejoined the main army lying quietly on the Chickahominy, and McClellan again telegraphed to the Secretary of War, saying: "I will do all that quick movements can accomplish, but you must send me all the troops you can, and leave me full latitude as to choice of commanders."

Three days afterward there were "quick movements" in the *Army of the Potomac*. General Johnston, perceiving McClellan's apparent timidity and the real peril of his army so injudiciously divided by the fickle Chickahominy, marched boldly out from his intrenchments in front of Richmond, to attack the Nationals on the city side of the stream. On the 31st of May he fell with great vigor upon the National advance under General Silas Casey, lying upon each side of the Williamsburg road, half a mile beyond a point known as the Seven Pines, and six miles from Richmond. General Couch's division was at Seven Pines, his right resting at Fair Oaks Station. Kearney's division

RUINS OF ARSENAL AT HARPER'S FERRY

of Heintzelman's corps was near Savage's Station, and Hooker's division of the latter corps was guarding the approaches to the White Oak Swamp. The country around was quite level and mostly wooded.

President Lincoln Visiting Camp at Antietam

General Longstreet led the Confederate advance, and fell suddenly upon Casey. A most sanguinary battle ensued. Casey fought valiantly until full one-third of his command was disabled, and he was driven back by overwhelming numbers. Keyes sent troops to aid him, but they could not withstand the

THE "WHITE HOUSE"

pressure, and the whole body was pushed back to **Fair** Oaks Station on the Richmond and York Railway. Reinforcements sent by Heintzelman and Kearney were met by fresh Confederates, and the victory seemed about to be given to the latter, when General Sumner appeared with the divisions of Generals Sedgwick and Richardson. Sumner had seen the peril, and without waiting orders from McClellan, had moved rapidly to the scene of action. He was just in time to check the Confederate advance. The battle still raged furiously. General Johnston was severely wounded and borne from the field; and early in the evening, a bayonet charge by the Nationals broke the Confederate line into confusion. The fighting then ceased for the night, but it was resumed in the morning (June 1, 1862), when General Hooker and his troops took a conspicuous part in the struggle, which lasted several hours. Finally, the Confederates withdrew to Richmond, and the Nationals remained masters of the battle-field of Fair Oaks, or Seven Pines, as it is sometimes called. The losses were nearly equal on both sides, and amounted to about seven thousand each. In that conflict General O. O. Howard lost his right arm.

The *Army of the Potomac* lay on the borders of the Chickahominy, in a most unhealthy position, for nearly a month after the battle of Fair Oaks, quietly besieging Richmond; and the public expectation was continually fed by the frequent announcement that the decisive battle would be fought "to-morrow." General Robert E. Lee had succeeded the wounded Johnston in the command of the Confederate troops, and had been joined by Generals Jackson and Ewell from the Shenandoah Valley. Thus strengthened, Lee prepared to strike the Nationals a deadly blow. A large body of his cavalry under the dashing leader General J. E. B. Stuart, rode all around McClellan's army. He had fifteen hundred mounted men, and four pieces of horse-artillery. He swept around almost to the "White House;" seized and burned fourteen wagons and two schooners laden with forage, in the Pamunkey, above the "White House;" captured and carried away one hundred and sixty-five prisoners and two hundred and sixty mules and horses; rested three hours, and during the night crossed the Chickahominy and returned to Richmond by the Charles City Road, on the morning of the 15th of June. This raid, the first of similar and more destructive ones by both parties during the war, produced great commotion in the *Army of the Potomac.* In the meantime reinforcements had been called for by McClellan, and sent, yet that commander hesitated to strike.

CHAPTER XVIII.

Battles of Mechanicsville and Gaines's Mill—Transfer of the Army to the James River—Battles at Savage's Station, White-Oak Swamp and Glendale—Battle at Malvern Hill—The Army at Harrison's Landing—"Army of Virginia"—Battle of Cedar Mountain—Washington in Danger—McClellan and the Government—Flank Movement—Battles at Groveton, Bull Run and Chantilly—Call for Volunteers—Barbara Frietchie—Battles on South Mountain and Antietam Creek—Burnside Succeeds McClellan—The Army at Fredericksburg and Battle There.

THE RUINS OF THE "WHITE HOUSE"

GENERAL LEE put General McClellan on the defensive when, on the 26th of June (1862), he sent "Stonewall Jackson," with a considerable force from Hanover Courthouse, to turn the right wing of the National army and fall upon their base of supplies at the "White House." Jackson had been quietly withdrawn from the Shenandoah Valley, and at the proper time made the aggressive movement with much celerity. At the same time a heavier force, under General Longstreet and others, crossed the Chickahominy near Mechanicsville, and attacked McClellan's right wing commanded by General Fitz John Porter. Near Ellison's Mill, not

GENERAL FITZ JOHN PORTER, STAFF AND SCENES

far from Mechanicsville, a terrific battle was fought that day, in which the Confederates were defeated with a loss of between three and four thousand men. The Nationals, advantageously posted, lost about four hundred. This event is known in history as the battle of Mechanicsville.

By this victory, Richmond was placed at the mercy of the National troops; but McClellan, considering his army and stores in peril, immediately prepared to transfer both to the James River. This movement was so secretly and skillfully made, that Lee was not certified of the fact until twenty-four hours after it was actually begun on the morning of the 27th of June. McClellan ordered his stores at the White House to be destroyed if they could not be taken away; and the duty of protecting them in their removal was assigned to the corps of Fitz John Porter. That corps was also charged with the duty of carrying away the siege guns and covering the army in its march for the James River. These troops were accordingly arranged on the rising ground near Gaines's Mill, on the arc of a circle between Cold Harbor and the Chickahominy, where they were attacked in the afternoon (June 27) by a heavy Confederate force led by Generals Longstreet and Hill. The battle that ensued was very severe. Hard pressed, Porter sent to McClellan, who was on the opposite side of the river, for help; but the latter, believing Magruder's twenty-five thousand men at Richmond to be sixty thousand, sent only

COMMANDER R. C. P. RODGERS, U.S.N.

Slocum's division of Franklin's corps. Finding that the battle still raged with great fury, and doubtful of the issue, the commander-in-chief then sent the brigades of Richardson and Meagher across the river. They arrived just in time to save Porter's corps from destruction. His shattered column was falling back in disorder, closely pressed, when the shouts of the fresh troops checked the pursuers and so inspirited the fugitives that they rallied and drove the Confederates back to the field they had won. So ended the battle of Gaines's Mill, with a loss to the Nationals of eight thousand men, and to the Confederates of about five thousand. Porter also lost twenty-two siege guns. During the night succeeding the battle his corps withdrew to the right side of the Chickahominy, destroying the bridges behind them.

Before the dawn of the 28th the National army moved toward Turkey Bend of the James River. General Keyes led the way through White Oak Swamp, followed by Porter's shattered corps. Then came a train of five thousand wagons laden with ammunition, stores and baggage, and a drove of twenty-five hundred head of beef cattle. This movement was so skillfully masked that General Lee, who suspected McClellan was about to give battle on the northern side of the Chickahominy, in defence of his stores at the "White House," or was preparing to retreat down the Peninsula, was completely deceived; and it was late in the night of the 28th (June, 1862) when the astounding fact was announced to him that the *Army of the Potomac* were far on their way toward a new position on the James River. He had then just been informed that a large portion of the stores at the "White House" had been removed, and that the remainder, with the mansion itself, were in flames. To overtake and destroy the retiring army was now Lee's first duty, and he prosecuted the effort with so much vigor, that the Nationals had a desperate struggle to escape.

The divisions of Sedgwick, Richardson, Heintzelman and Smith, of Franklin's corps, were at Savage's Station, under the general command of Sumner. These formed McClellan's rear-guard. There they were assailed by a Confederate force under Magruder, whom Lee had sent for the purpose, and who first attacked Sedgwick at about nine o'clock on the 29th. Then a battle of great severity was fought, and it ended only at evening, after darkness had come on. Magruder was repulsed by the brigade of General Burns, supported by those of Brooke and Hancock. The Nationals fell back to White Oak Swamp covered by French's brigade, leaving twenty-five hundred of them wounded at Savage's Station, who became prisoners to the Confederates. By five o'clock the next morning the entire army had passed the Swamp, and destroyed the bridge behind them that spanned a creek which they had crossed in the passage.

There were severe contests on the morning of the 30th of June, at the main bridge in White Oak Swamp and at Glendale, near by. McClellan's main army had then reached the open country in the region of

GENERAL HUGER, C. S. A.

Antietam Bridge

Method of Destroying Railroads to Prevent Transportation

Malvern Hill. General Franklin had been left with a rear-guard to protect the passage of the bridge and cover the withdrawal of the wagon-trains from that point, and it was with him that the Confederate pursuers had a sharp contest which lasted nearly all day. The latter were kept back; and that night,

GENERAL J. K. F. MANSFIELD
KILLED AT THE BATTLE OF ANTIETAM

the Nationals, having destroyed the bridge, withdrew, leaving behind them three hundred of their sick and wounded and some disabled guns. While the strife was going on there, a sanguinary battle was fought at Glendale, not far off, between the Nationals and a column of Confederates led by Longstreet and Hill. In that conflict, Pennsylvania troops, under General McCall, suffered much. That leader was captured, and General Meade was severely wounded. Fresh troops under Hooker, Meagher and Taylor, arrived in time to give the victory at Glendale to the Nationals; and the next day (July 1, 1862) the *Army of the Potomac*, united for the first time since it was divided by the Chickahominy, were in a strong position on Malvern Hill, within the reach of National gunboats on the James River. But General McClellan thought the position not a safe one, notwithstanding it is a high plateau, with a bold bank sloping toward the river and flanked by deep ravines; and on the morning of the first of July he went down the James River on the gunboat *Galena* and selected a spot at Harrison's Landing, not far from Malvern Hill, as a secure place for his army and base of supplies.

By vigorous movements, Lee compelled the Nationals to fight while their chief leader was away. The Confederates were concentrated at Glendale, and were moved, in a heavy line under Lee's best generals, to carry Malvern Hill by storm. They fell with intense fury upon the Nationals, and one of the most terrible battles of the war was there fought. The brunt of it was borne by the troops of Porter, Couch and Kearney, until toward evening, when Meagher and Richardson came to their aid with fresh soldiers. The Confederates were sorely smitten by well-directed bomb-shells from the gunboats.

This fierce contest continued, with varying fortunes for both parties, until nine o'clock in the evening, when the Confederates were driven to the shelter of the woods and swamps, utterly broken and dispirited. The victory for the Nationals was so decisive that their leaders expected to pursue Lee's shattered army in the morning, and march into Richmond within twenty-four hours. Their disappointment was grievous when General McClellan, who had been on board the *Galena* nearly all day while the army was fighting, ordered that army to fall back and encamp at Harrison's Landing. The chief officers felt that the prize for which they were contending, namely, the defeat of Lee's army and the capture of Richmond, now within their grasp, was snatched from them by a timid hand, and obedience was reluctantly but promptly given. It seemed to be a fitting ending of a campaign which had been a series of signal failures, with little fruit, excepting the loss since the 23d of May of more than fifteen thousand men. The army lingered long among the malarious vapors of the James River, until many more had fallen victims of disease.

When Halleck succeeded McClellan as chief of the armies, he arranged the troops for the defence of Washington in three corps; and placing them under the command of General John Pope, who had been called from the West, named these forces the *Army of Virginia*. These corps were commanded respectively by Generals McDowell, Banks and Sigel. When McClellan had retreated to Harrison's Landing, the Confederates at Richmond, satisfied that no further attempts to take that city would be made at that time, ordered Lee to make a dash on Washington. Having information of Lee's preparations for a raid to the northward, Halleck ordered Pope, at the middle of July, to meet the invaders at the outset of the raid. National cavalry were first sent by General Rufus King, at Fredericksburg, who made excursions to within thirty or forty miles of the Confederate capital, and destroyed railway tracks and bridges.

At that time "Stonewall Jackson" was at Gordonsville with a heavy force, and Pope's main army was near Culpepper Court-House. The former, by Lee's orders, crossed the Rapidan; and at the foot of Cedar Mountain, a few miles west of the Court-House, he was met by General Banks toward the evening of the 9th of August. There occurred one of

GENERAL I. P. RODMAN KILLED AT THE
BATTLE OF ANTIETAM

Scenes at the Battlefield of Antietam

Miller's House, Antietam

the most sanguinary battles of the war.   Some of the time the struggle was carried on hand-to-hand, under an awful pall of smoke which, after nightfall, obscured the light of the moon.   Banks was pressed back by overwhelming numbers, and sorely pressed, until the timely arrival of Rickett's division of McDowell's corps, which checked the pursuers.   In this conflict Banks was ably assisted by Generals Crawford, Augur, Geary and others.   The battle ceased at nine o'clock in the evening, though cannonading was kept up until midnight.   "I have witnessed many battles during the war," wrote a newspaper correspondent, "but I have seen none where the tenacious obstinacy of the American character was so fully displayed."   The National loss was about two thousand men, killed and wounded, and that of the Confederates was about the same.

GENERAL O. O. HOWARD

Jackson held fast to his mountain position until the night of the 11th (August, 1862) when, hearing of the approach of National troops from the Rappahannock, he fell back behind the Rapidan.   Pope took position along the line of that stream, where Le was reinforced by troops from the Carolinas under Generals Burnside and Stevens.   The Confederates were now concentrated for a march on Washington, in heavy columns.   Halleck, meanwhile, perceiving possible danger to the capital, had issued a positive order to McClellan, on the 3d of August, for the immediate transfer of the *Army of the Potomac* to the vicinity of Washington.   That commander instructed his superior officer that "the true defence of Washington" was "on the banks of the James."   The order was repeated with urgency; but it took twenty days to accomplish the transfer.

In the meantime there had been stirring events in the direction of the capital.   Alarmed at the force which Lee had concentrated on his front, Pope retired behind the forks of the Rappahannock.   Lee pushed forward to that river with heavy columns, and on the 20th and 21st of August, a severe artillery duel was fought above Fredericksburg, for seven or eight miles along that stream.   Finding that they could not force a passage of the river, the Confederates took a circuitous route toward the mountains to flank the Nationals, when Pope made skillful movements to thwart them.   But danger to the National Capital increased every hour.   Troops were coming with tardy pace from the Peninsula; and on the 25th, when those of Franklin, Heintzelman and Porter had arrived, Pope's army, somewhat scattered, numbered about sixty thousand men.   On that day, Jackson, leading the great flanking force, crossed the Rappahannock.   By a swift march he went over the Bull Run Mountain at Thoroughfare Gap, and at daylight the next morning he was at Manassas Junction on the railway between the *Army of Virginia* and the National Capital.   Pope took measures for the capture of Jackson or to prevent his uniting with Longstreet, then coming to support him; but the latter event soon occurred at Groveton, not far from the Bull Run battle-ground.   There, on the 29th of August (1862), the combined Confederates fought the whole of Pope's army excepting Banks's troops.   The struggle was severe but indecisive. The loss in the battle at Groveton was about seven thousand men on each side.

Not doubting that he would be instantly reinforced by McClellan, who was at Alexandria, Pope prepared to renew the conflict the next morning. He confidently expected rations and forage from Alexandria, for McClellan had been ordered to supply them; but on the morning of the 30th, when it was too late to retreat and perilous to stand still, Pope received an astounding note from General Franklin, written by direction of McClellan, that "rations and forage would be loaded into the available wagons and cars" as soon as he (Pope) *should send a cavalry escort for the train!*   It was impossible.   Assured that he would not receive support from McClellan, Pope was compelled to fight under great disadvantages. Deceived by what appeared to be a retreat of Lee's army, he was drawn into an ambuscade on a part of the former battle-ground of Bull Run, not far from Groveton, and there a most sanguinary conflict ensued. The Nationals were defeated; and flying across Bull Run to Centreville, they were there reinforced by the troops of Franklin and Sumner.   Pope had labored hard under many difficulties; and he complained bitterly of a lack of co-operation with him, in his later struggles, by McClellan

GENERAL PHIL KEARNEY

MAJOR-GENERAL N. P. BANKS

GENERAL W. B. FRANKLIN

GENERAL E. V. SUMNER AND STAFF

and some of his subordinates.   After the most strenuous efforts of the President and General Halleck to have the *Army of the Potomac* join the *Army of Virginia* in confronting Lee, Pope was joined by only about twenty thousand of the ninety-one thousand who were at Harrison's Landing.   McClellan seemed more ready to give advice than to obey orders.   "I am not responsible for the past, and cannot be for the future," he wrote to Halleck, "unless I receive authority to dispose of the available troops according to my judgment."   And after, by delays, he had thwarted the efforts of the government to get Franklin's corps in a position to give Pope much-needed aid on the 29th, and Halleck had urged him to act promptly in finding out where the enemy was, for he was "tired of guesses," McClellan telegraphed to the President, saying: "I am clear that one of two courses should be adopted.   First to concentrate all our available forces to open communication with Pope;   second, *to leave Pope to get out of his scrape*, and at once use all our means to make the Capital safe."

Lee was afraid to attack the Nationals at Centreville, so he sent Jackson on another flank movement which brought on a battle at Chantilly, north of Fairfax Court-House.   It was fought in a cold and drenching rain.   For a while the conflict was very severe, and in it Generals Philip Kearney and Isaac A. Stephens perished.   The losses on each side were large.   The Nationals, under General Birney, held the field that night, and the next day the broken and demoralized army was sheltered behind the fortifications around Washington city. Pope now repeated, with great earnestness, a request to leave the *Army of Virginia* and return to the West.   His desire was gratified.   Then the *Army of Virginia* disappeared as a separate organization and became a part of the *Army of the Potomac*, and McClellan was placed in command of all the troops defending the Capital.   The disasters which had befallen the armies of the *Potomac* and of *Virginia* caused a momentary gloom to fall

upon the spirits of the loyal people, but it was soon dispelled.   Public opinion throughout the loyal states demanded that it was time for more aggressive work; the vexatious delays had become unbearable.

At the request of the governors of many States, the President, on the first of July (1862), called for three hundred thousand volunteers to serve during the war; and in August he called for three hundred thousand more, for three months, with the understanding that an equal number would be drafted from the citizens who were between eighteen and forty-five years of age, if they did not appear among the volunteers.   These calls were cheerfully responded to; and the Confederate government, alarmed, ordered General Lee to make a desperate effort to capture Washington city before the new army should be brought into the field.   Lee was immediately reinforced. Perceiving the folly of making a direct attack upon the well-fortified National Capital, he crossed the Potomac above that city (near the Point of Rocks) into Maryland to assail Baltimore, and if successful, to fall upon Washington in the rear.   He made the passage with almost his entire army, and on the 7th of September was encamped at Frederick, on the Monocacy.   There, on the 8th, he issued a stirring appeal, in the form of a proclamation, to the people of Maryland, and raised the standard of revolt.   He did not doubt that thousands would resort to it; on the contrary, he lost more men by desertion than he gained by recruiting there.

When General McClellan heard of Lee's invasion of Maryland, he left General Banks, with some troops, to defend Washington, and crossing the Potomac above the National Capital, with about ninety thousand men, he advanced cautiously toward Frederick, which Lee evacuated at their approach.   There McClellan discovered Lee's plan for seizing Washington.   It was to take possession of Harper's Ferry and open communication with Richmond by way ot the Shenandoah Valley, and then marching toward Pennsylvania, entice McClellan far in that direction. At a proper moment Lee was to turn suddenly, smite and defeat his antagonist, and then march upon Washington.

It is related that when the head of Lee's army led by "Stonewall Jackson" entered Frederick, Barbara Frietchie, a very old woman, in defiance of an order for hauling down every Union flag, kept one flying from the dormer window of her house near the bridge over the Monocacy Creek, in the town.

GENERAL JOSEPH HOOKER AND STAFF

GENERAL HOOKER'S HEADQUARTERS DURING BATTLE OF ANTIETAM

GENERAL JOSEPH HOOKER

Seeing it, Jackson ordered his riflemen to shoot away the staff.   When it fell the patriotic Barbara snatched it up, and leaning, says Whittier,

"Far out on the window sill,
  She shook it forth with a royal will;
'Shoot, if you must, this old gray head,
  But spare your country's flag,' she said.
A shade of sadness, a blush of shame,
  Over the face of the leader came:
The nobler nature within him stirr'd
  To life at that woman's deed and word;
'Who touches a hair of yon gray head,
  Dies like a dog! March on!' he said.
All day long through Frederick street
  Sounded the tread of marching feet.
All day long that free flag tost
  Over the head of the rebel host."

The Nationals followed the Confed-federates from Frederick, in two columns, over the South Mountain into the beautiful valley of the Antietam Creek.   The right and centre of the Nationals moved by the way of Turner's Gap, Burnside leading the advance; and the left, composed of Franklin's corps, by way of Crampton's Gap, on the same range, nearer Harper's Ferry.   At Turner's Gap,

MAJOR-GENERAL D. N. COUCH
MAJOR-GENERAL GEORGE STONEMAN
MAJOR-GENERAL W. F. SMITH   MAJOR-GENERAL SILAS CASEY

Burnside fought a desperate battle on the 14th of September; and at the same time Franklin was trying to force his way at Crampton's Gap, to get between General Lee and Harper's Ferry, where Colonel Miles, a Marylander, was in command of National troops.   The strife at Turner's Gap ceased at dark, with a loss to the Nationals of about fifteen hundred men, of whom a little more than three hundred were killed.   Among the latter was the gallant General Reno.   The Nationals intended to renew the battle in the morning; but the Confederates withdrew under cover of the night, and Lee concentrated his forces on Antietam Creek, near Sharpsburg.   Franklin, in the meantime, had fought his way over the Mountain into Pleasant Valley; and on the evening of the 14th (September) was within six miles of Harper's Ferry, which was then invested by a strong force under "Stonewall" Jackson.   The Confederates held the advantageous positions of Maryland and Loudon Heights on each side of the Potomac, which commanded the post at Harper's Ferry, and the latter could be preserved from capture only by help from outside.   This Franklin was about to give; but before he could do so, Miles surrendered the post to Jackson, after sending away his cavalry.   This unfortunate and unnecessary movement deprived the Nationals of a vast advantage which they might have gained by the apparently easy possession of Harper's Ferry, at that time.   Miles's conduct was such, that his loyalty to the Republic was justly suspected.

On the 16th of September, the Confederate army was well posted on the heights near Sharpsburg, on the western side of the Antietam Creek.   The Confederates had been followed from South Mountain cautiously, for McClellan professed to believe them to be in overwhelming numbers on his front.   But Lee's army then numbered only sixty thousand, while McClellan's effective force was eighty-seven thousand.   The latter hesitated to attack; and when he was put upon the defensive by a sharp artillery assault by Confederate cannon, the crisis had passed before he was ready to respond.   Then the brave and energetic Hooker was permitted to cross the Antietam with a part of his corps, commanded by Generals Ricketts, Meade, and Doubleday.   This passage was made on the extreme right of the Confederates, where he had a sharp and successful combat with the foe led by General Hood. Hooker's men lay upon their arms that night.   Other National troops passed over under cover of the darkness.   These were the divisions of Williams and Greene, of Mansfield's corps, who bivouacked a mile in Hooker's rear.

The best of McClellan's generals, expecting a heavy engagement in the morning, awaited these movements with great anxiety.   In this feeling the army of Lee concurred.   At dawn on the morning of the 17th (September, 1862), Hooker opened the battle by assailing the Confederate left with about eighteen thousand men.   The enemy were led by Jackson.   Hooker had Doubleday on his right, Meade on his left, and Ricketts in the centre.   With varying fortunes the contest raged on that wing of the army and along the centre until late in the afternoon.   The National chief, with a lofty faith that all would be well, did not leave his room at Pry's (his headquarters) that morning until eight o'clock, when

the hills had been echoing the cannon-thunder for hours. Then he went out and viewed the progress of the battle from the opposite side of the Antietam, where he held Porter's corps, with artillery, and Pleasanton's cavalry in reserve until toward evening, when he sent some troops to assist the fighters.

Meanwhile General Burnside, with the left wing of the Nationals, had been holding in check, and fighting the Confederate right under Longstreet, since eight o'clock in the morning, with varying success; and he was on the point of gaining a victory there, when the Confederates were reinforced by General A. P. Hill's division, which had hurried up from Harper's Ferry to the support of Lee. Darkness ended the struggle, which had lasted from twelve to fourteen hours. Both armies were severely smitten. The Nationals lost twelve thousand four hundred and seventy men, and McClellan estimated the Confederate loss to have been much greater. The advantage was decidedly with the Nationals that night. Lee's army, shattered and disorganized, and his supplies nearly exhausted, was without reinforcements near; while McClellan's was joined the next morning by fourteen thousand fresh troops. A vigorous movement on his part, that morning, might have put the whole Confederate force into McClellan's hands as prisoners of war; but with chronic hesitation and indecision, he refused to allow his army to pursue the retreating foe until thirty-six hours after the battle. His reasons for his dilatoriness were given in an apologetic tone, in his report, as follows: "Virginia was lost, Washington was menaced, Maryland invaded—the National cause could afford no risks of defeat:"

GENERAL IRVIN MCDOWELL AND STAFF

When, on the morning of the 19th of September, McClellan advanced, Lee had fled, under cover of the night, and was with his shattered army behind strong batteries on the Virginia side of the Potomac. A feeble pursuit was attempted and abandoned. Two brigades crossed the river, and were surprised and driven back into Maryland, when Lee, counting upon McClellan's habitual slowness, moved leisurely up the Shenandoah Valley. McClellan took possession of abandoned Harper's Ferry, and called for reinforcements and supplies to enable him to pursue the fugitives; and ten days afterward, when the news was hourly expected that the *Army of the Potomac* were in swift pursuit of Lee's shattered columns, the commander of the National army proclaimed that he intended to hold his troops where they were, and "attack the enemy should he attempt to cross into Maryland." The President, astounded by this declaration, hastened to McClellan's headquarters, in person, to ascertain the true state of the case. He was so well satisfied that the army was capable of a successful pursuit at once, that he ordered McClellan (October 6, 1862) to cross the Potomac immediately for that purpose. Twenty precious days were afterward spent in correspondence between the disobedient general and his patient superiors, before the former obeyed, during which time Lee's army was thoroughly recruited in every way, and his communications with Richmond were well established.

The beautiful month of October passed away. The roads in Virginia were never in a finer condition; and the loyal people were becoming exceedingly impatient, when, on the 2d of November, McClellan announced that his great army was once more on the soil of Virginia, prepared to move southward on the east side of the Blue Ridge instead of up the Shenandoah Valley, as he had been ordered to do. The patience of the Government and its friends was now exhausted. They had lost faith in McClellan's ability or disposition to achieve a decisive victory over the Confederates, and on the 5th of November he was superseded in the command of the *Army of the Potomac* by General Ambrose E. Burnside, of Rhode Island. So ended General McClellan's unsuccessful military career. He then entered the field of politics in opposition to the administration, and was equally unsuccessful there.

The *Army of the Potomac* was now about one hundred and twenty thousand in number. It was reorganized by Burnside; and he took measures for the early seizure of the Confederate capital rather than for the capture or destruction of the Confederate army. He made Aquia Creek, on the Potomac, his base of supplies; and he hastened to place his army at or near Fredericksburg, on the Rappahannock, from which he might march on Richmond. Lee, in the meantime, had gathered about eighty thousand

BATTERY IN ACTION AT FREDERICKSBURG

REMOVING WOUNDED AFTER BATTLE OF FREDERICKSBURG

BATTLEFIELD OF FREDERICKSBURG FROM MARYE'S HEIGHTS

men on the Heights in the rear of Fredericksburg, with three hundred cannon, and had destroyed all the bridges that spanned the Rappahannock in that vicinity.

It was the second week in December when the opposing great armies in Virginia were lying in parallel lines within cannon-shot of each other, with a narrow river between them. Sixty thousand National troops, under Generals Sumner and Hooker, lay in front of Fredericksburg, with one hundred and fifty cannon on Stafford Heights under the chief direction of General Hunt; and the corps of Franklin, about forty thousand strong, was encamped about two miles below. The troops could cross the river only on pontoons or floating bridges; and on the 11th of December, early in the morning, the engineers went quietly at work to construct five of them. These men were assailed and driven away by sharp-shooters concealed in buildings on the opposite shore. The batteries on Stafford Heights then opened a heavy fire on the town to drive out the enemy, and the city was set on fire, in many places, by the shells; but the sharp-shooters remained. Then a party of volunteers went across the river in open boats, in the face of flying bullets from Mississippi rifles, to dislodge the sharp-shooters. A drummer-boy from Michigan, named Hendershot, begged leave to go along, but was refused permission. Then he asked and obtained permission to push off one of the boats, when he allowed himself to be dragged into the water. Clinging to the vessel, he was conveyed to the opposite shore. Several men in the boat were killed; and when the boy was climbing the bank, his drum was torn in pieces by a flying fragment of an exploded shell. Then he seized the musket of a slain companion, and fought gallantly until the sharp-shooters were driven away or captured. The bridges were finished, and by the evening of the 12th a greater portion of the National army occupied Fredericksburg.

MARYE'S HOUSE ON MARYE'S HEIGHTS

On the morning of the 13th the National army made a simultaneous assault all along the National line, where a most sanguinary battle occurred, which ended with a repulse of Burnside's forces with a loss of almost fourteen thousand men. In this struggle, Generals Franklin, Couch, Hooker, Sumner, Meade, Doubleday, Howard, Humphrey, Wilcox, Hancock, French, Sturgis, Getty, Meagher and others were conspicuous. In the fight, the Confederates lost about half as many as the number lost by the Nationals. Burnside, anxious to gain a victory, was disposed to renew the battle the next day, but was dissuaded by some of his best officers, and his troops remained on the city side of the river until the night of the 15th unmolested by the Confederates. Then, under cover of darkness, they crossed the stream with all their cannon, taking up the pontoons behind them.

This failure produced some dissatisfaction, and Burnside was soon afterward superseded in the command of the *Army of the Potomac* by General Joseph Hooker. It was the misfortune, not the fault of the gallant Burnside, that he did not succeed at Fredericksburg. The *Army of the Potomac* now went into winter quarters on the borders of the Rappahannock.

Hooker's first care was to prevent desertion, secure the return of absentees on furlough, and to weed noxious materials out of the army. Disloyal officers were dismissed as soon as they were discovered; and the evils of idleness were prevented by keeping the soldiers employed. The express trains in the service of the Government were regularly searched, and all property belonging to private citizens was confiscated or destroyed. The army was comfortably hutted; and important changes were made in its organization and its staff department. The cavalry, hitherto scattered among the grand divisions and without organization, as a corps, were consolidated, and were soon placed in a condition of greater efficiency than had ever before been known in the service; and to improve them, they were sent out upon raids within the Confederate lines whenever the condition of the roads would permit. The region between Bull Run and the Rapidan became the theatre of many daring exploits by the horsemen of both armies.

PART OF COMPANY OF MAINE INFANTRY AFTER CHARGE AT MARYE'S HEIGHTS, FREDERICKSBURG

RUINS IN FREDERICKSBURG AFTER THE BATTLE

CHAPTER XIX.

National Rule in the Southwest—Guerrillas—Invasion of Kentucky—Cincinnati Saved—Battle at Mumfordsville and Perryville—
Army of the Cumberland—Battle at Iuka Springs—General Ord's Movements—Battle at Corinth and Operations near—Capture
of Baton Rouge—Destruction of the "Arkansas"—Operations in Arkansas and Louisiana—Battle at Murfreesboro'—Emancipation
Proclamation—The Confederate Government—Davis President—Doings of the Confederate Congress—British Sympathy with
the Confederates—The "Alabama"—Operations against Vicksburg—Operations on the Mississippi—Battles at Port Gibson, Raymond, Jackson, Champion Hills and Big Black River—Vicksburg Invested.

THE Lower Mississippi, from its mouth to New Orleans, was in the possession of the National
military and naval forces under General Butler and Commodore Farragut, at the beginning of
the summer of 1862. So, also, was the same river, from Memphis to St. Louis, controlled by
the Government troops and vessels; while the National forces held sway over southern Tennessee, and
northern Alabama and Mississippi.

Although the great armies of the Confederates had been driven from Kentucky and Tennessee,
the absence of any considerable Union force excepting on the southern border of the latter State, permitted
a most distressing guerrilla warfare to be carried on within the borders of those commonwealths by
mounted bands, who, with gallant leaders, hovered upon the rear and flanks of the National forces, or roamed at will over the whole country, plundering the Union inhabitants. One of their leaders was John Morgan, a bold Alabamian, at the head of dashing mounted men, who appeared in Kentucky, and raiding through that State prepared the way for the advance of an invading army from Chattanooga, led by General Braxton Bragg. Another mounted force, led by N. B. Forrest, was sweeping over a portion of Tennessee for the same purpose at the same time; and at the middle of July he threatened the Union post at Nashville, then in command of General Negley. In the meantime, General Bragg

BVT. MAJ.-GENERAL J. R. BROOKE
MAJ.-GENERAL J. SEDGWICK   BRIG.-GENERAL W. W. BURNS

was pushing toward Kentucky by a route eastward of Nashville, while General Buell was moving in the
same direction, on a parallel line, to foil the invaders.

General E. Kirby Smith, a native of Connecticut, leading the van of Bragg's army, entered Kentucky
from East Tennessee, and pushed on rapidly to Lexington, fighting and defeating a National force, on
the 30th of August, under General M. D. Manson, near Richmond in that State. The Secessionists
of Kentucky warmly welcomed the invaders, and swelled their ranks at every step. The alarmed Legislature of Kentucky, sitting at Frankfort, fled to Louisville, while Smith pressed vigorously on in the
direction of the Ohio River, with the intention of capturing and plundering Cincinnati. He was unex-
pectedly confronted on the southern side of the Ohio by strong fortifications and a considerable National
force under the energetic General Lewis Wallace, who had proclaimed martial law in Cincinnati,
Covington and Newport, and in a stirring proclamation, demanded the instant co-operation of the
people. "Citizens for the labor—soldiers for the battle," was the principle announced. The response
was wonderful. In the course of a few hours he had at his command an army of workers and fighters
forty thousand strong. The invader recoiled; and falling back to the Kentucky State capital (Frankfort),
seized it, and there awaited the arrival of Bragg, who crossed the Cumberland River and entered Kentucky
on the 5th of September, with forty regiments and forty cannon.

Bragg's advance, eight thousand strong, under General J. R. Chalmers, encountered a National
force under Colonel T. J. Wilder, at Mumfordsville, on the 14th of September. It was on the line of
the Nashville and Louisville Railway. A battle began at dawn and lasted about five hours, when the
Confederates were repulsed; but two days afterward a stronger force under General (Bishop) Polk fell
upon Wilder, and after a severe struggle he was compelled to yield to vastly superior numbers. Bragg
was elated by this success, and joining Smith, at Frankfort, he prepared to make a supposed easy march

Panoramic Views.

View from Tyler's Battery.

Lower End of Town.

House on Maryes Heights Showing effect of Shells.

Houses Showing Effects of Shells Dec. 13. 1862

FREDERICKSBURG

VIEWS OF FREDERICKSBURG

to Louisville, his destination. His army then numbered about sixty-five thousand effective men, and the movements of Buell seemed too tardy to promise serious impediments. Bragg was mistaken. Buell, who had kept abreast of Bragg, suddenly turned upon him with about sixty thousand men, and near the little town of Perryville, in Boyle county, they had a fierce combat on the 8th of October. In that battle the Nationals lost about four thousand three hundred and fifty men; but the invaders were so

roughly handled that they fled in haste, that night, toward East Tennessee, followed by their marauding bands, who had plundered the inhabitants in every direction. They started in their retreat with a wagon-train of stolen property, forty miles in length, but were compelled to leave a large portion of it behind. The whole expedition seems to have had no higher aims than that of a plundering raid. It proved disastrous to Bragg's army, and would have caused its total ruin if that army had been vigorously pursued. Soon afterward, General Rosecrans, who had won substantial victories in northern Mississippi, succeeded Buell in the command of the *Army of the Ohio*, and its name was changed to that of the *Army of the Cumberland*.

While General Bragg was plundering the Kentuckians, bands of Confederates were raiding through western Tennessee to

FUGITIVE NEGROES AND RAPPAHANNOCK STATION

draw attention from the invaders; and the army in northern Mississippi, now led by General Beauregard, had advanced toward Tennessee under Generals Van Dorn and Price. General Rosecrans was then in command of the *Army of the Mississippi*, charged with the duty of holding the region lately repossessed by the Nationals in consequence of the evacuation of Corinth and the valor of Mitchel.

Rosecrans was at Tuscumbia when General Grant informed him that danger was gathering westward of him; and when he moved toward Corinth, Price advanced toward Iuka Springs, a summer watering-place in northern Mississippi, to meet him. Near the village of that name, Rosecrans and Price met on the 19th of September, and fought a most severe battle. The disparity in numbers was very great. Price had full eleven thousand men, while Rosecrans did not have more than three thousand men actually engaged in the struggle. During the battle, which was extermely fierce, there was a desperate contest for the possession of an Indiana battery which the Confederates had seized after all the horses belonging to it, and seventy-two of its artillerymen, were killed. It was fought for hand-to-hand. Charges and counter-charges were made; until, at length, the Confederate soldiers dragged the cannon off the field, with ropes. But the Confederates were so badly beaten in the battle, that they fled southward in great haste and confusion. The National loss was nearly eight hundred; that of the Confederates over fourteen hundred. Meanwhile General Ord, whom Grant had sent to aid Rosecrans, had been watching the movements of a body of the Confederates who were making feints against Corinth. He had, according to orders, marched within four miles of Iuka; instructed to wait there until he should hear Rosecrans's great guns. A high wind from the north prevented their sounds reaching him. Ord lay there until the next morning, when he pushed on toward Iuka and found Rosecrans a victor and his foe departed. Then Ord retired to Bolivar, between Corinth and Memphis, while Rosecrans concentrated his troops at Corinth and prepared to meet an impending attack by the combined forces of Van Dorn and Price. These, about forty thousand in number, were united at Ripley, and at the close of September they moved on Corinth. At that place the opposing armies battled fiercely on the 3d and 4th of October, when the result was the repulse of the Confederates, the pursuit of them to Ripley, and a loss on the part of the Nationals of more than twenty-three hundred men. The Confederates lost about nine thousand men, including prisoners. On their retreat a part of Van Dorn's troops fought the forces of Ord at the Hatchee River, where the latter was severely wounded. For a while after this event there was comparative repose in General Grant's department.

The only obstructions to the free navigation of the Mississippi River, in the spring of 1862, were at Vicksburg and at Port Hudson below. Vicksburg, a city of Mississippi, situated on a group of high

GROUP OF CONFEDERATES AT FREDERICKSBURG

BETHEL CHURCH, HEADQUARTERS OF GENERAL BURNSIDE, AND OTHER VIEWS

eminences known as the Walnut Hills, on the eastern bank of the Mississippi River, at a bold turn in the stream, was a point of great military importance, for it had been fortified by the Confederates and was daily growing stronger. It promised to become impregnable for those who were opposing the grand scheme of the National Government for gaining the absolute control of that great stream, and thus securing important portions of the Confederacy. Toward the seizure of that point, operations in the southwest were soon tending. To remove these obstructions, Farragut, in command of National vessels, bent his energies. So early as the 7th of May (1862), Baton Rouge, the capital of Louisiana, had been captured by the National forces by land and water, when Farragut went up the river to Vicksburg and there held

GENERAL I. B. RICHARDSON

GENERAL G. W. MORRELL

communication with the commanders of gunboats above. Finally, he attacked the batteries there (June 26); and he also attempted to cut a canal across a peninsula in front of Vicksburg, so as to avoid the Confederate guns at the city altogether; but he failed in his undertakings, and descended the river with his vessels. This movement was followed, early in August, by an attack upon Baton Rouge, by a Confederate force led by General J. C. Breckinridge. The post was then in command of General Thomas Williams. There was a desperate struggle for about two hours, in which the Twenty-first Indiana Regiment was conspicuous. It lost all of its field officers before the end of the action. Seeing this, General Williams placed himself at its head, exclaiming, "Boys, your field-officers are all gone; I will lead you!" They gave him three hearty cheers, when a bullet passed through his breast and he fell dead. He had just issued orders for the line to fall back, which it did, in good order, with Colonel Cahill of the Ninth Connecticut in chief command. The Confederates, dreadfully smitten, also fell back, and then retreated.

The insurgents had constructed a formidable "ram," which they named *Arkansas*. With it they expected to sweep every National vessel from the Mississippi, and "drive the Yankees from New Orleans." It did not arrive at Baton Rouge in time to engage in the attack upon the National forces there; but on the morning after the battle, Commodore Porter, with the gunboat *Essex*, accompanied by the *Cayuga* and *Sumter*, went up the river to meet her. They found her five miles above Baton Rouge. After a short and sharp fight, she became unmanageable, and was headed toward the river bank and set on fire. Just as she touched the shore her magazine exploded, and the monster was blown into fragments.

During the summer and autumn of 1862, there were some stirring events in Missouri and Arkansas. After the battle at Pea Ridge, Curtis marched eastward, with his army, to assist in military operations on the borders of the Mississippi River; but he remained some time at Helena, menacing Little Rock and smiting guerrilla bands that roamed that State. Missouri was equally infested with guerrillas; and in June (1862) that Commonwealth was erected into a separate military district, with General J. M. Schofield at its head. He was vigilant and active; and with a force thirty thousand strong, scattered over the State in six divisions, he soon subdued, in a great degree, the numerous roaming bands that overran it. From April until September, about one hundred battles and skirmishes were fought in that State. Schofield drove out troops that came over the southern border to help the Missourians in arms, and these fugitives formed the nucleus of a force, about forty thousand strong, which gathered in Arkansas under General T. C. Hindman, formerly a member of Congress.

Leaving Curtis in command of the Missouri district, Schofield marched against Hindman, with eight thousand

GENERAL R. B. AYRES

GENERAL E. D. KEYES

A Michigan Regiment in Camp

General A. E. Burnside and Staff

troops under General J. G. Blunt, in southern Missouri. With these he sought the shy Confederates in the vicinity of the Ozark Mountains. Blunt attacked a portion of them at Fort Wayne, near Maysville, on the 22d of October, and drove them into the Indian country. A week later a cavalry force, under General F. T. Herron, struck another portion on the White River, eight miles from Fayetteville, and drove them into the mountains. Soon after this, ill health compelled Schofield to leave the field, when the command devolved upon General Blunt.

Hindman now determined to strike a decisive blow for the recovery of his State from National control. Late in November he had gathered about twenty thousand men on the western borders of Arkansas. He moved against Blunt, and on the 28th his advance, composed of Marmaduke's cavalry, was attacked and defeated by Blunt, on Boston Mountains. The latter then took position at Cane Hill, when Hindman, with eleven thousand men, prepared to crush him. Blunt sent for General Herron, then just over the border, in Missouri, to come and help him. Herron promptly complied. and the combined forces fought and defeated Hindman at a little settlement called Prairie Grove. The Confederates were driven in confusion over the mountains.

Meanwhile there had been stirring events nearer the Gulf of Mexico, west of the Mississippi. Texas was then under Confederate rule. So early as May, 1862, Commander Eagle, with a small squadron of National vessels, appeared before Galveston, and demanded its surrender. There was a prompt refusal to comply; and so the matter remained until October following, when the civil authorities of that city surrendered it to Commodore Renshaw of the National navy. At the same time General Butler sent aggressive expeditions into the interior of Louisiana. The most important of them was led by General Godfrey Weitzel, who went with a strong force to "repossess" the rich La Fourche parish.

BRIG GEN. W. DWIGHT.

MAJ GEN. E. G. AUGUR.

BRIG GEN. GROVER.

LT. COM. R. L. LAW.

This was accomplished, after a severe engagement at Labadieville, on the 27th of October. Very soon afterward the eastern portions of Louisiana, along the borders of the Mississippi, were brought under National control. On the 10th of December following, General Butler was succeeded in the command of the Department of the Gulf by General N. P. Banks.

The year 1862 was now drawing to a close. General Grant had concentrated the bulk of his army at Holly Springs, in Mississippi, where he was confronted by Van Dorn; at about the same time, General Rosecrans, with a greater part of the *Army of the Cumberland*, was moving southward to attack Bragg at Murfreesboro', below Nashville. Rosecrans was assisted by Generals Thomas, McCook, Crittenden, Rousseau, Palmer, Sheridan, J. C. Davis, Wood, Van Cleve, Hazen, Negley, Mathews and others; and Bragg had, as his lieutenants, Generals Polk, Breckenridge, Hardee, Kirby Smith, Cheatham, Withers, Cleburne, and Wharton.

On the 30th of December, the two armies lay within cannon-shot of each other on opposite sides of Stone River, near Murfreesboro'. On the following morning a sanguinary battle was begun, and continued until evening, with varied success and fearful losses. Rosecrans had gallantly conducted the fight in person, and he and Bragg prepared to renew the contest on the following morning, the first of January, 1863. That day was spent in heavy skirmishing; but on the morning of the 2d a terrific struggle was begun. The batteries on both sides were massed, and they were worked with destructive energy. The dead and wounded strewed the ground over scores of acres, for the carnage was dreadful; and, at one time, it seemed as if the total destruction of both armies would be the result. At length seven National regiments made a simultaneous charge, by which the Confederate line was broken into fragments and scattered in confusion. These regiments were the Nineteenth Illinois; Eighteenth, Twenty-first, and Seventy-fourth Ohio; Seventy-eighth Pennsylvania; Eleventh Michigan, and Thirty-seventh Indiana. Victory remained with Rosecrans, and Bragg retreated southward to Tullahoma, while his antagonist occupied the battle-field and Murfreesboro'. The National loss in the battle of Stone River was twelve thousand men, and that of the Confederates ten thousand. The relative position of the two armies immediately after the battle remained so for several months afterward.

The war had now been going on for almost two years. It had been begun by the politicians of the

SANITARY COMMISSION AT FREDERICKSBURG AND OTHER VIEWS

slave-labor States for the purpose of perpetuating the slave-system, which gave to the Confederate cause the chief sinews of its strength. It nurtured a producing class that fed, by its labor, the armies arrayed against the life of the Republic; and only a very small proportion of that class were drawn from the pursuits of agriculture to the camps. Perceiving this, the President of the United States and the loyal people resolved to destroy the system by some method of abolition. The kind-hearted Lincoln proposed to give pecuniary aid to any State government which might provide for the abolition of slavery; but the interested friends of that system everywhere refused to listen. Congress proceeded to abolish slavery in the District of Columbia, over which that body had direct control; and, finally, they gave the President discretionary powers to de- clare the emancipation of the slaves in States wherein insurrection existed. Fi- nally, late in September (1862), President Lincoln issued a proclamation, in which he gave public no- tice that it was his purpose to declare such emancipation on the first of January, 1863, to take effect immediately wherever a state of insurrec- tion might then exist, un-

AT HARRISON'S LANDING

less the offenders should lay down their arms. This friendly warning—this forbearance to strike the blow that was to remove the manacles from millions of bondsmen—was treated by the masters of the slaves with scorn. It was sneered at by them, as an act of sheer impuissance. It was compared to "the Pope's Bull against the comet;" and, because of this menace, resistance to the Government was more rampant than ever. It was evident that the warning would be ineffectual. The President prepared a proclamation of emanci- pation. It was submitted to his cabinet and approved; and on the first of January, 1863, it was promul- gated with the whole force of the Republic—its army, its navy, and its judiciary; its Executive and Legislative powers—back of it to enforce its provisions. The moral force of that proclamation was tremendous. By that act the shackles were taken from the personal freedom of over three million slaves. From the hour of the promulgation of the proclamation of emancipation, the power of the enemies of the Government began to wane, and the star of their own future prosperity arose with beams of promise.

Early in 1862, the Confederate government was changed from a "provisional" to a "permanent one." The "provisional congress," made up of delegates chosen by conventions of politicians and legislatures of States, had been in continuous session from the 18th of November, 1861, until the 18th of February, 1862, when its term expired by limitation. On the same day a congress, professedly elected by the people, commenced its session under the "permanent constitution of the Confederate States." I say "professedly elected by the people." The following was the method pursued in Virginia, as presented in an editorial article in a leading Richmond journal, in carrying on a *popular* election:

"It being necessary to form a ticket of electors, and the time being too short to call a convention of the people, it was suggested that the Richmond editors should prepare a ticket, thus *relieving the people of the trouble of making selections.* The ticket thus formed has been presented." Here several of the nom- inees were named. "Every district in the State," said the journal, "is embraced in this editorial report."

Views on the Field Where General Sumner Charged, Showing Many Dead Confederates in the Trenches

In the permanent Confederate congress, all of the slave-labor States were represented excepting Maryland and Delaware. The oath to support the constitution of the Confederate States was administered to the senators by R. M. T. Hunter of Virginia, and to the representatives, by Howell Cobb of

Georgia. Thomas Bocock, of Virginia, was elected Speaker of the House. On the following day (February 19) the votes for president of the Confederacy were counted, and were found to be one hundred and nine in number, all of which were cast for Jefferson Davis. Three days afterward Davis was inaugurated president for six years. He chose for his cabinet Judah P. Benjamin of Louisiana, secretary of state; George W. Randolph of Virginia, secretary of war; S. R. Mallory of Florida, secretary of the navy; Charles G. Memminger of South Carolina, secretary of the treasury, and Thomas H. Watts of Alabama, attorney-general. Randolph resigned, and James A. Seddon, a wealthy citizen of Richmond, who was conspicuous in the famous "Peace Convention" at Washington, was chosen to fill his place.

Measures were adopted by the Confederate Congress to prosecute the war against the Union with vigor. It was declared, by joint resolution, that it was the unalterable determination of the people of the Confederate States "to suffer all the calamities of the most protracted war;" and that they would never, "on any terms, politically affiliate with a people who were guilty of an invasion of their soil and the butchery of their citizens." With this spirit they prosecuted the war on land; and with the aid of the British aristocracy, ship-builders and merchants, and the tacit consent of the British government, they were enabled to keep afloat, on the ocean, some active vessels for plundering American com-

BRIG.-GEN. ISAAC I. STEVENS

merce. The hoped-for and expected result was the driving of the carrying-trade between the United States and Europe into British bottoms, and so enriching the British shipping merchants. This was the end to be accomplished, and it was effected.

The most formidable of these Anglo-Confederate plunderers of the sea was the *Alabama*, which was built, armed, manned and victualled in England. She sailed under the British flag, and was received with favor in every British port that she entered. In the last three months of the year 1862, she destroyed by fire twenty-eight helpless American merchant vessels. While these incendiary fires, kindled by Englishmen in a ship fitted out as a sea-rover by Englishmen commanded by a Confederate leader, were illuminating the bosom of the Atlantic Ocean, a merchant ship (the *George Griswold*), laden with provisions as a gift for starving English operatives in Lancashire, who had been deprived of work and food by the Civil War in America, and whose necessities their own government failed to relieve, was sent from the city of New York, *convoyed by a national war vessel to save her from the fury of the British sea-rover!* The sequel of the *Alabama* story will be told hereafter.

At the beginning of 1863, the National Government had more than seven hundred thousand soldiers in its service; and up to that time the loyal people had furnished twelve hundred thousand troops, mostly volunteers, for the salvation of the life of the Republic. The theatre of war had become co-extensive with the slave-labor States; and at that time the capture of Vicksburg and Port Hudson, on the Mississippi

River, was a chief object of the Government. Only between these places was that river free from the patrol of National gunboats; and it was desirable to break this connection between the insurgents on each side of the stream. To this end General Grant concentrated his forces near the Tallahatchee River, in northern Mississippi, where Generals Hovey and Washburne had been operating with troops whom they had led from Helena, in Arkansas. Grant had a large quantity of supplies at Holly Springs. These, through carelessness or treachery, fell into the hands of Van Dorn on the 20th of December (1862), and Grant was compelled to fall back to Grand Junction to save his army.

MAJ GEN. G. W. GETTY.
MAJ GEN. J. GIBBON.
MAJ. GEN. D. B. BIRNEY.

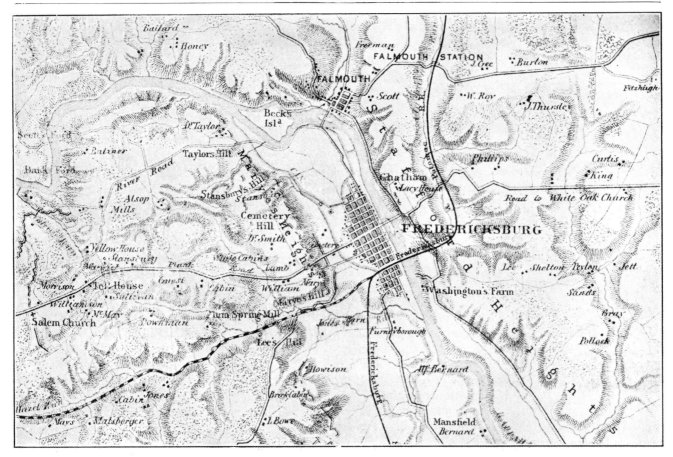

MAP OF FREDERICKSBURG AND VICINITY

VIEWS OF FREDERICKSBURG

CHRONOLOGICAL SUMMARY AND RECORD—Continued

NOVEMBER, 1863—*Continued from Section* 9

27—Cleveland, Tenn. 2d Brigade of 2d Cavalry Division. *Confed.* 200 captured.

Ringgold and Taylor's Ridge, Ga. Portions of Twelfth, Fourteenth, and Fifteenth Corps. *Union* 68 killed, 351 wounded. *Confed.* 50 killed, 200 wounded, 230 missing.

27 to 29—Fort Esperanza, Tex. Portions of 1st and 2d Divisions Thirteenth Corps. *Union* 1 killed, 2 wounded. *Confed.* 1 killed.

DECEMBER, 1863

1 to 4—Ripley and Moscow Station, Miss., and Salisbury, Tenn. 2d Brigade Cavalry Division of Sixteenth Corps. *Union* 175 killed and wounded. *Confed.* 15 killed, 40 wounded. *Union* Col. Hatch, commanding, wounded.

2—Walker's Ford, W. Va. 65th, 116th, and 118th Ind., 21st Ohio Battery, 5th Ind. Cav., 14th Ill. Cav. *Union* 9 killed, 39 wounded. *Confed.* 25 killed, 50 wounded.

7—Creelsboro, Ky., and Celina, Tenn. 13th Ky. Cav. *Confed.* 15 killed.

8 to 21—Averill's Raid in Southwestern Va. *Union* 6 killed, 5 wounded. *Confed.* 200 prisoners.

10 to 14—Bean's Station and Morristown, Tenn. Shackleford's Cavalry. *Union* 700 killed and wounded. *Confed.* 932 killed and wounded, 150 prisoners.

17 to 26—Rodney and Port Gibson, Miss. Miss. Marine Brigade. *Union* 2 killed.

19—Barren Fork, Ind. Ter. 1st and 3d Kan., Indian Home Guards. *Confed.* 50 killed.

24 and 25—Bolivar and Summerville, Tenn. 7th Ill. Cav. *Union* 3 killed, 8 wounded.

28—Charlestown, Tenn. Detachments of 2d Mo. and 4th Ohio Cav. guarding wagon train. *Union* 2 killed, 15 wounded. *Confed.* 8 killed, 39 wounded, 121 captured.

29—Talbot's Station and Mossy Creek, Tenn. 1st Brigade, 2d Division Twenty-third Corps, 1st Tenn. Cav., 1st Wis. Cav., 2d and 4th Ind. Cav., 24th Ind. Battery.

30—St. Augustine, Fla. 10th Conn., 24th Mass. *Union* 4 killed.

Greenville, N. C. Detachments of 12th N. Y., 1st N. C. and 23d N. Y. Battery. *Union* 1 killed, 6 wounded. *Confed.* 6 killed.

Waldron, Ark. 2d Kan. Cav. *Union* 2 killed, 6 wounded.

JANUARY, 1864

1 to 10—Rectortown and London Heights, Va. 1st Md. Cav., Potomac Home Brigade. *Union* 29 killed and wounded, 41 missing. *Confed.* 4 killed, 10 wounded.

3—Jonesville, Va. Detachment 16th Ill. Cav., 22d Ohio Battery. *Union* 12 killed, 48 wounded, 300 missing. *Confed.* 4 killed, 12 wounded.

7—Martin's Creek, Ark. 11th Mo. Cav. *Union* 1 killed, 1 wounded.

12—Mayfield, Ky. 58th Ill. *Union* 1 killed, 1 wounded. *Confed.* 2 killed.

13—Mossy Creek, Tenn. McCook's Cav. *Confed.* 14 killed.

14—Bealton, Va. One Co. 9th Mass. *Union* 2 wounded. *Confed.* 3 killed, 12 wounded.

16 and 17—Dandridge, Tenn. Fourth Corps and Cav. Division of Army of the Ohio. *Union* 150 wounded.

20—Tracy City, Tenn. Detachment 20th Conn. *Union* 2 killed.

23—Rolling Prairie, Ark. 11th Mo. Cav. *Union* 11 killed.

24—Baker Springs, Ark. 2d and 6th Kan. Cav. *Union* 1 killed, 2 wounded, *Confed.* 6 killed, 2 wounded.

Tazewell, Tenn. 34th Ky., 116th and 18th Ind., 11th Tenn. Cav., 11th Mich. Battery. *Confed.* 31 killed.

27—Fair Gardens or Kelly's Ford, Tenn. Sturgis's Cavalry. *Union* 100 killed and wounded. *Confed.* 65 killed, 100 captured.

28—Tunnel Hill, Ga. Part of Fourteenth Corps. *Union* 2 wounded. *Confed.* 32 wounded.

29—Medley, W. Va. 1st and 14th W. Va., 23d Ill., 2d Md., Potomac Home Brigade, 4th W. Va. Cav., Ringgold (Pa.) Cav. *Union* 10 killed, 70 wounded. *Confed.* 100 wounded.

FEBRUARY, 1864

1—Smithfield, Va. Detachments 99th N. Y., 21st Conn., 20th N. Y. Cav., 3d Pa. Artil., and marines from U. S. Gunboats *Minnesota* and *Smith Briggs*. *Union* 90 missing.

1 to 3—Bachelor Creek, Newport Barracks, and New Berne, N. C. 132d N. Y., 9th Vt., 17th Mass., 2d N. C., 12th N. Y. Cav., 3d N. Y. Artil. *Union* 16 killed, 50 wounded, 280 missing. *Confed.* 35 killed, 30 wounded.

1 to March 8—Expedition up the Yazoo River, Miss. 11th Ill., 47th U. S. Colored, 3d U. S. Colored Cav., and a portion of Porter's Fleet of Gunboats. *Union* 35 killed, 121 wounded. *Confed.* 35 killed, 90 wounded.

3 to March 5—Expedition from Vicksburg to Meridian, Miss., including Champion Hills, Raymond, Clinton, Jackson, Decatur, Chunky Station, occupation of Meridian, Lauderdale Springs, and Marion, Miss. Two Divisions of the Sixteenth and three of the Seventeenth Corps, with the 5th Ill., 4th Iowa, 10th Mo. and Foster's (Ohio) Cav. *Union* 56 killed, 138 wounded, 105 captured. *Confed.* 503 killed and wounded, 212 captured.

5—Qualltown, N. C. Detachment of 14th Ill. Cav. *Union* 3 killed, 6 wounded. *Confed.* 50 captured, including Maj.-Gen. Vance.

Cape Girardeau, Mo. 2d Mo. Militia Cav. *Confed.* 7 killed.

6—Bolivar, Tenn. Detachment of 7th Ind. Cav. *Union* 1 killed, 3 wounded. *Confed.* 30 wounded.

Morton's Ford, Va. Portion of Second Corps. *Union* 10 killed, 201 wounded. *Confed.* 100 missing.

7—Barnett's Ford, Va. Brig.-Gen. Merritt's Cav. *Union* 20 killed and wounded.

Vidalia, La. 30th Mo., 64th U. S. Colored, 6th U. S. Artil., Colored. *Confed.* 6 killed, 10 wounded.

9—Morgan's Mills, Ark. Detachments of 4th Ark., 11th Mo. Cav., 1st Neb. Cav. *Union* 1 killed, 4 wounded. *Confed.* 65 killed and wounded.

9 to 14—Barber's Place, St. Mary's River, Lake City and Gainesville, Fla. 40th Mass. Mounted Inft. and Independent (Mass.) Cav. *Union* 4 killed, 16 wounded. *Confed.* 4 killed, 48 wounded.

10 to 25—Smith's Raid from Germantown, Tenn., into Mississippi. Smith's and Grierson's Cav. Divisions. *Union* 43 killed, 267 wounded. *Confed.* 50 wounded, 300 captured.

12—Rock House, W. Va. 14th Ky. *Confed.* 12 killed, 4 wounded.

14—Ross Landing, Ark. 51st U. S. Colored. *Union* 13 killed, 7 wounded.

Brentsville, Va. 13th Pa. Cav. *Union* 4 killed, 1 wounded.

14 and 15—Waterproof, La. 49th U. S. Colored and U. S. Gunboat *Forest Rose*. *Union* 8 killed, 14 wounded. *Confed.* 15 killed.

19—Grosse Tete Bayou, La. 4th Wis. Cav. *Union* 2 wounded. *Confed.* 4 killed, 6 wounded.

Near Batesville, Ark. 4th Ark., 11th Mo. Cav. *Union* 3 killed, 4 wounded. *Confed.* 6 killed, 10 wounded.

20—Holston River, Tenn. 4th Tenn. *Union* 2 killed, 3 wounded. *Confed.* 5 killed, 10 wounded.

Olustee or Silver Lake, Fla. 47th, 48th and 115th N. Y., 7th Conn., 7th N. H., 40th Mass., 8th and 54th U. S. Colored, 1st N. C. Colored, 1st Mass. Cav., 1st and 3d U. S. Artil., 3d R. I. Artil. *Union* 193 killed, 1,175 wounded, 460 missing. *Confed.* 100 killed, 400 wounded.

22—Mulberry Gap, Tenn. 9th Tenn. Cav. *Union* 13 killed and wounded, 256 captured.

Drainesville, Va. Detachment of 2d Mass. Cav. *Union* 10 killed, 7 wounded, 57 captured. *Confed.* 2 killed, 4 wounded.

Johnson's Mills, Tenn. Detachment of 24 men 5th Tenn. Cav., captured and massacred by Ferguson's guerrillas.

23 and March 18—Calf Killer Creek, Tenn. 5th Tenn. Cav. *Union* 8 killed, 3 wounded. *Confed.* 33 killed.

25 to 27—Buzzard Roost, Tunnel Hill and Rocky Face, Ga. Fourth and Fourteenth Corps and Cavalry Corps Army of the Cumberland. *Union* 17 killed, 272 wounded. *Confed.* 20 killed, 120 wounded.

27 and 28—Near Canton, Miss. Foraging Detachments of 3d and 32d Iowa. *Union* 2 killed, 5 wounded. *Confed.* 3 killed, 15 wounded.

28 to March 4—Kilpatrick's Raid, Stevensburg to Richmond, Va. Kilpatrick's Cavalry. *Union* 330 killed, wounded and captured. *Confed.* 308 killed, wounded and captured.

MARCH, 1864

1—Stanardsville and Burton's Ford, Rapidan, Va. Custer's Cav. *Union* 10 wounded. *Confed.* 30 captured.

2—Harrisonburg, La. Porter's Miss. Squadron. *Union* 2 killed, 14 wounded.

5—Panther Springs, Tenn. One Co. 3d Tenn. *Union* 2 killed, 8 wounded, 22 captured. *Confed.* 30 wounded.

7—Decatur, Ala. Army of the Tennessee, commanded by Brig.-Gen. Dodge.

9—Suffolk, Va. 2d U. S. Colored Cav. *Union* 8 killed, 1 wounded. *Confed.* 25 wounded.

14—Fort De Russy, La. Detachments of Sixteenth and Seventeenth Corps and Porter's Miss. Squadron. *Union* 7 killed, 41 wounded. *Confed.* 5 killed, 4 wounded, 260 prisoners.

15—Clarendon, Ark. 8th Mo. Cav. *Union* 1 killed, 3 wounded.

17—Manchester, Tenn. 5th Tenn. Cav. *Confed.* 21 killed.

21—Henderson Hills, La. Detachments of Sixteenth Corps and Cavalry Division Nineteenth Corps. *Union* 1 wounded. *Confed.* 8 killed, 250 captured.

24—Union City, Ky. 7th Tenn. Cav. 450 men captured by Forrest.

25—Fort Anderson, Paducah, Ky. 122d Ill., 16th Ky. Cav., 8th U. S. Colored Artil. *Union* 14 killed, 46 wounded. *Confed.* 10 killed, 40 wounded. *Confed.* Brig.-Gen. Thompson killed.

26 to 30—Longview and Mt. Elba, Ark. 28th Wis., 5th Kan. Cav., 7th Mo. Cav. *Union* 4 killed, 18 wounded. *Confed.* 12 killed, 35 wounded, 300 captured.

28—Charleston, Ill. Attack on 5th Ill. by mob of Copperheads while returning to the front on veteran furlough. *Union* 2 killed, 8 wounded. *Confed.* 3 killed, 4 wounded, 12 prisoners.

29—Bolivar, Tenn. 6th Tenn. Cav. *Union* 8 killed, 35 wounded.

31—Near Snydersville, Miss. 3d U. S. Colored Cav. *Union* 16 killed, 3 wounded. *Confed.* 3 killed, 7 wounded.

APRIL, 1864

1—Augusta, Ark. 3d Minn., 8th Mo. Cav. *Union* 8 killed, 16 wounded. *Confed.* 15 killed, 45 wounded.

2—Spoonville, Ark. 29th Iowa, 9th Wis., 50th Ind., with 1st Mo. Cav. *Union* 10 killed, 35 wounded. *Confed.* 100 killed and wounded.

Crump's Hill or Piney Woods, La. 14th N. Y. Cav., 2d La., 2d Ill., and 16th Mo. Cav., 5th U. S. Colored Artil. *Union* 20 wounded. *Confed.* 10 killed, 25 wounded.

3—Okalona, Ark. 27th Wis., 40th Iowa, 77th Ohio, 43d Ill., 1st Mo. Cav., 13th Ill. Cav. *Union* 16 killed, 74 wounded. *Confed.* 75 killed and wounded.

4—Campti, La. 35th Iowa, 5th Minn., 2d and 18th N. Y. Cav., 3d R. I. Cav. *Union* 10 killed, 18 wounded. *Confed.* 3 killed, 12 wounded.

4 to 6—Elkins' Ford, Ark. 43d Ind., 29th and 36th Iowa, 1st Iowa Cav., Battery E 2d Mo. Light Artil. *Union* 5 killed, 33 wounded. *Confed.* 18 killed, 30 wounded.

5—Roseville, Ark. Seventy-five men of 2d and 6th Kan. Cav., in engagement with guerrillas. *Union* 19 killed, 11 wounded. *Confed.* 15 killed, 25 wounded, 11 captured.

Stone's Farm. Twenty-six men of 6th Kan. Cav., in engagement with guerrillas. 11, including Asst. Surg. Fairchild, captured and massacred.

(*Continued in Section* 11)

OLD RED CHURCH.

CHANCELLORS HOUSE,
REAR SHOWING SHELLS.

DONDALL'S TAVERN.

OLD WILDERNESS CHURCH.

ELY'S FORD ROAD.

VIEWS AT CHANCELLORSVILLE

CHAPTER XIX.—Continued.

TAKING advantage of this movement, a large force of Confederates gathered at Vicksburg under General J. C. Pemberton, for the protection of that post. On the day when Grant's supplies were seized at Holly Springs, about twenty thousand National troops, led by General W. T. Sherman, left Memphis in transports, with siege guns, to beleaguer Vicksburg. At Friar's Point they were joined by

CHANCELLORSVILLE

troops from Helena, and were met by Commodore Porter, whose fleet of gunboats were at the mouth of the Yazoo River, just above Vicksburg. The two commanders arranged a plan for attacking the city in the rear, and proceeded to execute it. The troops and fleet went up the Yazoo River to capture some batteries which disputed the way to that rear; but Sherman was repulsed after a sharp battle at Chickasaw Bayou (December 28), and the project was abandoned for a time.

General John A. McClernand, the senior of Sherman in rank, arrived at headquarters, near Vicksburg, early in January, 1863, and took the chief command. He and Porter went up the Arkansas River with their forces, and on the 11th captured the important Fort Hindman at Arkansas Post. In the meantime General Grant had arranged his army into four corps, and with it descended the river from Memphis to prosecute the siege of Vicksburg with vigor. He was soon convinced that it could not be taken by direct assault. He tried to perfect the canal begun by Farragut, but failed; and then he sent a considerable land and naval force up the Yazoo to capture batteries at Haines's Bluff, and so gain a footing in the rear of Vicksburg. These were repulsed at Fort Pemberton, near Greenwood, late in March. Other channels among the brimming bayous and small rivers were diligently sought by the indomitable Porter, to gain the rear of the foredoomed city, but in vain, and again the enterprise was abandoned. The details of these efforts of the army and navy, during the spring of 1863, form one of the most wonderful chapters in the history of the war. The waters were then redundant, and the voyages were sometimes wild and perilous, the gunboats sweeping on strong currents through overflowed swamps under lofty overarching trees draped with the trailing Spanish moss, and having their smoke-stacks leveled at times, and their wheels fearfully bruised.

While these operations against Vicksburg were in progress, there had been lively times on the bosom of the Mississippi. In February (1863), iron-clad vessels of Porter's fleet ran by the batteries at Vicksburg, and made considerable havoc among Confederate transports below that were supplying the troops there and at Port Hudson with stores. These venturesome National vessels were lost, and their crews were made prisoners. Later, when Grant had sent a strong land force down the west side of the river, Porter successfully ran by the batteries at Vicksburg with nearly his whole fleet and the transports, on the night of the 16th of April. Then Grant prepared for vigorous operations on the flank and rear of Vicksburg, on the line of the Big Black River. Porter also attacked and ran by the Confederate batteries at Grand Gulf, on the 27th of April, when Grant's army crossed the Mississippi a little below, pressed forward, and at Port Gibson gained a decisive victory in a battle fought there on the first of May.

In the meantime, Sherman, who had made another unsuccessful effort to capture the batteries at Haines's Bluff, by order of General Grant, marched down the west side of the Mississippi, crossed it, and joined the main army on the 8th of May. Then the whole force pushed rapidly toward Jackson, the capital of Mississippi, where General Joseph E. Johnston was in command of a Confederate army. After a severe battle

GENERAL JAMES S. NEGLEY

at Raymond, on the 12th of May, in which the Confederates were defeated, and another near Jackson, on the 14th, when the insurgents were driven northward, the Nationals seized the State capital, and

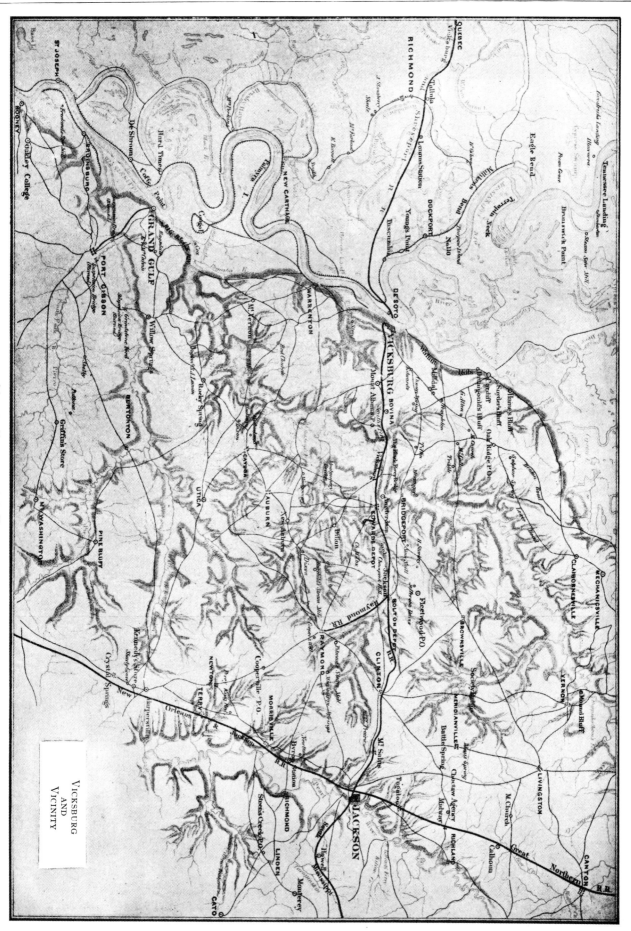

MAP OF VICKSBURG AND VICINITY

destroyed a large quantity of public property there.   Then the victorious army turned toward Vicksburg, and after defeating the Confederates under Pemberton at Champion Hills on the 16th of May, and at the passage of the Black River on the 17th, the National army swept on and closely invested Vicksburg, in the rear, on the 19th, receiving their supplies from a base on the Yazoo, established by Porter.   For a

fortnight the army had drawn its subsistence from the country through which it had passed.   It now rested for a brief space after a wonderful week's work.   Then, after two unsuccessful and disastrous assaults on Vicksburg, Grant began a regular siege of the works there, with the co-operation of Porter's fleet.

CHAPTER XX.

Investment and Siege of Vicksburg—Galveston—Banks in Louisiana—Siege and Surrender of Port Hudson—The Two Armies in Virginia—Peck and Longstreet at Suffolk—Moseby at Fairfax Court-House—Cavalry Battle—Cavalry Raids—Movements on Chancellorsville —Battle There—Death of "Stonewall Jackson"—Sedgwick's Escape—Retreat of the Army of the Potomac—Siege of Suffolk—The Confederate Army and Service—Power of the Confederates Abroad—Davis Recognized by the Pope—Napoleon, Mexico, and the Confederacy—Napoleon's Real Designs—Confederates Invade Maryland and Pennsyl- vania—Panic—Operations in Pennsylvania—Battle at Gettysburg—Seward's Circular.

GENERAL U. S. GRANT

FTER Grant's last assault on Vicksburg, his effective men did not exceed twenty thousand in number.   He determined to make the capture of Vicksburg an event of the near future, and called in reinforcements.   They came in such numbers, that by the middle of June the investment of Vicksburg was made absolute.   Sherman's corps was on the extreme right, McPherson's next and extending to the railway, and Ord's (late McClernand's) on the left, the investment in that direction being made complete by the divisions of Herron and Lanman, the latter lying across Stout's Bayou, and touching the bluffs on the river.   Parke's corps, and the divisions of Smith and Kimball, were sent to Haines's Bluff, where fortifications commanding the land side had been erected to confront any attempt that Johnston might make in that direction.   Meanwhile Vice-Admiral Porter had made complete and ample arrangements for the most efficient co-operation on the river, and his skill and zeal were felt throughout the siege, which continued until the first week in July.

Every day, shot and shell were hurled upon the city and the insurgent camps, from land and water. The inhabitants were compelled to seek shelter in caves dug out of the clay hills on which the city stands. In these, whole families, free and bond, lived for many weeks, while their houses without were perforated by the iron hail.   Therein children were born, and persons died, and soldiers sought shelter from the tempest of war.   Very soon famine afflicted the citizens.   Fourteen ounces of food became a regular allowance for each person for forty-eight hours.   The flesh of mules made savory dishes toward the end of the siege.   Finally the besiegers undermined one of the principal forts of the enemy, in the line of the defences on the land side, and it was blown up with fearful effect.   Other mines were made ready for the infernal work, when Pemberton, despairing of expected aid from Johnston, made a proposition to Grant to surrender the post and his army.   The generals met under the shadow of a live-oak tree in the rear of the town on the 3d of July to arrange the terms of surrender, and on the 4th the stronghold of Vicksburg, with twenty-seven thousand men and a vast amount of ordnance, and other public property, were surrendered to the leader of the National forces.

From the time of the battle at Port Gibson to the fall of Vicksburg, General Grant had captured thirty thousand prisoners (among them fifteen general officers), with arms and ammunition for an army of sixty thousand men; also steamboats, locomotives, railroads, a vast amount of cotton, etc.   He had lost, during that time, nine thousand eight hundred and thirty-three men, of whom one thousand two hundred and thirty-three had been killed.   By the experience of those few weeks, he had ascertained the real weakness of the Confederacy in that region.

On the night of the 4th of July (1863), the powerful fleet of Vice-Admiral Porter was lying quietly at the levee at Vicksburg, and in commemoration of that National holiday our troops regaled the citizens with a fine display of fireworks more harmless than those which, for more than forty nights, had coursed the heavens above them like malignant meteors.

Galveston had been recaptured by the Confederates on the first of January, 1863; but that victory was rendered almost fruitless by a close blockade of the port by National vessels.   From that time General Banks had been co-operating with General Grant, and making efforts to "repossess" Louisiana.

VIEWS OF VICKSBURG AND VICINITY

An expedition under General Weitzel and Commodore McKean Buchanan took possession of the remarkable Teche country in that State, when Banks concentrated his troops, about twelve thousand in number, at Baton Rouge (which was then held by General Grover), for the purpose of assisting Commodore Farragut in an attempt to pass the formidable batteries at Port Hudson, twenty-five miles up the Mississippi. That attempt was made on the night of the 13th of March, when a terrible contest occurred, in the darkness, between the vessels and the land batteries. Only Farragut's flag-ship (the *Hartford*) and another succeeded in passing by.

SCENE AT VICKSBURG

Banks now sent a large portion of his available troops into the interior of Louisiana, where General Richard Taylor was in command of a Confederate force. The Nationals were concentrated at Brashear City, on the Atchafalaya, and from that point they marched triumphantly to the Red River, accompanied by Banks in person. From Alexandria, early in May, that general wrote to his Government that the Confederate power in northern and central Louisiana was broken; and with this impression he moved eastward with his troops, crossed the Mississippi River, and late in May (1863) invested Port Hudson, then in command of the Confederate general, Frank Gardner. For forty days he besieged that post, during which time many gallant deeds were performed on each side. Banks was ably assisted by the squadron of Farragut—the *Hartford*, *Albatross*, *Monongahela*, *Richmond*, *Essex* and *Tennessee*, and some mortar-boats. Finally, at the close of June, the ammunition of the closely invested garrison was almost exhausted. When news of the fall of Vicksburg reached Gardner, he perceived that further attempts at resistance would be futile; and on the 9th of July he surrendered the post to Banks, with much spoil. The National loss during the siege was about three thousand men, and that of the Confederates, exclusive of prisoners, was about eight hundred. The loss of Vicksburg and Port Hudson was a severe calamity for the Confederates. It gave the final blow in the removal of the obstructions to the navigation of the Mississippi River by Confederate batteries, and thenceforth it was free. Powerful portions of the Confederacy were "repossessed" by the National Government, and wise men among the enemies of the Republic clearly perceived that their cause was hopeless.

At the moment when Vicksburg fell, the *Army of the Potomac* gained an equally important victory on the soil of Pennsylvania. We left that army on the northern side of the Rappahannock River, near Fredericksburg, in charge of General Joseph Hooker. From January to April (1863), he was engaged in preparing for a vigorous summer campaign. His forces remained in comparative quiet for about three months, during which time they were reorganized and well-disciplined; and at the close of April, his army numbered one hundred thousand effective men. General Lee's army, on the other side of the river, had been divided; a large force under General Longstreet being required to watch the movements of the Nationals under General Peck, in the vicinity of Norfolk. Lee had in hand about sixty thousand well-drilled troops, lying behind strong intrenchments extending twenty-five miles along the line of the Rappahannock. For the space of three months some cavalry movements only, disturbed the two armies. General W. H. F. Lee, with a mounted force, attacked National troops at Gloucester, opposite Yorktown, early in February; and at midnight of the 8th of March, Colonel Moseby, at the head of a band of guerrillas, dashed into the village of Fairfax Court-House and carried off the commander of the Union forces there. A little later National cavalry under General Averill and Confederate horsemen led by General Fitzhugh Lee, had a severe battle near Kelly's Ford, on the Rappahannock, in which the former were repulsed. That was the first purely cavalry contest of the war.

Hooker became impatient. The time of the enlistment of many of his troops would soon expire, and he determined to put his army in motion toward Richmond early in April, notwithstanding his ranks were not full. Cavalry, under General Stoneman, were sent to destroy railways in Lee's rear, but were foiled by the high water in the streams. After a pause, Hooker determined to attempt to turn Lee's flank, and for that purpose he sent ten thousand mounted men to raid in his rear. Then he threw thirty-six thousand troops of his own right wing across the Rappahannock, with orders to halt and intrench at Chancellorsville between the Confederate army and Richmond. This movement was so masked by a demonstration on Lee's front, by Hooker's left wing under General Sedgwick, that the

SCENES IN AND NEAR VICKSBURG

U.S. SIGNAL CORPS HEADQUARTERS.

U.S. PROVOST MARSHALL'S GUARD HOUSE.

U.S. QUARTERMASTER'S CAMP, SHOWING CONFEDERATE FORTIFICATIONS IN REAR OF CITY.

HOUSE OCCUPIED AS U.S. HEADQUARTERS.

BARRACKS 124TH ILLINOIS INFANTRY.

right was well advanced before Lee was aware of his peril.   These troops reached Chancellorsville in a region known as The Wilderness, on the evening of the 30th of April, when Hooker expected to see Lee, conscious of danger, fly toward Richmond.   He did no such thing, but proceeded to strike the National army a heavy blow, for the twofold purpose of seizing the communications between the two parts of

CONFEDERATE GUN "WHISTLING DICK"

BATTERY "SHERMAN"

CONFEDERATE FORTIFICATIOS.

that army and compelling its commander to fight at a disadvantage, with only a portion of his troops in hand. For this purpose, "Stonewall Jackson" was sent with a heavy force, early in the morning of the first of May, to attack the Nationals, when Hooker sent out his troops to meet them.   The Confederates moved upon Chancellorsville by two roads.   A sharp engagement ensued, when the Nationals were pushed back to a defensive position behind their intrenchments; but the efforts of Lee

to seize these works were foiled.

Both armies were now in a perilous position.   Hooker resolved to rest on the defensive; but Lee boldly detached the whole of Jackson's command, on the morning of the 2d of May, and sent it under cover of the forest-curtain of The Wilderness to make a secret flank movement and gain the rear of the Nationals.   It was observed by the latter.   Suddenly, Jackson burst from the woods with twenty-five thousand men, and falling upon Hooker's right, crumbled it, and sent the astounded column in confusion upon the remainder of the line.   A desperate battle, in which nearly all the troops on both sides participated, was the consequence.   It lasted until late in the evening, when Jackson fell, mortally wounded by a bullet sent by mistake, in the gloom, by one of his own men.   Jackson had been engaged in a personal reconnaissance with his staff and an escort; and when returning, in the darkness, to his lines, he and his companions were mistaken by their friends for Union cavalry.

Hooker now made disposition for a renewal of the conflict on the morning of the 3d.   He had called Reynolds's corps of more than twenty thousand men from Sedgwick, and these arrived late on Saturday evening (the 2d), swelling his army to sixty thousand.   Sedgwick, by Hooker's order, had crossed the Rappahannock, seized Fredericksburg and the Heights, and was pushing on toward Chancellorsville, when he was checked by troops sent by Lee, and compelled to retreat across the river at Banks's Ford, to save his army.   This was accomplished on the night of the 4th and 5th of May.   In the meantime there had been hard fighting at Chancellorsville.   At dawn on Sunday morning, the 3d of May, the dashing General Stuart, leading the column of the slain commander so much loved, shouted, when he saw the Nationals, "Charge, and remember Jackson!" and then fell heavily upon the troops commanded by General Sickles.   The conflict was desperate and soon became general; and the National army, after a long struggle, was finally pushed from the field to a strong position on the roads back of Chancellorsville.

Lee's army was now united; that of Hooker was yet divided; and hearing of Sedgwick's critical situation, the latter determined to retreat to the north side of the Rappahannock.   The *Army of the Potomac* passed the river in safety on the night of the 4th, when Lee, unable to follow, resumed his former position on the Heights of Fredericksburg.   Both armies had lost heavily—the Nationals over seventeen thousand men including prisoners, and the Confederates about fifteen thousand.   Meanwhile Stoneman's cavalry had been raiding on Lee's communications with Richmond, and a part of them, under Colonel Judson Kilpatrick, had swept down within two miles of that city.   They destroyed much property, but failed to break up the railway communication between Lee and the Confederate capital.   So far the raiding was a failure.

Longstreet, as we have observed, had been sent to confront General Peck in southeastern Virginia. The latter was strongly fortified near Suffolk, where he was besieged by Longstreet early in April, who

GENERAL U. S. GRANT'S BAGGAGE WAGON

GENERAL JOHN A. RAWLINS   GENERAL U. S. GRANT   COLONEL THEO. S. BOWERS

expected to drive the Nationals from that post, and seizing Norfolk and its vicinity, make a demonstration against Fortress Monroe.   He failed; and hearing of the struggle at Chancellorsville, he abandoned the siege and joined Lee with his large detachment.

Lee's army was now strong in material and moral force.   Recent successes had greatly inspirited it.   It was reorganized into three army corps, commanded respectively by Generals Longstreet, A. P. Hill, and Ewell. These were all able leaders, and each bore the commission of lieutenant-general. And at no time, probably, during the war was the Confederate army more complete in numbers, equipment and discipline, or furnished with more ample materials for carrying on the conflict, than it was at the middle of June, 1863. According to the most careful estimates made from the Confederate official returns, there were then at least *five hundred thousand* men on the army rolls, and more than *three hundred thousand* "present and fit for duty." Fully one-half of the white men of the Confederacy eligible to military duty were then enrolled for active service, while a large proportion of the other half were in the civil and military service in other capacities. Doubtless at least seven-tenths of the white adults were then in public business; while a large number of slaves, though legally emancipated, were employed in various labors, such as working on fortifications, as teamsters, etc.   The following is the form of a voucher held by the Confederate government as the employer of slaves for such purposes.   It is copied from the original before me:

MAJ. GEN. J. M. PALMER.   MAJ. GEN. G. M. DODGE.   BRIG. GEN. E. W. WHITTAKER.

"We, the subscribers, acknowledge to have received of John B. Stannard, First Corps of Engineers, the sums set opposite our names respectively, being in full for the services of our slaves on Drewry's Bluff, during the months of March and April, 1863, having signed duplicate receipts.

From whom hired	Name and occupation	Time employed.	Rate of Wages	Amount for each slave	Amount received	Signatures
J. G. Woodin..................	William, laborer	22 days	$16 a month		$13.33	Joseph G. Woodin
William E. Martin............	Richard, "	37 "	" "	$19.75		
William E. Martin............	Henry, "	37 "	" "	19.75	39.46	W. E. Martin

"I certify the above pay-roll is correct and just.

"JOHN B. STANNARD."

Richmond seemed secure from harm.   Charleston was defiant, and with reason.   Vicksburg and Port Hudson on the Mississippi, though seriously menaced, seemed impregnable against any force Grant or Banks might array before them; and the appeals of General Johnston, near Jackson, for reinforcements, were regarded as notes of unnecessary alarm.   The Confederates were encouraged by their friends in Europe with promises of aid; and the desires of these for the acknowledgment of the independence of the "Confederate States of America" were strongly manifested.   In England, public movements in favor of the Confederates were then prominent.   Open-air meetings, organized by members of the aristocracy, were held, for the purpose of urging the British government to declare such recognition; and in the spring of 1864 a "Southern Independence Association" was formed with a British peer (Lord Wharncliffe) as president, and a membership composed of powerful representatives of the Church, State, and Trade.

General E. O. C. Ord, Wife and Daughter

Generals Benj. Harrison, W. T. Ward, Don Dustin and Cogswall

But the British government wisely hesitated; and notwithstanding the unpatriotic Peace-Faction in the city of New York had, six months before (November, 1862), waited upon Lord Lyons, the British minister at Washington, with an evident desire to have his government interfere in our affairs, and thus secure the independence of the Confederates, and the emissaries of the conspirators were specially active in Europe, the British ministry, restrained by the good Queen, steadily refused to take decided action in the matter. Only the Roman Pontiff, then a temporal prince, of all the rulers of the earth officially recognized Jefferson Davis as the head of a real government.

JOHN C. BRECKENRIDGE, C. S. A.

At the same time, a scheme of the emperor of the French for the destruction of the Republic of Mexico, and the establishment there of a monarchy ruled by a man of his own selection, and pledged to act in the interests of despotism, the Roman Catholic Church and the promotion of the domination of the Latin race, was in successful operation, by means of twenty thousand French soldiers and five thousand allied Mexicans. In this movement, it is alleged, the leaders of the great insurrection were the secret allies of the emperor, it being understood that as soon as he should obtain a firm footing in Mexico he should, for valuable commercial considerations agreed upon, acknowledge the independence of the Confederate States, and uphold it by force of arms if necessary; it also being understood that the government which Davis and his associates were to establish at the close of hostilities should, in no wise, offend Napoleon's imperialistic ideas. The slave-holding class were to be a privileged one, and be the rulers, and the great mass of the people were to be subordinated to the interests of that class. Therefore, the triumphal march of the French invaders of Mexico, in the spring of 1863, was hailed with delight by the *government* at Richmond, while the great mass of the people were ignorant of the conspiracy on foot to deprive them of their sacred rights.

At the same time the perfidious emperor was deceiving the Confederate leaders concerning his real and deeper designs, which were both political and ecclesiastical. His political design evidently was to arrest the march of empire southward on the part of the United States. His religious design was to assist the Church party in Mexico, which had been defeated in 1857, in a recovery of its power, that the Roman Catholic Church might have undisputed sway in Central America. In a letter to the Spanish General Prim, in July, 1862, the Emperor, after saying that the United States fed the factories of Europe with cotton, and asserting that it was not the interest of European governments to have our country hold dominion over the Gulf of Mexico, the Antilles, and the adjacent continent, he declared that if, with the assistance of France, Mexico should have a "stable government"—that is, a monarchy—"*we shall have restored to the Latin race upon the opposite side of the ocean, its strength and prestige;* we shall have guaranteed then security to our colonies in the Antilles, and to those of Spain; we shall have established our beneficent influence in the centre of America; and in this influence, by creating immense openings to our commerce, will *procure to us* the *matter indispensable to our industry*"—that is, cotton. This contemplated blow against our great cotton interest was a prime element in Napoleon's scheme, for the consummation of which he coquetted with the Confederate leaders, and deceived them.

The Confederate government, greatly elated by the events at Chancellorsville, ordered Lee to invade Maryland again. His force was now almost equal in numbers to that of his antagonist, and in better spirits than were the *Army of the Potomac.* By a sudden flank movement, Lee caused Hooker to break up his encampment on the Rappahannock and move toward Washington, after some sharp cavalry fights above Fredericksburg. General Ewell, in command of Lee's left wing, was sent into the Shenandoah Valley through Chester Gap, and sweeping down toward the Potomac, drove General Milroy and seven thousand National troops across that stream, on the 15th of June. Meanwhile Longstreet, with a strong force, moved along the eastern bases of the Blue Ridge, watching for an opportunity to fall on Washington city; while Hooker moved in a parallel line to thwart him. Several cavalry engagements

GENERAL J. B. MCPHERSON

GENERALS GODFREY WEITZEL AND KAUTZ

MAJOR-GENERAL GODFREY WEITZEL AND GROUP OF OFFICERS

ensued; and fifteen hundred mounted Confederates dashed across the Potomac in pursuit of Milroy's wagon-train. They pushed up the Cumberland Valley as far as Chambersburg, plundering the people and causing intense alarm in all Pennsylvania.

Lee had, by skillful movements, kept Hooker in doubt as to his real object, until Ewell's corps had crossed the Potomac above Harper's Ferry on the 22d and 23d of June, and marched rapidly up the Cumberland Valley to within a few miles of the Susquehanna opposite Harrisburg, the capital of Pennsylvania. Another large body of Confederates, led by General Early, pushed on through Gettysburg to York, on the Susquehanna, levying contributions on friend and foe alike. Ewell and Early were speedily followed by Hill and Longstreet (June 25, 1863), and again the whole of Lee's army was in Maryland and Pennsylvania. It seemed, at one time, as if nothing could prevent that army penetrating to the Schuylkill and even to the Hudson. The panic north of the Potomac was intense. Valuable goods that were portable were sent from Philadelphia to points above the Hudson Highlands, for safety. The people flew to arms everywhere to oppose the invaders.

GOVERNOR ANDREW G. CURTIN
OF PENNSYLVANIA

The *Army of the Potomac* was now one hundred thousand strong. It was thrown across the river into Maryland, at and near Edwards's Ferry. Halleck (the general-in-chief) and Hooker differed most decidedly in opinions about some important military movements that were proposed, when the latter resigned and was succeeded by General George G. Meade, who held the command of that army until the close of the war. Meade entered upon his duties at Frederick (June 28) in Maryland, where the *Army of the Potomac* lay, ready to strike Lee's communications or to attack him, as circumstances might dictate.

Lee was preparing to cross the Susquehanna and push on to Philadelphia, when news reached him that the reinforced *Army of the Potomac* was threatening his flank and rear. Alarmed by this intelligence and the rapid gathering of the yeomanry on his front, he ordered the concentration of his army near Gettysburg, with the intention of crushing Meade's forces by a single blow, and then marching on Baltimore and Washington; or, in case of failure, to secure a direct line of retreat into Virginia. In the meantime Meade was pushing toward the Susquehanna with cautious movement; and on the evening of the 30th of June he discovered Lee's evident intention to give battle at once.

The National cavalry, meanwhile, had been carefully reconnoitering; and on the previous day, Kilpatrick's mounted men had a sharp fight at Hanover, a few miles from Gettysburg, with some of Stuart's cavalry, and, assisted by General Custer, defeated them. Buford's division of National cavalry entered Gettysburg the same day; and the next day the left wing of Meade's army, led by General J. F. Reynolds, arrived near there. At the same time the corps of Hill and Longstreet were approaching from Chambersburg, and Ewell was marching down from Carlisle in full force. That night Buford's cavalry, six thousand strong, encamped between Reynolds and Hill.

On the morning of the first of July, Buford met the van of Lee's army, led by General Heth, between Seminary Ridge, a little out of Gettysburg, and a parallel ridge a little further west, when a sharp skirmish ensued. Reynolds, who was a few miles distant, hastened to the relief of Buford, and in a severe battle that followed, he was killed, and General Abner Doubleday took command of his troops. In the meantime General O. O. Howard came up with his corps. Lee's troops were then concentrated there, and the battle soon assumed grander proportions. The Nationals were finally pressed back; and under the general direction of Howard, they took a strong position on a range of rocky hills near Gettysburg, of which Culp's Hill and Little Round Top were the two extremes of the line, and Cemetery Hill, at the village, was the apex. There the Nationals rested that night, and the Confederates occupied Seminary Ridge.

GENERAL JOHN McA. SCHOFIELD

General Meade, with the remainder of the *Army of the Potomac*, now hastened to Gettysburg, and he and Lee prepared cautiously to renew.

GENERAL JEFFERSON C. DAVIS AND STAFF

GENERALS RAWLINS, COMSTOCK, DUNN, GRANT, MORGAN, PARKER AND OTHERS

the battle.   It did not begin until the middle of the afternoon of the 2d, when Lee fell, with great weight, upon Meade's left wing commanded by General Sickles.   A most sanguinary battle ensued, extending to the centre on Cemetery Hill, where General Hancock was in command.   Heavy masses of Confederates were hurled against him, and these were thrown back with fearful losses on both sides.   Meanwhile there had been a terrible struggle on the right and centre of the Nationals, where Generals Slocum and Howard were in command, the former on Culp's Hill, and the latter on Cemetery Hill.   Against these a large portion of Ewell's corps had been sent.   The latter were pushed back by Howard, but seized and occupied the works of Slocum, on the extreme right of Culp's Hill, that night.   The battle ended at sunset on the left, but it was continued until about ten o'clock that night on the right.

Slocum renewed the battle at four o'clock on the morning of the 3d, when he drove the Confederates out of his lines after a hard struggle for four hours.   There he held Ewell in check, while the contest raged elsewhere.   Lee, perceiving the Little Round Top—a steep, rocky eminence—to be impregnable, proceeded, at a little past noon, to attack the more vulnerable centre.   Upon this he opened one hundred and forty-five heavy cannon, chiefly against Cemetery Hill and its vicinity, occupied by Meade's centre.   A hundred National great guns quickly answered; and for two hours a fearful cannonade that shook the country around was kept up.   Then the Confederates, in heavy columns, preceded by a cloud of skirmishers,

BODIES OF FEDERAL DEAD ON BATTLEFIELD, GETTYSBURG

swept over the plain and assailed the National line with great fury.   It was intended by Lee to give a crushing blow that should ensure victory.   A terrible struggle followed, that covered the ground with the slain—men and horses.   At sunset the Confederates were repulsed at all points; and the decisive battle of Gettysburg ended in triumph for the *Army of the Potomac*.   In that fearful struggle, the Nationals lost in killed, wounded and missing, over twenty-three thousand men; the Confederates lost about thirty thousand, including fourteen thousand prisoners.

On the evening of the day after the battle (July 4, 1863) Lee began a retreat toward Virginia, followed the next day by Meade, who pursued as far as the Potomac, which had been filled to the brim by heavy rains; but the Confederate leader, by skillful management, kept the Nationals at bay until he had made ready to cross that stream by pontoons and fording.   This he did with his shattered army, his artillery and trains, on the 14th of July, much to the disappointment of the loyal people.   Perceiving the battle to be a decisive one in favor of the Union cause, and believing it to be a turning point in the war, the President of the United States recommended the people to observe the 15th of August next ensuing as a day for public National thanksgiving, praise and prayer.   And the Secretary of State (Mr. Seward), satisfied that the insurrection would soon be ended by the discomfiture of its supporters, sent a cheering circular to the diplomatic agents of the Republic abroad, in which he recited the most important events of the war to that time; declared that "the country showed no sign of exhaustion of money, material or men"; that one loan was "purchased at par by our citizens at the rate of $1,200,000 daily"; and that gold was selling in our markets at 23 to 28 per centum premium.

GENERAL JOHN SEDGWICK AND STAFF

GENERAL GEORGE G. MEADE AND STAFF SHOWING GENERALS INGALLS, HUMPHREY PATRICK, AND OTHERS

CHAPTER XXI.

Partisan Opposition to the Government—Knights of the Golden Circle—The Draft Riots in New York—Colored Troops in New York—Morgan's Great Raid—Meade and Lee in Virginia —Operations of the Two Armies in Virginia—Raid in Western Virginia—Rosecrans and Bragg in Tennessee—Streight's Great Raid—Bragg Driven to and from Chattanooga—Burnside in East Tennessee—Battle of Chickamauga—The Army at Chattanooga—Division of Mississippi—Battle at Wauhatchie—The Mule Charge—Events in East Tennessee—Battle on Lookout Mountain and on Missionary Ridge—Operations against Charleston—Robert Small—Death of General Mitchel.

HILE the loyal people were rejoicing because of the great deliverance at Gettysburg, and the Government was preparing for a final and decisive struggle with its foes, leading politicians of the Peace-Faction, evidently in affiliation with members of the disloyal organization known as *Knights of the Golden Circle*, were using every means in their power to defeat the patriotic purposes of the National Administration, and to stir up the people of the free-labor States to engage in a counter-revolution.

The association called *Knights of the Golden Circle* was organized, it is said, as early as 1835, by some of the leaders who were engaged in the nullification movements in South Carolina two or three years before. Its chief objects were the separation of the Union politically, at the line between the free-labor and slave-labor States; the seizure of some of the richest portions of Mexico and the Island of Cuba, and the establishment of an empire whose corner-stone should be Slavery. The bounds of that empire were within a circle, the centre of which was at Havana, in Cuba, with a radius of sixteen degrees of latitude and longitude, reaching northward to the Pennsylvania border and southward to the Isthmus of Darien and even beyond. It would include the West India Islands and those of the Caribbean Sea, with a large part of Eastern Mexico and the whole of Central America. The limits of this empire the projectors called "The Golden Circle," and

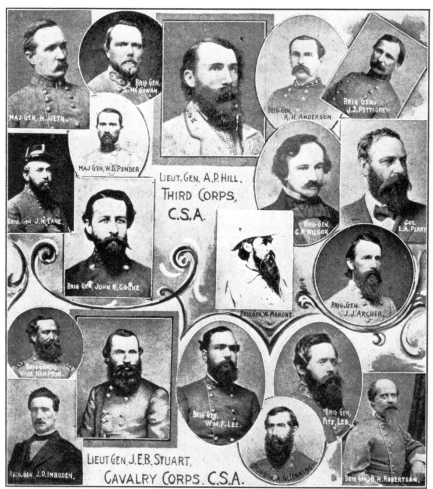

COMMANDERS OF THE THIRD CORPS AND CAVALRY CORPS, C. S. A., GETTYSBURG

the members of the association, "Knights of the Golden Circle," who formed the soul of all the "filibustering" operations before the breaking out of the Civil War, from 1850 to 1857. When these failed, their energies were put forth for the destruction of the Union. "Castles" or "lodges," with a secret ritual, were formed in various Southern States, and their membership included many active politicians north of the Ohio River, in 1863.

These disloyal men in the northern States, countenanced by the unpatriotic Peace-Faction, became very vehement in their opposition to the Government when, in the summer of 1863, a draft or conscription to fill up the ranks of the army, which had been authorized by Congress, was put into operation by the President. This act, the suspension of the privilege of the writ of habeas corpus, the arrest of seditious men, and other measures which the Government deemed necessary for the maintenance of the National authority, were denounced by the leaders of the party opposed to Mr. Lincoln's administration, as

MAJOR-GENERAL J. F. REYNOLDS AND OFFICERS AT GETTYSBURG

WHERE GENERAL REYNOLDS WAS KILLED AND OTHER VIEWS AT GETTYSBURG

unconstitutional and outrageous. Instigated by raving political leaders, inflammatory speeches, and the daily utterances of the press that was in sympathy with the opponents of the draft, a mob, composed largely of the lower class of the Irish population in the city of New York, entered upon a fearful riot there early in July. It prevailed for almost three days. The immediate pretext for the disturbance was the alleged oppression of the draft. The riot was begun by destroying the telegraph wires extending out of the city. Then the rioters paraded some of the streets and forced citizens to join them; and after first uttering cries against the draft, they yelled, "Down with the Abolitionists! Down with the nigger! Hurrah for Jeff Davis!" The special objects of their wrath were the innocent colored people and their friends. Arson and plunder, maiming and murder, were their business and recreation. Men and women were clubbed to death in the streets, hung on lamp-posts or butchered in their houses. The infuriated rioters laid in ashes an asylum for colored orphan children; and the terrified inmates, who fled in every direction, were pursued, and some of the poor children were cruelly beaten and maimed. The colored people throughout the city were hunted and treated as if they were noxious wild beasts, and many fled to the country. Finally the police, aided by troops, suppressed the insurrection in the city, but not until several hundred human lives had been lost, and property to the amount of at least $2,000,000 was destroyed.

GEN. MEADE'S HEADQUARTERS

GEN. MEADE'S HEADQUARTERS DISTANT VIEW SHOWING HORSES KILLED BY ARTILLERY FIRE.

GEN. LEE'S HEADQUARTERS ON NIGHT OF FIRST DAY NEAR CHAMBERSBURG PIKE.

THREE CONFEDERATE PRISONERS.

This riot seems to have been only an irregular manifestation of an organized outbreak in New York city simultaneously with a similar insurrection projected in some of the western cities. But the draft went on in spite of all opposition; and the Knights of the Golden Circle and the Peace-Faction were discomfited. The turn of affairs at Gettysburg made them more circumspect. They hesitated; and finally they postponed indefinitely an attempt to execute their scheme. And six months after the terrible "three days of July"—13th, 14th and 15th—in the city of New York, when no colored person's life was considered safe there, a regiment of negro soldiers, raised and equipped by the Loyal League of that city, marched down Broadway—its great thoroughfare—for the field of battle, escorted by many of the leading citizens of the metropolis, and cheered by thousands who covered the sidewalks and filled windows and balconies.

At about that time, the notorious guerrilla chief, John Morgan, made a famous raid through Kentucky, Southern Indiana and Ohio, entering Indiana from Kentucky, below Louisville, on the 8th of July, with about four thousand mounted men. This raid was intended as a signal for the uprising of the disloyal men in those States in favor of the Confederates. The lesson taught at Gettysburg was heeded, and they were quiet. But there was a marvellous uprising of sixty thousand loyal yeomen of Indiana and Ohio to capture or expel the invaders. Morgan went swiftly through the country, from village to village, plundering, destroying, and levying contributions. He first encountered stout resistance from Indiana militia, and was soon closely pursued by those of Ohio. Finally this bold raider was hemmed in and made a prisoner, with many of his followers, in southeastern Ohio, late in July, and the remainder were killed or dispersed.

Three days after General Lee escaped into Virginia, General Meade crossed the Potomac to follow his flying antagonist. The Nationals marched rapidly along the eastern base of the Blue Ridge, while the Confederates as rapidly went up the Shenandoah Valley, after trying to check Meade by threatening to re-enter Maryland. Failing in this, Lee hastened to avert the danger that menaced his front and

General George G. Meade in Camp

A Wounded Zouave

flank.   During that exciting race, several skirmishes occurred in the mountain passes; when Lee, by a quick and skillful movement while Meade was detained at Manassas Gap by a heavy skirmish, darted through Chester Gap, and crossing the Rappahannock, took a position between that stream and

the Rapidan. Meade advanced cautiously, and at the middle of September, he crossed the Rappahannock and drove Lee beyond the Rapidan, when the latter took a strongly defensive position. Meanwhile the National cavalry under Buford and Kilpatrick had been active between the two rivers, and had frequent skirmishes with Stuart's mounted troops.

Lee now attempted to turn the right flank of the *Army of the Potomac* to gain its rear and march rapidly

COMMANDING GENERALS OF THE THIRD ARMY CORPS, GETTYSBURG

on Washington.   He had moved some distance for this purpose before Meade discovered his peril.   Then a third race for the National Capital by the two armies over nearly the same course occurred.   The *Army of the Potomac* won it, reaching Centreville Heights on the 15th of October.   It was a race marked by the most stirring incidents, for there was much scouting and skirmishing on the way.   At Jeffersonton, the National cavalry under General Gregg were routed; and at Auburn, the seat of John Minor Botts, a prominent Virginia statesman, Stuart, with two thousand Confederate cavalry, came very near being captured.   From that point to Bristow's Station the race was sharp, for Centreville Heights was the goal.   At Bristow's, a severe engagement occurred between the corps of Generals Warren and Hill.   The latter was joined by that of Ewell; but before they could fall upon Warren, he withdrew in the night (October 14) and joined Meade at Centreville on the morning of the 15th.

The race was ended at Bristow's Station.   Lee was beaten, and fell back to the Rappahannock, destroying the railway behind him.   Meade repaired the road, and following Lee slowly, attacked him at Rappahannock Station early in November.   A very sharp battle ensued.   It was fought by detachments of the Fifth and Sixth corps, under General Sedgwick; and it was ended by a gallant charge on a redoubt and rifle-trenches.   These were carried in the face of a tempest of grape-shot and *minie* bullets, when the Nationals swept down to a pontoon bridge, cut off the retreat of the Confederates from the abandoned works, made over sixteen hundred of them prisoners, and drove Lee's army toward Culpepper Court-House.   There the latter had proposed to go into winter quarters; but this disaster alarmed him, and he sought safety from his pursuer behind the Rapidan.   His force was then fifty thousand strong, and Meade's numbered seventy thousand.   With these the latter crossed the Rappahannock and lay quietly between the two rivers until late in November, while Lee occupied a line of strong defences along Mine Run.

Feeling strong enough for the enterprise, Meade proceeded, on the 26th of November, to attempt a dislodgment of his antagonist.   He crossed the Rapidan on that day, and pushed on in the direction of his foe.   General Warren, in the advance, opened a battle; but Meade soon perceived that the Confederates were too strongly intrenched and weighty in numbers to give him hopes of success, and he withdrew.   The *Army of the Potomac* went into winter-quarters on the north side of the Rapidan: and so was ended the campaign of that army for the year 1863.

VIEWS OF LITTLE ROUND TOP AND TROSTLE'S BARN, BATTLE OF GETTYSBURG

There had been comparative quiet in Western Virginia since the autumn of 1861; but in the summer and fall of 1863, that quiet was broken by an extensive raid over that region by National cavalry led by General W. W. Averill, who, before the close of the year, nearly purged West Virginia of armed Confederates, and seriously interrupted railway communication between the army of Lee in Virginia and Bragg in Tennessee. We left the last-named officer and Rosecrans confronting each other in Tennessee, after the battle of Murfreesboro'; Bragg below the Duck River and Rosecrans at the scene of the battle. The two armies held that relative position from January to June, 1863; while the cavalry forces of each were active in minor operations. Confederate cavalry, four thousand strong, led by Generals Wharton and Forrest, attempted to capture Fort Donelson early in February, but failed. A little later General Van Dorn, with a considerable force of cavalry, was near Franklin, below Nashville, threatening Rosecrans's

supplies at the latter place. In March, General Sheridan drove Van Dorn south of the Duck River; and in the same month Morgan was operating with considerable effect eastward of Murfreesboro'. Van Dorn reappeared near Franklin, early in April, with about nine thousand Confederates; and on the 10th he attacked the Nationals there, who were commanded by General Gordon Granger. Van Dorn intended, if he won, to push on and seize Nashville; but he was repulsed, and retired to Spring Hill with a loss of about three hundred men.

In the meantime Rosecrans had sent out expeditions in various ways, the most remarkable of which was led by Colonel A. D. Streight, who left Nashville in steamers, debarked his troops at Fort Donelson, marched over to the Tennessee River, and moved up

First Corps C. S. A. at Battle of Gettysburg

that stream to the borders of Mississippi and Alabama, getting horses by the way for the purpose of mounting his men. The latter service was nearly completed at Tuscumbia; and from that point Streight, with his troopers, swept in a curve bending eastward, through Alabama into Georgia, in the rear of Bragg's army. Their chief objects were Rome, where the Confederates had extensive iron-works, and Atlanta, the centre of an important system of railroads. They were pursued by the cavalry of Forrest and Roddy, and these parties skirmished and raced until Streight was within a few miles of Rome, when his exhausted horses and his ammunition failed him. Many of the poor beasts died; and when, on the 3d of May (1863), the raiders were struck by their pursuers, the former were compelled to surrender. The captives were sent to Richmond and confined in the loathsome Libby Prison, from which Streight and one hundred of his officers escaped by burrowing under the foundations of that edifice.

The *Army of the Cumberland*, in three divisions, commanded respectively by Generals Thomas, McCook and Crittenden, began its march from Murfreesboro' to Chattanooga, in northern Georgia, late in June. Bragg was then strongly intrenched on the line of the Duck River, but was pushed back to Tullahoma; and when he saw Rosecrans seize the mountain passes on his front, and seriously menace his flank, he turned and fled without giving a blow, his antagonist pressing hard upon his rear. Having the advantage of railway communication, the retreating army very easily kept ahead of their pursuers, and passing rapidly over the Cumberland Mountains toward the Tennessee River, they crossed that stream at Bridgeport, destroying the bridge behind them, and made a rapid march to Chattanooga.

The expulsion of Bragg's army from Tennessee alarmed and disheartened the Confederates, and they felt that everything depended on their holding Chattanooga, the key to East Tennessee and northern Georgia. Toward that point the *Army of the Cumberland* moved slowly; and late in August it had crossed the mountains, and was stretched along the Tennessee River from above Chattanooga, many a league westward. On the 21st of August, National artillery placed on the eminence opposite Chattanooga awakened the mountain echoes with their thunder, and sent screaming shells over the Confederate camp. Bragg was startled by a sense of immediate danger; and when, soon afterward, Generals Thomas and

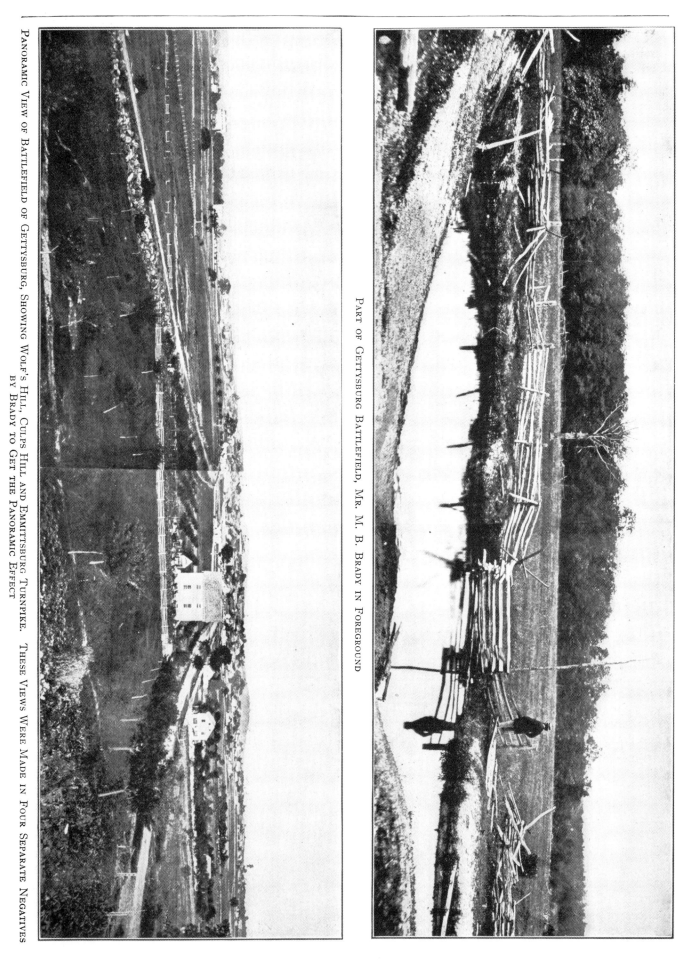

PANORAMIC VIEW OF BATTLEFIELD OF GETTYSBURG, SHOWING WOLF'S HILL, CULPS HILL AND EMMITSBURG TURNPIKE. THESE VIEWS WERE MADE IN FOUR SEPARATE NEGATIVES BY BRADY TO GET THE PANORAMIC EFFECT

PART OF GETTYSBURG BATTLEFIELD, MR. M. B. BRADY IN FOREGROUND

McCook crossed the Tennessee, with their corps, and took possession of the passes of Lookout Mountain on Bragg's flank, and Crittenden took post at Wauhatchie, in Lookout Valley, nearer the river, the Confederates abandoned Chattanooga, passed through the gaps of Missionary Ridge and encamped on

BRIG.-GENERAL J. KILPATRICK

the Chickamauga Creek near Lafayette, in northern Georgia, there to meet expected National forces when pressing through the gaps of Lookout Mountain and threatening their communications with Dalton and Resaca. From the lofty summit of Lookout Mountain, Crittenden had observed the retreat of Bragg from the Tennessee River, and he immediately led his forces into the Chattanooga Valley and encamped at Ross's Gap in Missionary Ridge, within three miles of the town.

General Burnside was then in command of the *Army of the Ohio*, and had been ordered to co-operate with Rosecrans. With twenty thousand men he climbed over the Cumberland Mountains into the magnificent Valley of East Tennessee, his baggage and stores carried, in many places, on the backs of pack-mules. On his entering the Valley, twenty thousand Confederates in East Tennessee, commanded by General Buckner, fled to Georgia and joined Bragg, when Burnside took a position near the Tennessee River, so as to have easy communication with Rosecrans at Chattanooga. The latter, meanwhile, erroneously supposing Bragg had begun a retreat toward Rome, had pushed through the mountain passes, when he was surprised to find that general, instead of retreating, concentrating his forces to attack the attenuated line of the Nationals, the extremities of which were fifty miles apart. Rosecrans proceeded at once to concentrate his own forces; and very soon the two armies were confronting each other in battle array, on each side of Chickamauga Creek, in the vicinity of Crawfish Spring, each line extending toward the slopes of Missionary Ridge. General Thomas, who was on the extreme left of the National line, opened the battle on the morning of the 19th of September. It raged with great fierceness until dark, when the Nationals seemed to have the advantage. That night General Longstreet, whom Lee had sent from Virginia to assist Bragg, arrived with fresh troops which swelled the Confederate army to seventy thousand men, and gave to it a far better soldier than the chief leader. Rosecrans's army did not then exceed, in number, fifty-five thousand men.

On the morning of the 20th the contest was renewed after a thick fog had risen from the earth. There was a fearful struggle. A furious charge upon the National right had shattered it into fragments, and these fled in disorder toward Chattanooga. This tide carried with it the troops led by Rosecrans, Crittenden and McCook; and the commanding-general, unable to join Thomas, and believing the whole army would speedily be hurrying pell-mell toward Chattanooga, hastened to that place to provide for rallying them there. Generals Sheridan and J. C. Davis rallied a part of these troops, and Thomas stood firm, frustrating every effort to turn his flank. Forty-eight hours after the battle the army, which had been withdrawn to Chattanooga, was strongly intrenched there.

Victory crowned the Confederates in the battle of Chickamauga, but at the fearful cost of about twenty-one thousand men killed, wounded, and made prisoners. The Nationals lost about nineteen thousand men. During the contest a

GENERAL J. KILPATRICK AND STAFF

COMMANDERS OF THE 11TH, 12TH AND CAVALRY CORPS AT BATTLE OF GETTYSBURG

little volunteer soldier named John Clem, then about twelve years of age, performed a deed of daring. He had been in the thickest of the fight when, separated from his companions, he was seen running with a musket in his hand by a mounted Confederate colonel, who called out, "Stop! you little Yankee devil!"

GENERAL J. C. PEMBERTON

The boy halted, with his musket to an order, when the colonel rode up to make him a prisoner. Young Clem, with swift motion, brought up his gun and shot the colonel dead. The boy escaped; and for this achievement he was made a sergeant, put on duty at the headquarters of the *Army of the Cumberland*, and placed on the roll of honor by General Rosecrans. He grew to manhood, married, and held a position in one of the departments of Government in Washington.

For a time the vanquished army suffered much at Chattanooga, for communication with their supplies by the Tennessee was cut off, the Confederates occupying Lookout Mountain and commanding that stream. Bragg hoped to starve his foes into submission. He strove to deprive them of all supplies, and severe struggles between detachments of the two armies were the consequences. Bragg failed. The National Government had determined to hold Chattanooga, and orders were given for the consolidation of the armies of the *Cumberland* and *Tennessee*, constituting the military division of the *Mississippi*, with General Grant as commander-in-chief. He had secured the free navigation of the Mississippi River, after the fall of Vicksburg and Port Hudson, by driving the Confederates, under Johnston, from the vicinity and strongly fortifying the first-named place; and when he took command of the new division, General Sherman was made the leader of the *Army of the Tennessee*, and General Thomas was placed in command of the *Army of the Cumberland*, Rosecrans having been ordered to St. Louis.

When Grant arrived at Chattanooga, he ordered Hooker, who was at Bridgeport, to advance to Lookout Valley, menace Bragg's flank, and protect the passage of supplies up the Tennessee to within a short distance from the famishing armies. This was promptly done. Hooker's main force took post at Wauhatchie, where he was attacked before daylight on the morning of the 29th of October. After a battle for three hours in the darkness, the Confederates were beaten and driven away. An amusing incident of this struggle occurred. When it began, about two hundred mules, frightened by the noise, broke from their tethers and dashed into the ranks of Wade Hampton's legion, and produced a great panic. The Confederates supposed it to be a charge of Hooker's cavalry, and fell back, at first, in great confusion. The incident was a theme for a mock-heroic poem of six stanzas in imitation of Tennyson's "Charge of the Light Brigade," two verses of which were as follows:

"Forward, the mule brigade—
Was there a mule dismay'd?
Not when their long ears felt
    All their ropes sundered.
Theirs not to make reply—
Theirs not to reason why—
Theirs but to make them fly—
On! to the Georgia troops
    Broke the two hundred.

"Mules to the right of them—
Mules to the left of them—
Mules all behind them—
    Paw'd, neigh'd, and thundered;
Breaking their own confines—
Breaking through Longstreet's lines—
Testing chivalric spines,
Into the Georgia troops
    Storm'd the two hundred."

After this battle, the Tennessee was free for vessels with supplies for the National troops, and the two armies lay confronting each other, only about three miles apart.

Meanwhile there had been stirring events in the Valley of East Tennessee, where Burnside was trying to expel the Confederates. In these efforts he had spread his army considerably. Perceiving this, Bragg sent Longstreet to the Valley with a strong force to seize Knoxville and drive out the Nationals. He advanced swiftly and secretly; and on the 20th of October he struck a startling blow at Burnside's outposts at Philadelphia. In obedience to a command from Grant, the latter concentrated his forces (Ninth Army Corps), fell back to Knoxville, and there intrenched. Longstreet pressed forward, and after some

GENERAL PEMBERTON'S HEADQUARTERS

CEMETERY GATE.
LUNETTES THROWN UP TO PROTECT
GUN OF BATTERY B, U.S. ARTILLERY.

BRYAN'S HOUSE.
IN 2ND CORPS LINE
NEAR PICKETT'S CHARGE.

CEMETERY HILL, SHOWING POINT OF
ATTACK OF
LOUISIANA TIGERS.

SHOWING POSITION OCCUPIED
BY 9TH MASS. BATTERY AND
THEIR DEAD HORSES.

TROSTLE'S HOUSE.

GROUND OVER WHICH LOUISIANA TIGERS ADVANCED TO ATTACK
FROM STEVENS KNOLL.

CULPS HILL IN THE FOREGROUND BALTIMORE PIKE
AND LUNETTES PROTECTING GUNS OF REYNOLDS BATTERY.

SCENES AT THE BATTLEFIELD OF GETTYSBURG

fighting by the way, he began a regular siege of Knoxville at the middle of November. He continued it to the close of the month, when Generals Granger and Sherman were sent to the relief of Burnside, and caused the swift flight of Longstreet toward Virginia. By this blunder, Bragg had lost the support of this superior commander.

JOHN BURNS' COTTAGE AT GETTYSBURG

Hostilities had again occurred near Chattanooga. General Sherman arrived there, with his army, from the West. So strengthened, Grant determined to attack Bragg in the absence of Longstreet. On the 23d of November, General Thomas seized a commanding eminence in front of Missionary Ridge, called Orchard Knob, and fortified it; and Hooker was ordered to attack Bragg's left, on Lookout Mountain, the next morning, to divert attention from the movements of Sherman, who was to cross the Tennessee, above Chattanooga, and fall upon Bragg's right, on the Ridge. Hooker moved with vigor, fighting his way up the rugged wooded steeps of Lookout Mountain with musket, rifle and cannon, driving the Confederates before him. During the heaviest of the struggle the mountain was hooded in vapor that arose from the Tennessee and hid the combatants from the view of the anxious spectators at Chattanooga. They could hear the thunders of the artillery, but the warriors were invisible. It was literally a battle in the clouds. Finally the Confederates were driven to the summit; and that night they fled down the northern slopes to the Chattanooga Valley, and joined their commander on Missionary Ridge. In the crisp air and the sunlight, the next morning, the Stars and Stripes was seen waving over "Pulpit Rock," on the crest of Lookout Mountain, from which, a few days before, Jefferson Davis had harangued the troops, assuring them that all was well with the Confederacy.

Sherman, in the meantime, had crossed the Tennessee River and secured a position on the northern end of Missionary Ridge, on which Bragg had concentrated all his forces, and there the Confederates were attacked on front and flank on the 25th of November. Hooker came down from Lookout Mountain, and entering Ross's Gap, attacked Bragg's left, while Sherman was assailing his right. There was a fearful struggle, beheld with intense interest by General Grant, who stood on Orchard Knob and directed the movements of the National army. At length the centre, under General Thomas, moved up the declivities; and very soon the Confederates were driven from the Ridge, when they fled toward Ringgold, followed by a portion of the National army. At Ringgold, a sharp engagement occurred, when the Confederates retreated to Dalton, the Nationals fell back, and Sherman hastened to the relief of Burnside, as already mentioned.

General Grant reported the Union loss, in the series of struggles which ended in victory at Missionary Ridge, at five thousand six hundred and sixteen, in killed, wounded, and missing. The Confederate loss was about three thousand one hundred killed and wounded, and a little more than six thousand prisoners.

JOHN BURNS "THE HERO OF GETTYSBURG" SITTING IN FRONT OF HIS DOOR WITH RIFLE AND CRUTCHES.
SANITARY COMMISSION HEADQUARTERS.
SHATTERED ARTILLERY CAISSON NEAR PEACH ORCHARD.

LITTLE ROUND TOP AND BIG ROUND TOP

LITTLE ROUND TOP

FEDERAL ENTRENCHMENTS ON LITTLE ROUND TOP

"VALLEY OF THE SHADOW OF DEATH" OR THE SLAUGHTER PEN, BETWEEN THE TWO ROUND TOPS,

BIG ROUND TOP SHOWING FEDERAL ENTRENCHMENTS ON LITTLE ROUND TOP IN FOREGROUND

VIEWS ON THE BATTLEFIELD OF GETTYSBURG

CHRONOLOGICAL SUMMARY AND RECORD—Continued

APRIL, 1864—*Continued from Section* 10

6—Quicksand Creek, Ky. Co. I 14th Ky. *Confed.* 10 killed, 7 wounded.

7—Wilson's Farm, La. Advance Cavalry of Nineteenth Corps. *Union* 14 killed, 39 wounded. *Confed.* 15 killed, 40 wounded, 100 captured.

Near Port Hudson, La. Detachment 118th Ill., 3d Ill. Cav., 21st N. Y. Battery. *Union* 1 killed, 4 wounded.

8 and 9—Sabine Cross Roads and Pleasant Hills, La. Portions of Thirteenth, Sixteenth and Nineteenth Corps and Cavalry Division Army of Dept. of the Gulf. *Union* 300 killed, 1,600 wounded, 2,100 missing. *Confed.* 600 killed, 2,400 wounded, 500 missing. *Union* Maj.-Gen. Franklin and Brig.-Gen. Ransom wounded. *Confed.* Maj.-Gen. Moulton and Brig.-Gen. Parsons killed.

10 to 13—Prairie D'Ann, Ark. 3d Division Seventh Corps. *Union* 100 killed and wounded. *Confed.* 50 killed and wounded.

12—Pleasant Hill Landing, La. Seventeenth Corps and U. S. Gunboats *Osage* and *Lexington*. *Union* 7 killed. *Confed.* 200 killed and wounded.

13—Moscow, Ark. 18th Iowa, 6th Kan. Cav., 2d Ind. Battery. *Union* 5 killed, 17 wounded. *Confed.* 30 killed and wounded.

13 and 14—Paintsville and Half-Mount, Ky. Ky. Volunteers. *Union* 4 wounded. *Confed.* 25 killed, 25 wounded.

14—Smithfield or Cherry Grove, Va. 9th N. J., 23d and 25th Mass., 118th N. Y. *Union* 5 wounded. *Confed.* 6 wounded.

15—Bristoe Station, Va. 13th Pa. Cav. *Union* 1 killed, 2 wounded.

15 and 16—Liberty P. O., and occupation of Camden, Ark. 29th Iowa, 50th Ind., 9th Wis. *Union* 255 killed and wounded.

17—Decatur, Ala. 25th Wis. *Union* 2 wounded.

17 to 20—Plymouth, N. C. 85th N. Y., 103d Pa., 16th Conn. and the Navy. *Union* 20 killed, 80 wounded, 1,500 missing. *Confed.* 500 killed, wounded and missing. Lieut.-Com. Flusser, U. S. N., killed.

18—Poison Springs, eight miles from Camden, Ark. Forage train guarded by 18th Iowa, 79th U. S. Colored, 6th Kan. Cav. *Union* 113 killed, 88 wounded, 68 missing.

Boyken's Mills, S. C. 54th Mass., U. S. Colored. *Union* 2 killed, 18 wounded.

21—Cotton Plate, Cache River, Ark. 8th Mo. Cav. *Union* 5 killed, 2 wounded.

Red Bone, Miss., 2d Wis. Cav. *Union* 1 killed, 6 wounded.

22—Near Tunica Bend, Red River, La. Three Cos. 3d R. I. Cav. *Union* 2 killed, 17 wounded.

23—Nickajack Trace, Ga. Detachment of 92d Ill. *Union* 5 killed, 9 wounded, 22 taken prisoners, of whom 12 were shot down and 6 died from wounds.

23 and 24—Moneti's Bluff, Cane River and Cloutersville, La. Portion of Thirteenth, Seventh and Nineteenth Corps. *Union* 350 killed and wounded. *Confed.* 400 killed and wounded.

25—Mark's Mills, Ark. 36th Iowa, 77th Ohio, 43d Ill., 1st Ind. Cav., 7th Mo. Cav., Battery E 2d Mo. Light Artil. *Union* 100 killed, 250 wounded, 100 missing. *Confed.* 110 killed, 228 wounded, 40 missing.

25 and 26—Wautauga Bridge, Tenn. 10th Mich. Cav. *Union* 3 killed, 9 wounded.

26—Moro Creek, Ark. 33d and 40th Iowa, 5th Kan., 2d and 4th Mo., 1st Iowa Cav. *Union* 5 killed, 14 wounded.

29—Princeton, Ark. 40th Iowa, 43d Ill., 6th Kan. Cav., 3d Ill. Battery. Casualties not recorded.

30—Jenkins' Ferry, Saline River, Ark. 3d Division of Seventh Corps. *Union* 200 killed, 955 wounded. *Confed.* 300 killed, 800 wounded.

MAY, 1864

1—Jacksonville, Fla. 7th U. S. Colored. *Union* 1 killed.

1 to 8—Hudnot's Plantation and near Alexandria, La. Cavalry of Thirteenth and Nineteenth Corps. *Union* 33 killed, 87 wounded. *Confed.* 25 killed, 100 wounded.

2—Gov. Moor's Plantation, La. Foraging of Detachment of 83d Ohio and 3d R. I. Cav. *Union* 2 killed, 10 wounded.

3—Red Clay, Ga. 1st Division of McCook's Cav. *Union* 10 killed and wounded.

Richland, Ark. 2d Ark. Cav. *Union* 20 killed.

4—Doubtful Cañon, Ariz. Detachment of 5th Cav. and 1st Cal. Cav. *Union* 1 killed, 6 wounded. *Confed.* 10 killed, 20 wounded.

4 to 12—Kautz's Cavalry Raid from Suffolk, Wall's Bridge, Stoney Creek Station, Jarrett's Station, White's Bridge to City Point, Va. 5th and 11th Pa. Cav., 3d N. Y. Cav., 1st D. C. Cav., 8th N. Y. Battery. *Union* 10 killed, wounded and missing. *Confed.* 20 wounded, 50 prisoners.

4 to 13—Yazoo City expedition, including Benton and Vaughn, Miss. 11th, 72d and 76th Ill., 5th Ill. Cav., 3d U. S. Colored Cav., 7th Ohio Battery. *Union* 5 killed, 20 wounded.

5—Ram *Albermarle*, Roanoke River, N. C. U. S. Gunboats, *Ceres*, *Commodore Hull*, *Mattabesett*, *Sassacus*, *Seymour*, *Wyalusing*, *Miama* and *Whitehead*. *Union* 5 killed, 26 wounded, 57 captured.

Dunn's Bayou, Red River, La. 56th Ohio, on board U. S. Gunboat *Signal*, steamer *Covington* and transport *Warner*. *Union* 35 killed, 65 wounded, 150 missing.

5 to 7—Wilderness, Va. Army of the Potomac, Maj.-Gen. George G. Meade; Second Corps, Maj.-Gen. Hancock; Fifth Corps, Maj.-Gen. Warren; Sixth Corps, Maj.-Gen. Sedgwick; Ninth Corps, Maj.-Gen. Burnside and Sheridan's Cavalry. *Union* 5,597 killed, 21,463 wounded, 10,677 missing. *Confed.* 2,000 killed, 6,000 wounded, 3,400 missing. *Union* Brig.-Gens. Wadsworth, Hays and Webb killed. *Confed.* Gens. Jones and Pickett killed, and Longstreet, Pegram, Stafford, Hunter and Jennings wounded.

5 to 9—Rocky Face Ridge, Ga., including Tunnel Hill, Mill Creek Gap and Buzzard's Roost. Army of the Cumberland, Maj.-Gen. Thomas; Army of the Tennessee, Maj.-Gen. McPherson. Army of the Mississippi, Maj.-Gen. Sherman. *Union* 200 killed, 637 wounded. *Confed.* 600 killed and wounded.

6—James River, near City Point, Va. U. S. Gunboat *Commodore Jones*. *Union* 23 killed, 48 wounded.

6 and 7—Richmond and Petersburg Railroad, near Chester Station, Va. Portion of Tenth and Eighteenth Corps. *Union* 48 killed, 256 wounded. *Confed.* 50 killed, 200 wounded.

7—Bayou La Mourie, La. Portion of Sixteenth Corps. *Union* 10 killed, 31 wounded.

8—Todd's Tavern, Va. 2d Division Cavalry Corps Army of the Potomac. *Union* 40 killed, 150 wounded. *Confed.* 30 killed, 150 wounded.

8 to 18—Spottsylvania, Fredericksburg Road, Laurel Hill and Ny River, Va. Army of the Potomac, Maj.-Gen. Meade; Second Corps, Maj.-Gen. Hancock; Fifth Corps, Maj.-Gen. Warren; Sixth Corps, Maj.-Gen. Wright; Ninth Corps, Maj.-Gen. Burnside and Sheridan's Cavalry. *Union* 4,177 killed, 19,687 wounded, 2,577 missing. *Confed.* 1,000 killed, 5,000 wounded, 3,000 missing. *Union* Maj.-Gen. Sedgwick and Brig.-Gens. Rice, Owens, and Stevenson killed; Brig.-Gens. Robertson, Bartlett, Morris and Baxter wounded. *Confed.* Gens. Daniels and Perrin killed, Hayes and Walker wounded and Maj.-Gen. Ed. Johnson and Brig.-Gen. Stewart captured.

9—Varnell's Station, Ga. 1st Div. McCook's Cav. *Union* 4 killed, 25 wounded.

9 and 10—Swift Creek or Arrowfield Church, Va. Tenth and Eighteenth Corps. *Union* 90 killed, 400 wounded. *Confed.* 500 killed.

Cloyd's Mountain and New River Bridge, Va. 12th, 23d, 34th and 36th Ohio, 9th 11th, 14th and 15th W. Va., 3d and 4th Pa. Reserves. *Union* 126 killed, 585 wounded. *Confed.* 600 killed and wounded, 300 missing.

9 to 13—Sheridan's Cavalry Raid in Virginia, engagements Beaver Dam Station, South Anna Bridge, Ashland and Yellow Tavern. *Union* 50 killed, 174 wounded, 200 missing. *Confed.* killed and wounded not recorded, 100 prisoners. *Confed.* Maj.-Gen. J. E. B. Stuart killed and J. B. Gordon wounded.

12 to 16—Fort Darling, Drury's Bluff, Va. Tenth and Eighteenth Corps. *Union* 422 killed, 2,380 wounded, 210 missing. *Confed.* 400 killed, 2,000 wounded, 100 missing.

12 to 17—Kautz's Raid on Petersburg and Lynchburg Railroad, Va. *Union* 6 killed, 28 wounded.

13 to 16—Resaca, Ga. Fourth, Fourteenth, Twentieth and Cavalry Corps, Army of the Cumberland, Maj.-Gen. Thomas; Fifteenth and Sixteenth Corps, Army of the Tennessee, Maj.-Gen. McPherson, and Twenty-third Corps, Army of the Ohio, Maj.-Gen. Schofield. *Union* 600 killed, 2,147 wounded. *Confed.* 300 killed, 1,500 wounded, 1,000 missing. *Confed.* Brig.-Gen. Wadkins killed.

15—Mount Pleasant Landing, La. 67th U. S. Colored. *Union* 3 killed, 5 wounded.

New Market, Va. Maj.-Gen. Sigel's command. *Union* 120 killed, 560 wounded, 240 missing. *Confed.* 85 killed, 320 wounded.

Tanner's Bridge, Ga. 2d Division Cavalry, Army of the Cumberland. *Union* 2 killed, 16 wounded.

16 to 30—Bermuda Hundred, Va. Tenth and Eighteenth Corps, Army of the James. *Union* 200 killed, 1,000 wounded. *Confed.* 3,000 killed, wounded and missing.

17 and 18—Adairsville and Calhoun, Ga. Fourth Corps, Maj.-Gen. Howard. Casualties not recorded.

18—Rome and Kingston, Ga. 2d Division of Fourteenth Corps and Cavalry Army of the Cumberland. *Union* 16 killed, 59 wounded.

Bayou De Glaize or Calhoun Station, La. Portions of Sixteenth, Seventeenth and Cavalry of Nineteenth Corps. *Union* 60 killed, 300 wounded. *Confed.* 500 killed and wounded.

19 to 22—Cassville, Ga. Twentieth Corps, Maj.-Gen. Hooker. *Union* 10 killed, 46 wounded.

21—Mt. Pleasant, Miss. 4th Mo. Cav. *Union* 2 killed, 1 wounded.

23 to 27—North Anna River, Jericho Ford or Taylor's Bridge and Talopotomy Creek, Va. Second, Fifth and Ninth Corps, Army of the Potomac, Maj.-Gen. Meade. *Union* 223 killed, 1,460 wounded, 290 missing. *Confed.* 2,000 killed and wounded.

24—Holly Springs, Miss. 4th Mo. Cav. *Union* 1 killed, 2 wounded.

Wilson's Wharf, Va. 10th U. S. Colored, 1st D. C. Cavalry, Battery B U. S. Colored Artil. *Union* 2 killed, 24 wounded. *Confed.* 20 killed, 100 wounded.

Nashville, Tenn. 15th U. S. Colored. *Union* 4 killed, 8 wounded.

25 to June 4—Dallas, Ga., also called New Hope Church and Allatoona Hills. Fourth, Fourteenth, Twentieth and Cavalry Corps, Army of the Cumberland, Maj.-Gen. Thomas; Twenty-third Corps, Maj.-Gen. Schofield; Fifteenth, Sixteenth and Seventeenth Corps Army of the Tennessee, Maj.-Gen. McPherson—Army of the Mississippi, Maj.-Gen. Sherman. *Union* 2,400 killed, wounded and missing. *Confed.* 3,000 killed, wounded and missing. *Confed.* Maj.-Gen. Walker killed.

25—Cassville Station, Ga. 1st and 11th Ky. Cav. *Union* 8 killed, 16 wounded. *Confed.* 2 killed, 6 wounded.

26—Torpedo explosion on Bachelor's Creek, N. C. 132d and 158th N. Y., 58th Pa. *Union* 35 killed, 19 wounded.

26 to 29—Decatur and Moulton, Ala. 1st, 3d and 4th Ohio Cav., 2d Cavalry Division. *Union* 48 killed and wounded. *Confed.* 60 killed and wounded.

27 and 28—Hanoverton, Hawe's Shop and Salem Church, Va. 1st and Second Divisions Cavalry Corps, Maj.-Gen. Sheridan. *Union* 25 killed, 119 wounded, 200 missing. *Confed.* 475 killed, wounded and missing.

30—Hanover and Ashland, Va. Wilson's Cavalry. *Union* 26 killed, 130 wounded.

Old Church, Va. Torbett's Cavalry. *Union* 16 killed, 74 wounded.

JUNE, 1864

1 to 12—Cold Harbor, Va., including Gaines's Mills, Salem Church and Hawe's Shop. Second, Fifth, Sixth, Ninth and Eighteenth Corps and Sheridan's Cavalry. *Union* 1,905 killed, 10,570 wounded, 2,456 missing. *Confed.* 1,200 killed and wounded, 500 missing. *Union* Brig.-Gens. Brookes and Byrnes killed and Tyler, Stannard and Johnson wounded. *Confed.* Brig.-Gens. Doles and Keitt killed and Kirkland, Finnegan, Law and Lane wounded.

(*Continued in Section* 12)

U.S. ARTILLERY NEAR CULPEPPER SEPT. 1863.

DR. MURRAYS HOUSE NEAR AUBURN, VA.

GEN. MOTT AND OFFICERS CULPEPPER, OCT. 1863.

U.S. ARTILLERY NEAR CULPEPPER SEPT. 1863.

PONTOON BRIDGE ACROSS POTOMAC RIVER AT BERLIN.

GEN. PRINCE AND STAFF CULPEPPER. SEPT. 1863.

OFFICERS OF HORSE ARTILLERY CULPEPPER. SEPT. 1863.

OFFICERS 18TH N.Y. INFANTRY CULPEPPER. SEPT. 1863.

HEADQUARTERS OF THE ARMY OF THE POTOMAC, SEPTEMBER, 1863

CHAPTER XXI.—Continued.

GRANT had also captured forty pieces of artillery and about seven thousand small arms. In a letter to the victorious general, the President thanked him and his men for their skill and bravery in securing "a lodgment at Chattanooga and Knoxville." Congress voted thanks and a gold medal for Grant, and directed the President of the Republic to cause the latter to be struck, "with suitable emblems, devices, and inscriptions." The general was the recipient of other tokens of regard, of various kinds; and the legislatures of New York and Ohio voted him thanks in the name of the people of those great States.

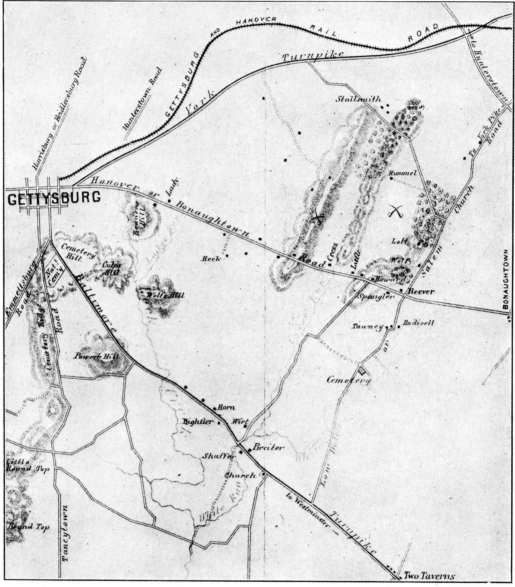

MAP OF THE BATTLEFIELD OF GETTYSBURG

During the first half of 1863, General J. G. Foster was in command of the National troops in North Carolina, with his headquarters at New Berne, from which point he sent out raiding parties to scatter Confederate forces who were gathering here and there to recover lost posts in that State. In these expeditions, many sharp skirmishes took place. The Nationals were generally successful, and confined their antagonists to the interior of the State. Finally, in July (1863), Foster was called to the command at Fortress Monroe, and left his troops in charge of General Palmer. Meanwhile there had been important occurrences in the vicinity of Charleston, South Carolina, the capture of that city being one objective of the National Government. Attempts had been made the previous year by General David Hunter (commanding the Department of the South) and Admiral Dupont, to seize that city, but failed. Dupont had received important information concerning military affairs at Charleston, from Robert Small, a slave, who was a pilot in the Confederate service. One night, in the middle of May (1862), assisted by some fellow-bondsmen, Small took the Confederate steamer *Planter* out of Charleston harbor, delivered her to Dupont, gave him valuable information, and entered the service of the Republic. Soon afterward the National land troops took a position on James Island, near Charleston; and at Secessionville,

CULPEPPER, VIRGINIA

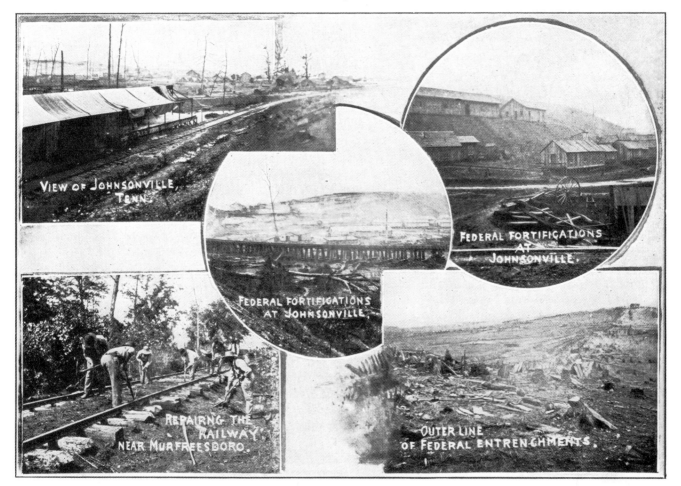

VIEWS AT MURFREESBORO AND JOHNSONVILLE

General Benham, with a small force, fought the Confederates at the middle of June, and was defeated. Further attempts to capture Charleston were then suspended.

Hunter was succeeded in the command of the department by General O. M. Mitchel, who, as we have observed, was called to Washington from Tennessee, where he chafed under Buell's command. He reached Hilton Head on the 16th of September, and with his usual vigor he devised plans and prepared to execute them for the public good. Hilton Head Island was swarming with refugee slaves, and he at once took measures for their relief, laying out a village, causing neat and comfortable log-houses to be built for their residences, and finding employment for them. He was preparing to use his military force with vigor in his department; but before his arrangements were completed, he was smitten with a disease similar to the yellow fever, when he was conveyed to the more healthy locality of Beaufort, where he

GENERAL GEORGE G. MEADE

died on the 30th of October. From that time, until the spring of 1864, very little of importance occurred in the Department of the South, of which Hunter again became the commander.

CHAPTER XXII.

Efforts to Capture Charleston—"The Swamp Angel"—Siege of Fort Wagner—Sumter in Ruins—Events West of the Mississippi—Invasion of Missouri—Lawrence Sacked—Events in Arkansas and in the Indian Territory—Raid into Missouri—Struggle for Louisiana—Grant in New Orleans—Designs against Texas—Forrest in Tennessee—Strength of the Nationals and Confederates Compared—High-Handed Measures—The British and the Confederates—Good Signs—Grant Lieutenant-General—Campaign of 1864—Sherman's Raid in Mississippi—Massacre at Fort Pillow—Forrest's Exploits—Red River Expedition—The Expedition Abandoned—Negro Troops.

ALTHOUGH Charleston had become a comparatively unimportant point in the grand theatre of the war, its possession was coveted by the National Government because of the salutary moral effect which such conquest would produce. A strong effort to accomplish that purpose was made in the spring of 1863. On the 6th of April, Admiral Dupont crossed Charleston Bar with nine "monitor" or turreted iron vessels, leaving five gunboats outside as a reserve, and proceeded to attack Fort Sumter, the most formidable obstacle in his way to the city. At the same time a co-operating force of land troops, four thousand strong, under General Truman Seymour, took a masked position on Folly Island. As Dupont approached, the cannon of the Confederates on Sumter and the adjacent batteries were silent until the vessels were entangled in an unsuspected network of torpedoes and other obstructions, when nearly three hundred guns opened a concentric fire upon the fleet, driving them back to the ocean and destroying the *Keokuk*, one of the smallest of the iron-clads. The land troops could do nothing until Fort Sumter was reduced, and the enterprise was a failure.

In June following, General Quincey A. Gillmore succeeded General Hunter in the command of the Southern Department. He found himself at the head of eighteen thousand men, with a generous supply of ordnance, small arms, and stores. An expedition against Charleston, by land and water, was immediately planned. Gillmore determined to seize Morris Island, on which was strong Fort Wagner that commanded Fort Sumter. That island and its military works in his possession, he might batter down Fort Sumter with heavy siege guns, and lay Charleston in ashes with his shells, if it was not surrendered. Dupont did not approve the plan; and early in July, Admiral John A. Dahlgren took his place. General Alfred H. Terry was sent with a force to James Island to mask Gillmore's intentions, when National troops were suddenly landed on Morris Island, and, with the aid of batteries on Folly Island, they drove the Confederates into Fort Wagner. Then Gillmore planted a line of batteries across Morris Island to confront that fort, which he found to be much stronger than he suspected. The Nationals assaulted it (July 11) and were repulsed, when a simultaneous bombardment by sea and land was determined on. This was done on the 18th of July, when a hundred great guns opened on the fort from the ships and the land-batteries. Meanwhile General Terry had been attacked by a force sent from Charleston, by Beauregard, to surprise him. But the vigilance of Terry never slept, and the Confederates were easily repulsed. The Nationals were then withdrawn from James Island and joined the main body of troops on Morris Island.

At sunset on the 18th, Gillmore's forces moved in two columns, to attack Fort Wagner. A violent

MILITARY RAILROAD TRESTLE BRIDGE AND PASS IN RACCOON RANGE, NEAR WHITESIDE.

ARMY TRANSPORTS ON TENNESSEE RIVER.

ARMY TRANSPORTS BRIDGEPORT ON TENNESSEE RIVER.

THE VALLEY OF RUNNING WATER CREEK, NEAR WHITESIDE.

HOUSE OF JOHN ROSE, NEAR BRIDGEPORT, GA.

Scenes Near Whiteside and Views on Tennessee River

thunder-storm was raging. One column was led by General Strong, the other by Colonel H. L. Putnam, acting as brigadier. The struggle was brief but fearful. Both columns of the Nationals were repulsed, with great slaughter in their ranks, losing, in the aggregate, full fifteen hundred men. Strong and Putnam

were mortally wounded; and Colonel Robert G. Shaw, who was at the head of the first regiment of colored troops organized in the free-labor States, was instantly killed. Because he commanded colored troops, Shaw was intensely hated by the Confederates; and they foolishly thought they had dishonored him when, as they proclaimed, they had buried his body "in a pit under a heap of his niggers."

Gillmore now abandoned the plan for capturing Fort Wagner by direct assault, and began a regular siege. With infinite labor a battery was constructed in a morass half-way between Morris and James islands, upon a platform of heavy timbers standing in the deep black mud. When a lieutenant of engineers was ordered to construct it he said, "It is impossible." His commanding officer replied, "There is no such word as impossible; call for what you need." The lieutenant, who was a wag, made a requisition on the quartermaster for "one hundred men eighteen feet high to wade in mud sixteen feet deep"; and he gravely inquired of the engineer whether these men might be spliced, if required. The lieutenant was arrested for contempt, but was soon released, and he built a redoubt with the services of men of ordinary height. Upon the redoubt

GENERAL PHIL SHERIDAN

was erected a Parrott gun, which they called "The Swamp Angel," that sent shells into Charleston, five miles distant. One of these entered St. Michael's Church near the roof, and destroyed the tablet on the wall that contained the ten commandments, obliterating all of them excepting two—"Thou shalt not kill. Thou shalt not commit adultery."

General Gillmore was ready for another attack on Forts Wagner and Sumter on the 17th of August, and on that day the guns of twelve batteries and of the fleet opened upon them. Before night the granite walls of Fort Sumter began to crumble and its cannons ceased to roar, under the pressure of Dahlgren's guns. The land troops pushed their parallels nearer and nearer Fort Wagner; while the fleet guns continually pounded away, day after day, until the 6th of September, when General Terry was prepared to storm the latter work. Then it was ascertained that the Confederates had evacuated it and fled from Morris Island. Gillmore took possession of Fort Wagner and turned its guns on Fort Sumter, battering it dreadfully and driving away (it was supposed) its garrison. But that sentinel, which had so long guarded the gate to Charleston harbor, only slumbered; and when, on the night of the 8th, an armed force from the ships, in small boats, attempted to take possession of it, a vigilant garrison that had been lying quietly there, suddenly arose and repulsed the assailants with great loss to the latter. Finally, late in October (1863), Gillmore brought his heaviest guns to bear on Sumter, and reduced the once proud fort to a heap

of ruins. Charleston now, as a commercial mart, had no existence. For months not a blockade-runner had entered its harbor, and its wealth and trade had departed. In a military point of view, as we have observed, it was absolutely of very little importance. Let us leave the Atlantic coast, and consider stirring events in the interior.

A thousand miles westward of the sea-coast the war was still going on, but more feebly than at first. The Confederates reoccupied all Texas in 1863, and carried on a sort of guerrilla warfare in Arkansas and Missouri during a part of that year. In the earlier months, Marmaduke was active with his mounted men. He rushed over the border from Arkansas into Missouri, and fell upon Springfield in January, but was repulsed with a loss of two hundred men. After some other

TROOPS BUILDING BRIDGE ACROSS NORTH FORK OF RAPPAHANNOCK RIVER

BODIES OF DEAD IN WOODS LITTLE ROUND TOP.

BODIES OF DEAD COLLECTED FOR BURIAL, Mc PHERSON'S WOOD'S.

DEAD CONFEDERATE SHARPSHOOTERS HOOD'S DIVISION:

Bodies of Dead, Battle of Gettysburg

reverses, he fell back; and at Little Rock, the capital of Arkansas, he planned a formidable raid into Missouri, chiefly for the purpose of seizing National stores at Cape Girardeau, on the Mississippi. He invaded the State with eight thousand men, and was met at the Cape by General McNeil, on the 20th of April, who, after a sharp engagement, drove Marmaduke out of Missouri. Other bands of Confederates, under various leaders, roamed over the western borders of Arkansas, and, at one time, seriously menaced Fort Blunt, in the Indian Territory. There was a sharp engagement at Honey Springs, in that Territory, on the 17th of July, between Nationals under General Blunt and Confederates in strong force led by General Cooper, in which the latter were defeated, and a part of them fled into northern Texas. Guerrilla bands in Blunt's rear did much mischief. One of them, led by a white savage named Quantrell, fell upon the defenceless town of Lawrence, in Kansas, on the 13th of August, and murdered one hundred and forty of the inhabitants. They also laid one hundred and eighty-five buildings in ashes, and escaped.

Earlier than this, the strongly fortified post of Helena, on the Mississippi, in eastern Arkansas, became

GROUP OF CONFEDERATE GENERALS

a coveted object; and on the 3d of July (1863) eight thousand Confederates, under General Price and others, ignorant of the strength of the post, attacked it. General Steele was in command there. After a sharp fight, the Confederates were repulsed with a loss of twenty per cent. of their number. That section of Arkansas was then abandoned by the Confederates; and on the 10th of August, Steele left Helena with twelve thousand troops and forty pieces of cannon, to attempt the capture of Little Rock. He pushed back Marmaduke, who confronted him; and early in September he moved on the State capital in two columns, one on each side of the Arkansas River. The Confederates there, after setting fire to several steamboats, abandoned the place on the evening of the 10th (September) and fled to Arkadelphia, on the Wachita River. Meanwhile General Blunt had been trying to bring the Confederates and their Indian allies in western Arkansas to battle, but had failed. He took possession of Fort Smith (September 1) and garrisoned it; and on the 4th of October, while he was on his way from Kansas to that post with an escort of one hundred cavalry, they were attacked near Baxter's Springs, on the Cherokee Reservation, and scattered, by six hundred guerrillas led by the notorious Quantrell, who plundered and burnt the accompanying train of the Nationals. Blunt's forces were nearly all killed or disabled in the conflict. The wounded were murdered; and Blunt and only about a dozen followers barely escaped, with their lives, to Little Fort Blair. Some of Blunt's escort fled, at first, without firing a shot. Had they acted more bravely, they could have driven off their assailants in ten minutes, Blunt declared.

Finding their supplies nearly exhausted, the Confederates in that region made a raid into Missouri as far as Booneville, at the close of September; but they were driven back into Arkansas by Generals E. B. Brown and McNeil. No other military movements of much importance occurred in Missouri and Arkansas for some time after this, excepting an attack made by Marmaduke upon Pine Bluff, on the Arkansas River, on the 25th of October, 1863. The little garrison there was commanded by Colonel Powell Clayton, and these, with the assistance of two hundred negroes in making barricades, fought the assailants (who were two thousand strong, with twelve pieces of artillery) for several hours, and drove them away. Quiet prevailed for some time afterward.

When General Banks left Alexandria, on the Red River, and marched to the siege of Port Hudson, General Taylor, whom he had driven into the wilds of western Louisiana, returned, occupied that abandoned city and Opelousas, and garrisoned Fort de Russy. Then he swept vigorously over the country in the direction of the Mississippi River and New Orleans. With a part of his command he captured

SCENES IN AND ABOUT CHATTANOOGA, TENN.

Brashear City on the 24th of June (1863), with an immense amount of public property, and made a thousand National troops prisoners. At about the same time another portion of the Confederates, under General Green, operating in the vicinity of Donaldsonville, on the Mississippi, were driven out of the district. Finally, at the middle of July, when Banks's troops were released, on the fall of Port Hudson, they expelled Taylor and his forces from the country eastward of the Atchafalaya. This was the last struggle of Taylor's forces to gain a foothold on the Mississippi.

General Banks now turned his thoughts to aggressive movements. General Grant visited him at New Orleans early in September, and was in that city when he was summoned to Chattanooga. There it was determined that Banks should make an attempt to recover Texas; and he speedily sent four

MAJOR-GENERAL N. P. BANKS AND STAFF

thousand troops under General Franklin, accompanied by four gunboats commanded by Lieutenant Crocker, to seize the Confederate post at Sabine Pass, on the boundary line between Louisiana and Texas. Owing to a premature attack by the gunboats, the expedition was a disastrous failure. Then Banks concentrated his land forces on the Atchafalaya, for the purpose of penetrating Texas from the east by way of Shreveport, on the Red River; but this design was abandoned for a time, and it was concluded to attempt to seize and hold the coast harbor of that Commonwealth. To mask this movement, General C. C. Washburne, with a considerable body of troops, moved across Louisiana toward Alexandria, when about six thousand other Nationals under General Dana, with some war-vessels, sailed for the Rio Grande. The troops landed, and drove Confederate cavalry up that river. The Nationals pressed on; and on the 6th of November encamped at Brownsville, opposite Matamoras. At the close of the year, the National troops occupied all the strong positions on the Texan coast excepting Galveston Island and a formidable work near the mouth of the Brazos; and the Confederates had abandoned all Texas west of the Colorado River. Meanwhile N. B. Forrest, who had become a noted guerrilla chief, had broken into western Tennessee, from Mississippi, with four thousand Confederate soldiers, and making Jackson, in the first-mentioned State, his headquarters (December, 1863), had sent out foraging parties in various directions. General Hurlburt, at Memphis, tried to catch him, but failed.

There were many hopeful signs of success for the defenders of the life of the Republic at the opening of the third year of the Civil War, 1864. The debt of the National Government was then more than $1,000,000,000; but the public credit never stood higher. The loyal people stood by the Government, and trusted it with a fidelity and faith that was truly sublime. At the same time the Confederate debt was at least $1,000,000,000, with a prospective increase during the year to double that amount. The Confederate Government had contracted loans abroad to the amount almost of $15,000,000, of which sum the members of the *Southern Independence Association* in England (composed chiefly of the British aristocracy) loaned a large share and lost it, the security offered for the Confederate bonds being cotton to be forwarded, and which was never delivered. The producers of the Confederacy, better informed than their English sympathizers, were unwilling to trust the promise of their government and withheld

Scene on the Orange and Alexandria Railroad Near Union Mills, Tenn.

Battlefield of Chickamauga, Union Mills, Tenn.

supplies, for they preconceived the worthlessness of the bonds and paper currency of the Confederates. The people there were no longer willing to volunteer for the military service; and Davis and his associates at Richmond, in their desperation, proceeded to the exercise of a despotic act that has no parallel in the history of civilized nations.   By the passage of a law they declared that *every white man in the Confederacy,*

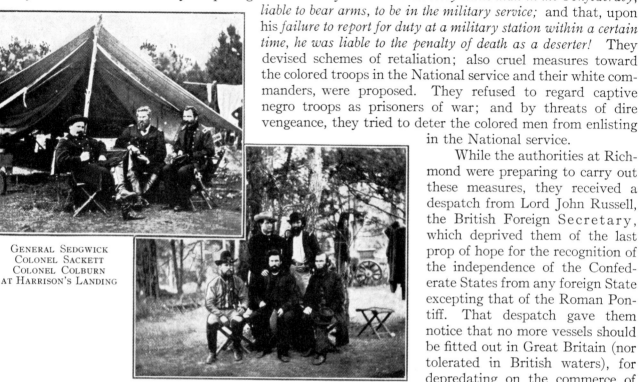

GENERAL SEDGWICK
COLONEL SACKETT
COLONEL COLBURN
AT HARRISON'S LANDING

GROUP OF OFFICERS OF THE IRISH BRIGADE

liable to bear arms, to be in the military service; and that, upon his *failure to report for duty at a military station within a certain time, he was liable to the penalty of death as a deserter!* They devised schemes of retaliation; also cruel measures toward the colored troops in the National service and their white commanders, were proposed. They refused to regard captive negro troops as prisoners of war; and by threats of dire vengeance, they tried to deter the colored men from enlisting in the National service.

While the authorities at Richmond were preparing to carry out these measures, they received a despatch from Lord John Russell, the British Foreign Secretary, which deprived them of the last prop of hope for the recognition of the independence of the Confederate States from any foreign State excepting that of the Roman Pontiff. That despatch gave them notice that no more vessels should be fitted out in Great Britain (nor tolerated in British waters), for depredating on the commerce of the United States by persons employed by the "so-called Confederate States." The last expression, which absolutely ignored the very existence of the "Confederate States" was very significant, and also very offensive to Davis and his associates. The latter replied sharply, protesting against the "studied insult;" and thenceforward the Confederates regarded the British government as their enemy. That government, perceiving the weakness of the Confederacy which it had tried to foster, stood firm, and so did our own. Regardless of the menaces of the Confederate leaders, the President determined to defend the colored troops against the vengeance of their late masters, and to prosecute the war with greater vigor. "The signs," he said, "look better." More than fifty thousand square miles of territory had already been recovered from the Confederates. There were about eight hundred thousand National troops in the field, while the Confederates had only about half that number; and the former were disposed to act on the offensive, while the latter were generally standing on the defensive.

Early in 1864, Congress created the office of lieutenant-general. The President nominated Ulysses S. Grant to fill it, and the Senate confirmed the nomination. Grant was made general-in-chief of the armies of the Republic, and he fixed his headquarters with that of the *Army of the Potomac.* He believed that mercy required that war should be made sharp and decisive, so as to end it speedily, and he acted accordingly. He believed his government to be right and its assailants wrong; and with all the zeal born of positive convictions, he prepared for the campaign of 1864. Two grand expeditions were planned —one for the capture of Richmond, the other for the seizure of the great railroad centre, Atlanta, in Georgia. To the *Army of the Potomac,* commanded by General Meade, was assigned the task of taking Richmond; and to General Sherman was given the command of the forces destined for Atlanta. Meanwhile important events had occurred in the Valley of the Mississippi.

When General Sherman was called to Chattanooga, he left General J. B. McPherson in command at Vicksburg; but soon after Bragg was driven southward from Chattanooga, Sherman suddenly reappeared in Mississippi; and at the head of twenty thousand troops, he made a most destructive raid (February, 1864) from Jackson to the intersection of important railways at Meridian, in that State. His object was to inflict as much injury as possible upon the Confederate cause and its physical strength. Like Grant, he believed in the righteousness and efficacy of making war terrible. The line of his march

GENERAL CORCORAN AND OFFICERS OF THE 69TH NEW YORK VOLUNTEERS—GENERAL CORCORAN ON EXTREME LEFT

from Jackson, eastward, presented a black path of desolation. No public property of the Confederates was spared. The station-houses and the rolling stock of the railway were burned. The track was torn up, and the rails, heated by the burning ties cast into heaps, were twisted and ruined; and were often, by bending them, while red-hot, around a sapling, converted into what the men called "Jeff. Davis's neckties." General Sherman intended to push on to Montgomery, Alabama, and then, if circumstances appeared favorable, to go southward and attack Mobile.

GENERAL TRUEMAN SEYMOUR

At Meridian, General Sherman waited for General W. S. Smith to join him with a considerable force of cavalry; but that officer was held back by Forrest and others. After waiting in vain for a week, Sherman laid Meridian in ashes and returned to Vicksburg with four hundred prisoners and five thousand liberated slaves. This raid spread great alarm over the Confederacy; for General (Bishop) Polk, in command of the insurgents in that region, made but a feeble resistance. General Joseph E. Johnston, in command of Bragg's army in northern Georgia, had sent troops to reinforce Polk; but was compelled to recall them when his own army was menaced by a National force under General Palmer, which had been sent down from Chattanooga. Johnston fought Palmer between Ringgold and Dalton (February, 1864), and drove him back to Chattanooga.

Some weeks later, General Forrest, having an enlarged command, made a rapid raid through Tennessee and Kentucky; and on the 13th of April he laid siege to Fort Pillow, on the Mississippi, above Memphis, which was garrisoned chiefly by colored troops. He assailed it successfully, with a cry of "No quarter"; and when the garrison threw down their arms and begged for mercy, they were nearly all slaughtered. "Forrest's motto," said Major Charles W. Gibson, of his command, to the writer, was, "War means fight, and fight means kill—*we want but few prisoners.*" An unsuccessful attempt was made to intercept him in his retreat from the scene of the massacre. Troops sent out from Memphis, a few weeks later, by General Smith, to hunt him up and beat him, in Mississippi, were defeated in a severe battle with him on the 10th of June, at Gun Town, on the Mobile and Ohio Railway, and were driven back with great loss. Twelve thousand men, led by General A. J. Smith, went out for the same purpose, and fought and defeated Forrest near Tupelo on the 14th of June, and then retreated to Memphis; and not long afterward, when Smith was in Mississippi with ten thousand men, the bold raider, at the head of three thousand cavalry, flanked him, dashed into Memphis in broad daylight, in search of National officers, and escaped into Mississippi.

At the beginning of 1864, another attempt was made to recover Texas, by an invasion by way of the Red River and Shreveport. General Banks was ordered to organize an expedition for the purpose, and General Sherman was directed to send troops to aid him. Admiral Porter was also directed to place a fleet of gunboats on the Red River to assist in the enterprise; and General Steele, at Little Rock, Arkansas, was ordered to co-operate with the expedition. Banks's column, led by General Franklin, moved from Brashear City by way of Opelousas, and reached Alexandria on the 26th of March. The detachment from Sherman's army, led by General A. J. Smith, had already gone up the Red River in transports, captured Fort de Russy, and taken possession of Alexandria on the 16th of March, followed by Porter's fleet of gunboats.

Banks moved forward with his whole force; and early in April the army was at Natchitoches, eighty miles further up the river, at which point Porter's vessels arrived, after encountering much difficulty in passing the rapids at Alexandria on account of low water. His larger gunboats could proceed no further than Grand Ecore. Banks pushed

GENERAL ROBERT S. FOSTER AND STAFF

BRIDGE OVER THE CUMBERLAND RIVER AT CHATTANOOGA

CHATTANOOGA, TENN., IN 1864

on toward Shreveport, and Porter's lighter vessels went up the river with a body of troops under E. Kirby Smith.   The Confederates had been gathering force under Generals Taylor, Price and Green, and were driven before the Nationals until they reached Sabine Cross Roads, where they made a stand on the 8th of April.   A sharp battle ensued between them and the advance of Banks's army.   There was a hard struggle for the mastery. Franklin's troops came to the aid of the latter late in the afternoon; but their antagonists fought so well and desperately that the whole body of the Nationals were routed, with heavy loss, and fled in some confusion. The fugitives were received three miles from the battle-field, at a place called Pleasant Grove, by the division of General Emory; and there another severe engagement took place, in which the Nationals were victorious.   The latter fell back, however, fifteen miles, pursued by the Confederates; and the next day (April 9) another heavy battle was fought at Pleasant Hill, which resulted in a victory for Banks.   That officer now wished to renew the march for Texas; but his associates counselled a still further retreat to the Red River, at Grand Ecore, where Porter's larger vessels lay.   There they were joined by the troops under E. Kirby Smith, that went up the river in transports, and had some sharp fighting.

GENERAL STIRLING PRICE, C. S. A.

The river was still falling.   Food and water for man and beast, in that region, could not be procured excepting with great difficulty, and it was determined to continue the retreat to Alexandria.   After much difficulty the fleet passed the bar at Grand Ecore on the 17th of April.   The army moved from that point on the 21st, and entered Alexandria on the 27th, after an encounter with the Confederates at the passage of the Cane River.   So many difficulties lay before the National army, that the expedition against Shreveport was abandoned, and the land and naval forces prepared to return to the Mississippi River.

A serious impediment to such a movement now presented itself.   The water in the rapids of the Red River at Alexandria was so shallow that the fleet could not repass them.   General Hunter had just appeared at Alexandria with orders to close the Red River campaign as speedily as possible, for the troops from General Sherman were wanted eastward of the Mississippi.   The call was urgent.   To get the fleet below the rapids was now the first work to be done.   It was proposed to dam the river above the rapids, and send the vessels over the rocks upon the bosom of a flood that might be set free through sluices.   Porter did not believe in the feasibility of such a project.   Banks did, and set Lieutenant-Colonel Joseph Bailey, of a Michigan regiment, to attempt it.   By skill and industry the work was accomplished; and every gunboat, great and small, reached the deep water below the rapids in safety, the crowd of spectators on the shores greeting the achievement with loud huzzas.   The whole expedition now pushed toward the Mississippi River, where Porter resumed the service of patrolling that stream.   General E. R. S. Canby took command of Banks's forces on the Atchafalaya; and General Smith, with his detachment, returned to Mississippi.   A strong confronting force of Confederates had kept Steele from co-operating with the

GROUP OF CONFEDERATE GENERALS

expedition.   He had moved from Little Rock with eight thousand men, pushed back the Confederates, and on the 15th of April captured the important post of Camden on the Wachita River; but after a severe battle at Jenkinson's Ferry, on the Sabine River, Steele abandoned Camden and returned to Little Rock.   So ended this disastrous campaign.

We have observed that colored troops were employed as soldiers in the National service, and that the Confederates were disposed to treat them and their white leaders with cruelty.   Let us take a hasty glance at the history of their employment in the army.

When the President called for troops, in April, 1861, to put down the rising insurrection, some colored men in the city of New York hired a room and began to drill in military tactics.   The

VIEWS ON LOOKOUT MOUNTAIN

sympathizers with the insurgents threatened them with violence; and the Superintendent of Police felt compelled, in order to secure the public peace, to order them to cease drilling.   So they waited until they were called for.

More than a year afterward, General Hunter, in command of the Department of the South, ordered the organization of negro regiments in his department.   This measure raised a tempest of indignation in the National Congress among the sympathizers with the insurgents.   On motion of Wickliffe of Kentucky, the Secretary of War was asked whether Hunter had organized a regiment of fugitive slaves, and whether the Government had authorized the act.   Hunter was allowed to make explicit answers himself.   To the first question he replied: "No regiment of 'fugitive slaves' has been or is being organized in this department.   There is, however, a fine regiment of persons whose late masters are fugitive rebels—men who everywhere fly before the appearance of the National flag, leaving their servants behind them to shift for themselves as best they can."   A few weeks later, Secretary Stanton, by special order, directed General Rufus Saxton, military governor of the sea-coast islands, to "arm, uniform, equip and receive into the service of the United States, such number of volunteers of African descent, not exceeding five thousand," as would be useful.

General G. W. Phelps, in command above New Orleans, in the summer of 1862, finding crowds of colored people flocking to his camp, asked permission of General Butler to arm and equip negro regiments.   Butler had no authority to do so.   He recommended Phelps to employ them in servile work on fortifications.   Phelps replied: "I am not willing to become the slave-driver you propose, having no qualifications that way," and throwing up his commission, returned to Vermont.   Soon afterward Butler called for negro volunteers from the free colored men in New Orleans, and regiments were formed.

GENERAL BRAXTON BRAGG, C. S. A.

Another year passed by, and yet very few of the thousands of colored men made free by the proclamation of emancipation were found in arms.   There was a universal prejudice against them; but as the war went on that prejudice, like others, gave way, and in the summer of 1863 the President was authorized by Congress to accept colored volunteers.   From that time such troops were freely enlisted wherever the Government authority prevailed; and nearly two hundred thousand of them fought in the ranks for the preservation of the Republic, and their own freedom.   Their brethren, who were yet in bondage, were then freely used by the Confederates, in the military service; not, however, with arms in their hands. The Confederates never armed them.   It might have been a fatal experiment.   They were organized under white leaders, and were "armed and equipped" with axes, shovels, spades, pick-axes, and blankets.

The natural docility of the negro made him an excellent man to discipline for a soldier; and his faithfulness and courage were never surpassed, in strength and endurance, by the white man's faithfulness and courage.   Their conduct throughout the war was most remarkable.   Their numbers, in some of the revolted States, were nearly equal to those of the white people; and in the absence of the men of the latter race, in the army, the whole region which they occupied was absolutely at their mercy.   There were, at first, apprehensions that the negroes, perceiving their opportunity and advantage, would rise in insurrection and assert their right to freedom.   On the contrary, they worked faithfully and patiently for their masters, on the plantations, and there is no record of an attempt, by individuals or in numbers, of that vast servile population, to gain their liberty.   Not a woman or child was injured by their slaves; on the contrary, they were the trusted protectors from violence, of the wives and children of the Confederate soldiers.   They had faith that God would, in his own good time, deliver them from bondage; and in that faith they patiently waited and suffered.   Because of their faithfulness and forbearance, when they might have filled the land with horror, the colored population of the South deserve the everlasting gratitude and good-will of the white people there, whose families they protected and by their labor supplied with food and clothing during the terrible Civil War.   History furnishes no parallel to the noble conduct of the negroes toward those who were making war for the purpose of perpetuating the slavery of their race.

MAJ. GEN. D. M. M. GREGG.   MAJ. GEN. J. BUFFORD.

PULPIT ROCK WHERE JEFF. DAVIS ADDRESSED THE ARMY

VIEW FROM NEAR THE ROLLING MILL

PULPIT ROCK WHERE JEFF. DAVIS ADDRESSED THE ARMY

NORTH SLOPE

Pulpit Rock and Views of Lookout Mountain

The Gorge—Lookout Mountain

CHAPTER XXIII.

Another Invasion of Missouri and Its Results—Morgan in East Tennessee—Morgan Killed at Greenville—Cavalry Operations against Richmond—Campaign of the Army of the Potomac Begun—Battles in the Wilderness and near Spottsylvania Court-House—Sheridan's Raid—Operations between Petersburg and Richmond—Kautz's Raid—Struggles of Grant and Lee—Battle at Cold Harbor—The Nationals Cross the James and Invest Petersburg—Confederate Invasion of Maryland—Salvation of Washington—A Plundering Raid to Chambersburg—Sheridan in the Shenandoah Valley—His Brilliant Campaign—Richmond Threatened—Siege of Petersburg—Capture of Fort Harrison—Medal to Colored Troops—Losses—Sherman's Campaign in Georgia.

THE Confederates were emboldened by the failure of the Red River expedition and the expulsion of Steele from the region below the Arkansas River; and raiding bands awed the Unionists into silence and inactivity. This state of things gave Price an opportunity early in the autumn to invade Missouri again, this time chiefly with a political object in view. Secret societies, in sympathy with the Knights of the Golden Circle, had been formed in Missouri and neighboring Southern States, whose object was to give aid to the Confederate cause and assist in the election of General McClellan (who had been nominated by the Democratic party) to the office of President of the United States. Price

GENERAL U. S. GRANT

had been promised twenty thousand recruits, if he should enter Missouri with a respectable military force. He and General Shelby went over the Missouri border late in September (1864), with twenty thousand followers, and pushed on to Pilot Knob, half-way to St. Louis. But the promised recruits did not appear. The vigilant Rosecrans, in command of the Department of the Missouri, had discovered the plans of the disloyalists, and by some arrests had so frightened them that they prudently remained in concealment. Price was sorely disappointed; and he soon perceived that a web of great peril was gathering around him. At Pilot Knob, General Ewing, with a brigade of National troops, struck him an astounding blow. Soon afterward, these, with other troops under Generals A. J. Smith and Mower, sent Price flying westward toward Kansas, closely pursued. The exciting chase was enlivened by severe skirmishes; and late in November, Price was a fugitive in western Arkansas, with a broken and dispirited army. This was the last invasion of Missouri.

When Longstreet retired from Knoxville, he lingered awhile between there and the Virginia border; but he finally went to the aid of Lee's menaced army. Morgan, the guerrilla chief, remained in East Tennessee until the close of the following May (1864), when he went over the mountains and raided through the richest portions of Kentucky. General Burbridge went after him, and soon drove him and his shattered columns back into East Tennessee. He was surprised at Greenville, where he was shot dead in a vineyard while attempting to escape. Soon afterward the region between Knoxville and the Virginia line became the theatre of some stirring minor events while General Breckenridge was in command of the Confederates there.

Let us now resume the consideration of the military movements against Richmond and Atlanta.

The campaign of the *Army of the Potomac* under General Meade, against the Army of Northern Virginia led by General Lee, in the spring of 1864, was preceded by some movements for the capture of Richmond and the liberation of Union soldiers confined in Libby Prison, and on Belle Isle in the James River at that city. Treachery defeated the purpose for which, in February, General B. F. Butler, in command of the Department of Virginia and North Carolina, sent fifteen hundred troops, foot and horse, under General Wistar, against Richmond. General Kilpatrick, with five thousand of his cavalry, came from the *Army of the Potomac* to co-operate with him. They swept within the outer lines of the defences of Richmond, on the first of March; and Colonel Dahlgren, son of the admiral of that name, with another portion of that cavalry, was repulsed the next day, and was killed. A few days later, General Custer, with his horsemen, threatened Lee's communications in the direction of the Shenandoah Valley. The movements of Wistar were made fruitless, owing to a deserter, who gave the Confederates warning of it, and they were prepared to meet it.

The grand movement of the *Army of the Potomac* began in May. When it crossed the Rapidan and tried to go swiftly by Lee's flank under cover of the dense woods of the Wilderness, and plant itself

CREST OF MISSIONARY RIDGE

PANORAMIC VIEWS OF MISSIONARY RIDGE

CONFEDERATE ARTILLERY CAPTURED AT MISSIONARY RIDGE.

PANORAMIC VIEWS OF MISSIONARY RIDGE

VIEWS OF MISSIONARY RIDGE

between the Confederate army and Richmond, the vigilant Lee discovered the movement and boldly attacked the Nationals. The two armies numbered, in the aggregate, about two hundred thousand men; and that mighty host fought desperately for almost two days (May 5th and 6th) on one of the most

MAJOR-GENERAL JOSEPH HOOKER

remarkable battlefields ever known. The ground was covered with a thick growth of pines, cedars, and scrub-oaks, with tangled underbrush and vines, wherein regular military movements were impossible. Cavalry could not contend; and no single vision could discern a thousand men at one time. In that mysterious land the brave General Wadsworth of the Genesee Valley was killed, and the slaughter of troops was fearful. Both armies were badly shattered; and there was no victory for either. The Confederates withdrew to their intrenchments; and the Nationals, led by General Warren, hastened to the open country near Spottsylvania Court-House.

Lieutenant-General Grant was the guiding-spirit in the National army. He was determined to flank Lee; but when his troops emerged from the Wilderness, he found the Confederates in heavy force and rapidly gathering athwart his path. Arrangements were immediately made for another battle, during which the gallant General Sedgwick, leader of the Sixth Corps, was killed by a Confederate sharp-shooter. Both armies were cautious in their movements; and finally, on the morning of the 10th (May, 1864), when all was in readiness, a furious conflict began and raged all day with dreadful losses on each side. On the following morning, General Grant sent to the President the famous despatch, in which he said: *"I propose to fight it out on this line, if it takes all summer."*

On the 12th, another sanguinary battle was opened. General Hancock, after the most gallant struggle, broke through the Confederate line and gained a great advantage; but the fierce conflict continued until twilight, and did not entirely cease until midnight, when Lee suddenly withdrew behind a second line of entrenchments, and appeared as strong as ever. Yet Grant, stubborn and bold, was not disheartened. He sent cheering despatches to the government; and pressing forward, fought another desperate battle on the Ny, not far from Spottsylvania Court-House. Lee was repulsed. Grant's flanking movement was temporarily checked, but he speedily resumed it. The losses on both sides, during about a fortnight, had been fearful. That of the *Army of the Potomac* was about forty thousand men, killed, wounded, and prisoners; and that of the *Army of Northern Virginia* was about thirty thousand.

In the meantime, General Sheridan had been raiding in Lee's rear with a greater part of the National cavalry. Like Kilpatrick, he swept down into the Confederate outworks at Richmond, but with more successful results, for he destroyed the railway communication between Lee's army and that city. At the same time there was a co-operating force in the Shenandoah Valley, first under General Sigel and then under General Hunter; but they did not accomplish much of importance besides destroying a vast amount of property. There was another co-operating force below Richmond, commanded by General Butler. He had been joined by Gillmore's troops, which had been ordered up from Charleston; and with about twenty-five thousand men he went up the James River in armed transports, seized City Point at the mouth of the Appomattox River, and took possession of the Peninsula of Bermuda Hundred. He cast up a line of intrenchments across it from the Appomattox to the James and destroyed the railway between Petersburg and Richmond, so cutting off direct communication between the Confederate capital and the South. At the same time General A. V. Kautz went up from Suffolk with three thousand cavalry, to destroy the railways south and west from Petersburg; but before he struck them, Beauregard, who had been called from Charleston, had filled that city with defenders. The withdrawal of Gillmore's troops relieved Charleston of immediate danger; and when Butler went up the James, Beauregard was summoned to Richmond. At Petersburg he received hourly reinforcements, and some of them he massed in front of Butler's forces, along the line of the railway. Finally, on the morning of the 16th of May, while a dense fog brooded over the

AN ARMY NEWS BOY

RINGOLD'S BATTERY

VIEW OF RINGOLD, GEORGIA

country, he attempted to turn Butler's right flank. A sharp conflict ensued, in which the Nationals had about four thousand men engaged, and the Confederates about three thousand. It ended by the retirement of Butler's forces within their intrenchments. For several days afterward there was considerable skirmishing in front of Butler's lines, when he received orders to send nearly two-thirds of his effective men to the north side of the James River to assist the army contending with Lee in the vicinity of the Chickahominy. Butler complied with the requisition, which deprived him of all power to make further offensive movements. "The necessities of the Army of the Potomac," he said, "have bottled me up at Bermuda Hundred."

GENERAL N. B. FORREST, C. S. A.

While General Butler's main army was making movements toward Richmond, Kautz was out upon another raid on the railways leading to that city from the south and southwest. He left Bermuda Hundred on the 12th of May, with two mounted brigades; passed near Fort Darling, on Drewry's Bluff, and sweeping on an arc of a circle by Chesterfield Court-House, struck the Richmond and Danville Railway eleven miles west of the Confederate capital. After again striking it at other points, he swept around eastward, divided his forces, and with a part of them crossed to the Southside Railway, while another portion proceeded to the junction of the Danville and Southside roads. Then he went eastward with his whole force, striking and destroying the Weldon Railway far toward the North Carolina line, and then made his way back to City Point. In this raid Kautz had seriously damaged the railroads that lay in his track, and took to City Point one hundred and fifty prisoners.

After the struggles near Spottsylvania Court-House, Grant moved steadily on toward Richmond, while Lee moved on a parallel line to thwart his antagonist's plans. At the passage of the North Anna, they fought a severe battle on the 23d of May. There, in close communication with the Central Virginia Railway, Lee had evidently determined to make a stand. Over that railway, Breckenridge, who had beaten Sigel in the Shenandoah Valley, was hastening to reinforce Lee, and Grant resolved to dislodge his antagonist before aid should reach him. This was accomplished, when Lee withdrew to a stronger position where Grant did not attack him. The *Army of the Potomac* pressed steadily forward, with Sheridan's cavalry in advance, and on the 28th of May, the entire force of the Nationals were south of the Pamunkey River, with an uninterrupted communication with their new base of supplies at the ruins of the "White House" near the mouth of that stream. Lee had moved by a shorter road, and occupied a strong position on the Chickahominy River, which commanded a turnpike and two railways that led to Richmond.

Across the Chickahominy River was the only direct pathway to the Confederate capital, and to pursue it, Lee must be dislodged. The cavalry of both armies had sharp engagements at the close of May, while reconnaissances were going on; when Grant, believing he could not successfully assail his antagonist in his strong position, began another flanking movement with the intention of crossing the Chickahominy near Cold Harbor where Sheridan had gained an advantageous foothold. There the army was reinforced by ten thousand men sent from Bermuda Hundred, led by General W. F. Smith; and there, from the 1st to the 3d of June (1864), there was a fearful struggle on the old battle-ground of Lee and McClellan two years before. On the 3d, one of the most sanguinary battles of the war was fought. It was brief, but terrible. Within the space of twenty minutes after the first shot was fired, ten thousand Union soldiers were killed or wounded. The battle ended at one o'clock in the afternoon, the Nationals holding their ground. They moved gradually to the left, and on the 7th of June that wing touched the Chickahominy River. Then Sheridan was sent to destroy the railways on Lee's left, which he did as far as Gordonsville.

General Grant now determined to transfer his army to the south side of the James River, cut off the chief sources of supply of men and provisions for Lee's army from the South, and attempt the capture of Richmond from that direction. At near the middle of June the whole army crossed the Chickahominy at Long Bridge, and moved to the James by

GENERAL BISHOP POPE, C. S. A.

way of Charles City Court-House. They crossed that river in boats and

FORT SANDERS, KNOXVILLE, TENN.

on pontoon bridges; and on the 16th of June, when the entire army was over, General Grant made his headquarters at City Point. A portion of the *Army of the James*, under General Butler, had made an unsuccessful attempt to capture Petersburg before Lee should send down troops to reinforce Beauregard, who had cast up strong lines of intrenchments around that city. These works were confronted by the *Army of the Potomac* on the evening of the 16th of June; and from that time until the 30th of July, there was much severe fighting, with great loss of life, in unsuccessful attempts of the Union troops to take the place by storm and destroy railway communications with it.

ADMIRAL J. A. DAHLGREN

There was a brief lull in the operations against Petersburg and Richmond, at about the beginning of July. During that time, General Early, with about fifteen thousand Confederate troops, swept down the Shenandoah Valley and across the Potomac at Williamsport, driving General Sigel before him, and penetrating Maryland to Hagerstown and Frederick. This formidable raid was designed to draw a large body of troops from Grant to the defence of the National capital; also for plunder. When Grant heard of it, he sent General Wright, with the Sixth corps, to protect Washington. General Lewis Wallace, then in command of the Middle Department, with his headquarters at Baltimore, proceeded from that city, with a few troops hastily collected, to confront the invaders, and on the 9th of July he met and fought Early's host on the Monocacy River not far from Frederick. Wallace had been joined by a portion of Rickett's brigade from the advance of the Sixth corps. This handful of warriors, after fighting overwhelming numbers eight hours, were defeated, with heavy loss, when Early pushed on toward Washington. But the vanquished troops had really won a victory for their country, for they detained the invaders long enough to allow the Sixth and Nineteenth corps to reach and secure the National Capital. When General Early perceived this, he pushed across the Potomac with a large amount of plunder, closely pursued by General Wright to the Shenandoah Valley, through Snicker's Gap, where, after a sharp conflict on the 19th (July), the invaders retreated up the Valley and the pursuers returned to Washington.

It was soon discovered that Early had not gone to join Lee, as was suspected, but remained in the Valley with all his force. Some of his troops were worsted in a fight with Nationals under General Averill, near Winchester, on the 20th; and they soon afterward pushed General Crook, in command of the *Army of Western Virginia*, back toward the Potomac, with considerable loss. Then Early sent General McCausland, Bradley Johnson and other officers, with three thousand followers, all mounted, on a plundering tour in Maryland and Pennsylvania. They swept, in eccentric lines, over the country, thereby distracting the armed defenders of it; and on the 30th of July entered the defenceless and almost deserted village of Chambersburg, in Pennsylvania, where they demanded a tribute of $200,000 in gold, or $500,000 in paper currency, to insure the town from destruction. It was impossible to give the tribute, and two-thirds of the village was laid in ashes. No time was given for the removal of the infirm, the sick, or the women and children. The incendiaries did not remain long enough to see the ruin they had initiated; for General Averill, who was ten miles distant, moved against them, and chased them back into Virginia. This raid

ADMIRAL DAHLGREN AND STAFF

caused the Sixth and Nineteenth corps, commanded respectively by Generals Wright and Emory, to be sent into the Shenandoah Valley, where the National forces, now thirty thousand strong, were placed under the chief command of General Sheridan, early in August.

At the middle of September, General Grant visited Sheridan, at Charlestown. He found him ready for action against Early. Satisfied that his plan of operations was feasible, the lieutenant-general said to the energetic leader, "Go in." In these two words the chief expressed his confidence in Sheridan's judgment and skill. He did "go in;" and very soon he sent Early "whirling up the Valley," as he expressed it. He fought and conquered him at Winchester on the 19th of September (1864), when the Confederates fell back to the strong position of Fisher's Hill, near Strasburg. Sheridan

DECK AND CREW OF MONITOR

DECK OF GUNBOAT AGAWAM AND OFFICERS

drove them from there on the 22d, at the end of a sharp battle, in which Early lost heavily, and was chased to Port Republic, near which the pursuers burned his wagon-trains. The National cavalry followed him to Staunton, where the Confederates took refuge in the ranges of the Blue Ridge. Sheridan's forces fell

THE "SWAMP ANGEL" AT MORRIS ISLAND

back to a strong position behind Cedar Creek, and that leader departed for Washington city with the belief that the Valley was purged of Confederates in arms. It was a mistake. A month later, Early, reinforced, fell with crushing weight upon the Nationals at Cedar Creek, commanded by General Wright, and, for a time, their destruction seemed inevitable. They fell back to Middletown and beyond, where they turned upon the pursuers, and a desperate battle ensued.

When the battle commenced, Sheridan was in Winchester on his way to the army. The sound of conflict fell upon his ear, and, mounting his powerful black horse, he pushed on toward Cedar Creek. Presently he met the van of fugitives hurrying from the lost battle-field, at that stream, who told him a piteous tale of disaster. Sheridan ordered the retreating artillery to be parked on each side of the turnpike, and telling his escort to follow, he dashed forward, his horse on a swinging gallop, and at that pace he rode nearly twelve miles to the scene of conflict. The fugitives became thicker and thicker every moment. But Sheridan did not stop to chide nor coax; but as his powerful black steed thundered over that magnificent stone road which traverses the Shenandoah Valley, he waved his hat and shouted to the tumultuous crowds: "Face the other way, boys; face the other way! We are going back to our camp to lick them out of their boots!" The man and the act were marvellously magnetic in their effects. The tide of disordered troops was instantly turned, and flowed swiftly in the wake of their young commander. As he dashed into the lines, and rode along the front of forming regiments, he gave to each most stirring words of cheer and encouragement, and declared in substance, "We'll have all those camps and cannon back again." The men believed him, and showing their faith by their works, secured a speedy fulfilment of the prophecy. General Wright had already brought order out of confusion. A very severe struggle ensued, and very soon Early was again sent "whirling" up the Valley. The National cavalry of Emory's corps, falling upon both flanks, caused the Confederates to flee in hot haste up the Valley pike, in great disorder, to Fisher's Hill, leaving the highway strewn with abandoned hindrances to flight. The road was clogged with masses of men, wagons, cannon and caissons, in utter confusion, and these were left behind. This short but brilliant campaign of Sheridan, which nearly annihilated Early's force, ended hostilities in the Shenandoah Valley.

Let us now turn again toward Petersburg and Richmond, for a moment.

General Butler had thrown a pontoon-bridge across the James River at Deep Bottom, within ten miles of Richmond, over which troops passed to the north side of that stream and menaced the Confederate capital. Lee was alarmed by the movement and withdrew a large force from Petersburg to defend Richmond, believing the latter city would be immediately attacked; and there it was that General Grant made the unsuccessful attempts just mentioned, to penetrate the Confederate lines before Petersburg. He had mined under one of the principal forts, and it was blown up on the morning of the 30th of July, with terrible effect. In the place of the fortification was left a crater of loose earth two hundred feet in length, full fifty feet in width, and from twenty-five to thirty feet in depth. The fort, its guns and other munitions of war, with three hundred men, had been thrown high in air, and annihilated. Then the great guns of the Nationals

THE "SWAMP ANGEL" AFTER BURSTING ON 36TH SHOT

SCENES AT MORRIS ISLAND

opened a heavy cannonade upon the remainder of the works, with precision and fearful effect, all along the lines; but owing partly to the slowness of motion of a portion of the assaulting force, the result was a most disastrous failure on the part of the assailants.

A fortnight later Grant sent another expedition to the north side of the James, at Deep Bottom,

EXTERIOR OF FORT SUMTER WHILE IN POSSESSION OF CONFEDERATE FORCES

composed of the divisions of Birney and Hancock, with cavalry led by General Gregg. They had sharp engagements with the Confederates on the 13th, 16th and 18th of August, in which the Nationals lost about five thousand men without gaining any special advantage excepting the incidental one of giving assistance to troops sent to seize the Weldon railway, south of Petersburg. This General Warren effected on the 18th of August. Three days afterward he repulsed a Confederate force who attempted to repossess the portion of the road held by the Unionists; and on the same day General Hancock, who had returned from the north side of the James, struck the Weldon road at Reams's Station, and destroyed the track for some distance. The Nationals were finally driven from the road with considerable loss.

For little more than a month after this, there was comparative quiet in the vicinity of Petersburg and Richmond. The National troops were moved simultaneously toward each city. General Butler, with the Tenth Army Corps under General Birney, and the Eighteenth corps under General Ord, moved upon Fort Harrison, on the north side of the James, and captured it on the 29th of September. These troops charged upon another fort near by, and were repulsed with heavy loss. Among the slain was General Burnham. General Ord was severely wounded. The captured Fort Harrison was named Fort Burnham in honor of the slain general. In these assaults the gallantry of the colored troops was so conspicuous, that General Butler presented to each of the more meritorious ones a silver medal, which bore a device commemorative of their valor.

In the meantime, General Meade had sent General Warren with two divisions of his corps, General Parke with two divisions of the Ninth corps, and General Gregg with his cavalry, to attempt the extension of the National left on the Weldon road. The chief object of the movement was to mask the more important operations of Butler at that time. But it resulted in severe fighting on the first and second days of October (1864), with varying fortunes for both parties.

Now there was another pause but not a settled rest for about a month, when the greater portion of the *Army of the Potomac* was massed on the Confederate right, south of the James; and on the 27th of October, they assailed Lee's works on Hatcher's Run, westward of the Weldon road. A severe struggle ensued. The Nationals were repulsed, and on the 29th they withdrew to their intrenchments in front of Petersburg. Very little of importance was done by the *Army of the Potomac* after that, until the opening of the campaign in the spring of 1865, excepting the extension of their line to Hatcher's Run. The losses of that army had been fearful during six months, from the beginning of May until November, 1864. The aggregate number in killed, wounded, missing and prisoners, was over *eighty-eight thousand* men, of whom nearly *ten thousand* were killed in battle. Add to these the losses in the *Army of the James* during the same time, and the sum would be full *one hundred thousand men*.

The command of the troops engaged in the campaign against Atlanta was, as we have observed, entrusted to General Wm. T. Sherman, who had succeeded General Grant in command of the Military Division of the Mississippi. With a force composed of the *Army of the Cumberland* led by General George H. Thomas, the *Army of the Tennessee* led by General J. B. McPherson, and the *Army of the Ohio* commanded by General J. M. Schofield, Sherman moved southward from the vicinity of Chattanooga on the 6th of May, 1864.

MAJ. GEN. G. C. STRONG.

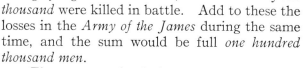

MAJ GEN GORDON GRANGER

MAJ GEN A. H. TERRY

INTERIOR VIEW.

SOUTH PARAPET.

GUARD MOUNTING.

INTERIOR VIEW.

INTERIOR VIEW. WITH QUARTERS OF FEDERAL GARRISON.

INTERIOR VIEW, WITH QUARTERS OF FEDERAL GARRISON.

INTERIOR VIEW, WITH QUARTERS OF FEDERAL GARRISON.

INTERIOR VIEW, WITH QUARTERS OF FEDERAL GARRISON.

VIEWS AT FORT WAGNER

CHRONOLOGICAL SUMMARY AND RECORD—Continued

JUNE, 1864—*Continued from Section* 11

2—Bermuda Hundred, Va. Tenth Corps. *Union* 25 killed, 100 wounded. *Confed.* 100 killed and wounded.

3 to 6—Panther Gap and Buffalo Gap, W. Va. Hayes's Brigade of 2d Division Army of West Virginia. *Union* 25 killed and wounded. *Confed.* 25 killed and wounded.

5—Piedmont, W. Va. Portion of Army of West Virginia, commanded by Maj.-Gen. Hunter. *Union* 130 killed, 650 wounded. *Confed.* 460 killed, 1,450 wounded, 1,060 missing. *Confed.* Gen. W. E. Jones killed.

6—Lake Chicot, Ark. Sixteenth Corps. *Union* 40 killed, 70 wounded. *Confed.* 100 killed and wounded.

9—Point of Rocks, Md. 2d U. S. Colored Cav. *Union* 2 killed.

Mt. Sterling, Ky. Burbridge's Cavalry. *Union* 35 killed, 150 wounded. *Confed.* 50 killed, 200 wounded, 250 captured.

9 to 30—Kenesaw Mountain, Marietta or Big Shanty, Ga., including general assault on the 27th, Pine Mt., Golgotha, Culp's House and Powder Springs. Fourth, Fourteenth and Twentieth Corps, Army of the Cumberland, Maj.-Gen. Thomas; Fifteenth, Sixteenth and Seventeenth Corps, Army of the Tennessee, Maj.-Gen. McPherson; Twenty-third Corps, Maj.-Gen. Schofield; Army of the Mississippi, Maj.-Gen. W. T. Sherman. *Union* 1,370 killed, 6,500 wounded, 800 missing. *Confed.* 1,100 killed and wounded, 3,500 missing. *Union* Brig.-Gens. Harker and McCook killed. *Confed.* Lieut.-Gen. Leonidas Polk killed.

10—Petersburg, Va. Portion of Tenth Corps and Kautz's Cav. *Union* 20 killed, 67 wounded.

Brice's Cross Roads, near Guntown, Miss. 81st, 95th, 108th, 113th, 114th and 120th Ill., 72d and 95th Ohio, 9th Minn., 93d Ind., 55th and 59th U. S. Colored, Brig.-Gen. Grierson's Cavalry, the 4th Mo., 2d N. J., 19th Pa., 7th and 9th Ill., 7th Ind., 3d and 4th Iowa, and 10th Kan. Cav., 1st Ill. and 6th Ind. Batteries, Battery F 2d U. S. Colored Artil. *Union* 223 killed, 394 wounded, 1,623 missing. *Confed.* 131 killed, 475 wounded.

Cynthiana and Kellar's Bridge, Ky. 168th and 171st Ohio. *Union* 21 killed, 71 wounded, 980 captured by Morgan's Raiders.

10 and 11—Lexington, W. Va. 2d Division Army of West Virginia. *Union* 6 killed, 18 wounded.

11—Cynthiana, Ky. Burbridge's Cav. Attack on Morgan's Raiders. *Union* 150 killed and wounded. *Confed.* 300 killed and wounded, 400 captured.

11 and 12—Trevilian Station, Va. Sheridan's Cavalry. *Union* 85 killed, 490 wounded, 160 missing. *Confed.* 370 missing.

13—White Oak Swamp Bridge, Va. Wilson's and Crawford's Cav. *Union* 50 killed, 250 wounded.

14—Lexington, Mo. Detachment 1st Mo. Cav. *Union* 8 killed, 1 wounded.

15—Samaria Church, Malvern Hill, Va. Wilson's Cav. *Union* 25 killed, 3 wounded. *Confed.* 100 killed and wounded.

15 to 19—Petersburg, Va. (Commencement of the siege that continued to its fall, April 2, 1865). Tenth and Eighteenth Corps, Army of the James, Maj.-Gen. B. F. Butler; Second, Fifth, Sixth and Ninth Corps, Army of the Potomac, Maj.-Gen. Geo. G. Meade. *Union* 1,298 killed, 7,474 wounded, 1,814 missing.

16—Otter Creek, near Liberty, Va. Hunter's Command in advance of the Army of West Virginia. *Union* 3 killed, 15 wounded.

17 and 18—Lynchburg, Va. Sullivan's and Crook's Divisions and Averill's and Duffie's Cav., Army of the West Virginia. *Union* 100 killed, 500 wounded, 100 missing. *Confed.* 200 killed and wounded.

19—Capture of the *Alabama*, off Cherbourg, France, by U. S. Steamer *Kearsarge*. *Union* 3 wounded. *Confed.* 9 killed, 21 wounded, 70 captured.

20 to 30—In front of Petersburg, Va. Fifth, Ninth, Tenth and Eighteenth Corps. *Union* 112 killed, 506 wounded, 800 missing. *Union* Gens. Chamberlain and Eagan wounded.

21—Salem, Va. Averill's Cav. *Union* 6 killed, 10 wounded. *Confed.* 10 killed and wounded.

Naval engagement on the James River, near Dutch Gap. Casualties not recorded.

Buford's Gap, Va. 23d Ohio. *Union* 15 killed.

22—White River, Ark. Three Cos. 12th Iowa, and U. S. Gunboat *Lexington*. *Union* 2 killed, 4 wounded. *Confed.* 2 killed, 3 wounded.

22 and 23—Weldon Railroad, Williams' Farm or Jerusalem Plank Road, Va. Second, Sixth and 1st Division of Fifth Corps, Army of the Potomac. *Union* 604 killed, 2,494 wounded, 2,217 missing. *Confed.* 300 wounded, 200 missing.

22 to 30—Wilson's Raid on the Weldon Railroad, Va. Kautz's and Wilson's Cav. *Union* 92 killed, 317 wounded, 734 missing. *Confed.* 365 killed and wounded.

23 and 24—Jones's Bridge and Samaria Church, Va. Torbett's and Gregg's Cavalry Divisions. *Union* 54 killed, 235 wounded, 300 missing. *Confed.* 250 killed and wounded.

25 to 29—Clarendon, St. Charles River, Ark. 126th Ill. and 11th Mo., 9th Iowa and 3d Mich. Cav., Battery D 2d Mo. Artil. *Union* 200 wounded. *Confed.* 200 wounded, 200 missing.

JULY, 1864

1 to 31—In front of Petersburg, including Deep Bottom, New Market, and Malvern Hill, on the 27th, and mine explosion on the 30th. Second, Fifth, Ninth, Tenth and Eighteenth Corps. *Union* 898 killed, 4,060 wounded, 3,110 missing. *Confed.* loss at Deep Bottom, 400 killed, 600 wounded, 200 missing.

2—Pine Bluff, Ark. 64th U. S. Col. *Union* 6 killed.

Fort Johnson, James Island, S. C. Troops of Department of the South. *Union* 19 killed, 97 wounded, 135 missing.

2 to 5—Nickajack Creek or Smyrna, Ga. Troops under command of Maj.-Gen. Sherman. *Union* 60 killed, 310 wounded. *Confed.* 100 killed and wounded.

3—Leetown, Va. 10th W. Va., 1st N. Y. Cav. *Union* 3 killed, 12 wounded.

Hammack's Mills, W. Va. 153d Ohio Natl. Guard. *Union* 3 killed, 7 wounded.

3 to 9—Expedition from Vicksburg to Jackson, Miss. 1st Division Seventeenth Corps. *Union* 150 wounded. *Confed.* 200 wounded.

4—Vicksburg, Miss. 48th U. S. Colored. *Union* 1 killed, 7 wounded.

4 to 5—Coleman's Plantation, near Port Gibson, Miss. 52d U. S. Colored. *Union* 6 killed, 18 wounded.

4 to 7—Bolivar and Maryland Heights. Maj.-Gen. Sigel's Reserve Division. *Union* 20 killed, 80 wounded.

5—Hagerstown, Md. 1st Md. Cavalry, Potomac Home Brigade. *Union* 2 killed, 6 wounded.

5 to 7—John's Island, S. C. Maj.-Gen. Foster's troops. *Union* 16 killed, 82 wounded. *Confed.* 20 killed, 80 wounded.

5 to 18—Smith's Expedition, La Grange, Tenn., to Tupelo, Miss. 1st and 3d Divisions Sixteenth Corps, one Brigade U. S. Colored Troops and Grierson's Cavalry. *Union* 85 killed, 567 wounded. *Confed.* 110 killed, 600 wounded.

6—Little Blue, Mo. 2d Col. Cav. *Union* 8 killed, 1 wounded.

6 to 10—Chattahoochee River, Ga. Army of the Ohio, Maj.-Gen. Schofield; Army of the Tennessee, Maj.-Gen. McPherson; Army of the Cumberland, Maj.-Gen. Thomas; Army of the Mississippi, Maj.-Gen. W. T. Sherman. *Union* 80 killed, 450 wounded, 200 missing.

7—Solomon's Gap and Middleton, Md. 8th Ill. Cav., Potomac Home Brigade and Alexander's Baltimore Battery. *Union* 5 killed, 20 wounded.

9—Monocacy, Md. 1st and 2d Brigades of 3d Division Sixth Corps, and Detachment of Eighth Corps. *Union* 90 killed, 579 wounded, 1,290 missing. *Confed.* 400 wounded.

11 to 22—Rosseau's Raid in Alabama and Georgia, including Ten Islands and Stone's Ferry, Ala., and Auburn and Chewa Station, Ga. 8th Ind., 5th Iowa, 8th Ohio, 2d Ky. and 4th Tenn. Cav., Battery E 1st Mich. Artil. *Union* 3 killed, 30 wounded. *Confed.* 95 killed and wounded.

12—Fort Stevens, Washington, D. C. Twenty-second Corps, 1st and 2d Divisions Sixth Corps, Marines, Home Guards, citizens and convalescents. *Union* 54 killed, 319 wounded. *Confed.* 500 killed and wounded.

Lee's Mills, near Ream's Station, Va. 2d Division Gregg's Cav. *Union* 3 killed, 13 wounded. *Confed.* 25 killed and wounded.

14—Farr's Mills, Ark. One Co. 4th Ark. Cav. *Union* 1 killed, 7 wounded. *Confed.* 4 killed, 6 wounded.

14 and 15—Ozark, Mo. 14th Kan. Cav. *Union* 2 killed, 1 wounded.

16 and 17—Grand Gulf, Port Gibson, Miss. 72d and 76th Ill., 53d U. S. Colored, 2d Wis. Cav. Casualties not recorded.

17 and 18—Snicker's Gap and Island Ford, Va. Army of West Virginia, Maj.-Gen. Crook and portion of Sixth Corps. *Union* 30 killed, 181 wounded, 100 missing.

18—Ashby's Gap, Va. Duffie's Cav. *Union* 200 killed and wounded.

19 and 20—Darksville, Stevenson's Depot and Winchester, Va. Averill's Cav. *Union* 38 killed, 175 wounded. *Confed.* 300 wounded, 300 captured.

20—Peach Tree Creek, Ga. Fourth, Fourteenth and Twentieth Corps, Maj.-Gen. Geo. H. Thomas. *Union* 300 killed, 1,410 wounded. *Confed.* 1,113 killed, 2,500 wounded, 1,183 missing. *Confed.* Brig.-Gens. Featherstone, Long, Pett's and Stevens killed.

22—Atlanta, Ga. (Hood's first sortie.) Fifteenth, Sixteenth and Seventeenth Corps, Maj.-Gen. McPherson. *Union* 500 killed, 2,141 wounded, 1,000 missing. *Confed.* 2,482 killed, 4,000 wounded, 2,017 missing. *Union* Maj.-Gen. McPherson and Brig.-Gen. Greathouse killed.

22—Decatur, Ga. 2d Brigade of the 4th Division of Sixteenth Corps. *Confed.* Maj.-Gen. Walker killed.

23 and 24—Kernstown and Winchester, Va. Portion of Army of West Virginia. *Union* 1,200 killed and wounded. *Confed.* 600 killed and wounded.

26—Wallace's Ferry, Ark. 15th Ill. Cav., 60th and 56th U. S. Colored Troops, Co. E 2d U. S. Colored Artil. *Union* 16 killed, 32 wounded. *Confed.* 150 wounded.

26 to 31—Stoneman's Raid to Macon, Ga. Stoneman's and Garrard's Cav. *Union* 100 killed and wounded, 900 missing.

26 to 31—McCook's Raid to Lovejoy Station, Ga. 1st Wis., 5th and 8th Iowa, 2d and 8th Ind., 1st and 4th Tenn., and 4th Ky. Cavalry. *Union* 100 killed and wounded, 500 missing.

27—Mazzard Prairie, Fort Smith, Ark. Two hundred men of 6th Kan. Cav. *Union* 12 killed, 17 wounded, 152 captured. *Confed.* 12 killed, 20 wounded.

28—Atlanta, Ga. (Second sortie at Ezra Chapel.) Fifteenth, Sixteenth and Seventeenth Corps, Maj.-Gen. Howard. *Union* 100 killed, 600 wounded. *Confed.* 642 killed, 3,000 wounded, 1,000 missing.

28 to Sept. 22—Siege of Atlanta, Ga. Army of the Military Division of the Mississippi, Maj.-Gen. W. T. Sherman. Casualties not recorded.

29—Clear Springs, Md. 12th and 14th Penna. Cav. *Confed.* 17 killed and wounded.

30—Lee's Mills, Va. Davis's Cav. *Union* 2 killed, 11 wounded.

Lebanon, Ky. One Co. 12th Ohio Cav. *Confed.* 6 killed.

AUGUST, 1864

1 to 31—In front of Petersburg, Va. Second, Fifth, Ninth and Eighteenth Corps. *Union* 87 killed, 484 wounded.

2—Green Springs, W. Va. 153d Ohio. *Union* 1 killed, 5 wounded, 90 missing. *Confed.* 5 killed, 22 wounded.

5—Donaldsonville, La. 11th N. Y. Cav. *Union* 60 missing.

5 to 23—Forts Gaines and Morgan, Mobile Harbor, Ala. Thirteenth Corps and Admiral Farragut's fleet of war vessels. *Union* 75 killed, 100 drowned by sinking of the *Tecumseh*, 170 wounded. *Confed.* 2,344 captured.

(*Continued in Section* 13)

Quarles Mill North Anna River.

Confederate Fortifications at Chesterfield Bridge.

Log Bridge across North Anna River at Quarles Mill.

Destroyed R.R. bridge across North Anna River.

Pontoon Bridges North Anna River.

SCENES OF GENERALS GRANT AND SHERIDAN'S CAMPAIGN, NORTH ANNA.

CHAPTER XXIII.—Continued.

THE aggregate number of Sherman's soldiers was about one hundred thousand men. These were confronted by about fifty-five thousand men, led by General Joseph E. Johnston, and arranged in three corps commanded respectively by Generals Hardee, Hood, and Polk. This army then lay at Dalton, at the parting of the ways, one leading into East Tennessee, and the other into West Tennessee. To strike

CHANCELLORSVILLE.

that position in front was impracticable, or, at least, perilous, for the Confederates were very strongly posted; and Sherman began there a series of successful flank movements. When he menaced the flanks of the Confederates at Dalton by seeking a passage through Snake Hill Gap, on the left, the insurgents fell back to a point near Resaca Station at the Oostenaula River, on the line of the railway between Chattanooga and Atlanta. At that place a sharp battle occurred on the 15th of May, when the Confederates were driven across the Oostenaula. Johnston fired the bridge that spanned that stream, cutting off direct pursuit immediately. Generals Thomas, Hooker, McPherson, Schofield, and other noted leaders were engaged in the fight; and as soon as a temporary bridge was constructed, the next morning, Thomas pursued Hardee (who covered the retreat) directly, while McPherson and Schofield kept on their flanks. The Confederates fled from post to post, burning bridges behind them, until they reached a mountainous region covering the Allatoona Pass. There Johnston halted, with the Etowah River between his troops and the National forces; and then both armies took a brief rest.

These flanking movements had resulted so favorably to the Nationals, that Sherman resolved to pursue them. He determined to flank Johnston out of his strong position at Allatoona Pass, by concentrating his forces at Dallas, westward of him. In attempting to thwart this movement, the Confederates brought on an engagement near Dallas, on the 25th of May. The battle was indecisive, and was followed by a very stormy night, during which Johnston's men used the pick-axe and spade so industriously that by morning Sherman found his antagonist strongly intrenched, with lines extending from Dallas to Marietta. Between these towns was a broken, wooded country, and in that region there was much severe fighting for several days. At length Johnston was compelled to evacuate Allatoona Pass (June 1, 1864), when it was garrisoned by Sherman and made his second base of supplies, the first being at Chattanooga. The burned bridges were rebuilt and well guarded, and full possession of the railway in his rear was obtained by Sherman. At Allatoona he was reinforced on the 8th by troops under General Frank Blair, which made his number of effective men nearly what it was when he moved from Chattanooga.

CHAPTER XXIV.

The Armies at Marietta—Death of Bishop Polk—Hood in Command—Battles around Atlanta—Thomas Sent to Nashville—Hood Chased into Alabama—Sherman's March to the Sea—Evacuation of Savannah—Events in Florida and North Carolina—Invasion of Tennessee—Hood's Defeats and Escape—Confederate Cruisers—Capture of the "Alabama"—Farragut near Mobile—Election of President—Sherman in the Carolinas—Evacuation of Charleston—Grierson's Raid—Capture of Fort Fisher—Battles at Averysboro' and Bentonville—Wilson's Raid—Capture of Mobile—Operations Below Petersburg—Sheridan's Raid—Lee's Attempt to Escape—Stoneman's Raid—Movements for Peace.

SOON after evacuating Allatoona Pass, General Johnston was compelled to abandon other posts before the approach of Sherman's strengthened army. The latter pressed vigorously forward toward the Kenesaw Mountains that overlook Marietta. Around these great hills and upon their slopes and summits, and also upon Lost and Pine Mountains, the Confederates had cast up intrenchments and planted

GENERAL E. KIRBY SMITH, C. S. A.

Major-General George G. Meade and Staff.

Generals Geo. A. Custer and Alfred Pleasonton.

signal stations; but after a desperate struggle—fighting battle after battle for the space of about a month, while rain was falling copiously almost without intermission—the Confederates were forced to leave all these strong positions. They fled toward the Chattahoochee River, in the direction of Atlanta, closely pursued by the Nationals. One of their corps commanders (Bishop Polk) had been instantly killed by a shell on the summit of Pine Mountain, and the insurgent armies had suffered fearful losses in that terrible struggle. So persistently did Johnston dispute the way from Dalton, in northern Georgia, to Atlanta, that when he reached the intrenchments at the latter place, he had lost nearly one-fourth of his army.

When, on the evening of July 2d, Sherman's cavalry threatened Johnston's flanks and menaced the ferry of the Chattahoochee, the Confederates abandoned the Great Kenesaw and fled; and at dawn the next morning, when National skirmishers planted the Stars and Stripes over the Confederate battery on the summit of that eminence, they saw the hosts of their enemies flying in hot haste toward Atlanta. At eight o'clock Sherman rode into Marietta, a conqueror, close upon the heels of Johnston's army. He hoped to strike the Confederates a fatal blow while they were crossing the Chattahoochee; but Johnston, by quick and skillful movements, passed that stream without mo-lestation, and made a stand along the line of it. General Howard laid a pontoon bridge two miles above the ferry

GENERAL CUSTER, WITH LIEUTENANT WASHINGTON,
A CONFEDERATE PRISONER.

where Johnston had crossed, and at the same time there was a general movement of Sherman's forces all along his line. The imperilled Confederates were compelled to abandon the works which they had thrown up near the Chattahoochee, and retreat to a new line that covered Atlanta, their left resting on the Chattahoochee and their right on Peach Tree Creek. Now, toward the middle of July, the two armies rested; and Johnston, an able and judicious leader, was succeeded by General J. B. Hood, of Texas, a dashing and less cautious officer than his predecessor. At that time (July 10), or sixty-five days after Sherman put his army in motion southward, he was master of the whole country north and west of the river on the banks of which he was resting (or nearly one-half of Georgia), and had accomplished one of the major objects of the campaign, namely, the advancement of the National lines from the Tennessee to the Chattahoochee.

The possession of Atlanta, the key-point of military advantage in the campaign in that region, was the next prize to be contended for. The Nationals advanced at a little past the middle of July, destroying railways and skirmishing bravely; and on the 20th the Confederates, led by Hood in person, fell upon

GENERAL GEO. A. CUSTER.

the corps of Howard, Hooker and Palmer, with heavy force. The assailants were repulsed after a sharp battle, in which both parties suffered severely.

There were now indications that Hood intended to evacuate Atlanta, when the Nationals moved rapidly toward the city, encountering strong intrenchments. Before these a part of Hood's army held their antag-
onists; while the main body, led by General Hardee, made a long night march, gained the rear of Sherman's forces on the morning of the 22d of July, and fell upon them with crushing weight of numbers that day. A terrific battle ensued, lasting many hours; and after a brief interval, one still more sanguinary was begun, which resulted in victory for the Nationals and the retreat of the Confederates to their works. During that day, General McPherson, who was at the head of the *Army of the Ten-
nessee*, while reconnoitering in a wood, was shot dead by a Confederate sharp-shooter (Major McPherson); and General Logan took his place in command. Yet another sanguinary battle was fought on the 28th of July, before Atlanta, when the Confederates were again driven to their lines, with heavy losses; and from that time until the close of August, hostilities in that region were confined, chiefly, to raids upon railways

Drewry's Bluff and Other Scenes.

and the interruption of the communications of each army with its supplies. Finally, on the 31st of August, the forces of Howard and Hardee had a severe battle at Jonesboro', twenty miles below Atlanta, in which the Confederates were defeated. When Hood heard of this disaster, he perceived his peril, and

GENERAL P. G. T. BEAUREGARD, C. S. A.

blowing up his magazine at Atlanta, formed a junction with Hardee, and with his whole army soon recrossed the Chattahoochee. By his rash acts, Hood had wasted nearly one-half of his infantry in the space of a few weeks. The Nationals entered Atlanta on the 2d of September, 1864.

The chief object of the Southern campaign was now in possession of the National forces. Much of September was passed in the reorganization of the two armies, with the Chattahoochee separating them. Satisfied that Hood was preparing to attempt the seizure of Tennessee, Sherman sent General Thomas to Nashville to organize new troops that were to be concentrated there. Meanwhile Hood had planned and attempted the seizure of stores at Allatoona Pass, but had been foiled. Sherman started after him and chased him into northern Alabama, and there relinquishing the pursuit, returned to Atlanta, destroying the railway behind him.

Late in October, Sherman prepared for his famous march from Atlanta to the sea. To General Thomas he assigned the absolute command of a large portion of his army, cut loose from all communications with the North, and on the morning of the 14th of November marched from Atlanta with sixty-five thousand men, in two columns, commanded respectively by Generals Howard and Slocum, preceded by General

Kilpatrick with five thousand cavalry. The army subsisted off the country, wherein they found ample supplies. They also met with very little opposition in its march of thirty-six days through the heart of Georgia. It was a military promenade, requiring very little military skill in the performance, and as little personal prowess. Finally, as the Nationals approached the Atlantic seaboard, they attacked and captured Fort McAllister, on the Ogeechee River. That was on the 13th of December; and four days afterward, the army being before Savannah, Sherman demanded its surrender. Hardee was there with fifteen thousand men, and on the 20th (December, 1864) they evacuated the city and fled to Charleston. On the following day, Sherman entered the city in triumph. By his march through Georgia, he had discovered that the Confederacy was a mere shell in that region. Here we will leave him, and consider events elsewhere.

Early in 1864, intimations came from Florida that its citizens desired reunion with the National Government, but were hindered by Confederate troops there, led by General Finnegan. General Gillmore, then holding Charleston tightly in his grasp, sent General Truman Seymour to assist the Floridians. At the head of six thousand troops, Seymour went up the St. John's River, drove the Confederates from Jacksonville, and pursued them into the interior. In the heart of a cypress swamp at Olustee Station, on a railway that crossed the Peninsula, Seymour encountered Finnegan strongly posted. A sharp battle occurred on the 20th of February (1864), when the Nationals were repulsed and retreated to Jacksonville, destroying Confederate stores valued at $1,000,000. At about the same time, Admiral Bailey destroyed Confederate salt-works on the coast of Florida, valued at $3,000,000.

In the spring of 1864, some stirring events occurred on the coast of North Carolina, the most notable of which was the capture of Plymouth (April 17), near the mouth of the Roanoke River, with sixteen hundred National troops, by the Confederate General Hoke. The Union troops were commanded by General Wessels. Hoke was assisted by the *Albemarle*, a powerful "ram." This vessel well guarded these waters for several months, when, on the night of the 27th of October, it was destroyed with a torpedo by Lieutenant Cushing of the National navy. The night was intensely dark. Cushing, with thirteen men, went into Plymouth harbor in a boat, with a torpedo, and made for the "ram" through a barricade of logs. When they were within twenty yards of the "ram," they were discovered; but in the face of a terrible shower of bullets, they thrust the torpedo under the *Albemarle*, and it exploded

GENERAL JUBAL A. EARLY, C. S. A.

In the Trenches at Petersburg.

Scenes near Petersburg.

with fatal effect. At that moment, a bolt from the "ram" went crashing through Cushing's boat. He and his men leaped into the water; but only himself and another escaped death from bullets and drowning, and were saved on a cutter that accompanied the torpedo boat. After that the war in that region consisted chiefly of skirmishes between detachments of the two armies. Gillmore's guns kept watch and ward over Charleston, while he and some of his troops, as we have observed, went to the James River.

General Hood, according to Sherman's expectations, pushed across the Tennessee River, near Florence, preceded by Forrest and his cavalry, who raided in lower Tennessee for some time, eluding National troops sent against him. He co-operated with Hood's army after its passage of the river, late in October; and at Johnsville, on the Tennessee, he destroyed National stores valued at $1,500,000. Hood had been reinforced by General Taylor, from Louisiana, and pushed vigorously on toward Nashville with fifty thousand troops. General Thomas was at that place with twenty thousand troops; and he had as many more under his command scattered over Tennessee and northern Alabama, in active service against the invading army.

General Schofield, who had advanced to the Duck River, first encountered Hood, and fell back gradually to Franklin, where he took a stand on the 30th of November, and cast up intrenchments. His chief care had been to impede the march of the invaders, and to cover his train until it should reach Nashville. Hood came up in the afternoon of that day and a desperate battle was fought, which raged until near midnight.

ADMIRAL DAVID B. PORTER, U. S. N

At the first onset, the Confederates drove the Nationals from their works and captured all their guns; but in a gallant counter-charge, all that the latter had lost were recovered, with ten battle-flags and three hundred captive insurgents as trophies of victory. Hood had lost one-sixth of his available force in the struggle. Schofield retreated to Nashville, with all his guns, closely pursued by Hood, who invested that post with forty thousand men at the beginning of December.

In the meantime, General Thomas had been reinforced by troops under General A. J. Smith, who had been driving Price out of Missouri. Hood's cavalry was superior to that of Thomas in numbers, and the latter kept the invaders in front of Nashville as long as possible, to enable him to collect there, horses and means for transportation. Finally, at the middle of December, the Nationals moved upon the Confederates. The Fourth corps, led by General T. J. Wood, attacked them vigorously and drove them back to the foot of the Harpeth Hills. The next day (December 16) the same troops and others advanced, and after a severe battle, the invaders were sent flying southward with great precipitation and much confusion, and were closely pursued several days, Hood turning to fight occasionally. At the close of the month, Hood, with his shattered army covered by Forrest's cavalry, escaped across the Tennessee, and he became no longer formidable. In the course of four months, Thomas had made eleven thousand

COMMODORE T. BAILEY, U. S. N.

five hundred Confederate prisoners of war, and captured seventy-two pieces of artillery. His own loss was about ten thousand men, or less than one-half that of his antagonists.

At the beginning of 1864, Confederate cruisers on the ocean had captured one hundred and ninety-three American merchant-ships, whose aggregate cargoes were valued at over $13,400,000. We have already noticed the depredations of the *Alabama*. Another rover, called the *Sumter*, after a short but destructive career, was blockaded and sold at Gibraltar, early in 1862. The *Florida* and *Georgia*, both built in Great Britain, captured and destroyed scores of ships; and in 1864, British shipyards furnished three other formidable cruisers for the use of the Confederates, in spite of the remonstrances of the American minister (Charles Francis Adams) in London.

The *Alabama* was the most formidable of them all. She was commanded by Captain Raphael Semmes, a native of Maryland, who died in August, 1877, in the sixty-ninth year of his age. She continued her depredations on the high seas, eluding the Government vessels, until the 19th of June, 1864, when she encountered the *Kearsarge*, Captain John A. Winslow, off the port of Cherbourg, France. They fought desperately

TOBACCO WAREHOUSE USED BY CONFEDERATES AS TEMPORARY PRISONS.

HOUSES SHOWING EFFECT OF FEDERAL BOMBARDMENT.

HOUSES SHOWING EFFECT OF FEDERAL BOMBARDMENT.

HOUSE SHOWING EFFECT OF FEDERAL BOMBARDMENT.

THE COURT HOUSE.

GRACE CHURCH.

RUINS OF WAREHOUSES NEAR RAILWAY CROSSING.

HOUSES SHOWING EFFECT OF FEDERAL BOMBARDMENT.

HOUSES SHOWING EFFECT OF FEDERAL BOMBARDMENT.

VIEW ON BOLINGBROOK ST. WALL OF HOUSE PERFORATED BY FEDERAL SHOT.

CITY OF PETERSBURG.   VIEWS TAKEN IN 1865, IMMEDIATELY AFTER THE CAPTURE.

for an hour, when the *Alabama*, badly bruised, began to sink. Her flag was struck, and twenty minutes afterward she went to the bottom of the sea, leaving her commander and his crew struggling for life in the water. At that moment the *Deerhound*, a yacht, with its owner (an English gentleman) and his family, appeared. The Englishman sympathized with the Confederates, and went out from Cherbourg ostensibly to see the contest, but really to bear away Semmes and his officers from the grasp of the Nationals should misfortune befall them. These officers, with a few of the crew, were rescued by the yacht and borne in safety to England, where the commander of the *Alabama* was honored with a public dinner (at Southampton); and Admiral Anson, of the royal navy, headed a list of subscribers to a fund raised for the purchase of an elegant sword to be presented to Semmes as a token of sympathy and esteem. The "common people" of the *Alabama* were saved by the boats of her antagonist, and some French vessels.

INTERIOR OF FORT AT PETERSBURG

The news of Winslow's victory was received with joy by the friends of the Government; and it was determined to close the ports of Wilmington and Mobile, the only ones open to blockade-runners. For that purpose Admiral Farragut appeared off the entrance to Mobile (August 5, 1864) with a fleet of eighteen vessels, four of them iron-clads. Five thousand troops under General Gordon Granger had been sent by General Canby from New Orleans, to co-operate with the fleet. The latter (the wooden vessels lashed together in couples) sailed in between the two forts that guarded the entrance—Fort Morgan on the main and Fort Gaines on Dauphin Island. In order to have a general oversight of all the movements, the admiral was fast-bound to the rigging at the maintop of his flag-ship (*Hartford*), that he might not be dislodged by the shock of battle. Through a tube extending from his lofty position to the deck, he gave orders clearly in the midst of the uproar of battle; and in that perilous situation he remained during the passage by the forts and the severe conflict with Confederate vessels that followed. In that passage one of his iron-clad gunboats (*Tecumseh*) was destroyed by a torpedo, but the rest of the fleet was only slightly bruised. When he had passed the forts, a formidable "ram" two hundred feet long, named *Tennessee*, was seen coming swiftly down the bay with other gunboats. These made a ferocious dash at the fleet; but after a sharp conflict, brief and decisive, the *Tennessee* was captured and victory remained with the Nationals.

The forts were now attacked by land and water, and were captured—Fort Gaines on the 7th of August, and Fort Morgan on the 23d. With these were surrendered one hundred great guns and over fourteen hundred men. The port of Mobile was effectually closed, and vigorous measures were adopted for ending the war. On the 3d of September the President called for three hundred thousand men to reinforce the armies in the field. A most cheerful response was made; and in view of omens of peace in the near future, the President issued a request that the people should, in their respective places of public worship, on a specified Sabbath-day, offer united thanksgivings to God for his blessings.

In the fall of 1864, a very exciting canvass for the election of President of the Republic occurred. President Lincoln had been nominated by the Republicans, with Andrew Johnson of Tennessee for Vice-President. The Democrats nominated General George B. McClellan of the army for President, and George H. Pendleton of Ohio for Vice-President. The sentiments of the Peace-Faction prevailed among the adherents of McClellan and Pendleton, and they had the support of all the sympathizers with the Confederates, in the free-labor States. The consequence was that only one of these States (New Jersey)

Mortar on Flat Car, Military Railroad, Petersburg

Mounting Mortars, Butler's Lines, Petersburg

gave them the electoral vote, and Lincoln and Johnson, supported by the loyal people, were chosen by an unprecedented majority.

We left General Sherman and his army at Savannah. After resting for about a month, they began a rapid march through South Carolina, in widely separated columns, and so distracted the Confederates that they did not concentrate a large body of troops anywhere. Incessant rains flooded the country, and the swamp-lands were overflowed; but Sherman pressed forward toward Columbia, the capital of the State, and captured it on the 17th of February, 1865. This disaster caused the Confederates to evacuate Charleston. Hardee and his troops fled into North Carolina and joined the forces there, commanded by General Joseph E. Johnston. Colored troops entered the abandoned city and put out the fires which the Confederates had kindled when they fled. A few weeks afterward, on the anniversary of the evacuation of Fort Sumter four years before, Major Anderson, with his own hand, raised over the ruins of that fortress the identical Union flag which he had carried away from it in April, 1861.

GENERAL E. O. C. ORD

Through the carelessness or folly of General Wade Hampton, who commanded the rear-guard at the evacuation of Columbus, the city was set on fire and a large part of it was laid in ashes. Sherman soon passed on to Fayetteville, in North Carolina, which place he reached on the 12th of March, leaving behind him a blackened path of desolation, forty miles in width. Most of the fighting on that march was done by the cavalry of Kilpatrick and Wheeler. From Fayetteville Sherman communicated with General Schofield, who was in command on the coast; and finding Johnston in front of him with forty thousand troops, he rested his army a few days.

At near the close of 1864, when Sherman was approaching the sea from Atlanta, a destructive raid through Northern Mississippi was made by General Grierson with twenty-five hundred well-mounted men. He left Memphis on the 21st of December, and pushed forward to the Mobile and Ohio Railway, which he struck at Tupelo and destroyed all the way to Okolona, burning Confederate stores and alarming the whole country. After a successful contest at Okolona, Grierson went westward, distracting his foes by feints. He struck the Mississippi Central Railroad at Winona Station, and after several skirmishes he made his way to Vicksburg with trophies consisting of five hundred prisoners, eight hundred beeves, and a thousand liberated slaves. During this raid Grierson destroyed ninety-five railway cars, three hundred wagons and thirty full warehouses.

It was late in 1864 when an attempt was made to close the port of Wilmington by the capture of Fort Fisher, at the mouth of the Cape Fear River. The expedition sent against that post was composed of a powerful fleet of war-vessels commanded by Admiral D. D. Porter, and land troops under the immediate command of General Godfrey Weitzel, accompanied by General B. F. Butler, who was in charge of the department whence the troops were taken. The attempt (December 25, 1864), was unsuccessful; but another made in February following, by the same fleet, and land troops led by General Alfred H. Terry, resulted in the capture of the fort and garrison on the 15th of that month. Terry was then joined by Schofield, who, being the senior officer, took the chief command. The fleet destroyed two Anglo-Confederate cruisers lying in the Cape Fear River, and the National army entered Wilmington as victors on the 22d of February.

Sherman's rest at Fayetteville lasted only three days. Then he moved his army forward in another distracting march that puzzled his antagonists. On the 16th of March, while moving eastward toward Goldsboro', his troops fought twenty thousand Confederates under General Hardee, at Averysboro', and defeated them. Two days afterward, a part of the army under General Slocum were attacked by the whole of Johnston's forces, near Bentonville. The conflict was terrible. Sherman's army had been surprised, and nothing but the most desperate efforts saved it from destruction. It received six distinct assaults by the combined forces of Hoke, Hardee and Cheatham, under the immediate command of General Johnston himself. The conflict ended at twilight. It had been conducted chiefly by General Jefferson C. Davis, of the Fourteenth Army Corps. Had the battle been lost by the Nationals, the results might have been most disastrous to the Union cause. Sherman's army might have been annihilated; so, also, might Grant's, at Petersburg, and the struggle would have been prolonged. It was won by the army of the Republic, and its enemies retreated hastily toward Raleigh, the capital of North Carolina.

Battlefield of Chicasaw Bluffs.

Poison Springs on Battlefield.

Chicasaw Bayou, Missisipi.

SCENES AT CHICASAW BLUFFS

Burnett's House near Cold Harbor.

Collecting remains of the dead on the battlefield of Cold Harbor months after the battle.

Camp in the woods at Cold Harbor.

Old Church Hotel near Cold Harbor

Photographers Camp at Cold Harbor.

Part of Battlefield of Cold Harbor

SCENES AT COLD HARBOR

Sherman was joined by Schofield and Terry at Goldsboro', when he hastened to City Point on the James River, by water, and there consulted the President and General Grant about future operations. He was back to his army three days after he left it.

After the sealing of Mobile harbor, arrangements were made for the capture of that city and gaining possession of Alabama. General Canby, in command of the Department of the Gulf, moved twenty-five thousand troops against Mobile, in March, 1865. At the same time General Wilson, of Thomas's army, with thirteen thousand horsemen and about two thousand foot-soldiers, swept down from the Tennessee to co-operate with Canby. In the space of thirty days, Wilson raided six hundred and fifty miles through Alabama and Georgia, meeting with scarcely any opposition but from Forrest's cavalry, whom he kept from assisting the besieged Confederates at Mobile. Wilson captured cities and towns and destroyed an immense amount of public property. Meanwhile Canby was reducing Mobile to submission; and on the 10th and 11th of April, General Maury, in command there, fled up the Alabama River with nine thousand troops, leaving five thousand men as prisoners, with one hundred and fifty cannon, in the hands of the victors. The war was now virtually at an end in the Gulf region.

GENERAL DAVID A. RUSSELL

During the winter of 1864-65, the *Armies of the Potomac* and of the *James* lay in comparative quiet in front of Petersburg and Richmond, holding the Confederate government and army so tightly in their grasp that the latter could not form a junction with Johnston's forces, nor interfere with Sherman's and Thomas's operations in the South and West. Early in December, Meade had sent Warren to destroy Lee's means of transportation of supplies over the Weldon Railway, near the North Carolina line; and early in February a heavy flanking column, horse and foot, stretched across that road beyond the Confederate right, to Dinwiddie Court-House, seeking an opportunity to turn the right flank of Lee's army. Severe struggles ensued, with heavy losses, and resulted in the permanent extension of the National line to Hatcher's Run, and the railway from City Point to that stream.

Grant now prepared to make a general and vigorous movement against Richmond; and late in February, he ordered General Sheridan to destroy all communications with that city north of the James River and to seize Lynchburg, a great depot of Confederate supplies. That officer was then in the Shenandoah Valley. With Generals Merritt and Custer, he left Winchester on the 27th, with ten thousand men, horse and foot; went up the Valley to Staunton, scattering Early's forces at Waynesboro'; and crossed the Blue Ridge and destroyed the railway as far as Charlottesville. Lynchburg was evidently too strong for him; so he divided his troops and sent one party to break up the railway toward that city, and the other to disable the James River Canal, by which large supplies of provisions entered the Confederate capital. Then Sheridan passed around the left of Lee's forces and joined the *Army of the Potomac* on the 27th of March. This destructive raid alarmed Lee, who saw that the salvation of his army and of the Confederacy now depended upon his forming a junction with Johnston's forces in North Carolina. For that purpose he concentrated his army near Grant's centre, in front of Petersburg, and made a furious assault (March 25, 1865) upon Fort Steadman, a strong point in the National lines, hoping to break through there; but he was repulsed with heavy loss, and his chances for reaching North Carolina were more remote than ever.

During the early part of the preceding winter, General Stoneman and his cavalry had made a campaign in southwestern Virginia; and early in February that commander was ordered to make a raid into South Carolina in aid of Sherman's movements. But that general was so successful that Stoneman's help was not needed, and he was directed to march eastward and destroy the Virginia and Tennessee Railroad as far toward Lynchburg as possible. When this was done, he turned southward and struck the North Carolina Railway between Danville and Greensboro'. Some of his troops penetrated to Salisbury, where the

GENERAL GEORGE CROOK

GENERALS DAVIS, GREGG, SHERIDAN, MERRITT, TORBETT AND WILSON

GENERAL W. S. HANCOCK AND STAFF

Confederates had many Union prisoners. There they destroyed a vast amount of public property; but the Union prisoners had been removed, and were not released. Then a part of Stoneman's force destroyed (April 19) by fire the magnificent railway bridge, eleven hundred feet long, of the South Carolina Railway, that spanned the Catawba River; while the leader and the main body went into East Tennessee. During this raid, the National cavalry captured six thousand prisoners, thirty-one pieces of artillery, and a large number of small arms.

GENERAL W. T. SHERMAN

It was evident in the early spring that a few more heavy blows would end the Confederacy and the war. Individuals had made efforts from time to time to secure a peace without conquering the enemies of the Republic by force of arms. In the summer of 1864, the late Horace Greeley made such an attempt. At about the same time, two other civilians made their way to Richmond, for the purpose; and at near the close of the year the venerable Maryland politician, the late Francis P. Blair, visited the Confederate capital on the same errand. He conferred with Jefferson Davis, who, in a letter addressed to him, expressed his willingness to "renew the effort to enter into a conference with a view to secure peace to the *two countries*." When Mr. Blair communicated the contents of this letter to President Lincoln, the latter expressed *his* willingness to receive any agent of the Confederacy to confer, with a view, he said, "to securing peace for the people of our *common country*." The latter expression showed Davis that he could not treat for peace on the basis of independence for the Southern States; nevertheless, so loud was the popular clamor for peace, that he appointed Alexander H. Stephens, John A. Campbell, and R. M. T. Hunter commissioners, who were permitted to proceed as far as Hampton Roads, by water, but were not allowed to land. There they were met by President Lincoln and Secretary Seward. The President assured the commissioners that peace might be secured only on the condition of absolute submission, everywhere within the bounds of the Republic, to the National authority; and that there could be no secession from the position taken on the subject of slavery. He told them that Congress had just adopted an amendment to the National Constitution, which would be ratified by the loyal people, for the prohibition of slavery in every part of the Republic.

The conference was fruitless except in obtaining a clearer definition of the views of the Government and the Confederate leaders. The result was very unsatisfactory to the latter. At a large public meeting held in Richmond on the 5th of February, Mr. Davis, speaking in reference to Mr. Lincoln's expression, "our common country," said: "Sooner than we should be united again, I would be willing to yield up everything I have on earth, and, if it were possible, would sacrifice my life a thousand times before I would succumb." And at a great war-meeting held on the 9th, at which R. M. T. Hunter presided, it was resolved that the Confederates would never lay down their arms until their independence was won. This being their determination, the National Government had no alternative, and was compelled to prosecute the war to a final dispersion of the armed forces seeking to destroy its existence.

The confidence assumed by Davis and his associates seems to have been inspired by hopes yet entertained of receiving foreign aid. Henry S. Foote, a member of the Confederate Congress (once United States Senator from Mississippi), says in his "War of the Rebellion": "The fact was well known to me that Mr. Davis and his friends were confidently looking for foreign aid, and from several quarters. It was stated, in my hearing, by several special friends of the Confederate president, that *one hundred thousand French soldiers* were expected to arrive within the limits of the Confederate States, by way of Mexico; and it was more than rumored that a *secret compact*, wholly unauthorized by the Confederate constitution, with certain Polish commissioners, who had lately been on a visit to Richmond, had been effected, by means of which Mr. Davis would now be supplied with some twenty or thirty thousand additional troops, then refugees from Poland, and sojourning in several European states, which would

GENERAL HOOD'S C. S. A. HEADQUARTERS AT ATLANTA.

VIEWS ON MARIETTA ST.

THE SLAVE MARKET.

VIEWS ON WHITEHALL ST.

VIEWS ON WHITEHALL ST.

THE RAILROAD DEPOT

VIEW OF THE CITY HALL 2ND MASS. INFANTRY.

VIEWS ON WHITEHALL ST.

THE RAILROAD ROUNDHOUSE

STREET VIEWS.

VIEWS ON MARIETTA ST.

Scenes at Atlanta

be completely at the command of the president for any purpose whatever." Mr. Foote adds, in that connection, that he was satisfied that Mr. Davis would, in sending peace commissioners, "so manacle their hands by *instructions,* as to render impossible all attempts at successful negotiation."

CHAPTER XXV.

A Desperate Struggle—Battle at the Five Forks—Assault on Petersburg—Panic in Richmond—Flight of the Confederate Government— Richmond on Fire—National Troops Enter It—Trophies and Confederate Archives—Rejoicings—Seward's Speech—Evacuation of Petersburg—Lee Becomes Despondent, is Defeated, and Surrenders at Appomattox Court-House—Lincoln in Richmond— Proclamation of Peace—Assassination of the President—The Assassin's Fate—Johnson President—A Murderous Plot—Proposal by the Confederate Leader Rejected by General Johnston—Surrender of General Johnston and Others—Capture of Jefferson Davis —Leniency toward Him.

AFTER Lee's effort to break through the National line at Fort Steadman, it was resolved to make a grand movement against the Confederate right. Large bodies of troops were drawn from the *Army of the James,* under General Ord. General Sheridan, with ten thousand horsemen, was placed on the extreme left of the National army. The Ninth corps, under General Parke, and the force commanded by General Weitzel, were left on the north side of the James to hold the extended line of

ALLATOONA PASS

the National intrenchments, then full thirty-five miles in length; and General Grant gave wide discretion to the commander on the left, concerning attacks upon the Confederate line during the contemplated grand movement. "I would have it particularly enjoined upon corps commanders," he said, "that in case of an attack from the enemy, those not attacked are not to wait for orders from the commanding officers of the army to which they may belong, but that they will move promptly, and notify the commander of their action." General Benham was in charge of the immense depository of supplies at City Point.

Two days after Sheridan's return from his great raid at the close of March, the forward movement was begun. Lee perceived his own imminent peril; and leaving Longstreet with eight thousand men to protect Richmond, he massed the remainder of his army at the point of most apparent danger. Then began a fierce and desperate struggle for the mastery. It was made on the part of the Nationals chiefly by the Fifth corps, under Warren, with the co-operation of Sheridan. The latter, holding a position called the Five Forks, was struck so suddenly and severely by troops under Pickett and Bushrod Johnson, that his force was driven back to Dinwiddie Court-House, in great confusion, hotly pursued. Warren was sent to Sheridan's aid; and near Five Forks a sanguinary battle was fought on the 1st of April. The Confederates were defeated and fled westward in great disorder, leaving five thousand of their comrades behind as prisoners of war. Many of the Confederates perished in the battle; and the loss of the Nationals was about a thousand men.

On the evening of the battle at the Five Forks, and before the shouts of victory there had reached the National line before Petersburg, General Grant had ordered his great guns all along that line to open a destructive cannonade upon the city and the Confederate works. The assault was kept up until four

No. 7 No. 8 No. 9

No. 10 No. 10 No. 11

No. 11 No. 12 No. 12

No. 13 No. 19 No. 19

FEDERAL FORTS.

Federal Forts at Atlanta

o'clock in the morning. It was an awful night for the few inhabitants remaining in Petersburg, and for the soldiers in the trenches. At dawn the works were assailed by infantry. Parke, with the Ninth corps, carried the outer works on his front, but was checked at an inner line; and the Nationals were successful on their extreme left, in crushing Lee's right wing. Longstreet had hastened down from Richmond to assist him, but he was too late. The Confederate right was shattered beyond recovery; and the Southside Railway, on which Lee placed great dependence, was struck by Sheridan at three different points.

Lee now perceived that he could no longer hold Petersburg, or the capital, with safety to his army, then reduced, by enormous losses in the space of a few days, to about thirty-five thousand men, and he resolved to maintain his position, if possible, until night, and then retreat with the hope of making his way to Johnston, in North Carolina, by way of the Danville railroad. He telegraphed to Davis at Richmond, in substance: "My lines are broken in three places; Richmond must be evacuated this evening." It was Sabbath morning, the 2d of April, and the message was delivered to Davis in St. Paul's Church. He quietly left the fane with deeply anxious features, and for a moment a painful silence prevailed. The religious services were closed; and before Dr. Minnegerode, the rector, dismissed the congregation, he gave notice that General Ewell, the commander in Richmond, desired the local forces to assemble at three o'clock in the afternoon.

For hours the people of the city were kept in the most anxious suspense, for the "government" was as silent as the sphinx. Panic gradually took the place of judgment; and when, toward evening, wagons were seen a-loading with trunks and boxes at the departments, and were driven to the Danville Railway station, and it became evident that Davis and his cabinet were preparing to flee, the wildest confusion and alarm prevailed. Prominent Confederates also prepared to fly, they knew not whither; and at eight o'clock in the evening, Davis abandoned his capital and sought personal safety in flight. This act was a marked commentary on his assertion made in a speech a few weeks before: "If it were possible, I would be willing to sacrifice my life a thousand times before I would succumb." His wife had fled to Danville a few days before, and there awaited his coming. At nine o'clock in the evening, the Virginia legislature fled. The Confederate congress had already gone, having left an order for the cotton, tobacco, and other property in the city, to be burned. At midnight, all signs of a "government" had disappeared; and at three o'clock in the morning, incendiary fires were lighted. There was a fresh breeze from the south, and very soon a large portion of the chief business section of Richmond was enveloped in flames. Drunken incendiaries fired buildings not in the pathway of the great conflagration; and until dawn the city was a pandemonium. Most of the Confederate troops had fled; and at an early hour in the morning, General Weitzel, in command of the forces on the north side of the James, entered Richmond with his colored regiments and put out the fires. Lieutenant Johnston Livingston De Peyster, of Weitzel's staff, ascended to the roof of the Virginia State-House and there unfurled the National Flag, where it had not been seen floating for four years.

Meanwhile, Davis and his associates fled to Danville, whither Lee hoped to follow. They had left the inhabitants of the capital defenceless and that city on fire; and they also abandoned five thousand of their sick and wounded in the hospitals, and a thousand soldiers, to become prisoners of war. They also left, as trophies for the victors, five hundred pieces of artillery, five thousand small arms, many locomotives and cars, and a large amount of other public property. They carried with them what gold they could seize in their haste; also the archives of the Confederate government, together with their

POTTER HOUSE AND OTHER SCENES, AT ATLANTA

KENESAW MOUNTAIN AND OTHER SCENES

great seal which had just arrived from England, but which was never stamped upon any public document. A part of the archives were captured by National troops, and the remainder were subsequently sold to our Government by the Confederate ex-minister to Mexico.

Tidings of the fall of Richmond went over the land on that memorable 3d of April, 1865, and produced great joy in every loyal bosom. Before sunset public demonstrations of delight and satisfaction were everywhere visible. At the National Capital, all the public offices were closed, and all business among those who were in sympathy with the Government was suspended. There was an immense gathering of people in Wall street, New York, on that day, to listen to the voices of patriotic orators; and from the tower of Trinity Church, which looks down upon that great mart of money-changers, the bells chimed

PART OF BATTLEFIELD, NEAR ATLANTA

music in airs consonant with the public feeling. The people lingered long; and a deep religious feeling, born of joy and gratitude, pervaded that almost innumerable throng. That feeling was remarkably manifested when thousands of voices joined in chanting the Christian Doxology to the grand air of Old Hundred.

In Washington city, the loyal people gathered in a great throng and visited Mr. Seward, the Secretary of State. They called for a speech, when he appeared and said: "I am now about writing my foreign despatches. What shall I tell the Emperor of China? I shall thank him, in your name, for never having permitted a piratical flag to enter a harbor of the empire. What shall I say to the Sultan of Turkey? I shall thank him for always having surrendered rebel insurgents who have taken refuge in his kingdom. What shall I say to the Emperor of the French? I shall say to him that he can go to Richmond to-morrow and get his tobacco, so long held under blockade there, provided the rebels have not used it up. To Lord John Russell, I will say, the British merchants will find the cotton exported from our ports, under treaty with the United States, cheaper than cotton obtained by running the blockade. As for Earl Russell himself, I need not tell him that this is a war for freedom and national independence, and the rights of human nature, and not a war for empire; and if Great Britain should only be just to the United States, Canada will remain undisturbed by us, so long as she prefers the authority of the noble Queen to voluntary incorporation in the United States. What shall I tell the King of Prussia? I will tell him that the Germans have been faithful to the standard of the Union, as his excellent minister, Baron Gerolt, has been constant in his friendship to the United States during his long residence in this country. To the Emperor of Austria, I shall say that he has proved himself a very wise man, for he told us at the beginning, that he had no sympathy with the rebels anywhere." In these few words, Secretary Seward revealed the fact that while Great Britain and France—Christian nations—were assisting the enemies of our Republic to destroy it, Pagan China and Mohammedan Turkey, animated by principles of right and justice, were its abiding friends.

View of Confederate Line.

View from Confederate Fort on Peach Tree St.

View of Confederate Line from Fort E.

View from Confederate Fort, looking east.

View of Confederate Fort "G"

View of Confederate Line.

View of Confederate Line.

View of Confederate Fort "G"

Views from Parapet of Confederate Works.

CONFEDERATE FORTS AT ATLANTA

Lee, after he had advised the evacuation of Richmond, perceiving that he could no longer hold Petersburg, abandoned it. He stole away so silently on the evening of the 2d, that the suspicions of the Union pickets were not awakened; and when, at dawn, it was discovered that the intrenchments of the Confederates in front of Petersburg had been abandoned, Lee's army were miles away to the westward, seeking to join the columns at Richmond, in a flight for safety. Lee concentrated his broken army at Amelia Court-House, where they might reach the Danville Railway. He had ordered stores to be sent from Danville to that point for the use of his army; but when, on Sunday afternoon, the loaded trains reached Amelia Court-House, a despatch reached the officer in charge, directing him to continue the train on to Richmond for the transportation of the "government" and the archives. The stupid officer

PART OF BATTLEFIELD, NEAR ATLANTA

did not leave the supplies at Amelia, but took them on to Richmond, and they were there destroyed in the conflagration. This was a fatal mistake; and when Lee reached Amelia Court-House, with his half-famished army, and found no supplies there, hope forsook him, for his plans were thwarted. He could not move on for want of provisions and forage; and in the meantime, Sheridan gained a position between the Confederates and Lee's avenue of escape. For several days the latter made desperate efforts to break through the National line, cavalry and infantry, that stood across his path, but failed. Finally, on the 9th of April, he made overtures for capitulation.

On the 7th, Grant had written a note to Lee, suggesting that the events of the past week should convince him of the hopelessness of further resistance on the part of the Army of Northern Virginia. "I feel that it is so," Grant wrote, "and regard it as my duty to shift from myself the responsibility of any further effusion of blood by asking of you the surrender of that portion of the Confederate States army known as the Army of Northern Virginia." To this, Lee replied, that he did not believe further resistance would be vain, but reciprocating Grant's desire to avoid useless effusion of blood, he said: "Before considering your proposition, I ask the terms you will offer on condition of its surrender." After dispatching his reply to Grant, Lee resumed his march westward toward Lynchburg, under cover of the darkness. He hoped to escape to the shelter of the mountains beyond Lynchburg. So silent was his retreat, that it was not discovered until the morning of the 8th, when the National army pushed on in pursuit of the fugitives.

On receiving Lee's answer, the lieutenant-general replied: "There is but one condition I would insist upon, namely, that the men and officers surrendered shall be disqualified for taking up arms against the Government of the United States, until properly exchanged;" and he proposed to meet Lee in person, or to delegate officers for the purpose of definitely arranging the terms of surrender.

Hoping to escape, after his uninterrupted night march, Lee sent a note to General Grant, saying he did not propose to surrender. "To be frank," he said, "I do not think the emergency has arisen to call

Etowah River bridge, and its defences.

Buzzard's Roost, Ga.

Chattachoocic River bridge, and its defences.

View of Kingston, Ga.

Pine Mountain, Ga.

Buzzard's Roost, and Other Views, near Atlanta

Views of Battlefield at Resaca, Ga.

for the surrender of this army." He then proposed to meet Grant on the morning of the 9th to confer upon the subject of peace. The lieutenant-general replied that he had no authority to treat on the topic of peace, and that a meeting for such a purpose would be useless. "The terms upon which peace can be had," he said, "are well understood. By the South laying down their arms, they will hasten that most desirable event, save thousands of human lives, and hundreds of millions of property not yet destroyed." In the meantime Sheridan had settled the question, and rendered further parley unnecessary. He stood across Lee's path on the morning of the 9th, near Appomattox Court-House. The latter saw that his only hope of escape was in cutting his way successfully through Sheridan's line. This he attempted at daybreak with his whole army, then numbering not more than ten thousand effective men. He failed again. Appalled, the Confederates staggered back, and displayed a white flag before the van of the troopers of General Custer. Then Lee wrote to Grant: "I received your note of this morning on the picket-line, whither I had come to meet you, and ascertain definitely what terms were embraced in your proposal of yesterday, with reference to the surrender of this army. I now ask an interview, in accordance with an offer contained in your letter of yesterday, for that purpose."

MAJOR-GENERAL J. M. SCHOFIELD

Grant sent Lee word that he assented to his request, and arrangements were made for an interview in the parlor of the neat brick dwelling of Wilmer McLean at Appomattox Court-House. There, at two o'clock on Palm-Sunday (April 9, 1865), the two commanders met, with courteous recognition. General Grant was accompanied by his chief aide-de-camp, Colonel Parker, a great-nephew of the celebrated Seneca chief, Red Jacket; General Lee, by Colonel Marshall, his adjutant-general, a great-grandson of Chief-Justice Marshall of the Supreme Court of the United States. The terms of surrender were discussed and settled. They were put in the form of a written proposition by Grant, and a written acceptance by Lee. Having been engrossed, they were signed by the generals, at half-past three o'clock, on a neat mahogany centre-table, with a marble top.

The terms prescribed by General Grant were extremely lenient and magnanimous, considering the circumstances. They required Lee and his men to give their parole of honor that they would not take up arms against their Government until regularly exchanged; gave to the officers their side-arms, baggage and private horses; and pledged the faith of the Government that they should not be punished for their treason and rebellion so long as they should respect that parole and be obedient to the laws. Grant even went so far, in his generosity, at Lee's suggestion, that he gave instructions to the proper officers to allow such cavalrymen of the Confederate army as owned their horses to retain them, as they would, he said, need them for tilling their farms.

When the terms of surrender were agreed upon, the Confederate soldiers were provided with food from the National stores; and on Wednesday, the 12th of April, 1865, they laid down their arms. Transportation and food were provided by the Government to large numbers of the troops on their journey homeward. The number paroled was about twenty-five thousand men, of whom not more than nine thousand men had arms in their hands. With the men were surrendered about sixteen thousand small arms, one hundred and fifty pieces of artillery, seventy-one stand of colors, about eleven hundred wagons and caissons, and four thousand horses and mules. The official announcement of the great victory was sent over the land with the speed of lightning, by the Secretary of War, and an order for a salute of two hundred guns at the headquarters of every army.

President Lincoln had been at City Point and vicinity, for several days before the fall of Richmond, anxiously watching the current of events. On the day after the Confederate capital was evacuated, he went up to that city on Admiral Porter's flag-ship, the *Malvern;* and while on his way to Weitzel's headquarters, at the late residence of Jefferson Davis, he was saluted with the loud cheers and grateful ejaculations of a vast concourse of emancipated slaves, who had been told that the "tall man" was their liberator. On the day of Lee's surrender, he

GENERAL JOSEPH E. JOHNSTON, C. S. A.

CONFEDERATE DEFENCES AT ATLANTA

CASEMENT BATTERY, CONFEDERATE LINES, NEAR WHITE HALL, TWO MILES SOUTHWEST OF ATLANTA

returned to Washington; and on the 11th he issued a proclamation, in which he demanded, henceforth, for our vessels in foreign ports, on penalty of retaliation, those privileges and immunities which had hitherto been denied them on the plea of according equal belligerent rights to the Republic and its internal

DEAD ON BATTLEFIELD

enemies. On the following day an order was issued from the War Department, putting an end to all drafting and recruiting for the National army, and the purchase of munitions of war and supplies. This virtual proclamation of the end of the war went over the land on the anniversary of the evacuation of Fort Sumter (April 14), while General Anderson was replacing the old flag over the ruins of that fortress. Preparations were a-making for a National Thanksgiving, and the beams of returning peace illuminated the Republic, so to speak, when suddenly a dark cloud appeared and overspread the firmament with a gloomy pall. Before midnight the telegraph flashed the sad tidings over the land that the President had been assassinated! He was sitting in a theatre (Ford's) at Washington, with his wife and friends, when John Wilkes Booth, an actor by profession, entered his box stealthily and shot Mr. Lincoln in the back of his head with a Derringer pistol. The assassin then rushed to the front of the box with a gleaming dagger in his hand, and shouted "*Sic semper tyrannis*"—so may it always be with tyrants—the motto on the seal of Virginia. Then he leaped upon the stage, booted and spurred for a night ride; and shouting to the audience, "*The South is avenged!*" he escaped by a back door, mounted a horse that was in readiness for him, dashed across the Anacosta and found temporary shelter among sympathizing Maryland slaveholders. Then he fled into Virginia, where he was overtaken by pursuers in a barn below Fredericksburg, which was set on fire; and as the assassin emerged from the flames he was shot by a sergeant named Boston Corbett.

The President expired early in the morning of the 15th of April. His body was taken, in solemn procession, to his home in Springfield, Illinois, by way of Baltimore, Philadelphia, New York, Albany and western cities, everywhere receiving tokens of the people's love and grief. Funeral honors were displayed in many cities in the land. Six hours after the demise of the Chief Magistrate, Andrew Johnson, the Vice-President, who was his constitutional successor, took the oath of office as President of the United States, administered by Chief-Justice Chase.

There seems to be a warrant for the belief, that the assassination of the President was only a part of a plan, in which the murder of the cabinet ministers, General Grant, and prominent Republicans, was contemplated; for on the same evening a murderous attack was made upon Secretary Seward, at his own house, by an ex-Confederate soldier. Secretary Stanton was absent from his home, and was not visited. It was a night of horrors at the capital; and President Johnson issued a proclamation early in May, signed by himself and Mr. Hunter, the Assistant-Secretary of State, in which he declared that there was "evidence in the Bureau of Military Justice" that there had been a conspiracy formed by "Jefferson Davis, Jacob Thompson, Clement C. Clay, Beverly Tucker, George N. Saunders and William C. Cleary, and other rebels and traitors against the Government of the United States, harbored in Canada," to assassinate the President and Secretary of State; and he offered a reward of $25,000 apiece for their arrest, excepting Cleary, a clerk, for whom $10,000 were offered.

With the surrender of General Lee at Appomattox, the war was virtually ended. But only the Army of Northern Virginia had surrendered. That of Johnston, in North Carolina, and smaller bodies elsewhere, were yet in arms. When Sherman heard of the evacuation of Richmond and Petersburg, he put his whole army in motion and moved on Johnston, who was at Smithfield, on the

DEAD ON BATTLEFIELD

RUINS OF RAILROAD AT ATLANTA

RAILROAD AND SHOPS DESTROYED BY CONFEDERATES AT ATLANTA

Neuse River, with full thirty thousand men, starting at daybreak on the 10th of April, for the purpose of striking his rear. Johnston had just heard of the surrender of Lee, and retreated through Raleigh, and along the course of the railway westward, toward Greensboro'. At the same time Davis and his

LIEUTENANT A. B. CUSHING.

cabinet, who had made Danville the seat of the Confederate government for a few days, had fled from that place to Greensboro', with anxious solicitude for themselves and their treasures. They had proposed to Johnston that he should disperse his army excepting two or three batteries of artillery, and as many infantry as he could mount, and with these should form a body-guard for the "government," and strike for the Mississippi and beyond, with Mexico as their final objective. Johnston, a man of honor, spurned this base and selfish proposal to desert his companions-in-arms far away from their homes and unprovided for, and subject the people in the region where the army would be disbanded to the sore evils of plunder, which lawless bands of starving men would engage in. Governed by the principles of justice and humanity, he had the moral courage to do his duty according to the dictates of conscience, and refused to fight any more in a hopeless cause. He stated frankly to the people of his military department, that "war could no longer be continued by them, except as robbers," and that he should take immediate steps to save the army and people from further evil and to "avoid the crime of waging a hopeless war." On the 26th of April, Johnston, and the army under his command, excepting a body of cavalry led by Wade Hampton, surrendered to Sherman, near Durham Station, in Orange County, North Carolina, on the same generous terms accorded to Lee and his troops. The number surrendered and paroled was about twenty-five thousand, with one hundred and eight pieces of artillery, and about fifteen thousand small arms. The whole number of his troops present and elsewhere was seventy thousand. On the 4th of May, General Taylor surrendered the Confederate forces in Alabama to General Canby, at Citronville; and the Confederate navy in the Tombigbee River was surrendered to Admiral Farragut at the same time. The last conflict in the terrible Civil War occurred near Brazos Santiago, in Texas, on the 13th of May, when hostilities entirely ceased.

Jefferson Davis, as we have observed, set up his "government" at Danville, after his flight from Richmond. On the 5th of April, he issued a proclamation from that place, in his usual style. "Let us but will it," he said, "and we are free. Animated by that confidence in spirit and fortitude which never yet failed me, I announce to you, my fellow-countrymen, that it is my purpose to maintain your cause with my whole heart and soul; that I will never consent to abandon to the enemy one foot of the soil of any one of the States of the Confederacy." This was followed a few days afterward by his proposition to Johnston to abandon his army and protect the "government" in its flight to Mexico. In his proclamation, Davis declared his purpose to defend Virginia, and that "no peace should ever be made with the infamous invaders of her territory;" now he ingloriously *abandoned* Virginia. When he heard of the surrender of Johnston's army, and the ring of Stoneman's sabres fell upon his ears, he and his cabinet, escorted by two thousand cavalry, fled across rivers and swamps, with their forces, toward the Gulf of Mexico; for the way to the Mississippi and beyond was barred. Rumors of Stoneman, of Wilson, and even of Sheridan being on their track quickened their flight; while their escort so rapidly dwindled that when they reached Washington, in Georgia, the troopers were not more than sufficient to make a respectable raiding party. There all the cabinet ministers but Postmaster-General Reagan, left Davis, whose wife and children, and Mrs. Davis's sister (Miss Howell) had accompanied the fugitive "government" from Danville. Now, for prudential reasons, this family took another but nearly parallel route for the shores of the Gulf of Mexico, traveling in wagons.

GATHERING THE DEAD ON THE BATTLEFIELD

SCENES AT SAVANNAH, GA.

CHRONOLOGICAL SUMMARY AND RECORD—Continued

AUGUST, 1864—Continued from Section 12

6—Plaquemine, La. 4th Wis. Cav., 14th R. I. Heavy Artil. *Union* 2 killed.

7—Moorefield, Va. 14th Penna., 8th Ohio, 1st and 3d W. Va., and 1st N. Y. Cav. *Union* 9 killed, 22 wounded. *Confed.* 100 killed and wounded, 400 missing.

7 to 14—Tallahatchie River. Abbeville, Oxford and Hurricane Creek, Miss. Hatch's Cav. and Mower's Command of Sixteenth Corps. Casualties not recorded.

9—Explosion of ammunition at City Point, Va. *Union* 70 killed, 130 wounded.

10 and 11—Berryville Pike, Sulphur Springs Bridge and White Post, Va. Torbett's Cav. *Union* 34 killed, 90 wounded, 200 missing.

13—Near Snicker's Gap, Va. 144th and 149th Ohio. *Union* 4 killed, 10 wounded, 200 missing. *Confed.* 2 killed, 3 wounded.

14—Gravel Hill, Va. Gregg's Cav. *Union* 3 killed, 18 wounded.

14 to 16—Dalton, Ga. 2d Mo. and 14th U. S. Colored.

14 to 18—Strawberry Plains, Va. Second and Tenth Corps and Gregg's Cav. *Union* 400 killed, 1,755 wounded, 1,400 missing. *Confed.* 1,000 wounded.

15—Fisher's Hill, near Strasburg, Va. Sixth and Eighth Corps and 1st Cav. Division Army of the Potomac. *Union* 30 wounded.

16—Crooked Run, Front Royal, Va. Merritt's Cav. *Union* 13 killed, 58 wounded. *Confed.* 30 killed, 150 wounded, 300 captured.

17—Gainesville, Fla. 75th Ohio Mounted Inft. *Union* 16 killed, 30 wounded, 102 missing.

Winchester, Va. New Jersey Brigade of Sixth Corps and Wilson's Cav. *Union* 50 wounded, 250 missing.

18, 19 and 21—Six-Mile House, Weldon Railroad, Va. Fifth and Ninth Corps and Kautz's and Gregg's Cav. *Union* 212 killed, 1,155 wounded, 3,176 missing. *Confed.* 2,000 wounded, 2,000 missing. *Confed.* Brig.-Gens. Saunders and Lamar killed and Claigman, Barton, Finnegan and Anderson wounded.

18 to 22—Kilpatrick's Raid on the Atlanta Railroad. *Union* 400 wounded.

19—Snicker's Gap, Pike, Va. Detachment of 5th Mich. Cav. *Union* 30 killed, 3 wounded (all prisoners taken, and the wounded, were put to death by Mosby).

Martinsburg, Va. Averill's Cav. *Union* 25 killed and wounded.

19—Pine Bluff, Tenn. River, Tenn. Detachment of Co. B 83d Ill. Mounted Inft. *Union* 8 killed, and mutilated by guerrillas.

21—Summit Point, Berryville and Flowing Springs, Va. Sixth Corps and Merritt's and Wilson's Cav. *Union* 600 killed and wounded. *Confed.* 400 killed and wounded.

Memphis, Tenn. Detachments of 8th Iowa, 108th and 113th Ill., 39th, 40th and 41st Wis., 61st U. S. Colored, 3d and 4th Iowa Cav., Battery G 1st Mo. Lt. Artil. *Union* 30 killed, 100 wounded. *Confed.* 100 killed and wounded.

21 and 22—College or Oxford Hill, Miss. 4th Iowa, 11th and 21st Mo., 3d Iowa Cav., 12th Mo. Cav. *Confed.* 15 killed.

23—Abbeville, Miss. 10th Mo., 14th Iowa, 5th and 7th Minn., 8th Wis. *Union* 20 wounded. *Confed.* 15 killed.

24—Fort Smith, Ark. 11th U. S. Colored. *Union* 1 killed, 13 wounded. Jones's Hay Station and Ashley Station, Ark. 9th Iowa and 8th and 11th Mo. Cav. *Union* 5 killed, 41 wounded. *Confed.* 60 wounded.

24 and 25—Bermuda Hundred. Va. Tenth Corps. *Union* 31 wounded. *Confed.* 61 missing.

24 to 27—Halltown, Va. Portion of Eighth Corps. *Union* 39 killed, 178 wounded. *Confed.* 130 killed and wounded.

25—Smithfield and Sheperdstown or Kearneysville, Va. Merritt's and Wilson's Cav. *Union* 20 killed, 61 wounded, 100 missing. *Confed.* 300 killed and wounded.

Ream's Station, Va. Second Corps and Gregg's Cav. *Union* 127 killed, 546 wounded, 1,769 missing. *Confed.* 1,500 killed and wounded.

27 and 28—Holly Springs, Miss. 14th Iowa, 11th U. S. Colored Artil., 10th Mo. Cav. *Union* 1 killed, 2 wounded.

29—Smithfield, Va. 3d Div. Sixth Corps and Torbett's Cav. *Union* 10 killed, 90 wounded. *Confed.* 200 killed and wounded.

31—Block House, No. 5, Nashville and Chattanooga Railroad, Tenn. 115th Ohio. *Union* 3 killed, *Confed.* 25 killed.

31 and Sept. 1—Jonesboro', Ga. Fifteenth, Sixteenth, Seventeenth and Davis's Cavalry Divisions of Fourteenth Corps. *Union* 1,149 killed and wounded. *Confed.* 2,000 killed, wounded and missing. *Confed.* Brig.-Gens. Anderson, Cummings and Patten killed.

SEPTEMBER, 1864

1 to 8—Rosseau's pursuit of Wheeler in Tenn. Rosseau's Cav., 1st and 4th Tenn., 2d Mich., 1st Wis., 8th Iowa, 2d and 8th Ind., and 6th Ky. *Union* 10 killed, 30 wounded. *Confed.* 300 killed, wounded and captured.

1 to Oct. 30—In front of Petersburg. Army of the Potomac. *Union* 170 killed, 822 wounded, 812 missing. *Confed.* 1,000 missing.

2—Fall of Atlanta, Ga. Twentieth Corps. *Confed.* 200 captured.

2 to 6—Lovejoy Station, Ga. Fourth and Twenty-third Corps. Casualties not recorded.

3 and 4—Berryville, Va. Eighth and Nineteenth Corps and Torbett's Cav. *Union* 30 killed, 182 wounded, 100 missing. *Confed.* 25 killed, 100 wounded, 70 missing.

4—Greenville, Tenn. 9th and 13th Tenn., and 10th Mich. Cav. *Union* 6 wounded. *Confed.* 10 killed, 60 wounded, 75 missing. *Confed.* Gen. John Morgan killed.

6—Searcy, Ark. Detachment 9th Iowa Cav. *Union* 2 killed, 6 wounded.

10—Capture of Fort Hell, Va. 99th Pa., 20th Ind., 2d U. S. Sharpshooters. *Union* 20 wounded. *Confed.* 90 prisoners.

13—Lock's Ford, Va. Torbett's Cav. *Union* 2 killed, 18 wounded. *Confed.* 181 captured.

16—Sycamore Church, Va. 1st D. C. and 13th Pa. Cav. *Union* 400 killed, wounded and captured. *Confed.* 50 killed and wounded.

16 and 18—Fort Gibson, Ind. Ter. 79th U. S. Colored and 2d Kan. Cav. *Union* 38 killed, 48 missing.

17—Belcher's Mills, Va. Kautz's and Gregg's Cav. *Union* 25 wounded.

19 to 22—Winchester and Fisher's Hill, Va. Sixth, Eighth and 1st and 2d Divisions of the Nineteenth Corps. Averill's and Torbett's Cav., Maj.-Gen. Phil. Sheridan. *Union* 693 killed, 4,033 wounded, 623 missing. *Confed.* 3,250 killed and wounded, 3,600 captured. *Union* Brig.-Gens. Russell and Mulligan killed, and McIntosh, Upton and Chapman wounded. *Confed.* Maj.-Gen. Rhodes and Brig.-Gens. Gordon and Goodwin killed, and Fitz-Hugh Lee, Terry, Johnson and Wharton wounded.

23—Athens, Ala. 106th, 110th and 114th U. S. Colored, 3d Tenn. Cav., reinforced by 18th Mich. and 102d Ohio. *Union* 950 missing. *Confed.* 5 killed, 25 wounded.

Rockport, Mo. 3d Mo. Militia Cav. *Union* 10 killed.

24—Fayette, Mo. 9th Mo. Militia Cav. *Union* 3 killed, 5 wounded. *Confed.* 6 killed, 30 wounded.

26 and 27—Pilot Knob or Ironton, Mo. 47th and 50th Mo., 14th Iowa, 2d and 3d Mo. Cav., Battery H 2d Mo. Lt. Artil. *Union* 28 killed, 56 wounded, 100 missing. *Confed.* 1,500 killed and wounded.

27—Centralia, Mo. Three Co.'s 39th Mo., massacred by Price. *Union* 122 killed, 2 wounded.

Marianna, Fla. 7th Vt., 82d U. S. Colored and 2d Maine Cav. *Union* 32 wounded. *Confed.* 81 missing.

28 and 30—New Market Heights or Laurel Hill, Va. Tenth and Eighteenth Corps and Kautz's Cav. *Union* 400 killed, 2,029 wounded. *Confed.* 2,000 killed and wounded.

29—Centreville, Tenn. 2d Tenn. Mounted Inft. *Union* 10 killed, 25 wounded.

29 and 30—Leesburg and Harrison, Mo. 14th Iowa, 2d Mo. Militia Cav., Battery H 2d Mo. Lt. Artil.

30 and Oct. 1—Poplar Springs Church, Va. 1st Div. Fifth Corps and 2d Div. Ninth Corps. *Union* 141 killed, 788 wounded, 1,756 missing. *Confed.* 800 wounded, 100 missing.

Arthur's Swamp, Va. Gregg's Cav. *Union* 60 wounded, 100 missing.

OCTOBER, 1864

2—Waynesboro, Va. Portion of Custer's and Merritt's Cav. *Union* 50 killed and wounded.

Saltville, Va. 11th and 13th Ky. Cav., 12th Ohio, 11th Mich., 5th and 6th U. S. Colored Cav., 26th, 30th, 35th, 37th, 39th, 40th and 45th Ky. Mounted Inft. *Union* 54 killed, 190 wounded, 104 missing. *Confed.* 18 killed, 71 wounded, 21 missing.

5—Jackson, La. 23d Wis., 1st Tex., and 1st La. Cav., 2d and 4th Mass. Battery. *Union* 4 killed, 10 wounded.

Allatoona, Ga. 7th, 12th, 50th, 57th and 93d Ill., 39th Iowa, 4th Minn., 18th Wis. and 12th Wis. Battery. *Union* 142 killed, 352 wounded, 212 missing. *Confed.* 231 killed, 500 wounded, 411 missing.

7—New Market, Va. 3d Div. Custer's Cav. *Union* 56 missing.

7 to 11—Jefferson City, California and Boonsville, Mo. (Price's Invasion.) 1st, 4th, 5th, 6th and 7th Mo. Militia Cav., 15th Mo. Cav., 17th Ill. Cav., Battery H 2d Mo. Lt. Artil.

7 and 13—Darbytown Road, Va. Tenth Corps and Kautz's Cav. *Union* 105 killed, 502 wounded, 206 missing. *Confed.* 1,100 killed and wounded, 350 missing. *Confed.* Gen. Gregg killed.

9—Tom's Brook, Fisher's Hill or Strasburg, Va. Merritt's, Custer's and Torbett's Cav. *Union* 9 killed, 67 wounded. *Confed.* 100 killed and wounded, 180 missing.

10—East Point, Miss. 61st U. S. Colored. *Union* 16 killed, 20 wounded.

11—Fort Donelson, Tenn. Detachment 4th U. S. Colored Heavy Artil. *Union* 4 killed, 9 wounded. *Confed.* 3 killed, 23 wounded.

12—Reconnaissance to Strasburg, Va. Maj.-Gen. Emory's and Crook's troops. *Union* 30 killed, 144 wounded, 40 missing.

13—Dalton, Ga. Troops under Col. Johnson, 44th U. S. Colored. *Union* 400 missing.

Buzzard Roost, Ga. One Co. 115th Ill. *Union* 5 killed, 36 wounded, 60 missing.

15—Glasgow, Mo. 43d Mo., and detachments of 17th Ill., 9th Mo. Militia, 13th Mo. Cav., 62d U. S. Colored. *Union* 400 wounded and missing. *Confed.* 50 killed and wounded.

19—Lexington, Mo. 5th, 11th, 15th and 16th Kan. Cav., 3d Wis. Cav. Casualties not recorded.

Cedar Creek, Va. (Sheridan's Ride.) Sixth Corps, Eighth Corps, and 1st and 2d Divisions Nineteenth Corps, Merritt's, Custer's and Torbett's Cav. *Union* 588 killed, 3,516 wounded, 1,801 missing. *Confed.* 3,000 killed and wounded, 1,200 missing. *Union* Brig.-Gens. Bidwell and Thorburn killed, Maj.-Gens. Wright, Ricketts and Grover and Brig.-Gens. Ketchem, McKenzie, Penrose, Hamlin, Devins, Duval and Lowell wounded. *Confed.* Maj.-Gen. Ramseur killed and Battle and Conner wounded.

21 and 22—Little Blue and Independence, Mo. Kansas Militia, 2d and 5th Mo. Militia, 2d Col. Cav., 5th, 7th, 11th, 15th and 16th Kan. Cav., 1st, 2d, 4th, 6th, 7th, 8th and 9th Mo. Militia Cav. Casualties not recorded.

23—Hurricane Creek, Miss. 1st Iowa and 9th Kan. Cav. *Union* 1 killed, 2 wounded.

26 to 29—Decatur, Ala. 18th Mich., 102d Ohio, 68th Ind., and 14th U. S. Colored. *Union* 10 killed, 45 wounded, 100 missing. *Confed.* 100 killed, 300 wounded.

27—Hatcher's Run, Va. Gregg's Cav., 2d and 3d Divisions Second Corps, Fifth and Ninth Corps. *Union* 156 killed, 1,047 wounded, 699 missing. *Confed.* 200 killed, 600 wounded, 200 missing

(Continued in Section 14)

The Blocakde Runner, "Teazer," after Her Capture

CHAPTER XXV.—Continued.

COMMODORE JOHN A. WINSLOW

INFORMATION soon reached Davis that some Confederate soldiers, believing that his wife had the treasure taken from Richmond with her, had formed a plot to seize all her trunks and search for it. He instantly hastened to the rescue of his family and property, and to provide for their protection. For this purpose he and a few followers rode rapidly eighteen miles and joined his family near Irwinsville, the capital of Irwin county, Georgia, nearly due south from Macon. They had just pitched tents for the night; and the wearied president of the ruined Confederacy lay down to rest, intending to retrace his steps in the morning.

One hundred thousand dollars had been offered by the Government for Davis's capture. Vigilance was thereby made keen and active. General Wilson was at Macon when he heard of Davis's flight toward the Gulf, and sent out two bodies of cavalry to intercept him. One was composed of Michigan men, under Lieutenant-Colonel Pritchard, and the others were from Wisconsin, led by Lieutenant-Colonel Hardin. Discovering Davis's halting-place, both parties approached the camp of the sleeping fugitives simultaneously from opposite directions, and, mistaking each other for enemies, in the gray light of early dawn, they exchanged shots. The noise aroused the slumberers. The camp was surrounded; and Davis, while attempting to escape partially disguised in a woman's water-proof cloak, and a shawl thrown over his head by Miss Howell, was captured by Pritchard and his men. The whole fugitive party were taken to Macon. Thence they were sent to Savannah, and conveyed by water to Fortress Monroe, where Davis was confined in comfortable quarters in a casemate. There he remained a long time, when he was admitted to bail. He was never tried, and lived an uncompromising enemy of the Republic which he tried to destroy.

CHAPTER XXVI.

WHEN the Civil War, waged by the armies in the field, had ended, the people turned to the pursuits of peace. There was joy and hope in every loyal bosom in the land; and the friends of the Union everywhere found expression to their feelings in the following hymn, composed by George H. Boker, and sung by the Loyal League of Philadelphia on the anniversary of the nation's independence, just four years after the National Congress met at the Capitol to provide for the suppression of the great insurrection and the salvation of the Republic:

> "Thank God the bloody days are past,
> Our patient hopes are crown'd at last;
> And sounds of bugle, drum and fife
> But lead our heroes home from strife!
>
> "Thank God there beams o'er land and sea
> Our blazing Star of victory;
> And everywhere, from main to main,
> The old flag flies and rules again!
>
> "Thank God! oh dark and trodden race,
> Your Lord no longer veils his face;
> But through the clouds and woes of fight
> Shines on your souls a brighter light!
>
> "Thank God! we see, on every hand,
> Breast-high the rip'ning grain-crops stand;
> The orchards bend, the herds increase,
> But oh, thank God! thank God for PEACE!"

BRIGADIER-GENERAL BENJ. H. GRIERSON

ADMIRAL FARRAGUT AND CAPTAIN DRAYTON ON THE UNITED STATES STEAMSHIP "HARTFORD"

GUNBOAT "GENERAL BURNSIDE"

Before this hymn was chanted, the soldiers of the great armies of the Republic who had saved the nation from political death, and, incidentally, had achieved the work of emancipation for an enslaved race, were making their way homeward. They were everywhere received with the warmest demonstrations of gratitude and affection. In almost every village and city there were public receptions of returning companies and regiments; and their tattered banners are cherished as precious mementoes of a noble work finished by those who bore them through the perils of the battle-field. With the exception of a few soldiers who were left in Virginia and North Carolina, those who confronted Lee and Johnston and achieved a victory over both were marched to the vicinity of the National Capital; and during two memorable days (May 22d, 23d, 1865) they moved through that city, in long procession, with tens of thousands of tear-moistened eyes gazing upon them, and passed in review before the Chief Magistrate of the nation and his ministers. Human vision had never beheld a spectacle like that, in all its aspects. Then began the work of disbanding the armies, by mustering out of service officers and men; and on the 2d of June (1865), the general-in-chief (Grant) issued the following address to them:

VIEW OF A GUNBOAT

"*Soldiers of the Armies of the United States:* By your patriotic devotion to your country in the hour of danger and alarm, and your magnificent fighting, bravery and endurance, you have maintained the supremacy of the Union and the Constitution, overthrown all armed opposition to the enforcement of the laws and of the proclamation forever abolishing slavery—the cause and pretext of the Rebellion—and opened the way to the rightful authorities to restore order, and inaugurate peace on a permanent and enduring basis on every foot of American soil. Your marches, sieges and battles, in distance, duration, resolution and brilliancy of results, dims the lustre of the world's past military achievements, and will be the patriot's precedent in defence of liberty and right in all time to come. In obedience to your country's call, you left your homes and families, and volunteered in her defence. Victory has crowned your valor, and secured the purpose of your patriotic hearts; and with the gratitude of your countrymen, and the highest honors a great and free nation can accord, you will soon be permitted to return to your homes and families, conscious of having discharged the highest duty of American citizens. To achieve these glorious triumphs, and secure to yourselves, your fellow-countrymen and posterity, the blessings of free institutions, tens of thousands of your gallant comrades have fallen, and sealed the priceless legacy with their blood. The graves of these, a grateful nation bedews with tears. It honors their memories, and will ever cherish and support their stricken families."

The Civil War in America was more extended in area and more destructive of life and property than any recorded in history. The whole number of men called into the military and naval service during the war, to save the Union, was 2,656,533, of whom nearly 200,000 were colored. About 1,400,000 men were in actual service, and 60,000 were killed in the field. There were 30,000 mortally wounded; and 184,000 died in hospitals and camps. Full 300,000 Union soldiers perished during the war, and it is supposed the Confederates lost an equal number. On both sides there were a large number more or less disabled for life. It is estimated that, during the war, 1,000,000 men, taken from the active pursuits of life, were sacrificed, to feed the ambition of a comparatively few men who wished to form an empire with human slavery as its corner-stone, and who tried to pull down our grand structure of free government, that they might build their forbidding fabric upon its ruins. That war burdened the industry of the whole nation with a loss and debt of over $6,000,000,000. But it gave freedom to about 4,000,000 slaves, and purged our National escutcheon of a monstrous stain.

BOW GUN ON GUNBOAT

The disbanding of the army went steadily on from the first of June (1865), and by the middle of November following, nearly 800,000 of the 1,000,000 of the soldiers whose names were on the rolls on the first of May had been mustered out of service and

Admiral David G. Farragut

returned to their several avocations. The wonderful spectacle was exhibited for the contemplation of the civilized world, of vast armies of men surrounded by all the paraphernalia of war, transformed, in the space of one hundred and fifty days, into a vast army of citizens engaged in the blessed pursuits of peace.

MAJOR-GENERAL GEORGE STONEMAN

No argument in favor of free institutions and a republican form of government, so conclusive and potential as this, was ever before presented to the feelings and judgment of the nations of the earth. The important political problem of the nineteenth century was solved by our Civil War. Our Republic no longer appeared as an *experiment*, but as a *demonstration*.

The National navy has an equal claim to the gratitude of the loyal people of our country, for its services during the war were of incalculable value. It attracted less attention than the army, because our vessels of war were engaged chiefly in the blockade service, or as auxiliaries of the army along the rivers and sea-coasts. In that service, especially in the latter portion of it, the labors of the officers and seamen were arduous in the extreme; and there were occasions for the display of prowess and skill equal to any required in the open ocean service. A history of the part performed by our gunboat squadron on the rivers would form a most marvellous chapter in the annals of the Civil War.

At the breaking out of hostilities, the navy was exceedingly weak, and by its geographical disposition, was, for a time, almost powerless, as we have already observed. It had been reduced during fifty years of peace to the smallest proportions, and was kept in existence only by the necessity of affording protection for the continually expanding commercial interests of the nation. Its men numbered only seven thousand six hundred at the beginning of 1861; and of its officers, three hundred and twenty-two proved treacherous in the day of trial, abandoned their flag, and entered the service of the enemies of their country. Under the able management of Mr. Fox, the energetic Assistant-Secretary of the Navy, the marine arm of the public service was speedily and wonderfully strengthened. Even while in its weakness, a decree went forth for the blockade of the Southern ports, in the face of the protests and menaces of foreign governments. Ingenuity and mechanical skill developed amazing inventions. The *Monitor*, with its revolving turret, was perfected and changed the mode of naval warfare. "Rams" were constructed for river service. Large numbers of vessels were built; others were purchased; and men from the merchant marine were invited to officer and man them. Dock-yards were enlarged and filled with workmen. The places of the treasonable deserters were soon filled. Volunteers flocked to the ships, and the number of seven thousand six hundred men that composed our navy when the war broke out, had increased to fifty-one thousand before it was ended. During the four years of the war, no less than two hundred and eight war-vessels were constructed and fitted out, and four hundred and fourteen vessels were purchased and converted into war-ships. Of these, three hundred and thirteen were steamers. Many of them were iron-clads; and the aggregate cost was $19,000,000.

The blockading service was performed with great vigor and success, under the triple stimulus of patriotism, duty, and the chances for personal emolument. While the British government professed to be neutral, swarms of swift steamers were fitted out by British merchants, and, laden with every kind of supplies for the insurgents, were sent to "run the blockade." The profits of such operations, if successful, were enormous, but the risks were equally so; and it is believed that a true balance-sheet would show that there were no profits left with these violators of law. Over fifteen hundred of these blockade-runners were captured or destroyed by our National vessels, during the war; and the aggregate value of property captured and condemned, as lawful prize, before November following the close of the war, was $22,-000,000. That sum was subsequently enlarged by new decisions. The value of the vessels so captured or destroyed, added to the value of goods in them, swelled the amount of loss to the British blockade-runners, to full $30,000,000.

GENERAL GEORGE A. CUSTER

Brig.Gen.H.G.Wright.

Brig.Gen.A.T.A.Torbert.

Brig.Gen.J.J.Bartlett.

Brig.Gen.D.A.Russell.

Col.L.A.Grant.

Brig.Gen.T.H.Neill.

Major Gen.John Sedgwick.

Brig.Gen.Frank Wheaton.

Brig.Gen.A.Shaler.

Col.H.L.Eustis.

GROUP OF FEDERAL GENERALS

GENERAL W. S. MERRITT AND STAFF

There is a dark chapter in the history of the Civil War, over which the writer would gladly draw the veil of forgetfulness, if it were possible. It relates to Union prisoners and their treatment. Soon after hostilities commenced and there were captives taken, the question was considered by President Lincoln's cabinet, Can the Government exchange prisoners with rebels against its authority, without acknowledging them as belligerents? Humanity took precedence of the law of nations, and an arrangement was made for an exchange. The business went on successfully until it was violently interrupted by Jefferson Davis at near the close of 1862. His anger had been kindled because of the employment of negroes in the military service, by the National Government; also by some proceedings of General Butler at New Orleans, already noticed. He first issued the savage proclamation (December 23, 1862) ordering Butler, and all commissioned officers serving under him, to be hanged, when caught, without trial, as outlaws. This was followed (January 12, 1863) by another proclamation, in which he announced his determination to deliver all officers of the National army commanding negro troops that might be captured after that date, to the respective State authorities to be hanged, and to treat those troops as rebels against their masters. The government paused. In Congress, measures for retaliation were proposed; but humanity and not policy bore sway, and such measures were not adopted. The exchange of prisoners, however, was interrupted; for the Confederate Commissioner, under instructions from Davis, refused to consider captive colored troops as prisoners of war. In several instances no quarter had been given them, in battle or afterward; and the black flag was carried against

JEFFERSON DAVIS, C. S. A.

officers commanding them. And when, in August, 1863, the National Commissioner (Meredith) demanded that negro troops and their officers should be treated as prisoners of war, the Confederate Commissioner (Ould) replied: "We will die in the last ditch before giving up the right to send slaves back into slavery." That determination, acted upon by Davis and his associates, caused an absolute cessation of the exchange of prisoners, for the Government would not be unjust toward any class of its defenders, especially the weaker. The consequence was that the number and sufferings of the Union prisoners fearfully increased, and the horrors of the prisons and prison-pens at Richmond, Salisbury, Charleston, Millen, and Andersonville occurred.

Well-supported facts seem fairly to warrant the unpleasant conclusion, that Davis's proclamations were made by him for the purpose of obstructing exchanges, that the Union prisoners might, by long and acute suffering, be rendered physically and mentally useless as soldiers thereafter. *The United States Sanitary Commission* appointed a committee, of which the eminent Dr. Valentine Mott of New York was chairman, to ascertain by inquiry and observation, as far as possible, into the matter of alleged cruelty to Union prisoners. They reported in September, 1864, saying: "It is the same story everywhere; prisoners of war treated worse than convicts; shut up either in suffocating buildings, or in out-door inclosures, without even the shelter that is provided for the beasts of the field; unsupplied with sufficient food; supplied with food and water injurious and even poisonous; compelled to live on floors often covered with human filth, or on ground saturated with it; compelled to breathe an air oppressed with an intolerable stench; hemmed in by a fatal dead-line, and in hourly danger of being shot by unrestrained and brutal guards; despondent even to madness, idiocy, and suicide; sick, of disease (so congruous in character as to appear and spread, like the plague) caused by the torrid sun, by decaying food, by filth, by vermin, by malaria, and by cold; removed at the last moment, and by hundreds at a time, to hospitals corrupt as a sepulchre, there, with a few remedies, little care and no sympathy, to die in wretchedness and despair, not only among strangers, but among enemies too resentful either to have pity or to show mercy. These are positive facts. Tens of thousands of helpless men have been, and are now being, disabled and destroyed by a process as certain as poison, and as cruel as the torture or burning at the stake, because nearly as agonizing and more prolonged. This spectacle is daily beheld and allowed by the rebel government. No

MAJOR-GENERAL H. W. SLOCUM

Evacuation of Port Royal, Rappahannock River

HORACE GREELEY

FIELD BATTERY

supposition of negligence, or indifference, or accident, or inefficiency, or destitution, or necessity, can account for all this. So many, and such positive forms of abuse and wrong cannot come from negative causes. *The conclusion is unavoidable, therefore, that these privations and sufferings have been designedly inflicted* by the military and other authorities of the rebel government, and cannot have been due to causes which such authorities could not control." One of the chief instruments employed in the infliction of cruelties upon Union prisoners was Brigadier-General John H. Winder, an inciter of the mob which attacked the Massachusetts troops in Baltimore. So notorious for his cruel acts had he become, that when (at the age of seventy years) he was sent to Georgia to carry on his horrid work at Andersonville, the *Richmond Examiner* exclaimed: "Thank God Richmond has, at last, got rid of old Winder! God have mercy upon those to whom he has been sent!"

Testimony given by Confederates themselves confirms the statements made by the prisoners. So early as September, 1862, Augustus R. Wright, chairman of a committee of the Confederate House of Representatives, made a report on the prisons at Richmond confining Union captives, to George W. Randolph, then the Confederate Secretary of War, in which report it was said that the state of things was "terrible beyond description;" that "the committee could not stay in the room over a few seconds;"

GENERAL SILAS CASEY AND STAFF

GENERALS OF THE SECOND CORPS, C. S. A.

GENERALS OF THE CONFEDERATE ARMY

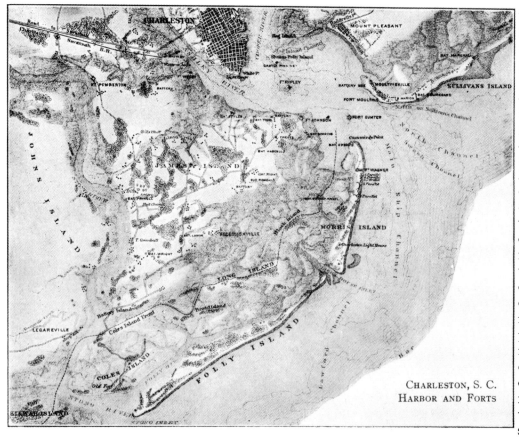

CHARLESTON, S. C.
HARBOR AND FORTS

that a change *must* be made, and that "*the committee makes the report to the Secretary of War, and not to the House, because, in the latter case, it would be printed*, and, for *the honor of the nation*, such things *must be kept secret*." In December, 1863, Henry S. Foote, a member of the Confederate House of Representatives, offered a resolution for the appointment of a committee of inquiry concerning the alleged ill-treatment of Union prisoners. His humane resolution was voted down. In the course of his remarks in its favor, Mr. Foote read testimony which, he said, was on record in the Confederate War Department, to prove that the charges of cruelty were true. Referring to Northrup, the Confederate Commissary-General, he said: "This man has placed our government in the attitude charged by the enemy, *and has attempted to starve the prisoners in our hands*." He cited an elaborate report made by the Commissary-General to the Secretary of War (Seddon), in which he used this significant language: "For the subsistence of a human Yankee carcase, a vegetable diet is the most proper," the terrible meaning of which is obvious. Foote, also, in a letter written at Montreal, in the spring of 1865, concerning the escape of Streight and his men from Libby Prison, by mining, declared "that a government officer of respectability" told him "*that a systematic scheme was on foot for subjecting these unfortunate men to starvation*." He further declared that Northrup's proposition was "endorsed by Seddon, the

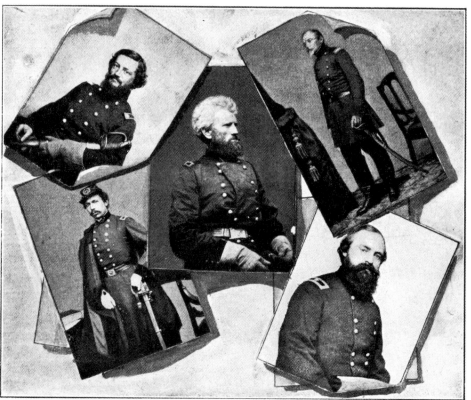

MAJ.-GENERAL T. L. KANE   BRIG.-GENERAL H. BOHLEN
                    MAJ.-GENERAL R. H. MILROY
MAJ.-GENERAL J. STAHL   BVT. MAJ.-GENERAL E. B. TYLER

Canvas Pontoon Bridges,
across
North Anna River.

Corps Ammunition Train
Crossing Pontoon Bridge.

N.Y. Engineers Constructing
road on South bank of
North Anna River.

N.Y. Engineers Constructing
Road on south bank of
North Anna River.

Chesterfield Bridge
North Anna River.

Canvas Pontoon Bridges Across North Anna River and Other Views

Secretary of War," who said substantially in that endorsement, that "the time had arrived for retaliation upon the prisoners of war of the enemy." In that letter Foote proved (1) that the starving of Union prisoners was known to the Confederate authorities; (2) that the Confederate Commissary-General proposed it; (3) that the Confederate Secretary of War approved and officially endorsed it; (4) that the Confederate Commissioner of Exchange knew it; and (5) that the Confederate House of Representatives knew of it, and endeavored to prevent an investigation. Foote said the positive proof was in the War Department. A greater portion of these documents were burned when the Confederate Gov-

EXCHANGED PRISONERS BELONGING TO THE 19TH INFANTRY, AT NEW ORLEANS

ernment fled from Richmond. Such is the testimony of one of the legislators of the Confederacy, who, it may be presumed, knew, personally, the facts of the case. And it is a matter of record, that a committee of the "United States Christian Commission" appeared before the lines of Lee's army and sought access to the Union prisoners in Richmond and on Belle Isle, in the James River there, to afford them relief, with the understanding that similar commissions would be allowed to visit Confederate captives. But they were not allowed to pass, because, as Confederate witnesses testify, the authorities at Richmond dared not let the outside world know, from competent witnesses, the horrible truths which such a visit would have revealed. But General Robert E. Lee (whose family resided on Franklin street in Richmond, from the rear gallery of whose residence he could, with his field-glass, have looked into the faces of the starving and freezing prisoners on Belle Isle, and who, after the autumn of 1863, was never a hundred miles from that city) testified before the National "Committee on Reconstruction," in February, 1866, that he was not aware of any bad treatment suffered by Union prisoners—not aware that any of them died of cold and starvation—that no report was ever made to him of the sad condition of Union prisoners anywhere—that he never knew who was in command at Andersonville, Salisbury, and other gathering-places of Union prisoners, until after the war, and that he "knew nothing in the world" of the alleged cruelties about which complaints had been made!

When the starvation plan had succeeded in reducing forty thousand Union prisoners to skeletons, generally no better for service than so many dead men, a proposition was made by the Confederate authorities for a resumption of exchanges. Again humanity took precedence of expediency, and these poor creatures in Confederate prisons were exchanged for as many prisoners who had been well fed and otherwise comfortably provided for in the North. This was attested by the Confederate Commissioner of Exchange, who, in a letter to

SURRENDER OF GENERAL ROBERT E. LEE TO GENERAL U. S. GRANT, APRIL 9, 1865

VIEWS ON THE APPOMATTOX RIVER

VIEWS ON THE JAMES RIVER

General Winder, from City Point, where exchanges had been resumed, said exultingly: "The arrangement I have made works largely in our favor. *We get rid of a set of miserable wretches, and receive some of the best material I ever saw.*"

Let us turn from the consideration of this unpleasant subject to that of the noble efforts made to relieve the suffering of soldiers in the field, the camp, and the hospital. It is just, however, before so doing, to ask the reader to remember, always, that the great body of the *Southern people* were not only entirely guiltless of the proven cruelties practised toward the Union prisoners, but were kept in profound ignorance of them. *The responsibility rests upon the few selfish political leaders in the great conspiracy and insurrection,* from the beginning to the end, who, whenever it suited their purposes, defied all moral and civil law. To these men belongs the responsibility of involving this happy and prosperous nation in a most destructive Civil War, with all its awful consequences; and to them our brethren of the late slave-labor States are indebted for whatever evil reports have affected them. A reign of terror under the

COUNCIL OF WAR.

MASSAPONAX CHURCH

COUNCIL OF WAR.

Richmond despotism crushed out all freedom of speech and action in the Confederacy, as Castle Thunder might testify. The *people* of the South, as good, benevolent, humane, refined, kind-hearted and Christian-like in character and deeds as any on the face of the earth, have unjustly suffered reproaches because of the wrongs committed by self-constituted political leaders who misrepresented them.

The arrangements by the Government for the care of the sick and wounded soldiers of the National army were ample and complete. When the war closed there were two hundred and four general hospitals fully equipped, with a capacity of nearly 137,000 beds. Besides these there were numerous temporary and flying hospitals, the former in camps and on vessels, and the latter on battle-fields. The report of the Surgeon-General (Joseph K. Barnes), at the close of the war, showed that from the beginning of hostilities in 1861, to July 1, 1865, there had been treated in the general hospitals alone, 1,057,423 cases, among whom the average rate of mortality was only eight per cent.; much smaller than had ever been known before in any army. That of the army of the United States in the war with Mexico was a little over ten per cent. Of the British in the Crimean campaign, it was nearly twenty per cent., and of their French allies there still greater.

The low rate of mortality in the Union army was due to several favorable circumstances, the chief of which was the employment, by the Government, of a sufficient number of skillful surgeons; a bountiful provision in all the hospitals of every necessity; the beneficent labors of the two powerful and popular organizations known as the *United States Sanitary Commission* and the *United States Christian Commission*, and the untiring labors of women everywhere. The latter worked with tenderness and devotion in hospitals, in camps, and even on or near the field of battle, as most efficient nurses. By their presence they continually brought images of home to the sick or wounded soldier, and cheered and consoled him with healing words more efficacious sometimes than the apothecary's medicine. To this catalogue of hygienic instrumentalities must be added the potent and benevolent influences of a hundred thousand army chaplains. As a class they were faithful servants of their Divine Master, and ever ready to "minister to a mind diseased." They formed a trusted link between the soldier and his home—a ladder for the angels of thought and affection between his Bethel and his heaven on earth—telling the bereaved, in written words, of the joy and hope of loved ones at the gate of death; or, better still, sending to anxious hearts the balm of consolation in sweet epistles giving the cheering news of convalescence. The most profound respect and gratitude are due by the people of our land to the chaplains of the hospitals of the army and navy.

Scenes Photographed at Headquarters Army of Potomac Nov 1862 June 1863

SCENES AT HEADQUARTERS OF THE ARMY OF THE POTOMAC, NOVEMBER, 1862, TO JUNE, 1863

GENERAL ROBERT E. LEE, C. S. A.

Allusion has been made to the origin of the *United States Sanitary Commission*, and to the *United States Christian Commission*. On the 16th of June, 1861, the Secretary of War (Mr. Cameron) issued an order appointing Henry W. Bellows, A. D. Bache, Jeffries Wyman, W. H. Van Buren, R. C. Wood, George W. Cullum and Alexander Shiras, in conjunction with such others as might associate with them, a "Commission of Inquiry and Advice, in Respect of the Sanitary Interests of the United States Forces." The functions of the Commission are indicated by the title. They appointed a board of managers, with Dr. Bellows (who may be regarded as the founder of the Commission) at its head. He submitted a plan of organization, to which the President and Secretary of War gave their sanction by affixing their signatures to it, and it became the constitution of the Commission. Its seal bore the words, "UNITED STATES SANITARY COMMISSION," with the date of its organization. Upon the face of the seal was an escutcheon, bearing the figure of Mercy, winged, with the symbol of Christianity upon her bosom and a cup of consolation in her hand, coming down from the clouds to visit wounded soldiers on the battle-field. Frederick Law Olmstead was chosen resident secretary, and became the general manager of the affairs of the Commission.

This Commission went to work most vigorously, to supplement the Government deficiencies in supplying comforts for the sick and wounded. They appealed to the people, and the response was marvellous. Supplies and money flowed in in sufficient volume to meet all demands. All over the country, men, women, and children, singly and collectively, were working for it, and contributing to it. Fairs were held in large cities, which turned immense sums of money into its treasury. With these funds it supplied

VIEW TAKEN NOV. 1864.

VIEW TAKEN NOV. 1864.

VIEW TAKEN APRIL 1865

VIEW TAKEN APRIL 1865

KEDGE BOAT SUNK BY CONFEDERATE SHELL

DUTCH GAP CANAL AND OTHER VIEWS

GENERAL GRANT'S BASE OF SUPPLIES, AT CITY POINT

QUARTERMASTER'S HEADQUARTERS, AT CITY POINT

the sick and wounded with delicacies, ice, stimulants, fruits, etc., and with trained nurses, while the Government supplied all regular rations. In a single fair, in the city of New York, the net receipts were $1,181,500. In the little city of Poughkeepsie, on the Hudson, whose population was then about 16,000, the net profits of the fair were over $16,000. Branches of the Commission were established; agents were employed; corps of nurses were organized; ambulances, army-wagons and steamboats of its own were employed in the transportation of the sick and wounded, and supplies. It followed the army closely in all campaigns. Its ear, always open, caught the first sounds of battle everywhere, and before the smoke of conflict was lifted from the field, there was the Sanitary Commission, like an omnipresent minister of good, with wagons, supplies, tents and nurses, ready to afford instant relief. Like a guardian angel it was always at the side of the soldier in moments of greatest need. When the war ceased, and the record of the work of the Sanitary Commission was made plain, it was found that the loyal people of the land

VIEWS IN WARRENTON, VA.

FORT DARLING, DREWRY'S BLUFF, JAMES RIVER

FIELD BATTERY

POWDER MAGAZINE ON THE LINES

had *given* to it supplies valued at about *five million dollars*.

The *United States Christian Commission* was a kindred organization, working in harmony with the *United States Sanitary Commission*, and performed great labors for the spiritual and temporal good of the soldiers. It had its origin in the Young Men's Christian Association of New York, and was first suggested by Vincent Colyer, an artist of that city, and an earnest worker in useful fields of benevolence. He, with Frank W. Ballard and Mrs. Dr. Harris, who represented the Ladies' Aid Society of Philadelphia, went to Washington City immediately after the first battle at Bull Run, to do Christian work in the camps and hospitals there. Every facility for visiting the camps was given to Mr. Colyer by the military authorities, and they even gave him permission to go to the Confederate camps if they would allow him to do so. He distributed Bibles, tracts, and hymn-books among the soldiers, held prayer-meetings, and labored most zealously, in many ways, for their spiritual good. Finally Mr. Colyer suggested the combination of all the Young Men's Christian Associations in the land, in the formation of a society similar to that of the *United States Sanitary Commission*. It was acted upon in September, 1861, when arrangements were made for holding a National Convention of such associations. A convention assembled in the city of New York on the 14th of November, and the *United States Christian Commission* was organized, with George H. Stuart of Philadelphia as president. Its specific work was to be chiefly for the moral and religious welfare of the soldiers, which was conducted by means of oral instruction and the circulation of the Bible and other proper books, with pamphlets, newspapers, etc., among the men in hospitals, camps, and ships.

This noble Commission, of which Vincent Colyer was the real founder, began earnest work at once on the same general plan of the other Commission. It did not confine its labors wholly to spiritual and intellectual ministrations, but also to the distribution of a vast amount of food, hospital stores, delicacies, and clothing. It, too, followed the great armies and co-operated efficiently with the chaplains of the army and navy, by supplying the soldiers and sailors with the scriptures and a vast number and variety of other good books. Chapels for religious labors and public worship were erected at permanent camps, and in many ways there was cast about the soldier a salutary religious influence. Money and supplies came to the Commission as a free-will offering from the patriotic people, mostly collected by the women of various denominations of the Christian Church, and amounted in value to *six million dollars*.

While the two great organizations here noticed were at work, others, in large numbers, but less conspicuous, were laboring for the same holy purpose. Associations for the relief of the freedmen, and for sailors, also for promoting enlistments for the military and naval service, were organized; and everywhere the most active and disinterested benevolence was manifested. High authority has said, "It is more blessed to give than to receive." If so, then the loyal people of our land were eminently blessed; for it is estimated that through these two great

BVT. MAJ.-GEN. W. S. HILLYER
BVT. MAJ.-GEN. J. A. RAWLINS
BVT. MAJ.-GEN. J. D. WEBSTER

GENERAL GRANT'S HEADQUARTERS, AT CITY POINT

COLONELS F. D. DENT, M. M. MORGAN, GENERALS J. G. BARNARD, J. A. RAWLINS, U. S. GRANT, M. R. PATRICK, SETH WILLIAMS AND RUFUS INGALLS; COLONEL E. S. PARKER, CAPTAIN H. C. ROBINETT, AT GRANT'S HEADQUARTERS AT CITY POINT
Picture taken April 12, 1865, after the surrender of Appomattox Courthouse, Va. Grant left that afternoon for Washington, D. C.
Identifications made by Colonel M. M. Morgan, of General Grant's Staff.

Commissions, various associations, and by private contributions, they made free gifts of their substance to the amount of *five hundred million dollars*.

While these associations were at work for the benefit of the Union soldiers, similar efforts, though not on so grand a scale, were put forth by the benevolent-minded in the slave-labor States for the benefit of the Confederate soldiers. They labored in the good work most zealously to the extent of their ability, and conferred vast benefits upon the sick and wounded soldiers of the Confederate army. We have no special reports of the result of their labors; but we know that it was a great blessing to the recipients of the kindly care, especially of the women of the South. Among the variety of organizations for benevolent purposes was one called *The Confederate Association for the Relief of Maimed Soldiers.* The object of that association was to supply artificial limbs gratuitously to soldiers who had lost their natural ones. An annual subscription of $10 constituted a member; of $300, a life-member; and of $100, an honorary director. Upon a certificate of membership, before me, is a rude wood-cut representation of the proposed seal of the Confederate States.

JOHN HAY, PRIVATE SECRETARY TO PRESIDENT LINCOLN, AFTERWARD SECRETARY OF STATE TO PRESIDENT MCKINLEY

CHAPTER XXVII.

Reorganization of the Union—President Johnson's Plan—Thirteenth Amendment—Character of the President—Justice for the Freedmen—Motives of Lincoln and Johnson Contrasted—A Pitiful Trick—Action in the Disorganized States—The Test Oath—"Reconstruction" Committee—President, Offended, Makes War on Congress—His Political Tour—His Vetoes—The President and Secretary Stanton—French Troops in Mexico—Napoleon's Designs and Perfidy—British Interference—Suffrage in the District of Columbia—President Threatened with Impeachment—Acts of Congress Vetoed and Passed—Extra Sessions—Unlawful Conduct of the President.

AFTER the terrible convulsions produced by the Civil War, by which State governments had been paralyzed, a hoary and deep-rooted social system had been overthrown, and throughout a number of the commonwealths of the Republic there had been a disruption of every kind of business, the powers of the National government were invoked to bring about a general reorganization of the disorganized elements, political, social, and industrial. There was nothing to be *reconstructed*, for nothing worth preserving had been *destroyed*. No State, as a component part of the Republic, had been severed from the others, for secession was an impossibility. When the war ended, the States, geographically and politically, remained as they were before it began. The insurrection against the authority of the National Government only placed the constitutions of some of the States in a condition of suspended animation. They needed only the stimulant of competent official authority exercised by the National Government to reanimate them. All the States were politically equal—living members of the great Commonwealth,

STEPHEN A. DOUGLAS

before, during, and at the close of the Civil War. Some of them, incapacitated for healthful functional action, were awaiting resuscitation at the hands of the only healer, the National Government. To that resuscitation—that reorganization and fitting them for active life—the General Government soon directed its efforts.

President Johnson took a preliminary step toward reorganization, on the 29th of April, 1865, when he proclaimed the removal of restrictions upon commercial intercourse between all the States. A month later (May 29) he issued a proclamation stating the terms by which the people of the paralyzed States, with specified exceptions, might receive full amnesty and pardon, and be reinvested with the right to exercise the functions of citizenship, supposed to have been destroyed by participation in the insurrection. This was soon followed by the appointment by the President of provisional governors for seven of those States which had formed the original fabric known as the "Confederate States of America," clothed with authority to assemble citizens in convention who had taken the amnesty oath, with power to reorganize State governments, and secure the election of representatives in the National Congress. The plan was to restore to the States named their former position in the Union without

CITY OF RICHMOND, VA., BEFORE BOMBARDMENT

CITY OF RICHMOND AFTER THE SIEGE.   RUINS OF STATE ARSENAL AND VIEW DOWN THE JAMES RIVER

any provision for securing to the freedmen the right to the exercise of citizenship which the amendment to the National Constitution, then before the State legislatures, would justly entitle them to. This amendment, known as the XIIIth, was adopted by Congress early in 1865, and was as follows:

"SECTION 1. Neither slavery nor involuntary servitude, except as a punishment for crime, whereof the party shall have been duly convicted, shall exist within the United States, or any place subject to their jurisdiction.

"SECTION 2. Congress shall have power to enforce this article by appropriate legislation."

This amendment was adopted by a large majority. When the result of the vote was known, the Republican members of the House of Representatives instantly sprang to their feet and applauded with cheers and clapping of hands. The spectators in the crowded galleries waved their hats and made the chamber ring with enthusiastic plaudits. Hundreds of ladies rose in their seats in the galleries and gave emphasis to their plaudits by waving their handkerchiefs and participating in the general demonstration of enthusiasm, and added to the intense excitement of a scene that will long be remembered by those who were fortunate enough to witness it. The amendment was sent to the several State legislatures for ratification and on the 18th of December following, the Secretary of State (Mr. Seward) declared that it had, by such ratification, become a part of the fundamental law of the land.

When Andrew Johnson was inaugurated President, there were painful apprehensions among men who knew him most intimately, that he would not be faithful to the trust reposed in him by the loyal people of the land. Notwithstanding the strength of our government had been made manifest by the shock of Civil War which it had survived, it was equally manifest that it was surrounded with great perils. A pilot was needed at the helm of the ship of state possessed of a combination of moral and intellectual forces of a rare order—sound morality, strong and unwavering convictions, firmness of will, sobriety of conduct, calmness of temper, a thorough knowledge of men, an accurate and impartial judgment, a willingness to take counsel, a clear perception of righteousness, and the acuteness of a true statesman. Circumstances had occurred which justly created a doubt in the public mind whether the new President

BEVEN'S BATTERY IN ACTION AT FAIR OAKS

RUINS OF RICHMOND

RICHMOND AFTER EVACUATION

SERGEANT BOSTON CORBETT, WHO SHOT WILKES BOOTH
CAPTAIN E. P. DOHERTY, OF 16TH NEW YORK CAVALRY,
WHO CAPTURED BOOTH

possessed all these qualities, so requisite at that critical time, and these doubts soon became settled convictions. His total disregard of the highest interests of the freedmen, and the fact that the President was making haste to pardon a large number of those who had been active in the service of the Confederates and would exercise a controlling influence in the States which he was equally in haste to reorganize on his own plan, startled the loyal men of the country, and made them doubt the sincerity of his vehement declaration of intentions to punish the leading enemies of our Government. To a delegation from New Hampshire, who waited upon him soon after his inauguration, he said: "Treason is a crime, and must be punished as a crime. It must not be regarded as a mere difference of political opinion. It must not be excused as an unsuccessful rebellion, to be overlooked and forgiven. It is a crime before which all other crimes sink into insignificance." Such, and even more severe language was used by the President when speaking of the leading Confederates; and, as we have seen, he charged Jefferson Davis and others with being accessories in the murder of Mr. Lincoln, and offered large rewards for their arrest. It was feared by some that the President would deal too harshly with the offenders; but events soon dispelled the illusion.

The poor freedmen relied with bright hopes upon the President's promise to be their "Moses" in leading them completely out of bondage; but they soon found that he was unwilling to do more than secure their personal freedom. He was unwilling to invest them with civil rights, which deprivation he knew would virtually remand them to slavery. The political party which had emancipated them and elevated Mr. Johnson to his high position, felt that justice, not expediency, should be the rule in the readjustment of the affairs of the Republic; and it was demanded, as an act of National honor, that the freedman, when made a citizen by the Constitution, should have equal civil and political rights and privileges with other citizens, such as the elective franchise. In the spring of 1864, President Lincoln suggested to the governor of Louisiana, the propriety of giving that franchise to the colored people. "They would probably keep," he said, almost prophetically, "in some trying time to come, the jewel of Liberty in the family of freedom." For an ignoble purpose, President Johnson proposed to his provisional governor of Mississippi to give the franchise to such of the freedmen as could read the National Constitution and possessed property worth two hundred and fifty dollars. He well knew that an extremely small number could avail themselves of the privilege, as the laws of Mississippi made it a punishable offence to teach a colored person to read; and in the condition of slavery, not one could hold property. It was a pitiful trick, which he was not ashamed to avow. In his letter to the governor, he said: "Do this, and, as a consequence, the radicals (in other words the most earnest Republicans), who are wild upon negro suffrage, will be completely foiled in their attempt to keep the Southern States from renewing their relations with the Union."

Within a hundred days after his inauguration, President Johnson took issue with the Republican party upon vital points of principle and policy; and at the close of 1865, it was plain to the comprehension of sagacious observers, that the Chief Magistrate was more friendly to the late enemies of his country than consistency with his professions, or the safety of the Republic, would allow. It was soon perceived that politicians

DAVID HEROLD

RUINS OF MAYO'S BRIDGE, RICHMOND, VA.

VIEWS OF RICHMOND IN RUINS

in the North who had sympathized with the Confederates during the war, and the newspapers in their interest which had advocated the cause of the insurgents, had assumed a belligerent tone toward Congress and the loyal people, which greatly disturbed the latter by unpleasant forebodings.

In the meantime measures had been taken for perfecting peaceful relations among the whole people of the Republic, by a revival of industrial pursuits and a restoration of harmony of interests. The order for a blockade of the Southern ports was rescinded late in June (1865); most of the restrictions upon inter-State commerce were removed in August; State prisoners were paroled in October; and on the first day of December, the first important measure adopted, after the assembling of Congress, was the repeal of the act suspending the privilege of the writ of habeas corpus.

During that period (June to December), Johnson's provisional governors had been diligent in carrying out his plan of reorganization before Congress should meet, and, possibly, interfere with it. Before the first of December five of the disorganized States had ratified the XIIIth amendment of the Constitution, cited on page 442. They had, also, caused the formation of constitutions for their respective States and the election of representatives in the National Congress. The President had hurried on his work, by directing the provisional governors to resign their powers into the hands of others who had been elected under the new constitutions. Some of these governors-elect had been active

BOX AT FORD'S THEATRE, WHERE PRESIDENT LINCOLN WAS ASSASSINATED

participants in the insurrection; and some of the Congressmen-elect in these States had been, it was said, active workers against the Government. These facts greatly disturbed the loyal people. They had witnessed with great anxiety the evident usurpations of power by the President, the exercise of which, as he had done, belonged exclusively to the functions of the representatives of the people in Congress assembled. The prescriptions of the Constitution are clear on that point. Yet the people waited patiently for the meeting of Congress in December, with the quieting knowledge that a majority of loyal men would be there, and that each House had the right to judge of the qualifications of its own members. It was a settled belief that disloyal men would not be allowed to enter either House over the bar of a test-oath prescribed by law, passed on the 22d of July, 1862. That law required every member to make oath that he had not "voluntarily borne arms against the United States since he had been a citizen thereof," or "voluntarily given aid, countenance, counsel or encouragement to persons engaged in hostilities thereto," and had never "yielded voluntary support to any pretended government, authority, power, or constitution within the United States, hostile or inimical thereto."

The subject of reorganization was among the first business of the Thirty-ninth Congress which assembled on the 4th of December, 1865. On the first day of the session, by a vote of 133 against 36, Congress agreed to a joint resolution to appoint a joint committee to be composed of nine members of the House and six of the Senate, to "inquire into the condition of the States which formed the so-called

CHAIR OCCUPIED BY PRESIDENT LINCOLN ON NIGHT OF ASSASSINATION

Confederate States of America, and report whether they, or any of them, are entitled to be represented in either House of Congress, with leave to report at any time, by bill or otherwise; and until such report shall have been made and finally acted upon by Congress, no member shall be received in either House from any of the so-called Confederate States; and all papers relating to the representatives of the said States shall be referred to the said committee." This body was known by the misnamed "*Reconstruction* Committee." It should have been "*Reorganization* Committee."

This action of Congress was a virtual condemnation of the President's usurpations. It was a legitimate interference of the representatives of the people with his chosen policy of reorganization, and he was highly offended. He soon manifested open and violent hostility to the legislative branch of the Government, and maintained that position during the whole of his administration.

PRESIDENT LINCOLN AND "TAD"

MRS. LINCOLN

ROBERT LINCOLN

"TAD" LINCOLN IN UNIFORM

CHRONOLOGICAL SUMMARY AND RECORD—Continued

OCTOBER, 1864—*Continued from Section 13*

27 and **28**—Fair Oaks, Va. Tenth and Eighteenth Corps and Kautz's Cav. *Union* 120 killed, 783 wounded, 400 missing. *Confed.* 60 killed, 311 wounded, 80 missing.

28—Destruction of the rebel ram *Albemarle*, by Lieut. Cushing and thirteen marines. *Union* 3 wounded, 11 captured.
Morristown, Tenn. Gen. Gillem's Cav. *Union* 8 killed, 42 wounded. *Confed.* 240 missing.

28 and **30**—Newtonia, Mo. Col. Blunt's Cav. in pursuit of Price. *Confed.* 250 wounded.

29—Beverly, W. Va. 8th Ohio Cav. *Union* 8 killed, 25 wounded, 13 missing. *Confed.* 17 killed, 27 wounded, 92 missing.

30—Near Brownsville, Ark. 7th Iowa and 11th Mo. Cav. *Union* 2 killed.

NOVEMBER, 1864

1 to **4**—Union Station, Tenn. 10th Mo. Cav. *Union* 2 killed, 2 wounded, 26 missing.

5—Fort Sedgwick or Fort Hell, Va. Second Corps. *Union* 5 killed, 10 wounded. *Confed.* 15 killed, 35 wounded.

9—Atlanta, Ga. 2d Division, Twentieth Corps. *Confed.* 20 killed and wounded.

12—Newtown and Cedar Springs, Va. Merritt's, Custer's and Powell's Cav. *Union* 84 wounded, 100 missing. *Confed.* 150 missing.

13—Bull's Gap, Tenn. 8th, 9th and 13th Tenn. Cav. *Union* 5 killed, 36 wounded, 200 missing.

16—Lovejoy Station and Bear Creek Station, Ga. Kilpatrick's Cav. *Confed.* 50 captured.

17—Bermuda Hundred, Va. 209th Pa. *Union* 10 wounded, 120 missing. *Confed.* 10 wounded.

18—Myerstown, Va. Detachment 91st Ohio. *Union* 60 killed and wounded. *Confed.* 10 killed and wounded.

20—Macon, Ga. 10th Ohio Cav., 9th Pa. Cav., 92d Ill. Mounted Inft., 10th Wis. Battery.

21—Griswoldville, Ga. Walcott's Brigade, 1st Division, Fifteenth Corps and 1st Brigade 3d Division Cav. *Union* 10 killed, 52 wounded. *Confed.* 50 killed, 200 wounded, 400 missing.
Rood's Hill, Va. Torbett's Cav. *Union* 18 killed, 52 wounded.
Lawrenceburg, Campbellville and Lynnville, Tenn. Hatch's Cav. *Union* 75 killed and wounded. *Confed.* 50 killed and wounded.

26—Saundersville, Ga. 3d Brigade 1st Division Twentieth Corps. *Union* 100 missing. *Confed.* 100 missing.

26 to **29**—Sylvan Grove, Waynesboro', Browne's Cross Roads. Kilpatrick's Cav. *Union* 46 wounded. *Confed.* 600 killed and wounded.

29 and **30**—Spring Hill and Franklin, Tenn. Fourth and Twenty-third Corps and Cavalry. *Union* 189 killed, 1,033 wounded, 1,104 missing. *Confed.* 1,750 killed, 3,800 wounded, 702 missing. *Union* Maj.-Gens. Stanley and Bradley wounded. *Confed.* Maj.-Gen. Cleborne, Brig.-Gens. Adams, Williams, Strahl, Geist and Granberry killed, Maj.-Gen. Brown and Brig.-Gens. Carter, Manigault. Quarles, Cockerell and Scott wounded.

30—Honey Hill or Grahamsville, S. C. 25th Ohio, 56th and 155th N. Y., 26th, 32d, 35th and 102d U. S. Colored, 54th and 55th Mass. Colored. *Union* 66 killed, 645 wounded.

DECEMBER, 1864

1—Stony Creek Station, Weldon Railroad, Va. Gregg's Cav. *Union* 40 wounded. *Confed.* 175 captured.
Twelve miles from Yazoo City, Miss. Detachment of 2d Wis. Cav. *Union* 5 killed, 9 wounded, 25 missing.

1 to **14**—In front of Nashville, Tenn. Fourth, Twenty-third and 1st and 2d Division of Sixteenth Corps and Wilson's Cav. *Union* 16 killed, 100 wounded.

1 to **31**—In front of Petersburg. Army of the Potomac. *Union* 40 killed, 329 wounded.

2 and **3**—Block-house No. 2, Mill Creek, Chattanooga, Tenn. Detachment 115th Ohio, 44th and two Cos. 14th U. S. Colored. *Union* 12 killed, 46 wounded, 57 missing.

3—Thomas's Station, Ga. 92d Ill. Mounted Inft. *Union* 2 killed, 1 wounded.

4—Block-house No. 7, Tenn. Gen. Milroy's troops. *Union* 100 wounded. *Confed.* 100 killed and wounded.

5 to **8**—Murfreesboro', Tenn. Gen. Rosseau's troops. *Union* 30 killed, 175 wounded. *Confed.* 197 missing.

6—White Post, Va. Fifty men of 21st N. Y. Cav. *Union* 30 wounded.

6 to **9**—Deveaux's Neck, S. C. 56th and 155th N. Y., 25th and 107th Ohio, 26th, 33d, 34th and 102d U. S. Colored, 54th and 55th Mass. Colored, 3d R. I. Artil. and U. S. Gunboats. *Union* 39 killed, 390 wounded, 200 missing. *Confed.* 400 killed and wounded.

7 to **9**—Eden Station, Ogeechee River, Ga. Fifteenth and Seventeenth Corps right wing of Sherman's Army.

7 to **11**—Weldon Railroad Expedition. Fifth Corps, 3d Division of Second Corps, and 2d Division Cavalry Corps, Army of the Potomac. *Union* 100 wounded.

8 and **9**—Hatcher's Run, Va. 1st Division, Second Corps, 3d and 13th Pa. Cav., 6th Ohio Cav. *Union* 125 killed and wounded.

8 to **28**—Raid to Gordonsville, Va. Merritt's and Custer's Cav. *Union* 43 wounded.

10 to **21**—Siege of Savannah, Ga. Fourteenth, Fifteenth, Seventeenth and Twentieth Corps of Sherman's Army. *Union* 200 wounded. *Confed.* 800 missing.

12 to **21**—Stoneman's Raid from Bean's Station, Tenn., to Saltville, Va., including Abingdon, Glade Springs and Marion. *Union* 20 killed, 123 wounded. *Confed.* 126 wounded, 500 missing.

13—Fort McAllister, Ga. 2d Division of Fifteenth Corps. *Union* 24 killed, 110 wounded. *Confed.* 250 missing.

14—Memphis, Tenn. 4th Iowa Cav. *Union* 3 killed, 6 wounded.

15 and **16**—Nashville, Tenn. Fourth Corps, 1st and 3d Divisions Thirteenth Corps, Twenty-third Corps, Wilson's Cav., and Detachments colored troops, convalescents. *Union* 400 killed, 1,740 wounded. *Confed.* 4,462 missing.

17—Franklin, Tenn. Wilson's Cav. *Confed.* 1,800 wounded and sick captured.

17 to **19**—Mitchell's Creek, Fla., and Pine Barren Creek, Ala. 82d and 97th U. S. Colored. *Union* 9 killed, 53 wounded, 11 missing.

20—Lacey's Springs. Custer's Cav. *Union* 2 killed, 22 wounded, 40 missing.

25—Fort Fisher, N. C. Tenth Corps and North Atlantic Squadron. *Union* 8 killed, 38 wounded. *Confed.* 3 killed, 55 wounded, 280 prisoners.

28—Egypt Station, Miss. 4th and 11th Ill. Cav., 7th Ind., 4th and 10th Mo., 2d Wis., 2d N. J., 1st Miss. and 3d U. S. Colored Cav. *Union* 23 killed, 88 wounded. *Confed.* 500 captured. *Confed.* Brig.-Gen. Gholson killed.

JANUARY, 1865

2—Franklin, Miss. 4th and 11th Ill. Cav., 3d U. S. Colored Cav. *Union* 4 killed, 9 wounded. *Confed.* 20 killed, 30 wounded.

2 and **3**—Nauvoo and Thornhill, Ala. 15th Pa. Cav., Detachments of 10th, 12th and 13th Ind. Cav. and 2d Tenn. Cav. *Union* 1 killed, 2 wounded. *Confed.* 3 killed, 2 wounded, 95 captured, and Hood's supply and pontoon train destroyed.

11—Beverly, W. Va. 34th Ohio and 8th Ohio Cav. *Union* 5 killed, 20 wounded, 583 missing.

12 to **15**—Fort Fisher, N. C. Portions of Twenty-fourth and Twenty-fifth Corps and Porter's Gunboats. *Union* 184 killed, 749 wounded. *Confed.* 400 killed and wounded, 2,083 captured.

14 to **16**—Pocataligo, S. C. Seventeenth Corps. *Union* 25 wounded.

16—Explosion of the magazine at Fort Fisher, N. C. *Union* 25 killed, 66 wounded.

25 to **Feb. 9**—Combahee River and River's Bridge, Salkahatchie, S. C. Fifteenth and Seventeenth Corps. *Union* 138 killed and wounded.

FEBRUARY, 1865

5 to **7**—Dabney's Mills, Hatcher's Run, Va. Fifth Corps and 1st Division Sixth Corps and Gregg's Cav. *Union* 232 killed, 1,062 wounded, 186 missing. *Confed.* 1,200 killed and wounded. *Union* Brig.-Gens. Morrow, Smyth, Davis, Gregg, Ayres, Sickels and Gwynn wounded. *Confed.* Gen. Pegram killed and Sorrell wounded.

8 to **14**—Williston, Blackville and Aiken, S. C. Kilpatrick's Cav. *Confed.* 240 killed and wounded, 100 missing.

10—James Island, S. C. Maj.-Gen. Gilmore's command. *Union* 20 killed, 76 wounded. *Confed.* 20 killed and 70 wounded.

11—Sugar Loaf Battery, Federal Point, N. C. Portions of Twenty-fourth and Twenty-fifth Corps. *Union* 14 killed, 114 wounded.

15 to **17**—Congaree Creek and Columbia, S. C. Fifteenth Corps. *Union* 20 killed and wounded.

18—Ashby Gap, Va. Detachment 14th Pa. Cav. *Union* 6 killed, 19 wounded, 64 missing.

18 to **22**—Fort Anderson, Town Creek and Wilmington, N. C. Twenty-third and Twenty-fourth Corps and Porter's Gunboats. *Union* 40 killed, 204 wounded. *Confed.* 70 killed, 400 wounded, 375 missing.

22—Douglas Landing, Pine Bluff, Ark. 13th Ill. Cav. *Union* 40 wounded. *Confed.* 26 wounded.

27 to **March 25**—Sheridan's Raid in Virginia. 1st and 3d Divisions Cavalry Corps. *Union* 35 killed and wounded. *Confed.* 1,667 prisoners.

MARCH, 1865

6—Olive Branch, La. 4th Wis. Cav. *Union* 3 killed, 2 wounded.
Natural Bridge, Fla. 2d and 99th U. S. Colored. *Union* 22 killed, 46 wounded.

8 to **10**—Wilcox's Bridge, N. C. Palmer's, Carter's and Ruger's Divisions. *Union* 80 killed, 421 wounded, 600 missing. *Confed.* 1,500 killed, wounded and missing.

16—Averysboro', N. C. Twentieth Corps and Kilpatrick's Cav. *Union* 77 killed, 477 wounded. *Confed.* 108 killed, 540 wounded, 217 missing.

19 to **21**—Bentonville, N. C. Fourteenth, Fifteenth, Seventeenth and Twentieth Corps and Kilpatrick's Cav. *Union* 191 killed, 1,168 wounded, 287 missing. *Confed.* 267 killed, 1,200 wounded, 1,625 missing.

20 to **April 6**—Stoneman's Raid into Southwestern Va. and North Carolina. Palmer's, Brown's and Miller's Cavalry Brigades.

22 to **April 24**—Wilson's Raid, Chickasaw, Ala., to Macon, Ga. *Union* 63 killed, 345 wounded, 63 missing. *Confed.* 22 killed, 38 wounded, 6,766 prisoners.

25—Fort Steadman, in front of Petersburg, Va. 1st and 3d Divisions Ninth Corps. *Union* 68 killed, 337 wounded, 506 missing. *Confed.* 800 killed and wounded, 1,881 missing, assault of the Second and Sixth Corps. *Union* 103 killed, 864 wounded, 209 missing. *Confed.* 834 captured.

26 to **April 9**—Siege of Mobile, Ala., including Spanish Fort and Port Blakely. Thirteenth and Sixteenth Corps and U. S. Navy. *Union* 213 killed, 1,211 wounded. *Confed.* 500 killed and wounded, 2,952 missing and captured.

29—Quaker Road, Va. Warren's Fifth Corps and Griffin's 1st Division, Army of the Potomac. *Union* 55 killed, 306 wounded. *Confed.* 135 killed, 400 wounded, 100 missing.

31—Boydton and White Oak Roads, Va. Second and Fifth Corps. *Union* 177 killed, 1,134 wounded, 556 missing. *Confed.* 1,000 wounded, 235 missing.
Dinwiddie C. H., Va. 1st, 2d and 3d Cavalry Divisions Army of the Potomac. *Union* 67 killed, 354 wounded. *Confed.* 400 killed and wounded.

(Continued in Section 15)

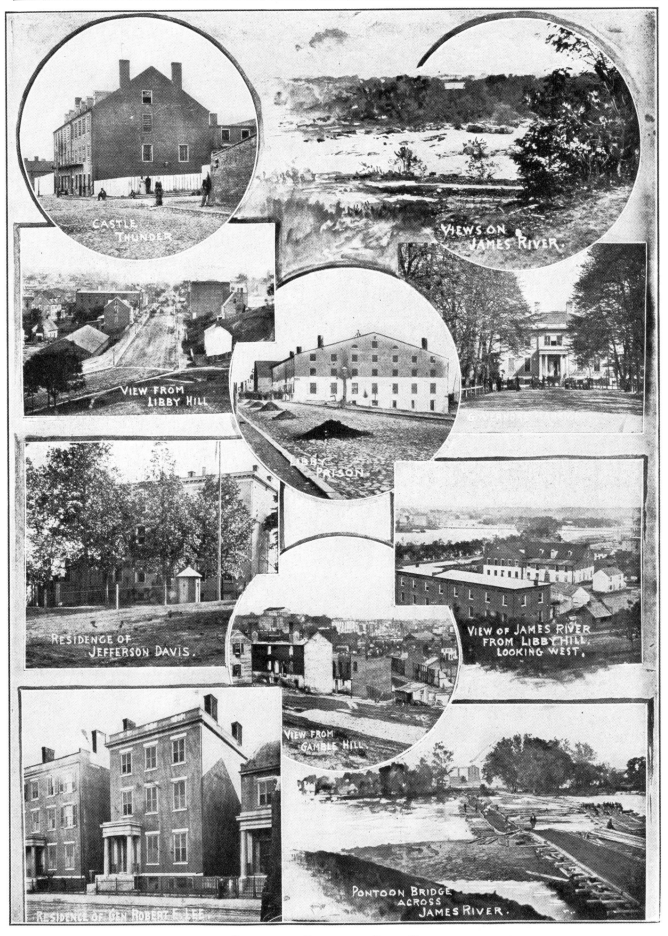

CASTLE THUNDER

VIEWS ON JAMES RIVER.

VIEW FROM LIBBY HILL

LIBBY PRISON

RESIDENCE OF JEFFERSON DAVIS.

VIEW OF JAMES RIVER FROM LIBBY HILL, LOOKING WEST.

VIEW FROM GAMBLE HILL.

RESIDENCE OF GEN. ROBERT E. LEE.

PONTOON BRIDGE ACROSS JAMES RIVER.

Confederate Prisons and Other Views

CHAPTER XXVII.—Continued

ANDERSONVILLE PRISON

IN a speech to the populace of the capital on the 22d of February, 1866—a speech which every good American would gladly blot from memory and from the records of our country, if possible—the President, evidently under the malign influence of an unfortunate habit, forgetting the dignity of his station, and insensible to the gravity of the question at issue, actually denounced by name leading members of Congress, and the Republican party which had given him their generous confidence.

But this exhibition was a small matter compared with what occurred later in the year (August and September, 1866) when the President and a part of his cabinet, with the pretext of honoring the memory of Senator Douglas by being present at the dedication of a monument to his memory erected at Chicago, on the 6th of September, made a political tour by a circuitous way through several States, to that city and beyond. He harangued the people by the way, in language utterly unbecoming the Chief Magistrate of a nation, and attempted to sow the dangerous seeds of sedition, by denouncing Congress as an illegal body because some of the disorganized States were not represented in it; declaring that it deserved no respect from the people, and that a majority of the members were traitors, "trying to break up the Government." That journey of the President, so disgraceful in all its features—its low partisan object, its immoral performances, and its pitiful results—forms a dismal paragraph in the history of the Republic.

That tour was suggested and its performances were inspired by the gathering in convention, at Philadelphia, on the 14th of August (1866), chiefly of men who had been engaged in the insurrection, and their sympathizers at the North. Their object was to form a new party, with President Johnson as their standard-bearer; but so discordant were the elements gathered there, that no one was allowed to debate questions of public interest, for fear of producing a disruption and the consequent failure of the scheme. It did utterly fail. Soon afterward a convention of loyal men from the South was held at Philadelphia, in which representative Republicans in the North participated. The President's journey being wholly for a partisan purpose, members of the latter convention followed in his track, making speeches in many places in support of the measures of Congress for effecting reorganization. They applied the antidote where the President had administered poison, and neutralized its effects.

So disgraceful was the conduct of the President when at Cleveland and St. Louis, in the attitude of a mere demagogue making a tour for a partisan purpose, under a false pretense, that the Common Council of Cincinnati, on his return journey, refused to accord him a public reception. The Common Council of Pittsburg, in Pennsylvania, did the same; and when, on the 15th of September, Mr. Johnson and his party returned to the Capital, the country felt a relief from a sense of deep mortification.

Having, soon after the meeting of Congress, laid aside the mask of assumed friendship for those who had

LIEUT. G. A. MORRIS, COMMANDANT OF THE "CUMBERLAND"
REAR ADMIRAL J. SMITH

OLD CAPITAL PRISON, WASHINGTON. PAT WIRZ, IN CHARGE OF ANDERSONVILLE PRISON, WAS EXECUTED HERE IN 1865

GUNBOAT MENDOTA ON THE JAMES RIVER

labored most earnestly for the suppression of the insurrection and for the good of the freedmen, the President used the veto power—his most efficient weapon—in trying to thwart the representatives of the people in their efforts to reorganize the disorganized States, and to quickly secure a full and permanent restoration of the Union on the basis of equal and exact justice.   In February, 1866, he vetoed an act for enlarging the operations of the Freedmen's Bureau, which had been established for the relief of freedmen, refugees, and for the cultivation of abandoned lands.   In March he vetoed an act known as the Civil Rights Law, which was intended to secure to *all* citizens, without regard to color or previous condition of slavery, equal civil rights in the Republic.   These acts became laws in spite of his veto, by the Constitutional vote of two-thirds of each House in their favor.   The President's uncompromising warfare upon the legislative branch of the Republic disgusted his ministers, who could not agree with him, and they resigned with the exception of Edwin M. Stanton, the Secretary of War.   The friends of the Republic urged him to remain, believing his retention of the bureau at that critical period in the life of the nation would be conducive to the public benefit.   He did so, and became the object of the mad President's bitter hatred.

ADMIRAL JOHN RODGERS, U. S. N.

Congress worked assiduously in efforts to perfect the reorganization of the Republic; and on the 29th of July, after a long and laborious session, adjourned.   On the 2d of April, the President, in a proclamation, had formally declared the Civil War to be at an end; and the first fruits of the Congressional plan of reorganization was seen by the restoration of the State of Tennessee to the Union, six days before the adjournment of the National Legislature.   Meanwhile notable events in the foreign relations of the Government had occurred.   The Emperor of the French had been informed by Secretary Seward that the continuation of French troops in Mexico was not agreeable to the United States; and on the 5th of April (1866) Napoleon's Minister for Foreign Affairs gave assurances to our Government that those troops would be withdrawn within a specified time.   This was done; and the Grand Duke Maximilian, of Austria, whom Louis Napoleon had, by military power, placed on a throne in our neighboring republic, with the title of Emperor, was deserted by the perfidious ruler of France.   The deceived and betrayed Maximilian, after struggling against the native republican government for a while, was captured and shot; and his loving wife, Carlotta, overwhelmed by her misfortunes and grief, became a hopeless lunatic.   Such was the sorrowful ending of one of the schemes of the Emperor of the French for the gratification of his ambition.   He had itched to aid the Confederates, with a hope that the severance of our Union would give him an opportunity to successfully defy the "Monroe Doctrine," and extend the domination of the Latin race and the Latin church on the American continent, as well as monarchical institutions.   As a pretext for sending soldiers to our frontiers, primarily to be ready to assist the enemies of the Republic should expediency warrant the act, the Emperor of the French picked a quarrel with Mexico, overturned its republican government, established a monarchy and supported it by French bayonets until the strength of our Union was made manifest to him.

The British ministry, too, as we have seen, itched to help the Confederates destroy our Republic, and had done so in a large degree, until they were satisfied of the enormous reserved power of our Union against the combined and cowardly attacks of European powers and of internal foes, when they abandoned the insurgents whom they had deceived with false promises, and sneeringly called their political organization the "so-called Confederate States of America."   Notwithstanding this faithlessness to their traditions, and fairly

FIELD HOSPITAL AT SAVAGE STATION, JUNE, 1862

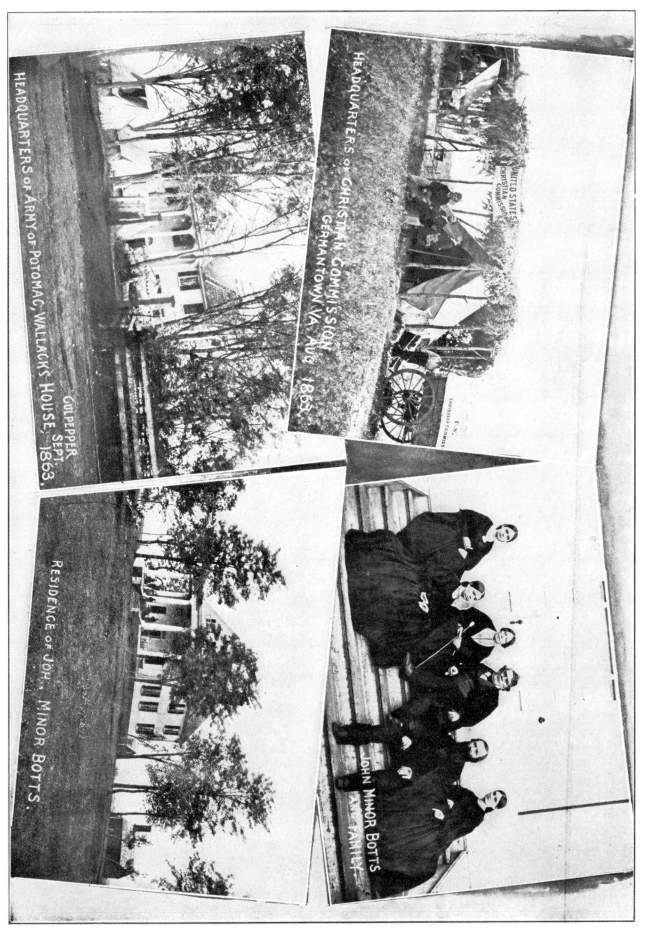

HEADQUARTERS OF CHRISTIAN COMMISSION GERMANTOWN VA. AUG. 1863.

UNITED STATES CHRISTIAN COMMISSION

U.S. CHRISTIAN COMMISS.

HEADQUARTERS OF ARMY OF POTOMAC, WALLACK'S HOUSE, SEPT. 1863. CULPEPPER.

RESIDENCE OF JOH. MINOR BOTTS.

JOHN MINOR BOTTS AND FAMILY.

HEADQUARTERS OF THE CHRISTIAN COMMISSION AND OTHER VIEWS

MISS CLARA BARTON

A nurse during the Civil War. Organized the American Red Cross Society in 1881. Died in Washington, April, 1912.

implied, if not absolutely stated, treaty stipulations on the part of the rulers of Great Britain, our Government was faithful to them all. When, in the spring of 1866, a military organization of Irish residents in our country, known as the Fenian Brotherhood, associated for the avowed purpose of freeing Ireland from British domination, made a movement, in May and June, for a formidable invasion of the neighboring British Province of Canada, the United States Government, instead of investing them with "belligerent rights," was true to its pledges to Great Britain concerning neutrality laws, interfered, and suppressed the warlike movement. But these are now things of the past, and should not be held in remembrance with any unkind feelings. At about the same

WALT WHITMAN AS A NURSE
IN THE CIVIL WAR

time a peaceful bond of union was formed with Great Britain, by the successful establishment of permanent telegraphic communication between England and the United States. An account of the first efforts toward this end will be given hereafter.

Notwithstanding the State elections in the autumn of 1866 indicated the decided approval by the

BVT. MAJ GEN. J. N. PALMER.

BVT MAJ GEN. VAN CLEVE.

BVT MAJ GEN. T. J. WOOD

MAJ GEN. F. T. HERRON.

BVT MAJ GEN. A. P. BLUNT

GROUP OF FEDERAL GENERALS

EXECUTIVE COMMITTEE OF THE SANITARY FAIR. PORTRAIT OF JOSEPH CHOATE AND OTHERS

GENERAL JOHN A. DIX AND SANITARY FAIR COMMISSION

CAMP OF THE 50TH NEW YORK ENGINEERS

people of the United States of the measures adopted by Congress for the restoration of the Union, the President persisted in his warfare with the National Legislature, and upon members of his cabinet who would not approve of his acts. The majority in Congress, feeling strengthened by the popular verdict upon their conduct, went steadily forward in perfecting measures for the restoration of the Union. They took steps for restraining the action of the President, who, it was manifest, had determined to carry out

BRIG.-GENERAL J. J. PETTIGREW, C. S. A.

GENERAL G. J. RAINS, C. S. A.   MAJOR-GENERAL W. MALONE, C. S. A.
LIEUT.-GENERAL D. H. HILL, C. S. A.   MAJOR-GENERAL R. E. RODER, C. S. A.

HEADQUARTERS OF THE SANITARY COMMISSION, RICHMOND

HEADQUARTERS OF THE CHRISTIAN COMMISSION, RICHMOND

GENERAL GEORGE SYKES AND STAFF

his own policy of reorganization, in defiance of Congress. Unmindful of his conduct, that body plainly indicated their general policy concerning suffrage, by passing a bill on the 14th of December (1866), by a large majority of both Houses, for granting the elective franchise in the District of Columbia (over whose affairs the National Legislature has direct control) to persons "without any distinction on account of color or race." The President vetoed the bill on the 7th of January, 1867, when it was immediately re-enacted by the vote of both Houses.

The course of the President in continually opposing his veto and casting obstacles in the way of the despatch of legislative business, now appeared so essentially and purely factious, and was, withal, so mischievous, that it was resolved to make an effort to put an end to it. On the same day when Johnson vetoed the District of Columbia Suffrage bill, Mr. Ashley, a representative from Ohio, arose in his place, and charged "Andrew Johnson, Vice-President and Acting President of the United States, with the commission of acts which, in the estimation of the Constitution, are high crimes and misdemeanors, for which he ought to be impeached." Mr. Ashley offered the following specifications, in which he charged him with usurpations and violations of law: (1) in that he has corruptly used the appointing power; (2) in that he has corruptly used the pardoning power; (3) in that he has corruptly used the veto power; (4) in that he has corruptly disposed of public property of the United States; and (5) in that he has corruptly interfered in elections, and committed acts which, in contemplation of the Constitution, are high crimes and misdemeanors. Mr. Ashley also offered a resolution, instructing the Committee on the Judiciary to make inquiries on the subject. This resolution was adopted by 137 to 38, forty-five members not voting. It was the first movement in the matter of the impeachment of the President, which resulted in his trial in May, 1868.

At a former session of Congress, bills were passed for the admission of the Territories of Colorado and Nebraska, as States of the Union. The President had interposed. Now similar bills were passed prescribing, as a preliminary to admission, a provision in their constitutions granting impartial suffrage to all citizens, and the ratification of the amendment to the National Constitution. As usual the President vetoed them; when that for the admission of Nebraska was passed over his veto. Colorado was compelled to wait ten years and six months for admission, while Nebraska took its place in the galaxy of States on the first of March (1867), making the thirty-eighth State.

An act was now passed for the purpose of limiting the authority of the President in making official appointments and removals from office. Among other provisions of the act was one that took from him the power to remove a member of his cabinet without permission of the Senate; declaring that they should hold office "for and during the term of the President by whom they may have been appointed, and for one month thereafter, subject to removal by and with the consent of the Senate." This law, known as the "Tenure of Office Act," was vetoed by the President, when it was passed over his negative by a large majority. Another bill was passed and vetoed and was made a law notwithstanding, repealing so much of an act passed in July, 1862, as gave the President power to grant amnesty and pardon to those who had been engaged in rebellion. A bill was also passed, with the same opposition of the President, for the military government of the disorganized States, which were divided into five military districts, Virginia comprising the *first;* North and South Carolina the *second;* Georgia, Florida and Alabama, the *third;* Mississippi and Arkansas, the *fourth;* and Louisiana and Texas, the *fifth.*

The Thirty-ninth Congress closed its sessions at mid-day, on the 4th of March, 1867, and twelve hours afterward the first session of the Fortieth Congress was begun. The country was greatly disquieted by the

GENERAL RUGGLES, C. S. A.

Camp of Sanitary Commission and Other Views

factious conduct of the President, which created painful forebodings of evil should that obstinate and angry man be left without restraint from March until December. The majority in Congress shared in this feeling, believing that the President was ready, if he should deem it expedient, to plunge the country into a revolution, and attempt, by a reactionary movement, to undo all that the war for the Union had done for the preservation of the Republic. For that reason, provision had been made by the Thirty-ninth Congress for the immediate assembling of the Fortieth on the expiration of its predecessor. That first session continued until the 30th of March, when, with the same lack of confidence in the

COLONEL TOWNSEND

LIEUT.-COLONEL G. K. WARREN

LIEUT. JOHN TROUT GREBLE
(Killed in the Battle of Big Bethel)
COLONEL BENDIX

COLONEL WARREN

COLONEL ABRAM DURYER

GENERAL EDWARD FERRERO AND STAFF. THIS IS NEGATIVE NO. 1 IN THE WAR DEPARTMENT

GENERAL A. T. A. TORBERT AND STAFF

MAJOR-GENERAL W. B. FRANKLIN　　　　　GENERAL E. D. KEYES
BVT. BRIG.-GENERAL O. H. HART

patriotism of Johnson, both Houses adjourned to meet on the 3d of July following.

Among the acts of the expiring Congress was one for the establishment of a National Bureau of Education which has become a most valuable auxiliary in the work of popular instruction. Also an act to establish a uniform system of bankruptcy throughout the United States; and another for the abolition of peonage—a system of slavery—in the Territory of New Mexico and other parts of the United States wherever it might exist.

Congress reassembled on the 3d of July, and adjourned on the 20th to the 21st of November. The principal business of this short session was to remove impediments which President Johnson had cast in the way of the reorganization of the Union. A bill supplementary to the act of March, for the military government of the disorganized States, became a law, notwithstanding it was vetoed by the President; and it was hoped

MAJOR-GENERAL W. H. FRENCH　　　BVT. MAJOR-GENERAL G. H. GORDON　　　MAJOR-GENERAL G. L. HARTSUFF

SCENES AT HEADQUARTERS OF THE ARMY OF THE POTOMAC, JUNE, 1863

and believed that Johnson would refrain from further acts that were calculated to disturb the public peace and impede the prosperity of the country. This expectation was not realized. When the members of Congress had returned to their homes, the President proceeded, in defiance of the acts of that body, and in positive violation of the Tenure of Office Act, to remove the Secretary of War (Mr. Stanton) and put General Grant in his place. On the 5th of August (1867) the President sent a note to Mr. Stanton, in which he said: "Grave public considerations constrain me to request your resignation as Secretary of War." Mr. Stanton, sharing in the general suspicion that the President contemplated reactionary measures in the absence of Congress in favor of the defeated enemies of the Republic, and was seeking a means for using the army for that purpose, immediately replied: "Grave public considerations constrain me to remain in the office of Secretary of War until the next meeting of Congress."

BRIG. GEN. J. M. SHACKLEFORD.

BRIG GEN. J. T. WILDER.

BRIG.-GEN. A. D. STRAIGHT

Only a week had elapsed after this correspondence, when Johnson directed General Grant to assume the position and duties of the Secretary of War. Grant, as a dutiful soldier, obeyed the commands of his superior, when Stanton, satisfied of the firmness and incorruptible patriotism of the general-in-chief of the armies, withdrew, under protest. This change was followed by such arbitrary acts on the part of the President, that the country was thoroughly alarmed. In the face of the most earnest protests of General Grant, in the War Office, Johnson removed Generals Sheridan and Sickles from the command of the Fifth and Second Military Districts. By this act the country was given to understand that the most faithful officers, who were able and willing to work for the speedy restoration of the Union, would be deprived of the power to be useful. He also issued, in defiance of law, a proclamation of amnesty for nearly the whole white population of the Southern States. These, and other unlawful acts, made the loyal inhabitants impatient for the reassembling of Congress, upon whom they relied in that dark hour of seeming peril.

Patriotic men of the opposition party, and even personal friends of the erring President, were amazed and mortified by his unwise conduct; and some of the latter charitably attributed these paroxysms of blind obstinacy to the effects of an unfortunate habit into which Mr. Johnson had fallen, and which appalled them at the time when he took the oath of office as Vice-President, in March, 1865. One of these friends—a distinguished politician—writing from Washington just after the removal of Sheridan and Sickles, said: "The President must be crazy. Does he suppose the country will much longer tolerate this unseemly warfare upon the Legislative branch of the Government? You and I know that he has not a single legitimate ground for his conduct, and that several of his acts are pure usurpations for which he may be impeached. It is neither just nor prudent for the Democratic party to countenance them; and it is in the highest degree impolitic for them to do so at this crisis. It is the best policy always to do right, for, in the long run, the right will prevail."

CHAPTER XXVIII.

THE second session of the Fortieth Congress commenced on the 2d of December, 1867. The President's annual message was so offensive in tone and temper, that when the usual resolution to print it was offered in the Senate, Mr. Sumner took fire and vehemently denounced it as a "libel," an "insult to Congress," and an "incendiary document, calculated to stimulate the rebellion once more, and to provoke Civil War. It is a direct appeal," he said, "to the worst passions and the worst

GENERALS GRANT, BADEAU, RAWLINS, COMSTOCK AND PORTER AND COLONELS DUFF, F. D. DENT, ROBINETT AND PARKER

GENERAL CHARLES GRIFFIN AND OFFICERS

prejudices of those rebels who, being subdued on the battle-field, still resist, through the aid of the President of the United States. It is an evidence of a direct coalition between the President and the former rebels." Senator Wilson, wiser and less impulsive than his colleague, while he as decidedly condemned "the tone and temper and doctrines of the message," saying in calm and dignified language that the President seemed to "have forgotten that we have had any rebellion at all," and pointing out the flagrant inconsistency of his conduct, nevertheless opposed a departure from the ordinary practice of the Senate in ordering the President's Message to be printed, and it was done.

A majority of the Judiciary Committee, to whom the charges against the President had been referred, for inquiry, reported the following resolution on the 5th of December: "*Resolved*, That Andrew Johnson, President of the United States, be impeached of high crimes and misdemeanors." In the course of the debate that ensued, Mr. Boutwell, of the majority of the Committee, submitted facts which proved that Mr. Johnson had long contemplated a desertion of the party that had elevated him; that while on his way to Washington to be inaugurated Vice-President of the Republic, he had confidentially avowed to an old Democratic partisan with whom he had acted before the war, that he preferred the party opposed to the administration of Mr. Lincoln, and that the country could yet be saved from ruin through that party only. It was also proven

ENGLISH OFFICERS

STAFF OFFICERS

TOPOGRAPHICAL ENGINEERS AT GENERAL
McCLELLAN'S HEADQUARTERS

that he and his friends had declared that his policy toward the enemies of his country and the freedmen before June, 1865, was only temporary and for a special object, and that he had since persistently pursued a course calculated to place the country under the control of those who had tried to destroy the Union. Notwithstanding this attitude of the President, so menacing to the good of the Republic, was well established, the House, hoping he might cease his impotent warfare upon Congress, hesitated to adopt extreme measures toward the erring Chief Magistrate, unless he should yet commit some flagrant act of disobedience to law. The resolution was, therefore, rejected by a decided majority.

A week later the President sent to Congress a message, in which he gave his reasons for the removal of Secretary Stanton. The reasons were not satisfactory; and, a month later (January 13, 1868), the Senate reinstated the former Secretary of War, when General Grant quietly retired from the office. This act enraged the President, and he reproached the general-in-chief for yielding to the implied commands of the Senate to retire. He charged him with having broken his promises; and Johnson tried to injure Grant's reputation as a citizen and a soldier. In the correspondence between them, which found its way to the public, a question of veracity between the President and the general-in-chief arose; and, finally, the latter felt compelled to say to the irate Chief Magistrate: "When my honor as a soldier and my integrity as a man have been so violently assailed, pardon me for saying that I can but regard this whole matter, from beginning to end, as an attempt to involve me in the resistance of law for which you hesitated to assume the responsibility in orders, and thus to destroy my character before the country." The President did not deny the truth of this damaging charge, and the correspondence ceased.

Congress now steadily advanced in the adoption of measures for the restoration of the Union on the basis of justice, by providing for conventions of the people in the disorganized States for forming new revising old constitutions, and electing representatives in the National Legislature. They had also, by law, given enlarged powers to the general-in-chief for the administration of military government in those States, and had deprived the President of power to interfere in the matter, when Mr. Johnson startled the country by an act bolder in aspect than any he had yet attempted. It was the issuing of an order on

OFFICERS AT HEADQUARTERS.

OFFICERS OF SIGNAL CORPS.

GROUP OF OFFICERS.

WAGONS AND HORSES. QUARTERMASTER'S REPAIR SHOP.

QUARTERS OF Gen. PATRICK. PROVOST MARSHAL GENERAL.

HEADQUARTERS OF NEW YORK HERALD IN THE FIELD.

OFFICERS 93RD N.Y. INFANTRY.

STAFF OFFICERS 93RD N.Y. INFANTRY.

HEADQUARTERS OF THE ARMY OF THE POTOMAC AND OTHER VIEWS

the 21st of February (1868) directing Mr. Stanton to vacate the office of Secretary of War; also another order to Adjutant-General Lorenzo B. Thomas, to enter and take the place of the deposed Secretary. These orders were officially communicated to the Senate on the same day, and drew from that body a resolution that the President had no authority, under the Constitution, for his act. Meanwhile Thomas had proceeded to the War Department and demanded the seals and the authority with which the President had invested him. Mr. Stanton, his official superior, refused to yield them, and ordered Thomas to return to the duties of his proper office. The President, satisfied that he would not be permitted to use military force to eject Mr. Stanton, did not attempt it, and that officer retained his place.

The patience and forbearance of Congress were now exhausted. This action of the President was such a flagrant violation of law and open defiance of the Legislature, that on the following day (February 22, 1868) the House of Representatives, by a vote of 126 to 47—an almost strictly party vote (only two Republicans voting with the minority)—"*Resolved*, That Andrew Johnson, President of the United States, be impeached of high crimes and misdemeanors." A week later, a committee of the House, appointed for the purpose, presented articles of impeachment, nine in number; and these, with slight alterations, were accepted.

They charged: (1) Unlawfully ordering the removal of Mr. Stanton, as Secretary of War, in violation of the provisions of the Tenure of Office Act; (2) unlawfully appointing General Lorenzo B. Thomas, as Secretary of War *ad interim;* (3) substantially the same as the second charge, with the additional declaration that there was, at the time of the appointment of General Thomas, no vacancy in the office of the Secretary of War; (4) conspiring with one Lorenzo Thomas, and other persons to the House unknown, to prevent, by intimidation and threats, Mr. Stanton, the legally appointed Secretary of War, from holding office; (5) conspiring with General Thomas and others to hinder the execution of the Tenure of Office Act, and, in pursuance of this conspiracy, attempting to prevent Mr. Stanton from acting as Secretary of War; (6) conspiring with General Thomas and others to take forcible possession of the property in the War Department; (7) and (8) substantially the charge of conspiring to prevent the execution of the Tenure of Office Act, and for taking possession of the War Department; (9) charged that the President called before him the commander of the forces in the Department of Washington, and declared to him that a law, passed on the 30th of June, 1867, directing that "all orders and instructions relating to military operations, issued by the President or Secretary of War, shall be issued by the General of the Army, and in case of his inability, through the next in rank," was unconstitutional, and not binding upon the commander of the Department of Washington; the intent being to induce the commander to violate the law.

Thaddeus Stevens of Pennsylvania, Benjamin F. Butler of Massachusetts, John A. Bingham of Ohio, George S. Boutwell of Massachusetts, James F. Wilson of Iowa, Thomas Williams of Pennsylvania, and John A. Logan of Illinois, were appointed managers of the impeachment case, on the part of the House of Representatives. The chief management of the case was intrusted to Mr. Butler. At this stage of the proceedings the Democratic members of the House, to the number of forty-five, entered a formal protest against the whole action in the matter.

On the 3d of March (1868) the managers presented two additional charges against the President, which were adopted by the House, as a part of the impeachment indictment. The first charged that the President had, by inflammatory speeches during his journey, already mentioned, attempted, with a design to cast aside the authority of Congress, to bring that body into disgrace, and to excite the odium and resentment of the people against Congress and the laws they enacted. The second charged that in August, 1866, the President, in a public speech at Washington, declared that Congress was not a body authorized

SENTRY DUTY IN WINTER

SUMMER CAMP SCENE

by the Constitution to exercise legislative powers. They then specified many of the President's offences in endeavoring, by unlawful means, to prevent the execution of laws passed by Congress.

These preliminary proceedings toward impeachment filled the loyal heart of the nation with the most profound satisfaction. Letters and telegrams covered the desks of members of Congress, all urging the most speedy and vigorous action toward impeachment. Appended is a copy of a despatch from Governor Oglesby, of Illinois, which is a fair specimen of the tone of the communications and expressive of the feelings of the people. It is dated "Springfield, Illinois; Executive Mansion, February 22, 1868," and is as follows:

GENERAL JOHN B. GORDON, C. S. A.

"The usurpations of Andrew Johnson have created a profound sensation in this State. His last act is that of a traitor. His treason must be checked. The duty of Congress seems plain. The people of Illinois, attached to the Union, I firmly believe demand his impeachment, and will heartily sustain such action by Congress. The peace of the country is not to be trifled with by this presumptuous demagogue. We know the National Congress will proceed wisely and cautiously; but let it proceed. Millions of loyal hearts are panting to stand by the Stars and Stripes. Have no fear. All will be well. Liberty and order will again triumph."

On the 25th of February, Messrs. Stevens and Boutwell appeared before the Senate in behalf of the managers, and in the name of the people of the United States, impeached "Andrew Johnson of high crimes and misdemeanors," and demanded of that body an order for the accused President to answer the impeachment. The Senate, by a provision of the National Constitution, composes a jury for the trial of such cases; and on the 5th of March (1868) it was organized as such, with Chief-Justice Salmon P. Chase as president of the court. The accused was summoned to appear at the bar on the 7th; but the Senate was not formally opened as a High Court of Impeachment until the 13th, when he did so appear, by his counsel, who asked for a delay of forty days wherein to prepare an answer to the indictment. Ten days were granted, and the answer was presented on the 23d, when the House of Representatives, which was the accuser, solemnly denied every averment of that answer. Then the President's counsel asked for a postponement of the trial for thirty days, but only seven were allowed.

On the 30th of March the trial was begun. Public feeling was profoundly excited by the event, and there was danger that the reason and judgment of the Senate might be swayed by unwise influences. Fortunately there were men in that body whose prescience clearly comprehended the future, and they were governed by that more than by their feelings or the mandates of present expediency. All through the trial, these men counselled moderation, and their advice was heeded. They pointed out the danger, that a verdict of guilty might create greater evils than the foolish President could possibly inflict, in his comparatively helpless state. When, after an examination of witnesses, which was concluded on the 22d of April, the presentation of the arguments of counsel, which continued until the 5th of May, and the debates, which consumed twenty days more, the votes of the fifty-four Senators present were taken on the verdict, *thirty-five* of them were for conviction, and *nineteen* were for acquittal. Some of the latter votes were by Republicans. As two-thirds of the votes were necessary for conviction, the President was acquitted by one vote.

This verdict caused Secretary Stanton to send a letter to the President, informing him that as the resolution of the Senate reinstating the Secretary had not been supported by two-thirds of that body present and voting upon the articles of impeachment, he had relinquished the office; whereupon Mr. Johnson nominated General John M. Schofield to be Mr. Stanton's successor. The President, in his communication nominating General Schofield, said he was to succeed "E. M. Stanton, removed." The Senate adopted the following preamble and resolution: "Whereas, the order of the President removing Secretary Stanton from office was unconstitutional and illegal; but on account of Mr. Stanton having, on Tuesday, relinquished said office, therefore, *Resolved*, That the Senate do advise and consent to the appointment of General Schofield."

BRIG.-GENERAL L. C. BAKER OF THE
SECRET SERVICE

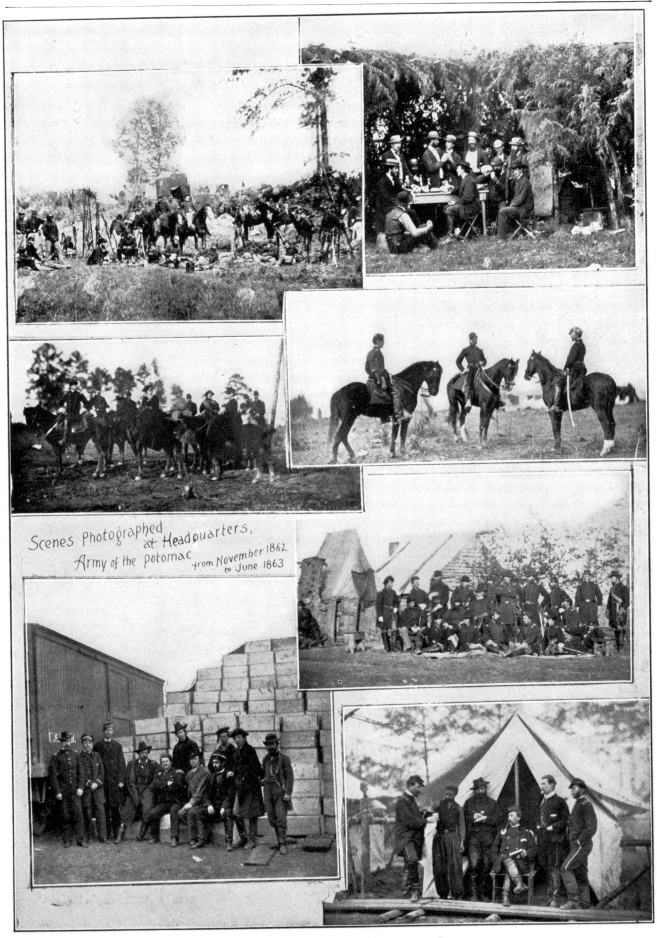

Scenes photographed at Headquarters, Army of the Potomac, from November 1862 to June 1863

SCENES AT HEADQUARTERS OF THE ARMY OF THE POTOMAC

The brilliancy and intrinsic value of General Grant's military services in behalf of the Republic, and his firmness and patriotism in defeating the designs of President Johnson at the capital, endeared him to the loyal people; and on the 19th of June (1868) the Republicans, in National Convention assembled at Chicago, nominated him for President of the United States, and Schuyler Colfax of Indiana for Vice-President. On the 4th of July following, a National Convention of representatives of the Democratic party met in Tammany Hall, in the city of New York, and nominated Horatio Seymour of the State of New York for President, and Francis P. Blair of Missouri for Vice-President. Wade Hampton, N. B. Forrest, and other prominent Confederate leaders, were members of that Convention, and were controlling architects of the platform there adopted, in which the acts of Congress for the reorganization of the Union were declared to be "usurpations, unconstitutional, revolutionary and void."

AT MESS

A few days before the meeting of the Convention, General Blair, the nominee for Vice-President, wrote a letter to James O. Brodhead, to be used at the Convention. In that letter he said, in contemplation of the election of the nominees: "There is but one way to restore the Government and the Constitution, and that is for the President-elect to declare these acts of Congress null and void; compel the army to undo its usurpations at the South; disperse the carpet-bag State governments (governments established under the authority of Congress); allow the white people to organize their own governments, and elect Senators and Representatives. The House of Representatives will contain a majority of Democrats from the North, and they will admit the Representatives elected by the white people of the South; and with the co-operation of the President, it will not be difficult to compel the Senate to submit, once more, to the obligations of the Constitution."

This revolutionary scheme—a scheme for inaugurating another Civil War—was so acceptable to the Convention, that its author was nominated for the second office in the gift of the people. But it was so distasteful to vast numbers of the patriotic and thinking members of the Democratic party, that the nominees were defeated at the polls by an overwhelming vote that elected Grant and Colfax.

During the unfortunate and unseemly controversy between President Johnson and the National Congress, the work of reorganization, according to the plans of the latter, had been going forward vigorously in spite of the factious interference of the Chief Magistrate. A Fourteenth Amendment had been proposed by a joint resolution of Congress, adopted on the 13th of June, 1866. This amendment had been ratified by a sufficient number of States to make it a part of the supreme law of the land, in July, 1868, and on the 28th of that month the fact was officially promulgated by the Secretary of State. That amendment secured the rights of citizenship to all persons "born or naturalized in the United States and subject to the jurisdiction thereof"; politically disabled a certain class of chief offenders in the insurrection; declared the validity of the National debt; and forbade the payment of any part of the so-called "Confederate" debt. Refer to the National Constitution, in the Appendix, for the text of this amendment.

Seven of the disorganized States, namely, North Carolina, South Carolina, Georgia, Alabama, Mississippi, Louisiana and Texas, had ratified the amendment; and having, by that act, by the adoption of State constitutions approved by Congress, and by the election of National Senators and Representatives, complied with the prescriptions of Congress, they took their places as revived States of the Union. But the perfect reorganization was not effected until the spring of 1872, when, on the 23d of May, the remaining three States having taken their places with their sisters, every seat in Congress was filled, for the first time since the winter of 1861, when members from several of the slave-labor States abdicated them. On the previous day (May 22, 1872) an Amnesty Bill was passed for removing the political disabilities imposed by the third section of the Fourteenth Amendment of the Constitution, from all persons excepting members of the Thirty-sixth Congress, heads of

GENERAL MANSFIELD LOVELL, C. S. A.

The "Commander Barney" Used as a Gunboat

Camp Butler Near Springfield, Ill.

departments, members of diplomatic corps, and officers of the army and navy, who had engaged in the rebellion.

At a little past midsummer (1868), when all but three States had been reorganized and civil government had been established in the restored States, the general-in-chief issued a proclamation (July 28)

declaring that so much of the "reconstruction" acts as provided for military rule in the South, had become inoperative. At the same time the President continued to display his factious spirit in a most ludicrous and futile manner. He asserted that the State governments in the South, established by an illegal Congress, were illegal, and, consequently, their ratification of the Fourteenth Amendment was of no effect, and it was not ratified. In order to forestall and weaken the operation of a part of that amendment, he issued a proclamation on the 4th of July (1868) declaring general and unconditional pardon and amnesty for all who had been engaged in acts of rebellion, excepting a few who were under presentment or indictment for the offence. This conduct of the President was so foreboding of mischief, that when Congress took a recess in August, it was agreed to meet again in September, should the public good require; but the Presidential election absorbed so much of the attention of Mr. Johnson and the whole people, that there was a lull in the war between the Executive and Legislative branches of the Government, and the recess continued until the regular session in December. Very soon after Congress met, the President made another foolish onslaught upon the authority of that body when, on Christmas day, he issued a proclamation which declared, in defiance of the provisions of

GENERAL JAMES LONGSTREET, C. S. A.

the Fourteenth Amendment, unconditional and unreserved pardon to *all and every person* who had participated in the late rebellion.

Before the adjournment of Congress for the recess, the Senate had ratified an important treaty with China, which Anson Burlingame, the American ambassador in that country, had negotiated. It established mutual intercourse between the citizens of the United States and those of China, and secured to each mutual and equal privileges of trade, travel, education, and religion. This was a concession never before made by the Chinese to any nation. Mr. Burlingame brought the treaty with him, and was accompanied by several high Chinese officials. He had won the entire confidence of the government, and had been appointed by the Emperor a general Commissioner to several of the Christian powers.

The result of the Presidential election gave increased strength to the Republican party. This condition implied increased responsibility, and the need of wisdom and sound judgment in the management of public affairs. The incidents of the war had produced causes of irritation between the governments of the United States and Great Britain, and most delicate questions of national responsibility had been raised. At home, that chronic evil, war with the Indians, was then raging on the great Western Plains; and there was a wide difference of opinion in the public mind as to the best methods of putting an end to the strife. There was great exasperation on both sides, along the frontiers. There was an abiding sense of mutual injury; while all well-informed persons had a clear conviction that the deep-rooted animosity of the Indians toward the white people was occasioned by the rank injustice which the former had suffered at the hands of the latter. With this conviction there was a widespreading desire that a policy toward the barbarians, founded on justice and kindness, should be pursued. But military leaders in the war, contemplating the barbarians from a point of view opposite to that occupied by the Christian philanthropist, recommended the most vigorous and unrelenting measures toward them, and for that purpose it was proposed to vest the entire control of the Indians in the War Department. "Indian tribes," said a distinguished general, "should not be dealt with as independent nations; they are wards of the Government, and should be made to respect the lives and property of citizens. The Indian history of this country for the last three hundred years shows that of all the great nations of Indians, only remnants have been saved. The same fate awaits those now hostile; and the best way for the Government is to

GENERAL WILLIAM MAHONE, C. S. A.

HOUSE USED AS HOSPITAL FOR HOOKER'S DIVISION

SICKLE'S BRIGADE COMING INTO LINE.

HOUSE NEAR WHICH OVER 400 SOLDIERS WERE BURIED

QUARLES HOUSE

HOUSE USED AS HOSPITAL

EARTHWORKS AT EXTREME FRONT.

THE BATTLEFIELD OF FAIR OAKS AND OTHER VIEWS

make them poor by the destruction of their stock, and then settle them on the lands allotted them." Another general, equally distinguished, formulated the estimate of the Indian character by the average frontiersmen, by saying, "The only good Indian is a dead Indian."

These indefensible propositions and this unjust judgment have been too long the inspiration of our methods of treating the Indians. Fortunately the ethics of the mailed hand—Might makes Right—does not wholly prevail, and a more humane policy has been adopted. President Grant, soon after his inauguration in the spring of 1869, recommended the appointment, as Indian agents, of several members of the Society of Friends, or Quakers, who are noted for their uprightness and peaceful principles and conduct. Congress approved the recommendation of the President, and early in April (1869) sixteen Friends were chosen to carry out the policy of justice.

The radical defect in the general policy of the Government is in its treatment of the barbarians, namely, holding them as *foreigners instead of as citizens*, and mak-

RETURNING TROOPS, WASHINGTON, 1865

ing formal treaties with them; or as *children* having no legal rights. The peace-policy has not yet had a fair trial. Its excellent fruits are seen in many places, and give abundant evidence that if it could be faithfully carried out, under a wiser political plan, it would solve the great problem by pacifying the Indians, and tend to their rapid advancement in civilization. Evidences abound in the later reports of the Commissioner of Indian Affairs, of a rapid advancement of the arts of peace, especially of agriculture, among the Indian tribes. Commissioner E. P. Smith, in his report for 1875, says: "The civilization of the Indians is not only entirely possible, but is fairly under way." He reported that out of the entire Indian population within the domain of the United States (278,963 souls), 40,638 men and boys supported themselves by the labor of their own hands. About one-sixth of the barbarian population in our Republic had become producers! "Five years ago," said the Commissioner, "10,329 Indian families were living in houses. This year shows 19,902; a gain of 92 per cent." He also reported that the number of children attending school was 10,600.

These facts show that our barbarian brethren are capable, not only of civilization, but of becoming orderly and valuable citizens. As a savage hunter, the Indian is expensive. During only six years— 1870 to 1876—our Government made appropriations for the support of the Indians on their reservations (exclusive of the cost of military movements to keep them from "picking and stealing") of the large

RETURNING TROOPS ON PENNSYLVANIA AVENUE, WASHINGTON, 1865

sum of nearly $44,000,000. Treat the Indian as a *man* and a *citizen*, and wars and unprofitable expenditures on his account would cease.

Immediately after the assembling of Congress in December, 1868, Mr. Cragin of New Hampshire offered an amendment of the National Constitution, for securing the elective franchise to the freedmen. The proposition was debated for several weeks, and on the 26th of February, 1869, Congress adopted a joint resolution recommending the following, as a Fifteenth Amendment of the Constitution:

"SECTION 1. The right of citizens of the United States to vote shall not be denied or abridged by the United States, or by any State, on account of race, color, or previous condition of servitude.

"SECTION 2. The Congress, by appropriate legislation, may enforce the provisions of this article."

This amendment was immediately submitted to the authorities of the several States for action, and was ratified by the requisite number. Before the close of that

PRESIDENT JOHNSON, GENERAL GRANT AND OTHERS VIEWING RETURNING TROOPS TO WASHINGTON

STORE-HOUSES AT CITY POINT

session, an important financial bill was adopted, of which the following was the chief provision: "The faith of the United States is solemnly pledged to the payment, in coin, or its equivalent, of all interest-bearing obligations of the United States, except in cases where the law authorizing the issue of any such obligations has expressly provided that the same may be paid in lawful money or other currency than gold and silver." This act was not only just, but expedient. It was intended to strengthen the credit of the Government at home and abroad, and that was accomplished.

LIEUT.-COLONEL HORACE PORTER
OF GRANT'S STAFF

The turbulent administration of Mr. Johnson closed on the 4th of March, 1869, when Ulysses Simpson Grant was inaugurated the eighteenth President of the United States. The oath of office was administered by Chief-Justice Chase, and the Senate confirmed his cabinet appointments, after some necessary changes, as follows: Hamilton Fish, Secretary of State; George S. Boutwell, Secretary of the Treasury; John A. Rawlins, Secretary of War; Adolph E. Borie, Secretary of the Navy; Jacob D. Coxe, Secretary of the Interior; A. J. Creswell, as Postmaster-General; and E. Rockwood Hoar, as Attorney-General.

On the day when Johnson retired from the chair of state, he issued a long address to his countrymen in vindication of his course as Chief Magistrate. He recited his most prominent acts, declaring the necessity for them; and having done this he assailed the majority of the Congress with his usual vehemence of tone, accusing them of acting in "utter disregard of the Constitution." "Since the close of the war," he said, "they have persistently sought to influence the prejudices engendered between the sections, to retard the restoration of peace and harmony, and by every means to keep open and exposed to the poisonous breath of party passion the terrible wounds of a four years' war. They have prevented the return of peace and the restoration of the Union; in every way rendered delusive the purposes, promises and pledges, by which the army was marshalled, treason rebuked, and rebellion crushed, and made the liberties of the people and the rights and powers of the President objects of constant attack."

This public exhibition of the retiring President's weakness; his inaccuracy of statements; his unjust and untrue accusations, and his manifestation of blind anger, mortified his real friends and elicited a smile of pity from those who were assailed. He seemed to forget that he was the *executive* and not the *legislative* or *judicial* branch of the Government; that it was the duty of Congress to make laws, and his to see that they were executed; that after he had expressed his reasons for the disapproval of an act, in a veto message, and that act became a law by a constitutional vote, it was his solemn duty to enforce that law; and that the Supreme Court, and not the Executive, was the sole judge of the constitutionality of an enactment.

The career of Andrew Johnson exhibits a peculiar phase in our social system—the possibilities that wait upon citizens of the most humble origin. Mr. Johnson was born in Raleigh, North Carolina, late in 1808. His parents were poor and lowly; and at the age of four years he was bereft of his father. Without an hour's schooling, he was apprenticed to a tailor at the age of ten years; and during that service he taught himself to read. With his own hands he supported his mother, and with her he moved to Greenville, East Tennessee, when he was eighteen years of age. There he soon married an excellent girl, who taught him to write. The energy of his character, his sobriety and strength of mind, commended him to the citizens, and he was elected alderman of Greenville at the age of twenty, and mayor when he was twenty-one.

GENERAL J. B. HOOD, C. S. A.

Mr. Johnson was possessed of a certain kind of rugged and ready oratory that made him very popular; also the elements and aspirations of an adroit politician; and he made his way upward in the path of distinction by his own indomitable will, passing successively through the offices of alderman, mayor, member of both houses of the Legislature of Tennessee, presidential elector, member of Congress, governor of Tennessee, national Senator, Vice-President, and Acting-President of the United States. His moral nature was more feeble than his ambition, and yielded to it; and in his career as President that weakness prevented his achieving most enviable fame as a patriot and a benefactor of his race.

GAINE'S MILLS, VA.

UNBURIED DEAD ON BATTLEFIELD GAINE'S MILLS.

ELLISTON MILLS, MECHANICSVILLE.

MECHANICSVILLE, VA.

UNBURIED DEAD ON BATTLEFIELD, GAINES MILLS 6

Battlefield of Gaines' Mills and Other Views

CHRONOLOGICAL SUMMARY AND RECORD—Continued

(Continued from Section 14)

APRIL, 1865

1—Five Forks, Va. 1st, 2d and 3d Cavalry Divisions and Fifth Corps. *Union* 124 killed, 706 wounded. *Confed.* 3,000 killed and wounded, 5,500 captured.

2—Fall of Petersburg, Va. Second, Sixth, Ninth and Twenty-fourth Corps. *Union* 296 killed, 2,565 wounded, 500 missing. *Confed.* 3,000 prisoners.

3—Namozin Church and Willicomack, Va. Custer's Cavalry. *Union* 10 killed, 85 wounded.

3—Fall of Richmond, Va. *Confed.* 6,000 prisoners, of whom 5,000 were sick and wounded.

5—Amelia Springs, Va. Crook's Cav. *Union* 20 killed, 96 wounded.

6—Sailor's Creek, Va. Second and Sixth Corps and Sheridan's Cav. *Union* 166 killed, 1,014 wounded. *Confed.* 1,000 killed, 1,800 wounded, 6,000 prisoners.

High Bridge, Appomattox River, Va. Portion of Twenty-fourth Corps. *Union* 10 killed, 31 wounded, 1,000 missing and captured.

7—Farmville, Va. Second Corps. *Union* 655 killed and wounded.

8 and 9—Appomattox C. H., Va. Twenty-fourth Corps, one Division of the Twenty-fifth Corps and Sheridan's Cav. *Union* 200 killed and wounded. *Confed.* 500 killed.

9—Lee surrendered to the Armies of the Potomac and James; Lieut.-Gen. U. S. Grant. *Confed.* 26,000 prisoners.

17—Surrender of Mosby to Maj.-Gen. Hancock. *Confed.* 700 prisoners.

26—Johnson surrendered to the Armies of the Tennessee, Georgia and Ohio; Maj.-Gen. W. T. Sherman. *Confed.* 29,924 prisoners.

MAY, 1865

10—Capture of Jefferson Davis at Irwinsville, Ga. 1st Wis. and 4th Mich. Cav. *Union* 2 killed, 4 wounded, caused by the pursuing parties firing into each other.

Tallahassee, Fla. Surrender of Sam Jones's command to Detachment of Wilson's Cav.; Maj.-Gen. McCook. *Confed.* 8,000 prisoners.

11—Chalk Bluff, Ark. Surrender of Jeff. Thompson's command to forces under Gen. Dodge. *Confed.* 7,454 prisoners.

13—Palmetto Ranche, Tex. 34th Ind., 62d U. S. Colored and 2d Tex. Cav. *Union* 118 killed and wounded.

26—Surrender of Kirby Smith to Maj.-Gen. Canby's command. *Confed.* 20,000 prisoners.

STATISTICAL EXHIBIT OF DEATHS IN THE UNITED STATES ARMY DURING THE CIVIL WAR

STATES, ETC.	Killed in action		Died of wounds received in action		Died of disease		Total, including causes not previously enumerated		Aggregate
	Officers	Men	Officers	Men	Officers	Men	Officers	Men	
Alabama	3	16	1	30	1	249	6	339	345
Arkansas	9	225	5	66	12	1,250	28	1,685	1,713
California	4	69	2	33	8	336	21	552	573
Colorado	4	114		35	3	117	9	314	323
Connecticut	81	1,021	58	787	58	3,010	204	5,150	5,354
Dakota		2				4		6	6
Delaware	18	189	11	165	10	421	40	842	882
District of Columbia	3	25	1	12	5	189	9	281	290
Florida		8		10	2	187	2	213	215
Georgia						13		15	15
Illinois	339	5,535	212	3,808	310	22,476	915	33,919	34,834
Indiana	244	4,028	156	2,815	213	17,572	640	26,032	26,072
Iowa	119	1,946	82	1,393	107	8,906	318	12,683	13,001
Kansas	24	494	9	210	27	1,647	66	2,564	2,630
Kentucky	95	1,390	39	954	121	7,122	271	10,503	10,774
Louisiana	4	125	5	80	3	636	12	933	945
Maine	115	1,658	90	1,321	59	5,739	271	9,127	9,398
Maryland	33	494	15	367	25	1,782	78	2,904	2,982
Massachusetts	248	3,457	120	2,290	66	6,947	446	13,496	13,942
Michigan	156	2,642	73	1,577	78	9,459	319	14,434	14,753
Minnesota	21	373	11	221	26	1,810	63	2,521	2,584
Mississippi				3		66		78	78
Missouri	102	2,089	66	1,060	118	9,350	317	13,568	13,835
Nebraska	1	29		5	2	158	3	236	239
Nevada		2				29		33	33
New Hampshire	84	990	43	786	37	2,684	166	4,716	4,882
New Jersey	114	1,550	38	876	28	2,806	189	5,565	5,754
New Mexico	3	54		16	5	139	13	264	277
New York	772	11,329	371	6,613	345	24,200	1,530	45,004	46,534
North Carolina	4	25		14	4	261	9	351	360
Ohio	402	6,433	239	4,514	274	21,447	957	34,518	35,475
Oregon	1	9		1		21	1	44	45
Pennsylvania	608	8,743	276	5,638	188	15,713	1,092	32,091	33,183
Rhode Island	18	278	10	154	16	716	45	1,276	1,321
Tennessee	25	441	16	262	44	5,192	99	6,678	6,777
Texas		8		4	1	101	1	140	141
Vermont	64	997	34	714	32	3,051	136	5,088	5,224
Virginia		4		6		29		42	42
Washington					2	10	2	20	22
West Virginia	61	717	20	449	20	2,475	103	3,914	4,017
Wisconsin	115	2,270	76	1,341	105	7,963	302	11,999	12,301
Indian Nations	4	82	1	20	18	757	23	995	1,018
Veteran Reserve Corps		1		26	26	1,398	30	1,642	1,672
U. S. Veteran Volunteers			1	3		79	4	102	106
U. S. Volunteer Engineers and Sharpshooters	9	158	5	91	3	269	17	535	552
U. S. Volunteer Infantry		6	1	5	2	200	4	239	243
General and general staff officers, U. S. Volunteers	50		35			143		239	239
U. S. Colored Troops	100	1,615	43	1,136	138	29,618	324	36,523	36,847
Miscellaneous U. S. Vols.		13		3		202		232	232
Regular Army	85	1,262	59	877	107	2,985	260	5,538	5,798

RECAPITULATION

	Killed in action		Died of wounds received in action		Died of disease		Total, including causes not previously enumerated		Aggregate
	Officers	Men	Officers	Men	Officers	Men	Officers	Men	
Total non-prisoners	4,142	62,916	2,124	38,816	2,712	197,008	9,365	320,665	330,030
Total prisoners			99	1,973	83	24,783	219	29,279	29,498
Grand aggregate	4,142	62,916	2,223	40,789	2,795	221,791	9,584	349,944	359,528

The quartermaster-general reports the total number of graves under the supervision of his department as 315,555, only 172,400 of which number have been identified. The remainder, 143,155, lie in graves the headstones of which are marked Unknown.

Number of United States troops captured during the war, 212,608; Confederate troops captured, 476,169.

Number of United States troops paroled on the field, 16,431; Confederate troops paroled on the field, 248,599.

Number of United States troops who died while prisoners, 29,725; Confederate troops who died while prisoners, 26,774.

FORT SAUDERS, SHOWING GROUND OVER WHICH CONFEDERATE ASSAULT ADVANCED.

FORT SAUDERS EXTERIOR VIEW.

RAILWAY BRIDGE ACROSS PLATT CREEK.

STRAWBERRY PLAINS BRIDGE

STRAWBERRY PLAINS BRIDGE.

VIEW FROM HEIGHTS

BATTLEFIELD OF STRAWBERRY PLAINS

VIEWS IN THE VICINITY OF KNOXVILLE, TENN.

MAKING GABIONS IN FRONT OF PETERSBURG

CHAPTER XXIX.

Public Affairs—"Alabama" Claims—Financial Affairs—National Debt, Banking and Currency—Suspension and Resumption of Specie
Payments—Proposed Amendment of the Constitution—Pacific Railway—Inter-Oceanic Ship Canal Considered—Difficulties with
Cuba and Spain—The "Virginius" Affair—The San Domingo Question—Samana Bay Company—Joint High Commission—Tribunal
of Arbitration and Its Award—Decision about Boundary on the Pacific—Electro-Magnetic Telegraph—Ligitations—Marine Teleg
raphy—Appliances of the Telegraph—Weather Signaling—Revelations of the Census—New Apportionment—Pensions.

AUSPICIOUS omens of peace and prosperity appeared at the beginning of President Grant's
administration. The condition of public affairs, at home and abroad, seemed to promise a bright
official career for the new Chief Magistrate. The only cloud seen in the firmament of our foreign
relations that betokened future difficulties, was the irritation felt concerning the depredations of the
Alabama under the tacit sanction of the British government. The Government of the United States
claimed for its citizens payment for the damages inflicted upon them by that Anglo-Confederate cruiser.

To effect a peaceful solution of the difficulty, Reverdy Johnson of Maryland was sent to England, in
1868, to negotiate a treaty for that purpose; but his mission did not have a satisfactory result. The treaty
agreed to was almost universally condemned by his countrymen, and it was rejected by the Senate by a
vote of fifty-four against one. Mr. Johnson was recalled, and J. Lothrop Motley, the historian, was
appointed American Minister to the British court, charged with the negotiation of another treaty for the

GENERALS GRANT, RAWLINS, DUFF, BADEAU, BOWERS, BARNARD, PARKER, BABCOCK AND MOULTER AND COLONEL DENT.
IDENTIFIED BY GENERAL MORSA FROM BROKEN BRADY NEGATIVE

GENERALS THOS. H. NEIL, RUSSELL AND MARTINDALE, 6TH ARMY CORPS

same purpose. Mr. Motley was no more successful in that particular mission than was his predecessor, and General Grant recalled him in 1870. The matter was finally settled by arbitration, as we shall observe presently.

COMTE DE PARIS

The financial aspect in the public affairs of our country, at the time of the accession of President Grant, was encouraging because of a prospect of a steady reduction of the enormous debt which the Civil War had imposed upon the nation. On the first of August, 1865, or three months after the close of the Civil War, in the field, that debt, including back-pay, bounties, over-due contracts, transportation, and a variety of other expenses incident to the closing of the war, was actually more than $3,000,000,000. On the first of March, 1869, it was $2,525,463,260, showing the remarkable fact that in the space of three years and eight months the National debt had been reduced over $600,000,000. This reduction has gone on gradually ever since until, on the first of October, 1877, the debt amounted to $2,051,587,254; while to 1905 it had been further reduced to $800,000,000.

It was during the Civil War that a radical and most salutary change was made in the banking system of our country. In 1860, on the eve of the breaking out of that war, the number of the banks in the Union was fifteen hundred and sixty-two, with an aggregate capital of almost $422,-000,000, and a circulation of about $207,000,000. At the same time they held nearly $84,000,000 in specie, and their aggregate deposits were almost $254,000,000. The necessity for a better National currency was conspicuous soon after the beginning of the war, but no provision was made for one until the 3d of June, 1864. A law was then passed providing for a separate bureau in the Treasury Department, the chief officer of which was called Comptroller of the Currency, whose office is under the general direction of the Secretary of the Treasury. It also provided for the formation of private banking associations, within defined limits, to have existence for twenty years, the stockholders to be equally liable to the extent of the stock for the debts and contracts of the bank. Every such association was required, preliminary to the commencement of banking, to transfer bonds of the United States to an amount not less than $30,000, and not less than the capital stock paid in. Then the association was entitled to receive from the Comptroller of the Currency circulating notes equal in amount to twenty per cent. of the current market value of the bonds transferred, but not exceeding ninety per cent. of the par value of such bonds. This made the Government of the United States the basis of security for the redemption of the paper currency, and that circulating medium was of equal credit in all parts of the United States. The latter feature of the system is of immense value to people in all financial transactions. The banking associations formed under this system are called National Banks; and at this time there are very few banks not included under that title.

By an act of Congress passed in 1875, banking under the National system is made free, without any restriction as to the amount of circulating notes that may be issued by the Comptroller of the Treasury to any part of the country; and the privileges attached to the National banks are open to individuals everywhere, making the proper deposit, for security, of United States bonds. Early in the Civil War, all of the banks in the Republic suspended specie payments, and up to 1877 they had not resumed, though Congress then provided for the taking of an initial step toward resumption on the first of January, 1879, at which time the Government itself stood pledged to resumption and to the final redemption and removal from the currency of the country of the legal-tender notes as fast as they shall be presented for redemption.

Resumption was really begun by the National Government in 1876, by calling in its fractional currency, and giving silver coin in exchange. The consequence

BRIG.-GENERAL ISAAC I. STEVENS AND STAFF

COMTE DE PARIS, PRINCE DE JOINVILLE, DUKE DE CHARTRESS AT MESS TABLE
ALSO THE ABOVE AND FOREIGN OFFICERS AT MCCLELLAN'S HEADQUARTERS

is that there is, at the present time (close of 1877), an excess of silver currency in circulation.

At an early period of Grant's administration, an important amendment to the National Constitution was proposed, by Mr. Julian of Indiana, for securing the ballot to women, in the following form:

"The right of suffrage in the United States shall be based on citizenship, and shall be regulated by Congress; and all the citizens of the United States, whether native or naturalized, shall enjoy this right equally, without any distinction or discrimination whatever, founded on sex."

As the first section of the Fourteenth Amendment declares that "all persons, born or naturalized in the United States, and subject to the jurisdiction thereof [without an allusion to sex] are citizens of the United States, and of the State wherein they reside," this amendment clearly gives to women the rights and privileges of citizens. No action has since been taken by Congress on the subject; but organizations

PEABODY FUND COMMISSION
ADMIRAL FARRAGUT, GEORGE PEABODY, HAMILTON FISH, GENERAL GRANT,
GOVERNOR AIKEN, S. C.: ROBERT WINTHROP, SAMUEL WETMORE

for effecting that object exist, and the matter will not be allowed to slumber indefinitely, for justice demands such a fundamental law. The right to the exercise of the elective franchise is guaranteed to our colored citizens; do women less deserve the privilege?

A most important event occurred in our country, in May, 1869, which has had a powerful effect already upon commerce, the arts and civilization, national and international. It was the completion of an uninterrupted railway communication, for freight and passengers, across our continent, between the Atlantic and Pacific oceans, thereby opening a way for a vast trade, for our countrymen, with China, Japan, and the islands of the sea. The ceremony of laying the last "tie" and driving the last "spikes," took place on the 10th of May (1869), in a grassy valley near the head of the Great Salt Lake, in Utah. It was performed in the presence of many hundred people of various nationalities, including some of our dusky barbarian brethren. That "tie" was made of laurel-wood brightly polished, its ends bound with silver bands. The "spikes" were three in number. One was of solid gold, sent from California; another was of solid silver, sent from Nebraska; and a third, composed of gold, silver and iron, was furnished by citizens of Arizona. These were driven, after some religious ceremonials; and when the work was completed, the fact was communicated to the people of our continent and across the seas, with the speed of the lightning's flash. That great railway crosses nine distinct mountain ranges, in its passage of about three thousand four hundred miles between New York and San Francisco, by way of Chicago; and the greatest elevation attained in the route is at Rattle Snake Pass, west of the Laramie Plains, where the road is seven thousand one hundred and twenty-three feet above the sea. Other railways—one more northerly and one more southerly—for connecting the two oceans by a bond of iron have been projected.

At the close of the Civil War, the subject of a ship-canal across the Isthmus of Darien to connect the waters of the two great oceans, was brought prominently before the American people. Explorations under the auspices of our Government, for such a purpose, had been attempted long before; but, for a time, nothing had been done. By a treaty concluded on the 14th of January, 1869, between our Government and that of the United States of Colombia, the former was empowered to survey and construct a canal at any point across the great isthmus, excepting along the route of the Panama Railroad, unless with the consent of the owners of that highway. Under the provisions of that treaty, the Government of the United States ordered surveys to be made, and two exploring expeditions were sent out in 1870. One, led by Commander T. O. Selfridge of the Navy, was sent to the lower portion of the Isthmus of Darien. Another, under Captain Shufeldt of the Navy, was sent to the Isthmus of Tehuantepec, further south.

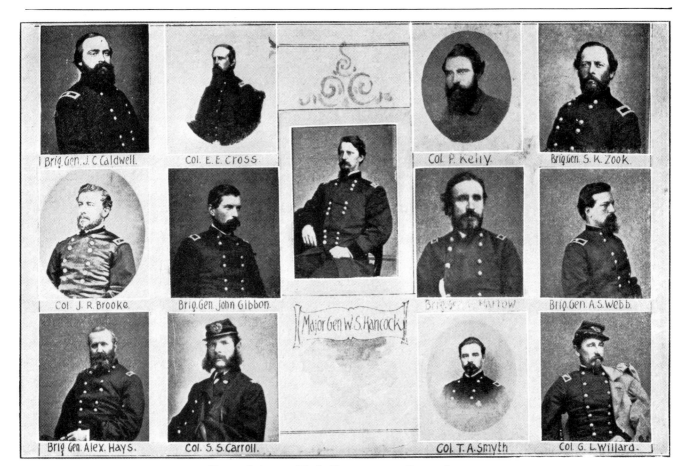

Major-General W. S. Hancock and Other Officers

Major-General George Sykes and Other Officers

The report of Captain Shufeldt showed that no extraordinary engineering would be required on the Tehuantepec route; but that an elevation of about six hundred and eighty feet would have to be reached

by means of locks. By this route the distance between New Orleans and Hong-Kong would be nine thousand miles less than by the way of Cape Horn, and over twelve hundred miles less than by the narrowest part of the Isthmus of Darien.

Commander Selfridge explored three routes across the Darien isthmus at its narrower part, all of which he reported to be impracticable. He also explored a route by way of the Atrato River and the Napipi, one of its tributaries, which he regarded as the best and most feasible in all that region. It includes one hundred and fifty miles of river navigation, and a canal less than forty miles in length, which would terminate at the mouth of the Limon River in Cupica Bay on the Pacific coast. The estimated cost of a canal by that route, including three miles of rock-cutting one hundred and twenty-five feet in depth, is $124,000,000. The highest point of the canal would be one hundred and thirty feet above the sea; and it may be fed by the Napipi River.

Selfridge made his report in 1871; and the next year the President appointed Major-General Humphreys, Professor Benjamin Pierce, Captain Daniel Ammen, commissioners to examine all plans and proposals for an inter-oceanic ship-canal across the isthmus. The vast importance of such a work is conceded. The advantage to the commerce of the world is obvious. That commerce demands its speedy completion. The route to the East Indies, even from Liverpool, would be much shortened by it.

REAR ADMIRAL HENRY H. BELL, U.S.N.

So early as 1850, our Government had difficulties with the authorities of Cuba, growing out of attempts to secure the independence of the Creoles. In 1869, an insurrection there had assumed such formidable proportions, and received so much moral support from the citizens of the United States, that again serious troubles, if not actual war with Spain, seemed inevitable. The American people naturally sympathize with others who are struggling against despotism and for the right to exercise local self-government, and are not always restrained by a wise prudence. Native Cubans and sympathetic Americans fitted out

expeditions, under the general directions of a "Cuban Junta" in the city of New York, for the purpose of carrying men and war-material to the insurgent camps. Then our Government, determined to observe the strictest neutrality and impartiality, felt compelled to notice this flagrant violation of law, and took measures to suppress all *fillibustering* movements, and to keep faith with foreign governments. At times, these peculiar relations between our people and those of the neighboring Spanish colony caused much irritation, and promised a disruption of the peaceful relations between the United States and Spain. Finally, late in 1873, war between the two countries seemed to be inevitable. The steamship *Virginius*, flying the flag of our Republic, suspected of carrying men and supplies to the Cubans, was captured by a Spanish cruiser off the coast of Cuba, taken into port, and many of her passengers, and her captain and some of the crew, were publicly shot by the local military authorities. This outrage produced intense excitement throughout our country. There was, for a while, a hot war-spirit in the land; but wise men in the control of the governments of Spain and the United States, calmly considered the international questions involved, and settled the matter by peaceful diplomacy. There were rights to be acknowledged by both parties. The *Virginius* was surrendered to the United States authorities, and ample reparation for the outrage was offered. While the vessel was on its way to New York, she sprung a leak off Cape Fear, and went to the bottom of the sea. So, by wise diplomacy, peace with all the world, with one notable and brief exception, has been maintained since the close of our Civil War.

SENATOR JAMES LANE OF KANSAS AND WIFE

SCENES AT AQUIA CREEK LANDING, ARMY OF THE POTOMAC, NOVEMBER, 1862, TO JUNE, 1863

For full twenty years the governments of Western Europe have suspected the United States of designs to gain a controlling influence among the West India Islands, by obtaining possession of Cuba, or some other territory. The suspicion was first aroused by the declarations of the infamous "Ostend Mani-

GENERAL JOHN M. CORSE

festo." It was allayed by the manifest determination of our Government to suppress all unlawful military expeditions against that island, or any other territory. It was again excited by movements on the part of our Government to obtain possession, by annexation, of the island of Hayti or San Domingo. The wants of commerce, and political considerations, had created a strong desire of the American people for our Republic to have a territorial possession among the West India Islands. Movements, with that object in view, were made in 1869. President Grant was decidedly in favor of a scheme for the annexation of San Domingo; and late in the autumn of that year, a treaty for the purpose was conducted between our Government and that of Hayti. There was opposition to the measure in Congress. More exact information concerning the physical aspects of the island and the disposition of the people was demanded; and a Commission, consisting of judicious men, was sent to San Domingo for observation. Their report, although it was favorable, did not lead to a ratification of the treaty by our Senate, and the project has slumbered ever since. Then a private treaty was made by a stock company with the authorities of San Domingo, by which the government of that commonwealth ceded to the association a large portion of the island, with valuable privileges. All the public lands on the peninsula of Samana were so ceded.

In the year 1870, the claims of the Government of the United States upon that of Great Britain, for damages inflicted upon the American shipping interest by the depredations of the *Alabama*, and other Anglo-Confederate cruisers, occupied a large share of public attention. Two efforts to effect a treaty had been made and failed. Much diplomatic correspondence ensued. Finally, late in January, 1871, Sir Edward Thornton, the British minister at Washington, under instructions from his government, proposed, in a letter to Secretary Fish, a Joint High Commission, to be appointed by the two governments respectively, to settle a serious dispute which had arisen concerning the fisheries, and so to establish a permanent friendship between the two nations. Mr. Fish, in reply, proposed that the Commission should embrace, in its inquiries, the matter of the "*Alabama* claims," and other subjects of dispute, so that nothing should remain to disturb the relations of friendship which might be established. The suggestion was approved by the British minister, and each government proceeded to appoint its commissions. President Grant appointed Hamilton Fish, the Secretary of State; Samuel Nelson, Associate-Justice of the United States Supreme Court; Robert C. Schenck, minister to England; E. Rockwood Hoar, late Attorney-General of the United States; and George H. Williams, United States Senator from Oregon. Queen Victoria appointed George Frederick Samuel, Earl de Grey and Earl of Ripon; Sir Stratford Henry Northcote; Sir Edward Thornton, the British minister; Sir Alexander Macdonald, a member of the Privy Council of Canada, and Attorney-General of that Province; and Montague Bernard, Professor of International Law in the University of Oxford.

The commissioners of the United States were instructed to consider (1) the fisheries; (2) the navigation of the St. Lawrence River; (3) reciprocal trade between the United States and the Dominion of Canada; (4) the Northwest water boundary and the Island of San Juan; (5) the claims of the United States against Great Britain for compensation for injuries committed by rebel cruisers; and (6) claims of British subjects against the United States for losses and injuries arising out of acts committed during the recent Civil War.

On the 27th of February (1871), the Commission had their first meeting, in Washington city. Lord Tenterden, Secretary of the British Commission, and J. C. Bancroft Davis, Assistant-Secretary of State of the United States, were chosen clerks of the Joint High Commission. They held many meetings and the subjects were fully discussed, when a

COLONEL JAMES P. McMAHON OF THE
164TH NEW YORK VOLUNTEERS

GENERAL CHARLES DEVENS AND STAFF

GENERAL O. B. WILCOX AND STAFF

REAR ADMIRAL J. SMITH, U. S. N.

treaty was agreed to, which provided for the settlement, by arbitration, by a mixed commission, of all claims on both sides for injuries by either governments to the citizens of the other, during the Civil War, and for the permanent settlement of all questions in dispute between the two nations. This treaty was signed on the 8th of May, 1871, and was speedily ratified by the two governments.

The conclusion of the treaty was followed by the appointment of arbitrators. The United States appointed Charles Francis Adams; and Great Britain, Sir Alexander Cockburn. The two governments jointly invited the Emperor of Brazil, the King of Italy, and the President of the Swiss Confederation, each to appoint an arbitrator. The

REAR ADMIRAL THOS. O. SELFRIDGE

Emperor appointed Baron d'Itazuba; the King chose Count Frederick Sclopis; and the President of the Swiss Confederation appointed James Stæmpfli. J. C. Bancroft Davis was appointed agent of the United States; and Lord Tenterden, of Great Britain. These gentlemen formed what was termed the "Tribunal of Arbitration."

On the 15th of December, 1871, the "Tribunal" assembled at Geneva, in Switzerland, where Count Sclopis was chosen to preside. After two meetings, it was adjourned to the middle of June, 1872. A final meeting was held in September, the same year; and on the 14th of that month, its decision on the *Alabama* claims was announced. That decision decreed that the government of Great Britain should pay to the Government of the United States the sum of $15,500,000 in gold, to be given to citizens of the latter for losses incurred by the depredations of the *Alabama* and other Anglo-Confederate cruisers. That amount was paid into the Treasury of the United States, a year afterward, through the agency of the banking firms of Drexel, Morgan & Co. and Jay Cooke & Co., who made a contract with the British government to pay this award on or before the 10th of September, 1873. This transaction was performed in the following manner, without moving a dollar of coin:

The contracting bankers, from time to time, bought bills of exchange, which they deposited in comparatively small amounts, and received coin or gold certificates for such deposits, and purchased United States bonds. Those bonds and coin certificates they finally exchanged with the Secretary of the Treasury for a single certificate for $15,500,000, which reads as follows: "It is hereby certified that fifteen million five hundred thousand dollars have been deposited with the Treasurer of the United States, payable in gold, at his office, to

RAILROAD DEPOT. CONFEDERATE PRISONERS WAITING FOR TRANSPORTATION

FORT SHERMAN

INDIAN MOUND IN MONUMENT GARDEN

RAILROAD DEPOT. LOOKOUT MOUNTAIN IN DISTANCE

THE CRUTCHFIELD HOUSE

VIEWS OF CHATTANOOGA, TENNESSEE

VIEWS OF BURNSIDE BRIDGE

COMMODORE C. S. BOGGS, U. S. N.

CAPTAIN ALEX GIBSON, U. S. N.

Drexel, Morgan & Co., Morton, Bliss & Co., and Jay Cooke & Co., or their order." This was endorsed by these parties to pay the amount to the British minister at Washington, and the British Consul-General at New York. The minister and consul endorsed it with an order to pay the amount to Hamilton Fish, Secretary of State; and he, in turn, endorsed it with an order to pay it to W. A. Richardson, Secretary of the Treasury. The money was invested in the new five per cent. bonds of the United States of the funded loan, redeemable after the first day of May, 1881; and a commission was appointed to distribute the award among the just claimants for damages.

The question of boundary on the Pacific coast between our country and the British possessions was referred to the Emperor of Germany, who decided in favor of the claims of the United States, which gave to our territory the island of San Juan, the domain in dispute. So was settled by the peaceful and just method of arbitration, most exciting questions, which, at one time, threatened to be referred to the arbitrament of the sword.

Allusion has been made to the electro-magnetic telegraph, and the first establishment of communication between America and Europe by it. That invention, conceived more than a century ago, was first brought to perfection and made a medium for the transmission of language instantly over great spaces, by Samuel Finley Breese Morse of New York, and was first presented to public notice in the year 1838. He filed a caveat at the Patent Office in the autumn of 1837, and gave a private exhibition of its marvellous power, in the New York University, in January, 1838, when intelligence was instantly transmitted through a circuit of ten miles of wire, and plainly recorded on a cylinder.

Professor Morse applied to Congress for pecuniary aid to enable him to construct an experimental line of telegraph between Washington and Baltimore. He was unsuccessful, and for four years he waited for the tardy action of his government. Then, in the spring of 1842, Congress appropriated $30,000 for his use; and two years afterward Professor Morse transmitted from Washington to Baltimore, a distance of forty miles, the first message, furnished him by a young lady—"What hath God wrought!" The first public message was the announcement of the nomination of James K. Polk for President of the United States, by a Democratic convention sitting at Baltimore, in May, 1844.

Others claimed to be the authors of the great invention, and Professor Morse was put upon the defensive. Infringements of the patents he had obtained ensued, and years of costly litigation. He triumphed. His rights were fully and finally established by the careful sifting of testimony by the courts, and a decision was made from which there could be no just appeal, that Professor Morse was the original and sole inventor of the electro-magnetic recording telegraph system, known by his name. Its value was soon perceived. Monarchs bestowed *orders* and pecuniary gifts upon the inventor, and colleges conferred honorary degrees upon him.

Professor Morse originated marine telegraphy. He suggested the possibility of telegraphic communication between America and Europe, by means of a submarine cable, in a letter to the Secretary of the Treasury in the summer of 1843; and in 1858 he participated in the labors and honors of achieving it. In the summer of that year a cable was laid between Valencia in Ireland and the shore of Trinity Bay, Newfoundland, over the great ocean plateau discovered by Professor Maury of the National Observatory. The first intelligent communication was made on the 13th of August. Early in the morning of the 17th, a message was received from

FACSIMILE OF PASS ISSUED BY PRESIDENT LINCOLN. MR. BRADY CARRIED THE ORIGINAL IN HIS POCKETBOOK FOR MANY YEARS

Burial Scene After the Battle of Fredericksburg

Captain Wiley's Camp, Quartermaster at Stonington Station

BATTERY NO. 4 IN FRONT OF YORKTOWN

the Queen of Great Britain, for the President of the United States, and an answer was immediately returned, when the cable ceased its functions. It was dumb until the summer of 1866, when communication was re-established, and has been permanent ever since. There now seems to be no impediment to its utterances by a pathway under the sea, and over the land, between nearly all the countries of the civilized world.

Many new functions of this great invention have been discovered, and its powers seem to be in their infancy of manifestation. Messages are now sent by a single wire, each way, at the same instant of time. The human voice and the melody of musical instruments may now be transmitted over hundreds of miles of space, and even impressions of handwriting and the living features of the human face may now be sent by friend to friend, from State to State, from ocean to ocean. Commerce and agriculture are receiving vast benefits from its use in meteorological observations and scientific predictions of future events.

In the year 1870, Congress authorized the establishment of a Weather-Signal Service, under the control of the War Department, which was designed to collect information and give notice by signals or by telegraph, of *any* approaching danger; in time of peace, of dangers to arise from storms in their progress, or other atmospheric disturbances. This peculiar service was invented and organized by General Albert J. Myer, who has been at the head of it from the beginning. The system, as arranged by General Myer, permits the forecasting of atmospheric phenomena for twenty-four hours in advance; and to such perfection is the system brought, that almost ninety per cent. of the predictions are verified by actual results.

GENERALS DAVID S. McCALLUM AND
STEPHEN A. HURLBURT

MONITORS AND GUNBOATS ON THE JAMES RIVER

RUINS OF NORFOLK NAVY YARD

Simultaneous weather reports from simultaneous observations, taken at different places, are transmitted to the Signal Office at Washington. Three of these simultaneous reports are made in each twenty-four hours, at the same instant of time, at intervals of eight hours; and warnings are given by signals, maps, bulletins, and official despatches, furnished by the Signal Office three times each day, to nearly all the newspapers of the land. So thoroughly is this work done, by means of the telegraph, and by the perfect organization of the system and the discipline of the operators, that it is estimated one-third of all the families in our country are in possession, each day, of the information at the Signal Office in Washington. The value of this service to commerce and agriculture is incalculable. A storm raging in any part of the country may be known to ports and districts in its track many hours before it can reach such points; and deductions from known meteorological laws enable the Signal Bureau to predict the probable state of the weather in every part of the country with great accuracy. The advantages of such a service are obvious. The invention and operations of the electro-magnetic telegraph furnish a marvellous chapter in the history of our country.

In the year 1870 the ninth enumeration or census of the inhabitants of the United States and their productions was begun; but it was not completed until late in the next year. The revelations of that census concerning the growth of our country in population, development of its resources and its various industries, were wonderful. It showed the remarkable fact that the inhabitants of this comparatively young country, with its immense out-of-doors, were not a pre-eminently agricultural people. When the first enumeration was taken in the year 1790, and the population was about four million, the value of the annual products of our agriculture was reported at $150,000,000. That of our manufactures was then quite small. The assessed wealth of the people then was estimated at $497,293,000. Sixty years after that enumeration (1850), the value of the annual products of agriculture was given at $1,070,000,000, and of manufactures at $1,019,000,000, and the assessed wealth at $2,276,000,000. Our population then was little more than twenty-three millions. Twenty years later, or at the decennial enumeration, 1870, when our population was almost forty million, the value of the annual agricultural products, including that of the farms, orchards, forests, buildings and live-stock, was estimated at almost $3,000,000,000. At the same time the value of the annual product of our manufactures was estimated at $4,232,325,000, or $1,232,325,000 more than the total value of the agricultural products of our country. This showed an increase in the value of the products of our manufactures, in the previous twenty years, of over three hundred per cent.

After this enumeration of the inhabitants, and the final restoration of the Union, in May, 1872, a new apportionment in representation was established, making the ratio one hundred and thirty-seven

A SHORE BATTERY

GENERAL MARTIN T. McMAHON AND STAFF

TAB'S HOUSE, YORKTOWN

thousand, instead of ninety thousand. A new Pension bill was also adopted, giving eight dollars a month to all surviving officers, enlisted men, and volunteers in the wars of the Revolution and of 1812, or their surviving widows.

GENERAL STEWART WOODFORD

CHAPTER XXX.

Propositions of National Interest Rejected—Public Park—National Conventions—Distinguished Visitors—Inauguration of Grant—His Cabinet—Acts of Congress—Salaries—Aspect of Public Affairs—The "Panic'—Indians and Indian Wars—The Modocs—Cheap Transportation—"Patrons of Husbandry"—Disturbances in the South—"White League"—The Sioux and Their Reservation Expedition against the Sioux—Destruction of Custer and His Command —Custer's Remains Taken to West Point—Escape of Sitting Bull—Admission of Colorado—Indian Territory and Alaska—Inhabitants of Indian Territory.

THE year of grace 1872 was a "Presidential year"—a year when the Chief Magistrate of the Republic is chosen—and that subject naturally occupied much of the public attention during the summer and fall; yet there were, besides, projects of a national character, of great interest, presented for consideration. One of these was a proposition to place the telegraph system of our country under the control of the National Government, and make it a part of the postal system of the United States. Another project was the enlargement of the land-locked navigation, by means of canals, from the extreme eastern portion of the Union to the Gulf of Mexico, and from the Mississippi River to various ports on the Atlantic coast. The governor of Virginia proposed that the State debts should be assumed by the National Government—an act that was wise and just when our Government first went into operation, for the State debts had been incurred chiefly by expenditures during the war for independence, for the general good. The present State debts have all been incurred for the benefit of each State separately. These various propositions failed to secure the popular favor.

By an act of Congress a large tract of the public domain, about forty miles square, lying near the head-waters of the Yellowstone River, on the northeastern slopes of the Rocky Mountains, was set apart for a public park. It is withdrawn from sale, settlement and occupancy, and is dedicated to the "pleasure and enjoyment of the people of the United States."

Early in the year 1872, several political national conventions were held for the purpose of nominating candidates for the Presidency. The first was that of the "Labor-Reform Party," held at Columbus, Ohio, in February, when David Davis of Illinois, one of the judges of the Supreme Court of the United States, was nominated. Mr. Davis declined, and finally Charles O'Conor of the City of New York was nominated by that party. In April, a "Colored National Convention" was held in New Orleans; but they refrained from nominating a President. A movement, begun in Missouri in 1870, for a union of Democrats and so-called "Liberal Republicans," culminated, in the spring and summer of 1872, in the fusion of these two political elements. A convention of "Liberal Republicans" assembled at Cincinnati on the first day of May (1872), and nominated the late Horace Greeley for President, and B. Gratz Brown of Missouri for Vice-President. The regular Republican Convention assembled at Philadelphia on the 5th of June, and nominated President Grant for re-election and Senator Henry Wilson of Massachusetts for Vice-President. On the 9th of July the Democratic Convention assembled at Baltimore, and adopted the nominees of the "Liberals" (Messrs. Greeley and Brown) by an almost unanimous vote. The Opposition party expected much strength from the coalition; but Grant and Wilson were elected, the majority of the former being much greater than he received in 1868.

Distinguished visitors came to the United States in 1872. An imposing embassy of twenty-one persons came from Japan to make inquiries about the renewal of former treaties between the two governments; but, not having sufficient delegated power to

GENERAL DICK BUSTED AND DRUMMER BOY

BATTERY NO. 1 IN FRONT OF YORKTOWN

make such renewals, the matter was not then settled. Relations between the United States and Japan are cordial in the extreme; and the commerce, politics, and society of the two nations are rapidly becoming more intimate with each other. The same year the Grand Duke Alexis, son of the Emperor of Russia, made a tour through our country, and was graciously received everywhere.

President Grant's second term of office began on the 4th of March, 1873. It was an intensely cold day at the National Capital; but the inaugural ceremonies were performed, as usual, in the open air, at the east front of the Capitol. Chief-Justice Chase administered the oath of office; and it was one of the latest public acts of that distinguished jurist. His health had been failing for some time, in consequence of a paralytic stroke in 1872, and he died two months after these imposing ceremonies. The Senate immediately confirmed President Grant's nomination of constitutional advisers, which were as follows: Hamilton Fish, Secretary of State; William A. Richardson, Secretary of the Treasury; William W. Belknap, Secretary of War; George A. Robeson, Secretary of the Navy; Columbus Delano, Secretary of the Interior; John A. J. Creswell, Postmaster-General; and George H. Williams, Attorney-General. Changes in the *personnel* of the cabinet afterward took place, and only Mr. Fish retained his position during the eight years of President Grant's administration.

EDWIN M. STANTON, SECRETARY OF WAR

The third session of the Forty-second Congress closed on the 4th of March, 1873, at noon. Among the numerous acts passed during that session was one to abolish the grades of Admiral and Vice-Admiral in the United States navy. Another abolished the Franking privilege; and another fixed the pay of certain officers of the Government and members of Congress. The salary of the President of the United States was raised from $25,000 a year to $50,000, payable in monthly installments. The salary of the Vice-President was fixed at $10,000; of the Chief-Justice of the Supreme Court, $10,500; and the Associate-Justices, $10,000 each. That of the heads of the several departments, and of the Attorney-General, was fixed at $10,000; of the Speaker of the House of Representatives, $10,000; and of Senators and Representatives, $7,500 each, a year, and no allowance made for traveling expenses, the mileage system having been abolished.

At the beginning of the second term of President Grant's administration, the future of our country, in all its aspects, appeared brighter than ever before, since the end of the Civil War. There seemed to be a steady improvement in the tone of public feeling after the irritations caused by the Civil War and the measures adopted for the restoration of the Union. The Government, in its dealings with the leaders in the insurrection, had been exceedingly lenient. Of the thousands of our citizens who consciously and willingly committed "treason against the United States," as defined by Article III, Section 3, Clause 1, of the National Constitution, not one had been punished for that crime; and only Jefferson Davis, the acting head of the Confederacy, had been indicted, and he was released from jail (illegally) by President Johnson's proclamation of Amnesty on Christmas day, 1868, already mentioned, and has never been called to account.

JOHN LOTHROP MOTLEY

There was, also, a gradual lightening of the burdens of taxation which the war had imposed. The amount was reduced by many millions annually, while the revenue had increased from $371,000,000 in 1869 to $430,000,000 in 1873. The exports showed an increase, as compared with 1859, of more than twenty-five per cent., while there had not been an equal increase in the value of imports.

Emigration from Europe poured, in an immense volume, upon our shores that year (1873), reaching the unprecedented number of souls that came, of 473,000. Never before nor since have so many aliens come to the United States, adding vastly to our material wealth. Efforts have been made to ascertain the capital value of the average emigrant who comes here, as a producer. Dr. Edward Young, the chief of our National Bureau of Statistics, Commerce and Navigation, has computed it at $800, not counting the money the emigrant brings with him, which, he calculates, is spent by him in preparing to become a producer. If, then,

INFANTRY ON PARADE

SCENE ON THE SEVERN RIVER, NEAR ANNAPOLIS, MARYLAND

we take the number of aliens who have come to our shores since the taking of the census in 1870, until the year 1877, amounting in round numbers to say 2,000,000, we have an aggregate sum of $1,600,000,000 added to our wealth within these seven years, by emigration alone. It is estimated by Dr. Young, that previous to 1870, there have been added to our wealth from the same source, $6,243,880,800; making a total increment from emigration alone of $7,843,880,800. It is estimated that sixty per cent. of all the emigrants who arrive are in the prime of life, and ready to enter at once into their several industrial pursuits.

COLONEL DIXON A. MILES

Dr. Young, writing in 1875, says: "As regards nationality, more than one-half of those who have thus far arrived in the United States are British, and come from the United Kingdom, or from the British possessions of North America. These speak our language, and a large part are acquainted with our laws and institutions, and are soon associated with and absorbed into our body politic.

"The German element comes next, and embraces nearly two-thirds of the remainder, being at once an industrious and an intelligent people, a large proportion settling in rural districts, and developing the agricultural resources of the West and South; while the remainder, consisting largely of artisans and skilled workmen, find profitable employment in the cities and manufacturing towns.

"The influx of Scandinavians, who have already made extensive settlements in the northwestern States, constitutes a distinctive feature of the movement; and though but a few years since it received its first impetus, it is already large and rapidly increasing. Industrious, economical and temperate, their advent should be especially welcomed.

"Asiatic emigration [Chinese], whatever views may be entertained of its influence upon our industries and customs, has not yet reached such proportions as to excite alarm in the most apprehensive, and falls short of what has been represented, never having reached, in a single year, the number of 15,000; forming only about four per cent. of our total immigration. So small a number can easily be absorbed into a population (1870) of 40,000,000, and no injury result, if the movement be confined to *voluntary* immigration. A peculiarity of the Chinese immigration is the small number of females, not exceeding seven per cent. of the whole, a fact which seems to preclude a large increase of the pure race.

"The Latin nations contribute very little to our population, and the Sclavic still less; while to-day, as from time immemorial, the different branches of the great Teutonic trunk are swarming forth from the most populous regions, to aid in the progress of civilization.

REAR ADMIRAL CADWALADER RINGOLD,
U. S. N.

"While a brief review of the ethnic derivation of the millions who have transferred their allegiance from the Old World to the New, exhibits a favorable result, other elements of their value to this country require consideration. The wide contrast between skilled and unskilled labor, between industry and laziness, between economical habits and unthrift, indicates a marked variation in the capital value of the immigrant to this country. The unskilled laborers, who at once engage in subduing the forests, or cultivating the prairies, are of far more value to the country than those who remain in the large cities."

The "panic," the great tide of business revulsion that swept over the country in the autumn of 1873, prostrating thousands of commercial and manufacturing establishments, and so paralyzing various industries that the wages of hundreds of thousands of laborers were cut off or greatly reduced, caused a sudden check to emigration. The great depression in the business of the country, which immediately ensued, caused a reflux tide of emigration. In 1874, the number of immigrants who returned to Europe, was 72,346, and in 1875 the number was 92,754. That business depression continued to 1877, but a gradual improvement was visible, with sure signs of returning prosperity. The reflux tide of

GRAND REVIEW OF THE RETURNING TROOPS, IN WASHINGTON, D. C., MAY, 1865

emigration has almost ceased to flow, and the inflowing of a foreign population goes steadily on.

Over the firmament of the future of our country, at the time of President Grant's second inauguration, dark clouds soon appeared floating, and they have hung there almost ever since, more or less foreboding of evil in their aspect. In some of the late slave-labor States there have been fitful evidences of existing discontent and rebellious feeling, the manifestations of which have given the National Government much anxiety and trouble. "Indian hostilities" have continued as a sort of chronic disturber of the tranquillity of the nation, and especially of the settlements in mid-continent on the frontier borders of civilization.

TREES SHOWING BULLET MARKS

Owing to the unwise feature of the "Peace-policy" inaugurated by President Grant, of a continuance of the vicious system of treating our barbarian population as foreigners, keeping them on reservations, and so making necessary the employment of agents and contractors, who are too frequently unscrupulous speculators, continually worrying the Indians and exciting their righteous anger, that policy, as we have observed, has not worked so well as its friends had hoped it would. There are nearly one hundred reservations upon which about one hundred and eighty thousand Indians are seated. The aggregate area of these reservations is about one hundred and sixty-eight thousand square miles. Thirty-one of these are east of the Mississippi River, and upon the Pacific Slope are nineteen. The remainder are between these. There are about forty thousand Indians who have no lands awarded them by treaty, but they have reservations set apart for them upon the public lands of the United States, fifteen in number, and aggregating about sixty thousand square miles.

We have remarked that Indian wars have continued to disturb the repose of the Government and the frontier settlements. It is estimated that the potentially hostile tribes, at this time, number about sixty-four thousand; but they are widely scattered over a vast territory. War with such an enemy is exceedingly costly in men and money. War with the Cheyennes in 1864 caused about eight thousand troops to be taken from the armies engaged in suppressing the great insurrection, to fight the Indians. The result of the year's campaign was the killing of fifteen or twenty of the barbarians, at a cost of about one million dollars a-piece, while hundreds of soldiers lost their lives, and many border settlers were butchered! This and subsequent wars with the Indians have cost our Government over $100,000,000. How much cheaper and Christian-like it would have been to treat them with justice and kindness, as men and women possessed of souls and the qualities of common humanity, than as ravenous wild beasts, deserving only to feel the power of ball and sabre.

In the spring of 1873, difficulties occurred with the Modoc Indians who, for twenty years, had shown a hostile feeling toward the white people. A treaty had been made with them in 1864, which provided for the setting apart for them of seven hundred and sixty-eight thousand acres of land in Southern Oregon. Some of the tribe settled there; others, led by a chief known as "Captain Jack," a conspicuous warrior, preferred to remain where they were; but sullenly consented to go. Troubles with other Indians there

CAPTURED ARTILLERY

caused the Modocs to leave the reservation and begin anew their depredations. It was finally determined to compel them to go to their reservation, when the Indians, under the immediate leadership of Captain Jack, broke out into open war late in 1872, and on the same day eleven citizens were murdered.

In January, 1873, a severe engagement occurred between the National troops and the Modocs, who were strongly intrenched among rocks and vast lava-beds. All attempts to dislodge them were made in vain, and a peace commission was appointed to confer with them. That commission reported, on the 3d of March, that the Modocs had agreed to surrender their arms and go to the reservation. On the following day they were compelled to report that the barbarians had changed their minds, and had rejected all propositions for a removal, and refused to go to the reservation. Then another peace commission was appointed, composed of General Canby, the Rev. Dr. Thomas, and others.

Viewing the Return of Troops from the Capitol at Washington

Grand Review of the Army in Washington, 1865

They found the Modocs under the influence of Captain Jack very insolent in their bearing, and showing unmistakable signs of hostile feeling. Finally, on the 11th of April, 1873, while they were engaged in a council with the Indians, General Canby and Dr. Thomas were murdered by them, the savage warriors stealing upon them in a most cowardly manner.

This treachery caused the Government to make the most vigorous war upon the Modocs; and before the first of June they were driven from the lava-beds and were completely subdued. Captain Jack was deserted by most of his followers, and was finally captured, with several of the participants in the murder. They were tried by a court-martial, in August, and six of them were condemned to death. Captain Jack and three of his companions were hanged on the 3d of October following, at Fort Klamath, in Oregon.

In 1873, public attention, especially in the teeming West, was much occupied with the subject of cheap transportation along the courses of commerce from west to east. The matter was brought before the National Legislature, when it was decided by competent authority that Congress had, under an express provision of the Constitution, power to regulate commerce carried on by railroads. A bill was introduced, and passed the House of Representatives in March, 1874, for the institution of a board of commissioners (representing the nine judicial districts of the Republic) for the regulation of commerce carried by railroads among the several States. Nothing more was done. In that movement, a new organization, known as the "Patrons of Husbandry," took a conspicuous part. It was a secret order for the promotion of the various interests of agriculture, and had then become powerful in numbers and influence. Its growth had been marvellous. It was divided into local associations known as "Granges." There was a central or parent organization, called the National Grange, established at the capital of the Republic. State Granges were formed, with subordinate Granges in towns and counties. The membership consisted of men and women interested in agricultural pursuits.

These Granges first appeared in 1870. Their wonderful growth began in 1871, when there were only ninety in the whole country; in 1876, when they reached their maximum in strength, there were *nineteen thousand*. As the organization grew into immense proportions, politicians tried to seduce the Granges to their support; but the imperative rule of the Order, that no political or religious topics should be discussed at their meetings, foiled the politicians. In its aim, the organization was an admirable one; and it was the first of the secret societies (for it had secret pass-words and methods of admission) which has admitted women to full membership. How could the Patrons of Husbandry do otherwise, when the work and influence of women in the business of agriculture in our country are so important? The value of their exertions may be estimated, in a degree, when we consider the vast amount of mental and physical labor now performed, directly or indirectly, by women in the food production of our country, as in all others. In the annual production here of more than *six hundred million* pounds of butter and *two hundred and fifty million* pounds of cheese, a very large proportion is the result of woman's labor, besides their attention to poultry, the gathering of honey, and the products of the garden and orchard. In the Great West, and especially among the foreign-born population, women do a vast amount of planting, weeding, cultivating, haying, harvesting, and even caring for live-stock.

The Indian, whose dusky visage has appeared prominent on almost every page of our national history, from the time of the arrival of the Northmen until now, became a conspicuous object again at the beginning of 1875. All through that year there were either threatened or actual hostilities on the part of the barbarians. General George A. Custer had been sent into the region known as the Black Hills, with a military force, to examine and report upon the state of affairs there. It is a region that had been set apart, by our Government, as a reservation for the powerful and warlike Sioux Indians. They are the most numerous of all the tribes, and more difficult to conquer than any body of barbarians within our domain. It is estimated that if they should rally all their strength, they might muster ten thousand warriors. The Black Hills, which had been assigned to them, occupy portions of the Territories of Dakota and Wyoming. Custer was charmed with the beauty and apparent fertility of that region of country. He reported it to be another Florida in the exuberance of its floral beauty, and also extremely rich in precious metals. The cupidity of frontiermen was excited, and very soon prospecting miners appeared on the Sioux domain. Instructed by past experience of the bad faith of our Government, the Indians saw in these movements a sure sign of their final dispossession of these fair lands. Their jealousy was aroused. Their suspicions were well founded; for near the close of 1874, a bill was introduced into Congress which provided for the extinguishment of the Indian title to so much of the Black Hills reservation as lay within the Territory of Dakota.

In the spring of 1875, Mr. Jenny, Government geologist, was sent to the Black Hills country to make a survey of that region. He was escorted by six companies of cavalry and two of infantry. This invasion of their reservation, and the significant presence of surveyors, confirmed the suspicions of the Sioux, of the

VIEWS AT WEST POINT

design of our Government to deprive them of these lands; and all through that year they showed such unmistakable signs of preparations for war to defend their domain, that early in 1876 a strong military force was sent into the region of the Yellowstone River, in Montana Territory and the adjoining region, to watch the movements of the barbarians. Finally, a campaign against them was organized. The general plan was for the military force to make a simultaneous movement, under experienced leaders, in three columns—one from the Department of the Platte, led by General Crooke; one from the Department of Dakota, commanded by General Terry; and a third from the Territory of Montana, led by General Gibbon. The latter was to move with his column down the Valley of the Yellowstone, to prevent the Sioux from escaping northward; General Custer, at the same time, pushing across the country from the Missouri to the Yellowstone to drive the Indians toward General Gibbon; while General Crooke was to scout the Black Hills and drive out any of the hostile Sioux that might be found there. The expedition was under the chief command of General Alfred H. Terry, a brave, judicious, and experienced officer. He and his staff accompanied Custer from Fort Abraham Lincoln to the Yellowstone River. On their arrival in the vicinity, at about the first of June (1876), and communicating with General Gibbon, they found that Indians were in that neighborhood, in large numbers, and well supplied with munitions of war.

The reports of scouts caused a belief that the Indians, with their great movable village, were in the meshes of the net prepared for them near the waters of the Big and Little Horn, Powder and Tongue rivers (tributaries of the Yellowstone), and Rosebud Creek. The concentrated troops began to feel for themselves. On the 17th of June, Crooke had a sharp fight with a superior force of Sioux, who were thoroughly armed and equipped, and was obliged to retreat. Terry and Gibbon met at the mouth of the Rosebud. Custer was there, at the head of the stronger column, consisting of the whole of the Seventh regiment of cavalry, composed of twelve companies, and he was ordered to make the attack. He and Gibbon marched toward the vicinity of the Big Horn River. Custer arrived first and discovered an immense Indian camp on a plain. He had been directed to await the arrival of Gibbon, to co-operate with him, before making an attack; but inferring that the Indians were moving off, he directed Colonel Reno to attack them at one point with seven companies of the cavalry, while he dashed off with five companies (about three hundred men) to attack at another point. A terrible struggle ensued on the 25th of June, 1876, with a body of Indians, in number five to one of the white men. They were commanded by an educated, bold and skillful chief named "Sitting Bull." Custer and almost his entire command were slain. Two hundred and sixty-one were killed and fifty were wounded.

With General Custer perished two of his brothers, a brother-in-law, and other gallant officers. Many of them had doubtless been murdered after they had been captured, and their bodies were horribly mutilated. The body of the general was afterward found and fully identified. It was taken to Fort Abraham Lincoln, in Dakota Territory, where provision was made for its conveyance to West Point, on the Hudson River, for interment. It was at first sent to Poughkeepsie, at midsummer, 1877, and deposited in the receiving vault of the Rural Cemetery there, where it remained until the 10th of October following, when it was conveyed to West Point, with a certificate from the post-surgeon of Fort Lincoln, that the burial casket contained "the remains of General George A. Custer, lieutenant-colonel Seventh cavalry, killed at the battle of Big Horn River, June 25, 1876." The casket containing the remains was escorted to the steamboat that conveyed it to West Point, by Poughkeepsie military, followed by the mayor and common council of that city, and a large number of citizens in carriages and on foot. It was received at West Point by a guard of honor, and buried with imposing ceremonies, religious and military.

The news of the destruction of Custer and his command produced much excitement throughout the country; and the Government immediately ordered a large military force into the region of the Black Hills, for the purpose of utterly crushing the power of the Sioux. Sitting Bull and his followers, anticipating severe chastisement, at length withdrew into the British possessions, where they remained until the summer of 1881.

Arsenal Reservation, Washington, D. C., Showing Site of War College Where the Brady Negatives Are Now Preserved. Photographed by Brady in 1865. The Extreme Right Shows White Wall Behind Which the Conspirators Were Hanged.

U. S. MILITARY FORCES DURING WAR OF 1861-1865.

Condensed from official reports from the War Department.

January 1, 1861, the military forces of the United States consisted of a regular army numbering 14,663 present, 1,704 absent, making an aggregate of 16,367 officers and men.

April 15, 1861, the President issued a call for 75,000 three months' militia, under which the States furnished a total of 91,816 men.

May 3, 1861, and under the acts of Congress of July 22 and 25, 1861, the President issued a call for 83,000 three years' men.

In May and June, 1861, by special authority, 15,007 men were enlisted for three months.

Under the call of July 2, 1862, for 300,000 men for three years, 421,465 officers and men were furnished.

Under the call of August 4, 1862, for 300,000 militia for nine months, only 87,588 men were furnished.

Under the President's proclamation of June 15, 1863, for militia for six months, 16,361 men were furnished.

Under the call of October 17, 1863, which embraced men raised by draft in 1863, and under the call of February 1, 1864, the two calls being combined, and for 500,000 men for three years, 317,092 men were furnished, 52,288 men paid commutation, making a total of 369,380 men.

Under the call of March 14, 1864, for 200,000 for three years, 259,515 men were furnished, 32,678 paid commutation, making a total of 292,193 men.

Between April 23 and July 18, 1864, there were mustered into the service, for 100 days, 113,000 militia.

Under the call of July 18, 1864, for 500,000 men for one, two, three, and four years' service there were furnished: 223,044 men for one year; 8,430 men for two years; 153,049 men for three years; 730 men for four years; 1,298 men paid commutation, making a total of 386,461 men; this call was reduced by excess of credits on previous calls.

Under the call of December 19, 1864, for 300,000 men for one, two, three, and four years, the States furnished: 151,363 men for one year, 5,110 men for two years, 54,967 men for three years, 312 men for four years; 460 men paid commutation, making a total of 212,212 men.

One hundred and eighty-two thousand two hundred and fifty-seven volunteers and militia were furnished by States and Territories, not called upon for their quota, 166,848 of whom were for three years, and the balance for periods from sixty days to one year.

The grand aggregate of troops called for is 2,763,670 men, and there were furnished by the States and Territories 2,772,408 men, and 86,724 paid commutation, making an aggregate of 2,859,132 men. This aggregate, reduced to a three years' standard, would make a total number of 2,320,372.

Some of the States and Territories, to whom no quotas were assigned, as already stated, furnished men, which fact will account for the apparent excess, in some instances, of the men furnished over the number called for. There were in the service of the U. S.:

July 1, 1861

Present Regulars	14,108	
Present Volunteers	169,480	183,588
Absent Regulars	2,214	
Absent Volunteers	849	3,063
Grand total		186,651

January 1, 1862.

Present Regulars	19,871	
Present Volunteers	507,333	527,204
Absent Regulars	2,554	
Absent Volunteers	46,159	48,713
Grand total		575,917

March 31, 1862.

Present Regulars	19,169	
Present Volunteers	514,399	533,568
Absent Regulars	3,723	
Absent Volunteers	99,419	103,142
Grand total		636,710

January 1, 1863.

Present Regulars	19,169	
Present Volunteers	679,632	798,801
Absent Regulars	6,294	
Absent Volunteers	263,095	269,389
Grand total		1,068,190

January 1, 1864.

Present Regulars	17,237	
Present Volunteers	594,013	611,250
Absent Regulars	7,399	
Absent Volunteers	242,088	249,487
Grand total		860,737

January 1, 1865.

Present Regulars	14,661	
Present Volunteers	606,363	621,024
Absent Regulars	7,358	
Absent Volunteers	331,178	338,536
Grand total		959,560

March 31, 1865.

Present Regulars	13,880	
Present Volunteers	643,867	657,747
Absent Regulars	7,789	
Absent Volunteers	314,550	322,339
Grand total		980,086

May 1, 1865.

Present Volunteers		787,807
Absent Volunteers		202,709
Grand total		990,516

THE END.